CLARENDON LAW SERIES

Edited by

PAUL CRAIG

D1235443

CLARENDON LAW SERIES

War

ANDREW CLAPHAM

Professor of International Law
Graduate Institute of International and Development Studies

OXFORD
UNIVERSITY PRESS

OXFORD
UNIVERSITY PRESS

Great Clarendon Street, Oxford, OX2 6DP,
United Kingdom

Oxford University Press is a department of the University of Oxford.
It furthers the University's objective of excellence in research, scholarship,
and education by publishing worldwide. Oxford is a registered trade mark of
Oxford University Press in the UK and in certain other countries

First Edition published in 2021

Impression: 1

Published in the United States of America by Oxford University Press
198 Madison Avenue, New York, NY 10016, United States of America

British Library Cataloguing in Publication Data

Data available

Library of Congress Control Number: 2021933130

ISBN 978–0–19–881046–9 (hbk.)
ISBN 978–0–19–881047–6 (pbk.)

DOI: 10.1093/law/9780198810469.001.0001

Printed and bound by
CPI Group (UK) Ltd, Croydon, CR0 4YY

Preface

This is a book about how the concept of war affects the application of law. The idea of war often operates to legitimate something that would otherwise be illegal. Killing people is normally outlawed; destroying property is normally something that ought to be punished or compensated; seizing property is normally theft; locking people up should be justified through elaborate procedures. But when one can claim 'there's a war on', the justifications for killing, destroying, seizing and interning become self-evident.

Moreover, the idea of war operates in people's minds in other ways. When I asked a group of refugees from South Sudan why they had fled to a neighbouring country, their answers invariably pointed to 'the war'; their hopes were for peace and an end to the war. Here the idea of war encapsulates horror, terror and a precarious existence; and at the same time, war is seen in contrast to a future peace. The end of war is accompanied by political agreement, the rule of law and the prospect of a life lived with dignity.

While the victims of war remain traumatized by their perception of war, the notion of war occupies the minds of leaders in very different ways. One gets a fictional insight into how the Commander in Chief of the United States might think about war from the recent book written by Bill Clinton and James Paterson. Threatened with a computer virus that could delete data from computer files across America, the President says that should the virus detonate, 'we will consider it an act of war'. He starts preparing for 'military strikes on Russia, China, North Korea – whoever is behind the virus'. The fictional President speaks of 'retaliation' and proclaims 'In the coming days ... we will find out who are America's friends and who are America's enemies. Nobody will want to be an enemy.'[1] War in this narrative triggers thoughts of retaliation (even including the use of nuclear weapons), a binary world of friends and enemies and of course the punishment of traitors.

---

[1] *The President is Missing* (2018) at 297, 350 and 398. For an overview of the thinking in the United States over the threat from cyberattacks, the appropriate responses and recent use of cyberweapons, see Sanger, *The Perfect Weapon: War, Sabotage, and Fear in the Cyber Age* (2018), who considers (ibid at xiv) that 'daily cyber conflict [is] now under way – the short of-war-attacks ... have become the new normal'. For him, 'Cyber conflict remains in the gray area between war and peace' (ibid at xv).

Most recently, faced with the coronavirus, we have seen various leaders referring to the 'frontlines in our war against the global pandemic';[2] our being at war, and calling for a general mobilization against an advancing invisible enemy;[3] and even stating that 'in this fight we can be in no doubt that each and every one of us is directly enlisted'.[4] Invoking wartime powers, legislation and spirit has been a way of stressing the seriousness of the situation, demanding sacrifices and rallying people together against a common foe.

One thesis of this book is that, for all the horrors of the fact of war, we should also consider that war is also sometimes *a state of mind*. I do not mean that war is imaginary; wars exist, and we should speak of them as such. Nevertheless, the idea of war can generate not only excuses and justifications for various actions, but also a state of mind where concepts such as loyalty, treason, enemies, victory and defeat crowd out other ideas. Inevitably, human enemies are demonized, even dehumanized, destroying not only human lives but also the prospects of living together in the near future.

As we shall see, the idea of war has recently ushered in concepts such as 'war powers over enemy combatants', and the notion that 'war-sustaining economies' can be targeted as military objectives. It almost goes without saying that the phrase 'war on terror' has been deployed, not only to garner support for counter-terrorism efforts, but also with the effect of creating an environment where the treatment of detainees amounts to war crimes. This book, however, looks beyond the rhetorical value of expressions referencing war, and examines how the actual legal concept of war has evolved, and what consequences flow from something being an actual *War* in the legal and technical sense (capital letter intended), rather than a riot, a terrorist attack or simply an armed conflict.

The present book appears in the Clarendon Law Series that was launched with HLA Hart's *The Concept of Law*. In that book, Hart claimed that, in trying to convince sceptics that 'international law can be called "law"', some theorists have exaggerated by claiming that war is a 'legislative act'. The idea is that the peace treaty that follows war could ensure that the defeated state cede territory. So war creates new law. Hart uses this example to show why national law is different from international law. In his words: the former usually does not, and the latter does, 'recognize the validity of agreements extorted

---

[2] President Trump, 18 March 2020.

[3] President Macron, 16 March 2020: 'Nous sommes en guerre, en guerre sanitaire, certes: nous ne luttons ni contre une armée, ni contre une autre Nation. Mais l'ennemi est là, invisible, insaisissable, qui progresse. Et cela requiert notre mobilisation générale.'

[4] Prime Minister Johnson, 23 March 2020.

by violence.[5] The present book will show that international law no longer recognizes the validity of coerced treaties or the validity of territory acquired by force. So one apparent 'salient difference' between national law and international law has evaporated.

Hart then highlights what he considers to be a second difference between national and international law. He contrasts legally regulated sanctions in national law with 'decentralized sanctions' in international law. He concludes that, in the absence of a compulsory jurisdiction equivalent to a national court, there is no one to investigate the rights and wrongs of states sanctioning other states through 'self-help'. On this he is of course right, although the International Court of Justice now plays a much bigger role than at the time he was writing. What is telling, however, is that Hart's example of legitimate self-help by a state claiming that its rights under international law have been violated is to 'resort to war or forceful retaliation'.[6] As this book will show, states are no longer entitled to resort to war or forceful retaliation to vindicate their rights. The thesis of the present book is that the legal conception of war is changing, and this has very concrete legal effects. At one point I had even toyed with the idea of suggesting the title *The Concept of War* in a clumsy attempt to bounce off Hart. But in the end I realized such a title would promise more than I could deliver, so I narrowed my ambitions and plumped for one of the shortest book titles I know: *War*.

Throughout the book we will consider how contemporary discussions adopt and adapt the notion of war beyond the older narrow confines of a technical 'State of War' strictly speaking. We will cover war powers, war crimes and even, in what ought to be a chilling phrase but has unfortunately become a commonplace expression, 'rape as a weapon of war'. This is a book not only about the laws of war, but also about how the concept of war is permeating legal thinking in new ways, presenting new challenges. Although the legal status of war is sometimes thought to belong to a faraway period, war as a concept is still being put to work with dramatic effects.

For an example of the complex use of the word 'war' by a political leader, we could consider a speech by President Obama where he uses the word 'war' over 20 times, starting with the Civil War, the Cold War, going to war with Al-Qaeda after September 11, the war in Iraq, and then turning to suggest that most terrorism is based on the lie that there is a conflict with the United States but in fact, he concluded, 'the United States is not at war with Islam'.

---

[5] *The Concept of Law*, 3rd edn (2012) at 232.
[6] Ibid at 233.

Obama identified the need to define the effort beyond Afghanistan, 'not as a boundless "global war on terror", but rather as a series of persistent, targeted efforts to dismantle the specific networks of violent extremists that threaten America'. He nevertheless justified the action as 'just war' to the same audience at the National Defense University:

> Under domestic law, and international law, the United States is at war with al Qaeda, the Taliban, and their associated forces. We are at war with an organization that right now would kill as many Americans as they could if we did not stop them first. So this is a just war – a war waged proportionally, in last resort, and in self-defense.

While Obama promises that in targeting individual terrorists, 'before any strike is taken, there must be near-certainty that no civilians will be killed or injured – the highest standard we can set' – when civilians are killed, it is war that is the idea that excuses these deaths. As Obama explains, 'Nevertheless, it is a hard fact that U.S. strikes have resulted in civilian casualties, a risk that exists in every war'. President Obama then goes on to refer to the need to discipline our thinking and definitions to avoid being drawn into 'more wars we don't need to fight'. Lastly, for Afghanistan, he speaks of bringing 'law of war detention to an end'.[7] The idea of war is used, then, simultaneously descriptively and as justification, but the speech also opens up the idea that wars might be unnecessary.

The rhetoric of war and its related concepts are all around us, but few contemporary law books address the topic of war as such. Of course the term 'war' is often used loosely in these contexts, and even in other areas such as the war on drugs and the war on poverty, but this only reinforces the need to ask ourselves – what is it about the idea of war that retains such a hold on us? Moreover, how exactly are appeals to 'war' and 'the laws of war' being used to shape the legal rights and responsibilities applicable to situations of armed violence?[8]

---

[7] *Remarks by the President at the National Defense University* (23 May 2013).

[8] For a thoughtful overview of how the very notions of 'war' and who is a warrior are constructed, contested and instrumentalized, see Berman, 'Privileging Combat? Contemporary Conflict and the Legal Construction of War', 43 *Columbia Journal of Transnational Law* (2004) 1–71; the book *La tropa. Por qué mata un soldado (The troop. Why a soldier kills)* (2019) by Rea and Ferri (in Spanish) looks at how the war on drugs became a war on drug-traffickers in Mexico, and how the language of war affects training and perceptions of, among other things, the sense of a nation fighting an enemy. I am grateful to Antonio García Madrigal for pointing out the pertinence of the authors' findings in the context of the present book.

Perhaps the example of those being held and tried in Guantánamo Bay can help to illustrate the point. The terrorist attack on the United States on 11 September 2001 led to US airstrikes on Afghanistan and its invasion by the United States and others. At the same time the United States denied prisoner of war status under the Third Geneva Convention to the armed forces in Afghanistan (the Taliban) that resisted the invasion, and they were instead detained alongside those suspected of being Al-Qaeda. This treatment, it was argued, was pursuant to the laws of war, but ironically with no recognizable law of war status or formal legal protection under the Geneva Conventions.[9] At one level it was thought that, by denying the law of war's protection to these individuals, one could engage in torture and expedited justice without repercussions under war crimes law. The 'gloves came off', and those captured in this new 'global war on terror' were tortured and detained without trial.[10]

A few years later it was decided to prosecute some of the same detainees for war crimes in a specially convened Military Commission in Guantánamo Bay. One such detainee is Al-Nashiri, who is accused, *inter alia*, of attacks on the US warship USS *Cole* in the year 2000. He faces the death penalty. His case turns in part on whether there was indeed a war/armed conflict when that attack in Yemen took place. The stakes are high. No war or armed conflict should mean no war crimes – and no jurisdiction for the Military Commission in Guantánamo Bay over these crimes. While Al-Nashiri points to the fact that the US authorities at the time stated there was no war, the Prosecution will point to the 1996 'declaration of war' by Osama bin Laden, and the Judge has ruled that Al-Qaeda's sense of war is part of the evidence to be evaluated:

> Whether hostilities existed on the dates of the charged offenses necessarily is a fact-bound determination; moreover, whether a state of hostilities existed is as much a function of the will of the organization to which the accused is alleged to belong to as the U.S. government. In determining whether hostilities exist or do not exist, the enemy gets a vote. Whether

---

[9] For an authoritative piece explaining the law that should have been applied to determining prisoner of war status, see Aldrich, 'The Taliban, Al Qaeda, and the Determination of Illegal Combatants', 96 *AJIL* (2002) 891–98. The issue is discussed in section 9.1.2.

[10] For a gripping explanation of how the lawyers sought to exclude detainees from the protection of the Geneva Conventions, and thereby officials on their own side from the scope of war crimes law, see Sands, *Torture Team: Deception, Cruelty and the Compromise of Law* (2008) esp at 39 and 212.

Al Qaeda, the organization of unprivileged enemy belligerents to which the accused is alleged to be a member, considered itself to be at war with the United States on the date of the alleged law of war violations is a factor among many to be considered by the trier of fact and is as relevant as any judgments made or withheld by the President or the Congress.[11]

This issue is slowly working its way through the appeal courts,[12] and the movement to close Guantánamo remains stalled.[13]

Although the detainees in Guantánamo succeeded in convincing the US Supreme Court that the writ of *habeas corpus* (the right to challenge the legality of their detention) should apply to those detained there, when it came to challenges with regard to detainees in Afghanistan in Bagram the lower courts declined jurisdiction, referring, first, to the idea of the Supreme Court that the reasoning should be different where the detainees are 'located in an active theater of war' and, second, to the idea that 'Detention decisions made at Bagram are inextricably a part of the war in Afghanistan. Reviewing those decisions would intrude upon the President's war powers in a way that reviewing Guantanamo detentions does not.'[14] Reframing places and decisions as related to wartime and war powers takes people into places where exceptional powers are exercised with fewer checks and balances.

The word 'war' has such a powerful hold that it can easily be deployed and defined in order to justify not only detention, but also killing. Consider the controversy over UK Government Ministers' claiming that British jihadis in Syria should be killed rather than allowed to return to Britain. Melanie Phillips, a well-known columnist from *The Times*, deploys the logic of war to

---

[11] *USA v Al Nashiri*, Order AE 104F, 15 January 2013, at 2, Judge Pohl. In a related appeal concerning those accused of aiding and abetting the 19 hijackers on 11 September 2001, the Prosecutor promises to ground jurisdiction on either the bin Laden 1996 declaration of war or the initial 2001 attack as the outbreak of hostilities. According to the transcript the Prosecution said that although at trial it will 'show that the armed conflict with al Qaeda began as early as 1996 when Usama bin Ladin publicly declared war against the United States, even had he not, even if there had been no warning, no declarations of war, that the attacks of September 11, 2001, even if the first attack, would have been hostilities in and of itself prosecuted – prosecutable by military commission as a violation of law of war'. *United States v Khalid Shaikh Mohammad, et al*, unofficial/unauthenticated transcript 15723 (15 May 2017).

[12] For the background on the issue of the start of the armed conflict with Al-Qaeda and some of the detail on Al Nashiri's case, see Blank and Farley, 'Identifying the Start of the Conflict: Conflict Recognition, Operational Realities and Accountability in the Post-9/11 World', 36 *Michigan Journal of International Law* (2015) 467–539.

[13] For an analysis of the political obstacles to closing Guantánamo see Abel, *Law's Wars: The Fate of the Rule of Law in the US 'War on Terror'* (2018) Ch 3.

[14] *Al Maqaleh v Hagel*, US Court of Appeals, 24 December 2013, at pp 28 and 38.

defend in quasi-legal terms the killing of these individuals and flatly contradict those who claim such action could be illegal:

> Terrorists are people such as the IRA, committing acts of violence for limited political ends. Terrorism like this is treated as a crime and dealt with through arrest, prosecution and imprisonment. By contrast, war involves identifying an enemy to be killed and thus defeated. War is conventionally defined as taking place between states and involving soldiers wearing the uniform of their country. Jihadis are non-state actors and don't wear any uniform. So their violence is branded terrorism. But this is not accurate. By their own account, jihadis are engaged in holy war. We should accept this definition of their activities because it is true. Holy war is not a figure of speech. It is a type of warfare.
>
> The definition of war is complex. What is generally accepted, though, is that war has a strategic aim whereas terrorism is tactical. To put it another way, terrorism uses violence in order to intimidate or coerce a government or institution to deliver an objective. War identifies an enemy to be destroyed altogether. The jihadis aren't killing western civilians because they want to force British or western governments to change their policies. They want to kill British and western people as 'unbelievers' and wipe out western civilisation altogether.
>
> The IRA used the murder of British soldiers and civilians to try to achieve a united Ireland. If their aim had been instead to murder as many British people as possible and replace British democracy by a global Catholic theocracy – and were seeking out weapons of mass destruction to do so – Britain would have viewed them as waging war, not committing terrorist crimes. Accordingly, it would have sent in the military not to help the civil power enforce the criminal law, as happened in Northern Ireland, but to kill those warmongers first. What matters is intention. Jihadis don't kill the innocent as a means to a political end. Killing the innocent *is* the political end. Terrorism is the method. But the aim of this holy war could not be more strategic.[15]

I have reproduced such a lengthy passage as I think it illustrates rather well the manoeuvre with which this book is concerned. Claiming that what a government wants to do is being done in a war not only makes it right, it gives

---

[15] 'It's Right to Use Lethal Force Against Jihadis', *The Times* (11 December 2017).

it rights. Phrasing the problem as one of war creates an existential threat, which 'accordingly' allows the state to deploy draconian measures. The commentator accepts that war is conventionally understood to refer to two states fighting each other through their armed forces in uniform, but in order to achieve the end of proving an assumed power to kill people, crime and terrorism are said to morph into war due to the aims and intentions of the individual targets. A claim by terrorists to be at war apparently triggers the rights of states at war, and would seem to eliminate any human rights those individuals may have had. This view has been vociferously challenged,[16] and yet, as we shall see, it remains remarkably easy for governments both to claim to be relying on the principles of the laws of war and, nevertheless, at the same time, deny that they are really in a state of war.

Clearly this is an area where language matters, or we would not need to use quotation marks around expressions such as the 'war on terror', or revert to the expression 'so-called Islamic state'. I am suggesting that the notion of war is again centre-stage in politics, ethics, philosophy and law. The conflicts in Iraq, Afghanistan, Syria, Libya and Ukraine have all thrown up challenges to our understanding of what law covers such wars. Controversy continues around the now increasingly discredited concept of the 'war on terror' and the so-called 'declarations' of war by Al-Qaeda. There was even the presumption that the 2016 attacks by the so-called Islamic state on a church in France constituted a declaration of war on France.[17]

But bemoaning the increasing references to being at war will not get us very far. As I said at the start, the victims of war may need to reference the fact of war as part of their expectation that they can struggle for a life without war. Our focus is on the ways in which wars have become illegitimate. Turning to the expression 'civil war', we find it comes with its own history, as Armitage's

---

[16] Anthony Dworkin, 'The Problem with Western Suggestions of a "Shoot to Kill" Policy Against Foreign Fighters', *The Times* (13 December 2017); and in more detail Dworkin, 'Individual, Not Collective: Justifying the Resort to Force against Members of Non-State Armed Groups', 93 *International Law Studies* (2017) 467–525.

[17] References to Al-Qaeda's 'declarations of war' are not limited to the judicial proceedings in Guantánamo Bay referred to above; for an early reference by the FBI to Congress, see https://archives.fbi.gov/archives/news/testimony/al-qaeda-international. And see *9/11 Commission Report* (New York: Norton, 2004) at 47, 59 and 10, which refers to Bin Ladin's 'declaration of war'. For more on the 1996 *fatwa* (Declaration of Jihad on the Americans Occupying the Two Sacred Places (published in *Al Quds al Arabi*, 23 August 1996) and the 1998 *fatwa* (The World Islamic Front's Statement Urging Jihad Against Jews and Crusaders, published in *Al Quds al Arabi*, 23 February 1998, see Gunaratna, *Inside Al Qaeda: Global Network of Terror*, 2nd edn (2003) at 40–48; President Hollande considered that attacks by ISIS were a declaration of war on France – http://edition.cnn.com/2016/07/26/europe/france-normandy-church-hostage/index.html .

scholarly study illustrates: 'Following the age of revolutions, civil war was supposed to have become an illegitimate form of struggle, a throwback to the turbulent rule of kings or to the recurrent instability of republican Rome – an ancient curse that enlightened modern times had lifted.'[18] In his words, 'We should be suspicious by now that the words "civil war" could ever be used without political intent or ideological baggage.'[19] Although the term may be loosely used today in legal circles, we should pause to consider some further insights that reveal what is, and is not, included in the normative framework. As Armitage explains, 'Civil wars spring from deep and deadly divisions but they expose identities and commonalities. To call a war "civil" is to acknowledge the familiarity of the enemies as members of the same community: not foreigners but fellow citizens.'[20] But Dudziak asks us to remember who gets left out as the legal framework develops around such a civil war. Referencing the massacre of American Indians from the Cheyenne and Arapaho Tribes at Sand Creek, she explains:

> They were thought to be of a different character than the white Northerners and Southerners fighting the Civil War. They were the kind of barbarians that, thanks to the Lieber Code, the Union Army could distinguish itself from through honourable combat. The Code's limits did not apply to people thought of as savages. The Indian Wars were not treated like the Civil War as battles between peoples for sovereignty – although that is what in part they were. They were conceptualized by US military leaders as battles on behalf of civilization against the savage threat.[21]

Similarly, as revealed by Mégret, Colonial Powers in the second half of the 19th century considered that the rules of civilized warfare did not apply to uncivilized 'savages' as they were incapable of applying such rules, and recast the warfare as police action or the maintenance of law and order.[22]

War is perhaps seen as the antithesis of law, but wars (in the sense of what are usually now described as armed conflicts in the realm of books on

---

[18] Armitage, *Civil Wars: A History* (2017) at 163.

[19] Ibid.

[20] Ibid at 12, for a discussion in this book of the understanding of lawyers when using the expression 'civil war' see Section 6.1.

[21] Dudziak, 'On the Civil-ness of Civil War: A Comment on David Armitage's *Civil War Time*', 111 *Proceedings of ASIL* (2017) 14–19 at 17–18 (footnotes, referencing Kinsella, *The Image before the Weapon*, 2011 omitted).

[22] Mégret, 'From "Savages" to "Unlawful Combatants": A Postcolonial Look at International Humanitarian Law's "Other"', in Orford (ed), *International Law and its Others* (2006) 265–317.

international law) are more regulated by international law than almost any other form of human activity. Most books on armed conflict or international humanitarian law today avoid the language of war. After the 1945 UN Charter outlawed aggressive war and all forms of inter-state use of force, focusing on the laws of war seemed to many authors and organizations inappropriate, as if one were developing a regime for how to wage war properly.[23] Indeed, by 1966 McNair and Watts wrote in the fourth edition of their book on *The Legal Effects of War* that 'Today the term "war" is out of fashion.'[24]

Half a century later, the term 'war' may remain unfashionable in certain legal circles, but my aim is to give the reader a sense of how casual recourse to various notions of war is affecting decision-making in multiple fora. Recourse to the language of war not only affects the perceived legitimacy of any use of force or detention by states, it also shapes the conduct of warfare, the protection of the victims of war and the prosecution of war crimes. The book therefore covers the rules on recourse to force by states (*jus ad bellum*) and the law of armed conflict (*jus in bello*), and ends by considering the law on accountability related to the post-conflict phase, which sometimes is covered by the expression *jus post bellum*.

The law governing the relevant rights and obligations in armed conflict is now under increasing strain. For some time, the attention given by non-governmental organizations and the United Nations to respect for law in times of armed conflict has given rise to concern in certain circles that law is getting in the way of fighting, or is being misapplied and abused. This heady mixture of law and war has led to several scholars and policy makers to focus on the use of 'law as a weapon of war'.[25] Dubbed 'lawfare' or 'legal warfare', there is increasing attention to the deployment of law rather than traditional weapons of war, not only to achieve political objectives but also to hinder the military.

Let me then summarize my reasons for focusing on war. First, it is remarkable how easily politicians and others in the contemporary world resort to the language of war. Leaders today are heard to complain of acts of war; they invoke a state of war for political effect to mobilize support and justify

---

[23] Fortin's research highlights how this suggested turn from codifying the law of war to developing the law of peace can already be found in commentary on what should be the tasks for the new League of Nations in 1920, 'Complementarity between the ICRC and the United Nations and International Humanitarian Law and Human Rights Law, 1948–1968', 94 *IRRC* (2012) 1433–54 at fn 19.

[24] McNair and Watts, *The Legal Effects of War*, 4th edn (1966) at vii.

[25] Kittrie, *Lawfare: Law as a Weapon of War* (2016).

exceptional measures; and they cut short any opposition as treason. Invoking war can in subtle ways suggest leaving law behind and appealing to the need for self-preservation. The warning by McNair and Watts of course remains relevant here: 'where leading political figures of a country engaged in hostilities refer to their country being "at war" caution must be exercised before concluding therefrom that a war exists in any legal sense, since the references may prove to be more of emotional and political significance than legal'.[26] But even lawyers need to be aware of the emotional and political significance of words used by leaders.

A second reason to highlight 'war' is the emergence of lines of contemporary legal argument that seek to justify detention and targeting by reference back to the idea of war. As we saw with regard to the appeal from a Guantánamo detainee, recourse to the notion of '*law of war* detainees' can imply that this status provides the international legal grounds for their detention, thereby deflecting human rights concerns about prolonged arbitrary detention.[27] Similarly, as we shall see, when it comes to targeting, the language of war is influencing the concept of what can be destroyed. The latest US *Law of War Manual*, interpreting the concept of 'military objective', reads as follows:

> It is not necessary that the object provide immediate tactical or operational gains or that the object make an effective contribution to a specific military operation. Rather, the object's effective contribution to the war-fighting or war-sustaining capability of an opposing force is sufficient.[28]

The question, to be examined in detail later, is whether labelling a refinery as contributing to the *war-sustaining* capability of the Islamic state in Syria really does make it targetable under the law. It obviously makes it sound to the public and those doing the targeting as if it should be targeted, but ought we simply to accept this? Adding the word 'war' in front of whom you want to detain or what you want to destroy should not necessarily mean you have the

---

[26] McNair and Watts, *The Legal Effects of War* (n 24) at 8.

[27] The United States, in its follow-up to the priority recommendations of the UN Human Rights Committee, explains: 'The United States continues to have legal authority under the law of war to detain Guantanamo detainees until the end of hostilities, consistent with U.S. law and applicable international law, but it has elected as a policy matter, to ensure that it holds them no longer than necessary to mitigate the threat they pose.' Diplomatic Note 038-15, 31 March 2015, at para 24.

[28] See US Department of Defense, *Law of War Manual* (December 2016) at para 5.6.6.2; see also 10 US Code § 950p(a)(1).

right to act in that way. One hope for this book is that when readers in future find the word 'war' deployed to diffuse their concerns, they might critically reflect on whether such a deployment is legally sensible, or simply designed to distract and disarm.[29]

Third, the vocabulary of war is not just a way of outweighing humanitarian demands; referring to war triggers the idea that some decisions to use force abroad have constitutional implications. The expression 'War Powers' is of obvious relevance in multiple countries. In the United States in recent years both the Obama and Trump Administrations have sought to use force abroad (in Libya, Yemen and Syria) and argue that such force falls short of 'war' so that Congressional approval is not necessary under the Constitution; while at the same time reports have been presented to Congress on US involvement in 'hostilities' under the War Powers Resolution. Here the language of war is downplayed in order to resort to warfare under the law. Beyond the debates in the United States, other countries are looking to develop parliamentary control over engaging their troops to fight abroad. These are inevitably referenced in English as 'war powers'.

Fourth, some national laws still remain dependent on whether or not the government considers it is in a State of War (formally speaking). In the United Kingdom, for example, when determining whether trading with the enemy legislation applies, the question of whether war has been declared can be critical. The UK's Trading with the Enemy Act 1939 defines the enemy as 'any State, or Sovereign of a State, at war with His Majesty'. As we shall see, several constitutions around the world refer to what can or not happen in time of War. Such texts were often conceived in a different era, and we have to ask what sort of war is needed before these laws apply today?

Lastly, we must mention the implications of the terminology of war for human rights generally, and the human rights to life and liberty in particular. The tension between human rights and war is multifaceted. War was invoked under constitutional law in order to override fundamental rights when Solidarity challenged the regime in Poland in 1981.[30] States

[29] For a key document that explains the Presidential powers to use force and the role of the War Powers Resolution with regard to Afghanistan, Iraq and Syria, Yemen, Libya and Somalia, see the Obama White House's *Report on the Legal and Policy Frameworks Guiding the United States' Use of Military Force and Related National Security Operations* (December 2016), which also discusses and approves (at 23–24) the targeting of 'objects that make an effective contribution to the enemy's war-fighting or war-sustaining capabilities' such as refineries.

[30] Mikos-Skuza provides the interesting historical example that 'when martial law was introduced in Poland in 1981 to prevent the "Solidarity" workers' movement from overthrowing the regime, the regime officially proclaimed a "state of war"'. Under the Constitution at the time,

that join treaties abolishing the death penalty allow for reservations related to the use of the death penalty in 'wartime'.[31] As we shall see, there are multiple skirmishes over where the boundary between the law of human rights and the laws of war should be drawn. Although we will be demonstrating that human rights law continues to apply during wartime, there is a strain of the doctrine that insists that 'the law of war serves a radically permissive function: to legally sanction the killing of other human beings'.[32] When authors and officials want to legalize a killing, they usually appeal to the laws of war (rather than 'humanitarian law'); from there it is a short step to claiming that human rights are designed for peacetime and 'impracticable', 'impossible' or 'inappropriate' in times of war.[33]

In deciding to write this book, I became amazed by the way in which the word 'war' works to trigger emotions and organize thoughts. The word 'war' somehow makes its way into book titles with particular resonance. Starting with Sun Tzu's *The Art of War* (5th century BCE), on to Machiavelli's *The Art of War* (1521) and Clausewitz's *On War* (1832), through to Tolstoy's *War and Peace* (1869) and Forsyth's *Dogs of War* (1974), we get not only bestsellers, but enduring cultural references too. In thinking about war, one will also keep bumping up against significant titles from radio, TV, theatre and film, such as *The War of the Worlds*, *The War Game*, *Oh What a Lovely War!*, *War Horse*, *Star Wars*, *The War of the Roses*, *The War at Home*, *Lord of War* and *The Warlords* (to mention just a handful).[34] And then we come to the contemporary academic catalogues: *Just and Unjust Wars*, *More on War*, *New Wars*, *Power Wars*, *Wartime*, *Frames of War*, *Killing in War*, *War! What is it Good For?*, *The Ethics of War*, *Borderless Wars*, *Drone Wars*, *Privatizing War*, *Power Wars*, *Men at War* and *The Unwomanly Face of War*. We will be referencing several of these as we progress.

So, whether one sees the concept of war as old-fashioned and redundant, or modern and scarily omnipresent, I suggest we do need to know what

---

this allowed for 'more drastic steps than those that were allowed in case of a "state of emergency"'. Mikos-Skuza, 'International Law's Changing Terms: "War" becomes "Armed Conflict"', in O'Connell (ed), *What is War? An Investigation in the Wake of 9/11* (2012) 19–29 at 20.

[31] These provisions are examined in detail in Ch 1.

[32] Ohlin, *The Assault on International Law* (2015) at 171.

[33] See further Clapham, 'Human Rights in Armed Conflict: Metaphors, Maxims, and the Move to Interoperability', 12 *Human Rights and International Law Discourse* (2018) 9–22.

[34] For reflection on the changing portrayal of war in film and other media, see Winter, *War Beyond Words: Languages of Remembrance from the Great War to the Present* (2017).

this word can mean and what it does and does not entitle people to do.[35] Of course, we need to inquire into how the notion of war has to adapt,[36] but I am insisting on reiterating that the victims of war risk losing out as the laws of war are adapted to suit the needs of those adapting them. I am suggesting that we go back to looking at what it is exactly that war entitles you to do.

I am aware that some commentators will see this as coming close to wanting to 'try to jam war back into its old box'. According to Rosa Brooks (an academic who worked as a counsellor in the US Department of Defense), this is 'a waste of time and energy – and an exercise in self-deception. We can argue all we want about category errors and the importance of ridding ourselves of the "war paradigm", but events march inexorably on.'[37] Brooks wants us to see that war and peace lie on a continuum rather than as binary opposites, and she is of course right that things are complicated today. But I suspect she is cautioning against simply thinking that the solution to all our legal concerns can be remedied by reminding everyone to stop using the word 'war' when to do so would be legally illiterate. Nevertheless, I think we have to admit that the actual law in this field should remain of crucial importance. It cannot be that, as events unfold, the law simply adjusts to become an apology for what some states feel

---

[35] Clark makes the point 'What matters here is not solely the act of killing, but its social evaluation. War is a patently practical activity, often expressed through acts of violence resulting in death. It represents also, however, a diverse set of ideas drawing on cultural, legal, and ethical assumptions. Of central concern is whether and how we can differentiate between killing in war and murder.' *Waging War: A New Philosophical Introduction*, 2nd edn (2015) at 1.

[36] The idea that academics need to look forwards rather than backwards in this field is the concluding thought in a wide-ranging book review essay by Mark Mazower: 'If there is a single collective lesson to be drawn from these books, it is that in the sphere of war, as in so many other areas of contemporary life, the world is changing so fast that academics are having difficulty keeping up. Many of them are still more comfortable discussing the prehistoric or ancient past than the present. Nothing dates as fast as the study of the future. Yet we badly need help thinking though, in the most rounded way possible, the consequences of war's coming transformation.' 'War or Peace', *Financial Times* (15/16 April 2017), review of Armitage, *Civil Wars* (n 18); Grayling, *War: An Enquiry* (2017); van Creveld, *More on War* (2017); and Gat, *The Causes of War and the Spread of Peace: But Will War Rebound?* (2017). Readers might be interested to discover further recent non-legal scholarship that takes as its starting point the idea of war. Relevant recent publications include: Butler, *Frames of War: When Is Life Grievable?* (2009); Strachan and Scheipers (eds), *The Changing Character of War* (2011); Dudziak, *War Time: An Idea, Its History, Its Consequences* (2012); Kaldor, *New and Old Wars: Organized Violence in a Global Era*, 3rd edn (2012); Bourke, *Wounding the World: How Military Violence and War-Play Invade Our Lives* (2014); and Bartelson, *War in International Thought* (2018), who studies the historical ontology of war from the 17th to the 19th centuries and concludes at one point (at 134) that 'as much as war needs international law to exist as a meaningful category of thought and action, international law needs war in order to maintain its autonomy as a field of inquiry'.

[37] Brooks, *How Everything Became War and the Military Became Everything: Tales from the Pentagon* (2016) at 344.

they need to do. There is a danger that the law of war is simply invoked in a rather casual way to explain away questions about the morality, wisdom and legitimacy of all sorts of activity. My aim is to give a realistic picture of what the law might be in these fields; I am rejecting the idea that the law of war is simply in flux and ill-adapted to new forms of asymmetric warfare, etc. As Brooks herself eloquently puts it:

> If we can't figure out whether or not there's a war – or where the war is located, or who's a combatant in that war and who's a civilian – we have no way of deciding whether, where, or to whom the law of war applies. And if we can't figure out what legal rules apply, we lose any principled basis for making the most vital decisions a democracy can make: What is the appropriate sphere for the military? When can a government have 'secret laws,' and when must government decisions and actions be submitted to public scrutiny? Which communications and activities can be monitored, and which should be free of government eavesdropping? What matters can the courts decide, and what matters should be beyond the scope of judicial review? Who can be imprisoned, for how long, and with what degree, if any, of due process? When can lethal force be used inside the borders of a sovereign country? Who is a duck and who is a rabbit?

> Ultimately: Who lives, and who dies?[38]

Andrew Clapham
Geneva
January 2021

---

[38] Ibid at 342.

Acknowledgements

The Graduate Institute of International and Development Studies in Geneva has been a stimulating environment in which to test ideas and develop thoughts. I am especially appreciative of the support I received for my recent sabbatical from the Institute's Director, Philippe Burrin, which enabled me to find space for writing these chapters. I am a firm believer in quite a few things: one of them is the importance of taking sabbaticals to write, read and reflect (not necessarily in that order). Thanks also to Martine Basset and Marie-Pierre Flotron from the Institute's library, whose tireless efforts ensured I had almost instant access to whatever text I was obsessively trying to track down (often last thing on a Friday afternoon). I am also grateful to the librarians of the Middle Temple Library in London for directing me to the right stacks in the basement, where I located the details I was missing concerning the 1939 Declaration of War.

This book has benefitted from discussions with graduate students and PhD researchers over many years. In the autumn semester in 2020 I was lucky to get specific comments and suggestions from dozens of my students at the Graduate Institute who were reacting to draft chapters of the present book. Thank you to all of you. A number of students offered detailed suggestions on the eventual draft, and I should like to thank them for their insights and for sharing their expertise from their home countries around the world: Juan Pappier, Louise Oftedal, Alessandra Spadaro, Hibiki Urano, Rodolfo Ribeiro Coutinho Marques, Antonio García Madrigal, Sarthak Roy, Daniel Ricardo Quiroga Villamarin, Jose Antonio Aleman, Zoi Lafazani, Marishet Mohammed Hamza, Ryan Mitra, Himanil Raina, Julio Veiga-Bezerra, Maeve Céline Grange, Perrine Cavenne, Ralph Ian Loren Eisendecher, Clara Palmisano, Marisa Giustiniani and Alessandro Marinaro.

In addition, I have been fortunate to have worked with a series of teaching assistants and others, each of whom has not only assisted but also contributed ideas and shaped my approach in recent years. I should like to thank: Michelle Healy, Fiona Le Diraison, James Fry, Armelle Vessier, Elise Hansbury, Céline Bauloz, Oana Ichim, Ben Shea, Klara Polackova Van der Ploeg, Ilia-Maria Siatitsa, Tom Gal, Elisabeth Boomer, Lucy Richardson, Aliki Semertzi, Ana Beatriz Balcazar Moreno, Francesco Romani, Giulia Raimondo, Bianca

Maganza, Alfredo Crosato Neumann, Ka Lok Yip, Pavle Kilibarda, George Dvaladze, Anastasia Smirnova, Hiruni Nadezhda Alwishewa, Peter Kobina Otoo and Fred Kusim Awindaogo.

David Rodin kindly gave two guest classes on just war in the contemporary world, and I am especially grateful for all the insights I have picked up from him in the classroom and in our conversations. In the final stages, I was introduced by Hibiki Urano to Professor Yuji Uesugi from the Waseda University in Japan, and I am grateful to both of them for pointing me to recent changes with regard to the regulation of Japan's use of force abroad.

I should like to thank Eric Steinmyller for his introduction to the former Commissaire général Jean-Louis Fillon, from the French Navy, who in turn supplied detailed answers to my questions concerning France and the law on blockade and prize. I am also particularly grateful to Mitch Robinson for his thoughts and for facilitating my trip to the Guantánamo Bay Naval Base in Cuba and the Military Commission there at Camp Justice. Thanks also to Sharon Weill and Ney Ramati for expert help with the translations from Hebrew with regard to the Israeli Prize Cases.

Huge thanks to my fellow Commissioners on the UN Commission for Human Rights in South Sudan, Yasmin Sooka and Barney Afako, and all the secretariat from the Commission for constant inspiration on how to think about the victims of war. Particular thanks to Peter Katoneene Mwesigwa and Yousufuddin Syed Khan, who engaged with me on specific issues related to this book.

I am especially grateful to Sandesh Sivakumaran, Oona Hathaway, Katharine Fortin, Robin Geiss, Annyssa Bellal and Abhimanyu George Jain for reading and commenting in detail on various draft chapters. Peter Haggenmacher has been a constant friend and sounding board, from the very conception of this project through to its latest iteration. His support and wise counsel have helped at every stage. Other colleagues who have been more supportive than perhaps they even realize include Susan Marks, Conor Gearty, Georges Abi-Saab, Steven Haines, Paola Gaeta, Marco Sassòli and Mariya Nikolova. Particular thanks go to Daniel Warner for all his encouragement over the last few years, and for helpfully sending me two books by PJ O'Rourke – *Give War a Chance* and *Peace Kills* – thanks Danny.

More seriously, I am very conscious that my work is parasitic on the long list of scholars who have toiled to produce their insights and critiques of the law of war over centuries. As the bibliography for my book mushroomed, we decided it would be better to make this file available online in order to slim down the printed volume. The bibliography includes extra details on the references in the footnotes as well as a number of publications that I had no opportunity to reference. Some books have been marked with an asterisk* where I thought they would be particularly rewarding for general readers looking for accessible further reading . The bibliography can be found at www.oup.com/clapham.

The team at Oxford University Press have accompanied me very skilfully through every stage. Thank you to Merel Alstein, Alex Flach and John Louth for their early enthusiasm and very helpful suggestions. I should also mention the useful insights from the anonymous reviewers. In the later stages, the manuscript was professionally prepared by Jack McNichol and Arokia Anthuvan Rani, and meticulously polished by Catherine Minahan, whose eye for detail and ear for syntax have saved me from inflicting various errors and clunky phrases on the reader.

Of course all remaining errors and problematic passages are my responsibility alone.

Lastly, I must thank my extended family, who contributed in concrete and diffuse ways. Until I started working on the topic of war, I had not realized how much I may have been shaped by war stories handed down and discussed in multiple contexts. Today, the war on COVID may edge out thoughts about other wars for many, but as I was writing on this topic, I found that family stories started to seem less about half-remembered stories and more about the terror and devastation of war. I recalled hearing about hiding from air raids, bombed-out houses, house demolitions, quartering soldiers, internment camps, conscientious objection, volunteering, occupation, checkpoints, enemy alien status, enemy property, requisitioned property, confiscated property, reparations, refugees, deportations, statelessness and concentration camps. The present book tackles the legal significance of some of these phenomena and many others. At one point I was reminded of how these experiences are lived by the book *Voices from the Second World War: Witnesses Share Their Stories with the Children of Today* (2016). Among the stories is an interview conducted by my nephews and niece, Chester, Wilfie and Dora. Thank you to all my family for their involvement and curiosity in my ruminations on war. My book, however, is not a plea to remember any particular war or group of victims, but rather to think about the legitimacy of any resort to warfare anywhere. Our best chance of determining the boundaries of what should be acceptable is when we imagine how we would feel if such action were to be taken against our own families.

My constant companion on this journey has been my wife, Mona Rishmawi. Her insights and experience have enhanced my understanding at every stage. Her love is wondrous and I dedicate this book to her.

Contents

Table of Cases

For the benefit of digital users, table entries that span two pages (e.g., 52–53) may, on occasion, appear on only one of those pages.

INTERNATIONAL

Table of International Instruments and National Legislation

Note to the Reader

A bibliography for this volume is available online and can be accessed at www.oup.com/clapham.

In order to distinguish between armed conflicts in general and situations that can be considered as constituting a State of War under international law, this book distinguishes between war with a small 'w' and War with a big 'W'. Where the book cites other authors or official documents the capitalization is from the original which may or may not be drawing this distinction. An introduction to the situations where different legal consequences flow depending on whether one is in the presence of a war or a War comes in Chapter 1. A suggested definition of what constitutes War with a capital W is set out in Section 1.3.

1

The Multiple Meanings of War

1.1 Meanings of War Today

As we have just seen in the Preface, politicians, prosecutors, novelists, journalists and terrorists may all invoke the concept of war to achieve their aims. Talking about war can be used to get people to rally round to face a common enemy, to justify exceptional measures that would not be acceptable in peacetime, and to claim powers to kill and capture enemies while destroying or capturing their property. 'This is war' can be a statement of fact, it also reflects a state of mind.

But is there something out there that we can agree qualifies as a war with legal consequences? As we shall see, international law abolished war as an acceptable way for states to settle their disputes. Nevertheless, fights still break out and texts still reference war as something that might trigger rights and obligations. Before looking at how the concept of war has evolved over the centuries, let us start with some everyday situations where we may need to know whether it is war or not.

There are some situations where your legal rights are determined by whether or not there really is a war. At a day-to-day level, should you care to read the small print, you will discover, as I did, that the table you ordered over the internet will not be delivered in case of 'war'. Check out the terms and conditions of your travel insurance, and you will invariably find that 'You are not covered for claims arising out of loss or damage directly or indirectly occasioned by, happening through or in consequence of war.' Such clauses all assume that everyone knows what a war is, but the line between a war and some other sort of violence has been blurred and disputed for centuries. What should become clear in the course of this chapter is that the meaning of 'war' will depend on the context. And each context brings with it different policy implications for finding there is a war on.

Let me illustrate some contexts by considering a selection of decisions from the US courts in three different areas: life insurance claims; military discipline for US military personnel; and environmental liability. A few key cases concern insurance companies' refusal to pay out where personnel were killed at Pearl Harbour during the attack by Japanese aircraft. Some US courts held that, as War was only actually declared the next day, there was no War at the time of the attack, and so the insurance company had to pay as the claims were not excluded due to death resulting from War. Other US courts held that there was a War on the day of the attack.[1] Reasonable judges could come to different conclusions.

Similarly, there can be confusion about when a War has ended. Some insurance contracts excluded a pay-out where the insured was part of the armed forces of any country engaged in War, including undeclared war. Lewis Durham was killed outside his home in September 1945 (after the unconditional surrender of Germany and Japan). The same practically-minded Judge who had held there was a war during the Pearl Harbour attack, even in the absence of declared War, concluded that even if no official act had announced the termination of the War, the hostilities were terminated and so the full life insurance sum of $5,234 should be paid. Lewis Durham was not at the time in the service of a country 'engaged in war'.[2]

The US courts were similarly divided over whether, for similar insurance claims, the Korean conflict was a war. Some considered that the conflict was indeed a war, while the Supreme Court of Pennsylvania held the opposite, finding there was merely a dispatch of forces in accordance with the 'recommendations of the Security Council'. Of course it is not hard to understand that some judges may be keen to apply a construction that reads the term 'war' in favour of the insured.[3] In these life insurance claims, considering the situation a war means that the bereaved family gets no money.

Turning to our second topic, military justice, this law may not always be so tilted in favour of individuals. In the US military justice system, various provisions apply in 'time of war'. A situation of war can mean that the punishment for violations of the military code may include the death penalty. So various cases, for example concerning sleeping on sentry duty, have explored what 'time of war' means in this context. The same system also lifts the statute of limitations on offences such as desertion in 'time of war'. So one could be punished many years later for desertion if there was a 'war', but if there was

---

[1]   Cohan, 'Legal War: When Does It Exist, and When Does It End?', 27 *Hastings International and Comparative Law Review* (2004) 221–318 esp 294–395; the following account draws heavily on Cohan's detailed article. *Savage v Sun Life Assurance Co of Canada* 57 F Supp 620 (WD La 1944) 10 November 1944; see also *New York Life Insurance Co v Bennion*, 158 F2d 260, 265 (10th Cir 1946), 6 November 1946, Judge Murrah.

[2]   *New York Life Ins Co v Durham*, 166 F2d 874 (10th Cir 1948) Judge Murrah.

[3]   *Beley v Pennsylvania Mutual Life Insurance* Co 373 Pa 231 (1953) 231 at 237.

no war one could go free. The relevant Courts of Military Appeals found that both the Korean and Viet Nam conflicts were 'wars' for these purposes, stressing the needs of the military faced with armed conflict (and despite the absence of any Declaration of War by Congress or any suggestion from the executive authorities that these were Wars).[4] Considering the situation a war leads to enhanced disciplinary measures.

In this military context, courts might look to the actual fighting rather than the formal status of the conflict. So in cases where the offences occurred after the armistice in Korea, it was held that these were not committed in 'time of war'. But as Lieutenant Commander Romero explains in a wide-ranging re-view of the case-law:

> This is not to say the court relied on the 'legal nicety' of the armistice alone. On the contrary, it was of critical importance in the court's analysis that '[a]rmed combat ended and battlefield conditions ceased; there was no more shooting and there were no battle casualties; a Demarcation Line and Demilitarized Zone were established; and war prisoners were repatriated.'[5]

Romero poses some interesting questions in the contemporary con-text: how to classify the global war on terror? And against which groups would the wartime provisions apply? Romero was forced to conclude in 2005 that, even in the technical realm of the application of the 'time of war' provi-sions in the Uniform Code of Military Justice, 'In effect, we could be "in time of war" ad infinitum.'[6]

Third, let us consider claims brought to determine liability for cleaning up environmental damage. One claim concerned a site in California that was contaminated with hazardous waste associated with the production of avi-ation fuel during the Second World War. Shell and the other oil companies 'operated aviation fuel refineries in the Los Angeles area during the war and dumped their waste at the McColl site'.[7] The United States and the State of California sued the companies for the cost of the clean up. There is a defence under the legislation that states that there shall be no liability for a person, otherwise liable, who can show that the release of the hazardous substance

---

[4] Cohan 'Legal War' (n 1) at 276–91.

[5] Romero, 'Of War and Punishment: "Time of War" in Military Jurisprudence and a Call for Congress to Define its Meaning', 51 *Naval Law Review* (2005) 1–52 at 25, discussing *United States v Shell*, 7 CMA 646 (CMA 1957).

[6] Ibid at 48.

[7] *United States v Shell Oil Company*, 294 F3d 1045, 28 June 2002, at 1048.

and damage were caused solely by an 'act of God' or an 'act of war'.[8] The Court of Appeals references the fact that the court below 'noted that the term "act of war" appears to have been borrowed from international law, where it is defined as a "use of force or other action by one state against another", which "[t]he state acted against recognizes . . . as an act of war, either by use of re-taliatory force or a declaration of war".[9] And the opinion goes on to justify a narrow reading of the expression 'act of war' in policy terms – the legislation's having been designed for strict liability. The oil companies were liable for the cost of the clean-up; there was no defence of act of war.

A different Court of Appeals, interpreting the same legislation, was faced with the question whether the airline companies, and others, could rely on the 'act of war' defence, when they were sued for the cost of the environmental clean-up after the attacks of September 11, 2001. The Court concluded that the 9/11 attacks were 'acts of war', and explained that this

> contextual reading comports with the plain meaning of 'act of war' not-withstanding that the September 11 attacks were not carried out by a state or a government. War, in the CERCLA context, is not limited to opposing states fielding combatants in uniform under formal declarations.[10]

It accepted that the international law definition of 'war' had been referenced by the other Court of Appeals in finding no act of war for the California clean-up, but it also relied on the fact that Congress had passed legislation in the aftermath of the 9/11 attacks that referenced the 'War Powers Act', and that the President had addressed a joint Session of the Congress with the words 'On September 11th, enemies of freedom committed an act of war against our country.' And it similarly noted that the Supreme Court had deferred to these declarations when it stated that it did 'not question the Government's position that the war commenced with the events of September 11, 2001'.[11]

These examples concern only a few discrete aspects of US national law, but they highlight how an understanding of war may oscillate between a strict formal understanding based on duly promulgated Declarations of War against nation states, and something much more pragmatic based on contemporary challenges. The international law understanding of war may or

---

[8] 42 US Code § 9607 – Liability para (b)(1) and (2).

[9] *United States v Shell Oil Company* (n 7) at para 79.

[10] *Re September 11 Litigation*, Docket 10-4197, decided 2 May 2014. CERCLA refers to the Comprehensive Environmental Response, Compensation, and Liability Act.

[11] *Re September 11 Litigation* (n 10) quoting *Hamdan v Rumsfeld*, 548 US 557, 599 n 31 (2006).

may not be relevant. At the same time, the cases also highlight that we need to consider why we are arguing about whether something is war or not. Is it about denying someone their life insurance or extending effective military justice to deserters? How exceptional was the damage that the companies are expected to clean up? Interpreting the word 'war' as a matter of law is going to be very dependent on the circumstances and context.

Outside the United States, national courts have faced similar dilemmas in constitutional and contract law cases. In one case a complaint was made against Ireland that the permissions granted to the US armed forces to overfly Ireland, and land and refuel at Shannon Airport, on the way to the 2003 conflict in Iraq, breached Ireland's duty under its Constitution not to participate in war.[12] In a second case, similar overflight and refuelling activity was complained about in the context of US military action in Afghanistan in response to the 9/11 attacks.[13] The Irish Government in argument saw the attack on Iraq as a war, and action in Afghanistan as something else:

> Unlike the position in Afghanistan, the events which took place in Iraq in relation to the 2003 invasion of that country constituted a war in the classic sense of the word because the regime there was recognised as constituting the lawful government of Iraq, recognised by the international community as such.[14]

The Irish Government contended

> that the Taliban regime in Afghanistan was not recognised by the international community as the government of Afghanistan. The Taliban, if it had a status, had some type of de facto control over parts of Afghanistan and to that extent were recognised only by three other states. On the other hand the Taliban was not recognised by this State at all. So far as this State is concerned, and having regard to terms of resolution 1368, what occurred was not only in accordance with the wishes of the Security Council but also with the consent of the lawful government of Afghanistan against a de facto regime which operated in parts of Afghanistan.[15]

---

[12] *Horgan v An Taoiseach et al* [2003] IEHC 64, ILDC 486 (IE 2003).
[13] *Dubsky v Government of Ireland et al* [2005] IEHC 442, ILDC 485 (IE 2005).
[14] Ibid at para 50.
[15] Ibid.

The applicant on the other hand argued that war in this context meant armed conflict.

The Judge decided that he could not, and did not need to, determine whether there was a war. But this passage from his judgment helps us see how a judicial body perceives the concept of war in the contemporary context:

> What is remarkable is that, notwithstanding all the argument, no party was in a position to refer to any accepted legal definition of what is meant by war in national or international law. It is equally true that, among the several general dictionaries opened, the word is defined as having a variety of meanings, but these cannot be accepted as constituting a clear legal definition of the word either.[16]

The Judge considered he did not need to resolve the definitional issue because, whether or not Ireland had duties of neutrality, and whether or not there was a war, any breach of those international principles through overflight and landing could not constitute participation in a war.[17]

When we move to mentions of war in private contracts, the British courts have been clear. The meaning of war in the contract depends on the context, and what the parties would have intended. The meaning of war is not dependent on whether there was a declared War, or whether the Executive considered there was a War.[18] In 1937, Japan and China were engaged in hostilities involving serious fighting. The UK Government chose not to issue a certificate stating whether there was a war or not. The Court of Appeal, in a famous case, found that there was a war for the purposes of enforcing the terms of a contract that stipulated that the contract would be cancelled 'if war breaks out involving Japan'. As explained by Sir Wilfred Greene, the Master of the Rolls, 'in the particular context in which the word "war" is found in this charterparty, that word must be construed, having regard to the general tenor and purpose of the document, in what may be called a common

---

[16] Ibid at para 84.

[17] Ibid at para 90.

[18] See McNair and Watts, The Legal Effects of War, 4th edn (1966) at 201 (footnote omitted): 'It is important to recognize that when the parties to a contract use the expression "war", "warlike operations" or some similar expression, the problem before the Court is to decide not whether there exists what international law or English municipal law would regard as "war", but to assign to the expression the ordinary meaning which a person of common sense would assign to it in the relevant context.' For frustration of contracts in the context of war, including abrogation or suspension, see ibid Ch 5 and the House of Lords judgment in *Arab Bank v Barclays Bank* [1954] AC 495.

sense way'.[19] The absence of a Declaration of War, or the failure of the fighting parties to break off diplomatic relations, was not considered determinative. Similarly, the English courts have been happy to extend the meaning of 'war risks' in contracts to cover situations such as the Spanish civil war.[20] Today, the expression 'civil war' is often reserved for significant armed conflicts between armed groups or between such a group and a government. No particular legal consequences flow from terming an armed conflict a civil war.[21]

A further example from the French courts, by contrast, takes a more formalistic approach. The French Military Penal Code contained a provision that stated that self-mutilation in the presence of the enemy was an 'aggravating circumstance', as opposed to ordinary self-mutilation. The defendant had been in the French Army, and was serving in the UN Force in Korea. He deliberately shot himself (self-mutilation). The Prosecution argued that the armed forces of North Korea and China were the enemy, and so the penalty

---

[19] *Kawasaki Kisen Kabushiki Kaisha of Kobe v Bantham Steamship Company, Ltd* [1939] 2 KB 544 at 559; see also *Tsakiroglou v Noblee & Thorl* [1961] 1 Lloyd's Rep 329, relating to the conflict with Egypt and the closure of the Suez Canal, accepting an earlier finding that '[t]here were hostilities but not war in Egypt at the material time', per Viscount Simonds at paras 111–112.

[20] See *Pesquerias y Secaderos De Bacalao De Espana v Beer* [1949] 16 ILR 363 at 372 per Lord Morton, who said 'in my view the word "war" in a policy of insurance includes civil war unless the context makes it clear that a different meaning should be given to the word'; *Spinneys (1948) Ltd v Royal Insurance Co Ltd* [1980] 1 Lloyd's Rep 406 (finding that the situation in Lebanon in 1976 had not gone beyond massive civil strife to civil war); and *IF P and C Insurance Ltd v Silversea Cruises Limited et al* [2004] EWCA Civ 769, considering whether the 9/11 attack was an act of war (but not deciding either way), Rix LJ mentioning (at [143]) in this context a distinction between 'acts of war' and 'war': 'For instance, I wonder whether a *casus belli*, which it might be argued that 9/11 was, in as much as it led within a month to the invasion of Afghanistan, is a candidate for an act of war?' Ward LJ did not consider there was an act of war, or a war or an armed conflict with Al-Qaeda (at [147]–[148]). A leading case in the United States determined that the war exclusion clauses did not apply to a claim for the hijacking and destruction of a Boeing 747 in 1970 by the Popular Front for the Liberation of Palestine. The insurers failed to bring the cause of the loss within what the Court referred to as an 'approximately increasing scale and organization of violence, "riot," "civil commotion," "insurrection," "military or . . . usurped power," "rebellion," "revolution," "civil war," "warlike operations," and "war" exhaust the possibilities, and that the cause of the loss must be described by at least one of the terms. However, each of the exclusionary terms has dimensions besides the level of violence. For example, for there to be a "riot" three or more actors must gather in the same place; for there to be an "insurrection" there must be an intent to overthrow a lawfully constituted regime; for there to be a "war" a sovereign or quasi-sovereign must engage in hostilities.' *Pan American v Aetna Casualty* 505 F2d (1974) 989 at 1005; followed more recently by the Ninth Circuit in denying that Hamas firing rockets into Israel would be covered by the war exclusion clause with similar wording: *Universal Cable Productions, LLC v Atlantic Specialty Insurance Co*, No 17-56672 (9th Cir, 12 July 2019), available at http://cdn.ca9.uscourts.gov/datastore/opinions/2019/07/12/17-56672.pdf.

[21] Lawyers tend to think of civil wars as those conflicts that would reach the threshold demanded by Additional Protocol II to the Geneva Conventions; see, eg, Gray, *International Law and the Use of Force*, 4th edn (2018) at 85; De Wett, *Military Assistance on Request and the Use of Force* (2020) at 17–19.

should be the more severe option due to the aggravating circumstance. The defendant argued that there was no war between France and those two states, and so they were not the 'enemy'. The Court of Appeal agreed with the soldier, finding that there had been no Declaration of War under international law, nor had there been a vote authorising a Declaration of War in the French Assembly, as required by the Constitution;[22] and in addition it held that 'a state of war can only exist between States which have recognized each other', and that neither North Korea nor the Chinese People's Republic were 'countries . . . . recognised by the French Government'.[23]

The Supreme Court of India more recently considered whether an attack on the Indian Parliament in December 2001 by five heavily-armed individuals could constitute the crime of waging war against the Government of India under the Indian Penal Code. The Court stated:

> War, terrorism and violent acts to overawe the established Government have many things in common. It is not too easy to distinguish them, but one thing is certain, the concept of war imbedded in Section 121 is not to be understood in the international law sense of inter-country war involving military operations by and between two or more hostile countries. Section 121 is not meant to punish prisoners of war of a belligerent nation.[24]

The Court then explained the factors that led it to conclude that the attack on Parliament could be considered as waging war:

> [T]he fire power or the devastating potential of the arms and explosives that may be carried by a group of persons may be large or small, as in the present case, and the scale of violence that follows may at times become useful indicators of the nature and dimension of the action resorted to. These, coupled with the other factors, may give rise to an inference of waging war.
>
> The single most important factor which impels us to think that this is a case of waging or attempting to wage war against the Government of India

---

[22] For the practice concerning such Declarations (which are very rare) see Zoller, 'The War Powers in French Constitutional Law', *ASIL Proceedings* (1996) 46–51.

[23] *War in Korea (Self-Mutilation Case)*, French Court of Appeal, 10 December 1953, 20 ILR 591; *Dalloz* (1954) *Jurisprudence* 155. See for further cases on the meaning of war before national jurisdictions Avram, *The Evolution of the Suez Canal Status from 1869 up to 1956: A Historico-Juridical Study* (1958) esp 109–142; Green, *Essays on the Modern Law of War*, 2nd edn (1999) 75–129.

[24] *State (NCT of Delhi) v Navjot Sandhu @ Afsan Guru and Shaukat Hussain Guru v State (NCT of Delhi)*, MANU/SC/0465/2005, at section xi, 'waging war'.

is the target of attack chosen by the slain terrorists and conspirators and the immediate objective sought to be achieved thereby. The battle-front selected was the Parliament House Complex. The target chosen was the Parliament – a symbol of sovereignty of the Indian republic. Comprised of peoples' representatives, this supreme law-making body steers the destinies of vast multitude of Indian people. It is a constitutional repository of sovereign power that collectively belongs to the people of India. The executive Government through the Council of Ministers is accountable to Parliament. Parliamentary democracy is a basic and inalienable feature of the Constitution. Entering the Parliament House with sophisticated arms and powerful explosives with a view to lay a siege of that building at a time when members of Parliament, members of Council of Ministers, high officials and dignitaries of the Government of India gathered to transact Parliamentary business, with the obvious idea of imperilling their safety and destabilizing the functioning of Government and in that process, venturing to engage the security forces guarding the Parliament in armed combat, amounts by all reasonable perceptions of law and common sense, to waging war against the Government.[25]

Although we have barely scratched the surface with our examples, they suffice to show that context is everything when it comes to interpreting the legal meaning of war. Each national jurisdiction will most likely determine the meaning of war in the context of its own legal traditions and constitutional order, including the national arrangements for declaring war. And each jurisdiction too will be aware of the policy implications of the decision at hand, even in a specialized field such as marine insurance.[26] As the idea of

---

[25] *State (NCT of Delhi) v Navjot Sandhu* (n 23) at section xi, 'waging war'. See also *The State of Maharashtra v Mohammed Ajmal Mohammad Amir Kasab @ Abu Mujahid*, Confirmation Case No 2 of 2010 in Sessions Case No 175 of 2009, Criminal Appellate Jurisdiction Bombay, 21 February 2011, where the same reasoning regarding waging war was applied to the attack on hotels and the railway station in Mumbai in 2008 (esp para 571). I am grateful to Sarthak Roy for pointing me to these cases and other materials.

[26] See Hudson, 'Effect on Commercial Law of Non-Declaration of War', in Rowe (ed), *The Gulf War 1990–91 in International and English Law* (1993) 333–47, who suggests (at 346) that 'even in the absence of specific legislation, British underwriters would not be required to pay for marine or aviation losses caused by an opponent in an undeclared war by British or co-belligerent military action . . . even payment on non-war risk might be regarded as contrary to public policy'. For the unenforceability of insurance contracts in time of Declared War under trading with enemy rules at Common Law, see Beale (ed), *Chitty on Contracts: General Principles*, 31st edn (2012) vol 1 at para 16–026 and the references therein. For the history of the role of government in maritime insurance in time of War, as well as using insurance 'as an instrument of war', see Lobo-Guerrero, *Insuring War: Sovereignty, Security and Risk* (2012). For the UK Government's present role in insuring for war risks, see the Marine and Aviation Insurance (War Risks) Act 1952, s

declaring war in an official form becomes less and less likely, we should expect a continuing multiplicity of interpretations of the word 'war', and what it means in any one national legal context. Such a flexible approach to what might constitute war has not always been so obvious: being at war had multiple legal effects in the past. The law may have changed, but, as we shall see, these older conceptions of the concept of war continue to exert considerable influence.

1.2   Early War and Just War

War has been primarily conceived as organized violence between two political entities. For the ancient Greeks, or the Chinese, the notion of war implied fighting foreigners, not those from the same civilization.[27] The separate

10(1) of which states that '"war risks" means risks arising from any of the following events, that is to say, hostilities, rebellion, revolution and civil war, from civil strife consequent on the happening of any of those events, or from action taken (whether before or after the outbreak of any hostilities, rebellion, revolution or civil war) for repelling an imagined attack or preventing or hindering the carrying out of any attack, and includes piracy'. In the United States, see 46 USC §539. In the private sector, 'war risk' insurance is taken out as additional insurance and conditions may be determined by the Joint War Committee, which keeps a 'war list' directing shipping away from certain zones. This list does not refer to states at war but rather to multiple threats from terrorists, armed robbers, pirates, etc. See, eg, JWLA-024, available at https://www.lmalloyds.com/LMA/Underwriting/Marine/JWC/JW_Bulletins/JWLA024.aspx. The Institute War Clauses Cargo 2009 insurance (and the clause is replicated in most contracts) covers loss or damage caused by '1.1 war civil war revolution rebellion insurrection, or civil strife arising therefrom, or any hostile act by or against a belligerent power 1.2 capture seizure arrest restraint or detainment, arising from risks covered under 1.1 above, and the consequences thereof or any attempt thereat 1.3 derelict mines torpedoes bombs or other derelict weapons of war'. The clause for insurance for the hull of the ship is similar but excludes, *inter alia*, loss, etc from 'the outbreak of war (whether there be a declaration of war or not) between any of the following countries', ie UK, USA, France, Russia and China (01/11/1995, at para 5.1.1). See also para 6.2.1 for termination on the outbreak of war between the 'five powers'. For other contracts with different states beyond these five which have been included in contracts in case of outbreak of war, see Bundock, *Shipping Law* Handbook, 6th edn (2019), eg charterparty contract at 1088; see also Rose, *Marine Insurance: Law and Practice*, 2nd edn (2013) esp paras 17.29, 17.38-40 and 17.80-83. See further Davey, Davey and Oliver, *Miller's Marine War Risks*, 4th edn (2020) Ch 6 for a discussion of cases concerning the conflicts between Japan and China (1937), the Spanish civil war, Korea, Falklands/Malvinas, Gulf war (1991), Germany as part of NATO in Kosovo, and the 9/11 attacks.

[27]   Plato (attributed to Socrates): 'Accordingly the Greeks being their own people, a quarrel with them will not be called a war. It will only be civil strife, which they will carry as men who will some day be reconciled. So they will not behave like a foreign enemy seeking to enslave or destroy, but will try to bring their adversaries to reason by well-meant correction. As Greeks they will not devastate the soil of Greece or burn the homesteads; nor will they allow that all the inhabitants of any state, men, women, and children, are their enemies, but only the few who are responsible for the quarrel. The greater number are friends whose land and houses, on all these

concept of civil war, where the fighting is internal, is perhaps not as modern as is sometimes presumed, and Armitage's recent scholarship carefully traces it to Sulla's advance on Rome in 83 BCE.[28] What interests us here is not so much whether there were events that were considered war, or civil war, but whether there were rules that determined when one resorted to war in the legal sense, rather than simply engaging in violence.

There is evidence of certain war rituals before battle from early history, and Stephen Neff's superb book *War and the Law of Nations* points to a number of traditions of fair play in war in Ancient China (Confucian tradition), Ancient India (the Mahabharata and the Code of Manu), Ancient Greece (Plato) and Ancient Rome (Camillus and Cicero).[29]

Religious beliefs have set parameters for war. Sinha explains that 'Hinduism, like most religions, believes that war is undesirable because it involves the killing of fellow human beings and hence should be avoided as a means of settling disputes.' He continues:

> Ancient India developed a method in four successive stages for the settlement of disputes between States: the first stage is called peaceful negotiation (*sama*); the second stage consists of offering gifts (*dana*) to appease the enemy; the third is a veiled threat (*bheda*); and the last stage allows the use of force (*danda*). The clash of arms in battle is therefore clearly undesirable

accounts, they will not consent to lay waste and destroy. They will PURSUE the quarrel only until the guilty are compelled by the innocent sufferers to give satisfaction.' *The Republic of Plato*, tr Cornford (1941) at 170 [v 470, orig c 380 BCE]. It has been suggested that one explanation why Sun Tzu's classic *The Art of War* (roughly 5th century BCE) is addressed only to war between rulers is that any sort of rebellion against the Emperor would have been seen as disturbing the cosmic order and simply criminal: Van Creveld, *More on War* (2017) at 175; but the story of the Duke of Sung's refusal to attack the forces of the state of Chu until they were ready suggests that some restraints related to a concept of war operated in the so-called 'Warring States Period'. See Grayling, *War: An Enquiry* (2017) at 13ff; Armitage has pointed to a Chinese conception of 'internal war', *Civil Wars: A History* (2017) at 23; and Neff suggests that operations carried out by the Chinese central government would have been seen as a counterpart to what other societies saw as foreign war, citing the Yellow Turban Revolt of AD 184, *War and the Law of Nations* (2005) at 20.

[28] Armitage, *Civil Wars: A History* (n 27) at 56.

[29] Neff has some of the best coverage of the meaning of war from a legal perspective. He identifies how four features of war mark it out as a distinct legal phenomenon: it is a violent conflict between collectivities; it is waged against foreigners rather than domestic enemies; it is usually rules-based; and it is time bound, in that there is a time of war and then there is a time of peace: *War and the Law of Nations* (n 27) at 15.

as long as it can be avoided. The policy of conciliation and making gifts should be tried first before engaging in war.[30]

War was long understood as part of a dispute settlement system containing the ultimate option of self-help.[31] In Roman times (from circa 6th century BCE) the *fetiales* (the priests in charge of war) would determine whether there was a just cause for war. Draper lists the just causes as: violation of Roman dominiums; violation of ambassadors; violation of treaties; and support to an enemy of Rome by a hitherto friendly state.[32] The proceedings were as follows:

> The *fetial* priest, in full ceremonial garments, travelled to the border of the offending state, proclaimed his purpose at the border and swore to its truth. Then he crossed the border, repeated his claim and oath to the first person he met, repeated the claim and the oath to the gate keeper of the offending city, entered the city and went to the forum where he repeated his claim and oath to the magistrates and then conferred with them. If they agreed to give recompense he left as a 'friend', but if they needed to confer he granted them ten days, and he would grant two additional ten-day periods when needed. If, at the end of 30 days, they had not agreed – or if they had refused out-right – he would return to the Roman Senate and announce that Rome had the right to go to war.[33]

An important aspect to this procedure, and influential beyond Roman times, is the belief that 'battles are decided by providential interference and that victory is a gift of the gods who thereby legitimatize the conquests made in war'.[34] A war started in accordance with these rules was legally correct and

---

[30] Sinha, 'Hinduism and International Humanitarian Law', 87 *IRRC* (2005) 285–94 at 287; see further, with regard to other religions, Popovski, Reichberg and Turner (eds), *World Religions and Norms of War* (2009).

[31] Some authors emphasise how hunting evolved into warfare as leaders emerge and slaughter switches from animal trophies to war captives, eg, Bryant, *A World History of War Crimes: From Antiquity to the Present* (2016) Ch 1. Others have stressed that aggression originally stems from feeling to be the victim of predators, for further discussion on the early origins of the idea and practice of war see Green (n 23) 41–74. See also Dyer, *War* (2017). Our focus is less on the emergence of the phenomenon of war and more on the early sense that war could be used to resolve disputes.

[32] Meyer and McCoubrey (eds), *Reflections on Law and Armed Conflicts* (1998) at 5.

[33] Bradford, *War: Antiquity and Its Legacy* (2015) at 85–86.

[34] von Elbe, 'The Evolution of the Concept of Just War in International Law', 33 *AJIL* (1939) 665–88 at 666.

justum, and sanctified by religion and so *pium.*[35] The label of a just and pious war was nevertheless more a convenience than something we would consider today as justified. As Wehberg explains, because the *pater patratus* who had summoned the hostile state to make reparation 'never investigated, and because – on account of the preponderance of the state over religion in ancient Rome – he was forbidden to investigate whether in any individual case the Roman claim for reparation was justified, the fiction arose that Rome always waged just wars'.[36]

Texts from the Middle Ages that sought to set out an international law on when war could be waged can be quite confusing, for they included in the concept of war conflicts between individuals. In 1360, Giovanni da Legnano, who has been credited with providing much that is comparable 'in a rudimentary way, to an International Law of War',[37] divided war into celestial spiritual war, human spiritual war, universal war, particular corporal wars, war for the defence of a mystical body (reprisals) and war for compurgation – also known as a 'duel'.[38] Space does not permit us to delve into the sometimes explicitly metaphysical aspects of these categories, or the approach in Islam;[39] suffice to say that categorizing different types of war, along with the justifications for them, was quite a science in the 14th century.

The theological tradition of developing conditions for just war is often traced by western scholars to Saint Augustine, for whom a just war avenged wrongs when a state had refused to make amends, or restore what it had unjustly seized. As Neff explains, theologians developed a complex set of rules from roughly 1050 to 1300.[40] There were several main principles for just war, and the following description draws heavily on Neff's scholarly explanation.

First, *auctoritas,* or right authority, meaning that the war needed to be waged on the command of a sovereign. Neff adds that this *auctoritas* was 'necessary on *both* sides of the conflict, and not only on the just side. This requirement had the effect of excluding domestic law-enforcement

---

[35] Ibid at 666–67.
[36] Wehberg, *The Outlawry of War* (1931) at 1; for more on this early period, see Cox, 'The Ethics of War up to Thomas Aquinas', in Lazar and Frowe (eds), *The Oxford Handbook of Ethics of War* (2018) 101–21.
[37] Holland, 'Introduction', in Giovanni da Legnano, *Tractatus de Bello, de Represaliis et de Duello (1360)*, ed Holland, tr Brierly (1917) at xxxii.
[38] Giovanni da Legano, *Tractatus de bello* (n 37) at 217.
[39] See also Bassiouni, *The Sharīʿa and Islamic Criminal Justice in Time of War and Peace* (2014) esp Ch 4 and Appendices A and B for the history concerning Islamic states and the prohibitions on aggression.
[40] Neff, *War and the Law of Nations* (n 27) 49–53.

operations against bandits, pirates and the like from the category of just wars.'[41] Giovanni da Legnano has long and complicated passages explaining the Pope's authority to declare war on infidels, and how from this one can infer the Emperor's justification for declaring war against enemies. But for him war could not be declared by others except for a prince (sovereign). The prince 'alone may declare war by his own authority, since he has no superior to whom he may resort to obtain justice.'[42]

Second, *personae* 'meant that only certain categories of person were entitled to engage in armed conflict'. So 'women, children and the aged or infirm were excluded by the dictates of nature', while ecclesiastics were excluded as their profession 'was incompatible with the shedding of blood'.[43]

Third, *res* meant that there had to be a thing that was the object of contention. This could be disputed title over a territory, or a demand for compensation.

Fourth, *justa causa* meant there had to be a valid legal claim. This included the idea of necessity, meaning that

> a war would not be just if an alternative and non-forcible way of resolving the crisis was available. There was also, if only implicitly, a requirement of proportionality – that a war should not be waged if the good which was expected to flow from it was outweighed by the evils that it would entail.[44]

Fifth, *animus*, meaning that one had to have the right intention and that personal hatred of the enemy had no place in just war; one could hate the wrongdoing but not the wrongdoer. Neff reports that 'Augustine made an analogy with a father applying corporal punishment to a son for corrective purposes, with a motive of love'.[45]

By 1360 Giovanni da Legnano was employing medical metaphors to explain how just as 'in the small world' we might 'turn to a doctor, who operates by a remedy which is extrinsic and poisonous', in the 'great world' the 'Most High Creator, and doctor of the universe [. . .] uses the remedy of war to exterminate vices and excesses, and to reduce . . . to the proper temperature'.[46] And in 1386 de Bonet likens 'a just war to the administration of medicine to

---

[41] Ibid at 50.
[42] Giovanni da Legano, *Tractatus de bello* (n 37) at 234.
[43] Neff, *War and the Law of Nations* (n 27) at 50.
[44] Ibid at 51.
[45] Ibid at 52.
[46] Giovanni da Legano, *Tractatus de bello* (n 37) at 225–26.

the sick – painful and unpleasant in the short term, but done for the good of the patient himself'.[47]

It is this fifth element of right intention that continues to raise problems in ethics and law. Right intention allows for the idea of accidental, incidental or collateral casualties, known in this context as the law of 'double effect'. Right intention in just war theory only prohibited what was 'intended'; one was not blamed for the unintended side-effects..[48]

Vitoria (1480–1546) and Suárez (1548–1617) added further requirements: war can only be a last resort after having failed to resolve the matter by any other method; that the innocent should be immune from direct attack; and that due proportion should be observed at the beginning of, during and after the war.[49]

The concept of the meaning of 'just' in 'just war' was, at one stage, adapted to the related idea of the word 'just' meaning that the war was 'regular' in the formal legal sense.[50] While the idea of 'regular war' may have existed in parallel alongside 'just war' since the time of Cicero, the movement from the idea of just war to regular war came to a head in the western tradition with the work of Grotius.

In Grotius's ambitious work, *On the Law of War and Peace* (1625), we are introduced to the distinctions between public war, private war and mixed war. The first is waged by someone who has lawful authority to wage it; the second is waged by someone who does not have such lawful authority; and a mixed war is one where one side is public and the other private. Then there is the distinction in public war between formal (complete) and less formal wars. A formal war requires, under the law of nations, that it be waged with the authority of the sovereign power of the state, that there be a declaration of war and that it be waged in accordance with the laws of war.[51] A less formal

---

[47] Neff, *War and the Law of Nations* (n 27) at 52.

[48] The modern rule on collateral damage is discussed in detail in section 7.2.

[49] Bailey, *Prohibitions and Restraints in War* (1972) at 12; These three ideas are today known as necessity, distinction and proportionality: see Ch 7. For a detailed look at this period, see Schwartz, 'Late Scholastic Just War Theory', in Lazar and Frowe (eds), *The Oxford Handbook of Ethics of War* (2018) 122–44; see also Kalmanovitz, 'Early Modern Sources of the Regular War Tradition' ibid at 145–64.

[50] Haggenmacher, 'Just War and Regular War in Sixteenth Century Spanish Doctrine', 32 *International Review of the Red Cross* (1992) 434–45, esp at 443, relying on the work of Balthazar de Ayala (1582).

[51] Grotius, *On the Law of War and Peace* (1625) tr Kelsey (Oxford: Clarendon Press, 1925) Book I, Ch 1, §2; Ch 3, §§ 1, 4, 5; Book III, Ch 3. Note, it has been pointed out that *bellum solemne* (formal war) has sometimes been mistranslated as 'public war': Onuma, 'War', in Onuma (ed), *A Normative Approach to War: Peace, War, and Justice in Hugo Grotius* (1993) 57–121 at 98 fn 138. Readers looking for a carefully abridged version of Grotius's book with helpful notes are directed to Neff (ed), *Hugo Grotius: On the Law of War and Peace* (2012).

war, Grotius says, may be waged against private persons on the authority of any public official, but he says that almost every state has laws that limit the power to wage war to the one who has the sovereign authority.[52] Grotius also provides us with a distinction between perfect and imperfect wars.[53] For Grotius, the latter involved conduct in the absence of a declaration of war between states, but authorized by the sovereign by way of reprisal against nationals of another state who had committed a wrong against the sovereign's own national. This authorization would be contained in what were called 'letters of reprisal'.[54]

The first principles of nature are said by Grotius to accord with war, and the justifiable causes for undertaking war are famously listed as including: 'defence, the obtaining of that which belongs to us or is our due, and the inflicting of punishments'.[55] He then has detailed sections on defence of property and defence of self (which relate mainly to private war and the right of individuals to defend themselves): 'if an attack by violence is made on one's person, endangering life, and no other way of escape is open, under such circumstances war is permissible, even though it involve the slaying of the assailant';[56] 'The danger, again must be immediate and imminent in point of time.'[57] When applying these principles to public war between states, he rejects the idea of a war to weaken another power that poses a future potential source of danger: 'that the possibility of being attacked confers the right to attack is abhorrent to every principle of equity'.[58] Subsequent chapters cover the acquisition of property, binding promises, contracts, oaths, treaties and punishments. Wars that are neither justifiable nor with persuasive cause are 'wars of savages'; and wars that have persuasive causes but not justifiable ones are 'wars of robbers'.[59]

---

[52] Grotius (n 51) Book I, Ch 3, § 4 para 2.

[53] Grotius (n 51) Book III, Ch 2, §2.

[54] 'What is envisaged is that a private citizen commits a wrong against a foreigner, with the citizen's ruler then committing the additional wrong of refusing to provide just redress to the foreigner. In such a case, the injured foreigner could obtain from his own sovereign a licence, known appropriately as a "letter of reprisal". With this letter, he could proceed, in the jurisdiction of the ruler who granted it, to take property from subjects of the wrong-doing sovereign for the loss he suffered.' As explained by Neff (ed), *Hugo Grotius* (n 51): *On the Law of War and Peace* at 338–39. For other uses of the expressions perfect and imperfect war, see Neff, *War and the Law of Nations* (n 27): *A General History* (2005) at 119–20, 155–56, 181 and 215.

[55] Grotius (n 51) Book II, Ch 1, §2 (Heading) tr Kelsey (Oxford: Clarendon Press, 1925) at 171.

[56] Grotius (n 51) Book II, Ch 1,, § 3 at 172.

[57] Grotius (n 51) Book II, Ch 1, § 5 at 173 (footnote omitted).

[58] Grotius (n 51) Book II, Ch 1, § 17 at 184.

[59] Grotius (n 51) Book II, Ch 22, §§2 and 3 (Headings) at 547.

These categorizations, and in particular the triptych of justifiable causes for war – defence, righting a wrong and punishment – have been carried over by other scholars as authoritative, and they remain quite influential. Just war for self-defence is referenced in some detail in the Catechism of the Catholic Church[60] and in the Basis of the Social Concept of the Russian Orthodox Church,[61] is influential in the writings of certain military leaders from the UK,[62] has been invoked by political leaders such as Barack Obama and Tony Blair,[63] and is often presented as providing the framework for discussion in the realms of contemporary military science, ethics and philosophy.[64] Politicians and others might find it useful to appeal to just war to garner support, justify departure from international law, or lay claim to territory, but we would suggest the concept of just war should be treated with caution in the 21st century.

Jürgen Habermas, the German philosopher, has rejected the approach of philosophers such as Rawls and Walzer, who present a modern take on just war theory to map out their moral blueprints for action.[65] For Habermas, 'we no longer have just or unjust wars, only legal or illegal ones, depending on whether they are justified or unjustified under international law'.[66]

[60] Catechism of the Catholic Church, paras 2302–2317, available at http://www.vatican.va/archive/ENG0015/__P81.HTM.

[61] See esp paras VIII.3 and VIII.2, available at https://mospat.ru/en/documents/social-concepts/viii/.

[62] General Sir Michael Rose offers this insight as to how Generals view the legality of war based on 'just war' thinking: 'Yet, when NATO went to war against Serbia in 1999, it not only went to war without the authorization of the United Nations, but it also did so before exhausting all other political options. At Rambouillet in January 1999, Milošević had acceded to all NATO's demands except one: that NATO troops should have full freedom of movement not only in Kosovo but throughout Serbia. In spite of going to war, NATO never succeeded in achieving this unnecessary and provocative demand. Going to war was certainly not the action of last resort and by ignoring this necessary requirement of just war, NATO allowed itself to become involved in an illegal war.' Rose, 'Meaning of War', in O'Connell (ed), *What is War? An Investigation in the Wake of 9/11* (2012) 167–76 at 170. See also Guthrie and Quinlan, *Just War: The Just War Tradition: Ethics in Modern Warfare* (2007).

[63] Obama, 'A Just and Lasting Peace' (10 December 2007, Oslo); Blair, 'Doctrine of the International Community' (24 April 1999, Chicago, IL).

[64] Reichberg, 'Historiography of Just War Theory', in Lazar and Frowe (eds), *The Oxford Handbook of Ethics of War* (2018) 58–79; Schulzke, *Just War Theory and Civilian Casualties: Protecting the Victims of War* (2017); Grayling, *War: An Enquiry* (2017) Ch 6; Rodin and Shue (eds), *Just and Unjust Warriors: The Moral and Legal Status of Soldiers* (2008).

[65] Walzer, *Just and Unjust Wars*, 5th edn (2015); Rawls, *The Law of Peoples* (1999). Habermas takes issue with the fact that neither author is prepared to see international institutions control when states can exercise what Rawls calls 'the right to war'; we might add here that Rawls (at 98), borrowing a concept from Walzer, allows for something called a 'Supreme Emergency Exception', which would permit civilians' 'being directly attacked in war'. Rawls admits that this departs from just war theory or natural law. He would not, however, allow for a derogation from the rule that prohibits the torture of prisoners of war.

[66] Habermas, *The Divided West*, ed and tr Cronin (2006) at 102.

Religious leaders and others may appeal to the rules of just war, pointing to a morality beyond international law. This could be helpful in order to limit recourse to war (for example, by demanding that there be right authority from the United Nations, or highlighting that the proposed course of action cannot qualify as a war of last resort).[67] And it could also be helpful to recall the need to restrict the conduct of the war (for example, by pointing to the need for proportionality in targeting decisions). The problem comes when just war theory is invoked by theologians and others to justify not just action in self-defence, but also war in order to right a wrong. Modern defenders of war reach back to just war theory and invoke its ideas of retribution. Nigel Biggar thinks of retribution

> merely as a hostile response to wrongdoing, which might and should be proportionate. Retribution is important because wrongdoing needs to be contradicted, fended off, and reversed. Not to contradict it and fend it off and try to reverse it is to imply that it does not matter and, therefore, that its victims do not matter. Just war is an extreme form of retributive punishment.[68]

This is problematic, as contemporary international law no longer allows for wars to punish wrongdoing. Perhaps even more problematic is that this kind of defence of this sort of just war goes on to explain that killing in such a war is therefore morally justified at the level of the individual soldier. 'Since just war is basically a punitive response to grave injustice, whether directed at one's own people or another's, it follows that the justification for killing enemy combatants is paradigmatically that they are capable of objective injustice, or presumably so'.[69] At the individual level the soldier is absolved from guilt in killing by shifting the discussion to intention. Biggar concludes that causing objective injustice is not sufficient for an enemy combatant to lose their right not to be harmed: 'What is also necessary is that those who kill them do not intend (that is maliciously want) their deaths, that they kill only as a last resort, and that they do so with proportionate reason'.[70] The manoeuvre here is to take inspiration

---

[67] Rowe gives examples of the Bishop of Oxford in the House of Lords and Mr Douglas Hogg MP in the House of Commons arguing that the conditions for just war were not satisfied in 2003 for the conflict with Iraq Rowe, *Legal Accountability and Britain's Wars 2000–2015* (2016) at 71.

[68] Biggar, *In Defence of War* (2013) at 11.

[69] Ibid at 212.

[70] Ibid at 213. The paragraph continues 'Thus will wrongdoers be rendered the respect that is due. Thus will the harshness they suffer be made kind.'

from a strain of just war theory to defend a war fought to right a wrong, and remind how compliance with just war principles can be used to re-assure soldiers that their killing is ethical.[71]

Biggar is responding to contemporary theorists who have challenged the assumptions of just war. David Rodin has questioned whether it is al-ways morally justifiable to kill based on arguments of defence of national sovereignty.[72] He suggests that soldiers fighting on the unjust side should find themselves 'held responsible for unjust killing after the conflict'.[73] Jeff McMahan, along with Rodin, has suggested that killing in war has to be justified by the threat the soldiers pose. He makes the point that if we ex-pect soldiers to disobey an order to commit war crimes, why not then ex-pect disobedience in the context of being asked to fight in an unjust war?[74] But in the end he seems to concede that one would need an independent 'source of guidance', and this would be best achieved at the international level.[75] The assumption of McMahan and others is that, to address this problem, including as it relates to conscientious objection, one would need legal rules 'that are plausibly and more determinately applicable than the present broad generalizations of international law about aggression and defense'.[76]

The next three chapters consider when the resort to force by one state against another is legal under international law. This may be considered guidance for some, and will certainly go beyond broad generalizations; how-ever, we should be careful about slipping into the trap of thinking that just be-cause the resort to the use of force or armed conflict can be considered legal as a matter of international law, it is to be considered wise or appropriate.

---

[71] For further discussion of just cause in just war theory that goes beyond what is permissible under international law, see Coates, *The Ethics of War*, 2nd edn (2016).

[72] Rodin, *War and Self-Defense* (2002).

[73] 'The Moral Inequality of Soldiers: Why *jus in bello* Asymmetry in Half Right', in Rodin and Shue (eds), *Just and Unjust Warriors: The Moral and Legal Status of Soldiers* (2008) 44–68 at 46.

[74] McMahan, *Killing in War* (2009) at 98.

[75] 'Can Soldiers be Expected to Know Whether their War is Just?', in Allhof, Evans and Henschke (eds), *Routledge Handbook of Ethics and War: Just war theory in the 21st century* (2013) 13–22 at 22.

[76] McMahan, *Killing in War* (2009) at 99.

1.3 Some Well-Known Definitions of War

A particularly influential early non-legal definition of war that I kept coming across during the writing of this book was that of Jean-Jacques Rousseau. He wrote his definition in the 1750s, and separates out 'state of war', from 'war', and 'legitimate war'.

> I say then that war between two Powers is the result of a settled intention, manifested on both sides, to destroy the enemy State, or at least to weaken it by all means at their disposal. The carrying of this intention into act is war, strictly so called; so long as it does not take shape in act, it is only a state of war.
>
> I foresee an objection. As, on my principles, the state of war is the natural relation of one Power to another, why do I say that the intention from which war results requires to be manifestly displayed? My answer is that, in the passage referred to, I was speaking of the natural state and that I am now speaking of that which is legitimate; and I shall show hereafter that, to be legitimate, war requires to be declared.[77]

Rousseau's thoughts on war are today remembered, however, more for the idea that because war is fought between states and not between individuals, we should not consider the individuals from the other side our enemies.[78] In his later publication, *The Social Contract* (1761), he stated:

> War, then, is not concerned with the relation between man and man, but between State and State, in which individuals are only enemies accidentally, not as men, nor even as citizens, but as soldiers; not as members of the fatherland, but as its defenders. Ultimately, States can only have other

---

[77] Rousseau, *A Lasting Peace Through the Federation of Europe and the State of War* [circa 1756] tr Vaughan (1917) at 121–22.

[78] The passage continues: 'If there never was and never could be such a thing as a war between individuals, who then are those between whom war takes place and who alone can truly be called enemies? I answer that they are public persons. And what is a "public person"? I answer that it is that moral creation called a Sovereign, which owes its existence to a social compact and all the decisions of which go by the name of "laws". Applying here the distinctions made above, we are entitled to say, when considering the results of war, that it is the Sovereign which causes the injury and the State which suffers it. And if war is possible only between such "moral beings" it follows that the belligerents have no quarrel with individual enemies and can wage war without destroying a single life.'

States, and not men, as enemies, since we cannot establish a real relation between things which are different in nature.[79]

This well-known passage does not necessarily reflect how international lawyers were treating the concept of War. Writing at the same time, the influential Swiss jurist Emer de Vattel confidently takes a different tack in his *Law of Nations*. He separates out public Enemies and individual enemies (capitals in the original[80]). The nation engages in open War with Enemies (capital E). He further explains, 'The Latins of Ancient Rome had a specific term (*hostis*) to designate a public Enemy, distinguished from an individual enemy (*inimicus*).'[81] He is keen to explain the difference:

> Our language uses the same term for two types of persons who really ought to be distinguished. An individual enemy is someone who seeks to do us harm and takes pleasure in it: a public Enemy makes claims against us, or rejects our own claims, and maintains its real or imagined rights through armed force.[82]

But Vattel extended the concept of enemy to those individuals on the other side in time of War. The next paragraph goes on:

> When the ruler of a State, the Sovereign, declares War on another Sovereign, we understand that the Nation has declared War on another Nation.... The two Nations are then enemies, and all the subjects of one are thence the enemies of all the subjects of the other. The practice here conforms with principles.[83]

---

[79] Book I, Ch IV, author's translation. The original reads (footnote omitted): 'La guerre n'est donc point une relation d'homme à homme, mais une relation d'Etat à Etat, dans laquelle les particuliers ne sont ennemis qu'accidentellement, non point comme hommes, ni même comme citoyens, mais comme soldats; non point comme membres de la patrie, mais comme ses défenseurs. Enfin chaque Etat ne peut avoir pour ennemis que d'autres Etats & non pas des hommes, attendu qu'entre choses de diverses natures on ne peut fixer aucun vrai rapport.'

[80] I became aware of this point thanks to Taira Nishi 'Enemy and Criminal: Analysis of the Different Structures of Legal Protection', 55 *Japanese Yearbook of International Law* (2012) 403–39 at 404–5.

[81] The capitalization of the 'Ennemi public' can be seen in the first edition of 1758. Book III, Ch V para 69. *Le droit des gens, ou Principes de la loi naturelle, appliqués à la conduite et aux affaires des Nations et des Souverains* (said to be published in London but the publisher is not clear) 2 vols. This translation and most of those in this chapter are the author's own and use the original capitalizations of words by Vattel.

[82] Ibid.

[83] Ibid at para 70.

Vattel continued this separation of the 'necessary law of nature' (also known as natural law) from the 'voluntary law of nations' (now known as positive law). The former is for the 'conscience of sovereigns', the latter represents what a nation may require of other states.[84] Vattel pointed out that just war morality could not provide the certainty that the law required. Under just war morality, only the sovereign on the side of justice had 'a right to make war', and 'he alone is empowered to attack his enemy, to deprive him of life, and wrest from him his goods and possessions'.[85] But Vattel saw that, in the absence of a judge to determine who had the right to resort to war, no one would be able to adjudicate whether a killing was justified as opposed to an act of injustice, or whether victories would be 'so many murders'.[86] Similarly, the seizing of property in war took place where there was no one to determine the justness of the cause. For Vattel, 'until some acknowledged judge (and there is none such between nations) shall have definitively pronounced concerning the justice of the cause . . . things so acquired will ever remain liable to be claimed, as property carried off by robbers'.[87] His solution: to leave the issue of the justness of the cause to the conscience of sovereigns and declare that '*regular war, as to its effects, is to be accounted just on both sides*'.[88] He then shifted the focus to the legality of the means used during the war and away from the cause of the war – which for him could not be resolved in the absence of an international judge.

This key shift, from concern over the just causes of war to a concentration on the legal effects of war, is nicely captured by Quincy Wright (who spent a lifetime thinking about war and the law):

> The conception of war underwent changes. Instead of an instrument of justice, it came to be considered an instrument of policy. Vattel, who wrote in the middle of the eighteenth century, assumed that, although princes should satisfy themselves that they had a just cause before they initiated war, no one else could pass judgment on the matter. States with no direct interest in the controversy should be neutral, although qualification of that neutrality by treaties already in existence and by consideration of national

---

[84] Vattel, *The Law of Nations: Or, Principles of the Law of Nature, Applied to the Conduct and Affairs of Nations and Sovereigns (1797)*, eds Kapossy and Whatmore (2008) Book III, Ch 12 at para 189 (p 590).

[85] Ibid at para 188 (p 589).

[86] Ibid.

[87] Ibid.

[88] Ibid; and at para 190 (p 591) (original emphasis).

interest was permitted. War was a trial by battle or duel whose results determined the merits of the controversy, not the execution of a judgment made after rational consideration of the merits, as it had been in the system of Grotius. The initiation of war became for third states, therefore a question of fact, not of law. The legal interest of such states lay not in the circumstances of the war's origin but in the legal changes its initiation brought about.[89]

So, even if the early Christian doctrine of just war starts with the idea of righting a wrong, the later idea of a voluntary law between nations, a positive international law separate from any natural law and ethics, meant that under the law of nations there were no legal conditions for resort to war.[90] By the 19th century, this law of nations becomes known as international law. Emmanuelle Jouannet explains in very clear terms:

> [F]rom the eighteenth century onwards, when international law truly emerged, the law of war was radically transformed. It was a time when the old idea of just war was definitely abandoned by jurisconsults and European powers. The recourse to war remained lawful but only for sovereign states . . . the expression 'just war' was soon to be replaced by 'formal war' or 'regulated war', fought solely between states and lawful by that fact alone.[91]

For some, resort to war from the 19th century until the end of the First World War was best explained by saying that it was neither legal nor illegal but rather extra-legal – 'just as an event occurring in nature can be extra-legal (earthquake, flood, etc)'.[92] Others, such as Jouannet, consider that there were continuing rules that determined the parameters of resort to war but, in the absence of outside control, it was simply left to the states themselves to determine whether these rules had been complied with.[93]

---

[89] Wright, *A Study of War* (abridged), 2nd edn (1964) at 367.

[90] This is not to say that away from the law textbooks there was no commitment to the imagined morality of war. Margaret MacMillan quotes a British military journal from before the First World War asking whether war is not 'the grand scheme of nature by which degenerate, weak or otherwise harmful states are eliminated from the concerted action of civilized nations, and assimilated to those who are strong, vital, and beneficial in their influences': MacMillan, *War: How Conflict Shaped Us* (2020) at 107.

[91] Jouannet, *A Short Introduction to International Law* (2014) at 13.

[92] Tucker, 'The Interpretation of War under Present International Law', 4 *ICLQ* (1951) 11–38 at 13.

[93] See Jouannet, *The Liberal-Welfarist Law of Nations* (2012) at 41–2 and 129–31, where she explains (at 130) that one should not infer 'that states had the right to trigger war at any time. Nothing could have been more mistaken. In classical international law – as in the modern law

Moreover, a distinction in the 19th century was indeed drawn in some quarters, particularly in Colonial Great Britain, between 'small wars' and wars between regular troops. The widely studied manual on the topic explained that a small war 'comprises the expeditions against savages and semi-civilised races by disciplined soldiers, campaigns to suppress rebellious and guerrilla warfare in all parts of the world where organized armies are struggling against opponents who will not meet them in the open field'.[94] Such small wars were divided into three classes: 'campaigns of conquest or annexation, campaigns for the suppression of insurrections or lawlessness or for the settlement of conquered or annexed territory, and campaigns to wipe out an insult, to avenge a wrong, or to overthrow a dangerous enemy'.[95]

Different tactics were counselled depending on the objective, the type of armaments used by the opposition and the terrain. However, as the defeat of the hostile army was not the main objective – as it was with regular warfare – a different logic applied. So, for example, 'Expeditions to put down revolt are not put in motion merely to bring about a cessation of hostility, their objective is to ensure a lasting peace. Therefore in choosing the objective the overawing and not the exasperation of the enemy is the aim to keep in view'.[96] While some of the same rules might have been considered applicable, the manual simply states that instead of defeating a regular army, 'operations are sometimes limited to committing havoc which the laws of regular warfare do not sanction'.[97]

The idea that small wars fought against irregular forces demand different tactics, even different rules, finds its modern mirror in the discussion over what is today sometimes termed 'asymmetric warfare',[98] to which we will

---

of nations – the right to resort to war was no more the right to do just anything than sovereignty itself was absolute. On the eve of the First World War it was even very strictly bounded. The problem at the time was therefore not the absence of legal limits on the right to resort to war, but rather the lack of *control* over states' exercise of their option of subjectively interpreting the situation and therefore deciding to resort to war.'

[94] Callwell (Maj), *Small Wars: Their Principles and Practice* (1899) at 1.

[95] Ibid at 5–6.

[96] Ibid at 21.

[97] Ibid. For a discussion on the extent to which the laws of war were not considered to apply in such contexts, see Mégret, 'From "Savages" to "Unlawful Combatants": A Postcolonial Look at International Humanitarian Law's "Other"', in Orford (ed), *International Law and its Others* (2006) 265–317.

[98] One aspect that troubles ethicists is that a technologically superior party, using unmanned drones, is taking no risks and there is no fair fight in such an asymmetric war; see, for an introduction, Galliott and Galliott, 'Asymmetry in Modern Combat: Explaining the Inadequacy of *Jus ad bellum* and *Jus in bello*', in Galliott (ed), *Force Short of War in Modern Conflict* (2019) 13–35; for further meanings of asymmetric warfare, see section 1.6 below.

return later. Regular war, as opposed to these so-called 'small wars' in the colonies, meant recognized nation states with regular armies resolving a dispute through force and often invoking the legal institution of a 'State of War'.

While some rules for the *conduct* of war in the just war tradition find some modern equivalence in the contemporary humanitarian law of armed conflict,[99] the older ideas of *just cause* for just war, and the winnings that flowed from victory in war, can no longer find any reflection in contemporary law. First, war was considered in the past as a way to ensure that wrongs were righted, some scholars restricting this to the right of an injured party to go to war to punish the wrongdoer, others seeing this resort to war more as a way of ensuring order and harmony in a world with no superior authority. Neither justification applies in the modern world. The idea that it was permitted to go to War to resolve legal disputes, or as part of a national policy, was eventually abandoned with the Peace Pact of Paris in 1928. Furthermore, in 1945, resort to any use of force by one state against another was outlawed in the UN Charter, with exceptions for self-defence and force authorized by the United Nations. Today no state can rely on a breach of international law to justify resorting to war.

Second, war (or the laws of war[100]) can no longer give the victor new rights to territory,[101] to enslave and kill the defeated enemy, to acquire all enemy

---

[99] As Haggenmacher explains, the law on the conduct of war had a separate life during this period. 'Although the just war tradition was more conspicuous in the lofty sphere of moral philosophy, owing to the prestige enjoyed by theology as the unqualified queen of sciences, the lawyers' regular war tradition was doubtless more effective on the ground, as it was in tune with the practice of a whole class of persons for whom war represented a way of living and a means of living. It bore various names such as the law of arms (*ius armorum*) or the law or usage of war (*ius belli, usus belli*). Its chief function was to settle the numerous disputes arising from warfare as to booty, ransom and similar questions. It mainly consisted of customary rules, feudal law, canon law, and not least Roman law. It was indeed Roman law which formed its backbone by stating equal rights of war for both belligerents, provided these were proper "enemies", ie independent powers.' Haggenmacher, 'On the Doctrinal Origins of *Ius in Bello*: From Rights of War to the Laws of War', in Maruhn and Steiger (eds), *Universality and Continuity in International Law* (2011) 325–58 at 332.

[100] As highlighted by Haggenmacher the origins of the legal concept of regular war had its focus on the equality of the parties. The 'effects of war had nothing to do with *ius in bello* in the modern sense of a humanitarian code of conduct. They were *iura belli* in the old way, allowing each party to make whatever gains it could in the form of booty or ransom or territorial conquest. If anything, those rights of war should be named *ius ex belli*. War in this perspective, apart from its political finalities, appeared as a kind of legal mechanism for the transfer of property.' Ibid at 333-4; for the full explanation see Haggenmacher, *Grotius et la doctrine de la guerre juste* (1983) Ch VIII.

[101] The Prime Minister of Israel, Benjamin Netanyahu, recently claimed 'Israel won the Golan Heights in a just war of self-defense': Press conference, Washington, 25 March 2019. This idea and the ideas later expressed to journalists are invalid as a matter of contemporary international law. Netanyahu is quoted as later saying that 'There is a very important principle in international life . . . When you start wars of aggression, you lose territory, do not come and claim it afterwards.

property or the chance to coerce new treaties from the vanquished. What remains of the legal institution of war is radically changed.

Let us turn now to contemporary international law to see what is left of the 'status of War in the legal sense' and contrast this with 'war in the material sense'.[102] In order to facilitate my explanation I shall continue (wherever possible) to use a capital 'W' to signify that we are discussing War in this legal sense, and a small 'w' for war where we are simply describing an armed conflict. At the end of this section I will offer a definition of what the conditions are for the existence today of a War in the legal sense.

Part of the reason that the legal category of war was so important in the past was that, once states went to war, this had some very concrete legal consequences for them and for third states. In antiquity it was fairly clear that war entitled one to take prisoners for ransom and as slaves, enemy property could be destroyed or seized, and in some periods the loser even had to pay for the cost of the winner's war expenses.

Later, in the 18th century, with the development of the international law rules on neutrality, states that were not parties to the War (as understood as a State of War in international law) would take on the rights and duties of Neutral states, and the states at War acquired 'Belligerent Rights' and duties to respect the rights of Neutral states.[103] The law of naval warfare developed complex rules for dealing with 'contraband of War' aboard neutral ships, and for seizing enemy merchant ships and enemy cargo. When such ships or their cargoes were seized, issues of title and compensation were dealt with in special courts under the 'Law of Prize'. As the Law of Prize only applied to ships and goods seized in War, the rules covering the beginning and end of Wartime, or the existence of a State of War, became essential to the parties contesting these claims. We will consider what are left of these Belligerent Rights in naval warfare later;[104] the point here is that whether something was

It belongs to us . . . . Everyone says you can't hold an occupied territory, but this proves you can. If occupied in defensive war, then it's ours.' Halbfinger and Kershner, 'Netanyahu Says Golan Heights Move "Proves You Can" Keep Occupied Territory', *New York Times* (26 March 2019). The actual international law is discussed in section 3.6 below.

[102] This distinction has a long pedigree – see, eg, Kotzsch, *The Concept of War in Contemporary History and International Law* (1956) 54ff; for a continuing use, see Dinstein, *War, Aggression and Self-Defence*, 6th edn (2017) at 17: 'War is a hostile interaction between two or more States, either in a material sense or in a purely technical sense. War in the purely technical sense is a formal status produced by a declaration of war. War in the material sense is generated by actual use of armed force, which is comprehensive on the part of at least one Belligerent Party.'

[103] I am using a capital N here to emphasize that the rights and obligations flow from the formal State of War between the Belligerent states at War, see further section 2.3.

[104] See Ch 8.

a War or not mattered for states and their nationals, and perhaps, just as importantly, for other non-belligerent or Neutral states and their nationals.[105] The sums of money involved were not trivial. We are not here dealing with an undelivered table or an unpaid life insurance payment. International trade depended on merchant shipping. A State of War would cripple businesses and economies as cargoes were blockaded, captured, diverted or left to perish through delays.

In the 19th century one can find disputes, such as the litigation that ended in the US Supreme Court in the *Prize Cases*,[106] where the rights and duties of the parties, and the property of their nationals, might be determined by the existence or not of a State of War. Engaging in Blockade, or a clear Declaration of War by one side or the other, would be enough to confirm a State of War, with the starting date perhaps being backdated to the initial act of War. In this period scholars speak of War as an 'institution of international law'. Let me illustrate by looking at the Pastry War dispute.

The 'Pastry War', or *Guerre des Pâtisseries*, owes its name to a complaint in 1832 by a French pastry chef that his shop on the outskirts of Mexico City had been looted by Mexican officers during civil disturbances. This complaint to the French King was amalgamated with other claims concerning the mistreatment of French nationals in Mexico, and France demanded from Mexico the sum of 600,000 Pesos.[107] France's demands were backed with the threat of War. The demands went unmet and the French first blockaded the ports, then opened fire on Fort de Saint-Jean-d'Ulloa and captured the Mexican fleet of warships anchored in front of the Fort. Mexico declared War, and engaged in the mass expulsion of French citizens living in Mexico. A peace treaty was negotiated within a month, and two issues were submitted to international arbitration. First, whether the warships and other ships captured by the French during the Blockade and after the Declaration of War should be returned to

---

[105] Moving from a state of war to a state of peace transformed illegal acts into acts that could no longer give rise to claims under international law. As Wright explains: 'An act of war is an invasion of territory or an attack on public forces and so normally illegal. Such an act if not followed by war gives grounds for a claim which can be legally avoided only by proof of some special treaty or necessity justifying the act. But if the act inaugurates war or is preceded by a declaration of war, there is no basis for a claim, in the absence of express treaty, unless the act was in violation of the law of war. The incidence of an act or declaration converting the state of peace into a state of war establishes a division in time before which acts of war are illegal and after which they are legal between belligerents if within the law of war.' 'Changes in the Conception of War', 18 *AJIL* (1924) 755–67 at 756–57(fn omitted).

[106] See US Supreme Court, *Prize Cases*, 67 US (1862) 635, discussed in section 6.4.

[107] A considerable sum at the time, the pastry shop itself being estimated at less than 1,000 Pesos.

Mexico or indemnified. Second, whether France should be indemnified for the damage suffered by French citizens as a result of the expulsion order.[108] The Arbitrator, Queen Victoria of the United Kingdom, determined that neither side should be indemnified as the acts on both sides were justified by the State of War that existed between them.[109]

Resorting to War relieved states from obligations they would normally owe to other states. Being at War meant that under international law, warring parties could, for example, keep enemy ships seized from the other side. A definition of War was needed for the purposes of knowing whether states were in a State of War, but not at that time for prohibiting recourse to War.

There are more or less well-known definitions of war that reflect their times or context. Oppenheim's definition, first introduced in 1906, remains widely referenced: 'War is a contention between two or more States through their armed forces, for the purpose of overpowering each other and imposing such conditions of peace as the victor pleases.'[110] When Oppenheim was first writing, the idea was common that war brings with it an apparent inherent justification for the violence used.[111] Oppenheim's treatise, in the 1952 version, continues later to explain the purpose of war, which is imposing a 'defeat which compels the vanquished to comply with any demand'.[112] The book continues 'Victory is necessary in order to overpower the enemy; and it is this necessity which has been invoked as justifying all the horrors of war, the sacrifice of human life, and the destruction of property and devastation of territory.'[113]

I will be arguing this definition and logic can no longer stand. By the end of this book I hope to have shown that all action in war (in either the technical or the non-technical sense) has to be justified under a specific rule, and that, on its own, the quest for victory in war can no longer justify anything.

---

[108] See Lapradelle and Politis, *Recueil des Arbitrages Internationaux*, vol 1: *(1798–1855)* (1905) 545–79 at 554.

[109] Ibid at 558–59, *France v Mexico*, 1 August 1844: 'Nous sommes d'avis que ni les sujets français, les Mexicains, n'ont droit à la moindre indemnité, les actes des deux pays se trouvant justifiés par l'état de guerre qui existait entre eux.'

[110] Lauterpacht (ed), *Oppenheim's International Law: a Treatise (Disputes, War and Neutrality)*, 7th edn (1952), vol II at 202. There may be indirect consequences in national law where a state of War is a prerequisite under national law for triggering certain laws.

[111] In an earlier edition of this treatise one also finds the sentence 'As war is a struggle for existence between States, no amount of individual suffering and misery can be regarded; the national existence and independence of the struggling State is a higher consideration than any individual well-being.' Oppenheim, *International Law: A Treatise* (1906) at 64–65, and .

[112] Lauterpacht (ed) (n 110) at 208; Oppenehim's first edition states (at 73) 'the purpose of war is always the same . . . namely, the overpowering and utter defeat of the opponent'.

[113] Lauterpacht (ed) (n 110) at 209.

It is only in the 20th century that we start to find limits on the resort to force for the settlement of grievances. In 1907, Hague Convention II prohibited states from resorting to force to recover debts on behalf of their nationals.[114] Following the First World War, the League of Nations Covenant (1919) sought further to limit recourse to War. Members of the League were obliged first to seek a peaceful settlement of their dispute before engaging in War. But ambiguity swirled around whether states could avoid their conflict's being categorized as a War by denying any *intention* to be *at War*.

While the Covenant sought to regulate the procedure for going to War,[115] the member states sought, nevertheless, during the League of Nations period to avoid the new rules by defining their actions as 'measures short of War' (however warlike they might appear to be). The focus in the inter-war years was often on the definition of War, because the sanctions regime in the Covenant was automatically addressed to the state that had resorted to War in breach of the procedures in the Covenant.[116] This might have been a time to define exactly what was meant by War in international law. The League of Nations organs, however, left many questions unanswered,[117] even when faced with direct demands for clarification, as with the follow-up to the bombardment of occupation of Corfu by Italy in 1923.[118] Commentators such as Eagleton insightfully argued at the time that the point of the League was to ensure peace by preventing the use of force by one state against another, and therefore no useful purpose would have been served by separating out the concept of War from other forms of inter-state violence. Moreover the League was to ensure peace through organized military sanctions against the offender. If all use of force were to be defined as War, he argued, the League would itself be accused of engaging in War – the very thing it was supposed to be preventing! He suggested, therefore, 'it is desirable to eliminate the

---

[114] See Art 1: 'The Contracting Powers agree not to have recourse to armed force for the recovery of contract debts claimed from the Government of one country by the Government of another country as being due to its nationals. This undertaking is, however, not applicable when the debtor State refuses or neglects to reply to an offer of arbitration, or, after accepting the offer, prevents any compromis from being agreed on, or, after the arbitration, fails to submit to the award.'

[115] League of Nations Covenant Arts 10–16.

[116] See Art 16 of the Covenant.

[117] For references to the doctrinal debates over whether the Covenant prohibited measures short of War, see Kolb, 'Article 15' in Kolb (ed), *Commentaire sur le pacte de la Société des Nations* (2015) 599–692 esp at 611–16.

[118] See section 3.3 below.

word [war], with all its unpleasant psychology, from the vocabulary of international affairs'.[119]

1.4 The Significance Today of a State of War in the International Legal Sense

By 1928, as we shall see when we cover the Kellogg-Briand Pact (also known
as the Paris Peace Pact), key states had agreed to 'condemn recourse to war
for the solution of international controversies, and renounce it, as an instrument of national policy in their relations with one another'.[120] Resorting to
War was now outlawed, at least for those states that remained in the Peace
Pact. And by 1945, with the adoption of the UN Charter, all forms of non-
defensive force against another state were outlawed, and the legal institution
of War seemed to be coming to an end. If all forms of the use of force against
another state were outlawed, the distinction between force short of War and
actual War seemed to lose its pertinence.

At the same time it became even clearer, with the adoption of the 1949
Geneva Conventions, that one should not be able to avoid the laws for the
conduct of war by claiming there was no War. These laws, designed for the
protection of victims of war, have to apply to armed conflicts, irrespective
of whether the conflict constitutes a formally declared War between states.
War crimes must still be prosecuted even in the absence of a formal War; it
is enough that there is a connection to an armed conflict. Today the need to
determine whether or not there is a War, as such, seems to many observers
to have evaporated. But I would suggest the distinction between 'War' in the
technical sense and 'war' in the material sense remains important. Let me
first outline how we can identify a State of War in the legal technical sense,
before setting out the areas where this remains relevant.

McNair's definition remains a good starting point:

---

[119] Eagleton, 'The Attempt to Define War', 15 *International Conciliation* (March 1932) 237–87
at 286. Arguably, Art 16 of the Covenant avoids this result by separating out 'resort to war' and
the consequence that this be deemed 'an act of war against all other Members of the League'. See
also Eagleton, 'Acts of War', 35 *AJIL* 2 (1941) 321–26, where he concludes (at 325) that the expression 'act of war' 'has no technical significance in international law'. He showed how 'act of
war' was used for acts of force short of legal War, acts performed after the War had started, and to
refer to acts that could be legitimate only under the status of War.

[120] Art 1.

A state of war arises in International Law (a) at the moment, if any, speci-fied in a declaration of war; or (b) if none is specified, then immediately upon the communication of a declaration of war; or (c) upon the commis-sion of an act of force, under the authority of a State, which is done *animo belligerendi*, or which, being done *sine animo belligerendi* but by way of re-prisals or intervention, the other State elects to regard as creating a state of war, either by repelling force by force or in some other way: retroactive effect being given to this election, so that the state of war arises on the com-mission of the first act of force.[121]

We could synthesize these ideas for today: a State of War in International Law means that *a state has either declared War on another state, or that the in-tention of one or more of the states means that a State of War is being asserted and exists as a matter of international law*.[122]

I would suggest there are at least four areas where a State of War remains relevant: either in the form of a declared War, or because a state asserts that a State of War exists as a matter of international law.

First, national law may require a formal State of War for the prosecution of certain crimes, such as treason or trading with the enemy.[123]

Second, even in the absence of fighting or violence, the Geneva Conventions of 1949 and their First and Third Additional Protocols apply to all cases of declared War.[124] A number of other treaties are dependent on these treaties, or repeat the declared War formula, for determining their ap-plication.[125] Therefore, we may need to understand what constitutes a formal Declaration of War in this context. In brief, we can state that a 'declared War'

---

[121] McNair, 'The Legal Meaning of War, and the Relation of War to Reprisals', 11 *Transactions of the Grotius Society* (1925) 29–51 at 45.

[122] This seems not dissimilar in substance to the definition offered by Verri: 'Not all violent actions between States are wars. A distinction is made between (a) events involving the use of armed force but taking forms that do not interrupt the state of peace because any desire to end that state is lacking, and (b) the typical forms of war, ie, war in its violent form characterized by the will to make war and the consequences of that will de facto or by a formal declaration, viz, the state of war with all its legal consequences including application of the law of armed conflict.' ' "War" should not be confused with hostilities', *Dictionary of the International Law of Armed Conflict* (1992) at 123.

[123] We will deal with this law in Ch 5.

[124] ICRC, *Commentary on the First Geneva Convention*, 2nd edn (2016) at paras 200–209.

[125] So, for example, a declaration of war would trigger the applicability of the Convention on Prohibitions or Restrictions on the Use of Certain Conventional Weapons Which May be Deemed to be Excessively Injurious or to Have Indiscriminate Effects (1980) and its annexes. See also the Hague Convention for the Protection of Cultural Property in the Event of Armed Conflict (1954) Art 18.

means a formal unilateral Declaration has been issued by the appropriate authority of a state declaring War on another state. There is no particular form that such a Declaration of War need take, but political statements will not today be assumed to be the equivalent of a Declaration of War.[126]

Third, the assumption still operates for several states, and for some authors, that a formal State of War is needed for the full scope of the obligations related to neutrality[127] and institutions of the State of War such as Blockade, the right to search neutral ships and seize contraband of war, and the right to acquire rights over this and other property through the institution of Prize Law administered through Prize Courts.[128]

Fourth, some treaties (beyond the laws of armed conflict) include provisions that refer to war in ways that indicate something other than armed conflict more generally. Human rights treaties, on the abolition of the death penalty, allow for states to make provisions in their laws that foresee the death penalty 'in respect of acts committed in time of war or of imminent threat of war'.[129] Here it is said that the term 'war' seems to refer to a formal State of War. The late Professor Sir Nigel Rodley noted, with regard to the 6th Protocol to the European Convention (1980), that 'the formula refers to "war" rather than "armed conflict"'.[130] For him, '"War" is a legal status,

---

[126] See *Eritrea/Ethiopia Arbitration* 26 RIAA, 19 December 2005, Partial Award, *Jus Ad Bellum – Ethiopia's Claims 1–8*, at para 17, discussed in section 6.1 below. The same Arbitration Commission also chose, in the context of determining which principles to apply in awarding damages, to distinguish its finding that Eritrea had violated Art 2(4) of the UN Charter and the rules prohibiting the use of force, and yet it did not find 'that Eritrea had waged an aggressive war': Decision No 7, 27 July 2007, para 32; an aggressive war would presumably have led to findings of more extensive financial responsibility: see para 5, and para 312 of the *Final Award: Ethiopia's Damages Claims*, 17 August, 2009, where Eritrea's violation of the *jus ad bellum* is contrasted with the Second World War, the invasion of South Korea, and Iraq's invasion and occupation of Kuwait. So here we find a distinction being drawn between an armed conflict and an aggressive war.

[127] See Heintschel von Heinegg, with regard to the scope on the law on neutrality: 'While some states continue to regard a declaration of war as a precondition, others base their assessment on the extent and intensity of the armed conflict.' 'Maritime Warfare', in Clapham and Gaeta (eds), *The Oxford Handbook of International Law in Armed Conflict* (2014) 145–81 at 171. See also Bothe, 'The Law of Neutrality', in Fleck (ed), *The Handbook of International Humanitarian Law*, 2nd edn (2007) 573–604 at 578–79, para 1106; compare Greenwood, 'Scope of Application of Humanitarian Law', ibid 39–63 at 54, para 20; Greenwood, 'Comments', in Dekker and Post (eds), *The Gulf War of 1980–1988* (1992) 212–16 at 212–13; and Bothe, 'Neutrality at Sea', ibid at 205–09.

[128] Discussed in detail in Ch 8.

[129] Protocol No 6 to the European Convention on Human Rights (1980) Art 2; see also Second Optional Protocol to the International Covenant on Civil and Political Rights (1989) Art 2; Protocol to the American Convention on Human Rights to Abolish the Death Penalty (1990) Art 2.

[130] Rodley with Pollard, *The Treatment of Prisoners under International Law*, 3rd edn (2009) at 292.

normally declared by at least one of the parties, conferring rights and duties both upon the belligerents and upon third parties in their relations with the belligerents.' He concluded, after referencing the difference between declared War and armed conflicts in Common Article 2 to the Geneva Conventions, that it is 'reasonable to assume that "war" in the Protocol is intended to exclude other armed conflicts'. He also concluded that the word 'war' here would preclude a declared civil war, even one giving rise to Belligerent Rights under international law. The reasoning is worth citing here:

> In practice, the word 'war' is so pervasively used in the sense of 'international armed hostilities' that it would be perverse not to refer specifically to civil war if it had been intended to include this within the article 2 exception. Moreover, the effect of concluding that 'war' includes 'civil war' would be that 'imminent threat of war' includes 'imminent threat of civil war'. This would mean that states could bring within the exception so great a range of circumstances as radically to vitiate the basic abolitionist rule laid down in article 1.[131]

Ten years later, the 2nd Optional Protocol to the International Covenant on Civil and Political Rights, aiming at the abolition of the death penalty (1989) allowed for reservations, providing 'for the application of the death penalty in time of war pursuant to a conviction for a most serious crime of a military nature committed during wartime'. Rodley, who would have been very involved at all stages of drafting both these treaties, concluded again 'that the war in question must be a formally declared war between states, not a civil war. Such interstate wars are now in fact the rare exception rather than the rule; however many states have left unabrogated laws that entered their statute books when such wars were more prevalent.'[132] Another expert on the death penalty, Schabas, concludes that 'The argument that "state of war" should be construed narrowly, applying only to international armed conflict declared by at least one of the belligerents, is therefore a persuasive one.'[133]

We might add that this last treaty, and the Inter-American Protocol to the American Convention on Human Rights to Abolish the Death Penalty (1990), both state that the state party has to notify the depository of the

---

[131] Ibid.

[132] Ibid at 288.

[133] Schabas, *UN Covenant on Civil and Political Rights: Nowak's CCPR Commentary*, 3rd edn (2019) at 1089.

beginning or end of any 'state of war'. This requirement further suggests that it is not the fact of an impending or actual armed conflict that allows for reservations and the use of the death penalty, but rather the drafter's concern to allow states to join the treaty while leaving intact existing national legislation providing for 'wartime' executions. In this way a state could ratify the Protocol on abolition of the death penalty, while admitting that capital punishment remained on the books for a 'most serious crime of a military nature' in the context of the prospect of a War in the sense of a legal State of War.

A perusal of the reservations formulated by states reinforces this conclusion. While states such as Malta and Spain withdrew their reservations, which related to 'times of war', the reservation formulated by El Salvador references its Constitution, which refers to the use of the death penalty prescribed by military law during a state of international War: 'durante el estado de Guerra internacional'.[134] The Brazilian Constitution similarly states 'there shall be no punishment . . . of death, save in case of declared war'.[135]

1.5 The Meaning of the Word 'War' in a Selection of Other Treaties

Another human rights treaty, the 1966 Civil and Political Rights Covenant, states 'Any propaganda for war shall be prohibited by law.' One might assume that the word 'war' here was to be interpreted widely, covering all sorts of large-scale armed conflict. But such an interpretation would mean that states parties were expected to prohibit support for the use of force authorized by the UN Security Council, or national action taken in the legitimate exercise of self-defence.

In fact, the UN Human Rights Committee has opined that this prohibition on 'propaganda for war' only covers propaganda for 'an act of aggression or breach of the peace contrary to the Charter of the United Nations', and therefore the Civil and Political Rights Covenant does not 'prohibit advocacy of the sovereign right of self-defence or the right of peoples to self-determination and independence in accordance with the Charter of the United Nations'.[136] Propaganda for defensive war, an armed conflict authorized by the UN

---

[134] Art 27.

[135] Art 5 (XLVII) (a). War can only be declared by the President; see Art 83 (XIX).

[136] General Comment 11, 1983, para 2. See also Schabas, *U.N. Covenant* (n 133) 576–83 and 590–91.

Security Council, or for a war of national liberation would not apparently be prohibited by this provision, in which war is construed very narrowly. Essentially, in this treaty, 'propaganda for war' means propaganda for the side waging an illegal international armed conflict. According to the commentary, 'internal "civil wars" were not meant to fall under its scope of application, so long as they do not develop into international conflict'.[137] And 'what is decisive is that the propaganda aims at creating or reinforcing the willingness to conduct a war of aggression'.[138]

Turning to a last example, the European Convention on Human Rights (1950) refers not only to derogations in 'time of war or other public emergency',[139] but also, rather ambiguously, to a valid derogation to the right to life being permitted for 'lawful acts of war'.[140] Some commentators here read 'war' in this last phrase in a wider sense, beyond War in the technical sense, as covering armed conflicts where the laws of war apply.[141] Others restrict 'war' here to inter-state conflict of a certain intensity (war in the material sense),[142] or simply refer to international armed conflicts.[143] An examination of the records of the drafting reveals little.[144]

In his *Commentary*, Schabas, while he considers it is possible that 'lawful acts of war' refers to any acts lawful under the law of armed conflict, has suggested that the context of the drafting after the Second World War means that

---

[137] Schabas, *U.N. Covenant* (n 133) ibid at 581.

[138] Ibid at 582.

[139] Directorate of the Jurisconsulte of the Council of Europe, 'Guide on Article 15 of the European Convention on Human Rights' (2020) with regard to Article 15(1) of the European Convention, at para 7: 'The Court has not been required to interpret the meaning of "war" in Article 15 § 1; in any case, any substantial violence or unrest short of war is likely to fall within the scope of the second limb of Article 15 § 1, a "public emergency threatening the life of the nation".'

[140] Art 15(2) ECHR.

[141] Landais and Bass, 'Reconciling the Rules of International Humanitarian Law with the Rules of European Human Rights Law', 97 *IRRC* 900 (2015) 1295–311 at 1299. Note also the Document produced by the Directorate of the Jurisconsulte of the Council of Europe (2018) (n 139) makes no comment on the meaning of 'lawful acts of war'.

[142] Pettiti, Decaux and Imbert (eds), *La Convention européenne des droits de l'homme: commentaire article par article*, 2nd edn (1999) at 497.

[143] Doswald-Beck, 'The Right to Life in Armed Conflict: Does International Humanitarian Law Provide All the Answers?', 88 *IRRC* (2006) 881–904 at 883, who considers that the word 'war' in this context limits such a derogation to international armed conflicts, insurgencies being covered elsewhere in Art 2 ECHR.

[144] It was suggested at one point that that 'in time of war', a state could not be strictly bound by 'obligations assumed under a convention' (Information Note dated 22 May 1956, DH (56)4 at para 37); and it was also suggested that a reference to the UN Charter would clarify that 'war was recognised only in cases of self-defence or for other reasons consonant with the Charter' (ibid at para 43).

a valid derogation could require that the resort to armed conflict by one state against another be lawful at the outset:

> [T]o avail of the 'lawful acts of war' exception to killing in the course of armed conflict, the use of force itself must be consistent with international law. In other words, a declaration of derogation from the right to life by a State with respect to the use of force against another State that is not in the exercise of the inherent right of self-defence or authorized by the Security Council would be ineffective.[145]

So even within human rights treaty law, 'war' may mean very different things. First, when it comes to exceptions allowing for the death penalty, the law may demand a declared formal State of War. Second, when outlawing propaganda for war, the 1966 Covenant may be referring only to supporting the aggressor in a war of aggression (declared or not), or an illegal resort to international armed conflict. Third, when referring to lawful acts of war, there may be an assumption that one is referring to a state's respecting the prohibition on the use of force in the UN Charter. This multiplicity of meanings is inconvenient but not really incoherent. Sometimes states want to allow for certain action only in times of War in the technical sense. At other times, things might be prohibited for a wider range of armed conflicts. The key is to understand that we have moved on from a situation when every type of war was perceived by some as permitting every type of behaviour.

One last example from the field of international trade law highlights how difficult it is for an international body to determine whether or not one is in the presence of a war. In a dispute between Russia and Ukraine, the word 'war' has recently been interpreted widely to include *all forms of armed conflict*. The issue turned on an interpretation of a clause in the General Agreement on Tariffs and Trade (1994) that allows a contracting party to take any action it considers necessary for the protection of its essential security interests, 'taken in time of war or other emergency in international relations'.[146]

---

[145] Schabas, *The European Convention on Human Rights: A Commentary* (2015) at 602, he also covers the possibility of considering 'lawful acts of war' from the perspective of the international law covering the conduct of hostilities and *jus in bello* more generally. See also Milanovic, 'The Lost Origins of *Lex Specialis*: Rethinking the Relationship between Human Rights and International Humanitarian Law', in Ohlin (ed), *Theoretical Boundaries of Armed Conflict and Human Rights* (2016) 78–117.

[146] GATT Art XXI(b)(iii).

The dispute turned in part on whether the World Trade Organization (WTO) Panel could determine whether or not there was 'a time of war or other emergency in international relations'. Russia had argued that

> the Panel, and the WTO more generally, 'being trade mechanisms are not in a position to determine whether sovereign states are at war. Similar logic applies to "other emergency in international relations". Only sovereign states may declare the status of their relations with other sovereign states.'[147]

The Panel considered the use of the word 'war' in its context in the treaty meant it was an objective fact and not a subjective state of affairs or something that was self-judging:

> [A]s for the circumstances referred to in subparagraph (iii), the existence of a war, as one characteristic example of a larger category of 'emergency in international relations', is clearly capable of objective determination. Although the confines of an 'emergency in international relations' are less clear than those of the matters addressed in subparagraphs (i) and (ii), and of 'war' under subparagraph (iii), it is clear that an 'emergency in international relations' can only be understood, in the context of the other matters addressed in the subparagraphs, as belonging to the same category of objective facts that are amenable to objective determination.
>
> The use of the conjunction 'or' with the adjective 'other' in 'war *or other* emergency in international relations' in subparagraph (iii) indicates that war is one example of the larger category of 'emergency in international relations'. War refers to armed conflict. Armed conflict may occur between states (international armed conflict), or between governmental forces and private armed groups, or between such groups within the same state (non-international armed conflict).[148]

Bearing in mind these various contexts and the shifting meanings of the word 'war' in treaties, contracts and national law, we cannot therefore always simply assimilate war with armed conflict,[149] or even international armed conflict. We can only offer the interim working explanation: the word 'war'

---

[147] Russia – Measures Concerning Traffic in Transit Report of the Panel, WT/DS512/R, 5 April 2019, fn 67.

[148] Ibid at paras 7.71–7.72.

[149] This distinction is highlighted in Starke's manual as 'war in the traditional sense' and 'non-war armed conflicts'; see Chs 18 and 19 of Shearer, *Starke's International Law*, 11th edn (1994).

has to be interpreted in its context. Or, in the words of Pierre Lalive's famous Arbitral Award, ' "war" may have various meanings for different purposes'.[150]

1.6 Talking about War away from the World of Law

In closing this chapter on the meaning of war, let us consider other ways of discussing what constitutes war away from the legal context. First, to add to our confusion, political scientists and historians have their own definitions of what a war is, and these are commonly reproduced and cited in writing across all disciplines. Particularly influential in political science is the Correlates of War Project, which facilitates the use of quantitative data and which analyses 'wars', defined as 1,000 battle-related deaths per year.[151] Similarly the Uppsala Conflict Data Program covers conflicts with at least 25 deaths a year and reserves the term 'war' for conflicts with 1,000 deaths in a calendar year.[152]

Strachan, as a historian, answers the question 'what is war?' as follows:

> First, it involves the use of force. . . . [Although] a state of war can exist between two opponents without there being any active fighting. . . . Second, war rests on contention. War is not a one-sided activity, but assumes resistance. . . . Third, a war assumes a degree of intensity and duration to the fighting. . . . Fourth, those who fight do so not in a private capacity, but

---

[150] *Dalmia Cement Ltd v National Bank of Pakistan*, (1976) 67 ILR 611 at 627.

[151] The Correlates of War Project has various categories of war and explains the calculation of battlefield deaths as follows: 'The current requirement for all categories of wars is for 1,000 battle-related deaths per year (twelve-month period beginning with the start date of the war) among all the qualified war participants. Battle-deaths include not only those armed personnel killed in combat but also those who subsequently died from combat wounds or from diseases contracted in the war theater. In determining if the war battle-related death threshold has been reached, civilian fatalities are excluded regardless of which type of war is under consideration.' Meredith Reid Sarkees, 'The COW Typology of War: Defining and Categorizing Wars (Version 4 of the Data)', available at http://www.correlatesofwar.org/data-sets/COW-war/cow-war-list/at_download/file.

[152] The Uppsala Conflict Data separates out state-based conflict from non-state conflicts and one-sided violence, see further at http://ucdp.uu.se/. The term 'war' distinguishes state-based conflicts (at least one government involved) with more than 1,000 battle-related deaths in one calendar year from 'minor' state-based conflicts with between 25 and 1,000 battle-related deaths in one calendar year. There is a related debate over whether or not the data allow one to conclude that violence and war are declining. Obviously this depends on how one quantifies the suffering associated with war. See, for part of the argument, John Gray, 'Steven Pinker is Wrong about Violence and War', *Guardian* (13 March 2015); Pinker, *The Better Angels of Our Nature: Why Violence Has Declined* (2011); Krause, 'From Armed Conflict to Political Violence: Mapping and Explaining Conflict Trends', 145 *Daedalus* (2016) 113–26.

as public servants. . . . Fifth, war is not fighting for its own sake: it has an aim.[153]

He admits that Clausewitz would be comfortable with this, but that the criteria fail 'to embrace many conflicts we might wish to see as wars'.[154]

Turning to moral philosophy, some ethicists may be simply content to assume that 'war involves physical force or other means (such as germ warfare, mind control, etc) to control or destroy an opponent, offensively or defensively, on a large scale'.[155] Or even more succinctly, war 'means large-scale armed conflicts between organised groups'[156].

The advent of cyberwarfare has given rise to appeals to move beyond conventional thinking about war and self-defence that depend on the concept of an 'armed attack'.[157] The expression *hybrid warfare* is used by different authors to cover multiple ideas: from the ancient idea of mixing conventional and non-conventional forces,[158] to the newer notion used by the European Union, NATO and Western politicians to refer to threats from Russia involving a combination of cyber-attack, mass communication and the use of unattributable armed forces.[159] One sometimes finds the label *hybrid, asymmetric* or *grey zone* attached to a conflict to suggest that the ordinary law of armed conflict is inapplicable. As we shall see, these labels, and others such as *political warfare, irregular warfare* and *ambiguous warfare*, may help us to understand the phenomenon, but they do not in themselves alter the legal

---

[153] Strachen, *The Changing Character of War* (Oxford: Europaeum, 2007) at 10–11.

[154] Ibid at 11.

[155] Kamm, *The Moral Target: Aiming at Right Conduct in War and Other Conflicts* (2012) at 3.

[156] Lazar, 'War', in Zalta (ed) *The Stanford Encyclopedia of Philosophy* (Spring 2020 Edition), <https://plato.stanford.edu/archives/spr2020/entries/war/>. At fn 1.

[157] William Hague, 'Nato must confront Putin's stealth attacks with a new doctrine of war of its own', 'Military leaders need to integrate all this into their thinking ... so that they plan for taking action without knowing whether they are, in a conventional sense, at war.' *Daily Telegraph* (19 March 2018). He explains, 'A new doctrine would make clear that the case of a hybrid and undeclared attack would trigger a collective response from the alliance [NATO] – a response that can be scaled up or down, and like the attack itself, stop short of all-out war.'

[158] Murray and Mansoor (eds), *Hybrid Warfare: Fighting Complex Opponents from the Ancient World to the Present* (2013).

[159] Hague (n 157): 'But what if the attack takes the form of vital services being disrupted, communications mysteriously cut off, millions of messages on social media discrediting the country's armed forces, and men without uniforms raiding the border – all while RT [Russia Today] pours scorn on the very idea it could be anything to do with Moscow? Does that trigger Article 5 or not? And if it does, do tanks roll and bombers take to the air, starting a full-scale conflict?'

frameworks.[160] And as Sari points out, the hybrid warfare concept 'carries the risk of turning everything into an act of warfare'.[161]

In ending this chapter on the meaning of war, we might refer to the etymology of the word 'war'. Freedman explains it the following way:

> The Latin word for war, *bellum*, survives when we talk of people inclined to war as being bellicose or belligerent. The wordsmiths of the first millennium, however, considered *bellum* to be inappropriately close to the word for beauty, *bellus*, and so looked for alternatives. An old English word *Gewin*, meaning struggle or strife, was replaced by the German *werren*, which meant something similar, and is linked to *worse*. *Werran* became *weeorre* and then *warre* in English, and *guerre* in French. As originally used it seems to have referred to confusion or discord.[162]

---

[160] From time to time it is suggested that because groups such as Al-Qaeda, or ISIS or the Taliban are not regular opponents and do not apply the laws of war, the conflict is asymmetrical, and so the lack of reciprocity could remove the obligations on states to apply the laws of war. These ideas are regularly refuted by lawyers; see further Heintschel von Heinegg, 'Asymmetric Warfare – How to Respond?', 41 *Israel Yearbook on Human Rights* (2011) 31–48; Paulus and Vashakmadze, 'Asymmetrical War and the Notion of Armed Conflict – A Tentative Conceptualization', 91 *IRRC* (2009) 95–125.

[161] 'Hybrid Warfare, Law and the Fulda Gap', in Ford and Williams (eds), *Complex Battle Spaces* (2019) 161–90 at 190.

[162] Freedman, 'Defining War', in Lindley-French and Boyer (eds), *The Oxford Handbook of War* (2012) 17–29 at 17.

2

Declarations of War and Neutrality

2.1 Declarations of War

The institution of a Declaration of War has ancient roots. From across the world and throughout time one can find reports of one side sending another a challenge to fight. These challenges can take various forms. A study by Davie lists examples from all five continents. We could just highlight the following: a boomerang with a shell attached (the shell to be broken and the boomerang sent back if the other side declines the challenge and accepts defeat); bamboo shoots with symbols explaining the grievances; a broken spear; or a bundle of arrows wrapped in rattlesnake skin. Davie's examples illustrate a sense that one should not only give the other side the chance to prepare, but that the details of the missive might explain the nature of the grievance, and give the other side a chance to avoid war. They also indicated the timing and scale of the war. Davie finds accounts that suggest that, for example, in Mexico it was believed to be 'cowardly and unworthy of valiant men to surprise the enemy'.[1] Such declarations of war help us to understand some of the early logic of the declaration.

In *The Laws of War in the Late Middle Ages*, Keen cautions against treating the early 'law of arms as if it were a modern international law'.[2] This older customary military law amounted to rules of honour rather than anything rational or humanitarian. The signs used nevertheless had legal significance. First, they could be an indication of the rules that would be observed in battle. So there were distinctions between *guerre mortelle*, which was war to the death, *bellum hostile* or open war between Christian sovereigns, where men might take the spoils and prisoners for ransom, and *guerre couverte*, covered or feudal war, where 'men could wound and kill without blame, but could not burn or take spoil'.[3] To signify a war to the death one would fly a red flag or

---

[1] Davie, *The Evolution of War: A Study of its Rôle in Early Societies* (1929) Appendix L at 293–96.
[2] Keen, *The Laws of War in the Late Middle Ages* (1965) at 108.
[3] Ibid at 104.

banner; for open or public war the Prince's banner would be unfurled and a State of War occurred as a matter of law. The State of truce was signified by a white flag, and the Heralds carried white wands as a sign of their immunity.[4]

The significance of such a State of War was that men would not be punished for killing, burning and theft – for these acts would no longer be crimes but rather justified as 'done under the right of war'.[5] For the crime of arson, Saint Raymond of Pennaforte wrote that 'an incendiary is one who, out of hate or ill-will or for the sake of revenge sets fire to a town, or to a village or to a house or vines or anything of that kind. But if he does this at the command of one who has the power to declare war, then he is not to be judged an incendiary'.[6] As Keen explains: 'It was the same with other crimes, such as spoliation of a man's goods. In time of peace this was robbery, but in time of war it might be the basis of a legal title to possession, because in war it is not unjust or unreasonable to despoil the goods of the enemy'.[7]

From the 14th century to the 19th century one finds that Declarations are crafted to reinforce and explain why the War is justified, and as von Elbe explains, even within the Declaration, states were 'wont to express the hope that justice of their cause will procure Divine assistance'.[8] Separate from the text of a Declaration of War were 'war manifestos'. These have recently been subjected to renewed scholarly attention. More than 350 manifestos for war spanning five centuries (1492–1945) have been collected and analysed by a project at Yale University and are now freely available.[9] In contrast to a Declaration of War, a manifesto would enter into pages of detail concerning the background reasons for war and why it was now necessary to resort to war. According to the Yale study:

---

[4] Ibid at 105–09.

[5] Ibid at 65.

[6] Quoted by Keen, ibid at 64–65. *Summa de Poenitentia* (1224–26) Lib II, 5§5.

[7] Keen, *The Laws of War* (n 2) at 65. See also Joseph-Mathias Gérard de Rayneval: '[A] war without a prior declaration is truly pillage and robbery: it is a war of pirates and filibusters.' Allain, *The Last Waltz of the Law of Nations: A Translation of the 1803 Edition of The Institutions of Natural Law and the Law of Nations by Joseph-Mathias Gérard de Rayneval* (2019) Book III, Ch III, § 1, 'On Declarations of War' at 149. A *filibustier* was the name given to a French pirate or freebooter in the Americas.

[8] von Elbe, 'The Evolution of the Concept of Just War in International Law', 33 *AJIL* (1939) 665–88, at 685 fn 157, where he gives multiple examples, including the Duke of Milan's so declaring in taking up arms against the Duke of Savoy, 'confident in the Divine mercy which always favours the just cause' (1427).

[9] See Hathaway et al, 'War Manifestos', 85 *Chicago Law Review* (2018) 1139–1225, and their War Manifestos Database containing all known war manifestos issued by sovereigns between 1492 and 1945, available at http://documents.law.yale.edu/manifestos.

The sovereign issuing the manifesto generally explains that he has attempted to negotiate with the other side or remedy the situation through diplomatic means. Because those efforts have not yielded the desired results, the sovereign concludes, he has no choice but to go to war.[10]

Some of the earliest attempts to define the rules on Declarations of War go into excruciating detail as to the various categories of war and the limits on who could make such Declarations and against whom.[11] But by the end of the 19th century, it seems clear that there were no real obligations to issue a declaration before hostilities, nor even at any stage. As Neff explains:

> In an era in which war was seen frankly as a matter of policy rather than of law or morals, and in which nationalistic sentiments were playing an increasing role, it is not surprising that the dryly polite style of declarations of previous centuries went out of fashion. In its place came elements of bombast, emotion and patriotic self-righteousness.[12]

Wars have existed even in the absence of formal Declarations, and even when Declarations have been issued, they may refer to wars that have already started. Although reference is sometimes made to Grotius (writing in the 16th century), stating that a Declaration was required to produce the legal effects that flowed from the institution of War, there are multiple examples of Wars from the 16th century to the middle of the 20th century where no Declaration was ever made.[13] Castrén mentions that between '1700 and 1870 declarations of war prior to hostilities occurred in one case out of ten, and such declarations were very rare after war had been commenced'.[14] Where

---

[10] Hathaway et al, 'War Manifestos' (n 9) at 1151.

[11] da Legnano, in his *Treatise on War*, set out a variety of types of wars and then 'what law allows the Church to declare war against infidels, and to invade their territories' and 'who are the emperors against whom war may be declared', 'whether universal war may be declared by others than a prince'. *Tractatus de Bello, de Represaliis et de Duello (1360)*, ed Holland, tr Brierly (1917) at 231–34. For an overview of how other writers treated the need for Declarations, see Ballis, *The Legal Position of War: Changes in its Practice and Theory from Plato to Vattel* (1937).

[12] Neff, *War and the Law of Nations: General History* (2005) at 185, where he offers a wonderful example in the form of the Emperor of Austria's announcement of War with Prussia in 1866.

[13] Westlake, *International Law: Part II War* (1907) 18–26; see also Eagleton, 'The Form and Function of the Declaration of War', 32 *AJIL* (1938) 19–35 and for later examples see Castrén, *The Present Law of War and Neutrality* (1954) at 97.

[14] Castrén, *The Present Law of War and Neutrality* (n 13) at 96; see the study by Maurice, *Hostilities without a Declaration of War: An Historical Abstract of the Cases in Which Hostilities Have Occurred Between Civilized Powers Prior to Declaration or Warning* (1883) at 4, which found that from 1700 to 1870, from the 107 instances analysed, 'less than ten' involved a Declaration

an ultimatum was issued, and the conditions were not met, War would start from the time when the demanded conditions were not met; in this way the ultimatum would become seen as a formal Declaration of War.

2.1.1 The Obligation to Declare War as a Matter of International Law

The move to generate an international obligation to declare War before the start of hostilities can be traced to the undeclared outbreak of the War between Russia and Japan in 1904, and the subsequent work of the Institut de droit international and its 1906 Resolution on the topic. The members of this private organization for the study and development of international law (which had been awarded the Nobel Peace prize two years earlier) suggested that states should issue either a declaration *'pure et simple'*, or an ultimatum, which would be duly notified to the adversary, and that hostilities should not start before sufficient time had elapsed to show that the other side was aware.[15] The subsequent Hague Convention III of 1907 referenced the need for neutral powers to be aware of the beginning of war, and added that the Declaration must give reasons for the War. The treaty is still in force for the 36 states parties, and most recently, in 2015, Ukraine notified that it considered itself a party as a successor state to the Soviet Union.

Article 1 of the Hague Convention III states: 'The contracting Powers recognize that hostilities between themselves must not commence without previous and explicit warning, in the form either of a declaration of war, giving reasons, or of an ultimatum with conditional declaration of war.' Failure to duly declare War with reasons, and to notify neutral states, would be a violation of the treaty, but could not be used to avoid the law of war.

The Tokyo International Military Tribunal was careful to include in its definition of crimes against peace 'the planning, preparation, initiation or waging of a declared or undeclared war of aggression, or a war in violation of international law, treaties, agreements or assurances'. Moreover, entering into

---

of War before hostilities. This study was requested by a Trade Committee looking into the issue of 'the Channel Tunnel' (!) and responded to a concern to know whether 'war would be declared against us, as we might say out of a clear sky, without any previous strain or notice that a quarrel was impending' (ibid at v).

[15] Available at http://www.idi-iil.org/app/uploads/2017/06/1906_gand_02_fr.pdf.

an armed conflict without fulfilling the requirements for a Declaration of War was, at one point, considered relevant to individual criminal charges in Tokyo. The indictment[16] against the Japanese defendants states that there was no 'declaration of War against China', for the force used against Nangking in 1932 and 1937, and the absence of a declaration of War for the attack on the USSR in 1938, the attack on Mongolia in 1939, and the 1941 surprise attacks on the British Commonwealth at Singapore, Hong Kong and Shanghai, and the attack on the Philippines. The indictment also considered that the document delivered to the United States after the attack on Pearl Harbour did not amount to a Declaration of War.

The Tokyo Tribunal listed the violation by Japan of Article 1 of the Hague Convention III ('Hague III'), concerning the need for a Declaration of War, as relevant not only for the prosecution of crimes against peace, ie a war in violation of international treaties, but also for simple charges of murder. The idea was that these killings 'resulted from the unlawful waging of war'.[17] The Judgment later explained:

> In all cases the killing is alleged as arising from the unlawful waging of war, unlawful in respect that there had been no declaration of war prior to the killings (counts 39 to 43, 51 and 52) or unlawful because the wars in the course of which the killings occurred were commenced in violation of certain specified Treaty Articles (counts 45 to 50).[18]

In the end, the Judges did not look at the idea of murder as a result of a violation of the obligation to issue a Declaration of War under Hague III or any other treaty, as they concentrated on the waging of aggressive wars as such.[19] The Judges found they could convict for conspiracy to wage wars of aggression, or actual waging of wars of aggression, and saw no need to look at wars otherwise in violation of international law or treaties.[20] The Majority explained: the waging of wars of aggression 'is the major crime, since it involves untold killings, suffering and misery. No good purpose would be served by

---

[16] The Indictment is reproduced in Boister and Cryer (eds), *Documents on the Tokyo International Military Tribunal: Charter Indictment and Judgments* (2008); for the references, see ibid at 32, 35, 36, 42, 45.

[17] Ibid at 86, para 48,452 of the Majority Judgment.

[18] Ibid.

[19] Ibid at paras 48,452–48,453, and esp paras 49,576–48,581.

[20] Ibid at para 49,772.

convicting any defendant of that major crime and also of murder [by that name].'[21]

In sum, states do enter into hostilities with other states without a Declaration of War, and for states parties to Hague III this could constitute a violation of that treaty. Fighting an undeclared War, or indeed any form of armed conflict, does not relieve the parties or any individuals of their obligations under the law of war.

2.1.2 Authority to Declare War under National Law

Different states will have different rules for determining which body or officeholder can declare War. As we shall see, under the US Constitution, only Congress can declare War. In France (and many other states), it is up to Parliament to authorize a Declaration of War, even if the decision is actually taken by the Executive.[22] Germany, Italy and Japan have constitutional prohibitions on war as an instrument of aggression. The Japanese Constitution is particularly emphatic:

> Aspiring sincerely to an international peace based on justice and order, the Japanese people forever renounce war as a sovereign right of the nation and the threat or use of force as means of settling international disputes. In order to accomplish the aim of the preceding paragraph, land, sea, and air forces, as well as other war potential, will never be maintained. The right of belligerency of the state will not be recognized.[23]

---

[21] Ibid at para 49,576. See Ch 7 in this book for a discussion by certain contemporary just war theorists that individual soldiers should indeed be held accountable for murder in an aggressive war.

[22] Berramdane, 'La Constitution de 1958 et l'autorisation de déclaration de guerre', *Revue de droit public et de la science politique en France et à l'étranger* (1995) 1221–43.

[23] Japanese Constitution Art 9. For detail on the new legislation in force since 2016, which sets out what measures are permitted for self-defence or to support states engaged in operations for peace and security, see Ministry of Defense (Japan) *Defense of Japan 2017* Ch 3 available at <https://warp.da.ndl.go.jp/info:ndljp/pid/11591426/www.mod.go.jp/e/publ/w_paper/2017.html>. The right of belligerency clause is read as meaning not the right to self-defence but rather the 'various rights that a belligerent nation has under international law, including the authority to inflict casualties and damage upon the enemy's military force and to occupy enemy territory.' Japan draws a distinction here so 'Occupation of enemy territory, however, would exceed the minimum necessary level of self-defense and is not permissible.' *Defense of Japan 2016* at 166 available at <https://warp.da.ndl.go.jp/info:ndljp/pid/11591426/www.mod.go.jp/e/publ/w_paper/2016.html>.

But pointing to all such arrangements is now rather misleading. The Executive may justify its use of force not as war, but as part of a collective security operation, a UN authorized peace operation, or urgent intervention taken in self-defence or even to rescue individuals in imminent danger. To many people such military operations will look like war.

Such decisions to fight in something not labelled 'war' may still be subject to democratic control. France has introduced the need for parliamentary authorization where its armed forces intervene abroad and the intervention lasts more than four months, and Germany requires parliamentary approval for the deployment of armed forces, with the Constitutional Court playing an important role in determining what constitutes a deployment.[24] Japan and Italy have new legislation regulating participation in international operations.[25]

Interestingly, the Italian law allows for the authorization of 'exceptional humanitarian interventions' by participation in operations of international organizations, where Italy is a member of the organization. The same law nevertheless requires conformity with international law and the Constitution, which states that 'Italy rejects war as an instrument of aggression against the freedom of other peoples and as a means for the settlement of international disputes.'[26] Curiously, the default internal military justice law to be applied is the military penal code for peace, but the military penal code for war can be applied for a particular mission under a special procedure involving Parliament.[27] The Italian Constitution nevertheless retains a number of provisions that relate to a 'state of war' or 'time of war', and Article 78 provides that 'Parliament has the authority to declare a state of war and vest the necessary powers into the Government.'[28]

---

[24] Peters, 'Military Operations Abroad Under the German Basic Law', in Bradley (ed), *The Oxford Handbook of Comparative Foreign Relations Law* (2019) 791–809; Forteu, 'Using Military Force and Engaging in Collective Security: The Case of France', ibid at 811–27.

[25] Mori, 'Decisions in Japan to Use Military Force or Participate in Multilateral Peacekeeping Operations', in Bradley (n 24) at 829–42.

[26] Art 11 of the Italian Constitution (1948), Archives and Publications Office of the Senate Service for Official Reports and Communication; see the new law, Legge 21 July 2016, n 145, Disposizioni concernenti la partecipazione dell'Italia alle missioni internazionali (GU n 178 del 1 August 2016); for comment, see Ronzitti, 'Missioni all'estero, arriva la legge', 10 January 2017, *Affari Internazionali*, available at https://www.affarinternazionali.it/2017/01/missioni-allestero-arriva-la-legge/.

[27] Legge 21 July 2016 (n 26), n 145, Arts 2(2) and 19(2).

[28] For further analysis, see Ronzitti, *Diritto internazionale dei conflitti armati*, 6th edn (2017) Ch 4 and 155–60.

2.1.3   The Future of Declarations of War

The World Wars of the 20th century included multiple Declarations of War. There were therefore 52 situations of a State of War (formally understood) between different states in the First World War, and 164 situations of a State of War in the Second World War,[29] the last Declaration of War being the Soviet Union's made on Japan on 8 August 1945 (two days after the dropping of the nuclear bomb on Hiroshima).[30] But today, although recently there may be claims that this or that action by the United States represents an 'Act of War' for Iran[31] or a 'Declaration of War' for North Korea,[32] such statements are not considered as actually creating a State of War in the formal legal sense.

Even if the language of war is all around, states do not resort to their constitutional arrangements for going to war. The Executive in many cases, as we shall see, usually considers its use of force abroad to be authorized or required by the United Nations, or to be at the request of another state fighting insurgents or terrorists, or action justified by self-defence. Because the idea of a State of War seems incongruous with the collective security arrangements put in place by the United Nations (which limit any use of force to self-defence or Security Council-authorized operations), the paradox is that, today, even massive uses of force (such as the 1991 'Gulf War') are not strictly speaking Declared Wars. Of course, as we shall see, the laws of war most definitely apply, and violations could be war crimes, and in inter-state conflicts there could be prisoners of war, but for 70 years there have probably been no unequivocal Declarations of War leading to a recognized State of War as such. Whilst being at War may no longer be admitted as a strict matter of law, the same levels of violence can ironically be unleashed in many cases without

---

[29] Berramdane, 'La Constitution de 1958 et l'autorisation de déclaration de guerre', *Revue de droit public et de la science politique en France et à l'étranger* (1995) 1221–43; ibid at 1233 fn 22, for the references that contain the lists of these 216 separate Wars in the two World Wars; see *Revue générale de droit international public* (1918) 84–92 for lists of the Declarations for the First World War, and *Recueil de textes à l'usage des conférences de la paix* (1946) 243–47, which contains matrices showing which states were in a State of War with which other states, along with the relevant Declarations of War for the Second World War.

[30] For the text, see at https://avalon.law.yale.edu/wwii/s4.asp.

[31] For example, see the quotes, tweets, etc in Cole, 'Trump's Order to Kill Iran's General is "Act of War" Says Tehran's UN Envoy: "There Will Be Harsh Revenge" (4 January 2020) available at https://www.newsweek.com/trump-iran-general-act-war-tehran-united-nations-revenge-1480392.

[32] Fish, 'The Long History of North Korea's Declarations of War', *The Atlantic* (25 September 2017). See also the 'Full War Declaration Statement from DPRK' published by North Korea, available at http://live.reuters.com/Event/North_Korea/70001409.

the constitutional controls that have to be exercised before a Declaration of War can be issued.

The question can arise as to how a declaration of war made by an unauthorized body would be seen. Eagleton's study gives some examples of declarations that were unauthorized but nevertheless treated as valid. He suggests 'if the President of the United States should, without Congressional authority, declare war against another state, there is little doubt that that state would consider itself at war with the United States'.[33] He also suggests that proclamations by commanders or admirals may equally establish a State of War. Because war can exist without a declaration, one could see declarations as redundant, but he nevertheless goes on to suggest some uses for the Declaration of War:

> Internally, it could furnish authority for legislative or executive acts which depend upon the existence of war; it could furnish a guide for domestic court action – if its authority and implications were clearly stated; it could state the reasons for the entry into war, both to arouse popular support at home and to win favor abroad. More important, it could give notice to neutral states of the coming into force of a different legal status, with its consequent variation of rights and duties; and it could fix the exact time at which this new legal status should go into effect, for the benefit of individuals and of foreign states.[34]

More recently, Charles Dunlap, a retired Major General from the US Air Force, has highlighted how the US Supreme Court has drawn a distinction in the past between a 'general war' and a 'limited war', also described as the difference between a 'perfect war' and an 'imperfect war'. Focusing on the 1952 decision of the US Supreme Court to strike down President Truman's seizure of steel mills in the interests of national security against the background of the hostilities in Korea, he refers to Chief Justice Rehnquist's book, in which Rehnquist writes 'I think that if the steel seizure had taken place during the Second World War, the government probably would have won under the constitutional grant of war powers to the president'.[35] Dunlap concludes that

---

[33] Eagleton, 'The Form and Function of the Declaration of War', 32 *AJIL* (1938) 19–35 at 38.

[34] Ibid at 34.

[35] Dunlap, 'Why Declarations of War Matter', *Harvard National Security Journal* (30 August 2016) available at http://harvardnsj.org/2016/08/why-declarations-of-war-matter/ quoting Rehnquist, *The Supreme Court* (2002) at 191. Rehnquist continues, 'but I also have the distinct feeling that if the American objectives and strategy in Korea had been less uncertain, the

'where there is a declaration of war, we may find that the Court is more deferential to presidential actions, even if not explicitly backed by law or clear Article II [of the US Constitution] authority'.[36] From a practical point of view he goes on to make the point that a declaration of war can generate support for a conflict and

> energize the citizenry towards winning it. That kind of overt national commitment could strengthen military morale . . . having troops in the field uncertain about the legality of their actions is plainly inimical to the kind of morale and discipline that facilitates military success.

We can now see that the Declaration of War is relevant at various levels. First, the failure to issue a warning in the form of a Declaration of War or an ultimatum can constitute a violation of Hague Convention III (1907). Such a violation will not now, however, be relevant for the prosecution of individuals for crimes against peace (if it ever was); the contemporary crime of aggression is defined without reference to this treaty.[37] Second, a Declaration of War could legalize certain measures where the treaty provisions or national rules specify that powers only flow from a valid Declaration of War.[38] Third, the judicial branch may arguably offer more deference where there is a clear situation of Declared War and there is a need to exercise exceptional executive war powers. Fourth, a Declaration can explain the reasons and objectives of a War and motivate support for it; at the same time, those acting to oppose the War can be tainted with treason, disloyalty or lack of patriotism (discussed in section 5.6). Lastly, we should explain that should any state, that had not been attacked, make a Declaration of War against another state, this would be most likely seen as a threat of the use of force and therefore be in violation of the UN Charter.[39] Moreover, a state would not be entitled to

---

government would probably have fared better in the Supreme Court even without being able to resort to the president's war power': *The Supreme Court* (2002) at 191.

[36] Dunlap 'Why Declarations of War Matter'.

[37] See Ch 4 below.

[38] See Ch 1 above for examples from treaties, and Ch 5 below for examples in national law; Ch 6 starts with some examples of arbitrators determining that certain statements did not constitute Declarations of War.

[39] Wehberg, 'L'interdiction du recours à la force: le principe et les problèmes qui se posent', 78 *RCADI* 1 (1951) 1–121 at 73.

react with the use of force to such a Declaration, as self-defence has to be in response to an armed attack and not a simple threat.[40]

2.2 The End of War: Peace Treaties, Armistices, Cease-Fires, Truces and Agreements with Non-State Actors

It is often assumed that a State of War leads to the termination of treaties, or at least their suspension, until a formal Peace Agreement is signed. While it may indeed be the case that, in the past, states did seek to avoid labelling their disputes as Wars in order to preserve their legal and diplomatic relations, and that treaties (then mostly bilateral) would be abrogated, there is a presumption today that multilateral treaty provisions continue even in time of war or armed conflict.[41] There would be an expectation that states would follow the procedures for the termination of treaties should they wish to alter their legal obligations. Although some of the treaty provisions may be inapplicable in certain contexts, or not intended to apply in time of conflict,[42] state practice suggests that even bilateral 'Friendship Treaties' may continue, and that certain rights of foreign nationals from the enemy state may even be preserved.[43] It is also clear that treaties concerning diplomatic and consular relations continue, and the treaties specifically require that even where diplomatic or consular relations are severed, the host state has to respect and protect the diplomatic or consular premises of the other state 'even in case of armed conflict'.[44]

A peace agreement thus is important to understanding when the war is over, and what obligations may flow, but such a treaty does not simply automatically restore terminated or suspended obligations from the time of peace.

---

[40] Ibid at 81, and more recently confirmed by Dinstein, *War, Aggression and Self-Defence*, 6th edn (2017) at 223: 'The crux of the issue is that anticipatory use of force today, in response to sheer threats rather than an armed attack, would not be in compliance with the text of Article 51 of the UN Charter.'

[41] For the details, see the work of the International Law Commission and its Draft Articles on the Effects of Armed Conflicts on Treaties (2011). The Draft Articles make no distinction between an armed conflict and a War: *Ybk ILC* (2011), Vol II, Part Two, 108–30.

[42] For examples us suspension during the Second World War of some multilateral treaties (unconnected to the law of armed conflict) under the supervision of the League of Nations see Brandon and Leriche, 'Suspension of Rights and Obligations Under Multilateral Conventions Between Opposing Belligerents on Account of War', 46 *AJIL* (1952) 532–37.

[43] *Ybk ILC* (2011),Vol II, Part Two, 108–30, at 123–26.

[44] Vienna Convention on Diplomatic Relations 1961 Art 45; and Vienna Convention on Consular Relations 1963 Art 27.

The peace agreement, like a Declaration of War, can set out when exactly the war is considered to be over. This could be back-dated, or apply on signature or set some date in the future. Such dates could be important for any national rules that are dependent on the existence of a formal State of War. This has meant that the end of the War may need to be defined quite precisely. For the First World War,

> declarations of war were general and it was officially made known when peace was re-established. In many of the more than fifty declarations of war the day, hour, and minute when war would begin was made known. For France the official period of the war was from '6.45 pm on August 3, 1914,' to '4.15 pm on January 10, 1920.'[45]

Today, as the institution of War fades and the focus shifts to the legal category of armed conflict, the significant date is more likely to turn on the end of the conflict, perhaps through an armistice, a cessation of hostilities, cease-fire or truce. Treaties and scholars have separated out these terms over the years, but they are not used today with any consistency. Readers would be advised to consider the context and intentions of the actors, rather than rely on the title that any agreement is given. Dinstein has tracked the evolving nature of terms such as 'peace treaty', 'armistice' and 'truce', and concludes that the 'passage of time has brought about alterations in international legal terms of art'.[46] He considers that the Panmunjom Armistice Agreement (ending the Korean conflict) would fit the 'modern meaning of an armistice agreement as an end to war'.[47] Just as armistices are the new peace treaties, in turn Dinstein suggests that the rules covering armistices in the Hague Regulations 'must be deemed applicable to present-day cease-fires (as opposed to modern armistices)'.[48]

One can still find references by states in formal settings to 'acts of war' or being in 'a state of war',[49] but the rules on the beginning and end of the

---

[45] Wilson, 'Use of Force and Declaration of War', 32 *AJIL* (1938) 100–1, at 100.

[46] 'The Initiation, Suspension, and Termination of War', 75 *International Law Studies* (2000) 131–59 at 153.

[47] Ibid at 143

[48] Ibid at 147; but Dinstein has emphasized the continuing 'state of war' between Israel and Iraq (since 1948), and describes 'a number of rounds of hostilities' between Israel and Egypt and Syria as belonging to one war since 1967: *War, Aggression and Self-Defence* (n 40), esp 41, 51–52, 61, 64 and 227. See further the conclusion to the present book for a rejection of such an approach.

[49] In the 21st century there are hardly any official references that could be seen as evidence of the continuing international legal relevance of War. Such references as exist do not seem to be designed to trigger any particular legal effect. See UN Doc A/60/937-S/2006/515 for a letter

application of the laws of armed conflict mostly operate independently from the question of War, and we will tackle these thresholds in Chapter 6. For now, the possible remaining significance of a State of War or a State of Peace may be the implications for the rights and duties arising from the laws related to Neutral Status, and the historical legacy associated with Belligerent Rights connected to naval warfare involving search and seizure of neutral shipping on the high seas.

2.3 War and Neutrality

Just as with the notion of war, where we separated formal Wars involving a State of War from wars more generally, if we are interested in the legal rights and duties that flow from neutrality we may have to distinguish on the one hand between casual references to being 'neutral' and, on the other hand, the international law that flows when a state relies on rights and obligations that flow from its Neutral Status as a matter of international law. I will use a capital 'N' here to try to distinguish those states that have assumed Neutral Status under international law from those neutral states that are merely not participating on either side of an inter-state armed conflict. Such a non-participating state is now also known as a 'non-belligerent state'.

Commitments to neutrality made by humanitarian agencies raise a completely different set of duties. Organizations such as the International Committee of the Red Cross (ICRC) define themselves as 'neutral',[50] but the contours of what this means here, or for other humanitarian organizations abiding by a principle of neutrality, are more operational and ethical than legal, and the meaning of 'neutral' here is not uniform across all organizations. For example, some humanitarian organizations would consider that

from the Israeli Permanent Representative to the UN, stating that Hezbollah rockets constituted a 'clear declaration of war' and that 'Responsibility for this belligerent act of war lies with the Government of Lebanon', but no particular belligerent rights beyond the right of self-defence under the UN Charter were claimed. See also Israel's references to being engaged in a conflict 'short of war' in its submission to the Sharm el-Sheikh Fact-Finding Committee, 28 December 2000, at paras 18, 286, 323. It is not clear what was intended by the expression 'short of war' in this context.

[50] Statutes of the ICRC (2017), Preamble, Art 4(1)(a)(d) and (2); and see the Statutes of the International Red Cross and Red Crescent Movement (2006), which commit the movement to seven principles, including neutrality: 'In order to continue to enjoy the confidence of all, the Movement may not take sides in hostilities or engage at any time in controversies of a political, racial, religious or ideological nature.'

neutrality should not preclude 'undertaking advocacy on issues related to accountability and justice'.[51]

But to keep to the main focus of this book, let us try to separate out the rights and obligations that apply where states elect to rely on a recognized Neutral Status[52] from the rules that apply to all states that have chosen not to join another state in an inter-state armed conflict. In other words, I think we should consider two sets of obligations: one applying to states that have assumed Neutral Status, and another set of rules that applies to all non-participating states in all international armed conflicts.[53]

2.3.1 The Obligations and Rights of Neutral and Belligerent States

The state of neutrality law has been described by one scholar as not only *chaotic*, but also in *crisis*, with the legal writing leaving only a picture of *confusion*.[54] Much of the confusion is due to the fact that no multilateral treaties have specifically addressed Neutral Status as such since 1907.[55] This is compounded by the near absence of authoritative decisions of international judicial bodies,[56] and the careful ambiguity with which states treat the question of Neutral Status. States with powerful navies might have once seemed keen to limit the rights of neutral shipping when they were engaged as Belligerent

---

[51] Schenkenberg van Mierop, 'Coming Clean on Neutrality and Independence: the Need to Assess the Application of Humanitarian Principles', 97 *IRRC* (2016) 295–318 at 298, explaining the process leading to the Common Humanitarian Standard.

[52] On the the relevance of Declarations of Neutrality and recognition of Neutral Status in the 19th century, see Upcher, *Neutrality in Contemporary International Law* (2020) Ch 1 esp at 12ff.

[53] Not everyone would agree with such a dichotomy; see, eg, the approach taken by Upcher ibid, and Verlinden, 'The Law of Neutrality', in Wouters, De Man and Verlinden (eds), *Armed Conflicts and the Law* (2016) 75–106. Both would apply the obligations of Neutral Status to all international armed conflicts.

[54] Gioia, 'Neutrality and Non-Belligerency', in Post (ed), *International Economic Law and Armed Conflict* (1994) 51–110.

[55] See, for regional treaties, the Convention on Maritime Neutrality (1928) for the Americas, and the Stockholm Declaration Regarding Similar Rules of Neutrality (1938) for the five Nordic countries. For the history and scope of neutrality law as well as early treaties whereby states committed to remain neutral, see Verzijl, *International Law in Historical Perspective: Part IX-B The Law of Neutrality* (1979).

[56] For a rare example, see *The SS 'Wimbledon', United Kingdom and ors v Germany*, PCIJ, Judgment 17 August 1923, which held that the Versailles Peace Treaty obligations on Germany meant the Kiel Canal was an international waterway for ships from states at peace with Germany. Art 380 of the Treaty reads 'The Kiel Canal and its approaches shall be maintained free and open to the vessels of commerce and of war of all nations at peace with Germany on terms of entire equality'. But see the Dissenting Opinions by Anzilotti, Huber and Schücking.

States at War, yet those same states, having abandoned recourse to War, or the prospect of naval warfare, may now see the need to protect their own neutral shipping in times of armed conflict. At the same time, some states that might have championed the rights of neutral trade may later find themselves dominant naval powers.[57]

As an illustration, the United States adopted complex rules on neutrality starting in 1794, some of them applying beyond what was commonly understood by neutrality at the time.[58] Presidential proclamations on the subject were not questioned in the courts, as they were considered 'political questions'. The United States essentially wanted to keep out of European Wars and did not want to give European powers an excuse to go to War with them. Much later, in the First World War, the German naval attacks on US merchant ships were explained by Germany in terms of US deviation from the duties derived from Neutral Status through its assistance to the United Kingdom.[59] Neutrality came to be seen by some in the United States as a liability rather than merely a way for ensuring peace. By the time of the Neutrality Act of 1939, it was explicitly stated that proclamations of Neutrality could only be triggered by the President or Congress, where they found that there existed a State of War between foreign states and that it was 'necessary to promote the security or preserve the peace of the United States or to protect the lives of the citizens of the United States'.[60] As Quincy Wright illustrated in 1940, the

---

[57] For the ways in which the attitudes of the different naval powers changed over time, see Neff, *The Rights and Duties of Neutrals* (2000). Of course the vast majority of states that exist today were not included in the formation of the rules that applied between the major powers in the centuries leading to the eventual creation of the United Nations. The 1909 London Naval Conference was only open to the following powers: Austria-Hungary, France, Germany, Italy, Japan, Netherlands, Russia, Spain, UK and USA. The resulting Declaration was never ratified.

[58] Interestingly, with regard to the *Caroline* incident (to be discussed in section 4.1.1), America was taking steps at that time to bolster her role as a state with Neutral Status in other people's Wars, and under international law that also meant that Belligerents from those Wars had to respect its rights that flowed from its Neutral Status. Strictly speaking, the fight in 1837 between the Canadian insurgents and Great Britain could not be considered a War in the technical sense but rather as something closer to a civil war. However, from the US perspective at that time, Neutrality obligations should apply to civil wars, and their own Neutrality Acts were adjusted in 1818 so that the provisions indeed applied to civil wars as well. Wani, *Neutrality in International Law: From the sixteenth century to 1945* (2017) at 58–59. Indeed, two of the ringleaders organizing the use of the *Caroline* for the insurgency were convicted for violating these Neutrality Acts in the years following the incident. Forcese, *Destroying the Caroline: The Frontier Raid that Reshaped the Right to War* (2018) at 251 and 253.

[59] On the failure by the United States to respect strict laws of neutrality in the first year of the War, see Coogan, *The End of Neutrality: The United States, Britain, and Maritime Rights 1888–1915* (1981).

[60] Explained and discussed by Wright, 'The Power to Declare Neutrality under American Law', 34 *AJIL* (1940) 302–10; in the inter-war years there was a stream of opinion that suggested

United States and others were willing in the inter-war years simply to pick out those conflicts where they would declare Neutrality; and in other instances they would consider a state's action as aggression, or a violation of treaties, and go on to choose to aid the victim state.[61]

After the Second World War, the creation of the United Nations suggested that there would now be collective security measures, and states could no longer choose to remain neutral in the face of an aggression in violation of the UN Charter. The scholarly debate in the middle of the 20th century, over what was left of the law on neutrality, ebbed and flowed depending on the context, and statements from state representatives were either too casual, or too cautious to be conclusive. Scholars in the 1950s and 1960s usually assumed that the United Nations would do one of two things: either identify who the aggressor was (thus making it illegal to take sides), or oblige states to support the United Nations' policing action to restore the peace (thus overriding any neutrality obligations). These scholars would then often adhere to the idea that in the absence of such UN action, remaining neutrality rights and obligations depend on a State of Declared War.

But of course during the Cold War the United Nations was unable either to condemn aggression, or to authorize the use of force to restore the peace. Castrén (in his 1954 book-length study on neutrality) saw that it may be difficult to determine whether there is an actual War or 'merely some other kind of armed activity'; his solution was that the parties to the conflict should 'make their attitude known and notify it to outside States in order for them to take appropriate measures'.[62] By 1979 Schindler was concluding that 'State practice since 1945 shows that, in a state of war, third parties generally do not act in a different way than in that of an armed conflict without war.'[63] He then went beyond the simple elimination of the distinction between War and armed conflict and suggested that 'This may lead to the conclusion that a duty of non-participants to apply the law of neutrality is no longer recognized, even when a state of war exists.'[64] For a permanently Neutral State such

that insisting on neutrality rights 'leads to ultimatums which inevitably lead to war'. Warren, 'Troubles of a Neutral', 12 *Foreign Affairs* (1934) 377–94 at 390.

[61]   Wright, 'The Present Status of Neutrality', 34 *AJIL* (1940) 391–415, esp at 403–07.
[62]   Castrén, *The Present Law of War and Neutrality* (n 13) at 423; and see Skubisczewski, 'Use of Force by States. Collective Security. Law of War and Neutrality', in Sørensen (ed), *Manual of Public International Law* (1968) 739–854 at 809, 'whenever the parties do not regard their armed conflict as war ... the law of neutrality does not apply at all'.
[63]   Schindler, 'State of War, Belligerency, Armed Conflict', in Cassese (ed), *The New Humanitarian Law of Armed Conflict* (1979) 3–20 at 15.
[64]   Ibid at 15.

as Switzerland, he admitted that such a state 'stands aside from all inter-State conflicts and not merely' some particular War.[65]

Brownlie, having researched in detail the reasons why states and the League of Nations sought to avoid categorizing a conflict as leading to a State of War, took a variegated approach. He admitted there needed to be different definitions of war for different contexts. So, for the humanitarian aspects of the laws of war there should be the 'widest possible application', while 'the law of neutrality with its far reaching effects on international relations should only be brought into operation when the hostilities have a degree of permanence and a scope which necessitate regulation of the belligerents and third states'.[66] Significantly, he also suggested that the now universal prohibition on the use of force allows a third state to avoid any obligations related to Neutral Status by arguing that it is responding to the illegal use of force with a countermeasure. Failure to observe such obligations can therefore be presented as a sanction, reprisal or countermeasure against the aggressor state, and this precludes the wrongfulness of the behaviour of the non-belligerent state. This was indeed part of the US argumentation to explain why its support for Britain before the United States entered the Second World War did not breach the law on neutrality.[67]

After the Iran–Iraq conflict in the 1980s, there was a new flurry of scholarly writing and more confusion based on the ambiguous behaviour of states.[68] By now, for many authors, it was clearer that, even faced with a major armed conflict, the Security Council, stymied by the Cold War, might be unable to come to clear decisions as to who the aggressor was, or what all member states must do. Schindler explains that, in such circumstances, 'A duty to remain neutral in case of uncertainty as to who is the aggressor does not exist.'[69] His conclusion was 'A third State may assist the victim of armed attack without regard to the existence of a state of war.'[70]

Similarly, scholars such as Gioia argued that state behaviour during the Iran–Iraq conflict suggested that 'States not wishing to enter into an armed

---

[65] Ibid at 449.

[66] Brownlie, *International Law and the Use of Force by States* (1963) at 400–01.

[67] Ibid at 79, 106–07 and 403, where he also points out that if a third state is entitled to join in collective self-defence against an aggressor, that state ought also to be able to refrain from fulfilling all its duties under the law of neutrality.

[68] Dekker and Post (eds), *The Gulf War of 1980–1988* (1992); Post (ed), *International Economic Law and Armed Conflict* (1994) 5–34.

[69] Schindler, 'Commentary to the 1907 Hague Convention XIII Concerning the Rights and Duties of Neutral Powers in Naval War', in Ronzitti (ed), *The Law of Naval Warfare: A Collection of Agreements and Documents with Commentaries* (1988) 193–222 at 212.

[70] Ibid at 213.

conflict are no longer under a legal duty to abide by the traditional laws of neutrality.'[71] And he went on to outline the legal relevance of states' having a choice to remain neutral, or take an intermediate position of 'qualified neutrality' or 'non-belligerence'.[72] Such an approach is not shared by all,[73] but it reflects in many ways the practice of states such as the United Kingdom and Italy, who have been more transparent than most in addressing their understanding of the law.[74]

Under this approach, only those states that declare themselves to have Neutral Status in a particular prolonged conflict (and this would include states with a status of Permanent Neutrality such as Switzerland) will take on the duties of Neutral Status 'in its strict sense'.[75] These are the duties of abstention, prevention and impartiality (dealt with below).

The 2007 *US Commander's Handbook on the Law of Naval Operations*, valid until 2017, stated that 'a neutral nation is defined as a nation that, consistent with international law, either has proclaimed its neutrality or has

---

[71] Gioia, 'Neutrality and Non-Belligerency', in Post (ed), *International Economic Law and Armed Conflict* (1994) 51–110 at 68; and see further examples of states favouring one side in the Iran–Iraq war in Gioia and Ronzitti, 'The Law of Neutrality: Third States' Commercial Rights and Duties', in Dekker and Post (eds), *The Gulf War of 1980–1988* (1992) 221–42 at 228–31.

[72] Gioia (n 71) at 86.

[73] See especially Heintschel von Heinegg, ' "Benevolent" Third States in International Armed Conflicts: The Myth of the Irrelevance of the Law of Neutrality', in Schmitt and Pejic (eds), *International Law and Armed Conflict: Exploring the Faultlines (Essays in Honour of Yoram Dinstein)* (2007) 543–68 at 555–56; and Heintschel von Heinegg, 'International Economic Relations and Armed Conflict', in de Guttry, Post and Venturini (eds), *The 1998–2000 War between Eritrea and Ethiopia* (2009) 371–87. Kleffner simply concludes that the law of neutrality applies to an international armed conflict even in the absence of a State of War: 'Scope of Application of International Humanitarian Law', in Fleck (ed), *The Handbook of Humanitarian Law in Armed Conflict*, 3rd edn (2013) 43–78 at 49.

[74] Ronzitti, 'Italy's Non-Belligerency During the Iraqi War', in Ragazzi (ed), *International Responsibility Today: Essays in Memory of Oscar Schachter* (2005) 197–207; Humphrey, 'Belligerent Interdiction of Neutral Shipping in International Armed Conflict', 2 *Journal of Conflict and Security Law* (1997) 23–44; Gray, 'The British Position in Regard to the Gulf Conflict', 37 *ICLQ* (1988) 420–28; Gray, 'The British Position in Regard to the Gulf Conflict (Iran–Iraq): Part 2', 40 *ICLQ* (1991) 464–73.

[75] Schindler, 'Commentary' (n 69) at 213. See also Shearer, *Starke's International Law*, 11th edn (1994) at 481: 'Assuming the hostilities are on a sufficiently extensive scale, the decision may be made ... to make a declaration of neutrality, irrespective of the intentions of the contestants. A third state, adopting this course, would be subject to the risk of the exercise of belligerent rights by either contestant, whose right to do so could not then be challenged. A non-war status could none the less still apply in the relations of the contestants inter se.' See also McNair and Watts, *The Legal Effects of War*, 4th edn (1966) at 10, and the definition offered by McNair, 'The Legal Meaning of War, and the Relation of War to Reprisals', 11 *Transactions of the Grotius Society* (1925) 29–51. Compare Wright, 'When Does War Exist?', 26 *AJIL* (1932) 362–68 at 365–67.

otherwise assumed neutral status with respect to an ongoing conflict.[76] More recently, the US *Manual on the Law of War* (2016) explains:

> Although the practice of issuing formal proclamations of neutrality has de-clined, States have continued to make public statements of neutrality to in-dicate their national policy and legal status in relation to an armed conflict. States may also communicate their neutral status through diplomatic chan-nels or use other means they deem appropriate.[77]

The *Manual* stops short of demanding that all non-participating states owe international obligations of neutrality, because it accepts its own idea, practised by the United States in the Second World War, of 'qualified neu-trality', whereby 'neutral States had the right to support belligerent States that had been the victim of flagrant and illegal wars of aggression'.[78]

It is contested whether and when the rights and duties that flow from Neutral Status apply outside such a formal proclamation of declaration. The German *Manual* suggests one should posit a threshold for triggering the obligations of Neutral Status by reference to the intensity or duration of the armed conflict.[79] In practice, for low-level conflicts the issue of neutral duties

---

[76] Version of 2007 at para 7.1. The 2017 version of para 7.1 has dropped this definition and simply states: 'The law of neutrality prescribes the legal relationship between belligerent States and neutral States. Belligerent States are those engaged in an international armed conflict, whether or not a formal declaration of war has been made, while neutral States are those that are not taking part in the armed conflict. A third term, "nonbelligerent" State, is also sometimes used to describe a State not participating in an armed conflict. ... The duties of neutral states to refrain from certain types of support to belligerent States are only triggered in international armed conflicts of a certain duration and intensity.'

[77] At para 15.2.1.4 (footnote with examples of declarations of neutrality omitted).

[78] At para 5.2.2 for the idea that the United States considered that it could adopt 'qualified neutrality' at the start of the Second World War as it was responding to aggression outlawed by treaties such as the 1928 Kellogg-Briand Pact of Paris. Today some experts consider that such 'qualified neutrality', ie the right to assist one side to the conflict, can only be claimed where the Security Council has determined in a binding decision who the aggressor is – see Boothby and Heintschel von Heinegg, *The Law of War: A Detailed Assessment of the US Department of Defense Law of War Manual* (2018) at 376; however, one might have to admit that in some cases the Security Council may not come to such a conclusion and yet a state would feel obliged to react to an obvious aggression by arming the victim state. If obligations of Neutral Status apply as a matter of international law then the easiest justification for the otherwise wrongful action would be for the assisting state to consider its breach of its obligations as a reprisal or countermeasure directed at the aggressor state.

[79] See the German *Law of Armed Conflict Manual*, Joint Service Regulation (ZDv) 15/2, May 2013, at para 209: 'In a state of war or any other international armed conflict, the law of neutrality may be applied to the relations between Parties to the conflict and States not participating in the conflict.' And at para 1202 (original emphasis): 'The neutrality of a State in an international armed conflict *begins* with the outbreak of an international armed conflict between other States which is of such *duration or intensity* that it requires the application of the law of neutrality.' See

under law may not arise. As Mancini concludes, having studied the evidence of the last few decades, 'so far the rules of neutrality have been applied only where there were extensive hostilities involving a large number of troops'.[80]

Upcher concluded his study by arguing that the obligations related to Neutral Status apply to all third states in all international armed conflicts (notwithstanding that they may sometimes act contrary to the obligations that flow from that Status).[81] But he nuances this by stating that the rights and duties change according to the scope of the conflict, so in the context of naval warfare the justifications for belligerents to interfere with neutral shipping will be greater as the conflict 'expands in intensity and reach', and at the same time the duties of neutrality become 'more onerous' as 'an international armed conflict expands'.[82]

For those taking this variegated approach, the full range of obligations applies only in *exceptional circumstances*. As Heintschel von Heinegg concludes:

> The position of some authors who apply the law of neutrality *in toto* to every international armed conflict is unsustainable in light of State practice. While it is true that the law of neutrality serves the interests of both belligerents and neutrals, this does not necessarily mean that the law of neutrality is applicable *in toto* in every international armed conflict. State practice supports the view that the law of neutrality applies automatically and comprehensively in exceptional cases only, regardless of whether the armed conflict in question amounts to a state of war or not. According to modern State practice, the applicability of the law of neutrality depends on functional considerations that will, in most cases, result in differential or partial applicability of that body of law.[83]

the US *Department of Defense Law of War Manual* (2016) at para 15.2.1.2: 'The duties of neutral States to refrain from certain types of support to belligerent States do not apply to all armed conflicts to which *jus in bello* rules apply; rather, such duties are only triggered in armed conflicts of a certain duration and intensity.'

[80] Mancini, 'The Effects of a State of War or Armed Conflict', in Weller (ed), *The Oxford Handbook of the Use of Force in International Law* (2015) 988–1013 at 1004.

[81] Upcher, *Neutrality* (n 52) at 30.

[82] Ibid at 51.

[83] Heintschel von Heinegg, ' "Benevolent" Third States in International Armed Conflicts' (n 73) at 561 (footnote omitted).

We seem, then, to have here an argument for a sort of sliding scale, where different rules on neutrality apply according to the extent of the conflict, while at the same time the old division between Wars and other forms of armed conflict is no longer as relevant as it once was.

I suggest that one way out of this confusion is to break down the rights and obligations associated with neutrality into four separate packages.

Let me try to sketch the outlines of the four packages before we embark on the excavation of the actual obligations:

- The expressions 'neutral states' or 'neutrals' are often used to describe states that are not parties to an armed conflict between other states.[84] We could call them 'non-participating states'. All such states have rights not to have their territory used by belligerent states as part of the conflict. Rather than seeing these rights as stemming from the law of war, it may be better simply to see them as flowing from states' sovereignty over their own territory.
- All non-participating states have certain obligations with regard to humanitarian protections for the victims of war under international humanitarian law, codified in the 1949 Geneva Conventions and their Protocols. The references in those treaties to 'neutral Powers' includes any state not participating in an international armed conflict.
- In some international conflicts, where the Security Council has not called for cooperation against a particular state, states may declare that that they will assume a Neutral Status in a strict sense and abide by the obligations in the Hague Conventions V and XIII of 1907. States with Permanent Neutrality, such as Switzerland, will automatically assume these obligations of Neutral Status from the outbreak of such hostilities between two states.
- There is a continuing sense in some quarters that a belligerent state should be able to assert against neutral ships and aircraft the sort of Belligerent Rights to engage in economic warfare at sea that states once assumed in time of a State of War. It is not at all clear what sort of conflict today would trigger the right to engage in such economic warfare, for

---

[84] See Commentary to the Draft Articles on the Effects of Armed Conflicts on Treaties, 2011, UN Doc A/66/10, Art 17, para 1, 'Article 17 is another "without prejudice" clause, which seeks to preserve the rights and duties of States arising from the laws of neutrality. It was felt that the reference to "neutrals" was, as a matter of drafting, imprecise, as it was not clear whether it referred to formal neutrality or mere non-belligerency.'

example seizing and confiscating neutral ships for carrying contraband, engaging in unneutral service or breach of blockade.

2.3.2 The Rights and Duties of All Third States to Have their Territory Protected from the International Armed Conflict

States engaged in an inter-state armed conflict are prohibited from using the territory (including the territorial waters) of all non-participating third states for the armed conflict. This means such a non-participating state is protected by law from the conflict. To be clear, this applies to all states irrespective of any declaration of war or neutrality. The International Court of Justice, when considering the legality of the use of nuclear weapons, confirmed that 'the principle of neutrality' applies 'whatever its content' and '(subject to the relevant provisions of the United Nations Charter) to all international armed conflict, whatever type of weapons might be used'.[85] The Court here was really only addressing this first rule, which would prohibit fighting or damage by belligerents on the territory of a third (non-participating) state.[86]

But this first package of rights and obligations remains important and applies in all international armed conflicts.[87] It protects all non-participating states and those that live there, and it can be seen as preventing the spread or escalation of the conflict. The non-participating state will have obligations to address harmful acts emanating from its territory.[88] The right of the non-participating (neutral) state is described in the US *Law of War Manual*:

[85] *Legality of the Threat or Use of Nuclear Weapons*, Advisory Opinion (1996) at para 89; but then the Court went on to conclude (at para 95) that it did not have the elements to conclude that the use of nuclear weapons would necessarily violate the principles and rules applicable in armed conflict 'in any circumstance'.

[86] See the detailed explanation in Dominicé, 'La question du droit de la neutralité', in Boisson de Chazournes and Sands (eds), *International Law, The International Court of Justice and Nuclear Weapons* (1999) 199–208 esp at 202–04, where he suggests that because the extension of damage onto the territory of the third state is itself a wrongful act, whether or not there is a conflict is in fact irrelevant. The rule is also reflected in Hague V (1907) Art 1 and Hague XIII (1907) Arts 1 and 25; see also Doswald-Beck (ed), *San Remo Manual on International Law Applicable to Armed Conflicts at Sea* (1995) paras 15 and 22; Harvard Program on Humanitarian Policy and Conflict Research, *Manual on International Law Applicable to Air and Missile Warfare* (2013) Section X.

[87] Boothby and Heintschel von Heinegg, *The Law of War* (n 78) at 375; and see *Department of Defense Law of War Manual* (2016) at para 15.2.1.2.

[88] See Heintschel von Heinegg, 'The Current State of the Law of Naval Warfare: A Fresh Look at the San Remo Manual', 82 *International Law Studies* (2006) 269–96 at 283; see also *Harvard Manual on Air Warfare* (n 86) Rule 168(a); the *Tallinn Manual 2.0 on Cyber Operations* (2017) Rule 153 provides 'If a neutral State fails to terminate the exercise of belligerent rights on its

The territory of neutral States is inviolable. The inviolability of neutral territory prohibits any unauthorized entry into the territory of a neutral State, its territorial waters, or the airspace over such areas by armed forces or instrumentalities of war.[89]

The *Manual* then goes on, however, to claim a right of a participating state to use force on the territory of the non-participating state in case of breaches by the non-participating state of its obligations:

> Should the neutral State be unable, or fail for any reason, to prevent violations of its neutrality by the forces of one belligerent entering or passing through its territory (including its lands, waters, and airspace), the other belligerent State may be justified in attacking the enemy forces on the neutral State's territory.[90]

There is a problematic conflation here between, on the one hand, a failure of a state to address the use of its territory by one of the belligerents, and, on the other hand, an implied authorization under international law to use force on the territory of the non-participating state. Today, I would suggest, it is not enough to point to a breach of neutrality in this way: all use of force is governed by the UN Charter,[91] as the latest UK *Manual* makes clear:

territory, the aggrieved party to the conflict may take such steps, including by cyber operations, as are necessary to counter that conduct.'

---

[89] US *Law of War Manual* (n 87) para 15.3.1.1. See also Art 1 of the Convention Respecting the Rights and Duties of Neutral Powers and Persons in Case of War on Land (1907) (Hague V); Art 1 of the Convention Concerning the Rights and Duties of Neutral Powers in Naval War (1907) (Hague XIII); see also *Harvard Manual on Air Warfare* (n 86) Rules 166 and 167.

[90] Para 14.4.2.

[91] 'As the use of force against the territory of another State is now regulated by the UN Charter, the cited rule of the law of neutrality is no longer applicable. The legality of armed countermeasures is to be judged on the basis of Article 51 of the Charter, the Charter taking precedence over the old law of neutrality.' Schindler, 'Transformations in the Law of Neutrality Since 1945', in Delissen and Tanja (eds), *Humanitarian Law* of Armed *Conflict – Challenges Ahead: Essays in Honour of Fritz Kalshoven* (1991) 367–86 at 382; see also Ingber, 'Co-Belligerency', 42 *Yale Journal of International Law* (2016) 67–120 and her assertion (at 89) that 'any right to use force in response to a violation of neutrality falling below an armed attack does not survive the UN Charter's regulation of the use of force'. See further the discussion and similar conclusion by Upcher, *Neutrality* (n 52) at 89–98. For the disagreements on this issue during the drafting of the *San Remo Manual* see Doswald-Beck (n 85) at 101–02. The *San Remo Manual* suggests (at para 22) 'If the violation of the neutrality of the State by the belligerent constitutes a serious and immediate threat to the security of the opposing belligerent and the violation is not terminated, then that belligerent may, in the absence of any feasible and timely alternative, use such force as is strictly necessary to respond to the threat posed by the violation.'

Neutral states must refrain from allowing their territory to be used by belligerent states for the purposes of military operations. If a neutral state is unable or unwilling to prevent the use of its territory for the purposes of such military operations, a belligerent state may become entitled to use force in self-defence against enemy forces operating from the territory of that neutral state. Whether or not they are so entitled will depend on the ordinary rules of the *jus ad bellum*.[92]

Attention has recently turned to how such rights and duties for non-participating states would apply with regard to cyberwarfare or in outer space. According to the *Tallinn Manual*, a '"Neutral State" denotes a State that is not a party to the international armed conflict in question.'[93] The *Manual* states that belligerents may not direct operations by cyber means against cyber infrastructure, or use neutral territory for cyber operations.[94] Furthermore, 'A neutral state may not knowingly allow the exercise of belligerent rights by the parties to the conflict from cyber infrastructure located in its territory or under its exclusive control.'[95] And as with the traditional rules, the *Manual* suggests that breaches can be met with appropriate countermeasures: 'If a neutral State fails to terminate the exercise of belligerent rights on its territory, the aggrieved party to the conflict may take such steps, including by cyber operations, as are necessary to counter that conduct.'[96]

The key point in concluding this section is that a non-participating state in an international armed conflict is protected from any other state's using its territory for the conflict. If the non-participating state fails to bring an end to such uses then another state can take steps to bring it back into compliance, but any use of force on the territory of the non-participating state

---

[92] UK Ministry of Defence, *The Manual of the Law of Armed Conflict* (2004) para 143(a). See also para 13.9E as amended in 2004 for violations of the regime of neutral waters. Compare the UK's 1958 *Manual of Military Law* at para 655: 'Should, however, one belligerent violate neutral territory by marching troops across it and the neutral state be unable or unwilling to resist the violation, the other belligerent may be justified in attacking the enemy there or in demanding compensation from the offending state.' The differences among experts are captured and described as 'doctrinal' in Doswald-Beck (ed) *San Remo Manual* (n 85) at 101-02.

[93] *Tallinn Manual 2.0 on the International Law Applicable to Cyber Operations* (2017) at 553.

[94] Ibid Rules 150 and 151.

[95] Ibid Rule 152.

[96] Ibid Rule 153. For outer space, it has been suggested by Heintschel von Heinegg that the core rules apply in all situations of armed conflict, and so 'the launching of belligerent military space objects from neutral territory constitutes a violation of neutrality'. But in his view, 'If the neutral State is unwilling or unable to terminate the violation of its neutrality and if the violation is serious, the aggrieved belligerent is entitled to use proportionate force to terminate the violation'. Heintschel von Heinegg, 'Neutrality and Outer Space', 93 *ILS* (2017) 526–47 at 538.

should today, I would say, be justified under the law on the use of force, and not by simple reference to some breach of neutral duties.[97]

2.3.3 The Humanitarian Protection Provisions for the Protection of Victims of War in Neutral States

The Geneva Conventions of 1949 (GC) and Additional Protocol I of 1977 (AP I) contain a number of protections for the victims of international armed conflicts. They contain duties for 'neutral Powers', and refer in addition to 'neutral or non-belligerent powers' as well as to 'neutral and other States not Parties to the conflict'.[98] We are here in the protective humanitarian branch of the laws of war, and there seems no reason to question the low threshold that would normally apply for the applicability for these treaties to an inter-state armed conflict. There is no need here to tangle up the humanitarian duties of neutral states with the onerous traditional duties associated with a State of War (discussed in the next package).

For an example of these protective humanitarian provisions consider Article 4 of the First Geneva Convention 1949, which demands that neutral states apply the provisions regarding the wounded and sick to individuals received in their own territory. Here the idea is to ensure protection for such persons in third neutral states beyond the territory of the states in conflict. The idea that such neutral states would only be bound if there were a formal Declaration of Neutrality or a conflict amounting to a War makes no sense.

The ICRC Commentary to the Additional Protocols confirms that the term 'neutral' in the Geneva Conventions can be interpreted as covering non-participation in conflicts in general.[99] It is also clear that all non-participating

---

[97] In his historical account, Verziij was unable to find historical examples of 'counter-action' by belligerents in response to neutral states violating their obligations towards belligerents. He details, however, the explicit references in the 1907 Hague Conventions that state that the use of force by a neutral state to suppress acts against its territory by a belligerent cannot be regarded as hostile acts. *International Law in Historical Perspective: Part IX-B The Law* of Neutrality (1979) at 38. See Arts 10 and 26 of Conventions V and XIII respectively. Art 24 of the Harvard Draft Convention on Rights and Duties of Neutral States in Naval and Aerial War (1939) foresaw reprisals by belligerent states against neutral states, but added 'a State is not to be charged with failure to perform its duties as a neutral State because it has not succeeded in inducing a belligerent to respect its rights as a neutral State': 33 *AJIL* (supplement) (1939) 175–203.

[98] See eg GC 1 Art 4; GC III Arts 4B(2); and AP I Art 2(c).

[99] Sandoz, Swinarski and Zimmermann (eds), *Commentary on the Additional Protocols of 8 June 1977 to the Geneva Conventions of 12 August 1949* (1987) at para 136; see further ICRC *Commentary GC I* (2016) Art 4 esp at paras 908–919; Sandoz, 'Rights, Powers, and Obligations of Neutral Powers under the Conventions', in Clapham, Gaeta, and Sassòli (eds), *The 1949*

states would continue to have these international humanitarian law obligations in relation to the wounded, even if the Security Council had called for
all states to take measures against a belligerent state.[100]

2.3.4 Rules Related to Neutral Status in a Strict Sense: Abstention, Prevention and Impartiality

A third package of obligations relates to what might be termed Neutral Status
in a strict sense (use of capitals deliberate). In contrast to the first two packages, whereby all non-participant states take on rights and obligations in
every international armed conflict, these duties may only apply under certain
conditions that flow from the older ideas of War. The duties that flow from
Neutral Status are traditionally said to be abstention, prevention and impartiality. They have been summarized by Schindler as follows:[101]

> Abstention means that the neutral State may not provide military assist-
> ance to belligerents. In particular it may not put at their disposal troops,
> war materials, territory, military intelligence and credits for war pur-
> poses (*cf*, Articles 5–8 of the Hague Convention V and Article 6, Hague
> Convention XIII).
>
> Under the duty of prevention, the neutral State is obliged to prevent belli-
> gerents from using its territory for war purposes. Neutrals may not tolerate
> on their territory acts of belligerents which are prohibited by the law of neu-
> trality (*cf*, Articles 5 and 10 of the Hague Convention V, Articles 8 and 25,
> Hague Convention XIII) [eg the movement of belligerents, munitions or
> supplies through the territory, the erection of radio equipment for commu-
> nication with belligerent forces, formation or recruitment of combatants].
>
> Finally, the duty of impartiality obliges the neutral State to apply equally
> to all belligerents the rules set up by itself with regard to its relations with

---

Geneva Conventions: A Commentary (2015) 85–108, at 92-3; for a discussion of the scope of the
obligations see Sassòli, *International Humanitarian Law* (2019) Ch 9.5.

[100] ICRC *Commentary GC I* (2016) para 918.
[101] Schindler, 'Transformations in the Law of Neutrality Since 1945', in Delissen and Tanja
(eds), *Humanitarian Law of Armed Conflict – Challenges Ahead: Essays in Honour of Fritz
Kalshoven* (1991) 367–86 at 379–80. For a very thoughtful detailed study, see Upcher, *Neutrality*
(n 52).

belligerents *eg* rules restricting the private export of war materials (*cf*, Article 9 of both Hague Conventions V and XIII).

The question for us now is when might these obligations still apply?

The law on Neutral Status now has to be adjusted to take into account the obligations undertaken by UN member states. Where the UN Security Council decides that a member state has to cooperate with a UN authorized use of force in an international armed conflict, or in the imposition of sanctions on certain goods, those obligations as a UN member state override any obligations that flow from that member state's Neutral Status.[102] Whether or not the Security Council can make such demands on a non-member state was of some interest before Switzerland joined the United Nations,[103] but it is now of limited interest. In fact the clearest modern practice on the issue of the obligations of a state with Neutral Status has emerged since Switzerland joined the United Nations.

The application of these rules related to Neutral Status, reflected in treaty law and sometimes considered customary,[104] emerges when one considers the way Switzerland carries out its obligations, which are not related to any particular conflict but stem from its status of Permanent Neutrality.[105] First,

---

[102] See esp Arts 25 and 103 of the UN Charter.

[103] See Thürer, 'UN Enforcement Measures and Neutrality: The Case of Switzerland' 30 *Archives du droit international* (1992) 63–85.

[104] See, eg, Hague V (1907) and Hague XIII (1907). The Irish cases mentioned in Ch 1 of this book considered whether Ireland (a non-party to these treaties) was bound by customary international law on neutrality. The results are contradictory. In *Horgan v An Taoiseach et al* ILDC 486 (IE 2003), the Judge found that there was a war and that customary international law on neutrality applied to Ireland as the operation was not 'UN led' (at paras 120–122 and 125): 'Despite the great historic value attached by Ireland to the concept of neutrality, that status is nowhere reflected in Bunreacht na hÉireann, or elsewhere in any domestic legislation. It is effectively a matter of government policy only, albeit a policy to which, traditionally at least, considerable importance was attached. Ireland is thus in a different position than certain other States, who have incorporated a permanent status of neutrality in their domestic laws. Without exhaustively requoting from the charters, conventions and writings relied upon by the plaintiff in this case, I am satisfied that there does still exist in international law a legal concept of neutrality whereunder co-relative rights and duties arise for both belligerents and neutrals alike in times of war in circumstances where the use of force is not "UN led". ... The court is prepared to hold therefore that there is an identifiable rule of customary law in relation to the status of neutrality whereunder a neutral state may not permit the movement of large numbers of troops or munitions of one belligerent State through its territory en route to a theatre of war with another.' In *Dubsky v Government of Ireland et al* ILDC 485 (IE 2005), the Judge concluded (at para 90) 'I do not accept that the applicant has established that the provisions of the Hague Convention as contended for, are sufficiently well established as a principle of international law as are necessarily included in Article 29 of the Constitution.'

[105] Seger, 'The Law of Neutrality' in Clapham and Gaeta (eds), *The Oxford Handbook of International Law in Armed Conflict* (2014) 248–70; Permanent Neutrality is explained ibid at 259–50; see also Bothe, 'Neutrality, Concept and General Rules', *MPEPIL* (2015) at para

one should understand that, from the perspective of a UN member state, once the Security Council has authorized the use of force and UN member states are bound by decisions of the Council in terms of what they must do to co-operate, then no duties related to Neutral Status apply. The non-participating state is simply obliged as a UN member state to do whatever the Security Council demands. As explained by the Swiss Federal Government in 2005, in its review of its policy with regard to the 2003 Iraq conflict, 'neutrality law is not applicable to military measures decided on by the UN Security Council in accordance with Chapter VII of the UN Charter'.[106]

But where an international armed conflict arises without any Security Council authorization and demands on the member states, the international law on Neutrality may apply to a state that has assumed Neutral Status. The detail has been helpfully explained by Seger, from the perspective of the Legal Advisor of the Ministry of Foreign Affairs of Switzerland. For example, in the context of the 2003 Iraq conflict, Switzerland officially declared the application of the Law on Neutrality and undertook its own obligations, from the 'beginning of the aerial attacks on Iraq on 20 March 2003'.[107] Similarly, Switzerland had denied overflight to belligerent states in the 1991 conflict with Iraq (when Switzerland was not yet a member of the United Nations),[108] and again in 1999 when it rejected requests by NATO for military over-flights and transit of military goods through its territory in the context of the Kosovo conflict. In the words of a Swiss brochure prepared by the Federal Government, 'As NATO's military operation took place without a UN mandate, the law of neutrality had to be observed.'[109]

15: 'Permanent neutrality a status under which a State undertakes in peacetime a legal obligation to remain neutral in case of an armed conflict between two other states.'

[106] Summary of Switzerland's neutrality policy during the Iraq conflict in response to the Reimann Postulate (03.3066) and to the Motion by the SVP Parliamentary Group (03.3050) of 2 December 2005 at para 3.1.1. So when the Security Council did later authorize the use of force, the report continues (at para 6) 'Security Council Resolution 1546 means that neutrality cannot legally be applied.'

[107] Seger, 'The Law of Neutrality' (n 105) at 254.

[108] See White Paper on Neutrality: Annex to the Report on Swiss Foreign Policy for the Nineties of 29 November 1993 at 18: 'As a matter of principle, Switzerland has never participated in military measures. When allied military Gulf War operations . . . began on January 17, 1991, the Federal Council decided not to allow countries involved in the military measures decreed by the UN to fly over Swiss territory with combat aircraft or airlifters carrying troops and ammunition. Already then, however, the Federal Council announced that it would re-examine Swiss practice in this area.'

[109] *Swiss Neutrality*, 4th edn (no date) at 8, available at https://www.eda.admin.ch/dam/eda/en/documents/aussenpolitik/voelkerrecht/Swiss%20neutrality.pdf.

The ending of the obligations that flow from the self-imposed Neutral Status is, according to Seger, something that can be determined by the state that has assumed this Status:

> Unless a formal armistice or peace agreement is signed between the warring parties, the determination of the appropriate moment to cease applying the law of neutrality is left to the appreciation of the neutral power. In the case of the Iraq war Switzerland considered this moment to have come on 16 April 2003 when the Iraq army was seen as defeated, and lifted the measures taken in application of the Hague Conventions of 1907. The issue of military occupation is left unanswered by the Hague Conventions. One may find arguments for and against the continued applicability of the law of neutrality: the fact that occupation is a direct consequence of the armed conflict and is still a military act speaks in favour. On the other hand, occupation is also the consequence of military defeat of the occupied power. Since the hostilities between the former belligerents have come to an end (at least provisionally), the law of neutrality which is intended for active war is no longer applicable.[110]

What about states that are not in the unambiguous situation of Switzerland with its Permanent Neutrality? Three possibilities are often suggested as triggering the obligations related to Neutral Status: there is a Declaration of War, and so non-participating states are on notice that they have duties under the law of Neutrality; there are Declarations of Neutrality, and such Declarations trigger Neutral Status with the attendant rights and obligations; or the scope of the conflict is so extensive that the rules relating to Neutral Status apply just as they would have done in the past in time of War. The doctrine produces no clear answer.

The late LC Green continued to make the following suggestion in the 2008 version of his book:

> So that third states may know when the duties of neutrality are expected of them, belligerents should notify non-parties to the conflict that a state of war exists, although if it is clear that this is a matter of public notoriety and they do in fact know of the state of affairs they cannot defend what would otherwise be unneutral conduct on the lack of notification. Regardless of

---

[110] Seger, 'The Law of Neutrality' (n 105) at 254.

notification, the rights and duties of neutrality come into effect with the outbreak of hostilities and it is usual, if no declaration of war has been announced or notifications thereof made for third states to issues declarations proclaiming their neutrality. Nevertheless, if the belligerents deny that a state of war exists, as did the United Kingdom at the time of the Suez conflict in 1956, they cannot complain if third states refuse to observe the rules of neutrality.[111]

Ultimately he has left the door open for non-participating neutral states to avoid the obligations that flow from Neutral Status in situations where the other states deny they are in a State of War. Should we insist today on more? Should the obligations of Neutral Status now apply to all states, irrespective of how the parties categorize their conflict? At one level it would seem a wise thing to expand the duties on non-participating states in this way. Duties of abstention in participation in the conflict could prevent the expansion or even the duration of the conflict, and this looks at first sight like a good thing. But the history of this topic suggests that things are not so simple.

Violations of the rights and duties of Neutral Status have themselves been historically used to justify the use of force and new Wars in their own right. Insisting on strict obligations connected to Neutral Status for every significant conflict could create more tension rather than less violence. It is said that it was the manner of the British denial of the right of the United States to trade with France that was one of the causes of the 1812 War.[112] Similarly, violations of the neutrality rights of the United States by Germany in the First World War were also a factor leading the United States to enter that War.[113] Such examples may seem irrelevant today, but the idea that the armed conflict can be taken to neutral states that are unwilling or unable to fulfil their neutral duties has some traction. It looks as though insisting on neutral duties could be another way to expand rather than reduce the use of force abroad.

In any event, as we saw above, a state that might have obligations that flow from some continuing idea of Neutral Status can apparently argue that it is

[112] For the detail of the background and further references to the official reasons in the Declaration of War, see Kert, *Prize and Prejudice: Privateering and Naval Prize in Atlantic Canada in the War of 1812* (1997).

[113] Neff, *The Rights and Duties of Neutrals* (n 57) at 162 suggests that the United States entered the First World War 'for the defence of its claimed neutral rights'; he also considers that concerns about neutral rights led to the US Declaration of War on the United Kingdom in 1812: Neff, 'A Tale of Two Strategies: Permanent Security and Collective Security', in Reginbogin and P Lottaz (eds), *Permanent Neutrality: A Model for Peace, Security, and Justice* (2020) 15–38 at 18.

breaching those obligations by way of reprisal in order to help a state that is the victim of an aggression by another state. We saw this with regard to the way the US *Manual* currently describes the idea of 'non-belligerency' by reference to its assistance to Great Britain in the early part of the Second World War.

Stepping back, we could ask, from a moral perspective, should we be encouraging aloofness or rather solidarity with the victims of aggression? An obligation of abstention for all states that were not participating in the War made sense when War was a duel to resolve a dispute or reclaim a debt and no international law prevented states from going to War in this way. But now that the recourse to force is forbidden, why should states be forbidden from acting in ways that punish the wrongdoing aggressive state and assist the innocent victim state?

Recent state action suggests that governments want to keep their options open. Italy chose to describe its position as one of non-belligerency with regard to the 2003 conflict with Iraq. Italy prohibited aircraft from taking off to bomb Iraq, but allowed troops not immediately engaged in combat activity to take off from Italian soil.[114] Ronzitti further explains how the strict obligations might have operated had Italy had Neutral Status rather than been simply 'non-belligerent'. A number of treaties between Italy and the United States regulate US military facilities in Italy: 'It would have been impossible to follow a strict policy of neutrality since it would have implied freezing NATO assets and interning American soldiers!'[115]

But the issues here, I would suggest, are more political than technical. As Ronzitti concludes, 'Non-belligerency could be an appropriate policy in those legal orders in which constitutional constraints limit the possibility of going to war.' As was seen in section 2.1.2, the Italian Constitution says that Italy rejects 'war as an instrument of aggression', but Ronzitti suggests that political or logistical support is not covered. Other NATO states, such as France, Germany and Turkey, all allowed overflight over their territory for this 2003 conflict with Iraq.[116] Some might see all this support as constituting violations of the obligations of Neutral Status.[117] The problem is that if such

---

[114] Ronzitti, 'Italy's Non-Belligerency During the Iraqi War', in Ragazzi (ed), *International Responsibility Today: Essays in Memory of Oscar Schachter* (2005) 197–207.

[115] Ibid at 200. Note Hague V (1907) Art 11, 'A neutral Power which receives on its territory troops belonging to the belligerent armies shall intern them, as far as possible, at a distance from the theatre of war.'

[116] Ronzitti, 'Italy's Non-Belligerency' (n 114) at 202.

[117] See Verlinden, 'The Law of Neutrality' (n 53) at 104.

obligations exist, states have ignored them.[118] There is little convincing evidence that states consider that the old law relating to Neutral Status applies to such a situation beyond the obligations of Permanent Neutrality adopted by Switzerland and others. It seems to me that the better view is that today Neutral Status is something that a state elects to have.[119] In sum, it seems fair to draw the partial conclusion that the duties attached to Neutral Status in a strict sense apply where states have formally declared themselves to have this Status.

As already noted, the content of the obligations that flow from Neutral Status are abstention, prevention and impartiality. Let us look into these obligations in a bit more detail.

The question of supplying arms is complicated. According to the abstention rule, Neutral Status means the state cannot supply either side with arms, etc,[120] and further rules cover the conversion of merchant ships to warships.[121] However, the Hague Conventions (1907) expressly state that 'A neutral Power is not called upon to prevent the export or transport, on behalf of one or other of the belligerents, of arms, munitions of war, or, in general, of anything which can be of use to an army or a fleet.'[122] This has been understood to mean that there is no obligation to ban *private* arms sales, even though the obligation remains to ensure that any restrictions are applied impartially. Switzerland expresses this as an obligation to 'ensure equal treatment for belligerent states in respect of the exportation of war material.'[123]

---

[118] 'In post-World War II international armed conflicts States not parties have rarely complied with the comparatively strict rules of the law of neutrality laid down in the 1907 Hague Conventions V and XIII. Instead, they have more or less openly supported one of the belligerent parties, either economically or militarily.' Heintschel von Heinegg, ' "Benevolent" Third States' (n 73) at 548.

[119] See in this direction Roberts and Guelff (eds), *Documents on the Laws of War*, 3rd edn (2001) at 86 (with regard to Hague V) and at 127–28 (with regard to Hague XIII): 'UN member states are free to be neutral or non-belligerent if, in an armed conflict, the UN does not call upon all members to take action involving the use of force under Chapter VII of the Charter.' Of course if two states went to War and insisted on other states abiding by the Neutrality obligations in the Hague Conventions V and XIII, those obligations could perhaps be seen as valid as a matter of treaty law, but this rather suggests that states retain the right to go to War and benefit from the Belligerent Rights associated with being at War. We will be questioning in Chapter 8 whether such Belligerent Rights should continue to exist.

[120] See Hague XIII (1907) Art 6.

[121] See Hague VII Convention Relative to the Conversion of Merchant Ships into War-ships (1907).

[122] See Hague V (1907) Art 7; Hague XIII (1907) Art 7.

[123] 'Neutrality', Directorate of International Law, Federal Department of Foreign Affairs, Switzerland, available at https://www.eda.admin.ch/eda/en/fdfa/foreign-policy/international-law/neutrality.html.

Today, however, arms exports are usually strictly regulated and export licences would be required from the state. The state's involvement in private arms supplies to a state involved in an international armed conflict is going to be such that the old laissez-faire idea of non-interference with the private sector's exports of arms makes little sense. Bothe is clear that, in his opinion, a new rule has emerged, which would consider a state's authorization of arms transfers from the private sector to violate the obligations of a state that has assumed Neutral Status:

> The separation of the state and the private armaments industry is nowadays artificial and does not correspond with political reality. Arms production and arms trade are in many ways managed, promoted, and controlled by the state. Therefore it would simply be unrealistic if one did not attribute to the state the exports of that state's 'official' arms industry. Modern state practice accords with the rule of non-separation. Where states took the view that the law of neutrality applied, they did not permit arms exports by private enterprise, nor did they rely on the artificial separation between state and private enterprise. According to the current state of customary law, the correct view is that a state's permission to supply war material constitutes a non-neutral service.[124]

Furthermore, in any event, all states will have obligations not to aid or assist violations of international law by the receiving state.[125] States parties to the Arms Trade Treaty (2013) will have additional obligations where the arms or ammunition would or could be used for certain violations of international law, including war crimes.[126]

Special rules apply in treaty law forbidding recruitment to assist the belligerents,[127] duties to intern the troops of belligerent armies on the territory of states with Neutral Status,[128] and obligations related to the fitting out or arming of ships in the jurisdiction of these states. A state with Neutral Status has an obligation to do what it can 'to prevent the fitting out or arming of

---

[124] Bothe, 'The Law of Neutrality', in Fleck (ed), *The Handbook of Humanitarian Law in Armed Conflict*, 3rd edn (2013) 549–80 at 562; see also Neff, *The Rights and Duties of Neutrals* (n 57) 201–02.

[125] See Art 16 of the ILC's Articles on State Responsibility (2001); and Jackson, *Complicity in International Law* (2015).

[126] For the details, see Casey-Maslen, Clapham, Giacca and Parker, *The Arms Trade Treaty: A Commentary* (2016).

[127] Hague Convention V (1907) Art 4.

[128] Hague Convention V (1907) Art 11.

any vessel within its jurisdiction which it has reason to believe is intended to cruise, or engage in hostile operations, against a Power with which that Government is at peace'.[129] A second connected rule for Neutral Status demands that such states prevent adapted ships leaving 'for use in war'.[130]

Lastly in this context, we can mention Seger's examination of what it means to ensure impartiality or equal treatment:

> [T]he principle of equal treatment only applies to acts of the neutral state which are of military relevance to the belligerents. It does not require the neutral to treat them impartially or equally in other areas, such as politics, human rights, or the media. For instance, a neutral state may criticize one party for resorting to armed force or for not respecting the laws of armed conflict without violating its neutrality.[131]

Switzerland has the status of 'Permanent Neutrality'. As Seger explains:

> [A] permanent neutral state fully respects its obligations if it practises a military neutrality and a 'political' neutrality is not required. As an example, a neutral power is entirely free to recognize other states, to establish diplomatic relations or not, and to take positions on violations of human rights or international humanitarian law.[132]

Beyond the legal obligations it has assumed, Switzerland has distinguished a separate neutrality policy. 'The policy of neutrality is not governed by law. It is a combination of all the measures a neutral state takes of its own accord to ensure the clarity and credibility of its permanent neutrality'.[133] There may be some international legal obligations that apply to a state with Permanent Neutrality even in peacetime. For example, such a state could not join a military alliance that demanded military assistance in the event that another member is attacked.

---

[129] Hague Convention XIII (1907) Art 8.

[130] Hague Convention XIII Art 8.

[131] Seger, 'The Law of Neutrality' (n 105) at 257; see also, on human rights law and neutrality, Schindler, 'Neutrality and Morality: Developments in Switzerland and in the International Community', 14 *American University International Law Review* (1998) 155–70.

[132] Segar (n 105) at 269.

[133] 'Neutrality', Directorate of International Law, Federal Department of Foreign Affairs, Switzerland, available at https://www.eda.admin.ch/eda/en/fdfa/foreign-policy/international-law/neutrality.html.

2.3.5 The Question of the Rights of a Belligerent State over Ships and Aircraft from Neutral States

We shall see in Chapter 8 that there are real questions to be answered when it comes to deciding if the traditional Belligerent Rights of a State at War should continue to be applied in a world where recourse to War has been abolished by law. There are also a number of new practical challenges that suggest that searching for, diverting, seizing, or even attacking or destroying ships flying neutral flags are no longer feasible courses of action in the modern world.[134]

The law of economic naval warfare, whether or not it has survived the outlawing of war and the arrival of the UN Charter, was developed and distorted in the two World Wars, with the result that hundreds of neutral merchant ships were destroyed and thousands of crew members and passengers lost their lives, as each side sought to demolish the economic life of their enemy. As Humphrey explains, this traditional law 'was developed for and clearly applicable to war, and war on a scale requiring the economic destruction of the opposition where the very survival of the state was at stake'.[135]

I will be suggesting that we may be making a fundamental error if we blithely transfer these Belligerents Rights for states at War to today's armed conflicts.

For the moment it is enough to highlight that when these rules for warfare at sea were last codified by experts in the *San Remo Manual* in 1994, the commentary concluded that, while it is clear that the 'protective rules of

---

[134] See Haines, 'War at sea: Nineteenth-century laws for twenty-first century wars?', 98(2) *IRRC* (2016) 419–47. The far-reaching belligerent rights that seem to remain on the books, such as blockade and capture of enemy goods, and even the destruction of enemy merchant shipping, have been similarly questioned by Haines in an earlier piece as not only 'out of fashion' and politically problematic, but also in some cases unacceptable and absurd. 'The idea that it would today be generally acceptable for belligerent warships to trawl the oceans in search of belligerent merchant shipping and, when finding it, to destroy it, for the simple reason that it was not convenient to escort back to their own ports as prize, is close to absurd.' S Haines, 'The United Kingdom's Manual of the Law of Armed Conflict and the San Remo Manual: Maritime Rules Compared', 36 *Israel Yearbook of Human Rights* (2006) 89–118 at 113–14. Greenwood has also questioned the extent to which the international community would tolerate the degree of interference that goes with visit and search, condemnation of contraband in prize, and the use of force against neutral shipping. For detail, see Greenwood, 'Self-Defence and the Conduct of International Armed Conflict', in Dinstein and Tabory (eds), *International Law at a Time of Perplexity: Essays in Honour of Shabtai Rosenne* (1989) 273–88 esp at 283, although he leaves open the possibility that the traditional law developed in the two World Wars could apply in the same way 'in a conflict on the massive scale of the two World Wars'. He also suggests (ibid at 286) that 'a decision by States to regard a conflict as war would be factual rather than legal. It would normally reflect the fact that the conflict was on a considerable scale and this in turn would have a bearing on the degree of force that could be regarded as reasonably necessary and proportionate in self-defence.'
[135] Humphrey, 'Belligerent Interdiction' (n 74) at 28.

humanitarian law' apply from the moment armed force is used by the parties to the conflict, it is 'less clear if all the traditional rules relating to the duties of neutral states automatically come into operation at the same time'.[136]

The *Manual* continues, however, to say that once the belligerent rights associated with economic warfare are imposed on neutral shipping and aircraft, then one applies the rules in the *Manual* applicable to the relationship between belligerents and neutral ships and aircraft. The question left unanswered is: when exactly does this point come?[137] The post-Second World War examples of states interfering with neutral shipping mostly seem to skirt an application of traditional Belligerent Rights in time of War, and rely instead on notions of self-defence, defensive quarantine, or interdiction.[138]

We will examine in detail the rights claimed by belligerents against neutral shipping in Chapter 8. For present purposes we can mention the following: the right to capture neutral ships carrying contraband (goods destined for military use by the enemy); the right to capture neutral ships for breach of blockade; and the right to attack neutral ships for resisting such capture or failing to stop.[139]

Traditionally these economic warfare rights to capture neutral ships and goods on the high seas were applied as of right by belligerent states in a State of War. Now that force has to be justified by the Security Council, or as a proportionate and necessary act of self-defence, I will suggest that any remaining belligerent rights to acquire neutral property at sea or use force against neutral shipping are constrained by the UN Charter and the parallel customary international law.

The UK *Manual of the Law of Armed Conflict* states that the UN Charter rule that force can only be used by a belligerent state where necessary and proportionate to the 'achievement of the goal for which force may be used' applies to the detailed conduct of maritime warfare. And according to this

---

[136] Doswald-Beck (ed), *San Remo Manual* (n 85) at 74.

[137] In the past Prize Courts in the Belligerent States would be granted jurisdiction over ships and goods seized from neutral states and their jurisdiction would be associated with the State of War. One might ask whether today non-participating states would accept the jurisdiction of a Prize Court answerable only to the belligerent capturing state (see section 8.5 for more detail on prize Courts). The proposals for an International Prize Court or compulsory jurisdiction for the Permanent Court of Arbitration have not borne fruit: see the Institut de droit international's *Règlement international des prises maritimes* (1897) paras 100–109; Hague Convention (XII) relative to the Creation of an International Prize Court (1907); the Harvard Draft Convention on Rights and Duties of Neutral States in Naval and Aerial War, 33 *AJIL* (supplement) (1939) 175–203, Art 113.

[138] Neff, *The Rights and Duties of Neutrals* (n 57) 210–17.

[139] *San Remo Manual* (n 85) at paras 67, 68, 146, 153.

Manual, in 'a conflict of limited scope' the belligerent states are 'constrained' to a greater extent than the traditional rules in the action they may lawfully take 'against the shipping or aircraft of states not involved in the conflict'.[140] The phrases 'conflict of limited scope' and 'states not involved in the conflict' suggest that we are speaking of something less than Declared War and something other than Neutral Status. The *Manual*, however, does not elaborate further, nor on how such constraints would operate, adding only 'In cases where those constraints apply, further guidance will be given by the Ministry of Defence.'

Humphrey, writing in 1997 when he was the UK's Chief Naval Judge Advocate, explains the consequences of demanding that belligerents apply not only the traditional law regarding interference with neutral shipping, but also the restraints of proportionality and necessity inherent in the law of self-defence:

> [I]t follows that the legality and extent of measures of economic interdiction are dependent on the intensity of the struggle in which they are sought to be implemented: in a large scale conflict or one in which the very survival of the state is in jeopardy the full range and extent of economic measures permitted by the traditional law would be justified; in a small conflict or one of less desperate intensity such full measures would be less justified or not justifiable at all.[141]

Although this approach, which builds the limits of self-defence into the tactical calculation of how much force can be used against neutral shipping, has been roundly rejected by some experts,[142] others (and a majority of those involved in the *San Remo Manual*[143]) are of the opinion that the

---

[140] See the UK Ministry of Defence, *The Manual of the Law of Armed Conflict* (2004) (as amended) at 348–49, paras 13.3 (for force used by a belligerent against shipping or aircraft of 'states not involved in the conflict') and 13.9E (for force used in neutral waters), and generally on neutrality paras 1.42–1.43; Greenwood, 'Scope of Application of Humanitarian Law', in Fleck (ed), *The Handbook of Humanitarian Law in Armed Conflict*, 2nd edn (2007) 45–78 at 54. See further Greenwood, 'Comments', in Dekker and Post (eds), *The Gulf War of 1980–1988* (1992) 212–16 at 216 and 'Comments' by Bring in Dekker and Post at 243–4; and see the US *Manual on the Law of War* at para 15.2.3.1 and the reference in fn 40; compare Doswald-Beck (ed), *San Remo Manual* (n 85) at 101–02 discussion on para 22;

[141] Humphrey, 'Belligerent Interdiction' (n 74) at 38.

[142] Heintschel von Heinegg, '"Benevolent" Third States in International Armed Conflicts' (n 73) esp 561–65.

[143] See Doswald-Beck, 'The San Remo Manual on International Law Applicable to Armed Conflict at Sea', 89 *AJIL* (1995) 192–208 at 197.

logical consequence of the prohibition on the use of force in inter-state relations means that 'Unless the belligerent has the right to self-defence
in the first place, it cannot validly act against the neutrals through the exercise of its claimed belligerent rights.'[144] This makes sense in the abstract,
but the problem remains that, today, it is rare that a state considers that it is
the aggressor, or that its actions are not somehow authorized under the UN
Charter. Rather than seeking to limit Belligerent Rights over enemy and neutral property to those exercising self-defence, perhaps we ought to admit that
these detailed rights and obligations for Belligerent and Neutral States were
developed for periods when there could be little doubt that states were at War
and that the regime would continue until the agreement of an armistice or a
peace treaty. In other words, rather than adjusting such Wartime Belligerent
Rights for the modern world, perhaps we should admit that they should no
longer exist.

The starting point for the codification of the law of seizing private property for War at sea was that the right of visit existed from the time when the
Declaration of War had been notified to states, and continued up until the
time of a peace treaty, armistice or truce.[145] One could make the case that
these Belligerent Rights over neutral shipping and aviation only apply in a
formal State of War (and this is why I have insisted in capitalizing Belligerent
Rights, they are directly derived from the old idea of a State of War and arguably have no other legitimacy). The expert and military manuals, however, have chosen to leave open the possibility of exercising such belligerent
rights in armed conflicts of a certain duration that look a bit like wars. Those
who continue to believe in belligerent rights in this context have avoided too
much detail on the threshold question by explaining that these claimed rights
in practice only occur from the moment that a belligerent state resorts to 'recognized methods and means by, for example interfering with neutral shipping and aviation'.[146]

---

[144] Orakhelashvili, 'Overlap and Convergence: The Interaction Between *Jus ad Bellum* and *Jus in Bello*', 12 *Journal of Conflict and Security Law* 2 (2007) 157–96 at 192; for the details of some of these claimed Belligerent Rights, see Ch 8.

[145] See the Institut de droit international's 'Traitement de la propriété privée dans la guerre maritime (1877) Zurich Session, para V : 'Le droit de visite peut être exercé depuis le moment où la déclaration de guerre a été notifiée jusqu'à la conclusion de la paix. Il est suspendu pendant une trêve ou un armistice.' The London Declaration concerning the Laws of Naval War (1909), which did not enter into force, was to apply under Article 66 in any war in which all the belliger-ents would be parties to the Declaration.

[146] Heintschel von Heinegg, '"Benevolent" Third States in International Armed Conflicts' (n 73) at 561.

As I will be arguing in Chapter 8 that no such belligerent rights should continue to exist over enemy or neutral ships and goods, there is no need for me here to add to the doctrine and try to develop a threshold for their application. There is no need to adapt the old ideas of economic warfare that allowed that a state at War can capture neutral ships and aircraft accused of unneutral service. One might recall the origin of some of these rules of unneutral service. The Rule of the War of 1756 is explained by Neff as stemming from the idea that colonial trading should be reserved for subjects of the colonial state. So when France opened its colonial trade in the West Indies to the Dutch, the British considered that neutral Dutch ships carrying French goods could be interfered with and the French goods seized as good prize. The justification for the Rule of 1756, according to Neff, was that the British considered that such seizures were justified, as neutrals were 'not allowed to enter a trade during wartime which was closed to them in peacetime.'[147] Belligerent Rights were in this case rights assumed by naval powers over the nationals from neutral states in order to retain their economic dominance.

Such seizures of neutral property could of course also be further justified as tackling neutral behaviour that is assisting the enemy. But today, why should a belligerent state engaged in an armed conflict have any rights over neutrals seeking to sail the high seas and engage in trade? The fact that naval powers enforced related rights for hundreds of years does not make it just. The idea of War (Declared or not) should no longer be used to capture neutral ships, planes and property, not least because it is a small step from a right to capture to a claimed right to destroy or attack neutral ships and aircraft.[148]

---

[147] Neff, *The Rights and Duties of Neutrals* (n 57) at 66.
[148] See further Ch 8; for the rights to attack, see *San Remo Manual* (n 85) paras 67 and 68, for the destruction of neutral vessels see ibid para 151.

3

Outlawing War

By considering the concept of war in historical perspective we have witnessed how the concepts associated with just war were really more about ethics, religion and chivalry than about law and sanctions in the temporal world. As explained by Lesaffer, 'the scope of the just war doctrine was theological because it was chiefly the product of theologians and canon lawyers. The just war doctrine was the answer to the question of what partaking in war did to one's eternal soul.'[1]

Even though just war doctrine was on the minds of those writing up the law of nations based on the behaviour of states, the influence of the religious element was receding, and at the same time the nature of war was changing:

> Whereas under the medieval just war doctrine, war had been conceived of as a limited law enforcement action by a prince and his adherents against the perpetrator of the injury which had caused the war, in Early Modern Europe, war became clashes between sovereign states in their entirety. By the late 16th century, it had become customary for belligerents, at the inception of war, to take a series of measures in relation to trade, enemy property, and personnel, which fundamentally disrupted normal peacetime relations. Thus, war became an encompassing state of affairs, which differed from the state of peace.[2]

Under the standard account, a State of War became a state of affairs, and the developing positive law of nations, realizing that each party would normally claim to be fighting for a just cause, set down no conditions for when a state could resort to War as recognized as an institution in international law. The eventual prohibition of War in the 1920s marks what many consider a radical shift from the previous period when, according to James Brierly, in

---

[1] Lesaffer, 'Too Much History: From War as Sanction to the Sanctioning of War', in Weller (ed), *The Oxford Handbook of the Use of Force in International Law* 35–55 at 38.
[2] Ibid at 41.

an oft-quoted turn of phrase, 'a state might go to war for any cause or for no cause at all without any breach of law'.[3]

Whether or not states were obliged to justify their resort to War,[4] the idea of war retained a powerful influence as an organizing idea or even ideal. In seeking to explain the relationship between war and law for a general audience, Brierly, writing in 1944, quoted the following passages from Heinrich von Treitschke (1834–96), the German politician and influential professor of history and political science:

> In this eternal conflict of separate states lies the beauty of history: the wish to do away with this rivalry is simply unintelligent. . . . When a state realises that existing treaties no longer express the actual relations between the Powers, then, if it cannot bring the other contracting state to acquiescence by friendly negotiations, there is nothing for it but the international lawsuit – War. . . . The justice of war depends simply on the consciousness of a moral necessity. Since there cannot be, and ought not to be, any arbitrary power above the great personalities which we call nations, and since history must be an eternal flux, war is justified. War must be conceived as an institution ordained by God.[5]

Brierly wryly comments 'Though modern international lawyers may not believe with Treitschke in the beauty and divine origin of war, most of

---

[3] Brierly, *The Law of Nations: An Introduction to the International Law of Peace*, 5th edn (1955) at 309.

[4] Recent scholarship, however, from Agatha Verdebout, has questioned this 'theory of indifference', and has stressed that even if states may have had various motives for resorting to the use of force, they were at pains to explain the causes and justification for such wars. Verdebout, 'The Contemporary Discourse on the Use of Force in the Nineteenth Century: A Diachronic and Critical Analysis', 1 *Journal on the Use of Force and International Law* (2014) 223–46 at 234, where she concludes that war and intervention were 'generally considered as prohibited as a logical consequence of the principle of the equal sovereignty of states'; compare Ruys, 'From *passé simple* to *futur imparfait*? A Response to Verdebout', 2 *Journal on the Use of Force and International Law* (2015) 3–16 at 14, who concludes 'neither state practice nor legal doctrine offers strong evidence to support the existence during the nineteenth century of a prohibition against the recourse to war *as a means of settling inter-state disputes*. There was no general prohibition against "offensive" wars.'

[5] Brierly, *The Outlook for International Law* (1944) at 19 quoting Davis, *The Political Thought of Heinrich von Treitschke* (1914) at 130 and 178. The words omitted after ;the international lawsuit – War' from the passage quoted by Brierly read (Davis at 178–79): 'Under such circumstances, a State declares war with the consciousness of fulfilling an absolute duty. No motives of personal gain are involved. The protagonists have simply perceived that existing treaties no longer correspond with their actual relations, and, since the matter cannot be decided peaceably, it must be decided by the great international lawsuit – War.'

them would not differ greatly from his view of its relation to the law.'[6] For Brierly, the majority, but not all, had chosen a 'realistic' approach, rather than relying on just war ideas, 'they regard war simply as a fact or an event, neither legal nor illegal, that occurs from time to time in the relations of states, and that the law tolerates because it can do nothing else about it.'[7] This meant that under the 'prevailing doctrine, we must accept the freedom to make war for any cause or for none as one of the prerogatives of every sovereign state.'[8]

There is today a real interest in unearthing how writers in the 19th century came to succeed in elevating state sovereignty as the ultimate value, at the same time eliminating or minimising the idea that international law had something to say about when a state could resort to War. Opinions differ on the extent to which the turn to positivism meant that an evidence-based approach to the behaviour of states really should lead us to the conclusion that states considered themselves unconstrained by the law of nations. In a fascinating new account, Jochen von Bernstorff highlights the writings and teachings of a group of German authors:

> But why Germany? For a significant part of the intellectual elite and civil servants in Germany, war was closely connected with the recent birth of the nation-state through the Franco-Prussian War of 1870–1871. In line with Hegelian philosophy and alleged historical experience, wars related to the ontology of the nation-state were thus a positive – a creative historical force. Yes, war came with sacrifice, but at the same time, it had the proven power to bring about national salvation for those nations who allegedly were more advanced both culturally and technologically than other nations.[9]

---

[6] Brierly, *The Outlook* (n 5) at 19; for the radical view on how the Covenant and the Kellogg-Briand Pact had turned the League and its sanctions into a mechanism for total wars of humanity against its enemies, see the discussion of Schmitt in Koskenniemi, *The Gentle Civilizer of Nations: The Rise and Fall of International Law 1870–1960* (2001) Ch 8.

[7] Brierly, *The Outlook* (n 5) at 22.

[8] Ibid. Similarly see Hall, *A Treatise on International Law*, 4th edn (1895) at 64–65: 'The obedience which is paid to law must be a willing obedience, and when a state has taken up arms unjustly it is useless to expect it to acquiesce in the imposition of penalties for its act. International law has consequently no alternative but to accept war, independently of the justice of its origin, as a relation which the parties to it may set up if they choose, and to busy itself only in regulating the effects of the relation.'

[9] von Bernstorff, 'The Use of Force in International Law before World War I: On Imperial Ordering and the Ontology of the Nation-State', 29 *EJIL* (2018) 233–60 at 244–45.

He also reminds us that this permissive regime for resorting to War came alongside the 'increasingly violent state practice' of the European powers fighting colonial wars, where 'no legitimate reasons for waging war were required'.[10] In addition, 'measures short of war' were being resorted to by the United States and European nations at what von Bernstorff calls the semi-periphery: Latin American, the Ottoman Empire and China. Here the justifications given were to right wrongs and recover debts, restore honour, dignity or equilibrium, or simply as part of a right of self-preservation.[11]

Let us consider one particular emblematic incident in Latin America, and the subsequent arbitration and attempt to outlaw such use of force through a multilateral treaty. Germany and Great Britain, joined by Italy, decided to take coercive measures against Venezuela for unpaid debts. Having issued a final demand and warning, the German and British naval forces eventually went through with their threat and seized the Venezuelan gunboats off the coast of Venezuela in December 1902. Venezuela responded by arresting over 200 British and German residents of Caracas. Then, following an incident where a mob seized a British merchant vessel and her crew, the British and Germans proceeded to shell the forts of Puerto Cabello. A later incident involved the German destruction of Fort San Carlos, with the loss of 25 civilian lives in a nearby town.

There was negative coverage in the British and US press, and despite what later became a Blockade (in the formal sense) and a situation of War (in the formal sense), the situation was eventually resolved by all sides' agreeing to arbitration.[12] In December 1902, as it became clear that Venezuela, under coercion, would agree to a series of arbitrations to settle the dispute, the Foreign Minister of Argentina, Luis Drago, wrote a letter containing ideas that would eventually come to be known as the Drago Doctrine, and which were partially enshrined in the first multilateral treaty to outlaw the use of force.

[10] Ibid at 245; on the absence of laws of war for the conduct of warfare, see Mégret, 'From "Savages" to "Unlawful Combatants": A Postcolonial Look at International Humanitarian Law's "Other"', in Orford (ed), *International Law and its Others* (2006) 265–317.

[11] For a critical look at the ways in which states denied the existence of war or an international law rule restraining the use of force, see Baty, 'Abuse of Terms: "Recognition": "War"', 30 *AJIL* (1936) 377–99.

[12] For detail on the background and the political forces at work, see Mitchell, 'The Height of the German Challenge: The Venezuela Blockade, 1902–3', 20 *Diplomatic History* (1996) 185–209; Brownlie, *International Law and the Use of Force by States* (1963) at 35–36 for the British admission that the blockade had created a 'state of war'.

3.1 Hague Convention (II) Respecting the Limitation of the Employment of Force for the Recovery of Contract Debts (1907)

In 1907, Hague Convention II included Drago's idea that debts could not be used as a justification for the use of force by one state against another. The Convention is also known as the Drago–Porter Convention, Porter being the delegate from the United States at the Hague Conference who negotiated the final version. Article 1 of the Convention begins:

> The Contracting Powers agree not to have recourse to armed force for the recovery of contract debts claimed from the Government of one country by the Government of another country as being due to its nationals.

Obviously this leaves open the possibility of using force to recover public debts owed by one state to another. Furthermore Article 1 continues:

> This undertaking is, however, not applicable when the debtor State refuses or neglects to reply to an offer of arbitration, or, after accepting the offer, prevents any compromis from being agreed on, or, after the arbitration, fails to submit to the award.

The Convention did not go as far as Drago had requested, and Argentina never became a party to the treaty. The treaty remains in force, however, and represents an important landmark on the legal landscape of treaties gradually circumscribing the legal possibilities for states to resort to force against another state. The arbitration clause reminds us that states were not ready to renounce the use of force in general, but rather only ready to submit to suspend the right to use force while attempts were made to settle their dispute in other ways. In fact, for most of the 19th century, peace movements in the United States and elsewhere had been formulating the idea of a World Court, which would arbitrate between states in order to replace war as the means for settling international disputes. In the words of Mark Janis, a number of key American lawyers 'genuinely believed that international law could make less likely War among nations, that the courtroom could come to replace the battlefield'.[13]

---

[13] Janis, *America and the Law of Nations 1776–1939* (2010) at 211; more generally on the peace movements and congresses in Europe, see Hippler and Vec (eds), *Paradoxes of Peace*

3.2 Hague Conventions (I) on the Pacific Settlement of Disputes (1899, 1907) and other Treaties Prohibiting Resort to War

The more general Hague Conventions on the Pacific Settlement of Disputes (1899 and 1907) were even less constraining on states. They created a weak set of obligations to avoid War or the use of force. They built on earlier treaties that similarly required that states consider mediation before resorting to force.[14] The 1907 version of Hague Convention I reads (emphasis added):

> Article 1. With a view to obviating *as far as possible* recourse to force in the relations between States, the Contracting Powers agree to use their best efforts to ensure the pacific settlement of international differences.

> Article 2. In case of serious disagreement or dispute, before an appeal to arms, the Contracting Powers agree to have recourse, *as far as circumstances allow,* to the good offices or mediation of one or more friendly Powers.

The later Bryan treaties were bilateral treaties between the United States and various nations that introduced the idea of Commissions of Inquiry. These Commissions would not only determine the facts in order to resolve a dispute where mediation had not worked, but they would also make recommendations. War was not prohibited; rather, states were subjected to what is now often referred to as a 'cooling-off period'. This form of dispute settlement through independent commissions was later incorporated into a number of multilateral treaties. A common clause reads as follows:

> The high contracting parties agree that all disputes between them, of every nature whatsoever, other than disputes the settlement of which is provided for and in fact achieved under existing agreements between the high contracting parties, shall, when diplomatic methods of adjustment have failed, be referred for investigation and report to a permanent international commission, to be constituted in the manner prescribed in the next succeeding

---

in Nineteenth Century Europe (2015); and Cooper, *Patriotic Pacifism: Waging War on War in Europe 1815–1914* (1991).

[14] See, eg, Treaty of Paris 1856 Art VIII (Peace Treaty between Great Britain, France, the Ottoman Empire, Sardinia and Russia).

article; and they agree not to declare war or begin hostilities during such investigation and before the report is submitted.[15]

The United States agreed such treaties with more than 20 states, starting with El Salvador, later including Great Britain and France, although not Germany. Many of the treaties are still in force. Other treaties provided for arbitration or conciliation. The establishment of the Permanent Court of Arbitration meant that the peaceful settlement of disputes could now in theory be preferred over War as a way of righting wrongs. Brownlie suggests, with some justification, 'It might also be argued that the obligation to use available means of peaceful settlement before going to war was one which was in process of becoming a customary rule before the Covenant appeared.'[16]

3.3 The Covenant of the League of Nations and the Prohibition of Resorting to War

The Versailles Peace Treaty that ended the First World War included a Covenant for a League of Nations. The arrangements for the League would combine the older dispute settlement techniques in a system that essentially sought to give states a chance to settle their differences without resorting to War. The Covenant combined this with the prospect of economic sanctions to be imposed on those who failed to abide by these dispute settlement procedures. The system had a built-in set of mechanisms that ensured the familiar 'cooling-off period' before resort to War. To some extent there was a collective approach to preventing War, first through authorizing members to take economic sanctions against other members and, second, through the League's Council taking responsibility for fact-finding inquiries, and even recommending military action by the member states. Sanctions against the wrongdoing state would, however, not be considered a resort to War.

The theory explaining why such sanctions were not acts of War was expressed in a 1927 Legal Position of the League.[17] This Legal Opinion came

---

[15] Treaty between Great Britain and the United States for the Advancement of Peace (1914) Art 1; the 'Bryan' treaties were named after William Jennings Bryan, the US Secretary of State. They provided for alternative ways of settling disputes between the United States and a number of different states; see Schlochauer 'Bryan Treaties 1913-14' <*MPEPIL*> (2007).

[16] Brownlie, *Use of Force* (n 12) at 56.

[17] See the 'Legal Position Arising from Enforcement in Time of Peace of the Measures of Economic Pressure Indicated in Article 16 of the Covenant, particularly by a Maritime Blockade', Report of the Secretary-General of the League submitted to the Council 15 June 1927, LNOJ (1927) 834 at 835.

in the context of doubts over the warlike nature of pacific blockades. In 1921 the League had passed a Resolution addressing the possibility of economic sanctions' constituting pacific blockade. As we saw with the blockade of Venezuela in 1902, such 'gunboat diplomacy' was difficult to distinguish from War, and indeed Prime Minister Balfour famously admitted in Parliament that the British blockade of Venezuela did involve a State of War,[18] even if the Germans had insisted up till then that it was a 'pacific blockade'. A study appended to the Legal Opinion listed over 20 pacific blockades since their establishment 'as an institution' in 1827: 'France comes first with thirteen blockades: England next with twelve. Italy has adopted this method on six occasions; Germany and Russia on four; Austria-Hungary on three.'[19]

The Legal Opinion concluded that a pacific blockade could be imposed by the League under the Covenant, whose legal validity 'should be recognised by third States'.[20] And it was suggested such a blockade gave a right to the League members to sequestrate ships and cargoes of the blockaded state as part of the operation, but then return them without compensation. The acquiescence of third states could be expected 'by their sense of the importance to the whole world of the observance of the methods of pacific settlement laid down by the Covenant'.[21]

In the event that the legitimacy of the blockade was not recognized, the Opinion foresees the possibility of the blockading powers issuing a formal Declaration of War in order to gain Belligerent Rights. There would be no need for actual hostilities, there would simply be a State of War. The fundamental point was that blockading states could not pick the rights they wanted from the regime of War and then at the same time seek to enjoy alternative rights from the regime of Peace. In the words of the study, 'There must either be a state of peace or a state of war. There can be no intermediate situation, a State cannot claim simultaneously the benefits of peace and war.'[22]

So War was considered ultimately necessary in order for member states to enforce the League's measures short of War. From the beginning it was the idea that the League could ultimately resort to War in order to uphold its Covenant that sustained some opposition to the League in the United States. This problematic idea – that, in the end, the new architecture for the peaceful

---

[18] Neff, *War and the Law of Nations: A General History* (2005) at 233, suggesting this was 'history's most off hand declaration of war'.
[19] 'Legal Position' (n 17) Appendix II at 841.
[20] Ibid at 838.
[21] Ibid.
[22] Ibid at 845.

settlement of disputes continued to rely on the ultimate sanction of War –
bolstered the alternative movement in the United States for the 'Outlawry of
War'. The American approach is engagingly and carefully revealed in the inspired book by Hathaway and Shapiro, *The Internationalists: And Their Plan
to Outlaw War*, in their telling::

> According to Article 16, a majority of states in the League Council
> had power to order member states to take up arms in defense of the
> Covenant. To solve the problem of war, the League's answer seems to have
> been . . . more war.
> War as a legal institution had been so central to international relations
> that even a bloodbath that devastated millions of lives, and wasted billions
> of dollars, could not shake it loose.[23]

Furthermore, it was precisely this idea that the League could draw the United
States into another War that worried a number of Republicans in the US
Senate,[24] even if a strict reading would suggest that the Covenant only pro-
vided for the League to *recommend* rather than *order* military action.[25]

Many accounts of the inadequacies of the Covenant's provisions on
preventing War focus on the so-called 'gaps' in the texts that allowed states
to resort to War (where, for example, there was no unanimity in the Council,
or the matter was determined under international law to be solely within the
domestic jurisdiction of a party to the dispute).[26] In addition to the problems

---

[23]   *The Internationalists: And Their Plan to Outlaw War* (2017) at 106.

[24]   Ibid at 111.

[25]   It was not universally accepted that Art 16 obliged member states to take up arms; according to the Covenant, the Council could only make recommendations; see Brierly, *The Law
of Nations* (1928) at 217, 'it would seem that the boycott provisions are intended to be automatic,
whereas the military provisions, since here the Council only has a power to *recommend* are not'.
Waldock, writing much later, considered that the Covenant 'did not compel any Member to accept even the unanimous decision of the Council or of other Members of the Assembly. The
decision to apply sanctions was for each State an individual decision.' Waldock, 'The Regulation
of the Use of Force by Individual States in International Law', 81 *RCDI* (1952) 451–517 at 479.
Compare Wehberg, *The Outlawry of War* (1931) at 82 (at 11), 'Article 16 contains the obligation
for members of the League to take up arms in the event of a forbidden war'.

[26]   See Art 15(7) and (8):

> (7) If the Council fails to reach a report which is unanimously agreed to by the members
> thereof, other than the Representatives of one or more of the parties to the dispute, the
> Members of the League reserve to themselves the right to take such action as they shall
> consider necessary for the maintenance of right and justice.
> (8) If the dispute between the parties is claimed by one of them, and is found by the
> Council, to arise out of a matter which by international law is solely within the domestic
> jurisdiction of that party, the Council shall so report, and shall make no recommenda-
> tion as to its settlement.

caused by these 'gaps', it became clear that the League's bodies were unable to decide whether something was War or not. The issue is not really about poor drafting or lack of imagination, the relevant states were just not ready to give up their perceived need to resort to War. As Brierly was at pains to point out at this time, whatever treaty arrangement might have been made, a state party determined to commit an act of aggression 'will either break the promise outright or find some disingenuous way of evading it'.[27]

We can see in the Covenant that the theological reasoning concerning just war was now less relevant than it ever had been. The Covenant did not seek to include the old just causes for War but rather regulated resort to War 'by reference to the failure of other methods of settlement'.[28] The Covenant allowed states to resort to War against a state that failed to carry out a decision of the relevant body of the League of Nations.[29] At this point the last restriction was the 'cooling-off period', whereby it was agreed that the states would in no case resort to War 'until three months after the award by the arbitrators or the judicial decision of the report by the Council'.[30]

3.3.1 Article 10: Respect for Territorial Integrity and the Emerging Crime of Aggression

Although Article 10 of the Covenant committed member states to respect the territorial integrity and political independence of all other members of the League, and preserve such integrity and independence from external aggression, this obligation was decoupled from the provision in the same Covenant that regulated the resort to War, and Article 10 seems to have been 'treated as being directed at preventing an aggressor from sticking to the fruits of a successful use of force'.[31] Article 10 was not used by the League to address the resort to force as such, even if multiple members appealed to the League on the grounds that Article 10 was violated.[32]

Although Article 10 is said to state a 'general principle that aggression was unlawful',[33] the Covenant contains no definition of aggression.[34]

---

[27] Brierly, *Outlook* (n 5) at 64.
[28] Waldock, 'Use of Force' (n 25) 517.
[29] Art 12.
[30] Ibid.
[31] Waldock, 'Use of Force' (n 25) at 469–70.
[32] Brownlie, *Use of Force* (n 12) 64-5.
[33] Ibid at 65.
[34] Art 10 reads: 'The Members of the League undertake to respect and preserve as against external aggression the territorial integrity and existing political independence of all Members of

Nevertheless, in 1925 the League Assembly passed a Resolution stating that it was 'Declaring afresh that a war of aggression should be regarded as an international crime.'[35] In the years leading up to this Resolution, two treaty texts (which never entered into force) had stressed that wars of aggression were criminal. But a careful reading reminds us that at that time the crime was considered to be a crime committed by states.[36] For example, the draft Treaty of Mutual Assistance (1923) stated 'The High Contracting Parties solemnly declare that aggressive war is an international crime and severally undertake that no one of them will be guilty of its commission.'[37] Its principal author, Lord Cecil, explained why the word 'crime' came to be used in this context:

> The first Article begins by a general condemnation of aggressive war as an international crime. That was put in, I say so quite frankly, very largely for this reason: that when I was in America I found a very large and a very honest body of opinion which brought great charges against the League and myself, that with all the attempts we had made on behalf of the League we had never condemned war, and that the first thing to be done was to condemn war. I argued that that really was implicit in the whole of the Covenant and that it did not seem to us in Europe worth while to condemn a thing which probably nine-tenths of us were united in condemning. But it was a stumbling-block, and it seemed to me that this was a good opportunity to show to these critics at any rate that the fact that we had not condemned it in terms did not mean that we did not condemn it in fact.[38]

the League. In case of any such aggression or in case of any threat or danger of such aggression the Council shall advise upon the means by which this obligation shall be fulfilled.'

[35] Resolution of 25 September 1925, reproduced in 'Report to the Seventh Assembly of the League on the Work of the Council, on the Work of the Secretariat and on the Measures taken to execute the Decisions of the Assembly', 1 June 1926.

[36] See, eg, Wehberg, *Outlawry of War* (n 25) at 82, '[t]he nation which undertakes a war of aggression is pronounced a criminal'.

[37] Art 1, Records of the Fourth Assembly, Minutes of the Third Committee, LNOJ (Special Supplement No 16) (1923) 203–06. One year later, the ill-fated Geneva Protocol had included the preambular paragraph that asserted 'that a war of aggression constitutes a violation of this solidarity and an international crime': Protocol for the Pacific Settlement of International Disputes, 2 October 1924 (this treaty never entered into force).

[38] 'The Draft Treaty of Mutual Assistance', 3(2) *Journal of the British Institute of International Affairs* (1924) 45–82 at 51–52; in 1921 the pamphlet published by the American Committee for the Outlawry of War called for a conference of all civilized nations to declare '1. The further use of war as an institution for the settlement of international disputes shall be abolished. 2. War between nations shall be declared to be a public crime, punishable by the law of nations.' Quoted by Hathaway and Shapiro, *The Internationalists* (n 23) at 113. For the background to the diverging peace movements in the USA and in Europe, see Ferrell, *Peace in their Time: The Origins of the Kellogg-Briand Pact* (1952) 1–51, who (at 35) recounts that Lord Cecil was given a 'headache' by

Interestingly, *wars* of aggression were later considered as being criminal in the sense that individuals could be prosecuted for an international crime at the International Military Tribunals established in Nuremberg and Tokyo after the Second World War.[39] *Acts* of aggression were sometimes considered something separate.[40] At one point some governments considered that the customary international *crime* of aggression was linked to the idea of a *war* of aggression (as opposed to a simple act of aggression),[41] but today the definition of the crime in the Statute of the International Criminal Court drops any reference to war, and the crime is related to 'an act of aggression which, by its character, gravity and scale, constitutes a manifest violation of the Charter of the United Nations'.[42]

Although the international definition of the crime of aggression before the International Criminal Court has now dropped the connection with the idea of war, some national laws may continue to reference wars of aggression. For example, Germany has a constitutional prohibition on preparing for 'a war of aggression', and has criminalized such preparation by anyone, with a penalty of life imprisonment or not less than 10 years.[43]

Levinson in Chicago in 1923 on the topic of the outlawry of war. For the earlier origins of these Anglo-American peace movements seeking to eliminate war through a Congress of Nations and various forms of arbitration, conciliation and a World Court, see Janis, *America and the Law of Nations* (n 36); for some of the problems, see Lovriæ-Pernak, 'Aim: Peace – Sanction: War, International Arbitration and the Problem of Enforcement', in Hippler and Vec (eds), *Paradoxes of Peace in Nineteenth Century Europe* (2015) 62–74.

[39] Although the legal significance of criminalizing state behaviour was uncertain before and after the Second World War, today the idea has been rejected as confusing in the light of the regime of individual criminal accountability under international law: ; although the legal significance of criminalizing state behaviour was uncertain then, and today the idea has been rejected as confusing in the light of the regime of individual criminal accountability under international law: Brownlie, *Use of Force* (n 12) at 150–55; Crawford, *The International Law Commission's Articles on State Responsibility: Introduction, Text and Commentaries* (2002) at 16–20.

[40] See also the UN General Assembly's Definition of Aggression annexed to UN Doc A/RES/29/3314 Res 3314 (1974) Art 5(2), 'A war of aggression is a crime against international peace. Aggression gives rise to international responsibility.'

[41] See, eg, Wilmshurst, 'Aggression', in Cryer, Friman, Robinson and Wilmshurst, *An Introduction to International Criminal Law and Procedure*, 2nd edn (2010) 312–33 at 321, and ibid, 3rd edn (2014) at 312; and see 'The customary crime remains as in the jurisprudence of Nuremberg, supplemented by the subsequent proceedings under Control Council Law No 10 and the Tokyo IMT.' Wilmshurs 3rd edn at 308. See also Cryer's revision of this chapter in ibid, 4th edn (2019) at 309: 'The crime of aggression under customary international law is generally regarded as being limited to participation in a "war" of aggression.'

[42] ICC Statute Art 8bis(1).

[43] Art 26 of the Basic Law of 1946 and Section 80 of the Criminal Code, discussed in relation to the German Prosecutor's decision not to open investigations with regard to Iraq in 2003 by Kreß, 'The German Chief Prosecutor's Decision Not to Investigate the Alleged Crime of Preparing Aggression against Iraq', 2 *JICJ* (2004) 245–64 at 255–59. For some authors the customary crime may be narrower than the ICC crime of aggression, thus leading to the possibility of arguments

3.3.2 The Covenant Scheme for Sanctioning
Illegal War

Article 11 of the Covenant made War a concern of the League, and set the scene for the League to play a role in preventing and sanctioning War.[44] But the details of how the League would sanction *illegal* resort to War as opposed to *legal* War are found in the subsequent articles. On paper the provisions today look rather quaint, allowing as they do for a *resort to War* following a three-month period following an award, judgment or report addressed to the peaceful settlement of the dispute. Nevertheless, the Covenant does make illegal and liable to sanctions *resort to War* against a state that has accepted an arbitral award, judicial decision or unanimous report of the League Council.

Here are the key paragraphs (with emphasis added):

Article 12

The Members of the League agree that, if there should arise between them any dispute *likely to lead to a rupture* they will submit the matter either to arbitration or judicial settlement or to enquiry by the Council, *and they*

---

before the ICC that *ex post facto* applications of the Court's jurisdiction could depend on the Prosecution's proving that the offence fits the customary definition related to a war of aggression; see the distinctions drawn by Milanovic, 'Aggression and Legality: Custom in Kampala', 10 *JICJ* (2012) 165–87 esp at 184–85, highlighting the idea that the customary definition of the crime based on a war of aggression requires specific collective intent 'directed to the conquest or subjugation of another state'. For another reference to war, see the Italian Constitution Art 11: 'Italy rejects war as an instrument of aggression against the freedom of other peoples and as a means for the settlement of international disputes.' For other instances of national law renouncing war and even criminalizing certain acts, see Brownlie, *Use of Force* (n 12) at 157–59. For an attempt to raise the customary international crime of aggression as part of national law, see *R v Jones* [2006] UKHL 16. See also on the customary international crime Dinstein, *War, Aggression and Self-Defence*, 6th edn (2017) at 142, but he seems to consider that the two definitions are now coterminous and that for him, 'only a fully fledged aggressive war could conceivably fit the combined conditions of "character gravity and scale" ' found in the ICC Statute definition of 'crime of aggression' (ibid at 144); see further Dinstein, 'The Crime of Aggression under Customary International Law', in Sadat (ed), *Seeking Accountability for the Unlawful Use of Force* (2018) 285–302.

[44] Under Art 11:

Any war or threat of war, whether immediately affecting any of the Members of the League or not, is hereby declared a matter of concern to the whole League, and the League shall take any action that may be deemed wise and effectual to safeguard the peace of nations. In case any such emergency should arise the Secretary General shall on the request of any Member of the League forthwith summon a meeting of the Council.

It is also declared to be the friendly right of each Member of the League to bring to the attention of the Assembly or of the Council any circumstance whatever affecting international relations which threatens to disturb international peace or the good understanding between nations upon which peace depends.

agree in no case to resort to war until three months after the award by the arbitrators or the judicial decision, or the report by the Council. In any case under this Article the award of the arbitrators or the judicial decision shall be made within a reasonable time, and the report of the Council shall be made within six months after the submission of the dispute.

Article 13 (paragraph 4)

The Members of the League agree that they will carry out in full good faith any award or decision that may be rendered, *and that they will not resort to war against a Member of the League which complies therewith*. In the event of any failure to carry out such an award or decision, the Council shall propose what steps should be taken to give effect thereto.

Article 15 (paragraph 6)

If a report by the Council is unanimously agreed to by the members thereof other than the Representatives of one or more of the parties to the dispute, *the Members of the League agree that they will not go to war with any party to the dispute which complies with the recommendations of the report.*

Article 16 explained:

Should any Member of the League *resort to war in disregard of its covenants* under Articles 12, 13 or 15, it shall ipso facto be *deemed to have committed an act of war against all other Members* of the League, which hereby undertake immediately to subject it to the severance of all trade or financial relations, the prohibition of all intercourse between their nationals and the nationals of the covenant-breaking State, and the prevention of all financial, commercial or personal intercourse between the nationals of the covenant-breaking State and the nationals of any other State, whether a Member of the League or not.

It shall be the duty of the Council in such case *to recommend* to the several Governments concerned what effective military, naval or air force *the Members of the League shall severally contribute to the armed forces to be used* to protect the covenants of the League.

So, as Brownlie explains in his detailed examination of the law during this period:

Articles 12, 13, and 15 introduced a new concept into international law: a distinction between legal and illegal wars based on the formal criterion of compliance or non-compliance with obligations to use procedures for pacific settlement of disputes.[45]

But the political will was not there to make this system work when faced with major incidents, such as the Italian invasion and annexation of Ethiopia, or the Japanese conflicts with China.[46] States did not care enough to engage in effective sanctions or military responses.

For our purposes we should note that there were particular reasons why states avoided determining that there had been a resort to War. First, a finding of a resort to War in the absence of respecting the dispute settlement procedures would trigger the prospect of sanctions under Article 16. Key states that could be the target of sanctions resisted this furiously, and the states that would have to impose sanctions seemed unenthusiastic.

Second, for a victim state, such as China at that time, it has been suggested that it would have been disadvantageous for China to have declared War (moving the situation from material war to a technical State of War) as this would have triggered Neutrality obligations for states such as the USA, making it harder for China to get access to arms.

Third, by the 1930s it was becoming clearer that even if the sanctions regime were triggered, the sort of sanctions states were prepared to take were ineffective and self-harming. So, defining a conflict as a War meant potentially undermining the credibility of the League as its eventual response to War could prove ineffective.

Even against this background, lawyers spent considerable energy debating the meaning of the relevant expressions found in the Covenant: 'war or threat of war', 'resort to war' and 'act of war'. For some scholars, such as Wright, such references remained linked to the 'existence of legal war'[47] or, as uniquely referenced by Waldock, 'full-dress war'.[48] While Brierly was ready to countenance that this reference to 'resort to war' covered 'acts which are intrinsically "warlike" in character, even though a "state of war" does not result from such acts owing to the refusal of the other State to treat them as having introduced

---

[45] Brownlie, *Use of Force* (n 12) at 57.

[46] For the way the League bodies dealt with the Japanese conflict with China over Manchuria, see Lauterpacht, ' "Resort to War" and the Interpretation of the Covenant during the Manchurian Dispute', 28 *AJIL* (1934) 43–60 at 58–59, where he concluded that the Covenant did not automatically render illegal all acts of armed force, it rather *authorized* the members of the League to treat such acts as illegal according to the circumstances, including their attitude to the collective enforcement of peace.

[47] Wright, 'When Does War Exist?', 26 *AJIL* (1932) 362–68 at 367.

[48] Waldock, 'Use of Force' (n 25) at 471–72.

it',[49] Lauterpacht sought a middle way, coining the term 'constructive state of war', which allowed for third states to consider that a state of War existed even in the absence of either belligerent having the intention to be at War.[50]

Refreshingly, Borchard appealed for us to 'clear away the morass into which legalistic definitions' have led the peace movement:

> The position is made even more awkward by the suggestion, presumably derived from Grotius, that there is no twilight zone between 'peace' and 'war', so that these violent acts by which one nation sought to impose its will upon another must be called 'peaceful', or at least not to have disturbed 'peace'. Reis Effendi expressed this idea astutely when, in speaking of the so-called Battle of Navarino, in which the Turkish and Egyptian fleets were annihilated by the French, British, and Russians with great loss of life but, in the opinion of some, without creating a state of war, he said: 'It is quite as if, in smashing a man's head, I assure him at the same time of my friend-ship'. . . .
>
> It is submitted that Grotius ought not to be taken too literally, and that it must be conceded that *de facto* war, with or without a full state of war, is one of the commonest of phenomena, and that it cannot be reconciled with a state of peace.[51]

This sharp difference among the scholars highlights how there was a period when we moved from an understanding that references to 'war' in the Covenant obviously meant War in the formal, legal, technical sense, to an appreciation that, when measures were designed to prevent war through pacific settlement of disputes, the legal texts could be considered as aimed at armed

---

[49] Brierly, 'International Law and Resort to Armed Force', 4 *CLJ* (1932) 308–19.

[50] 'The Covenant would to a large extent be deprived of its meaning if "resort to war" meant invariably war in its limited technical sense, ie, a state of hostilities accompanied by a manifested *animus belligerendi*. The interpretation of the Covenant must of necessity be a compromise between the two apparently conflicting elements, one of which represents the purpose of the Covenant as an instrument for the preservation of the peace, and the other which gives expression to the intention of the signatories of the Covenant to retain a substantial measure of freedom of action. Such a compromise would consist in a construction which, while not discarding the requirement of a legal state of war as a necessary element of the conception "resort to war," at the same time includes, as a possible element of this conception, what may be called a constructive state of war, ie, a state of war brought about by factors other than the *animus belligerendi* of the disputants and determined by the members of the League judging each case on its merits'. Lauterpacht, 'Resort to War' (n 46) 43–60 at 54.

[51] ' "War" and "Peace" ', 27 *AJIL* (1933) 114–7 at 115-6.

conflicts generally, without having to determine whether or not they were technically Wars as such.[52]

To understand this context better, let us look in some detail at one incident in 1923 that became seen in some quarters as emblematic of the failure of the Covenant to outlaw measures short of War, such as occupation, reprisals, intervention and peaceful blockade. I will go into some detail to illustrate how, even in the wake of the First World War, which had led to millions of people being killed and maimed, the international society of states maintained the idea that international law sanctioned states resorting to force against each other to right the wrongs they had suffered. International law supplied the righteous justification for more legalized killing.

3.3.3   The Italian Bombardment and Seizure of Corfu 1923 and Reprisals Short of War

This incident in 1923 was seen as illustrating the impotence of the League of Nations, and the fragility of the new rules that sought to restrain the resort to war by states large and small. As the crisis unfolded, the British representative in Athens wrote internally 'Great principles appear to me to be involved. Not only is the League of Nations but international relations and indeed the whole Law of Nations at stake.'[53]

A boundary commission had been established by an entity called the Conference of Ambassadors, unconnected to the League, to report on a boundary dispute between Greece and Albania. It was chaired by an Italian General, and during an on-site visit on the Greek side of the border, he and his party of four others (three from the Italian delegation and an Albanian

---

[52]   See Kotzsch, *The Concept of War in Contemporary History and International Law* (1956) 177–99 for details of the ways in which the League dealt with (or did not deal with) the question of War and resort to war with regard to conflicts related to: the Yugoslav incursion into Albania (1921), the Greco-Italian conflict (1923), the Polish-Lithuanian 'state of war', the Greco-Bulgarian incident (1925), the Chinese Eastern Railway conflict (1929), the Leticia dispute between Colombia and Peru (1932–35), the Chaco War (1932–35) between Bolivia and Paraguay, the Manchuria Incident (1931), the Ethiopian War (1935), the Sino Japanese War 1937–45, the German invasion of Poland (1939) and the Russo-Finnish war of 1939–40 (where he concludes that the League could only determine that there was a 'material war', and yet this could nevertheless meet the demands of Art 6 of the Convention on the Non-Fortification of the Aaland Islands (1921, still in force), which stipulated that Finland would have the right temporarily to lay mines 'in the event of a war affecting the Baltic Sea': ibid at 198).

[53]   Bentick, quoted in Yearwood, '"Consistently with Honour"; Great Britain, the League of Nations and the Corfu Crisis of 1923', 21 *Journal of Contemporary History* 4 (1986) 559–79 at 559.

interpreter) were attacked and killed near Janina. It was not particularly clear whether this had been carried out by Greeks or Albanians, but no property was taken, so it was clear that the mission had been targeted in connection with its boundary work rather than by robbers.

Mussolini, the Prime Minister of Italy, made a number of demands on Greece, and then bombarded and eventually seized part of Corfu. The following are excerpts from the letters of the respective Greek and Italian Representatives submitted to the League of Nations, and are reproduced in order to give a sense of the ways in which big powers would resort to force (or War) as reprisal and to avenge their rights and 'dignity' within the existing law:

> A deplorable event has just taken place on Greek territory. It has caused consternation throughout the whole country and raised a feeling of violent and unanimous indignation amongst the Greek people. The Italian delegation on the Commission set up by the Conference of Ambassadors for the delimitation of the southern frontier of Albania has been assassinated by unknown persons a few kilometres from the Greco-Albanian frontier.
>
> The moment it learned of this regrettable event, the Greek Government took energetic steps to discover the author of the crime, and spontaneously expressed to the Italian Government the profound regrets of the whole country. However, before any kind of proof was forthcoming as to the nationality of the aggressors or the motives and circumstances of the crime, the Italian Government, through its Legation at Athens, addressed to the Greek Government a note ... in which it threw the moral responsibility for the crime upon the Greek Government and demanded certain measures of satisfaction and reparation which are incompatible in several respects with the sovereignty of the Hellenic State and the honour of the nation.[54]

The summary of the Italian note demanded from the Greek Government:

(1) An unreserved official apology to be offered to the Italian Government at the Royal Legation at Athens through the supreme Military Authority of Greece.

(2) A solemn memorial service for the victims of the massacre to be held in the Catholic Cathedral at Athens, and all the members of the Government to be present.

---

[54] Politis, LNOJ (1923) 1412–13.

(3) Honours to be paid to the Italian flag, by the Greek Fleet in the port of the Piraeus represented by a naval squadron which will visit the Piraeus for this special purpose; these honours to consist of a salute of 21 guns fired by the Greek warships, which will hoist the Italian flag while firing the salutes.

(4) A drastic enquiry to be carried out by the Greek authorities at the place of the massacre in the presence of the Royal Italian Military Attaché, Colonel Perrone, for whose safety the Greek Government will be responsible; the enquiry to be carried out within five days of the acceptance of these demands.

(5) Capital punishment for all the authors of the crime.

(6) An indemnity of 50 million Italian lire to be paid within five days of the presentation of this note.

(7) Military honours to be paid to the bodies of the victims at the moment when they are placed on board an Italian vessel at Preveza.

The Greek Government rejected the demands in paragraphs (4), (5) and (6), which it considered constituted 'an infringement of the sovereignty and an injury to the honour of Greece'.[55] A few hours later, according to the Greek Representative addressing the Council,

> a portion of the territory of Greece was occupied by Italian detachments, and a cruiser entered the territorial waters of Corfu and proceeded immediately to a disembarkation of troops following upon an incident extremely painful and in certain respects inhuman. You have before you the message, addressed to the League of Nations by Dr Kennedy, its representative on the Commission for the Protection of Women and Children in the Near East; it is to the following effect:
>
> Italian bombardment of Corfu was carried out at shortest notice on Friday evening and directed against barracks containing Greek and Armenian refugee women and children, many of whom were wounded and about 15 killed.[56]

The Greek Government considered it had a duty to bring the matter to the Council of the League under Article 15. The relevant part of Article 15 read:

---

[55] LNOJ (1923) 1413.
[56] Politis, LNOJ (1923) 1277.

> If there should arise between Members of the League any dispute likely to lead to a rupture, which is not submitted to arbitration or judicial settlement in accordance with Article 13, the Members of the League agree that they will submit the matter to the Council.

And Politis, the representative of Greece, went on to invoke the relevant part of Article 16:

> Should any Member of the League resort to war in disregard of its covenants under Articles 12, 13 or 15, it shall *ipso facto* be deemed to have committed an act of war against all other Members of the League.

He referred to the fact that the Italian Government had described the violence committed against Greece as 'pacific acts of a temporary character',[57] and finished by stating that the Greek Government was 'inclined to profit by the doubt which might exist as to the character of the acts committed by the Italian Government in order not to take the initiative in asking for the application of Article 16'.[58]

The Italian response was immediate and vehement in its rejection of the idea that there had been any act of War, or that the League could get involved in sanctions through Article 16:

> No Italian Government could have acted otherwise than the present Government has done. When a people is subjected to a blow like this, which has struck the public conscience in Italy, it must first of all take the steps which are necessary to safeguard its honour.
>
> M Politis has declared that the Greek Government does not intend to appeal to Article 16 of the Covenant, but he mentioned that article. It would have been better perhaps in the interest of the intentions which M Politis has shown if he had not done so. Article 16 cannot be applied to Italy. As appears from the official declaration of the Italian Government, Italy did not intend to commit an act of war. No Power under these circumstances would tolerate the application of Article 16. I accordingly invite the representative of Greece not to mention that article but to confine himself to the other articles of the Covenant.[59]

---

[57] Ibid.
[58] Politis, LNOJ (1923) at 1278.
[59] Salandra, ibid.

Lord Cecil, the British Representative on the Council, said he did not want to prejudice anything, but felt

> that it seems to me very difficult to understand how the occupation of a portion of the territory of another State by armed forces, accompanied, so we are told by our own representative, by a bombardment which killed fifteen individuals and wounded others, can be regarded as a pacific measure. I feel great difficulty in understanding how that can be differentiated from an act of war.[60]

The subsequent resolution of the dispute took place outside the League, as requested by the Italian Government,[61] and this included the payment of the 50 million lire to Italy (about £30 million in today's terms), but the incident is remembered by international lawyers for the ambiguous report delivered by the specially established Commission of Jurists mandated to look into the following question:

> Are measures of coercion which are not meant to constitute acts of war consistent with the terms of Articles 12 to 15 of the Covenant when they are taken by one Member of the League of Nations against another Member of the League without prior recourse to the procedure laid down in those articles?

The answer came back after a few days:

> Coercive measures which are not intended to constitute acts of war may or may not be consistent with the provisions of Articles 12 to 15 of the Covenant, and it is for the Council, when the dispute has been submitted to

---

[60] Ibid at 1279.

[61] For some of the detail as to why resolution through the Conference of Ambassadors was considered by powers such as Britain and France to be expedient, see Yearwood, 'Consistently with Honour' (n 53). For a full study of the Conference and its dealing with the dual questions of the Italian occupation and the Greek responsibility for the Janina incident, see Pink, 'The Conference of Ambassadors (Paris 1920–1931)' 12 *Geneva Studies* 4–5 (1942) 15–293 esp at 207–46. He offers the important insight that the Council of the League and the Conference represented the new and the old methods of settling disputes; not only was the Conference composed of only certain major powers from the League Council and unencumbered by the presence of smaller states such as Greece, but the methods were also very different (ibid at 212–13): '[W]hile the Council worked under the pressure of public opinion, the Conference of Ambassadors reached its decisions behind closed doors. There was really a conflict between two methods: the new method of the League and the old diplomatic method as represented by the Conference of Ambassadors.'

it, to decide immediately having due regard to all the circumstances of the case and to the nature of the measures adopted, whether it should recommend the maintenance or the withdrawal of such measures.[62]

This seemed for some to leave the door ajar for armed reprisals short of War to be considered as still legal as countermeasures recognized by international law. It could nevertheless be argued that armed reprisals were likely to 'lead to a rupture', thereby triggering at least Articles 12(1) and 15(1). In this way other international lawyers would have considered such armed reprisals outlawed by the Covenant (although not equivalent to a resort to War).[63]

Today armed reprisals are in any event outlawed under the 1945 UN Charter, which abandoned references to resort to war in favour of a simple prohibition on the use of force.

3.4 The Kellogg-Briand Pact 1928

The Anti-War movement in the United States entered a new phase after the establishment of the League of Nations and the failure of the United States to join the League. The story of how Salmon Levinson, a corporate lawyer from Chicago, pursued his dreams of ending the war in Europe, and then outlawing War through the 'Anti-War Pact' (aka the Kellogg-Briand Pact[64]) has been brilliantly narrated in the book referred to already: *The Internationalists: And Their Plan to Outlaw War*.[65]

---

[62] LNOJ (1924) 524. The Council unanimously approved the report, although Sweden and Uruguay expressed some doubts about the conclusion that the use of armed force or coercion was compatible with the Covenant in such circumstances (ibid at 526).

[63] See in particular the explanation by de Visscher, a member of the Commission, as recounted in Wright, 'Opinion of Commission of Jurists on Janina-Corfu Affair', 18 *AJIL* (1924) 536–44 at fnn 21 and 22; and the later account of Visscher, 'L'interprétation du Pacte au lendemain du différend italo-grec', 5 *Revue de droit international et de législation comparé* (1924) 213–30 [part 1], and 377–96 [part 2]esp at 215 and 382: 'l'usage des représailles armées avant recours aux procedures de règlement pacifique est incompatible avec l'esprit et avec l'économie générale du Pacte'. de Visscher seems to be leaving room for economic or financial reprisals: ibid at 385ff; Brierly, 'International Law and Resort to Force' (n 49) at 316–17; and Waldock, 'Use of Force' (n 25) at 475–76 with references. For the opposite views, see the references in Brownlie, *Use of Force* (n 12) at 222 fn 2, according to whom 'reprisals involving the use of force virtually disappeared from international life in the period leading to the Second World War'.

[64] This is considered the most 'accurate title', although the treaty has no official title; the US Department of State informed Farrell that the 'proper designation' in accordance with the preamble is 'Treaty providing for the renunciation of war as an instrument of national policy'. Brownlie, *Use of Force* (n 12) at 222 fn 2.

[65] Hathaway and Shapiro, *The Internationalists* (n 23).

In the following pages we will concentrate on some of the analogies that were made by the activists at the time, to explain their logic of outlawing the legal institution of War. I have taken the liberty of reproducing at length some of their writings, as they provide, I feel, a sense of what it was about War as an institution of international law that was so objectionable during that period. Levinson launched his idea drawing on the analogy of the successful outlawing of duelling:

> [T]he whole history of the duel closely parallels the course of international law with respect to war. For centuries efforts were made in most countries to moderate and regulate duelling by 'Codes', fixing the terms and conditions, weapons, distance, duties of seconds, etc, etc. The code became more and more elaborate; more and more 'humane'. Seconds were morally bound to act as a 'council of conciliation'. But the whole thing rested on the premise of the legality of dueling. It assumed affairs of honor in which it was the obligation as well as the right of a gentleman to resort to the shedding of blood. An interesting volume might be written comparing the code of honor between Individuals with that called International law between nations, the Hague Conventions occupying the place of culminating futility in the latter. In one case as the other, we want not laws *of* war, but laws *against* war, just as we have laws *against* murder, not laws *of* murder.[66]

His colleague in the movement, Colonel Robins, had a well-deserved reputation for oratory:

> We do not half appreciate the costs of the Great War. Ten million dead on battlefields; five million permanent cripples; hundreds of billions of wealth destroyed; pestilence, famine and unemployment; world propagandas of mass hatred and fear; anarchy and the force-spirit over-riding with ruthless violence constitutional liberty and due process of law in all lands – these are some of the visible fruits of the World War. ...[67]

---

[66] 'The Legal Status of War', *The New Republic* (9 March 1918) 171–73 at 172.

[67] Robins, 'The Outlawry of War – The Next Step in Civilization', in *The Annals of the American Academy of Political and Social Science* (1925) 125–56, at 153.

Each nation is being equipped with invisible and odorless poison gas that is instantaneously deadly; with fleets of bombing airplanes controlled by wireless. We are now able to destroy whole populations in a night. There are no longer any non-combatants. Old and young, women and little children, animals and the fruitful earth itself, now suffer a common devastation and ruin under the action of modern war. ...[68]

Wars of liberation – revolutionary struggles such as our own in 1776 – are all illegal. Every patriot in revolt against tyranny is guilty of the capital crime – treason. All wars of aggression or conquest are legal. Why was the Kaiser never brought to trial? Because he is guilty of no crime known to international law. War-making is the legal exercise of sovereignty – 'the King can do no wrong.' If as an individual citizen I assault and kill a human being I am guilty of murder. If as a king or a diplomat I start a war that kills ten million lads I am guilty of no crime known to the law of nations . ...[69]

We can outlaw this war system just as we outlawed slavery and the saloon. We can make war a crime under the law of nations, and substitute law for war in compelling the settlement of international disputes. Human society has overthrown other powerful legal institutions that had grown to be a menace to human welfare. Piracy, the international slave trade, the code duello, the slave system, the liquor traffic – all were legal institutions, all were as old as history – all have been outlawed and their exercise made a public crime, in the progress of man-kind from barbarism up to liberty and security under law.[70]

Just as Levinson had disparaged the adoption of rules for a better regime for duelling, Robins recalls those who preferred to improve the necessary evil institutions of slavery and the saloon:

Such persons thought that slave owners should be required to feed their slaves well, provide sanitary quarters, allow them one day's rest in seven and give them some moral instruction; that the saloon should be heavily taxed, limited as to hours and days for operation and restricted

---

[68] Ibid.
[69] Robbins (n 67) at 154.
[70] Ibid.

to certain localities; and that this was all that could be done to relieve the acknowledged wrongs of either institution. Opposed only by the efforts of these persons and methods, slavery and the saloon grew in wealth and power.[71]

It is against this background, that Briand as French Foreign Minister engaged with the Americans, leading to the adoption in Paris of the Pact for the Renunciation of War (the Kellogg-Briand Pact) and its widespread acceptance in treaty form by over 63 states. It remains in force for many of these states, including the United Kingdom.[72]

The key parts of the treaty are as follows:

Persuaded that the time has come when a frank renunciation of war as an instrument of national policy should be made to the end that the peaceful and friendly relations now existing between their peoples may be perpetuated;

Convinced that all changes in their relations with one another should be sought only by pacific means and be the result of a peaceful and orderly process, and that any signatory Power which shall hereafter seek to promote its national interests by resort to war should be denied the benefits furnished by this Treaty;

...

Article I

The High Contracting Parties solemnly declare in the names of their respective peoples that they condemn recourse to war for the solution of international controversies, and renounce it, as an instrument of national policy in their relations with one another.

Article II

The High Contracting Parties agree that the settlement or solution of all disputes or conflicts of whatever nature or of whatever origin they may be, which may arise among them, shall never be sought except by pacific means.

---

[71] Robins (n 67) at 155–56.
[72] See the response of the Solicitor-General, Hansard HC, vol 572, Written Answers, 16 December 2013, col 482W.

The key points to understand are that:

(a) it was assumed, and evidenced through separate notes,[73] that the right to self-defence continued;[74]

(b) the reference in the preamble to a state that resorted to War losing the benefits of the treaty meant that not only could the attacked state resort to force against the wrongdoing state, but that other states parties could also act against the wrongful state in ways that would otherwise be a violation of the treaty;

(c) because Article II demanded the resolution of all conflicts through peaceful means, the treaty in fact prohibited not only resort to War, but also resort to other forms of force; and

(d) the background discussions suggested that this Peace Pact should not affect the obligations of states under treaties that foresaw military sanctions (for example the Covenant's Article 16, the Locarno Treaties and various non-aggression pacts).[75] Under those arrangements, states would still be entitled to engage in such acts of 'international

---

[73] The extent to which these notes, understandings and declarations, including the 'British Monroe Doctrine', which the Foreign Office described as a 'caveat', would have reserved the right to resort to self-defence in response to interference in 'certain regions' is made clear in para 10 of Sir Austen Chamberlain's note: 'The language of article 1, as to the renunciation of war as an instrument of national policy, renders it desirable that I should remind Your Excellency that there are certain regions of the world the welfare and integrity of which constitute a special and vital interest for our peace and safety. His Majesty's Government have been at pains to make it clear in the past that interference with these regions cannot be suffered. Their protection against attack is to the British Empire a measure of self-defense. It must be clearly understood that His Majesty's Government in Great Britain accept the new treaty upon the distinct understanding that it does not prejudice their freedom of action in this respect. The Government of the United States have comparable interests any disregard of which by a foreign power they have declared that they would regard as an unfriendly act. His Majesty's Government believe, therefore, that in defining their position they are expressing the intention and meaning of the United States Government.' The whole note is reproduced in Miller, *The Peace Pact of Paris: A Study of the Briand-Kellogg Treaty* (1928) at 196ff. That book also contains a set of all the drafts and notes from other states. At the Senate Hearings (7 December 1928) these were explained away as simply reiterating established rules of self-defence, available at http://avalon.law.yale.edu/20th_century/kbhear.asp. This was apparently related to a concern about Egypt and the Suez Canal; see Ferrell, *Peace in Their Time* (n 38) 180–82.

[74] Later the Lytton Report into the 1931 Manchukuo incident (covered in section 3.6 below) actually determined that Japan had not acted in self-defence; the report read: 'The military operations of the Japanese troops during this night . . . cannot be described as measures of legitimate self-defence. In saying this, the Commission does not exclude the hypothesis that the officers on the spot may have thought they were acting in self-defence.' Report of the Commission of Inquiry, 1 October 1932, C.663.M.320. 1932. VII at 71. This finding eventually led to Japan's leaving the League.

[75] Kellogg, 'The War Prevention Policy of the United States', 22 *AJIL* (1928) 253–61 at 259–60.

police' rather than War,[76] or, as some saw it, the 'intention was to forbid all unilateral resort to war for purely national objects *whether on just or unjust* grounds but to permit war as a collective sanction either under the Covenant or the Pact itself (and now under the Charter)'.[77]

But although the Pact had in a way made the institution of War illegal, it was not universally seen as having solved the problem of preventing armed conflict, and the idea of 'outlawing war' did not always translate well. The concept of 'outlawry' was dismissed as 'bunkum', the treaty undermined as a 'scrap of paper', and lawyers pointed to the absence of any mechanisms for enforcing this new rule through sanctions or a compulsory forum for the settlement of the dispute. Furthermore, there was no mechanism for deciding who had been the first to have recourse to War or aggression.[78] It was still argued that 'armed reprisals, not being war under customary law, were "pacific means"', and so not prohibited.[79] There was considerable disagreement as to whether third states not at War would be obliged, or at least entitled, to support the victim state and thus ignore the traditional rules on Neutrality Status.[80] But if one were entitled to assist one side, who would really determine whether that actually was the innocent side ?[81]

One apparent solution would be for the League to act as 'referee'.

[76]   Wright, 'The Meaning of the Pact of Paris', 27 *AJIL* (1933) 39–61 at 51: 'Acts of self-defence or of international police are not war in the legal sense. The only circumstances in which a state can legally go to war is against another state which has already begun a war.' For the exchange of correspondence at the time of the drafting, see Ferrell, *Peace in Their Time* (n 38) at 174.

[77]   Waldock, 'Use of Force' (n 25) at 474 (original emphasis).

[78]   See Ferrell (supra).

[79]   Waldock, 'Use of Force' (n 25) at 474; similarly and more forcefully, see Lauterpacht, 'The Pact of Paris and the Budapest Articles of Interpretation', 20 *Transactions of the Grotius Society* (1934) 178–204 esp at 183; *contra* Wright, 'The Meaning of the Pact of Paris', 27 *AJIL* (1933) 39–61 at 52, 'reprisals or other uses of force to enforce remedies, whether by a state or under authority of an organization of states, are barred except against a state which has gone to war in violation of the Pact'. Compare the Resolution of the Institut de droit international, 'Régime des représailles en temps de paix' (Paris, 1934), Art 4, 'Les représailles armées sont interdites dans les mêmes conditions que le recours à la guerre.'

[80]   For some of the key legal debates over the meaning and scope of the Pact, see Report of the International Law Association, 'The Effect of the Briand-Kellogg Pact of Paris on International Law', Budapest Conference, *ILA Reports* (1934) 1–70. For an interesting debate in the UK House of Lords on this report, see 'Budapest Articles of Interpretation of the Briand-Kellogg Pact of Paris' 38 *ILA Reports* (1934) 310–51. Lauterpacht, 'The Pact of Paris' (n 79).

[81]   As mentioned in Ch 2, the United States did indeed rely on the Pact to argue that it could support Great Britain without violating laws on neutrality before the United States itself entered the Second World War, detailed in Wright, 'The Lend-Lease Bill and International Law', 35 *AJIL* (1941) 305–14; see also Wright, 'The Present Status of Neutrality', 34 *AJIL* (1940) 391–415.

3.5 The League Determines Whether Italy has Resorted to War

The League's efforts to apply the Covenant scheme in the face of resort to War reached a high point with the Italian invasion of Ethiopia. Following attempts at conciliation, arbitration Committees were set up by the Council, the last of which was formed immediately after the Italian bombardment and landing of troops on 3 October 1935. Ethiopia requested the Council to declare that Italy was resorting to War in violation of the Covenant and that the resort to War brought about the sanctions regime foreseen in Article 16(1).[82] A Committee of Six was established (United Kingdom, Chile, Denmark, France, Portugal and Romania). The Committee reported back two days later.

The discussions in the Committee of Six are entertainingly imagined by Frank Moorhouse in his novel *Dark Palace*, centred on the fictional heroine Edith Berry, who at this stage has been promoted to Secretary of the Committee. The other characters are real people and their dialogue is constructed by Moorhouse from documentary sources referencing their original words. As the issues seem so apposite to our own story, I hope I can be indulged for reproducing some pertinent extensive excerpts from the dramatized meeting of the Committee in Geneva:

> In the afternoon, the meeting was addressed by Gaston Jèze, Professor of International Law at the Sorbonne, who had been employed by the Ethiopians to present their case.
>
> The Italians walked out of the room as he rose to speak.
>
> Sadly, Edith felt that Jèze did not do a good job for the Ethiopians. They were a shaky little nation – the Italians were right about that – but Emperor Haile Salassie was trying to modernise it, and to bring it up to the European standards. It couldn't be treated as land up for grabs.
>
> She was surprised to see Eden [British Minister and Delegate for the League of Nations] ask Laval, the French Prime Minister, outright in front of the others, whether the French would join with the British in enforcing sanctions on the Italians. Perhaps he was taking advantage of the absence of the Italians. ...
>
> She suspected that it was the first time a member of League Council had seriously proposed the use of this new economic weapon.

---

[82] LNOJ (1935) 1212–13.

'This is clearly a case for Anglo-French collaboration, Eden said. If we fail to stand together now, the consequences will be calamitous for the League.'

It placed France on the spot.

Laval agreed. I have a divided Cabinet, as you are well aware, but I will ask for a mandate to apply sanctions, yes.'

'They should be substantial sanctions.'

'I agree.'

Edith regretted the absence of the Italians. She would've liked them to hear this.

Someone would be reporting to them. They must have known they would learn what was said or they wouldn't have walked out.

Edith then felt she should both recover her position and enlarge it by speaking.

At first a question: men enjoyed answering questions from a lady. They would all rush to answer. 'Will Mussolini formally declare war? Or simply walk into Ethiopia?'

The men made comments which assumed that Italy would follow the convention of declaring war.

'I ask,' she said, 'because Italy, if she declares, would be then entitled to belligerent rights.'

Laval was astonished. 'I have never heard of such a thing. *Belligerent rights* – what are these? Laval didn't address the question to her, but to Eden.

Eden thought for a moment and said, 'Berry has a point. If war is declared, for example, under International law Italy could stop French ships if she thought they were aiding Italy's enemy.'

'No one stops a French ship,' Laval said. 'Least of all, Mussolini.'

Edith cut in. 'If war is "declared" the belligerent also is supposed to adhere to international rules of warfare.'

She continued, but I do not believe that a nation which has breached the League Covenant can legitimately exercise any belligerent rights.'

And she would say one more thing. 'Until now, technically, war didn't exist until "declared". We have a new situation where we, the League, can deem a conflict to be a "war" – and by so describing it we *declare* a war in that sense.'

'Very interesting' Léger [secretary-general of the French Foreign Ministry] said. 'Yes. You are probably right.'

She said lightly, though without smiling, 'Curiously we have legalised war – in the broadest sense.' . . . 'I suppose that international law tries to ensure that nations do as much good as possible in peace and as little harm in war as possible.'

She stopped. The men were still looking at her, but pointed out that the 'law of war' had really begun with the Geneva and Hague Conventions, before the League.

Professor Jèze rushed to display his historical knowledge by agreeing with Léger.

Edith kept her stiff face but inwardly beamed. The acknowledged master of French foreign policy had agreed with her, even if his agreement had contained a correction.

'True', she said. 'It did begin with the Geneva and Hague Conventions in the nineteenth century, but what has changed is that with the Existence of the League, we have for the first time a referee, as it were.'

She realised that the exchange was taking place between bureaucrats – Léger and her – not among the delegates. This was that other level of participation at a committee – where the experts were expected to supply such material to the lay people. She liked the role.

But she realised with slight embarrassment that she had answered her own question.

Laval excused himself to return to Paris, leaving Léger to represent France. Laval turned to Edith and said. 'Thank you Madame for your lesson.'

The meeting continued its discussion until Eden intervened and suggested that a report be prepared *now*.

That day.

'We must act with speed', Eden told the Committee, 'or we will lose the moment.' . . .

Night fell on the Committee. Sandwiches, cheese, and fruit and coffee arrived.

After several more hours a draft was ready.

Edith's contribution was for her the most exciting sentence she had ever written or perhaps that anyone had ever written – at least in the history of the League.

Edith's sentence was: 'The Committee has come to the conclusion that the Italian Government has resorted to war in disregard of its obligations under Article 12 of the Covenant of the League of Nations.'[83]

---

[83] *Dark Palace* (2000) at 154–57.

According to the actual historical record, the report was before the League Council the next day. The Committee had considered two questions:

(1) Does a state of war exist between Italy and Ethiopia?

(2) If so, has the war been resorted to in disregard of Articles 12, 13 or 15 of the Covenant?[84]

The final part of the report concluded:

(d) Without prejudice to the other limitations to their right to have recourse to war, the Members of the League are not entitled, without having first complied with the provisions of Articles 12, 13 and 15, to seek a remedy by war for grievances they consider they have against other Members of the League. The adoption by a State of measures of security on its own territory and within the limits of its international agreements does not authorise another State to consider itself free from its obligations under the Covenant.

(e) The Pact of Paris of August 27th, 1928, to which Italy and Ethiopia are parties, also condemns recourse to war for the solution of international controversies and binds the parties to the Pact to seek by pacific means the settlement or solution of all disputes or conflicts, of whatever nature or of whatever origin they may be, which may arise among them.

(f) The Ethiopian Government, at the meeting of the Council on October 5th, invoked Article 16 of the Covenant. Under the terms of that article, should any Member of the League resort to war in disregard of its covenants under Articles 12, 13 or 15, it shall *ipso facto* be deemed to have committed an act of war against all other Members of the League.

(g) When a Member of the League invokes Article 16 of the Covenant, each of the other Members is bound to consider the circumstances of the particular case. It is not necessary that war should have been formally declared for Article 16 to be applicable. . . .

After an examination of the facts stated above, the Committee has come to the conclusion that the Italian Government has resorted to war in disregard of its covenants under Article 12 of the Covenant of the League of Nations.[85]

---

[84]   LNOJ (1935) 1223.

[85]   LNOJ (1935) 1224–25; this report, together with the reports of the Committee of Five and the Committee of Thirteen, is available at 30 *AJIL* (1936) Supplement (1–41).

The Council then asked by roll-call the members of the Council whether they approved the report and the conclusions. Italy was the only one to state that it did not approve the conclusions. The president then announced, 'I take note that fourteen members of the League of Nations represented on the Council consider that we are in the presence of a war begun in disregard of the obligation of Article 12 of the Covenant.'[86]

The League's efforts to impose sanctions under Article 16, and oil sanctions in particular, were undercut by the Anglo-French attempt to compromise with Mussolini through territorial concessions while holding off sanctions. The failure to follow through with sanctions may well have been a missed opportunity. Mussolini was later reported by Hitler's interpreter as stating, during the banquet at Munich in 1938, ' "If the League of Nations had followed Eden's advice in the Abyssinian dispute," he said to Hitler, "and had extended economic sanctions to oil, I would have had to withdraw from Abyssinia within a week. That would have been an incalculable disaster for me." '[87]

Mussolini threatened that oil sanctions would be considered an act of War, and the sanctions later undertaken by the members of the League and the United States, such as they were, failed to reverse Italy's action.[88] Two years later, Italy left the League. Eden resigned as UK Foreign Secretary the same year over differences with the Prime Minister, Neville Chamberlain, regarding the way in which the British Government was intending to manage *de jure* recognition of Italy's claims over Ethiopia.[89] Let us now end this chapter by considering this topic of recognition.

---

[86] Council meeting 7 October 1935, LNOJ (1935) 1226; for the nuance that the Council did not actually take a decision, see Spencer, 'The Italian-Ethiopian Dispute and the League of Nations', 31 *AJIL* (1937) 614–41 at 624. The Committee of Six had concluded that Italy had resorted to war. See also the recommendation by the Assembly for the coordination of sanctions and the reference to the obligations of member states under Art 16. LNOJ (Special Supplement No 138) (1935) 113–14, 11 October 1935.

[87] Schmidt, *Hitler's Interpreter* (2016) at 67 and 125.

[88] For discussion of the difficulties facing the international legal framework for peace and security during this period, see Koskenniemi, 'History of International Law, World War I to World War II', *MPEPIL* (2011).

[89] For the detail, see Rose, 'The Resignation of Anthony Eden', 25 *The Historical Journal* (1982) 911–31; for the parallel Anglo-French initiative that sought to compromise with Mussolini over Ethiopia outside the League, see Robertson, 'The Hoare-Laval Plan', 10 *Journal of Contemporary History* (1975) 433–64.

3.6 Non-Recognition of Territory Taken or Ceded as the Result of Force

In September 1931, Japanese troops guarding the South Manchurian Railway reacted to an explosion, which they labelled a Chinese attack. In turn, the Japanese troops attacked a Chinese garrison and eventually occupied the area of Manchuria. In 1932, Japan created a 'puppet state' in Manchuria called Manchukuo. Although the League Council and Assembly referred to the action as aggression, and when the Assembly called for Japanese with-drawal this eventually led to Japan's leaving the League itself, the original incident sparked a new departure in terms of policies of 'non-recognition', and an emerging universal norm that would obligate states not to recognize a situation brought about by force.[90]

The letters written by US Secretary of State Stimson in January 1932 to the Japanese and Chinese Governments read as follows:

> In view of the present situation and of its own rights and obligations therein, the American Government deems it to be its duty to notify both the Government of the Chinese Republic and the Imperial Japanese Government that it cannot admit the legality of any situation *de facto* nor does it intend to recognize any treaty or agreement entered into between these governments, or agents thereof, which may impair the treaty rights of the United States or its citizens in China, including those which relate to the sovereignty, the independence or the territorial and administrative integrity of the Republic of China, or to the international policy relative to China, commonly known as the Open Door Policy; and that it does not in-tend to recognize any situation, treaty, or agreement which may be brought about by means contrary to the covenants and obligations of the Pact of Paris of August 27, 1928, to which treaty both China and Japan, as well as the United States, are parties.[91]

---

[90] Brownlie, *Use of Force* (n 12) at 411–13 references various texts that encapsulated the idea of non-recognition of the use of force, starting with a recommendation of the International Conference of American States in 1890 that cessions of territory made under threat of war should be void. Stimson is often credited with the idea of non-recognition, as exemplified in the identical diplomatic notes he wrote to the Japanese and Chinese Governments; the recent book-length study of non-recognition by O'Mahoney highlights diary entries by Stimson in which he refers to US President Hoover's idea of the United States not recognizing a treaty between China and Japan brought about under military pressure. O'Mahoney, *Denying the Spoils of War: The Politics of Invasion and Nonrecognition* (2018) at 38, referencing Stimson's diary of 9 November 1931. He also reveals (ibid) that 'Hoover tried to get Stimson to declare it instead the "Hoover Doctrine"'.

[91] As reproduced in Wright, 'The Stimson Note of January 7, 1932', 26 *AJIL* (1932) 342–48; for analysis, see McNair, 'The Stimson Doctrine of Non-Recognition', 14 *BYBIL* (1933) 65–74;

Two months later the League Assembly adopted a Resolution, in the context of the Manchuria dispute (with China and Japan abstaining), which proclaimed the binding nature of Article 2 of the Paris Pact to settle disputes and conflicts through peaceful means, as well as the Covenant obligation to respect the territorial integrity of member states, and went on to declare 'that it is incumbent upon the Members of the League of Nations not to recognise any situation, treaty or agreement which may be brought about by means contrary to the Covenant of the League of Nations or to the Pact of Paris'.[92]

Stimson explained the significance of the non-recognition idea in a key speech (excerpted below). If the legal consequences of a successful War could be done away with, one could prevent recourse to War once and for all. We could have what the outlawry movement had been striving for – in Stimson's words, a 'warless world'. If the Kellogg-Briand Treaty and the Covenant had more or less outlawed War then the non-recognition doctrine (perhaps not yet a rule), if applied by the international community, would remove the incentive to enter into such illegal Wars and would sanction those who nevertheless resorted to War. Once War was outlawed by international law, it made no sense for international law to recognize the outcome of such illegal activity. Stimson's speech highlighted how the legal response to War had, until then, been merely to erect Neutrality laws that would hinder third states from aiding the warring parties. But the parties were left alone to fight it out, just like the duellists from the previous century. Let us see how Stimson explained these ideas in his own words, in his speech to the Council on Foreign Relations in 1932:

> Prior to the World War many men had had visions of a warless world and had made efforts to accomplish the abolition of war, but these efforts had never resulted in any very general or effective combinations of nations directed towards that end. During the centuries which had elapsed since the beginnings of international law, a large part of that law had been a development of principles based upon the existence of war. The existence and legality of war were to a large extent the central facts out of which these legal

Turns, 'The Stimson Doctrine of Non-Recognition: Its Historical Genesis and Influence on Contemporary International Law', *Chinese Journal of International Law* (2003) 105–43.

[92] LNOJ (Special Supplement No 101) (1932) 87–88; at the time such a duty was not considered, at least by British academics, to be binding under international law; Smith, 'The Binding Force of League Resolutions', 16 *BYBIL* (1935) 157–59; Brierly, 'The Meaning and Legal Effect of the Resolution of the League Assembly of March 11, 1932', 16 *BYBIL* (1935) 159–60; Brownlie in his 1963 *Use of Force* (n 12) at 418 considered that Art 10 of the Covenant involved such a legal obligation of non-recognition.

principles grew and on which they rested. Thus the development of the doctrine of neutrality was predicated upon the duty of a neutral to maintain impartiality between two belligerents. This further implies that each belligerent has equal rights and is owed equal duties by the neutral. It implies that the war between them is a legal situation out of which these rights and obligations grow. Therefore, it is contrary to this aspect of international law for the neutral to take sides between belligerents or to pass a moral judgment upon the rightfulness or wrongfulness of the cause of either – at least to the extent of translating such a judgment into action. So long as a neutral exercised this strict impartiality, international law afforded to him, his commerce, and his property, certain rights of protection.

And during the generations which preceded the World War much of the growth of international humanitarianism was associated with attempts, not to abolish war but to narrow and confine its destructive effects by the development of these doctrines of neutrality. Their chief purpose was to produce oases of safety for life and property in a world which still recognized and legalized the destruction of human life and property as one of the regular methods for the settlement of international controversies and the maintenance of international policy. ...[93]

War between nations was renounced by the signatories of the Briand-Kellogg Pact. This means that it has become illegal throughout practically the entire world. It is no longer to be the source and subject of rights. It is no longer to be the principle around which the duties, the conduct, and the rights of nations revolve. It is an illegal thing. Hereafter when two nations engage in armed conflict either one or both of them must be wrongdoers – violators of the general treaty. We no longer draw a circle about them and treat them with the punctilios of the duelist's code. Instead we denounce them as lawbreakers.

By that very act we have made obsolete many legal precedents and have given the legal profession the task of re-examining many of its codes and treatises. ...[94]

When the American Government took the responsibility of sending its note of January 7 last, it was a pioneer. It was appealing to a new common

---

[93] Stimson, 'The Pact of Paris: Three Years of Development', 11 *Foreign Affairs* (Special Supplement No 1) (1931) i–ix at i–ii.
[94] Ibid at iv.

sentiment and to the provisions of a Treaty [Kellogg-Briand] as yet untested. Its own refusal to recognize the fruits of aggression might be of comparatively little moment to an aggressor. But when the entire group of civilized nations took their stand beside the position of the American Government, the situation was revealed in its true sense. Moral disapproval, when it becomes the disapproval of the whole world, takes on a significance hitherto unknown in international law. For never before has international opinion been so organized and mobilized.[95]

The idea of a duty not to recognize territorial acquisitions, treaties or situations brought about through War or the use of force, threats or coercion, was developed in 1934 by the International Law Association's Budapest Articles of Interpretation of the Kellogg-Briand Pact (which also included a right to deny Belligerent Rights to a state violating the Pact).[96] The duty of non-recognition is also, from this point on, enshrined in a number of treaties and other instruments, including the Anti-War Treaty of Non-Aggression and Conciliation (1933),[97] the Convention on the Rights and Duties of States (1933), the Charter of the Organization of American States (1948),[98] the UN General Assembly's Friendly Relations Declaration (1970)[99] and Definition of Aggression (1974).[100]

---

[95] Ibid at viii.

[96] 38 *ILA Conference Reports* (1934) at 67: 'In the event of a violation of the Pact by a resort to armed force or war by one signatory State against another, the other States may, without thereby committing a breach of the Pact or of any rule of International Law, do all or any of the following things:– (a) Refuse to admit the exercise by the State violating the Pact of belligerent rights, such as visit and search, blockade, etc; (b) Decline to observe towards the State violating the Pact the duties prescribed by International, Law, apart from the Pact, for a neutral in relation to a belligerent; (c) Supply the State attacked with financial or material assistance, including munitions of war; (d) Assist with armed forces the State attacked.' The Conference that finalized the text was chaired by Manley Hudson and included experts such as Colombus, McNair and Brierly. However, the idea that a state could choose not to abide by its obligations of neutrality in the face of a breach of the Pact is dismissed by Lauterpacht, 'The Pact of Paris' (n 79) at 190–94.

[97] Art 2 provides: 'They declare that as between the high contracting parties territorial questions must not be settled by violence, and that they will not recognize any territorial arrangement which is not obtained by pacific means, nor the validity of the occupation or acquisition of territories that may be brought about by force of arms.'

[98] Under Art 21, 'No territorial acquisitions or special advantages obtained either by force or by other means of coercion shall be recognized.' And see Art 3(g), 'The American States condemn war of aggression: victory does not give rights.'

[99] A/RES/25/2625, 'The territory of a State shall not be the object of acquisition by another State resulting from the threat or use of force. No territorial acquisition resulting from the threat or use of force shall be recognized as legal.'

[100] Art 5(3) A/RES/29/3314, 'No territorial acquisition or special advantage resulting from aggression is or shall be recognized as lawful.'

Waldock, in his 1952 Hague Academy specialized course, considered:

> Aggressive war being now an international crime the duty of non-recognition would certainly seem to be imperatively demanded by the public law of the international community. In point of fact, there is now abundant evidence in State-practice of the development of a customary rule imposing a duty not to recognise the fruits of aggression.[101]

The outlawing of war, the categorization of aggressive war as an international crime, the development of multilateral economic sanctions in response to a resort to war in violation of the Covenant, the growing possibility of settling territorial disputes through international adjudication and the consolidation of the non-recognition rule may all have combined to reduce the instances of recognized forcible territorial transfer.[102] But non-recognition has its limits,[103] and at some point states may choose to follow their interests even while condemning the resort to War.

So even though, as we saw above, the members of the League explicitly considered they were in the presence of a War started by Italy against Ethiopia, the incorporation of Ethiopia into Italy was later legally recognized by a significant number of the same League of Nations member states, probably 'as part of a strategy to enlist Italian support against Nazi Germany'.[104] Of course this situation was later reversed after 1941,[105] and Italy (under a new Government) recognized Ethiopia with the Paris Peace Treaty of 1947, as well as the legality of Ethiopian measures taken to annul those taken by Italy since 3 October 1934.[106] Decolonisation more generally, and the significance

---

[101] Waldock, 'Use of Force' (n 25) at 481.

[102] One might also mention the growth of democracy, the globalization of the economy, the advent of nuclear weapons and the costs of conquest; see further Hathaway and Shapiro, *The Internationalists* (n 23) 329–33.

[103] See in particular McNair, 'The Stimson Doctrine of Non-Recognition' (n 91); Dinstein, *War, Aggression and Self-Defence* (n 43) at 193–94.

[104] O'Mahoney, *Denying the Spoils of War* (n 90) at 204; see further ibid at 74–110, with a list of recognitions in 1938 at 105–06.

[105] Talmon, *Recognition of Governments in International Law: With Particular Reference to Governments in Exile* (1998) 290.

[106] Art 35 of the Treaty of Peace with Italy provides: 'Italy recognises the legality of all measures which the Government of Ethiopia has taken or may hereafter take in order to annul Italian measures respecting Ethiopia taken after October 3, 1935, and the effects of such measures.' Note also Art 37: 'Within eighteen months from the coming into force of the present Treaty, Italy shall restore all works of art, religious objects, archives and objects of historical value belonging to Ethiopia or its nationals and removed from Ethiopia to Italy since October 3, 1935.'

of the right to self-determination, also played a role in reversing the trend of territorial conquest and increased the relevance of non-recognition.[107]

Today states may avoid the issue of conquest by remaining in long-term occupation, and create 'facts on the ground' through the establishment of settlements, re-routing transport links and mounting security barriers and walls. This is obviously the case with regard to the Israeli occupation of Palestinian territories.[108] Suggestions by Israeli politicians that these territories could be annexed have been met with official protests from other states that this would be a violation of international law and the annexation would not be recognized.[109]

The annexation of Crimea by Russia stands out as a particularly thorny situation. The arguments about aggression, self-determination, humanitarian intervention and invitation by consent are complex, and are carefully set out in a recent appraisal by Mary-Ellen O'Connell.[110] We will cover these rules in the next chapter. Here we are only interested in the issue of non-recognition. In 2014, 100 states voted in favour of a UN General Assembly Resolution that

> *Calls upon* all States, international organizations and specialized agencies not to recognize any alteration of the status of the Autonomous Republic of Crimea and the city of Sevastopol on the basis of the above-mentioned referendum and to refrain from any action or dealing that might be interpreted as recognizing any such altered status.[111]

---

[107] See the findings by O'Mahoney, *Denying the Spoils of War* (n 90).

[108] We will deal with these issues under the law of occupation in Ch 9. See also the Advisory Opinion of the International Court of Justice of 9 July 2004, *Legal Consequences of the Construction of a Wall in the Occupied Palestinian Territory*, esp para 121, which addresses *de facto* annexation. On the question of when an occupation becomes illegal, see 'Report of the Special Rapporteur on the situation of human rights in the Palestinian territories occupied since 1967' A/72/556, 23 October 2017.

[109] Joint Statement by France, Germany, Belgium, Estonia, Ireland, Norway and the UK following UN Security Council VTC Meeting on the Middle East, 24 June 2020: '[I]f any Israeli annexation of the Occupied West Bank – however big or small – is implemented, it would constitute a clear violation of international law, including the UN Charter, as well as the UN Security Council resolutions. ... [A]nnexation would have consequences for our close relationship with Israel and would not be recognised by us.' See further Hofmann, 'Annexation', *MPEPIL* (2020). In a Joint Statement with the United States and the United Arab Emirates dated 13 August 2020, Israel stated that it 'will suspend declaring sovereignty over areas outlined in the President's Vision for Peace'. Israeli politicians refer to implementing or applying sovereignty over this land; see, eg, 'Israel, UAE Reach Historic Peace Deal: "We can make a wonderful future."' Jerusalem Post (14 August 2020).

[110] O'Connell, 'The Crisis in Ukraine – 2014', in Ruys and Corten (eds), *The Use of Force in International Law* (2018) 855–72. For some of the issues of international humanitarian law, see Bothe, 'The Current Status of Crimea: Russian Territory, Occupied Territory or What?', 53 *Military Law and the Law of War Review* (2014) 99–116.

[111] A/RES/68/262 para 6. See also the draft resolution of the Security Council that was vetoed by the Russian Federation, S/2014/189 para 5.

Such non-recognition has not so far affected the Russian position with regard to Crimea.

Hathaway and Shapiro, however, ask us to look at the bigger picture and see Crimea as an outlier. Let us consider some of their findings. They selected cases from 1816 to 2014 where territory changed hands as a result of conquest (as opposed to a peaceful transfer, or independence or dissolution). They found that from 1816 to 1928, 'The average amount of territory conquered during this period was 295,486 square kilometres per year. That is roughly *eleven* Crimeas per year for more than a hundred years.'[112] But their analysis highlights a sharp fall-off in permanent transfers in the following periods – 'between 1816–1928 and 1929–1948, the average amount of land that was permanently seized each year declined by 86 percent. After 1948, it fell another 59 percent.'[113] This leaves recognized acquired territory through conquest at around 6% of the previous levels: 'In contrast to the end of the First World War (and most wars before it), the losing states of the Second World War were not carved up and peeled out to the victors.'[114]

This fundamental shift concerning the institution of War is elegantly characterized by Hathaway and Shapiro as they relate this history to the present situation, suggesting that the Paris Pact ended the Old World Order, while the end of the Second World War ushered in a New World Order:

> The history we have told demonstrates that in a world of multiple sovereign states, there are a limited set of legal orders from which to choose. In one – represented by the Old World Order . . . – all states agree that war is legal, a tool to right wrongs. In that world, conquest is permissible, aggression is not a crime, neutrals must stay impartial (thus economic sanctions against aggressors are illegal), and agreements may be coerced. In the second – represented by the New World Order . . . – all states agree that war is illegal, and refuse to recognize it as a source of legal entitlements, even when used to right wrongs. In that world, conquest is illegal, aggression is a crime, economic sanctions are an essential tool of statecraft, and agreements cannot be coerced.[115]

---

[112] Hathaway and Shapiro, *The Internationalists* (n 23) at 314.
[113] Ibid at 320.
[114] Ibid at 321.
[115] Ibid at 421.

4

The Use of Force after the UN Charter

4.1 The UN Charter 1945 and the Prohibition on the Threat or Use of Force

In 1941, at the height of the Second World War, Churchill and Roosevelt agreed the Atlantic Charter. The final paragraph reads

> they believe that all of the nations of the world, for realistic as well as spiritual reasons must come to the abandonment of the use of force. Since no future peace can be maintained if land, sea or air armaments continue to be employed by nations which threaten, or may threaten, aggression outside of their frontiers, they believe, pending the establishment of a wider and permanent system of general security, that the disarmament of such nations is essential.

The drafting of the eventual UN Charter in 1945 glossed over the idea of disarmament for those states that might threaten aggression,[1] and we are left with a ban on threats to use force. The final version of Article 2(4) in the UN Charter adopted in San Francisco in 1945 prohibits both the threat of force and the use of force, and abandons the language of the League of Nations Covenant, which spoke of acts of war, resort to war and going to war. The UN Charter demands instead:

> All Members shall refrain in their international relations from the threat or use of force against the territorial integrity or political independence of any state, or in any other manner inconsistent with the Purposes of the United Nations.[2]

Rather than outlawing war, the focus now is on prohibiting the use of force. At this point many commentators simply consign the concept of war

---

[1] See Stürchler, *The Threat of Force in International Law* (2007) at 18–24.

[2] Art 2(4).

to the legal dustbin. One of the aims of this book, however, is to point out that this has not happened. We touched on some examples in Chapter 1 related to the death penalty in time of a State of War, and, as we shall see in the next chapter on war powers in national law, multiple provisions in national law may require a legal State of War before they are activated.

The UN Charter prohibition on the threat or use of force means that a Declaration of War by a member state in the absence of an armed attack will be illegal.[3] The Charter must also be read as prohibiting resort to the use of force for armed reprisals (formerly known as actions 'short of War'). The Charter includes no exception for such armed reprisals.[4]

What, then, constitutes an illegal use of force under the Charter? As with our definition of a 'State of War' in Chapter 1, there is a subjective element. Not every use of force is considered by states to be a violation of this rule. Troops mistakenly operating over the border, or even the firing of missiles in error, have not been treated as violations of this rule, even if there might be complaints concerning violations of sovereignty.[5] Nor is every deliberate use of force outside the territory necessarily a breach of this rule. Law enforcement operations at sea, or even on land as part of an operation against a fugitive from justice, where troops on the other side are not engaged, may be violations of sovereignty, or action against the inviolability of the territory of another state, but not necessarily treated as a use of force in violation of Article 2(4).

As Olivier Corten's study illustrates, context is everything, and the gravity of the force used and the means employed by the intervening state will be crucial: a simple abduction, or extraction of nationals in danger, might not be

---

[3] Wehberg, 'L'interdiction du recours à la force: le principe et les problèmes qui se posent', 78 *RCADI* 1 (1951) 1–121 at 73; Stürchler, *The Threat of Force* (n 1) 129.

[4] See the Friendly Relations Resolution of the General Assembly (1970), 'Declaration on Principles of International Law concerning Friendly Relations and Co-operation among States in accordance with the Charter of the United Nations', A/RES/25/2625: 'States have a duty to refrain from acts of reprisal involving the use of force.' See also the ILC Commentary on the Draft Articles on State Responsibility, paras 4 and 5, in the Commentary to Article 50 in Crawford, *The International Law Commission's Articles on State Responsibility: Introduction, Text and Commentaries* (2002) at 288–89; see also Brownlie, *International Law and the Use of Force by States* (1963) at 281–82. Dinstein, *War, Aggression and Self-Defence*, 6th edn (2017) at 274, speaks of 'defensive armed reprisals' but limits these to the situation where a state has the right to self-defence under Art 51 of the UN Charter. See also Institut de droit international (1934) Régime des représailles en temps de paix, Art 3, 'Les représailles armées sont celles qui comportent le recours à la force sous quelque forme que ce soit, militaire, navale ou aérienne.' ibid Art 4, 'Les représailles armées sont interdites dans les mêmes conditions que le recours à la guerre.' See also Gaeta, Viñuales and Zappalà, *Cassese's International Law*, 3rd edn (2020) 300.

[5] See the examples given by Corten, *The Law Against War: The Prohibition on the Use of Force in Contemporary International Law* (2010) 50–92.

treated as a violation of the rule. On the other hand, the invasion of Panama and the capture and trial of General Noriega by US forces was framed by other states in terms of a violation of this prohibition on the use of force.[6] In short, one cannot claim to be engaging in law enforcement when the reality is a serious use of armed forces.

Even after his detailed study of state practice, Corten admits that it is sometimes difficult to determine when things are serious enough to constitute a violation of Article 2(4).[7] Context counts. The factors Corten identifies include: Who ordered the use of force? Was it directed at the infrastructure of the other state or something else? And was there an engagement with the armed forces of the other state?[8] Of course the biggest contemporary controversy concerns air strikes on terrorist bases in other countries. These strikes are, however, not defended today as international police actions, or law enforcement, but rather under the justification of self-defence. The state carrying out the strikes will argue that it is defending itself from terrorist attacks, or that it has been invited to defend another state from such attacks.[9] So in order to know whether there has been a violation of the prohibition on the use of force, we need to know if the actions can indeed be justified as self-defence under international law.

---

[6] Ibid at 67, referencing GA Resolution 44/240 of 29 December 1989, which includes a reference to Art 2(4).

[7] Ibid at 73.

[8] Although Art 2(4) refers to a use of force 'against the territorial integrity or political independence of any state', arguments that force could therefore be permitted for other purposes have not been widely accepted; for example, it has been suggested that force was not aimed at another state's territorial integrity or political independence but rather was aimed at rescuing nationals abroad, or targeted for humanitarian purposes or for the sole purpose of upholding international law. For a reading of Art 2(4) that would allow for the use of force for purposes other than threatening territorial integrity or political independence, see Shearer, 'A Revival of Just War Theory?', in Schmitt and Pejic (eds), *International Law and Armed Conflict: Exploring the Faultlines (Essays in Honour of Yoram Dinstein)* (2007) 1–20. *Contra* Corten *The Law Against War* (n 5) at 488–511; and Dinstein, *War, Aggression and Self-Defence*, (n 4) at 93–94.

[9] The criticism could be made that the Charter, rather than outlawing war and circumscribing the use of force, 'legitimates state behaviour by legalizing it, making certain categories of war more rather than less possible': Hurd, *How to Do Things with International Law* (2017) at 81. There is a debate among philosophers as to whether drone strikes in particular should be covered by special rules. For some philosophers these strikes fit neither the warfare nor the law enforcement paradigms; see the collection of essays in Galliott (ed), *Force Short of War in Modern Conflict: Jus ad Vim* (2019).

4.1.1   Self-Defence under Article 51 of
the UN Charter

Much of the modern law on self-defence is being shaped by references to the oft-quoted correspondence between the United States and Great Britain over the *Caroline* incident. The *Caroline* was a US steamship that was being used by rebels seeking to move arms and men from the United States to foment a revolution in what was, in 1837, the British possession of Upper Canada. Supporters from New York, calling themselves 'Patriots', were helping the insurgents. Some hoped for an independent state free from British rule, others thought that the area could become eventually part of the United States. The incident concerned the sinking of the *Caroline* by a British Navy expedition of seven boats, with about 80 men from the British force stationed in Canada sent to 'cut out' this supply vessel.[10] The idea was to stem the arrival of men, arms and supplies leaving the US side of the river and reaching Navy Island, a British possession in the Niagara River, where the rebels were assembling, and from where shots had apparently been fired at a settlement on the Canadian side and on British vessels.[11] The British force found the *Caroline* in US waters and, after some fighting, towed the ship out into the open water and set fire to it, leaving it (or parts of it) to drift on over the Niagara Falls. One person was killed on the dockside, and there were reports of Billy the cabin boy perishing in the ship.

The resulting correspondence turned on the importance of respecting America's Neutrality and the necessity of the action that was taken.[12] At one point US Secretary of State Webster wrote to the British Envoy to Washington, requesting whether the British had any legal justification for the destruction of the *Caroline*. He included the oft-quoted sentence, 'It will be for that Government to show a necessity of self-defence, instant, overwhelming,

---

[10] The figures are from Palmerston's letter of 27 August 1941; in his account, the intention had been to tow the *Caroline* back to the British shore, but she was found to be too heavy and was instead set on fire and left to drift over the Niagara Falls. As explained by Forcese, the British commander of the forces sent to deal with the *Caroline* considered that burning the vessel better fitted the purpose than capture: *Destroying the Caroline: The Frontier Raid that Reshaped the Right to War* (2018) at 37–38. Palmerston's letter is in *Correspondence between Viscount Palmerston and Mr Stevenson* at 56–62, printed for the Cabinet and marked 'confidential' (1841) available at https://archive.org/details/cihm_460050.

[11] Noyes, 'The *Caroline*: International Law Limits on Resort to Force', in Noyes, Dickenson and Janis (eds), *International Law Stories* (2007) 263–305 at 267–68.

[12] See further Green, 'Docking the *Caroline*: Understanding the Relevance of the Formula in Contemporary Customary International Law Concerning Self-Defense', 14 *Cardoza Journal of International and Comparative Law* (2006) 429–80.

leaving no choice of means, and no moment for deliberation.'[13] As Robert Jennings (later President of the International Court of Justice) explained in his detailed law review article:

> It was natural that the elaboration of that concept should come from the American side, for elaboration meant limitation, and made it no longer possible for the British to talk vaguely of self-defence and self-preservation as if the mere utterance of the words excused any and every sin.[14]

To read the sentence in this letter from the US Secretary of State as if it related to the contemporary law of self-defence is, therefore, anachronistic. According to the eminent legal historian Peter Haggenmacher, any idea of self-defence in the minds of those dealing with the *Caroline* was derived from Vattel's right to security (also later known as 'self-preservation'). As he explains, 'self-defence did not properly become a subject of debate in international law before the time when States resolved to outlaw war . . . after World War I'.[15]

The Charter's unequivocal ban on the use of force ought to have shut down arguments about using force based on the idea of self-preservation. Most dramatically, the idea resurfaced in the International Court of Justice, at the end of the 20th century, that self-preservation would override any international law restrictions on using nuclear weapons. Such thinking has been robustly rubbished by Dinstein:

---

[13] Letter from Webster to Fox (24 April 1841), in 'Correspondence between Great Britain and The United States, respecting the Arrest and Imprisonment of Mr McLeod, for the Destruction of the Steamboat *Caroline*', 29 *British Foreign and State Papers* (1840–41) at 1137–38; See also Wood, 'The Caroline Incident – 1837', in Ruys and Corten (eds), *The Use of Force in International Law* (2018) 5–14; and see the two well-known works by Bowett, *Self-Defence in International Law* (1958) at 58–60 and 143–44, and Brownlie, *Use of Force* (n 4) at 42–43, 249–50, 258–64, 366–68 and esp at 429 (footnote omitted): 'Yet in the correspondence self-defence was equated with self-preservation and Webster's test is primarily verbal: it deals with the question of degree and in fact merely states that governments should exercise their discretion to act in defence of their vital interests with caution. In isolation Webster's test is no more informative than the crude formula that there must be necessity to act: there is the advice that there must be necessity to act in self-defence but no definition of the latter concept. Webster's formula is exceptionally elastic and necessarily permits anticipatory self-defence. Moreover, in the submission of the present writer to rely on it is to ignore the actual development of the state practice since 1920.'

[14] Jennings, 'The *Caroline* and McLeod Cases', 32 *AJIL* (1938) 82–99 at 89.

[15] Haggenmacher, 'Self-Defence as a General Principle of Law and Its Relation to War', in Eyffinger, Stephens and Muller (eds), *Self-Defence as a Fundamental Principle* (2009) 3–49 at 13.

The nexus between the use of nuclear weapons and the survival of a State is insupportable. Either nuclear weapons are lawful under certain conditions or they are not, but the fact that the very survival of a State is at stake cannot possibly affect that conclusion. If nuclear weapons are lawful, they are lawful to all States. If they are not lawful, the unlawfulness cannot be diminished only because the survival of a particular State is at stake. Otherwise, what we have here is a throwback to the outdated concept that self-preservation is a fundamental right of States, prevailing over all other considerations.[16]

But the idea of self-preservation retains a powerful hold on the imagination.[17] One argument we should address is the notion that *Caroline*-style anticipatory use of force against rebels, or in today's language 'terrorists', survives any UN Charter limits on self-defence. This argument relies on the wording of the Charter's Article 51, and on the reference in English to an 'inherent' right to self-defence.[18]

What exactly does the Charter prescribe? Article 51 reads:

Nothing in the present Charter shall impair the inherent right of individual or collective self-defence if an armed attack occurs against a Member of the United Nations, until the Security Council has taken measures necessary to maintain international peace and security. Measures taken by Members in the exercise of this right of self-defence shall be immediately reported to the Security Council and shall not in any way affect the authority and responsibility of the Security Council under the present Charter to take at

---

[16] Dinstein, 'Military Necessity', *MPEPIL* (2015) para 11.

[17] For the restrictions on this right based on the entry into force of the UN Charter, see Green, 'Self-Preservation', *MPEPIL* (2009). For harsh criticism of attempts to construct a customary right to self-defence that survives the Charter, see Brownlie, *Use of Force* (n 4) esp at 42–43, 249–50, 258–64, 366–68 and esp at 429; see also Corten, *The Law Against War* (n 5) at 409–10. For the contrary view, that the inherent or natural right of self-defence is left untouched by Art 51 of the Charter where the situation requires the urgent use of armed force against present-day instances of indiscriminate terrorism, see Rosenne, 'Self-Defence and the Non-Use of Force: Some Random Thoughts', in Eyffinger, Stephens and Muller (eds), *Self-Defence as a Fundamental Principle* (2009) 49–65.

[18] The suggestion is that even if the Charter demands an armed attack, its reference to an 'inherent' right revives an old right to preventive self-defence (even self-preservation in some versions) that requires no such armed attack. The International Court of Justice has stated that the reference in the Charter to the 'inherent' right to self-defence covers the customary rule, and 'its present content has been confirmed and influenced by the Charter'. See *Military and Paramilitary Activities in and against Nicaragua (Nicaragua v USA)*, ICJ Rep (1986) at para 176; see also ibid at para 181.

any time such action as it deems necessary in order to maintain or restore international peace and security.

Failure to notify the Security Council would not invalidate the right to self-defence, while notification makes it easier to justify, especially where, as in recent years, the details of the origin of the alleged armed attack form part of the notification.[19] For a state to claim to be acting in collective self-defence of another state that was the victim of an attack, there should be an explicit request from the victim state.[20] The right to self-defence continues until the Security Council has taken the relevant measures.[21]

If a state's right to self-defence is limited to responding to an armed attack, the next key question we need to address here is: What constitutes an armed attack?

4.1.2 Armed Attack as a Condition for Self-Defence

The question of what sort of armed attack will justify self-defence under international law is one of the most contested topics in international law and relations.[22] There are three related controversies. First, what sort of use of force constitutes an armed attack? Second, can support to an armed group fighting in another state constitute an armed attack? And, third, does it matter whether the actual attack itself comes from a state or a non-state actor?

On the first question, the International Court of Justice is often portrayed as stating that 'a mere frontier incident' by the armed forces of a state does not constitute an armed attack,[23] and one needs 'to distinguish the most grave forms of the use of force (those constituting an armed attack) from other less grave forms'.[24] The conclusion is then drawn that a state subjected to the

---

[19] Ibid at paras 195–199 and 232–270. Discussed by Gray, *International Law and the Use of Force*, 4th edn (2018) 176–90.

[20] *Nicaragua v USA* (n 18) at paras 195–199 and 232–270. Discussed by Gray (n 19) at 176–90.

[21] For Dinstein this means that the Council takes a clear decision that a state can no longer resort to force in self-defence: Dinstein, *War, Aggression and Self-Defence* (n 4) at 253–58; Gray, *Use of Force* (n 19) at 131–32 seems to consider that demands for a cease-fire or other action might be sufficient; *contra* Roscini, 'On the "Inherent" Character of the Right of States to Self-defence', 4 *Cambridge Journal of International and Comparative Law* 3 (2015) 634–60 at 653–59.

[22] See Ruys, *'Armed Attack' and Article 51 of the UN Charter: Evolutions in Customary Law and Practice* (2010); compare Dinstein, *War, Aggression and Self-Defence* (n 4) at 197–300; see also Lubell, *Extraterritorial Use of Force Against Non-State Actors* (2010).

[23] *Nicaragua v USA* (n 18) at para 195.

[24] Ibid at para 191.

lesser forms of force is not entitled to defend itself from certain less grave forms of force. It is not hard to imagine scenarios (gaps) where this leads to untenable results.[25]

But a careful reading of the Court's judgment, in its context, shows that the Court was looking at a particular and separate question. The Court found that arming a non-state group operating in another state constituted a use of force even if it did not constitute an armed attack. The Court was not determining a minimum threshold for a state's own use of force against another state to constitute an armed attack. In fact, in a later case, the Court determined that the threshold for triggering the right to self-defence can be quite low. In the *Oil Platforms case*, the Court considered that an intentional mining of a US military vessel at sea could trigger the right to self-defence,[26] and did not exclude that attacks on a merchant ship might allow the flag state to act in self-defence.[27]

Writing extrajudicially, Judge Yusuf from the Court has more recently suggested that when it comes to low-level conflict between the armed forces of two states on land, even minimal incidents would similarly represent armed attacks: 'It is, however, difficult to imagine how the alleged killing by the armed forces of one state of six members of the armed forces of another state, if proven, fails to rise to the threshold of an "armed attack", unless it was an unfortunate accident.'[28]

On the second question, the Court has carefully drawn a line between financing, arming and training armed groups (which constitutes an illegal use of force and intervention), and *sending* such groups over a border to engage in the use of force, which constitutes an armed attack. The distinction becomes crucial, because only in the latter case does a state have the right to engage in acts of self-defence against the sending state. What, then, is a victim state to do in the face of the illegal use of force by the state supporting the armed group, where this is confined to supporting rather than sending

---

[25] See, *inter alia*, Green, *The International Court of Justice and Self-defence in International Law* (2009); Dinstein, *War, Aggression and Self-Defence* (n 4) at 209–11.

[26] *Oil Platforms (Iran v USA)*, ICJ Rep (2003) at para 72.

[27] For a detailed look at the law concerning attacks on merchant ships and other non-military targets in the context of triggering the right to self-defence, see Ruys, *'Armed Attack'* (n 22) at 126–249.

[28] Yusuf, 'The Notion of "Armed Attack" in the *Nicaragua* Judgment and Its Influence on Subsequent Case Law', 25 *Leiden Journal of International Law* (2012) 461–70, at 469; see also Taft, 'Self-Defense and the Oil Platforms Decision', 29 *Yale Journal of International Law* (2004) 295–306 at 302: 'For its part, if the United States is attacked with deadly force by the military personnel of another State, it reserves its inherent right preserved by the UN Charter to defend itself and its citizens.' See also the US *Law of War Manual* (2016) at paras 1.11.5.2 and 16.3.3.1.

armed groups abroad?[29] In the *Nicaragua* judgment, it was suggested that there could be defensive countermeasures taken by the victim state against the supporting state, even though the Court was ambiguous on the nature of such countermeasures. Judge Yusuf tantalizingly hints at the direction a future Court would take when he concludes 'it could perhaps be reasonably assumed that [the Court] was referring to military countermeasures'.[30]

But this topic, developed as it was during a period of small-scale conflict through proxy armed groups as part of the Cold War, has been overtaken by the pressing issue of determining whether a terrorist attack can be classed as an armed attack as such, irrespective of the involvement of the state from where it is operating. If the armed group's attack is considered an armed attack under the Charter then the victim state can respond with justified self-defence.

Turning to the third question, does it matter whether the attack comes from a state or a non-state actor? again the legal discussion starts with the pronouncements of the International Court of Justice. The Court is usually seen as having suggested that the concept of armed attack is limited to action by states.[31] It is possible, however, to see the Court's judgments as focused on the responsibilities of the states in the dispute before it, and not really dealing with the question of what constitutes an armed attack. The failure of the Court to address this head-on was criticized by Judge Simma in his 2005 Separate Opinion in *Democratic Republic of Congo v Uganda*. He considered the terrorist attacks of September 11 had led to the favourable reception of 'claims that Article 51 also covers defensive measures against terrorist groups'. And he concluded that the Security Council resolutions at that time 'cannot but be read as affirmations of the view that large-scale attacks by non-State actors can qualify as "armed attacks" within the meaning of Article 51'.[32] This view is gaining ground among a number of legal experts, including current

---

[29] Sohn, 'The International Court of Justice and the Scope of Self-Defense and the Duty of Non-Intervention', in Dinstein and Tabory (eds), *International Law at a Time of Perplexity* (1989) 869–78.

[30] Yusuf, 'The Notion of "Armed Attack" ' (n 28) at 466.

[31] *Nicargua v USA* (n 18) para 195; *Armed Activities on the Territory of the Congo (Democratic Republic of the Congo v Uganda)*, ICJ Rep (2005) at paras 146–147, and see the Separate Opinions by Judges Simma and Kooijmans; for a detailed discussion of the ruling and its implications see Ruys, 'Armed Attack' (n 22) at 479–89. The other instance is the Advisory Opinion *Legal Consequences of the Construction of a Wall in Occupied Palestinian Territory*, ICJ Rep (2004) at para 139, and see the Separate Opinions of Judge Kooijmans at paras 35–36 and Judge Higgins at para 33, and the Declaration by Judge Buergenthal at paras 5–6.

[32] *Democratic Republic of the Congo v Uganda* (n 31) at para 11.

and former judges from the Court.[33] Others, such as Dire Tladi, a member of the International Law Commission, point to protests from a number of states.[34] He considers that responding to terrorist attacks abroad with the use of force risks giving 'the terrorists what they want from us', undermining the collective security system and rule of law in favour of 'the law of the jungle and, ultimately chaos and insecurity'.[35]

An alternative way to justify the use of force in response to an attack from a non-state actor has been to argue that force is used to respond to the failure of the host state to deal with the non-state actors. This has taken hold in parts of the doctrine. Kretzmer considers that it is a 'well accepted approach' that, 'if the host state does not curb the activities of the non-state actors in its territory, a state which has been victim to an armed attack by those non-state actors may use force against them in that territory'.[36] Some states have indeed taken to justifying their use of force in Syria under the rubric that Syria is 'unable or unwilling' to halt the attacks launched from there by the 'Islamic state'. Not all states, however, have made this test part of their claimed right to self-defence or endorsed others' use of this doctrine.[37] One can see why some states, not involved in the air strikes on the 'Islamic state', may understandably be wary about accepting a doctrine that would leave them vulnerable to attack on the subjective appreciation of another state that they have been unable or unwilling to control groups on their territory.[38]

---

[33] See also Yusuf, 'The Notion of "Armed Attack"' (n 28) at 470: 'There is no doubt that the notion of an "armed attack" has evolved since the decision in *Nicaragua* and in light of the UN Security Council Resolutions 1368 (2001), 1373 (2001) and 1377 (2001) adopted in the aftermath of the 11 September terrorist attacks in the United States, particularly with respect to its *ratione personae* aspects.' For a discussion involving former and future members of the Court as well as international lawyers from a wide range of countries, see the discussion at the Institut de droit international in 2007 and the eventual Resolution on Self-Defence, as well as the report of Roucounas, who concluded that 'Despite the discrepancy between recent Security Council practice and the ICJ's Opinion on the *Wall*, it would appear that doctrine and practice support the position that an armed attack, triggering self-defence as contained in Article 51, can be carried out by a non-State actor.' 72 *Annuaire de l'Institut de droit international* (2007) 75–236 at 171.

[34] Tladi, 'The Use of Force in Self-Defence against Non-State Actors, Decline of Collective Security and the Rise of Unilateralism: Whither International Law?' in O'Connell, Tams and Tladi, *Self-Defence against Non-State Actors* (2019) 14–89 at 78–79.

[35] Ibid at 89.

[36] Kretzmer, 'The Inherent Right to Self-Defence and Proportionality in *Jus Ad Bellum*', 24 *EJIL* 1 (2013) 235–82 at 237; see also Alston, 'Study on Targeted Killings', UN Doc A/HRC/14/24/Add.6 at para 35.

[37] For consideration of some of state practice on the question of self-defence against armed attack from non-state actors abroad, see Gill and Tibori-Szabó, 'Twelve Key Questions on Self-Defense against Non-State Actors', 95 *International Law Studies* (2019) 467–505 esp at 475–90.

[38] For a detailed study that emphasizes resistance to the idea, see Corten, '"The Unwilling or Unable" Test: Has it Been, and Could it be, Accepted?', 29 *LJIL* (2016) 777–99; for a detailed study of invocation of this concept and reactions to it, see Deeks, '"Unwilling or Unable": Toward a

The unwilling and unable test has been explicitly highlighted by the Legal Officers of the United Kingdom and United States when it comes to explaining the legality of air strikes against terrorists abroad.[39] But there is some ambiguity in these statements about the 'unwilling and unable' test. I would suggest that we should see 'unwilling or unable' not as a new justification for self-defence, but rather as a factor that goes to the question of the *necessity* of the self-defence in the face of an armed attack. There is a danger that in focusing on the ability and obligations of the host state, one veers away from the logic of self-defence and starts to enter zones that might suggest separate grounds to justify the use of force.[40]

Some of the doctrine seeks to suggest that states such as Syria or Pakistan, being unable to deal with the terrorists operating there, have somehow *impliedly* consented to armed intervention. Alternatively, scholars reach back to the obligations of Neutral Status to suggest, by analogy, that harbouring belligerents means that the state has lost its immunity from breaches of its

---

Normative Framework for Extraterritorial Self-Defence', 52 *Virginia Journal of International Law* (2012) 483–550, with an updated set of references available at https://www.lawfareblog. com/who-board-unwilling-or-unable#. For a detailed look at some of the negative reactions to older incidents where this argumentation was relied on, see Ruys, 'Armed Attack' (n 22) at 419–72, where he covers, *inter alia*, the Israeli attack on the PLO in Tunisia, the Rwandese incursions into the Democratic Republic of Congo in search of the Interhamwe, and Colombia's raid on the FARC in Ecuador. For the argument that the unwilling or unable doctrine evokes the colonial 'standards of civilization', see Tzouvala, 'TWAIL and the "Unwilling or Unable" Doctrine: Continuities and Ruptures', 109 *AJIL Unbound* (2016) 266–70.

[39] See Wright, 'The Modern Law of Self-Defence', 11 January 2017; Egan, 'International Law, Legal Diplomacy, and the Counter-ISIL Campaign', 92 *International Law Studies* (2016) 235–48.
[40] See the discussion by Deeks ' "Unwilling or Unable" ' (n 38), as well as her warnings about some of the dangers for human rights with the use of force being based on consent in 'Consent to the Use of Force and International Law Supremacy', 54 *Harvard International Law Journal* (2013) 1–60. See also Bethlehem, 'Principles Relevant to the Scope of a State's Right of Self-Defense Against an Imminent or Actual Attack by Nonstate Actors', 106 *AJIL* (2012) 770–77; Wilmshurst and Wood, 'Self-Defense Against Nonstate Actors: Reflections on the "Bethlehem Principles" ', 107 *AJIL* (2013) 390–95; Tladi, 'The Nonconsenting Innocent State: The Problem with Bethlehem's Principle 12' 107 *AJIL* (2013) 570–76; Bethlehem, 'Principles of Self-Defence: A Brief Response', 107 *AJIL* (2013) 579–85. For further discussion and references, see Kolb, *International Law on the Maintenance of Peace: Jus Contra Bellum* (2018) 376–85; on the connections with neutrality, see Ingber, 'Untangling Belligerency from Neutrality in the Conflict with Al-Qaeda', 42 *Texas International Law Journal* (2011) 75–114 and Deeks, '"Unwilling or Unable" (n 38) esp 496–506. For the idea that we consider self-defence in this context as a circumstance precluding wrongfulness, and that the violation of sovereignty could be compensated even if the state using force could rely on Art 21 of the ILC's Articles on State Responsibility, see Tsagourias, 'Self-Defence against Non-state Actors: The Interaction between Self-Defence as a Primary Rule and Self-Defence as a Secondary Rule', 29 *LJIL* (2016) 801–25; see also De Wett, *Military Assistance on Request and the Use of Force* (2020) Ch 6 and esp at 208–11 for a discussion of the relevance of Art 25 (necessity as a circumstance precluding wrongfulness) of the ILC's Articles on State Responsibility.

territorial integrity by a belligerent party. (We may recall that with regard to the *Caroline* episode, although there was no War that triggered neutrality obligations *sensu stricto*, both the United States and the United Kingdom saw the right to use force as part of ensuring respect for the principle of Neutrality.) But as we saw in Chapter 2, the better view is that, today, a state cannot respond to a breach of the obligations associated with neutrality with the use of force. Today force can be used only in self-defence. Once we leave the strict logic of self-defence in response to an attack, we lose the restrictions that accompany the right to self-defence, namely: immediacy, necessity, proportionality, reporting to the Security Council and the prospect that the right is extinguished once the Security Council takes the necessary action.

4.1.3 Anticipatory Self-Defence

Considerable controversy surrounds the idea that a state can use self-defence to *prevent* an attack. We can probably agree that a state might not have to wait until the missile lands before it can deploy force against its attacker (notwithstanding that the English text of the Charter says 'if an armed attack occurs').[41] But states have sometimes sought to develop a permission to engage in preventive self-defence, as opposed to anticipatory or pre-emptive self-defence. Here the analogies with natural law or the national law that applies to individuals again start to break down. For me to claim that I punched you in self-defence, I must be responding to an ongoing attack; I cannot thump you on the grounds that I am pretty certain you might hit me tomorrow.

But, as we saw when we considered the *Caroline* incident, states have accepted in the past that, at some point, there may be no choice left but to act, even if one is not at that point actually being attacked. The modern rule, however, is not based on the philosophy of self-preservation that prevailed at that time.[42] In 1946 the Nuremberg International Military Tribunal referenced the *Caroline* test, and rejected the argument that the German invasion of Norway was justified as preventive self-defence. At one point the judgment states:

---

[41] Compare the French, 'dans le cas où un Membre des Nations Unies est l'objet d'une agression armée'.

[42] Nor can self-defence be derived from any natural right of self-preservation for individuals; see Brierly, *The Law of Nations*, 5th edn (1955) at 317.

From all this it is clear that when the plans for an attack on Norway were being made, they were not made for the purpose of forestalling an imminent Allied landing, but, at the most, that they might prevent an Allied occupation at some future date.

When the final orders for the German invasion of Norway were given, the diary of the Naval Operations Staff for 23rd March 1940 records: 'A mass encroachment by the English into Norwegian territorial waters . . . is not to be expected at the present time.'[43]

The idea that the *Caroline* test has survived the UN Charter, and that it could now be expressed as an imminence test, was tackled by Waldock (later President of the International Court of Justice, 1979–81) in his 1952 Hague Academy Course. His articulation of what international law demands in terms of imminence became particularly influential (including in debates at the Security Council), and is worth repeating in full:

Nor does it seem that at San Francisco there was an intention to cut down the right of self-defence beyond the already narrow doctrine of the *Caroline* Incident. That doctrine allows and only allows a right of defence in face of imminent threat of attack – in face of an attack already impending over the defending State. Where there is convincing evidence not merely of threats and potential danger but of an attack being actually mounted, then an armed attack may be said to have begun to occur, though it has not passed the frontier. The Charter prohibits the use of force except in self-defence. The Charter obliges Members to submit to the Council or Assembly any dispute dangerous to peace which they cannot settle. Members have therefore an imperative duty to invoke the jurisdiction of the United Nations whenever a grave menace to their security develops carrying the probability of armed attack. But, if the action of the United Nations is obstructed, delayed or inadequate and the armed attack becomes manifestly imminent, then it would be a travesty of the purposes of the Charter to compel a defending State to allow its assailant to deliver the first and perhaps fatal blow. If an armed attack is imminent within the strict doctrine of the *Caroline*, then it would seem to bring the case within Article 51. To read Article 51 otherwise is to protect the aggressor's right to the first stroke. To cut down the customary right of self-defence beyond even the *Caroline* doctrine does not

---

[43] *Prosecutor v Goering et al*, Judgment of the IMT, 1 October 1946, Official Text, at 208.

make sense in times when the speed and power of weapons of attack has enormously increased.[44]

In 1981, when Israel used force against the Osirak nuclear reactor in Iraq, Israel claimed that it had 'performed an elementary act of self-preservation, both morally and legally. In so doing, Israel was exercising its inherent right of self-defence as understood in general international law and as preserved in Article 51 of the Charter'.[45] It was claimed by Israel that the reactor could be used to create nuclear weapons by 'the mid 1980s'.[46] The members of the Security Council felt, however, that there was insufficient evidence that Iraq was about to attack Israel.

The Mexican Ambassador, speaking at the end of the debate, suggested that a point of convergence was that it was

inadmissible to invoke the right to self-defence when no armed attack has taken place. The concept of preventive war, which for many years served as a justification for the abuses of powerful States, since it left to their discretion to define what constituted a threat to them, was definitively abolished by the Charter of the United Nations.[47]

Israel was then strongly condemned by a unanimous UN Security Council for a military attack in 'clear violation of the Charter of the United Nations and the norms of international conduct'.[48]

In the second half of the 20th century, states were cautious about allowing claims of preventive self-defence. It is only in the post-9/11 world that we find states, and in particular the United States, stressing the legality of preventive self-defence.[49] There have been multiple attempts by scholars and practitioners to flesh out what sort of anticipatory self-defence might be allowed in the age of terrorist attacks and weapons of mass destruction. The International Court of Justice has steered away from offering hints on the law of anticipatory self-defence. Suggestions in UN reports that imminent attacks are enough to justify self-defence have not been met with endorsement by

---

[44] Waldock, 'The Regulation of the Use of Force by Individual States in International Law', 81 *Collected Courses of the Hague Academy of International Law* (1952) 451–517, at 497–98 (footnote omitted).
[45] Debate in the Security Council, S/PV.2280, 12 June 1981 at para 58.
[46] Amb Blum, Israeli Permanent Representative S/PV.2280, 12 June 1981 at para 89.
[47] Debate in the Security Council, S/PV.2288, 19 June 1981 at para 115.
[48] SC Res 487 (1981).
[49] Gray, *International Law and the Use of Force* (n 19) at 170–75.

the vast majority of states.[50] The general practice of states suggests a very cautious attitude to extending the right to use force against another state beyond the exception allowed by Article 51 'if an armed attack occurs'.[51]

The challenge remains to circumscribe a rule so that it leaves little room for abuse. Despite the reference in Article 51 to an 'inherent' right to self-defence, it is unlikely that this can now be read as preserving the old right to defend legal interests by force in the absence of an armed attack.[52] A careful reading of Waldock does not actually suggest this (as is sometimes claimed), but rather demands that the attack be actually imminent, meaning that it is 'already *impending over the defending State*. Where there is *convincing evidence* not merely of threats and potential danger but *of an attack being actually mounted*, then an armed attack may be said to have begun to occur, though it has not passed the frontier'.[53] Such an understanding of anticipatory self-defence seems quite reasonable and in conformity with the demands of the Charter. In a similar vein, Dinstein has spent some time considering the contemporary legal framework, and his contemporary approach firmly rejects *preventive* self-defence as incompatible with the UN Charter, and yet he foresees a right for states to use self-defence in response to an armed attack at an *incipient* stage of the armed attack. For Dinstein:

> There is no need to wait for the bombs to fall – or, for that matter, for fire to open – if it is certain that the armed attack is under way (even in a preliminary manner). The victim State can lawfully (under Article 51) intercept the armed attack, with a view to blunting its edge.[54]

Orakhelashvili has a formula that stresses the irretrievable nature of the commitment to attack and would allow for self-defence only where there is 'an attack committed to in an irreversible way'.[55]

So we can conclude that if there is convincing evidence that it is certain an armed attack *is being irreversibly mounted or underway*, a state may be

[50] Ibid at 174–75, referencing the report *A More Secure World: Our Shared* Responsibility, A/59/565 (2004) at paras 188–92 and the SG's report *In Larger Freedom: towards development security and human rights for all*, A/59/2005 (2005) at para 124.

[51] Ruys, '*Armed Attack*' (n 22) ch 4 at 336ff; Corten, *The Law Against War* (n 5) 406–43; compare Walzer, *Just and Unjust Wars*, 5th edn (2015) at 80–85, who admits (at 84) that his moral argument for pre-emptive strikes is a 'major revision of the legalist paradigm'.

[52] See Brownlie, *Use of Force* (n 4); *contra* Bowett, *Self-Defence* (n 13).

[53] Waldock, 'Use of Force' (n 44) at 498 (emphasis added).

[54] Dinstein, *War, Aggression and Self-Defence* (n 4) at 228; see also Friman, *Revisiting the Concept of Defence in the Jus ad Bellum: the Dual Face of Defence* (2017).

[55] *Akehurst's Modern Introduction to International Law*, 8th edn (2019) at 457.

entitled to engage in self-defence. This conclusion will not satisfy those who consider that international law cannot get in the way of the interests of a state in protecting itself from a future attack, and some will say that it does not answer the demands of practitioners who have to advise on the legality of strikes in the modern world. In the 21st century, there has been a flurry of attempts by practitioners to set down policy guidance to determine when an attack can be considered *so imminent* that an armed response remains within the bounds of the UN Charter. These guidelines hardly provide new binding rules, but they do give us an insight into how legal advisors from the key western states engaging in counter-terrorism strikes consider the key concept of imminence in this context. The Leiden Policy Recommendations (2010) and the Chatham House Principles (2006) both link imminence to the idea that the state believes that this period represents a last chance to avert the forthcoming attack.[56]

4.1.4 Necessity and Proportionality of Self-Defence

In addition to the need for an armed attack, the law of self-defence also requires that any use of force in self-defence be necessary and proportionate.[57] As we have seen, the test for responding to the mounting of an imminent attack incorporates the idea of necessity through the idea of last resort. But necessity has a role to play beyond explaining last resort in anticipation. To satisfy the broad necessity requirement, a state will have to show two things. First, that non-forceful measures were not a viable alternative option. So, for example, if a state admits that its attack was aimed at someone else, or was launched in error, and offers to resolve the issue peacefully, it is not necessary for the victim state to respond with force, because the moment for self-defence is over. Such a use of force in retaliation is unnecessary.

Second, if the state under attack uses force against a target that is unrelated to the attack or the prospect of future attacks, that response could be

---

[56] Schrijver and van den Herik, 'Leiden Policy Recommendations on Counter-terrorism and International Law', 57 *NILR* (2010) 533–50 at 543 para 46; Wilmshurst, 'The Chatham House Principles of International Law on the Use of Force in Self-Defence', 55 *ICLQ* (2006) 963–72 at 967–68. See also Ohlin and May, *Necessity in International Law* (2016) at 55–58, for the suggestion that the governing concept for Attorney-General Holder in determining strikes on individual terrorists was 'immediate necessity' rather than imminence.

[57] Although these terms are not mentioned in Art 51, it is now clear that these requirements form part of customary international law and the law of the UN Charter. See *Nicaragua v USA* (n 18) at para 176; *Democratic Republic of the Congo v Uganda* (n 31) at para 147.

considered unnecessary for dealing with the attack. The use of force has to be necessary to forestall the future attacks.

Corten divides up the Court's cases on this point, explaining that necessity is seen as being bounded by three criteria, and that failure to respect any one criterion would render the use of force illegal. The three criteria are:

1. The temporal criterion: defensive force which comes too long after the original attack is illegal.
2. The geographical criterion: a response that is too extensive and goes beyond what is necessary to deal with the attack is illegal.
3. The coherence criterion: this criterion is gleaned from the approach of the Court in the *Oil Platforms* case and could also be called an 'effectiveness criterion'. There, the Court considered relevant the fact that United States had not complained about the military activities of the Oil Platforms to the Iranian authorities in connection with the claimed attacks. This led the Court to the conclusion that the destruction of the Oil Platforms was not necessary for self-defence. The Court memorably labelled such unnecessary use of force in self-defence as involving a 'target of opportunity'.[58] The coherence criterion therefore means that the use of force is unnecessary and illegal where there is an 'absence of any military benefit from the action undertaken in respect of its stated aim'.[59]

A separate issue is the amount of force used in self-defence. Sometimes excessive force could be considered unnecessary, but such an evaluation of the quantity of defensive force is perhaps better conceived of under the proportionality test. The demands of proportionality have led to considerable confusion. This is explained in part by the fact that there is a tendency to confuse different proportionality tests that apply to the use of force. Let me separate out four different norms:

1. A state's use of force in self-defence must be proportionate to the armed attack and necessary to respond to it (*jus ad bellum* proportionality).[60]

---

[58] *Oil Platforms* (n 26) at para 76.

[59] Corten, 'Necessity', in Weller (ed), *The Oxford Handbook of the Use of Force in International Law* (2015) 861–78 at 870; see also Corten, *The Law Against War* (n 5) at 488–93.

[60] This is customary international law and part of Art 51 of the UN Charter; see *Nicaragua v USA* (n 18) at para 176.

2. It is prohibited for any party to an armed conflict to attack a military objective where the expected incidental loss of civilian life, civilian injury or damage to civilian objects would be excessive in relation to the concrete and direct military advantage anticipated (*jus in bello* proportionality). Where an individual launches such an attack with the requisite knowledge, this can be a war crime.[61]

3. For law enforcement officials, the use of force used in law enforcement has to be proportionate to the seriousness of the offence and the objective to be achieved, and intentional lethal force can only be used where this is strictly unavoidable to protect life (human rights law proportionality for law enforcement).[62]

4. Just war doctrine has suggested that not only must the cause be just, but the harm caused must not outweigh the benefits the war is expected to bring. Put another way, 'proportionality primarily involved an assessment of whether the overall evil of resorting to war was balanced by the overall good that would ensue'.[63] In journalistic terms, 'any good that will follow must outweigh the inevitable pain and destruction'.[64] This is a philosophical and moral exercise and does not necessarily track the legal proportionality tests just listed; it looks at the overall *harm* (to military and civilian objects) and considers the *benefits* in very broad terms beyond the actual conflicts (just war theory harm–benefit proportionality).[65]

For now we will only be considering the first rule. But even here, there is some confusion.[66] There is often an assumption that the response has to be proportionate to the violence of the attack; this could be seen as tit-for-tat, or

---

[61] See Henckaerts and Doswald-Beck, *Customary International Humanitarian Law*, vol 1: *Rules* (2005) Rule 11, and for the war crime ibid at 576 (international armed conflict) and 599 (non-international armed conflict). See also AP I (1977) Arts 51(5)(b) and 85(3)(b).

[62] See Basic Principles on the Use of Force and Firearms by Law Enforcement Officials, Adopted by the Eighth United Nations Congress on the Prevention of Crime and the Treatment of Offenders (1990) esp principles 5(a) and 9; for detailed discussion, see Melzer, *Targeted Killing in International Law* (2008) at 177–211.

[63] Gardam, *Necessity, Proportionality and the Use of Force by States* (2004) at 9; see also Schulzke, *Just War Theory and Civilian Casualties: Protecting the Victims of War* (2017) at 57–58.

[64] 'Proportional to What', *Economist* (20 December 2008).

[65] For an introduction to a contemporary use of this just war theory concept of proportionality, see, eg, Forge, 'Proportionality, Just War Theory and Weapons Innovation', 15 *Science and Engineering Ethics* (2009) 25–38.

[66] For a very helpful account, see Christodoulidou and Chainoglou, 'The Principle of Proportionality from a *Jus Ad Bellum* Perspective', in Weller (ed), *The Oxford Handbook of the Use of Force in International Law* (2015) 1187–209.

an eye for an eye, but such a response would be better seen as *retaliation* rather than the right to self-defence. It might represent an emotional response, but retaliation is not how the contemporary legal test is framed. For force to be legal as proportionate in self-defence, the response must take into account what is necessary to deal with the attack, reverse any invasion and avert any upcoming attack. The right of self-defence would not justify a massive use of force designed to eliminate the prospect of any future attacks in the distant future. The authorities on this point are a bit opaque, but the Chatham House Principles make the point with considerable clarity:

> The force used, taken as a whole, must not be excessive in relation to the need to avert the attack, or bring it to an end. The physical and economic consequences of the force used must not be excessive in relation to the harm expected from the attack.[67]

We can also add that the International Court of Justice has confirmed that states

> must take environmental considerations into account when assessing what is necessary and proportionate in the pursuit of legitimate military objectives. Respect for the environment is one of the elements that go to assessing whether an action is in conformity with the principles of necessity and proportionality.[68]

This brings environmental considerations into this *jus ad bellum* type of proportionality test as part of the law of self-defence.[69]

Furthermore, the better view is that these proportionality tests continue throughout the conflict, so that for a state to remain within the law of self-defence it will have to ensure proportionality is satisfied in its conduct of hostilities. In Greenwood's words, this means this *jus ad bellum* rule provides 'an additional level of constraint upon a state affecting, for example, its choice of

---

[67] Wilmshurst, 'Chatham House Principles' (n 56) at 968.

[68] *Legality of the Threat or Use of Nuclear Weapons, Advisory Opinion* (1996) at para 30.

[69] Greenwood, '*Jus ad bellum* and *jus in bello* in the *Nuclear Weapons* Advisory Opinion', in Boisson de Chazournes and Sands (eds), *International Law, The International Court of Justice and Nuclear Weapons* (1999) 247–66, at 256; the environment is also to be taken into account as part of the second proportionally rule related to targeting in the context of the war crime in the ICC Statute Art 8(2)(b)(iv), as well as a matter of the conduct of hostilities see Oeter, 'Methods and Means of Combat', in Fleck (ed), *The Handbook of Humanitarian Law in Armed Conflict*, 3rd edn (2013) 115–230 at 126-9 and 211-223.

weapons and the targets and the area of conflict'.[70] Although an alternative view assumes that this proportionality assessment is merely made once and only once at the beginning of the conflict, and thereafter one looks exclusively to the *jus in bello* rules of armed conflict to determine the legality of targeting, I would suggest that the law now indeed requires that each targeting decision has to satisfy not only the rules of armed conflict, but also the proportionality rule that is found as part of the rules that bind a state acting in self-defence.

Gardam is clear that this sort of proportionality 'remains relevant throughout a conflict'.[71] Discussing the coalition's use of force against Iraq in 1991 (acting in collective self-defence on behalf of Kuwait), she states 'Each time a decision was taken as to the choice of targets, for example, the relationship between the destruction of the target or targets and the scope of collective self-defence would have required assessment.'[72] Greenwood finds that the International Court of Justice's approach to proportionality confirms the validity of his consistent claim that the *jus ad bellum* proportionality test continues alongside the *jus in bello* proportionality test, so that each act throughout the conflict has to satisfy both tests.[73]

Even in the field of moral philosophy, the just war conditions are considered by Helen Frowe to apply throughout the fighting, and not just as pre-conditions for entering a just war. She rejects the idea that *jus ad bellum* ideas of just cause and last resort apply only at the outset of the conflict:

> Meeting the conditions of *jus ad bellum* is not a single judgment made before the start of a war, but rather an ongoing judgment that must be made throughout the war. We can see this most clearly with respect to . . . just cause. One may not continue to fight a war after its just cause has been secured – not least because in the absence of just cause, no offensive can be militarily necessary for securing the just cause and thus any fighting is impermissible. But the other *ad bellum* conditions must also be satisfied throughout the war. If, for example, it becomes apparent during the course

---

[70] Ibid at 258.

[71] 'Necessity and proportionality in *jus ad bellum* and *jus in bello*', in Boisson de Chazournes and Sands (eds), *International Law, The International Court of Justice and Nuclear Weapons* (1999) 275–92 at 280.

[72] Ibid at 280–81.

[73] Greenwood, '*Jus ad bellum* and *jus in bello* in the Advisory Opinion' (n 69) at 258; see also Greenwood, 'The Relationship between *Ius ad Bellum* and *Ius in Bello*', 9 *Review of International Studies* (1983) 221–34 at 223: 'The terms in which Articles 2(4) and 51 are couched, however, also have the consequence that the modern *ius ad bellum* applies not only to the act of commencing hostilities but also to each act involving the use of force which occurs during the course of hostilities.'

of a war that one has no reasonable prospect of success, one may not continue to fight. Nor may one continue to fight if war has become unnecessary – if, say, the aggressor offers terms of peace that will secure the just cause.[74]

Recent international law studies have demonstrated that even in cases where the attacks were arguably in conformity with international humanitarian law (*jus in bello* proportionality), an application of this *jus ad bellum* proportionality rule should have precluded attacks on infrastructure as disproportionate or unnecessary to the goal of self-defence. Well-known examples of controversial excesses include the destruction of Iraqi infrastructure in the 1990–91 conflict for the defence of Kuwait, and the targeting of Lebanese dual-use objects by Israel in 2006.[75] The 'intuitive' idea that there should be symmetry between attack and defence does not hold as a matter of the contemporary international law of self-defence.[76] This first proportionality rule is now increasingly seen as demanding that the use of force in self-defence is proportionate and necessary to halting and repelling the attack.[77]

A nuanced way to comprehend the limits to self-defence may be that the scale of the original attack is relevant to understanding the necessity and type of response, while the design and execution of the response must be proportionate to the legitimate aims of self-defence.[78] In the words of the 2018 report of the International Law Association, the legitimate aims here are 'to halt any ongoing attack and prevent the continuation of further attacks'.[79] The same report explains that 'while self-defence cannot justify "all-out" war to destroy the enemy, the forcible measures can include the need to defend the

---

[74] 'On the Redundancy of *Jus ad Vim*: A Response to Daniel Brunstetter and Megan Braun', in Galliott (ed), *Force Short of War in Modern Conflict* (2019) 197–212 at 200–01 (footnote omitted).

[75] See the discussion and references in Green and Waters, 'Military Targeting in the Context of Self-Defence Actions', 84 *Nordic Journal of International Law* (2015) 3–28 esp at 24–55.

[76] Cannizzaro, 'Contextualizing Proportionality: *Jus ad Bellum* and *Jus in Bello* in the Lebanese War', 88 *IRRC* (2006) 779–92 at 783, who distinguishes a quantitative test that responds to the quantitative features of the original attack and a qualitative test that looks at whether the means employed in response are appropriate to the aims of the response.

[77] See the Chatham House and Leiden Principles (n 56), and more recently the Resolution adopted by the International Bar Association's Human Rights Institute on the Use of Drones for the Delivery of Lethal Weapons, 25 May 2017: 'The use of force must be necessary to halt and repel the attack, and proportionate to that necessity.'

[78] See particularly Christodoulidou and Chainoglou, 'The Principle of Proportionality' (n 66) at 1192; Lowe, ' "Clear and Present Danger": Responses to Terrorism', 54 *ICLQ* (2005) 185–96; and Etezazian, 'The Nature of the Self-Defence Proportionality Requirement', 3 *Journal on the Use of Force and International Law* (2016) 260–89 at 288.

[79] ILA, 'Final Report on Aggression and the Use of Force' (2018) at 12.

State from the continuation of attacks, and not only repel the attack of the moment'.[80]

Greenwood has considered the idea that where one is in a State of War, there would be no need to continue to take into account the criteria of necessity and proportionality in self-defence. He rejects this idea, and suggests that in the post-UN Charter world, even a declared War could not remove the need for respect for these additional limitations on the use of force:

Most conflicts between States since 1945 have not been characterized as war . . . [n]evertheless, it is suggested that the fact that one or more of the parties to a conflict chooses to regard itself as being in a state of war does not relieve it of the necessity to confine its actions to what is permissible in self-defence. . . . The special status of the Charter prohibition on force in the international legal order is such that the obligations it creates for States cannot be circumvented by the expediency of characterizing a particular situation as war.[81]

He argues that the designation by states that a conflict is a War would indicate the scale of the armed conflict, which would affect the degree of force that was considered necessary and proportionate.[82] An aggressor's Declaration of War may also be particularly pertinent: 'A declaration of war by the aggressor does, however, imply that the aggressor is committed to the destruction of his adversary and this will obviously be a relevant factor in determining what is a proportionate response.'[83] But the significant point here is that the characterization of the conflict as a war, or even a War in the technical sense, changes

---

[80] Ibid at 11.

[81] Greenwood, 'Self-Defence and the Conduct of International Armed Conflict', in Dinstein and Tabory (eds), *International Law at a Time of Perplexity: Essays in Honour of Shabtai Rosenne* (1989) 273–88 at 286 (footnote omitted). See also Greenwood, 'Historical Development and Legal Basis', in Fleck (ed), *The Handbook of Humanitarian Law in Armed Conflict*, 2nd edn (2007) 1-43 at 35–37; and O'Connell, 'Historical Development and Legal Basis', in Fleck (ed), *The Handbook of Humanitarian Law in Armed Conflict*, 3rd edn (2013) 1–42 at 35ff, who reiterates the point.

[82] According to Greenwood, 'Self-Defence' (n 81) at 286, 'the only significance of a decision by States to regard a conflict as war would be factual rather than legal. It would normally reflect the fact that the conflict was on a considerable scale and this in turn would have a bearing on the degree of force that could be regarded as reasonably necessary and proportionate in self-defence. The recognition of a conflict as war would thus reduce the practical importance of the limitations that have been examined here, since they are clearly at their most significant in low level conflicts, but it would not dispense with them altogether.'

[83] Greenwood, 'Scope of Application of Humanitarian Law', in Fleck (ed), *The Handbook of Humanitarian Law in Armed Conflict*, 2nd edn (2007) 45–78 at 50.

nothing as regards the need for targeting decisions to continue to respect the principles of necessity and proportionality in self-defence.[84] This point is central to the present book, as it highlights how much the legal regime covering all wars has changed since the Second World War.[85]

Dinstein takes another approach, and the idea of a conflict's becoming a war of self-defence seems to him to trigger the right to use massive force across a wide geographical scope until the enemy is totally defeated:

> [I]n the general practice of States a war of self-defence is not limited at all to a mere repulse of an armed attack: force is often used tenaciously, with a view to bringing about the utter collapse of the aggressor's armed forces.[86]

Dismissing as absurd the idea that the attacks of 11 September affected only a small part of the United States, and therefore that it might not be legitimate to use force against the whole country of Afghanistan and destroy the Government, he responds:

> Is it necessary to recall that the Japanese attack against Pearl Harbour in December 1941 – affecting an even smaller part of the United States – engendered the Pacific War with the United States, in which the whole Empire of Japan was embroiled and in the end dismembered, entire Japanese cities were pulverized, and the Japanese autocratic system of government was eradicated? Patently when an armed conflict brings about a war of self-defence, the attacker must realize the stakes are mortal. . . .

---

[84] Greenwood, ibid at 50.

[85] See also Greenwood, 'Historical Development and Legal Basis' (n 81) at 36: 'Prior to 1945, once a state was justified in going to war it was invariably entitled to seek the complete submission of its adversary and to employ all force, subject only to the constraints of humanitarian law, to achieve that goal. This is no longer permissible. Under the UN Charter, a state which is entitled to exercise the right of self-defence is justified only in seeking to achieve the goals of defending itself and guaranteeing its future security. It may therefore use whatever force is necessary (within the limits of humanitarian law) to recover any part of its territory which has been occupied as the result of its adversary's attack, to put an end to that attack and to remove the threat which the attack poses. In an extreme case the achievement of these defensive goals might be possible only by securing the complete submission of the adversary, but that will not generally be the case.' But see LC Green, 'Comment No 5 on Mr Greenwood's Report' in Heintschel von Heinegg (ed), *Visit, Search, Diversion and Capture: The Effect of the United Nations Charter on the Law of Naval Warfare* (1995) at 191–200; however Green includes proportionality as part of the law of armed conflict, meaning 'that action should never exceed that which is absolutely essential and, when taken in response to activities by an adverse party, should not be in any way excessive': *The Contemporary Law of Armed Conflict*, 3rd edn (2008) at 13.

[86] Dinstein, *War, Aggression and Self-Defence* (n 4) at 285.

War of self-defence, if waged as a response to an armed attack, need not be terminated when and because an aggressor is driven back; rather it may be carried on by the defending State until final victory. Particularly when engaged in a successful response to a large-scale invasion, the defending State – far from being bound to stop at the frontier – may pursue the retreating enemy forces, hammering at them up to the time of their total defeat.[87]

Dinstein therefore distinguishes war from what he calls 'defensive armed reprisals', which are 'measures of counter-force "short of war"'.[88] Such reprisals would not only have to be in conformity with the explicit requirements of Article 51 of the UN Charter (ie be in response to an armed attack), but also conform to the international requirements of necessity, proportionality and immediacy. Dinstein's concept of proportionality in this context is dependent on the law that was said to govern armed reprisals in the pre-Charter world, where retaliation was considered an appropriate response to a perceived violation of international law. Although he admits '[i]t is unrealistic to expect defensive armed reprisals to conform strictly and literally to the tenet of "an eye for an eye"', he suggests that 'A calculus of force, introducing some symmetry or approximation between the dimensions of the lawful counterforce and the original (unlawful) use of force is imperative.'[89]

In any event, the conflicts being fought today are not really responses to large-scale invasions, let alone 'total wars' such as the Second World War.[90] Even if a conflict is presented as part of a 'war on terror', the legal justification remains that of self-defence in response to terrorist attacks, and it should be clear that that the restrictive conditions for self-defence continue to apply. As stated above, I consider they apply to individual acts in self-defence and not at the overall level of what is needed to 'win the war'.

The use of force by the United States, the United Kingdom and others in Syria against the so called 'Islamic state' (ISIS) may be referenced with phrases about being at war with terrorists or in conflict with ISIS, but as long as states are not invited in by Syria, such a use of force has to be justified as self-defence. States do file such self-defence justifications with the

---

[87] Ibid at 286–87; see also Gill, 'Legal Basis of the Right of Self-Defence under the UN Charter and Under Customary International Law', in Gill and Fleck (eds), *The Handbook of the International Law of Military Operations* (2010) 187–98 at 196–97.

[88] Dinstein, *War, Aggression and Self-Defence* (n 4) at 264.

[89] Ibid at 268.

[90] Greenwood, 'Self-Defence and the Conduct of International Armed Conflict' (n 81) at 278.

Security Council, either on the grounds that ISIS has attacked Iraq, and Iraq has requested those states to assist in its self-defence, or that the state is acting in its own national self-defence against ISIS. This 'war' on ISIS is therefore constrained not only by the law of armed conflict, but also by the UN Charter law on self-defence, including the attendant rules on necessity and proportionality.[91]

4.2 Authorizations and Demands from the Security Council

4.2.1 Authorizations and Demands for Member States

As already mentioned, there are two exceptions to the prohibition on the use of force. The first is self-defence; the second is authorization by the Security Council. The UN Charter foresaw that armed forces and facilities would be placed at the disposal of the Security Council to carry out enforcement measures necessary to maintain or restore international peace and security.[92] These agreements never materialized: states remain wary of placing their armed forces at the disposal of the United Nations. Instead, the Security Council has come to authorize the use of force by a state or a group of states in particular circumstances. Under the Charter, such authorization takes place once the Security Council determines that there is a threat to the peace, a breach of the peace or an act of aggression, and that such measures are necessary to maintain or restore international peace and security.[93]

A key difference from the arrangements under the League and the Kellogg-Briand Pact is that under the UN Charter the Security Council can authorize the use of force whenever it considers that there is a threat to the peace and that such measures are necessary to restore international peace and security.

---

[91] For a military manual instructing compliance with necessity and proportionality in self-defence, see the Danish *Military Manual* (2016) at 36–37: 'An act of self-defence must be *necessary*, ie, it must be necessary to prevent or suspend the attack or new attacks that are assessed to follow. If conditions suggest that it has been a single attack only or if it is assessed that a diplomatic effort will be capable of settling the dispute, it should be considered whether an act of self-defence is necessary. At the same time, the act of self-defence is required to be *proportionate*. This implies a requirement of proportionality between the act of attack and the act of self-defence, allowing expectations of subsequent attacks to be taken into account in the assessment.'

[92] See Arts 42–49.

[93] See Arts 39–42.

It need not debate or determine whether an identified state is responsible for a threat of war, recourse to war or aggression.[94] It is enough that the Security Council determines a threat to the peace. Krisch's expert commentary to the Charter explains that the Security Council acts as the police and not as a judge or jury.[95] The focus is not on finding violations of international law, or even upholding international law, but on maintaining or restoring international peace. Krisch highlights that from the time of the preparatory work on the 'Purposes of the United Nations', set out in Article 1, the priority was given, first, to stopping wars and, second, to justice and law.[96]

The Security Council is surprisingly coy about its authorization of the use of force under Chapter VII of the Charter. It usually speaks in code, stating that it is authorizing 'all necessary means' or 'all necessary measures'.[97] But it is now nevertheless clear that these phrases refer to the use of force, and that such authorizations provide an exception to the prohibition on states using force against another state. Nevertheless, the states on the Security Council can be split on whether to authorize the use of force, and this has led to claims that some resolutions adopted under Chapter VII are deliberately ambiguous, and that the Council has implied an authorization to use force. In the context of the Iraq invasion in 2003, it was claimed by the United States and the United Kingdom that a material breach of one or more Security Council resolutions had revived the previous authorization to use force from 1990.[98] Alternatively,

---

[94] The Security Council has only rarely referred to acts of aggression (South Africa S/RES/387 (1976); S/RES/567/ (1985); S/RES/568/ (1985); S/5RES/571 (1985); S/574 (1985); Southern Rhodesia S/RES/455 (1979); Israel S/RES/573 (1985); S/RES/611 (1988)). The politics of the history of the prohibition of aggression under international law, and the definition of aggression adopted by the UN General Assembly in 1974, is expertly told by Sellars, 'Definitions of Aggression as Harbingers of International Change', in Sadat (ed), *Seeking Accountability for the Unlawful Use of Force* (2018) 122–53. The question of the individual crime of aggression is dealt with below.

[95] Krisch, 'Introduction to Chapter VII: The General Framework', in Simma, Khan, Nolte and Paulus (eds), *The Charter of the United Nations: A Commentary*, 3rd edn (2012) vol II, 1237–71 at 1245.

[96] Ibid at 1257.

[97] Exceptionally the Council calls for the use of force if necessary – see Resolution 221 (1966) concerning the situation in Southern Rhodesia at para 5: '*Calls upon* the Government of the United Kingdom of Great Britain and Northern Ireland to prevent, by the use of force if necessary, the arrival at Beira of vessels reasonably believed to be carrying oil destined for Southern Rhodesia, and empowers the United Kingdom to arrest and detain the tanker known as the *Joanna V* upon her departure from Beira in the event her oil cargo is discharged there.'

[98] Taft and Buchwald, 'Preemption, Iraq, and International Law', 97 *AJIL* 3 (2003) 557–63; 'Attorney-General's Advice on the Iraq War – Iraq 1441' 54 *ICLQ* 3 (2005) 767–78; for a detailed examination of all claims of 'Implied (or Revived) Authorization to Use Force' covering Iraq 1991–2002, Kosovo and Iraq 2003, see Gray, *International Law and the Use of Force*, 4th edn (2018) 361–77.

states have claimed that they are enforcing the implied will of the Council.[99] The situation arises because the permanent members of the Security Council may sometimes allow for ambiguity in order to preserve the idea that the Council is not completely fractured.[100]

The result has been that those members of the Security Council that have become concerned about such attempts to imply authorizations for the use of force have now become more cautious about authorizing Chapter VII actions. They may now be more likely to specify that Chapter VII action, for example involving embargoes, is being taken under Articles 40 or 41, in order to preclude arguments that the Resolution is based on Article 42 (which is the provision that is the legal basis for the Council's authorization of the use of force).[101]

In order for such an authorization to use force to be valid under the UN Charter, the Security Council will have, first, to 'determine the existence of any threat to the peace, breach of the peace, or act of aggression', and decide what measures shall be taken 'to maintain or restore international peace and security'.[102] Then, if the Council decides that non-forceful measures,[103] such as sanctions, 'would be inadequate or have proved to be inadequate', it may authorize the use of force, 'as may be necessary to maintain or restore international peace and security'.[104] There is here, then, *a double necessity test*: first, that the alternative of peaceful sanction is inadequate; and, second, that the force authorized is that which is necessary to restore peace and security. The fact that the mandate to use force is given for a defined end – to restore peace

---

[99] Johnstone, 'When the Security Council is Divided: Imprecise Authorizations, Implied Mandates, and the "Unreasonable Veto"', in Weller (ed), *The Oxford Handbook on the Use of Force in International Law* (2015) 227–50 at 244–48. According to a new account by Seldon, various leaders in the United Kingdom have referred to the need to have a 'UN moment'. He attributes this use of the phrase to multiple politicians starting with Tim Livesey, Chief of Staff of the Leader of the Opposition, and also to Prime Minister Cameron in a conversation with President Obama, as well to Nick Clegg, referencing Lord Ashdown, the former leader of the Liberal Democrats. 'Syria, Anthony Seldon on ten days that changed the world', *The Sunday Times* (12 August 2018); see also Douglas Alexander speaking to Cameron, Clegg and Hague – 'You are talking about this UN Security Council meeting as a moment, as theatre, not substance' – as reported in Seldon and Snowdon, *Cameron at 10: The Inside Story 2010–2015* (2015) at 337. The UK Attorney-General ruled out in 2003 the idea that an 'unreasonable veto' could legalize what would otherwise be an unlawful resort to force, 'So there are no grounds for arguing that an unreasonable veto would entitle us to proceed on the basis of a presumed Security Council authorisation.' See 'Attorney-General's Advice' (n 98) at 776–77.

[100] Johnstone (n 99) 244–48; see also Hakimi's very thoughtful study of the practice, 'The *Jus ad Bellum*'s Regulatory Form', 112 *AJIL* (2018) 151–90.

[101] Krisch, 'Introduction' (n 95) at 1267 MN 61; Johnstone (n 99) at 238–43.

[102] See Art 39 UN Charter.

[103] See Art 41 UN Charter.

[104] See Art 42 UN Charter.

and security – means that not only must the decision to use force be necessary for that end, but also the amount of force has to be proportionate to it and any specific ends detailed in the authorization.[105]

Controversies have arisen most recently over the force used against Libya following a limited authorization by the Security Council in 2011.[106] For our purposes the key point is that when the Security Council acts under Article 42, it is not authorizing war but rather force for a limited purpose. Gardam has traced the legal limits on Security Council authorizations in some detail, and recalls the controversy over General McArthur's advocating the destruction of North Korean forces rather than simply pushing them back from South Korean territory. She quotes a well-known study by Bowett: 'Whereas, traditionally, a State waging war was entitled to do so to the stage of complete annihilation and subjugation of the other side, it can scarcely be maintained that United Nations action can be pursued so far.'[107]

Under the UN Charter, decisions of the Security Council are binding on UN member states. While the Security Council often recommends action, or appeals to states to refrain from certain action, where there is a *decision* that states must cease hostilities or take some action, for example with regard to disarmament, this creates a binding obligation in international law. It is also understood that a 'demand' from the Security Council in the context of Chapter VII signals a legal obligation.[108]

So the Security Council can do two significant things: it can authorize states to use necessary force against another state; and it can demand that states cease hostilities or take some other action.

4.2.2 Authorizations for UN Forces

What we have been discussing so far are instances of the Security Council authorizing peace enforcement operations to be carried out by member states or regional organizations. A separate type of operation is the UN peacekeeping operation, whereby the United Nations creates a force under the command and control of the Secretary-General. From early on, the Secretary-General has often had to tread carefully to keep the Security Council and

---

[105] See ILA, 'Use of Force' (n 79) at 8.
[106] See Gray, *Use of Force* (n 19) 377–80.
[107] Gardam, *Necessity, Proportionality and the Use of Force* (n 71) Ch 6 at 210.
[108] Krisch, 'Introduction to Chapter VII' (n 95 at 1265 MN 56; see also Dinstein, *War, Aggression and Self-Defence* (n 4) 57–59.

the troop-contributing countries on board. As Abi-Saab's brilliant study of the 1960 Congo Crisis explains, the Secretary-General may have to side-step condemnations of illegal interventions by member states, and refer to situations rather than disputes, if the United Nations is to receive a mandate in order to restore order and attempt to prevent a civil war.[109]

These UN operations, which involve sending 'blue helmets', can have a variety of mandates, and not all operations were necessarily created by the Security Council nor with a Chapter VII mandate. In the early days of the United Nations, a doctrine developed that assumed that such forces operated with the consent of the host state, and that such forces would only use force in self-defence or defence of the mandate. These concepts were tested and strained during the conflicts in the Congo, former Yugoslavia and Rwanda.[110] In some cases, states considered the peacekeepers went too far; in other situations the United Nations was seen to stand by while innocents were slaughtered. From 1999, the Council started authorizing peacekeeping forces to 'take the necessary action' to protect 'civilians under imminent threat of violence'.[111] The practice is to regard civilians in a broad non-legalistic sense, and protection is offered beyond situations of armed conflict.[112] By now the vast majority of UN peacekeepers around the world (about 100,000) are deployed in missions with a protection of civilians mandate.[113]

The UN's own guidelines synthesize the traditions and doctrine surrounding peacekeeping operations and the use of force: consent of the parties, impartiality, and non-use of force except in self-defence and defence of the mandate.[114] With regard to the use of force, the guidelines explain:

A United Nations peacekeeping operation should only use force as a measure of last resort, when other methods of persuasion have been exhausted, and an operation must always exercise restraint when doing so. The ultimate aim of the use of force is to influence and deter spoilers

[109] Abi-Saab, *The United Nations Operation in the Congo 1960–1964* (1978) at 11–17.

[110] For a critical analysis see Sheeran, 'The Use of Force in United Nations Peacekeeping Operations', in Weller (ed), *The Oxford Handbook on the Use of Force in International Law* (2015) 347–74.

[111] Res 1270 (1999) para 14. The background is explained by Mamiya, 'A History and Conceptual Development of the Protection of Civilians', in Willmot, Mamiya, Sheeran and Weller (eds), *Protection of Civilians* (2016) 63–87.

[112] Ibid at 78–79.

[113] In 2018 the figure was listed at more than 95%: see at https://peacekeeping.un.org/en/infographics.

[114] *United Nations Peacekeeping Operations: Principles and Guidelines* (2008) (Capstone Doctrine) at 31.

working against the peace process or seeking to harm civilians; and not to seek their military defeat. The use of force by a United Nations peace-keeping operation should always be calibrated in a precise, proportional and appropriate manner, within the principle of the minimum force necessary to achieve the desired effect, while sustaining consent for the mission and its mandate. In its use of force, a United Nations peacekeeping operation should always be mindful of the need for an early de-escalation of violence and a return to non-violent means of persuasion. The use of force by a United Nations peacekeeping operation always has political implications and can often give rise to unforeseen circumstances. Judgments concerning its use will need to be made at the appropriate level within a mission, based on a combination of factors including mission capability; public perceptions; humanitarian impact; force protection; safety and security of personnel; and, most importantly, the effect that such action will have on national and local consent for the mission.[115]

Although peacekeeping operations are established with the consent of the host state, and so the adoption of Chapter VII is only necessary in case such consent is withdrawn, resolutions that authorize the use of force to protect civilians have been adopted under Chapter VII as a way of signalling the Council's determination. While there may be little continuing debate about the legal basis of the use of force in this context, other problems remain concerning the contours of the legitimate use of force by such peacekeepers.

Can self-defence, or defence of the mission, extend to the use of deadly force to protect property? What constitutes an *imminent* threat to civilians? What happens when the use of force turns the operation from peacekeeping to 'war fighting'?[116] The Commander of the UN Forces in Bosnia famously referred to such a shift as crossing the 'Mogadishu line', as he considered that 'it was in Somalia that such a line was crossed to the detriment both of the peace-keepers and the people of Somalia'. For him, 'greater clarity as to what constitutes peacekeeping and what constitutes war fighting will enable future UN missions to avoid the mistakes made in Bosnia'.[117]

The primary issue is that in order to engage in 'war fighting', there needs to be a different level of equipment, training and mandate. But there are

---

[115] Ibid at 35.

[116] Sheeran, 'Use of Force' (n 110).

[117] Rose, 'Meaning of War', in O'Connell, (ed) *What is War? An Investigation in the Wake of 9/11* (2012) 167–76 at 173–76.

secondary issues as well. Once the United Nations is seen as engaging in an armed conflict with only one party to a pre-existing conflict, it will be hard for the same United Nations to maintain the idea that it is impartial in that pre-existing conflict. As the doctrine explains, the use of force is to prevent harm to civilians, not to seek a 'military defeat'. Such protective action is better perhaps seen as a form of law enforcement than a new war. In addition, should the United Nations have to take on government forces, this could be seen as an international armed conflict, and the treaties that protect the United Nations from attack would no longer apply. Instead of an attack on the UN forces being considered a war crime, the attack can become a legitimate act of combat in armed conflict.[118] So again the policy will be to avoid action that would categorize such engagement as a new armed conflict.

Crossing into 'war fighting' is not just a question of losing impartiality and immunity from attack. As we have seen, the language of war suggests the total subjugation of the enemy. Even when UN troops cross the line into using force for the protection of civilians, it is extremely unlikely that the idea would be to defeat the government as such. The UN presence will ultimately depend on the consent of the authorities if it is to remain operational. Peacekeeping requires jettisoning the logic of war but keeping its new commitment to the protection of civilians.

More recently we have seen the exceptional measure of mandating 'robust peacekeeping' with the creation of a UN 'Intervention Brigade' in the Democratic Republic of Congo. This foresees a level of violence to be used against non-state actors, but does not really put the UN on a 'war footing', even if the laws of armed conflict could apply to these confrontations with the armed groups. The aim of the mandate is to support the Government and 'carry out targeted offensive operations',

> to prevent the expansion of all armed groups, neutralize these groups, and to disarm them in order to contribute to the objective of reducing the threat posed by armed groups on state authority and civilian security in eastern DRC and to make space for stabilization activities.[119]

In practice, whatever the legal limits on the use of force, the bigger problem may be that although there is apparent support for the protection

---

[118] Clapham, 'The Concept of International Armed Conflict', in Clapham, Gaeta and Sassòli (eds), *The 1949 Geneva Conventions: A Commentary* (2015) 3–26 at 8–10; and see Ch 6 below.
[119] Res S/RES/2098/2013 para 12(b).

of civilians in all peacekeeping mandates, states are not always ready, as Mona Khalil explains, to 'put their troops in harm's way' when 'peace is absent or elusive'.[120]

4.3 Intervention by Invitation and the Rule of Non-Intervention in Internal Affairs

4.3.1 Invitation from One Government to Another

The right of one government to intervene to help another government fight insurgents has often been invoked over the years. But suspicion of this 'invitation rule' means that the timing, nature and authority of such invitations have to be carefully scrutinized. In the past, there has been opposition to the idea that support was permitted to colonial powers or racist regimes denying a people's right to self-determination. The UN General Assembly affirmed the illegality of forcible action depriving a people of their right to self-determination, and at the same time affirmed the legality of assistance (in economic and political terms) to a people under colonial rule struggling for self-determination, or against foreign occupation or a racist regime; such assistance was not to be considered a violation of the rule on non-interference in internal affairs.[121]

In the post-colonial period, it is hard to discern whether there remains a rule that prohibits assisting a state engaged in an armed conflict against a group within the state.[122] The assistance given by Russia and Iran at the

---

[120] 'Legal Aspects of the Use of Force by United Nations Peacekeepers for the Protection of Civilians', in Willmot, Mamiya, Sheeran and Weller (eds), *Protection of Civilians* (2016) 205–23 at 222.

[121] Resolution 2625 (1970) and Resolution 3314 (1974) Art 7. See Cassese, *Self-Determination of Peoples: A Legal Reappraisal* (1995) 175–76 and 200.

[122] For an detailed overview of the situation up to 1985, see Doswald-Beck, 'The Legal Validity of Military Intervention by Invitation of the Government', *British Yearbook of International Law* (1985) 189–252; more recently, some scholars have concluded that the essence of the rule of non-intervention on either side in a civil war continues – see, eg, Ruys, 'Of Arms, Funding and "Non-lethal Assistance" – Issues Surrounding Third-State Intervention in the Syrian Civil War', 13 *Chinese Journal of International Law* (2014) 13–53 esp at 45 and 52; Bannier-Christakis, 'Military Interventions against ISIL in Iraq, Syria and Libya, and the Legal Basis of Consent', 29 *LJIL* (2016) 743–75 esp at 754–56, who makes an exception for fighting terrorism (at 745): 'External intervention by invitation is normally unlawful when its objective is to settle an exclusively internal political strife in favour of the established government. Military assistance on request can nonetheless be perfectly legal when the *purpose* of the intervention is to realize other objectives, including the joint fight against terrorism.' See also the Resolutions of the Institut de droit international from Wiesbaden (1975) and Rhodes (2011). These conclusions are, however, contested – see Hafner, 'Intervention by Invitation' 73

invitation of Syria in order to fight the insurgency there has been objected to, but no state has suggested that such assistance to Syria represents a violation of international law. This is hardly surprising when the Western states that might have such objections have been intervening for some time on the side of Iraq and Afghanistan at the invitation of those governments to fight against the insurgents there. Similarly, France has claimed that it has been invited by various African states, such as Mali, to intervene, while Saudi Arabia and its allies claim that they were invited to intervene in Yemen; Kenya has been intervening in Somalia at the request of a government; and for some time Syria claimed its presence in Lebanon was by invitation.[123]

When this issue of intervention by consent has been tangentially considered by the International Court of Justice, the Court has implied that an outside state's use of force at the invitation, or with the consent, of the host government means there is no violation of the international law concerning armed intervention or interference.[124] We have to conclude in light of this that there is now probably no rule prohibiting military or other forms of assistance to the government of a state – unless it is clear that the government is denying a people's right to self-determination.[125] Although we immediately have to add that should the assistance be given in the context of violations of human rights or international humanitarian law (which in most conflicts today is extremely likely), the assisting state

---

AIDI (2009) 298–477; Dinstein, *Non-International Armed Conflicts in International Law* (2014) 74–83; Nolte, 'The Resolution of the *Institut de droit international* on Military Assistance on Request', 45 *RBDI* (2012) 241–62.

[123] For a full discussion, see Gray, *Use of Force* (n 19) Ch 3; De Wett, *Military Assistance on Request* (n 40) Ch 3, who also includes South Sudan and examines forcible assistance by international organizations including SADC, ECOWAS and the AU; for further discussion in particular on Liberia, Syria, Ukraine and Yemen, see Casey-Maslen, *Jus ad Bellum* (2020) Ch 2.

[124] *Nicaragua v USA* (n 18) at para 246; *Democratic Republic of Congo v Uganda* (n 31) at paras 42–54; see also Lieblich, *International Law and Civil Wars: Intervention and Consent* (2013) Ch 6; and Nolte, 'The Resolution of the *Institut* on Military Assistance' (n 122) .

[125] This principle is easy to state, but of course the contours of which peoples are entitled to self-determination in such a context will be contested. See further Weller, *Escaping the Self-Determination Trap* (2008); see also Cassese, *Self-Determination of Peoples: A Legal Reappraisal* (1995) and, on the specific issue of assistance to a government in a civil war, Cassese, *International Law*, 2nd edn (2005) at 370–71. In the context of the Georgia–Russia conflict, the Independent Fact-Finding Mission on the Conflict in Georgia seemed to recognize the aspect of self-determination being claimed for South Ossetia, but concluded that 'the South Ossetian authorities could *not* validly invite Russia to support them by military means' (Report (2009) vol II at 280); at the same time it also seem to suggest that state practice does not support intervention upon invitation in wars of secession (ibid at 277), although this should perhaps be read as limited to struggles involving self-determination.

could find itself in violation of international law for providing such assist-ance.[126] Precautions should therefore be taken to ensure that assistance is not being given in a situation where it could contribute to violations of international humanitarian law or human rights.

A valid invitation to use force may mean that the state's sovereignty was not violated as such. But we should be concerned not only about sovereignty, but also about the rights of the individuals subjected to this force.[127] A host state can consent to force being used on its territory, but it cannot waive the human rights of the persons being targeted. In the absence of an armed con-flict between the invited state and the targets on the ground, such killings could constitute extra-judicial executions.

In the absence of an armed conflict, relying on consent or self-defence therefore is not enough. One official US justification offered has been that its strike was in response to an 'imminent threat of violent attack against the United States' and 'conducted in a manner consistent with law of war prin-ciples'.[128] In 2016, a UK Parliamentary Committee asked the Government to provide the grounds on which it 'considers the Law of War to apply to lethal force outside armed conflict'. The Government responded that it 'considers that in relation to military operations, the law of war would be likely to be re-garded as an important source in considering the applicable principles'.[129] The

---

[126] See Moynihan, *Aiding and Assisting: Challenges in Armed Conflict and Counterterrorism* (2016); see in particular Arts 16 and 41 of the ILC's Articles on State Responsibility, UN Doc A/Res/56/83, adopted 12 December 2001; De Wett, *Military Assistance* (n 122) Ch 4. See Corten and Koutroulis, 'The Illegality of Military Support to Rebels in the Libyan War: Aspects of *Jus contra Bellum* and *Jus in Bello*', 18 *JCSL* (2013) 59–93. Under the Arms Trade Treaty 2013, states parties are prohibited from authorizing transfers where the items would be used in the com-mission of various violations of the laws of war, genocide or crimes against humanity; for the arguments that there would also be restrictions on a state seeking to authorize exports to a state involved in aggression or a violation of the law prohibiting the use of force where this would undermine peace and security, see Casey-Maslen, Clapham, Giacca and Parker, *The Arms Trade Treaty: A Commentary* (2016) at 200 and 255. Section 6(3)(1) of the German War Weapons Control Act (2002) provides 'A licence *shall be* denied if . . . there is a danger of the war weapons being used for an act detrimental to peace, especially for a war of aggression.'

[127] See Hathaway, Crootof, Hessel, Shu and Werner, 'Consent is Not Enough: Why States Must Respect the Intensity Threshold in Transnational Conflict', 165 *University of Pennsylvania Law Review* 1 (2016) 1–47; International Law Association Committee on the Use of Force, 'Final Report on Aggression and the Use of Force' (2018) at 19–20; White, 'The Joint Committee, Drone Strikes and Self-Defence: Caught in No Man's Land', *Journal on the Use of Force and International Law* (2016) 1–7.

[128] US Attorney-General Holder, speaking at Northwestern University School of Law, 5 March 2012, cited by Corn, 'The *Jus ad Bellum*', in Corn, VanLandingham and Reeves (eds), *US Military Operations: Law, Policy, and Practice* (2016) 91–121 at 117.

[129] Joint Committee on Human Rights, 'The Government's policy on the use of drones for targeted killing: Government Response to the Committee's Second Report of Session 2015–16', Fourth Report of Session 2016–17, HC 747, HL Paper 49, 19 October 2016, Appendix 1 at 16.

Joint Committee on Human Rights was not satisfied with this answer, and felt that it came close to suggesting that once the Government had decided to employ military means, 'the relevant principles and standards are the Law of War, even if the military operation is carried out in an area which is outside armed conflict'.[130]

For many commentators it is self-evident that law of war principles should not be determining the legality of lethal targeting outside of war or armed conflict. The human rights of the individuals targeted, as well as those killed or injured as innocent bystanders, are part of the legal landscape and do not disappear just because a state has the consent of another state, or invokes law of war principles. The prospect of 'an administrative law of transnational executions' has been memorably described as a 'zombie', created to rid us 'of all legal constraints on state violence imposed by the law enforcement paradigm'.[131] In the United States, the idea that these actions taken in self-defence are clothed with neither the cloak of the laws of war nor the mantle of human rights law has been referred to as 'naked self-defence'.[132] These vivid metaphors betray just how desperate the situation has become. However the situation is dressed up, two things ought to be clear. Outside armed conflict these laws of war play no role. The people targeted have human rights.[133]

4.3.2 Assistance to Non-State Actors Fighting in an Internal Armed Conflict

It is clear that an opposition armed group cannot invite a foreign state to use force against the government it is fighting.[134] Of course there can be debates

---

[130] Ibid at 6, para 18.

[131] von Bernstorff, 'Drone Strikes, Terrorism and the Zombie: On the Construction of an Administrative Law of Transnational Executions', 5 *EJIL Reflections (online)* 7 (2018).

[132] See Watkin, *Fighting at the Legal Boundaries: Controlling the Use of Force in Contemporary Conflict* (2016) 311–22; Hessbruegge, *Human Rights and Personal Self-Defense in International Law* (2017) 233; Hathaway et al, 'Consent is not Enough' (n 127).

[133] Multiple authors have sought to draw the contours of human rights law applicable to drone strikes outside armed conflict; see, *inter alios*, Heyns, Akande, Hill-Cawthorne and Chengeta, 'The International Law Framework Regulating the Use of Armed Drones', 65 *ICLQ* (2016) 791–827; Ramsden, 'British Air Strikes against ISIS: Legal Issues under the European Convention on Human Rights', *EHRLR* (2016) 151–60; Pejic, 'Extraterritorial Targeting by Means of Armed Drones: Some Legal Implications', 96 *RIRC* 893 (2015) 67–106; Melzer, *Targeted* (n 62). And see International Bar Association's Human Rights Institute, 'The Legality of Armed Drones Under International Law', Background Paper, 25 May 2017.

[134] See Gray, *Use of Force* (n 19) at 86–100; Fox, 'Intervention by Invitation', in Weller (ed), *The Oxford Handbook of the Use of Force in International Law* (2015) 816–40 at 827ff.

as to who exactly represents the government of the state and who is the opposition in situations of civil war or colonial struggle. Sometimes the Security Council may actually identify whom the United Nations considers the actual government to be. This choice will, in some cases, be influenced by issues of legitimacy rather than simple questions of who has effective control.[135] Although there may have been different views during the colonial period, today, not surprisingly, all states seem to agree that only they can invite other states to help them fight civil wars, and no state advocates that insurgents can invite in foreign armed forces.

But what if the armed group is supplied with arms, funds and training from outside? In the well-known case brought by Nicaragua against the United States, the International Court of Justice held two things. First, a state's *sending armed groups* abroad to another state can constitute an armed attack triggering the right to self-defence if the 'operation, because of its scale and effects, would have been classified as an armed attack rather than as a mere frontier incident had it been carried out by regular armed forces'.[136] Second, the *mere arming and training of armed groups abroad* constitutes only a violation of the rule outlawing the use of force rather than an armed attack, and therefore such support does not trigger the right to self-defence.[137] The *mere supply of funds* would not amount to a use of force; it would nevertheless amount to an intervention in the internal affairs of the other state and constitute a violation of international law.[138] As with assistance to states, there are complex arguments about the contours of legal responsibility for those states and individuals that assist armed groups to commit violations of international law.[139]

---

[135] See Redaelli, *Intervention in Civil Wars: Effectiveness, Legitimacy, and Human Rights* (2021).

[136] See *Nicaragua v USA* (n 31supra) at para 195, referencing in particular the definition of aggression in GA Resolution 3314 Art 3(g); see further section 4.4.2 below.

[137] The International Court of Justice seems to have considered that there could be countermeasures in the form of arming another group in conflict with the state that was originally supplying arms. Such a supply of arms would it seems have to be proportionate to the original violation of international law. Ibid at 237.

[138] See *Nicaragua v USA* (n 31) at paras 195, 203–209, 228, 241 and 298; on the issue of the appropriate countermeasures to be taken by the victim state, see paras 201 and 249, discussed in Casey-Maslen et al, *Arms Trade Treaty* (n 126) at 195–99.

[139] Clapham, 'Detention by Armed Groups under International Law', 93 *International Law Studies* (2017) 1–44 at 35–43.

4.4 The Individual Crime of Aggression

4.4.1 From War of Aggression to Crimes Against Peace

We saw in the last chapter how under the League of Nations, wars of aggression were declared to be international crimes. But this was a reference to the opprobrium to be heaped on the governments concerned, and in 1923 not really a reference to any sort of individual criminal responsibility under international law. The subsequent Kellogg-Briand Pact of 1928 contained no enforcement mechanisms of its own, and made no reference to individual responsibility. Various non-binding texts in the inter-war period reference aggressive war as a crime, and there were already multiple discussions in different fora concerning the development of an international criminal court.[140] But even during the Second World War, when attention turned to the possibility of prosecuting war crimes, the idea of prosecuting individuals for starting the war was not widely countenanced. William Schabas has described how, initially, only a small minority of lawyers (from occupied countries) sought to argue that violations of the Kellogg-Briand Pact by the German, Japanese and other Axis leaders could be prosecuted as the 'crime of war (breach of the Kellogg Pact)'.[141] By 1945, the British and the United States came around to the idea, ultimately switching the terminology from 'crime of war' to 'crimes against peace' (even if the definitions for the Nuremberg and Tokyo Tribunals still centred on the idea of an aggressive *war* in violation of international law).[142]

---

[140] Grzebyk, *Criminal Responsibility for the Crime of Aggression* (2013) Chs 1–3.

[141] Schabas, 'Nuremberg and Aggressive War', in Sadat (ed), *Seeking Accountability for the Unlawful Use of Force* (2018) 58–79 at 63, quoting the Belgian Chair, Marcel de Baer, writing to members of Commission II of the London International Assembly, on the Trial of War Criminals, in a letter of 22 July 1942; and see the proposals of Ečer (from the Czech government in exile), concluding that 'aggressive war is a crime, and by its character an international crime, because it aims against peace and international order' ibid at 67. For the detail of the negotiations, see Grzebyk (n 140) at 86–97.

[142] For the detail see Schabas (n 141) at 76–77. The London Charter for the International Military Tribunal eventually contained the following provision (emphasis added) '6(a) *Crimes against peace*: namely, planning, preparation, initiation or waging of a *war* of aggression, or a *war* in violation of international treaties, agreements or assurances, or participation in a common plan or conspiracy for the accomplishment of any of the foregoing'. The Statute of the Tokyo Tribunal went a step further, clarifying that the war of aggression could be declared or undeclared, and including war in violation of international law (emphasis added), '5(a) *Crimes against Peace*: Namely, the planning, preparation, initiation or waging of a *declared or undeclared war* of aggression, or a *war in violation of international law*, treaties, agreements or assurances, or participation in a common plan or conspiracy for the accomplishment of any of the foregoing'. For a detailed look at the ways in which the judges determined that individuals could be

The idea of prosecuting (and executing) leaders for a crime, which may not have been strictly speaking a crime at the time it was committed, did play on the minds of the judges in Nuremberg (1946) and Tokyo (1948). Most concluded in the end that individuals could be prosecuted for these crimes against peace related to waging aggressive war as outlined in their Statutes. The dissenting judgments in Tokyo nevertheless objected that there was little evidence under traditional international law that resort to war constituted a crime for individuals.[143] As Judge Pal from India put it, 'In my judgment no category of war became a crime in international life up to the date of commencement of the world war under our consideration.'[144]

4.4.2 The Crime of Aggression in the Rome Statute

Sixty years later in 2010, the Kampala Conference adopted a definition of the 'crime of aggression' for the purposes of prosecution in the International Criminal Court. The definition finally separates out acts of aggression from the idea of waging war.

During the early drafting, the United Kingdom's representative had argued:

An act of aggression which is not part of an aggressive war (whether declared or undeclared) may give rise to State responsibility. But my delegation remains to be convinced that it constitutes a crime for an individual under international law.

---

prosecuted for these crimes (notwithstanding the absence of a definition of 'war of aggression' or 'war in violation of international law'), see Boister and Cryer, *The Tokyo International Military Tribunal: A Reappraisal* (2008) Ch 5.

[143] Röling upheld the charge of aggression, but he saw punishment as necessary for security rather than flowing from a criminal act as such; he explained this in his dialogue with Cassese, in which he said 'My point was that the concept of the crime of aggression did not exist at the relevant times when the accused were carrying out the acts said to constitute this crime.' Röling and Cassese, *The Tokyo Trial and Beyond* (1993) at 65. See his dissent discussed ibid at 45, 'As indicated above, aggression was not considered a true crime before and in the beginning of this war'. The dissent also carefully considers all the inter-War texts for their references to war as a crime of aggression and evaluated their significance. Available at www.legal-tools.org/doc/462134/pdf/.

[144] Tokyo Tribunal, Dissenting Judgment at 151, available at https://www.legal-tools.org/doc/1dfce4/pdf/. And see the discussion of all the dissents on this point by Cryer, 'The Tokyo International Military Tribunal and Crimes Against Peace (Aggression): Is There Anything to Learn?', in Sadat (ed), *Seeking Accountability for the Unlawful Use of Force* (2018) 80–102.

Later the statement continued, 'jurisdiction should be given to the Court only in respect of the crime of aggression in the context of full scale war, whether declared or undeclared'.[145]

But the final definition focuses on 'an act of aggression which, by its character, gravity and scale, constitutes a manifest violation of the Charter of the United Nations'. Excising war from the definition of 'crime of aggression' represents a departure of some significance.[146] As the US representatives to the Conference later explained:

> The absence of an explicit requirement that a state have waged a 'war of aggression' appeared to depart from customary international law and was another point that significantly concerned the United States.[147]

But for others, dropping the reference to war was entirely appropriate, as this move ensured that modern aggressions, which might not necessarily be considered wars, would nevertheless reach the gravity threshold for prosecution at the International Criminal Court.[148]

The 2010 definition of the 'crime of aggression' is now in force for nationals from the relevant states parties and within the jurisdiction of the International Criminal Court. The Statute of the Court (aka 'the Rome Statute') includes the following crime of aggression:

> 8bis 1.   For the purpose of this Statute, 'crime of aggression' means the planning, preparation, initiation or execution, by a person in a position effectively to exercise control over or to direct the political or military action of a State, of an act of aggression which, by its character, gravity and scale, constitutes a manifest violation of the Charter of the United Nations.

---

[145] Excerpted in Kreß, 'The State Conduct Element', in Kreß and Barriga (eds), *The Crime of Aggression: A Commentary*, vol 1 (2017) 412–563 at 516; Dinstein, *War, Aggression and Self-Defence* (n 4) at 144 continues to see war as the key to understanding the new threshold: 'Still, only a fully fledged aggressive war could conceivably fit the combined conditions of 'character, gravity and scale'. See also Dinstein, 'The Crime of Aggression under Customary International Law', in Sadat (ed), *Seeking Accountability for the Unlawful Use of Force* (2018) 285–302.

[146] For the history of the separation of wars of aggression from acts of aggression under the 1974 General Assembly Definition of Aggression, see Sellars, 'Definitions of Aggression' (n 94) at 143–45.

[147] Koh and Buchwald, 'The Crime of Aggression: The United States Perspective', 109 *AJIL* (2015) 257–95 at 270.

[148] Pellet, 'Response to Koh and Buchwald's Article: Don Quixote and Sancho Panza Tilt at Windmills', 109 *AJIL* (2015) 557–69 at 558.

2. For the purpose of paragraph 1, 'act of aggression' means the use of armed force by a State against the sovereignty, territorial integrity or political independence of another State, or in any other manner inconsistent with the Charter of the United Nations. Any of the following acts, regardless of a declaration of war, shall, in accordance with United Nations General Assembly Resolution 3314 (XXIX) of 14 December 1974, qualify as an act of aggression:

   (a) The invasion or attack by the armed forces of a State of the territory of another State, or any military occupation, however temporary, resulting from such invasion or attack, or any annexation by the use of force of the territory of another State or part thereof;

   (b) Bombardment by the armed forces of a State against the territory of another State or the use of any weapons by a State against the territory of another State;

   (c) The blockade of the ports or coasts of a State by the armed forces of another State;

   (d) An attack by the armed forces of a State on the land, sea or air forces, or marine and air fleets of another State;

   (e) The use of armed forces of one State which are within the territory of another State with the agreement of the receiving State, in contravention of the conditions provided for in the agreement or any extension of their presence in such territory beyond the termination of the agreement;

   (f) The action of a State in allowing its territory, which it has placed at the disposal of another State, to be used by that other State for perpetrating an act of aggression against a third State;

   (g) The sending by or on behalf of a State of armed bands, groups, irregulars or mercenaries, which carry out acts of armed force against another State of such gravity as to amount to the acts listed above, or its substantial involvement therein.

A number of key points can be made straight away. First, the need to find a manifest violation of the Charter rules out clearly lawful uses of force in self-defence, or force authorized by the UN Security Council under Chapter VII.

Second, mistakes and minor incidents involving any of the enumerated acts would not normally qualify as crimes of aggression due to the qualifier that the act through its 'character, gravity and scale, constitutes a manifest violation of the Charter'.[149]

Third, the definition refers to the 'use of armed force' and makes no mention of the 'threat' of force, which is separately outlawed under the UN Charter. So a simple threat of force, including even a Declaration of War, would not qualify as the crime of aggression under this definition.[150]

Fourth, the crime is limited to certain leaders of states, those 'in a position effectively to exercise control over or to direct the political or military action of a State'.

In a separate amendment to the Statute the rules on assisting others to commit crimes have been adjusted. Those who are not leaders cannot be prosecuted for aiding and abetting those leaders who are in fact charged with aggression.[151] So merely fighting in the armed forces of an aggressor state cannot be prosecuted at the International Criminal Court as assisting in the crime of aggression.

The leaders of armed groups that attack states cannot be prosecuted for aggression at the International Criminal Court. Aggression is defined in the Statute as the use of armed force by a state. Interestingly, treaties adopted by African states have defined aggression to include acts by non-state actors.[152] One treaty for the Great Lakes region includes an undertaking by the member states to criminalize such acts of aggression 'by individuals or groups operating in their respective states'.[153]

The idea that armed attacks by organized terrorist groups do not count as aggression for the purposes of the International Criminal Court, or under customary international law, will strike some as strange, and indeed influential scholars such as Pellet have argued that in the post-9/11 world there is

---

[149] See also the Understandings adopted in Annex III to Resolution RC/Res.6, 11 June 2010, especially Understandings 6 and 7.

[150] See Kreß, 'The State Conduct Element' (n 147) at 424.

[151] Art 25(3)bis: 'In respect of the crime of aggression, the provisions of this article shall apply only to persons in a position effectively to exercise control over or to direct the political or military action of a State.'

[152] See African Union Non-Aggression and Common Defence Pact (2005): '"Aggression" means the use, intentionally and knowingly, of armed force or any other hostile act by a State, a group of States, an organization of States or non-State actor(s) or by any foreign or external entity, against the sovereignty, political independence, territorial integrity and human security of the population of a State Party to this Pact, which are incompatible with the Charter of the United Nations or the Constitutive Act of the African Union.' The treaty also includes a longer list of acts that constitute aggression.

[153] Protocol on Non-Aggression and Mutual Defence in the Great Lakes Region (2006) Art 3(4).

support for the idea that attacks such as those by Al-Qaeda on that day constitute armed attacks. For him, by implication, these are acts of aggression.[154]

An examination of the procedural rules for the prosecution of aggression would take us too far beyond our focus on war. We can simply explain here that the final arrangements for prosecution by the Court do not require a finding of aggression by the Security Council before the Court's jurisdiction can be exercised. There is merely an auxiliary role for the Security Council in the process of the authorization of investigation.[155] Moreover, should the Security Council acting under Chapter VII decide to refer a situation to the Prosecutor, then the International Criminal Court will have jurisdiction over any person (of whatever nationality) the Prosecutor determines should be prosecuted. Of course, in political terms, this means that each of the veto-wielding members of the Security Council (China, France, Russia, the United Kingdom and the United States) will be able to ensure that such a referral is not used against their wishes.

In situations where the Security Council does not act to refer a situation, the Court is dependent on a state referral or the initiative of the Prosecutor. In these circumstances, the jurisdictional rules are quite restrictive. First, the amendment to the treaty agreed in 2010 provides that it is impossible for a national of a state that has not joined the Statute to be prosecuted. So, for example, at present, the leaders of states such as Armenia, Azerbaijan, China, Egypt, Eritrea, Ethiopia, India, Iran, Iraq, Israel, North Korea, Pakistan, Russia, Saudi Arabia, Syria, Turkey, the United Arab Emirates and the United States cannot be prosecuted for aggression by this Court.[156]

Second, the Assembly of States Parties has adopted a resolution that confirms that even the nationals of states parties cannot be prosecuted for the crime of aggression unless their state of nationality has accepted the treaty amendments and, in addition, the state which is the victim of the aggression has also accepted the amendments.[157] This excludes the nationals of states

---

[154] Pellet (n 148) at 561–62 and 568. Of course it bears repeating here that in the French version of the UN Charter, the expression 'armed attack' is translated as 'agression armée'.

[155] Art 15bis(6)–(9) ICC Statute.

[156] Art 15bis(5): 'In respect of a State that is not a party to this Statute, the Court shall not exercise its jurisdiction over the crime of aggression when committed by that State's nationals or on its territory.'

[157] Resolution ICC-ASP/16/Res.5, 14 December 2017, para 2: '*Confirms* that, in accordance with the Rome Statute, the amendments to the Statute regarding the crime of aggression adopted at the Kampala Review Conference enter into force for those States Parties which have accepted the amendments one year after the deposit of their instruments of ratification or acceptance and that in the case of a State referral or *proprio motu* investigation the Court shall not exercise its jurisdiction regarding a crime of aggression when committed by a national or on the territory of a State Party that has not ratified or accepted these amendments'.

such as France and the United Kingdom from being prosecuted for aggression as long as those states decline to accept the amendments in full.[158] In part the reticence of France and the United Kingdom to be bound by the amendments on aggression may relate to the ambiguity some consider surrounds the idea that humanitarian intervention should not constitute aggression. As we shall see in the next section, this tension was fully debated during the negotiations on the definition of the crime of aggression.

4.5 Humanitarian Intervention and Responsibility to Protect

The idea of intervening with force for humanitarian reasons, to protect a population in danger, is not new, and such 'humanitarian intervention' has been promoted and disparaged with equal vehemence.[159] The basic reasoning is fairly simple. International law and morality demand respect for human life and the prevention of massive killings, including those involving crimes against humanity and genocide. At the same time, international law only allows one state to use force against another state in self-defence or with the authorization of the Security Council. Where a state is ready to use force to protect people and enforce the first rule, it is met with the accusation that this will be a violation of the second rule.

Those who oppose an interpretation that would allow for such humanitarian intervention involving the use of force, point out that there are too many examples of powerful states cloaking their intervention with humanitarian motives while engaging in other more selfish pursuits. Goodman calls this a concern about 'pretext wars'.[160] Added to this must be the fact that

---

[158] The background to these negotiations is detailed by Kreß, 'On the Activation of the ICC Jurisdiction over the Crime of Aggression', 16 *JICJ* (2018) 1–17. It is possible to accept the amendment yet make a declaration excluding the jurisdiction of the Court under Art 15bis(4) ICC Statute.

[159] For a careful legal analysis of the situation up to the end of the 20th century, see Chesterman, *Just War or Just Peace? Humanitarian Intervention and International Law* (2001), who concludes after a careful analysis of state practice that there is no such right to use force under international law; similarly Dinstein, *War, Aggression and Self-Defence*, 6th edn (2017) at 75–76. For arguments in the literature that such a right exists, see Koh, 'The War Powers and Humanitarian Intervention', 53 *Houston Law Review* (2016) 971–1033 and Tesón, *Humanitarian Intervention: An Inquiry into Law and Morality*, 3rd edn (2005); see also Rodley, 'Humanitarian Intervention', in Weller (ed), *The Oxford Handbook on the Use of Force in International Law* (2015) 775–95. For an early significant publication on the topic, see Lillich (ed), *Humanitarian Intervention and the United Nations* (1973).

[160] Goodman, 'Humanitarian Intervention and Pretexts for War', 100 *AJIL* (2006) 107–41.

many military interventions will involve people getting killed. If the argument is based more on morality than legal entitlement, how does one make the moral argument that saving some people justifies killing others who are doing nothing wrong?

This longstanding debate needs to be seen against some recent history. Following the genocidal massacre in Rwanda, where hundreds of thousands lost their lives in the face of inaction by the 'international community', the blame was variously apportioned to the limits of peacekeeping, the divided UN Security Council, the inertia of the UN Secretariat, the caution of the US Administration and misunderstandings about genocide; and finally some saw the problem as international law and its reverence for sovereignty. In the aftermath of the failure to act there was some self-reflection on what had gone wrong, and considerable interest in circumscribing a right of humanitarian intervention.

Particular attention was focused on atrocities that could be described as genocide. Samantha Power explains how genocide was understood at the time. She reveals that General Dallaire, having made

> the mental leap from viewing the violence as war to viewing it as crimes against humanity, . . . had begun to employ the phrase 'ethnic cleansing' to describe the ethnically motivated killing, a phrase he was familiar with from having presided over the dispatch of Canadian troops to former Yugoslavia.

Power goes on to quote General Dallaire:

> I was self-conscious about saying that the killings were 'genocidal' because to us in the West, 'genocide' was the equivalent of the Holocaust or the killing fields of Cambodia. I mean millions of people. 'Genocide' was the highest scale of crimes against humanity imaginable. It was so far up there, so far off the charts, that it was not easy to recognize that *we* could be in such a situation. I also knew that if I used the term too early, I'd have been accused of crying wolf and I'd have lost my credibility.[161]

As we shall see, in fact genocide does not require the killing of massive numbers. But the confusion over genocide went further. There was a general sense that whatever the Genocide Convention actually demands, calling

---

[161] Power, "*A Problem from Hell*" (2003) at 358.

the situation a genocide would force military action. John Shattuck, at that time at the US State Department, quotes an internal government memorandum that stated that a 'genocide finding could commit the US government to actually "do something"'.[162] Michael Barnett, at the time closely involved on behalf of the United States in the Security Council discussion, later wrote 'Although the Genocide Convention does not require a military response to genocide, the Council did not expect a literal reading from the international public, who it imagined would treat anything less than military action as a whitewash.'[163] He recounts that the British Ambassador warned that the Security Council would be considered a 'laughing stock' should they call Rwanda a genocide and then fail to act.[164] Even after the UN Secretary-General described the situation as a genocide, and the Security Council approved a larger force, the slaughter continued, and no troops or equipment were sent in time.[165] Dallaire remains convinced that had the peacekeepers on the ground been reinforced, rather than reduced, they could have stopped the genocide.[166]

Then, five years later, in 1999, in the absence of Security Council authorization, NATO states engaged in an extensive bombing campaign in order, they said, to prevent a humanitarian catastrophe in Kosovo. It seemed to some that the time had come to adjust the rules so that such humanitarian interventions would be unambiguously legal. That year, UN Secretary-General Annan launched an intense debate about the role of sovereignty. Speaking in Geneva, as the NATO bombing of Serbia continued, he launched his own bombshell, telling the Human Rights Commission:

> Emerging slowly, but I believe surely, is an international norm against the violent repression of minorities that will and must take precedence over concerns of State sovereignty. . . . No government has the right to hide behind national sovereignty in order to violate the human rights or fundamental freedoms of its peoples. Whether a person belongs to the minority or the majority, that person's human rights and fundamental freedoms are sacred.[167]

---

[162] Shattuck, *Freedom on Fire*, 342–43.
[163] Barnett, *Eyewitness to a Genocide: The United Nations and Rwanda* (2002) 135.
[164] Ibid.
[165] Boutros-Ghali, *The United Nations and Rwanda 1993–1996* (1996) 50–52.
[166] Dallaire and Carrier, 'Rwanda', in Genser and Stagno Ugarte (eds), *The United Nations Security Council in the Age of Human Rights* (2014) 275–87 at 287.
[167] SG/SM/6949, 7 April 1999.

Later in the year, after the conclusion of the NATO bombing campaign, Kofi Annan argued for a reappraisal of the meaning of sovereignty. He suggested, first, that the state is now understood as 'the servant of the people' and, second, that individual sovereignty meant that the human rights of every individual were enhanced by a new consciousness that every individual had the right to control their destiny.[168] The next year he continued in the same vein: 'National sovereignty offers vital protection to small and weak States, but it should not be a shield for crimes against humanity.'[169]

The idea developed that the time was ripe to look again at questions of sovereignty and humanitarian intervention. The Canadian Government established the International Commission on Intervention and State Sovereignty in 2000. The members of the Commission sought to reorient the debate.[170] They eschewed the term 'humanitarian intervention', in part to avoid a perceived militarization of humanitarian work, and in part due to the mounting opposition among states to the development of any such exception to the prohibition on the use of force. The Commission instead called for recognition of a 'responsibility to protect'.[171] It stressed two principles: first, that sovereignty implies a responsibility of a state towards its people; and, second, that the principle of non-intervention yields to the international responsibility to protect where a population is suffering serious harm as a result of internal armed conflict, repression or state failure, and the state in question is unwilling or unable to stop this.[172]

This proposed right (or duty) to intervene in the context of humanitarian catastrophe was at the same time to be circumscribed. The Commission would propose a 'just cause threshold' involving large-scale loss of life or ethnic cleansing, and a 'right authority' criterion foresaw that in cases where the Security failed to act the UN General Assembly would consider the matter under the Uniting for Peace procedure.[173] World events, however, took a

---

[168] SG/SM/7136, 20 September 1999, aka the 'Two Concepts of Sovereignty' speech.

[169] SG statement to the GA, New York, 3 April 2000. See also Kofi Annan, 'The Legitimacy to Intervene: International Action to Uphold Human Rights Requires a New Understanding of State and Individual Sovereignty', *Financial Times* (31 December 1999)

[170] The Sudanese scholar Francis Deng and his co-authors had already by 1996 started to reconceptualize sovereignty as an issue of responsibility Deng, Kimaro, Lyons, Rothchild and Zartman, *Sovereignty as Responsibility: Conflict Management in Africa* (1996).

[171] *The Responsibility to Protect: Report of the International Commission on Intervention and State Sovereignty* (2001).

[172] Ibid, Basic Principles (1)A and B at xi.

[173] Ibid, Principles for Military Intervention (3)E at xiii. See further Binder, 'Uniting for Peace Resolution (1950)', *MPEPIL* (2017). It is doubtful that even in the face of a Security Council veto, the Uniting for Peace procedure can authorize the use of force; it can merely recommend

dramatic turn. The terrorist attacks of 11 September 2001, the subsequent invasion of Afghanistan, and the bombing and occupation of Iraq in 2003 all changed the context. These events, and the accompanying political climate, led the majority of states seriously to question the wisdom of opening up a new exception to the established prohibition on the use of force. Feelings of failure over Srebrenica and Rwanda were fading. Images of Western forces operating in Afghanistan and Iraq were now a part of the daily news.

The key passage in the eventual 2005 Summit Outcome, adopted by all UN member states, carefully leaves the Security Council as the gatekeeper for an authorization of the use of force for the protection of populations. Member states of the United Nations agreed

> we are prepared to take collective action, in a timely and decisive manner, *through the Security Council, in accordance with the Charter, including Chapter VII*, on a case-by-case basis and in cooperation with relevant regional organizations as appropriate, should peaceful means be inadequate and national authorities are manifestly failing to protect their populations from genocide, war crimes, ethnic cleansing and crimes against humanity.[174]

This idea of a responsibility to protect became a set of organizing principles rather than a justification to use force in circumstances that would otherwise be unlawful.[175]

The question of humanitarian intervention arose again in 2010 in the context of the Kampala Diplomatic Conference on the crime of aggression in the Statute of the International Criminal Court. Some government officials were keen to ensure that the new prospects for prosecuting aggression at the Court would not prevent states from acting to prevent a future humanitarian catastrophe threatening many lives. The US Government suggested to the 2010 Kampala Conference an 'understanding'. The draft understanding stated that 'an act cannot be considered to be a manifest violation of the United

---

enforcement action. See also Wood, 'International Law and the Use of Force: What Happens in Practice?', 53 *Indian Journal of International Law* (2013) 345–67 at 364–65.

[174] A/RES/60/1, 24 October 2005, at para 139 (emphasis added); see also paras 5, 6, 69–80 and 138. See also Evans, *The Responsibility to Protect: Ending Mass Atrocity Crimes Once and for All* (2008).

[175] See Bellamy, *The Responsibility to Protect: A Defense* (2015); Boisson de Chazournes, 'Responsibility to Protect: Reflecting Solidarity?' in Wolfrum and Kojima (eds), *Solidarity: A Structural Principle of International Law* (2010) 93–122; Orford, *International Authority and the Responsibility to Protect* (2011).

Nations Charter' if it would be evident that it was undertaken 'in connection with an effort to prevent the commission of any of the core crimes' in the Statute: genocide, crimes against humanity or war crimes.[176]

In Kampala, Professor Kreß, from the German delegation, was entrusted with the consultations on this proposed text. While he reports that some delegations gave this US proposal substantive support, it was met with resistance from other states, the most outspoken being Iran.[177] The tense atmosphere that developed signalled to many that there was too much suspicion at that time for there to be much chance of drafting some sort of humanitarian intervention exception to the crime of aggression. The proposed 'understanding' was not adopted.

Nevertheless, Kreß concludes that, based on the statements made throughout the drafting process, the customary international criminal law on aggression does not cover force 'used with the purpose of enforcing the *specific* international legal obligation *not to commit crimes under international law*'.[178] He highlights that for the new crime of aggression, there is no longer a requirement based on the Nuremberg and Tokyo precedents that there be 'a collective intent to *annex* or *occupy* or to pursue *another objective, which is unacceptable to the international community as a whole*'.[179] And he goes so far as to suggest that collective intent still plays a role where the 'use of force [is] carried out with the purpose of averting the commission of crimes under international law'.[180] In the end he is arguing that 'a use of force to avert a humanitarian catastrophe' is excluded from the definition of the crime of aggression in the Rome Statute.[181]

---

[176] The full text is excerpted in Kreß, 'The State Conduct Element' (n 145) at 524.

[177] For an Iranian perspective, see Momtaz and Hamaneh, 'Iran' in Kreß and Barriga (eds), *The Crime of Aggression: A Commentary*, vol 1 (2017) 1174–97.

[178] Kreß, 'The State Conduct Element' (n 145) at 533 (original emphasis).

[179] Ibid (original emphasis).

[180] Kreß, 'The State Conduct Element' (n 145) at 535; for a similar conclusion and further discussion on the elements of crimes, see also Trahan, 'The Crime of Aggression and the International Criminal Court', in Sadat (ed), *Seeking Accountability for the Unlawful Use of Force* (2018) 303–36; see also in the same direction the ILA Report, 'Use of Force' (n 79) at 24, which suggests that the 'existence of such minority opinions [by scholars] means, at least, that it is difficult to conclude that right of humanitarian intervention is unquestionably unlawful, a point that may well be of relevance with respect to whether a humanitarian intervention amounts to an "act of aggression" which by its character (. . .) constitutes a manifest violation of the Charter of the United Nations"' (original ellipsis). Part of the emphasis here is on the idea that the *character* of a genuinely humanitarian intervention would not meet the character test in the definition of 'crime of aggression'.

[181] Kreß, 'The State Conduct Element' (n 145) at 536.

Moving away from the specificities of the crime of aggression at the International Criminal Court, is there anything left in the idea that force by one state against another could be justified under the title 'humanitarian intervention'? One way to deal with humanitarian intervention is to argue that it may be illegal, but on a moral level it is 'legitimate' or 'justified', or, in a variation of this, that the sanction or punishment should be 'mitigated' where an illegal intervention was truly humanitarian. This may work for some at a political level, but legal scholars such as Andrea Roberts have concluded, after a careful study, that in going down this path we risk undermining the relevance of law, and that 'legitimacy is undefined and open to manipulation by powerful actors'.[182]

Similarly, Sir Michael Wood, writing from the perspective of a former legal advisor to the UK Foreign Office, disparages such an approach:

> 'Legitimacy is to be distinguished from legality (lawfulness), which means in this context conformity with international law.' To blur the two may sometimes seem like good politics. It is not good law. It is reminiscent of the view, expressed by some at the time of the action over Kosovo, that a use of force may be unlawful but justified. That may be so, but that is not a matter for legal assessment. Lawyers should confine themselves to law, or at least make it clear when they are stepping outside their field. And non-lawyers should not lightly assume they understand international law.[183]

Notwithstanding the conclusion of the UN Summit Outcome that forceful protection against atrocity crimes is to be limited to action authorized by by the Security Council, the United Kingdom has nevertheless continued to argue that customary international law allows for such a use of force. The UK legal position was articulated most recently in the context of the 2018 air strikes on Syria in response to the use of chemical weapons:

> The UK is permitted under international law, on an exceptional basis, to take measures in order to alleviate overwhelming humanitarian suffering. The legal basis for the use of force is humanitarian intervention, which requires three conditions to be met:

---

[182] Roberts, 'Legality vs Legitimacy: Can Uses of Force be Illegal but Justified?', in Alston and Macdonald (eds), *Human Rights, Intervention and the Use of Force* (2008) 179–213 at 212.

[183] Wood, 'International Law and the Use of Force: What Happens in Practice?', 53 *Indian Journal of International Law* (2013) 345–67 at 350 (footnotes omitted).

   (i)   there is convincing evidence, generally accepted by the international community as a whole, of extreme humanitarian distress on a large scale, requiring immediate and urgent relief;

  (ii)   it must be objectively clear that there is no practicable alternative to the use of force if lives are to be saved; and

 (iii)   the proposed use of force must be necessary and proportionate to the aim of relief of humanitarian suffering and must be strictly limited in time and in scope to this aim (ie the minimum necessary to achieve that end and for no other purpose).[184]

Although the former Legal Advisor of the US Department of State, Harold Hongju Koh, has argued that the United States should similarly articulate its conditions for using force under the heading of 'humanitarian intervention', and that under similar conditions such a use of force could be legal under international law,[185] only a few states have in recent decades come close to officially endorsing the idea of this sort of humanitarian intervention.[186] In the run-up to the Millennium summit in 2000, a large number of states from the Global South considered that there was no such right of humanitarian intervention under international law.[187] This has been reaffirmed several times in Summits of the Non-Aligned Movement of 120 states, most recently in 2019 at the Baku Summit.[188]

It is often suggested that it is human rights groups that lobby for military intervention. In fact such groups have rarely argued for the use of force to protect rights. As one study concludes, in fact 'they're more likely to be fending off state leaders trying to usurp rights in the name of war'.[189]

---

[184] Syria action – UK Government legal position, 14 April 2018, available at https://www.gov.uk/government/publications/syria-action-uk-government-legal-position/syria-action-uk-government-legal-position.

[185] Koh, 'The War Powers and Humanitarian Intervention', 53 *Houston Law Review* (2016) 971–1033; Koh, 'The Real "Red Line" Behind Trump's April 2018 Syria Strikes' 16 April 2018, available at https://www.justsecurity.org/54952/real-red-linebehind-trumps-april-2018-syria-strikes/.

[186] For a discussion of the position of Belgium stated before the ICJ in 1999, see Chesterman, *Just War* (n 159) at 46–47; see also the Danish position published in 2013 – Denmark referenced by the ILA Report, 'Use of Force' (n 79) at fn 161. See further Wood, 'International Law and the Use of Force' (n 183) esp 360–65; Rodley, 'Humanitarian Intervention', in Weller (ed), *The Oxford Handbook on the Use of Force in International Law* (2015) 775–95; see generally Henriksen, 'The Legality of Using Force to Deter Chemical Warfare', 17 April 2018, available at https://www.justsecurity.org/55005/legality-international-law-force-deter-chemical-warfare/.

[187] 'We reject the so-called "right" of humanitarian intervention, which has no legal basis in the United Nations Charter or in the general principles of international law.' Declaration of the South Summit, G77, Havana, April 2000, adopted by Heads of State and Government of the member countries of the Group of 77 and China, at para 54.

[188] Final Document, NAM 2019/CoB/Doc.1, at para 1012.

[189] Smith, *Human Rights and War Through Civilian Eyes* (2017) at 197; and see generally Ch 6.

5

War Powers in National Law

5.1 National Authorization of Deployment of Force Abroad

As we have seen, the formal institution of the Declaration of War, even where specifically provided for in constitutions, has been invoked on relatively few occasions. At the international level, for those states that have ratified it, the 1907 Hague Convention III requires such a Declaration of War (with reasons) be given in order to warn the other side (no timeline given). It also states that the 'existence of a state war must be notified to the neutral Powers without delay'. Few, if any, Declarations of War have been unambiguously made and unequivocally recognized since the Second World War. Bearing in mind that, in the absence of an armed attack or UN authorization, any Declaration of War involving a direct threat of force would constitute a violation of the UN Charter,[1] we should not be surprised that such Declarations have become rare.

At the national level, a number of states (such as Germany, Japan and Italy) have constitutional provisions rejecting war,[2] while multiple constitutions reserve the right to declare War to specific organs. For example, the US Constitution reserves to Congress the power to 'declare War'. As we shall see, a national legislature today will more likely be interested in national arrangements related to the authorization of deployment of forces abroad rather than resort to War. The most famous of these arrangements is the War Powers Resolution, passed by the US Congress in the wake of Viet Nam. Congress was attempting to gain more control over Presidential decisions, and at the same time seeking greater consultation between the President and the Congress. The Resolution was adopted as law, overriding the veto of President Nixon, who considered it unconstitutional. Reports submitted by the President to Congress about the use of force by US armed personnel abroad have been

---

[1] Stürchler, *The Threat of Force in International Law* (2007) 129.
[2] For discussion, see section 2.1.2 above.

careful to state that they were 'consistent with' the Resolution – rather than 'pursuant' to it.

In the following sections, after having outlined how the US Constitution is said to divide up what are known as the war powers, we will consider how the actual War Powers Resolution applies in practice, and the challenges it poses in the contemporary world. We will then see how similar provisions apply in other countries, and look in some detail at the fragile 'Parliamentary Convention' in the United Kingdom.

5.1.1 The US Congress's Constitutional Role in Declaring War and the President's Power to Make War

The US Constitution states that 'The Congress shall have Power . . . To declare War, grant Letters of Marque and Reprisal, and make Rules concerning Captures on Land and Water'.[3] The Constitution was careful to ensure that the individual States that made up the United States did not play a role in matters of international relations. The concern, as can be seen from the records,[4] was

---

[3] Art I, § 8, para 11. For a near contemporaneous definition of 'reprisals', see Vattel, *The Law of Nations: Or, Principles of the Law of Nature, Applied to the Conduct and Affairs of Nations and Sovereigns (1797)*, eds Kapossy and Whatmore (2008) Book II, Ch 18, para 342. Letters of Marque were issued to private individuals by the sovereign in order that they might engage in reprisals: ibid at para 346. By the end of the 18th century, orders for the taking of general reprisals or issuing Letters of Marque would have been seen as the equivalent of a declaration of war. Neff, *War and the Law of Nations* (2005) at 108. See also section 1.2 above for the early concept of reprisals in Grotius.

[4] James Jay, the President of the Constitutional Convention, wrote in the *Federalist Papers* (1787), no 3:

> As to those just causes of war which proceed from direct and unlawful violence, it appears equally clear to me that one good national government affords vastly more security against dangers of that sort than can be derived from any other quarter. Because such violences are more frequently caused by the passions and interests of a part than of the whole; of one or two States than of the Union. Not a single Indian war has yet been occasioned by aggressions of the present federal government, feeble as it is; but there are several instances of Indian hostilities having been provoked by the improper conduct of individual States, who, either unable or unwilling to restrain or punish offenses, have given occasion to the slaughter of many innocent inhabitants. The neighborhood of Spanish and British territories, bordering on some States and not on others, naturally confines the causes of quarrel more immediately to the borderers. The bordering States, if any, will be those who, under the impulse of sudden irritation, and a quick sense of apparent interest or injury, will be most likely, by direct violence, to excite war with these nations; and nothing can so effectually obviate that danger as a national government, whose wisdom and prudence will not be diminished by the passions which actuate the parties immediately interested.
>
> But not only fewer just causes of war will be given by the national government, but it will also be more in their power to accommodate and settle them amicably. They will

to reduce the chances of the United States' sliding into War with powerful foreign nations. At the same time there would have been a keen awareness of the need to control who in the Federal Government of the United States should be entitled to declare War, bearing in mind how various sovereigns in Europe had in recent years casually declared War with very selfish motives.[5]

So, under the Constitution, the Federal legislative branch (Congress) would control, together with the Executive (the President), such entry into conflict. Nevertheless, it was clear early on that this power to declare War did not inhibit any power of the President to repel an invasion by a foreign nation. Some commentators highlight how the original wording gave the Congress power to 'make war' and that this wording was changed to 'declare war', thus leaving the *waging* of war to the Executive, with the President as the Commander-in-Chief, and leaving the Executive 'the power to repel sudden attacks'.[6] Congress retains ultimate control through budgetary and other clauses, which gave it the right, *inter alia*, to provide and maintain a navy.[7]

In sum, the War Powers Resolution now states:

> The constitutional powers of the President as Commander-in-Chief to introduce United States Armed Forces into hostilities, or into situations where imminent involvement in hostilities is clearly indicated by the cir-cumstances, are exercised only pursuant to (1) a declaration of war, (2) spe-cific statutory authorization, or (3) a national emergency created by attack upon the United States, its territories or possessions, or its armed forces.[8]

---

be more temperate and cool, and in that respect, as well as in others, will be more in capacity to act advisedly than the offending State. The pride of states, as well as of men, naturally disposes them to justify all their actions, and opposes their acknowledging, correcting, or repairing their errors and offenses. The national government, in such cases, will not be affected by this pride, but will proceed with moderation and candor to consider and decide on the means most proper to extricate them from the difficulties which threaten them.

[5] See Chen, 'Restoring Constitutional Balance: Accommodating the Evolution of War', 53 *Boston College Law Review* (2012) 1767–806. She quotes, *inter alios*, John Jay in the *Federalist Papers* (1787–88) no 4 at 1773–74, 'absolute monarchs will often make war when their nations are to get nothing by it, but for purposes and objects merely personal, such as, a thirst for mili-tary glory, revenge for personal affronts; ambition or private compacts to aggrandize or support their particular families, or partizans'.

[6] According to Madison's notes (James Madison and Elbridge Gerry moved the amend-ment), detailed and explained by Chen, 'Restoring Constitutional Balance'(n 5) at 1772, see also Bradley, *International Law in the US Legal System*, 2nd edn (2015) esp at fnn 21 and 46.

[7] See Art 1, § 8, esp cls 10–18.

[8] 50 US Code § 1541 (c) (War Powers Resolution).

According to the US Congressional Research Service,

> there have been 11 separate formal declarations of war against foreign na-
> tions enacted by Congress and the President, encompassing five different
> wars – the War of 1812 with Great Britain, the War with Mexico in 1846, the
> War with Spain in 1898, the First World War, and the Second World War.[9]

The last Declaration of War was against Romania in 1942. In the 20th century, they 'all declare a "state of war" exists between the United States and the
other nation'.[10] And, starting in 1798, there have been authorizations by the
legislature for the President to use force without a formal Declaration of War,
the last being in 2002 for the use of force against Iraq.[11] There is considerable
controversy over the ways in which the congressional authorization for the
use of force in the wake of September 11 has been extended to fighting groups
that had little connection with the original attack.[12]

Of course in the 18th and 19th centuries there might have been very good
reasons to avoid a State of War, as this would have led to the abrogation of
treaties, states with Neutral Status would have to cease trading with the
warring states, and all warring states would thereby enjoy the right to seize
enemy property and exercise Belligerent Rights against merchant ships, their
crew and cargo.[13] The use of force short of War could, on the other hand,
ensure the continuation of commercial and diplomatic relations, and would
not affect the rights of third states and their nationals. Later, as we have seen,

---

[9] Elsea and Weed, *Declarations of War and Authorizations for the Use of Military Force*
(2014) at 1.

[10] Ibid at 3.

[11] The full list can be found in ibid Annex B; it covers France 1798, Tripoli 1802, Algeria 1815,
Piracy 1819–23, Formosa 1955, Middle East 1957, Southeast Asia 1964, Lebanon 1983, Iraq
1991, Terrorist Attacks 2001, Iraq 2002.

[12] The Authorization for the Unilateral Use of Military Force (AUMF) of 18 September (Public
Law 107–40) stated 'That the President is authorized to use all necessary and appropriate force
against those nations, organizations, or persons he determines planned, authorized, committed,
or aided the terrorist attacks that occurred on September 11, 2001, or harbored such organizations or persons, in order to prevent any future acts of international terrorism against the United
States by such nations, organizations or persons.' See further Bradley and Goldsmith, 'Obama's
AUMF Legacy', 110 *AJIL* (2016) 628–45. For the suggestion that Congress should only authorize
such a use of force in the future with a sunset clause (a provision that states that the authorization
would cease to have effect after a specific date), see Ackerman and Hathaway, 'Limited War and
the Constitution: Iraq and the Crisis of Presidential Legality', 109 *Michigan Law Review* (2010)
447–517.

[13] As we shall see in Ch 8, war booty for states involving enemy state property, and the capture
of enemy merchant vessels and aircraft, is still foreseen as a right for states in an international
armed conflict.

when resort to War was supposed to be regulated by the League of Nations (1919), and was eventually outlawed in the Paris Peace Pact (1928), states mostly avoided the terminology of War, even in the face of large-scale conflicts, at least until the outbreak of the Second World War.

A second set of reasons explain the reticence to resort to Declarations of War. Such a Declaration of War would trigger a number of draconian options for the government under its own domestic law: internment of enemy aliens, seizure of enemy property, surveillance powers and a multitude of quite obscure but far-reaching provisions that, in US law, come into effect following a Declaration of War.[14]

The Speaker of the US House of Representatives, Thomas Foley, explained in 1991 that they had refrained from a Declaration of War with regard to Iraq precisely to avoid the triggering of these domestic provisions:

> The reason we did not declare a formal war was not because there is any difference I think in the action that was taken and in a formal declaration of war with respect to military operations, but because there is some question about whether we wish to excite or enact some of the domestic consequences of a formal declaration of war – seizure of property, censorship, and so forth, which the President neither sought nor desired.[15]

Since the Second World War, and starting with the Korean conflict, there have been controversies between those who would see the Executive as having inherent rights to engage in armed conflict, and others who consider that such action requires the assent of Congress. A list of incidences when the United States has used force abroad includes hundreds of entries. Some are more like wars than others. In addition to the 11 actual Declarations of War (mentioned above), the Congressional Research Service gives eight examples of 'extended military engagements that might be considered undeclared wars', and states that 'With the exception of the Korean War, all of these conflicts received congressional authorization in some form short of a formal declaration of war.'[16]

---

[14] For the details, see Elsea and Weed, *Declarations of War* (n 9) at 27–68.

[15] Speaking at the National Press Club, 7 February 1991, cited in Weed, *The War Powers Resolution* (2019) at 23.

[16] Torreon, *Instances of Use of United States Armed Force Abroad, 1789–2017* (Washington, DC: Congressional Research Service, 2017) (summary). The examples given are 'the Undeclared Naval War with France from 1798 to 1800; the First Barbary War from 1801 to 1805; the Second Barbary War of 1815; the Korean War of 1950–1953; the Vietnam War from 1964 to 1973; the Persian Gulf War of 1991; global actions against foreign terrorists after the September 11, 2001, attacks on the United States; and the war with Iraq in 2003'.

The arguments used to explain why the President should have the power to use force in the absence of congressional authorization include that the action is required to fulfil international obligations or ensure respect for the law.[17] The Korean action was referred to as fulfilling US obligations to the United Nations rather than as a War. But Korea was perhaps an exceptional situation.[18] The hundreds of uses of force falling short of undeclared wars are usually justified as protecting national security interests, or as necessary for the protection of nationals and property abroad. Such rescue operations are sometimes known in the military as 'non-combatant evacuation operations'. This implied power for the Executive relating to nationals abroad can go beyond 'non-combatant' roles and has been part of the reasoning for well-known 20th-century operations in Iran (the failed attempt to rescue the Teheran hostages) and the invasions of Grenada and Panama.

When the President does resort to force, in the absence of a Declaration of War, this has been justified by the Executive in terms of the (implied/established) constitutional power to protect national interests. Such reasoning is revealed in the 2011 hearing concerning Libya in the Senate Foreign Relations Committee. Harold Hongju Koh, the Department of State Legal Advisor, explained on behalf of the Administration:

> Nor are we in a 'war' for purposes of Article I of the Constitution. As the Office of Legal Counsel concluded in its April 1, 2011 opinion, under longstanding precedent the President had the constitutional authority to direct the use of force in Libya, for two main reasons. First, he could reasonably determine that US operations in Libya would serve important national interests in preserving regional stability and supporting the credibility and effectiveness of the UN Security Council. Second, the military operations that the President anticipated ordering were not sufficiently extensive in 'nature, scope, and duration' to constitute a 'war' requiring prior specific Congressional approval under the Declaration of War Clause.[19]

---

[17] See Art II, § 3, under which the President 'shall take Care that the Laws be faithfully executed'.

[18] Other UN-authorized uses of force have also been taken as sufficient authorization for the use of force; see Ackerman and Hathaway, 'Limited War and the Constitution: Iraq and the Crisis of Presidential Legality', 109 *Michigan Law Review* (2011) 447–517 at 458 fn 35, who reference Liberia 2003 and Haiti 2004.

[19] Testimony on Libya and War Powers before the Senate Foreign Relations Committee, 28 June 2011, at 13, available at https://2009-2017.state.gov/documents/organization/167452.pdf.

Clearly, a 'nature, scope and duration' test can set a very high threshold before one encounters a constitutional argument that the President has overstepped his powers[20] and encroached on Congress's power to Declare War (what has been referred to as 'war in the constitutional sense'[21]). Even though, as we saw in the *Steel Seizure Case*,[22] the Supreme Court has been prepared to curb the assertion of war powers claimed by the President, the Court did not enter into the tricky area of whether the deployment of the forces aboard was constitutional, simply determining that the fact of being a party to the conflict in Korea could not give rise to the internal powers the President was claiming.[23]

American Presidents have jealously guarded their perceived constitutional power to use armed force abroad. The American courts have refrained from entering into the constitutional legality of Presidential action where there is neither Congressional supportive action, nor an expressed will of Congress to the contrary.[24] In this way Presidents have been able to rely on implied Congressional support for such a use of force abroad. Congress has rarely had a majority that could, or wanted unambiguously to, restrain the Executive in this context. There is nevertheless a normative framework that is designed to do just this: the War Powers Resolution.

---

[20] The earlier 1 April 2011 memorandum opinion for the Attorney-General signed by Caroline Krass, 'Authority to Use Military Force in Libya', had concluded that 'President Obama could rely on his constitutional power to safeguard the national interest by directing the anticipated military operations in Libya – which were limited in their nature, scope, and duration – without prior congressional authorization.' See 35 *Opinions of the Office of Legal Counsel* (2011) 1–14 at 14. This test had been applied with regard to the Haiti intervention in 1994, where it was found that war could be distinguished from anticipated operations of limited nature, scope and duration.

[21] See Lederman, 'Why the strikes against Syria probably violate the UN Charter and (therefore) the US Constitution', 6 April, 2017, available at https://www.justsecurity.org/39674/syrian-strikes-violate-u-n-charter-constitution/; and see also his '(Apparent) Administration Justifications for Legality of Strikes Against Syria', which includes a press guidance issued by the Administration, at https://takecareblog.com/blog/apparent-administration-justifications-for-legality-of-strikes-against-syria.

[22] Section 2.1.3 above.

[23] *Youngstown Sheet & Tube Co v Sawyer (Steel Seizure Case)*, 343 US (1952) 579 at 641–43.

[24] Some commentators have described this Congressional silence as leading to a 'Twilight Zone' after Jackson's phrase in the *Steel Seizure Case* (ibid at 637), where he stated that '[w]hen the President acts in absence of either a congressional grant or denial of authority, he can only rely upon his own independent powers, but there is a zone of twilight'; see, eg, Corn, Gurulé, Jensen and Margulies, *National Security Law* (2015) at 23 and 60ff. For hints by the courts on when there could be justiciability over these issues, see Hathaway, 'National Security Lawyering in the Post-War Era: Can Law Constrain Power?', 4 *UCLA Law Review* (2020) 4–115 esp at 105 fn 339.

5.1.2 The US War Powers Resolution 1973

In 1973, following disengagement from Viet Nam, Congress passed the War Powers Resolution (or War Powers Act), which is binding law, even if the courts have proved reluctant to rule on its application (invoking various reasons, such as the political question doctrine and lack of standing of those seeking to challenge the President's action). The Act is aimed at reasserting the role of Congress through *consultation* and *reporting*, before and after the introduction of armed forces into hostilities. With regard to consultation, the Act demands that:

> The President in every possible instance shall consult with Congress before introducing United States Armed Forces into hostilities or into situations where imminent involvement in hostilities is clearly indicated by the circumstances, and after every such introduction shall consult regularly with the Congress until United States Armed Forces are no longer engaged in hostilities or have been removed from such situations.[25]

And with regard to reporting, if there is no Declaration of War,

> in any case in which United States Armed Forces are introduced—
> (1) into hostilities or into situations where imminent involvement in hostilities is clearly indicated by the circumstances;
> (2) into the territory, airspace or waters of a foreign nation, while equipped for combat, except for deployments which relate solely to supply, replacement, repair, or training of such forces; or
> (3) in numbers which substantially enlarge United States Armed Forces equipped for combat already located in a foreign nation; the President shall submit within 48 hours to the Speaker of the House of Representatives and to the President pro tempore of the Senate a report, in writing, setting forth—
>> (A) the circumstances necessitating the introduction of United States Armed Forces;
>> (B) the constitutional and legislative authority under which such introduction took place; and
>> (C) the estimated scope and duration of the hostilities or involvement.[26]

---

[25] 50 US Code § 1542.
[26] 50 US Code § 1543(a)

There then follows the clause on the famous 60-day period (which can be extended a further 30 days), within which, in the absence of a Declaration of War or Congressional authorization of the use of force, 'the President shall terminate the use of force'.[27]

However, a few complications in this arrangement have left the President free from any meaningful restraint from the Congress under the Act. First, according to section 5(b), the 60-day period is only triggered where reports are filed under section 1543(a)(1), ie with regard to 'situations where imminent involvement in hostilities is clearly indicated by the circumstances' (paragraph (1) above). Out of 168 reports filed by the President, only one cited that paragraph, and in that case the operation was over by the time of the filing.[28] The Executive has therefore been careful to reserve for itself the idea that the use of force without congressional approval is not necessarily limited by Congress, and even were it to be so, the Executive will determine what constitutes 'involvement in hostilities' for these purposes.[29]

Second, the Act does not, on its face, bring greater control over covert operations or the use of personnel not properly described as 'Armed Forces', even after they are no longer secret.[30] Third, 60 days, renewable for a further 30 days, is a long time for the Executive to be conducting a war without any congressional approval or limitation on the geographical scope or identification of the enemy.[31] Members of the Congress have tended to show themselves to be unwilling or unable to question the Executive, and have used this period to let the use of armed force run its course.[32] Fourth, the judiciary have been unwilling to find that members of Congress have *standing* to demand adherence with the terms of the Act. Alternatively, the judiciary have protected the Executive from scrutiny through the 'political question doctrine'.

---

[27] 50 US Code § 1544(b)

[28] Weed, *The War Powers Resolution* (n 15) (summary) the one incident is the 1975 *Mayaguez* seizure, discussed at 10, 'in May 1975 President Ford ordered the retaking of a US merchant vessel, the SS *Mayaguez* which had been seized by Cambodian naval patrol vessels'.

[29] Although § 1544(b) allows for the idea, in that the President must terminate the use of the Armed Forces 60 days from the date that the § 1543(a)(1) report 'is required to be submitted', Congress has not determined that such reports were actually *required*, and it seems unlikely that it could do so without a separate Resolution that would require the approval of the President; see Ely, *War and Responsibility: Constitutional Lessons of Vietnam and its Aftermath* (1993) at 124–25.

[30] Ibid at 105–14; and see Chen, 'Restoring Constitutional Balance' (n 5).

[31] See Ely (n 29) at 127–28, who names the inclusion of this lengthy period a 'congressional responsibility-avoidance device', and suggests that the period be shortened to 20 days.

[32] Ibid at 48–49.

Ultimately, then, the Act ought to function to prevent the President from engaging in hostilities for longer than two to three months, where there has been no Congressional authorization. But in practice it does not. Of course, the long campaigns in Iraq and Afghanistan were indeed covered by the Congressional authorizations of 1991, 2001 and 2002. They were not therefore vulnerable to challenge under the War Powers Act, as they would be considered 'specific statutory authorization'. The controversies have in recent times concerned Kosovo, Libya and Syria, and most recently the assistance to Saudi Arabia over the conflict in Yemen. Let us consider each of these in turn.

In the Kosovo case, although members of the Congress tried to challenge President Clinton in the courts after the 60-day period had elapsed, the military campaign eventually finished before the end of the 90-day period. The Court of Appeals found that Congress could have acted but chose not to do so: 'It voted down a declaration of war 427 to 2 and an "authorization" of the air strikes 213 to 213, but it also voted against requiring the President to immediately end US participation in the NATO operation and voted to fund that involvement.' The Court concluded, '[i]n this case, Congress certainly could have passed a law forbidding the use of US forces in the Yugoslav campaign'.[33] On the substance, it seems to have been suggested and accepted that there was an implied authorization through Congressional approval of the spending.[34]

With regard to Libya we find a very elaborate argument over the meaning of 'hostilities'. Again Koh provides an insider's guide to what was happening. As the sixtieth day approached,

> quiet inquiry revealed that too many members of Congress who had felt politically burned by their votes on the 2003 Iraq War were reluctant to have to vote on war again. Accordingly, the leadership in Congress made clear that they would not pass legislation, expressing in every conceivable way that they wanted no votes.[35]

Faced with the prospect of having to stop the operation, Koh considered that the best alternative course was to argue that the US was not involved in 'hostilities'. He later explained the thought process:

---

[33] *Campbell et al v Clinton*, 203 F 3d 19 (2000) at paras 6 and 21.

[34] Explained in Koh, 'The War Powers and Humanitarian Intervention', 53 *Houston Law Review* (2016) 971–1033 at 979.

[35] Ibid at 983.

As a legal matter, there seemed to be consensus that the force actually being used was so limited in nature, scope, and duration that it did not constitute a 'war' in a constitutional sense. Weren't we also obligated to investigate whether the force actually being used was so limited in nature, scope, and duration that it did not even constitute 'hostilities' in a statutory sense? If such facts existed, couldn't we lawfully accept the constitutionality of the War Powers Resolution but determine that we were not, in fact, in 'hostilities' that would trigger the sixty-day durational limit?[36]

This was a bold manoeuvre: there was clearly an armed conflict ongoing, with no one doubting that the laws of war applied. But just as we concluded that the word 'war' can legitimately take on different meanings depending on the intended outcome, we meet the idea that a simple word like 'hostilities' can be said to play one role in one context and another role in a separate context. Koh was also thinking that he could make the case that 'even if the US military action may have exceeded the "hostilities" level at its outset, it had fallen below that level by the sixtieth day and was virtually guaranteed to stay at that lower level because of the limited nature of the mission'.[37]

Before the Senate Foreign Relations Committee, Koh, who as an academic had expertise on the nature of the Congressional limits on the executive use of force abroad, set out his case in some detail:

Having studied this legislation for many years, I can confidently say that we are far from the core case that most Members of Congress had in mind in 1973. The Congress that passed the Resolution in that year had just been through a long, major, and searing war in Vietnam, with hundreds of thousands of boots on the ground, secret bombing campaigns, international condemnation, massive casualties, and no clear way out. In Libya, by contrast, we have been acting transparently and in close consultation with Congress for a brief period; with no casualties or ground troops; with international approval; and at the express request of and in cooperation with NATO, the Arab League, the Gulf Cooperation Council, and Libya's own Transitional National Council. We should not read into the 1973 Congress's adoption of what many have called a 'No More Vietnams' resolution an intent to require the premature termination, nearly forty years later, of limited military force in support of an international coalition to prevent the

---

[36] Ibid at 986.
[37] Ibid at 996–97.

resumption of atrocities in Libya. Given the limited risk of escalation, exchanges of fire, and US casualties, we do not believe that the 1973 Congress intended that its Resolution be given such a rigid construction – absent a clear Congressional stance – to stop the President from directing supporting actions in a NATO-led, Security Council-authorized operation, for the narrow purpose of preventing the slaughter of innocent civilians.[38]

Although one could query this interpretation of the word 'hostilities' in this context, and it was not shared by all the US Government legal counsel,[39] Congress did not to challenge this reading of hostilities, and the War Powers issue became moot after the fall of the Gaddafi Government.[40] Koh, writing five years later as an academic, went so far as to predict that future, carefully limited humanitarian operations 'would not violate the War Powers Resolution if continued for more than sixty days'.[41]

The more recent air strikes in 2017 and 2018 on Syria under the Trump Administration were notified to Congress referencing the War Powers Act, and setting out the constitutional authority 'to conduct foreign relations and as Commander in Chief'. In the end, both operations were confined to hours rather than days.[42] There were complaints from some members of Congress about the lack of consultation, but these most recent strikes force us to reconsider the adequacy of the War Powers Act in the contemporary world.

If the future of warfare is less about passing the 60-day mark and more about a single hour's worth of conflict (albeit with over 100 missiles fired), the model seems badly in need of retuning. If the future of warfare is more about unmanned aerial vehicles (drones) targeting individuals and less about the sending of hundreds of thousands of troops into hostilities, the use of

---

[38] Testimony on Libya and War Powers, 28 June 2011, at 12.

[39] See Hathaway, 'How to Revive Congress' Law Powers', *Texas National Security Review* (November 2019) 41–58 at 45; she suggests (ibid at 47) that Congress should define hostilities in this context as armed conflict, in the sense of the international law definitions for the application of humanitarian law (as explained in Ch 6 below).

[40] Harvard Law Review (HLR), 'Recent Administrative Interpretation' 125 *HLR* (2012) 1546–53 at 1553.

[41] 'The War Powers and Humanitarian Intervention' (n 34) at 997.

[42] Letter from President Trump of 8 April 2017: 'I acted in the vital national security and foreign policy interests of the United States, pursuant to my constitutional authority to conduct foreign relations and as Commander in Chief and Chief Executive.' Letter of 15 April 2018: 'I acted pursuant to my constitutional authority to conduct foreign relations and as Commander in Chief and Chief Executive and in the vital national security and foreign policy interests of the United States to promote the stability of the region, to deter the use and proliferation of chemical weapons, and to avert a worsening of the region's current humanitarian catastrophe.'

oversight by the legislature conditioned on the prospect of hostilities seems to have lost its relevance.[43]

In fact, as has been pertinently pointed out, future wars are more likely to rely on cyberwarfare, which might slip through the cracks in the traditional understanding of the role of the War Powers Resolution.[44] The Resolution is dependent on the concepts of sending armed forces and campaigns running to over three months. Looked at like this, the checks and balances, such as they are, start to look very inadequate for anyone seeking greater consultation, transparency and the possibility to restrain the lethal use of force abroad.

In 2019 a Joint Resolution of the Senate and House of Representatives demanded for the first time under the War Powers Resolution an end to US military operations abroad. It found:

> Congress has not declared war with respect to, or provided a specific statutory authorization for, the conflict between military forces led by Saudi Arabia, including forces from the United Arab Emirates, Bahrain, Kuwait, Egypt, Jordan, Morocco, Senegal, and Sudan (the Saudi-led coalition), against the Houthis, also known as Ansar Allah, in the Republic of Yemen.

And

> Since March 2015, members of the United States Armed Forces have been introduced into hostilities between the Saudi-led coalition and the Houthis, including providing to the Saudi-led coalition aerial targeting assistance, intelligence sharing, and mid-flight aerial refueling.[45]

Congress directed

> the President to remove United States Armed Forces from hostilities in or affecting the Republic of Yemen, except United States Armed Forces engaged in operations directed at al Qaeda or associated forces, by not later

---

[43] Weed, *War Powers Resolution* (n 15) at 43 suggests that, in the light of the Libya reasoning, 'if it is accepted that the President's use of [unmanned aerial vehicles] UAVs for military attacks against terrorist targets abroad constitutes an action that is limited in scope and duration, and does not require introduction of US military forces directly and physically into "hostilities," then the War Powers Resolution, under this interpretation, does not apply to this presidential action, nor require congressional statutory authorization'.

[44] See Chen, 'Restoring Constitutional Balance' (n 5).

[45] SJ Res 7 – 116th Congress (2019–2020).

than the date that is 30 days after the date of the enactment of this joint resolution (unless the President requests and Congress authorizes a later date),
and unless and until a declaration of war or specific authorization for such
use of United States Armed Forces has been enacted.

President Trump vetoed the legislation as soon as he received it, and it seems
there were not enough votes in Congress for the necessary majority to override his veto.

The President explained that the Resolution was unnecessary and dangerous. Unnecessary because it was claimed the United States was not engaged in hostilities in Yemen. Dangerous because

Congress should not seek to prohibit certain tactical operations, such as
in-flight refueling, or require military engagements to adhere to arbitrary
timelines. Doing so would interfere with the President's constitutional authority as Commander in Chief of the Armed Forces, and could endanger
our service members by impairing their ability to efficiently and effectively
conduct military engagements and to withdraw in an orderly manner at the
appropriate time.[46]

In 2020, in the wake of the US killing in Iraq of Major General Qassim
Suleimani from the Iranian Islamic Revolutionary Guard, another Joint
Resolution found that 'Congress has not yet declared war upon, nor enacted
a specific statutory authorization for use of military force against, the Islamic
Republic of Iran.' And Congress directed 'the President to terminate the use
of United States Armed Forces for hostilities against the Islamic Republic of
Iran or any part of its government or military, unless explicitly authorized by
a declaration of war or specific authorization for use of military force against
Iran.'[47] This again met with the veto of President Trump, who labelled the
Resolution unnecessary and dangerous. Unnecessary because military force
was authorized in Iraq by Congress since 2002. Dangerous

because it could hinder the President's ability to protect United States
forces, allies, and partners, including Israel, from the continued threat
posed by Iran and Iranian-backed militias. The resolution states that it
should not 'be construed to prevent the United States from defending itself

---

[46] Presidential Veto Message to the Senate to Accompany SJ Res 7, 16 April 2019.
[47] SJ Res 68 – 116th Congress (2019–2020).

from imminent attack.' But this overlooks the President's need to respond to threats beyond imminent attacks on the United States and its forces.[48]

One is left with the impression that, however one interprets or reforms the War Powers Act,[49] it seems incapable of empowering Congress (short of the special two-thirds majority) to rein in the President's powers over modern instances of the use of force abroad. One experienced commentator in this area, Jack Goldsmith, who served as a lawyer in the US Attorney-General's Office as well as in the Department of Defense, comes to this sobering conclusion:

> In short, our country has – through presidential aggrandizement accompanied by congressional authorization, delegation, and acquiescence – given one person, the president, a sprawling military and enormous discretion to use it in ways that can easily lead to a massive war. That is our system: One person decides.[50]

5.1.3 Other Examples of Political War Powers in National Legislation

As with the discussion concerning the arrangements in the United States, we find that the historical concept of War played an important influence in the design of constitutional arrangements that gave other parliaments a pre-emptive veto over going to War. Nevertheless, resort to armed conflict, rather than War in the formal sense, remains, in many cases, the prerogative of the executive branch.

One leading study explains:

> [I]n several countries parliament has the right to declare (a state of) war but is not empowered to decide on any other use of the armed forces. The list of states concerned includes countries as varied as Australia, Colombia, Mongolia, Peru, Poland, Portugal, Slovenia, Spain and Thailand.[51]

---

[48] Presidential Veto Message to the Senate for SJ Res 68, 6 May 2020.

[49] Pomper, 'The Soleimani Strike and the Case for War Powers Reform', 11 March 2020, at justsecurity.org; see also Hathaway, 'How to Revive Congress' War Powers' (n 39).

[50] 'The Soleimani Strike: One Person Decides', 3 January 2020, at lawfareblog.com.

[51] Wagner, Peters and Glahn, *Parliamentary War Powers Around the World, 1989–2004: A New Dataset* (2010) at 26.

A similar study, that sought to categorize the intensity of parliamentary control over the executive in 25 European states, found 11 countries with very strong parliamentary war powers: Austria, Estonia, Finland, Germany, Hungary, Italy, Latvia, Lithuania, Luxembourg, Malta and Slovenia. The following were listed as having very weak parliamentary war powers: Cyprus, France, Greece and the United Kingdom.[52]

One might expect that, with increasing enthusiasm for democratic accountability, there would perhaps be an increasing level of democratic control over the use of force (even if the rules on resort to War as such might remain fossilized). But in fact the opposite seems to be the case, Japan being a notable exception.[53] This relaxation of national control over the use of force abroad is in part due to states' adjusting their laws so as to be better able to respond to any demands related to arrangements under international treaties (such as those related to membership of the EU and NATO). There may also be waivers of parliamentary scrutiny where operations have been approved by the United Nations.[54] Nevertheless, even where there are applicable rules, national courts are reluctant to entertain challenges to their own Executive over respect for these rules. In the end, even where meaningful rules exist, there have been few instances of serious divergences between the Legislature and the Executive over resorting to armed conflict in possible violation of any national war powers legislation.

In Israel, the Basic Law provides that 'The state may only begin a war pursuant to a Government decision.' This is followed by 'Nothing in the provisions of this section will prevent the adoption of military actions necessary for the defence of the state and public security.'[55] The Israeli Supreme Court

---

[52] See, eg, Dieterich, Hummel and Marschall, *Parliamentary War Powers: A Survey of 25 European Parliaments* (2010)

[53] The recent Japanese Legislation for Peace and Security, which entered into force in 2016, sets conditions for self-defence, including that the use of force has to be approved by the Diet (parliament); with regard to cooperation and support operations with other states engaged in operations for international peace and security, 're-approval is required in the case of a lapse of more than two years since the commencement of the response measures'. Ministry of Defense (Japan), *Defense of Japan 2017*, Ch 3 at 250. There are also new provisions on rescuing Japanese nationals and those with them, and on ship inspection operations. The conditions for self-defence are actually stricter that is required under international law, in that the legislation demands that in a case of collective self-defence there would have to be 'an armed attack against a foreign country that is in a close relationship with Japan which as a result threatens Japan's survival and poses a clear danger to fundamentally overturn the people's right to life, liberty and pursuit of happiness (a survival-threatening armed attack)' (ibid at 252); see further Nasu, 'Japan's 2015 Security Legislation: Challenges to its Implementation under International Law', 92 *ILS* (2016) 249–80.

[54] See Wagner et al, *Parliamentary War Powers* (n 51).

[55] Basic Law: The Government, s 40(a) and (b).

was petitioned in 2006 on the grounds that the Israeli operation in Lebanon had been started in violation of this provision relating to war. The Court held that 'In the circumstances that have arisen, the government is entitled to determine that the military operations that it decided to carry out do not constitute "starting a war" but merely military operations that constitute self-defence in response to aggression.'[56] Interestingly, the Court explains that

> in Israeli law there is also no binding connection between the existence of a state of war, with all of its legal ramifications, and an official declaration of the government to start a war. The expression 'war' appears in various pieces of legislation and the interpretation given to it depends on the purpose of the legislation and the legislative environment in which the expression appears, rather than on the formal proceeding of a declaration of starting a war ...[57]

So under this national law there can be a 'state of war' even in the absence of a Declaration of War. This could affect offences such as aiding the enemy in a war, or smuggling in war, which it seems would exist even in the absence of a Declaration of War. As the Court explains:

> Large-scale military operations, firing by hostile forces (including a terrorist organization) on a civilian population, the civil population's feeling of emergency and threat and the casualties suffered as a result of military operations on both sides of the border all lead to a security situation in which the State of Israel is regarded by the public as in a state of war.[58]

What, then, would constitute 'war' for the purposes of section 40(a), which prohibits the state from *beginning a war* without a government decision? The Court offered these suggestions:

> [T]he Basic Law did not define what constitutes 'starting a war' within the meaning of the section. This is a complex question that is multi-faceted. The definition of the concept of 'war,' when we are speaking of the government's powers with regard to military operations, cannot be separated from the

---

[56] *Beilin v Prime Minister*, 1 August 2006, HCJ 6204/06, *Israel Law Reports* [2006] (2) 99 at 108. The Court also held that in any event, the Government had carried out the procedure for consultation with the various bodies in the Knesset required by s 40(a) and (c).

[57] Ibid at 107.

[58] Ibid at 108.

foreign affairs of the state and the functioning of the government in the sphere of international relations. Therefore, the interpretation of the concept of 'war' in this context, which has ramifications in the international sphere, is based mainly on the rules of international law.[59]

The international law of armed conflict applies to all armed conflicts, whether or not there exists a Declaration of War – or State of War in this international law sense. And the UN Charter rules that prohibit the use of force make no distinction between the use of force or War. But the idea of War is still relevant in multiple contexts, as we have seen, and the Israeli Court's insight is pertinent: 'A decision of the government that can be interpreted as a declaration of war is likely to have extreme consequences in the sphere of international relations'.[60]

In 2018, the Israeli Government moved to amend the relevant provision of the Basic Law so that section 40(a) would also cover 'operations that would lead to war in a level of probability of near certainty'. In addition, the Government would be entitled in some circumstances of 'secrecy, national security or foreign relations' to delegate its powers related to beginning a war to the Cabinet, and in urgent situations the Prime Minister and Minister for Defence could delegate to a small number (unspecified) of Ministers. It is unclear why such a reform should have come at this time, but the direction is essentially decreasing political control over the Executive's resort to war. Commenting on the proposed legislative changes, Amichal Cohen points out that in any event, 'most current armed conflicts are not "wars" – at least do not start as such'.[61]

In sum, the Israeli Court has separated out the idea of beginning a War (meaning that they consider there are ramifications in international relations) from being in a state of war, which responds to the civilian population's fears and has ramifications in national Israeli law. Other states, such as Georgia, have similarly referred to being in a state of war in order to take certain measures within their national legal order.[62]

---

[59] Ibid at 107.

[60] Ibid.

[61] At www.lawfareblog.com/will-amendment-israels-national-security-law-change-rules-game

[62] Ordinance of the President of Georgia, 'On Declaration of the State of War on the Whole Territory of Georgia and Full Mobilization', 9 August 2008. Such a Declaration may have concrete effects in terms of national law but should be distinguished from the definition of a State of War, which takes place at the international level between states and is set out in section 1.3 above.

5.1.4 The War Prerogative in the United Kingdom and the Emergence of the Parliamentary Convention

In England, monarchs through the ages had jealously guarded the prerogative to conduct foreign relations, enter into Wars, and receive the necessary funds to govern and go to War. But in her detailed study *The War Prerogative*, Rosara Joseph shows that 'in the 1620s, the Commons challenged or ignored accepted practice and used its power of the purse to communicate its mistrust of the government's objectives and to influence the king's foreign policy decisions'.[63] In fact Joseph describes an 'extraordinary historical period' from 1642 to 1649, when powers over War and the conduct of foreign relations were exercised by Parliament or committees appointed by Parliament. She highlights that from then on, 'It was difficult for future monarchs to contend that any topic existed where Parliament had no authority to act, or had to wait for royal initiative before doing so.'[64] Nevertheless, the enduring idea of a Royal prerogative power over War, foreign policy and the conduct of all forms of war endures, although, of course, these powers came to be exercised by modern government 'in the name of the Crown'.

Joseph has also illustrated how the rationale for the War prerogative has involved a complex stream of ideas that have ebbed and flowed over the centuries.[65] War-making power was perceived to lie with the monarch by divine right in the 17th century, but the Glorious Revolution of 1688, and the assumption of power by Cabinet, ended the idea of an inherent power in the monarch. Even as it became clearer in the 19th century that it was a fiction to suggest that these powers were exercised by the Crown 'on the advice of her Ministers', Parliament had little or no role. This was constantly reinforced by the following ideas: that complex matters of foreign policy should be left to experts with experience in foreign affairs; that decisions may have to be taken quickly when it comes to War and the deployment of armed forces; and that a large deliberative body such as Parliament is unsuited to the task of deliberating such issues. Joseph quotes Chitty's *Treatise on the Law of the Prerogatives of the Crown* (1820): 'Wavering with doubts, and distracted by the jealousies and animosities of party, such assemblies would be discussing the propriety of the step after the opportunity and occasion for its adoption had transpired.'[66]

---

[63] Joseph, *The War Prerogative* (2013) at 80.
[64] Ibid at 50.
[65] Ibid at 15–51.
[66] Ibid at 39.

Parliament was informed of the reasons for War, and support was sought, but such sharing of information typically took place after the Government had already committed to War. Even in the post-Second World War era, parliamentary involvement came after a decision had been taken to participate, and sometimes following an announcement that hostilities had already started.[67]

It was the 2003 decision to recall Parliament, and to allow a vote on attacking Iraq, that changed the parameters of what is now expected or considered. Parliament approved the substantive motion by 412 votes to 149.[68] In the following years, various Parliamentary Committees examined the prerogative power. The House of Lords Constitutional Committee produced a report in 2006 entitled *Waging War: Parliament's Role and Responsibility*, in which it was stated:

> Our conclusion is that the exercise of the Royal prerogative by the Government to deploy armed force overseas is outdated and should not be allowed to continue as the basis for legitimate war-making in our 21st century democracy. Parliament's ability to challenge the executive must be protected and strengthened. There is a need to set out more precisely the extent of the Government's deployment powers, and the role Parliament can – and should – play in their exercise.[69]

By March 2011, the Government was stating that there was now a 'convention' that Parliament would be given the chance to debate a decision to commit troops to armed conflict before the troops were actually committed (unless there was an emergency situation).[70] The debate on participation in the Libya operation took place later that month, albeit after British participation had been announced and authorized by the UN Security Council. The motion approving the use of UK armed forces was approved in the House of Commons by 557 votes to 13.

---

[67] For detail on parliamentary consultation for Korea (1950), Suez (1956), the Falklands (1982), Iraq (1991), Kosovo (1999) and Afghanistan (2001), see Mills, *Parliamentary Approval for Military Action* (Briefing Paper 7166: House of Commons Library, 17 April 2018) 10–15.

[68] The motion is long, but for present purposes the relevant phrase states that the House of Commons 'supports the decision of Her Majesty's Government that the United Kingdom should use all means necessary to ensure the disarmament of Iraq's weapons of mass destruction'. Available, together with Prime Minister Blair's speech, at https://www.theyworkforyou.com/debates/?id=2003-03-18.760.0#g760.3.

[69] *Waging War: Parliament's Role and Responsibility*, vol I: *Report* (HL Paper 236-I, 27 July 2006) at para 104.

[70] For the details see Mills, *Parliamentary Approval for Military Action* (n 67) at 24–38.

In 2013 events took a dramatic turn. The Government asked the House of Commons to approve military action focused on saving lives and deterring further use of Syria's chemical weapons. The motion was defeated by 285 votes to 272. This vote, which disappointed the Government and was not necessarily expected, is sometimes said to have influenced decisions in the United States as to whether to use force in Syria at that time.[71] While there may have been multiple reasons why a majority of Members of Parliament voted against the motion, the sense that the proposed attack on Syria could be seen as illegal under international law was repeatedly mentioned in the parliamentary debates and the Government's private discussion with opposition leaders.[72]

In Parliament there were calls to see the detailed legal advice, given that 'so many legal experts are saying that without explicit UN Security Council reinforcement, military action simply would not be legal under international law';[73] and the Opposition had sought an amendment that the United Kingdom would only use force once there was 'a clear legal basis in international law for taking collective military action to protect the Syrian people on humanitarian grounds'.[74]

After the Government lost the vote, the press repeatedly highlighted that this was the first time since 1782 that a British Government had been defeated in the House of Commons over a question of the use of force. The issue at that time had been whether Great Britain should continue to fight in North America. The action in the House of Commons not only successfully demanded an end to 'offensive war',[75] but also considered as 'enemies' those who were against such an end to war, stating in a motion that

---

[71] For some detail of the discussions between the White House and Prime Minister Cameron before and after the vote, see Seldon and Snowdon, *Cameron at 10: The Inside Story 2010–2015* (2015) 332–43.

[72] Ibid at 332ff. For the Parliamentary Debate, see *Hansard* HC Deb vol 556 at https://publications.parliament.uk/pa/cm201314/cmhansrd/cm130829/debtext/130829-0001.htm.

[73] *Hansard* (n 72), Caroline Lucas, 29 August, col 1427.

[74] *Hansard* (n 72), Edward Miliband, 29 August, 1440.

[75] Resolution moved by General Conway, 27 February 1782: 'That it is the opinion of this House, that the further prosecution of offensive war on the continent of North America, for the purpose of reducing the revolted colonies to obedience by force, will be the means of weakening the efforts of this country against her European enemies, tends, under the present circumstances, dangerously to increase the mutual enmity, so fatal to the interests of both Great Britain and America, and by preventing an happy reconciliation with that country, to frustrate the earnest desire graciously expressed by his majesty to restore the blessings of public tranquillity.' *Parliamentary Register* (1782) vol vi at 316–17.

this House will consider as enemies to his Majesty and this country, all those who shall endeavour to frustrate his Majesty's paternal care for the happiness of his people, by advising, or by any means attempting, the further prosecution of offensive war on the continent of North America, for the purpose of reducing the revolted colonies to obedience by force.[76]

In 2014 the House of Commons voted again. This time the issue was the use of force against the so called 'Islamic state' in Iraq. Now there was no obvious question of this being an illegal use of force. As a matter of international law the Iraqi Government was asking for such military action on its own soil, so it was assumed there was no question of a violation of the UN Charter (see section 4.3.1). This time there was parliamentary support, and a motion passed by 524 votes to 43, approving UK airstrikes to support Iraqi and Kurdish security forces' efforts against the Islamic state in Iraq. And in 2015, the House of Commons voted 397 to 223 in favour of airstrikes against ISIS targets in Syria. All this, however, took place in the absence of any legislative framework covering such use of force abroad.

Despite a number of quite concrete proposals to entrench the 'Convention' more firmly, it had become apparent to some in Government that they preferred not to circumscribe the Government's power in any formal way. First, any rule would have to include exceptions for emergencies, self-defence and possibly obligations under membership of international organizations. Second, there remains a fear that any legislation would leave the Government open to challenge in the courts, and that decisions on resort to armed conflict are felt to be unsuited to review by judges. Of course, none of these problems is insurmountable, but the divisions in the House of Commons must have forced the realization that one could no longer take it for granted that elected representatives would rally round the Government in time of war or hostilities abroad.

In 2016 the Government announced that there would be no further entrenchment of the 'Convention', while at the same time seeming to spell out a little more its understanding of what that Convention is. The Secretary of State for Defence delivered the following written statement, which perhaps deserves partial reproduction here as this text now reveals the normative framework covering UK parliamentary control over the use of force abroad:

---

[76] Motion of General Conway, 4 March 1782, ibid at 347.

The Cabinet Manual states, 'In 2011, the Government acknowledged that a Convention had developed in Parliament that before troops were committed the House of Commons should have an opportunity to debate the matter and said that it proposed to observe that convention except where there was an emergency and such action would not be appropriate.'

The Prime Minister repeated this commitment in relation to Libya in Parliament on 16 March 2016. The convention relates to conflict decisions rather than routine deployments of the UK armed forces around the world. The exception to the Convention is important to ensure that this and future Governments can use their judgement about how best to protect the security and interests of the UK. In observing the Convention, we must ensure that the ability of our Armed Forces to act quickly and decisively, and to maintain the security of their operations, is not compromised. ...

We cannot predict the situations that the UK and its armed forces may face in future. If we were to attempt to clarify more precisely circumstances in which we would consult Parliament before taking military action, we would constrain the operational flexibility of the armed forces and prejudice the capability, effectiveness or security of those forces, or be accused of acting in bad faith if unexpected developments were to require us to act differently. This Government have demonstrated their commitment to the convention by the debates they have held in 2013, 2014 and 2015, and their respect for the will of Parliament on each occasion.

The convention does not apply to British military personnel embedded in the armed forces of other nations as they operate as if they were the host nation's personnel, under that nation's chain of command, while remaining subject to UK domestic, international and host nation law. ...

After careful consideration, the Government have decided that it will not be codifying the convention in law or by resolution of the House in order to retain the ability of this and future Governments and the armed forces to protect the security and interests of the UK in circumstances that we cannot predict, and to avoid such decisions becoming subject to legal action.

We will continue to ensure that Parliament is kept informed of significant major operations and deployments of the armed forces.[77]

In 2018, when the Government decided to join with the United States and France on airstrikes on Syrian government facilities connected to chemical

---

[77] Armed Forces Update, HCWS678, *Hansard* vol 608, 18 April 2016, col 10WS.

weapons, several Parliamentarians saw this as a breach of the Convention. The Prime Minister, however, stressed that 'it was a decision that required the evaluation of intelligence and information, much of which was of a nature that could not be shared with Parliament'. And she reiterated that the Government 'have always been clear that the Government have the right to act quickly in the national interest'. More than once she highlighted the part of the 2016 statement, described as 'the exception', which reads 'In observing the Convention, we must ensure that the ability of our Armed Forces to act quickly and decisively, and to maintain the security of their operations, is not compromised.' Prime Minister May also relied on the statement by Prime Minister Cameron in 2014, in which he said 'it is important to reserve the right that if there were a critical British national interest at stake or there were the need to act to prevent a humanitarian catastrophe, you could act immediately and explain to the House of Commons afterwards'.[78] There was no substantive vote.[79]

We could try to summarize the situation for the UK:

1. There is no legally binding obligation on the Government to get prior or subsequent approval from Parliament for any form of military action. The UK is bound by international law on the use of force, and Ministers are bound by the Ministerial Code, which includes an obligation to respect national and international law.[80]

2. The Parliamentary Convention (aka War Powers Convention)[81] covers the commitment of troops to combat situations, and suggests that the

---

[78] 'Syria', 16 April 2018, *Hansard* vol 639, col 68, available at https://hansard.parliament.uk/Commons/2018-04-16/debates/92610F86-2B91-4105-AE8B-78D018453D1B/Syria; see also the Prime Minister's statement, 'As the exception makes clear, there are also situations when coming to Parliament in advance would undermine the security of our operations or constrain our armed forces' ability to act quickly and decisively. In these situations, it is right for the Prime Minister to take the decision and then to be held accountable to Parliament for it': 'Military Action Overseas: Parliamentary Approval', *Hansard* vol 639, 17 April 2018, col 204, available at https://hansard.parliament.uk/commons/2018-04-17/debates/EF164C0A-E0F5-40B6-A718-DD8693A2490C/MilitaryActionOverseasParliamentaryApproval.

[79] There has been some speculation that a vote would not necessarily have endorsed the use of force. Rentoul, 'Theresa May Avoided a Vote in Parliament on Syrian Air Strikes Because She Knew She Would Lose', *The Independent* (14 April 2018), who also looks back over the absence of votes called by the Government over the Korean War in 1950, Suez in 1956, the Falklands War in 1982, the Gulf War in 1991, the bombing campaign of Iraq at the end of 1998 called 'Operation Desert Fox', and action over Kosovo in 1999 and Sierra Leone in 2000.

[80] The Court of Appeal confirmed in 2018 that the new Ministerial Code includes a duty to respect international law; see *R (Gulf Centre For Human Rights) v The Prime Minister et al* [2018] EWCA Civ 1855.

[81] Strong, 'The War Powers of the British Parliament: What has been Established and What Remains Unclear?', 20 *British Journal of Politics and International Relations* (2018) 19–34.

House of Commons has the chance to debate such a commitment before it occurs. The Convention is not considered to cover routine deployments or embedding troops as part of the armed forces of another state. The use of airstrikes is covered in principle, as is the use of unmanned aerial vehicles (drones).[82] Observers suggest that the use of covert or special forces would not be covered by the Convention.

3. The nature of air strikes, and the perceived need to be able to work with other nations on humanitarian or peace and security operations, leads many to believe that hard-and-fast rules demanding consultation, debate and transparency in Parliament are impracticable goals. To the extent that the Convention demands a debate in the House of Commons before any participation in conflict, there is plenty of room for the Executive to rely on the need to act first, where the alternative would compromise the security of any operation.

4. The prospect of a UK War Powers Resolution,[83] or even legislation in the form of an Act of Parliament, remains a possibility; but as long as military action takes the form of limited air strikes rather than the deployment of large numbers of troops, it looks likely that the role of Parliament may be confined in many cases to hearing from the Prime Minister after the fact, while nevertheless retaining the ultimate sanction of a vote of no-confidence.

5.2 Legal Effects in National Law of Declared War

In this section we look at some of the remaining areas in law where a distinction is still drawn between a declared War (understood as giving rise to a State of War in international law) and an armed conflict. Most of these rules have a long lineage and were developed at a time when the institution of War gave rise to particular rights for states that affected the rights of their own nationals as well as foreigners.[84]

---

[82] Prime Minister Cameron explained the use of drones in Syria in the absence of Parliamentary approval as necessitated by national security.

[83] Draft Resolution on Parliament's Role in Conflict Decisions prepared by the Political and Constitutional Reform Committee (HC 892, March 2014) annexed in Mills, *Parliamentary Approval for Military Action* (n 67) at 63.

[84] For some of the older rules, see Lauterpacht (ed), *Oppenheim's International Law*, 7th edn (1952) vol II at 326–35; the detailed rules on war booty and naval warfare are dealt with in Ch 8 below.

In the United States, the 1917 dictum that the 'the power to wage war is the power to wage war successfully' has continuously influenced the understanding of the scope of Congressional and Presidential war powers under the US Constitution.[85] And during the Second World War, against the background of what people called 'total war', the law was developed so as to ensure that the Government had a wide margin for manoeuvre in order to defeat the enemy. But along the way there were very controversial decisions. Most significantly, these include the orders that led to the internment of American citizens of Japanese descent. The US Supreme Court's refusal to find such measures unconstitutional caused considerable outrage. Eugene Rostow, at the time a young professor at Yale, in his influential article in 1945, saw that the response from the Supreme Court reflected fears about new forms of warfare that 'made all older thought on the subject of war obsolete'. He concluded that any such technological advances

> do not compel us to deny suspects the right of trial, to hold people for years in preventive custody, or to substitute military commissions for the civil courts. The need for democratic control of the management of war has not been reduced by advances in the technique of fighting . . . The war power is the power to wage war successfully, as Chief Justice Hughes once remarked. But it is the power to wage war, not a license to do unnecessary and dictatorial things in the name of the war power.[86]

The war power we are considering here is the power of the Executive to take measures that affect the rights and duties of individuals and companies. Some of these war powers under national law may still depend on a Declared War.[87] Others may reference a 'state of war', 'time of war', 'war declared by Congress' and so on. Although most accounts of the law of war gloss over these rules and concentrate on the battlefield, I feel that a survey of a selection of the existing rules and their application from a few relevant jurisdictions will flesh out our understanding of the ways in which references to war, wartime, state of war, etc can radically displace what might otherwise be seen as fundamental liberties or inalienable rights.

---

[85] See Waxman, 'The Power to Wage War Successfully', 117 *Columbia Law Review* (2017) 613–86.

[86] 'The Japanese American Cases – A Disaster', 54 *Yale Law Journal* (1945) 489–533 at 529–30.

[87] For detail under US law, see Elsea and Weed, *Declarations of War* (n 9) esp 27–75.

5.2.1   Enemy Aliens and the Procedural Incapacity to Sue in the UK Courts

In the English Common Law, an alien enemy has no right of access to an English court as a claimant or an actor.[88] The definition is complicated. An 'alien enemy' is a 'person irrespective of nationality who voluntarily resides or who carries on business in any enemy or enemy-occupied country during war in which the United Kingdom is engaged'.[89] In the event that the person, according to McNair and Watts, 'is deemed to have the permission of the Crown to be in this country and is said to be within the protection of the Crown: he is not an enemy for procedural purposes. We shall call him an enemy "in protection".'[90] Chitty suggests that the person becomes an 'alien friend for procedural purposes'.[91] Such 'enemies in protection' or 'alien friends' would have the same rights as a British citizen. They would have the same procedural rights: 'Hence the test of enemy character at common law is a territorial and not a national one. It is an objective test and depends on facts, not on the prejudices, passions, or patriotism of the individual concerned.'[92] The procedural bar to access to the courts would also cover 'a person of any or no nationality who is an enemy in the territorial sense', and this would include an enemy government.[93] An alien enemy in the territorial sense is someone 'voluntarily resident or present or carrying on business in territory owned or occupied by an enemy State'.[94]

The rules are complicated (especially for determining when a company is an alien enemy[95]). They have developed to some extent to adapt to issues of public policy.[96] For our purposes, it remains uncertain whether the rules could apply outside a state of Declared War, or indeed whether they might

---

[88]   Beale (ed), *Chitty on Contracts: General Principles*, 31st edn (2012) vol 1 at paras 11-027–11-031, explaining the exceptions and that an alien enemy may be sued as a defendant.

[89]   Ibid at para 11-024 (footnotes omitted); similarly McNair and Watts, *The Legal Effects of War* (1966) at 78.

[90]   McNair and Watts (n 89) at 78.

[91]   *Chitty* (n 88) at para 11-024.

[92]   Ibid.

[93]   McNair and Watts (n 89) at 79.

[94]   Ibid at 78.

[95]   'A company registered in an enemy or enemy-occupied country is an alien enemy, unless the control of its affairs is shifted to a country not occupied by the enemy. But a company registered in the United Kingdom and carrying on business here may acquire enemy character by reason of the hostile residence or activities of its agents or other persons in de facto control of its affairs.' Chitty (n 88) at para 11-025 (footnotes omitted).

[96]   Ibid Ch 3; see especially *Sovfracht (VO) v Gebr Van Udens Scheepvaart Agentuur Maatschappij* [1943] AC 203.

have to be (or are already) adjusted to bring them into line with modern human rights law.

The only recent case on this topic saw an attempt, in 2004, to prevent an Iraqi national resident in Iraq, Sadiqa Amin, from suing in the English courts a solicitor with regard to a property he was managing. The solicitor raised the plea that Sadiqa Amin could not sue him as she was an enemy alien as a result of the armed conflict between the UK and Iraq. He also argued that the flat was enemy property, and that Mrs Amin's solicitors were 'guilty of the criminal offence of trading with the enemy'.[97] Justice Lawrence Collins (as he then was) went over a number precedents, and explained the meaning of 'war' in the English law as it related to whether or not Mrs Amin could sue in an English court at that time. He held that she could sue. He held she was not an enemy alien as there had been no Declaration of War against Iraq. He did not extend the procedural bar on enemy aliens in English law to situations of modern armed conflict (even such a large one as the 2003 Iraq 'war'):

> I am satisfied that HMG's [Her Majesty's Government's] position is that there is not, and has not been, a state of war between the United Kingdom and the Republic of Iraq, and that it is therefore not necessary for me to ask any questions of the Foreign and Commonwealth Office. I am also satisfied that the disability of alien enemies is part of the rules of English law relating to the traditional laws of war, and that there is no warrant for extending it to modern armed conflict not involving war in the technical sense.[98]

Collins J sets out the rationale and the continuing scope of the rule. First:

> The basis of the rule is that the enemy subject in this country cannot come to sue in the courts any more than could an outlaw, and that the courts will give no assistance to proceedings which, if successful would lead to the enrichment of an alien enemy, and therefore would tend to provide his country with the sinews of war.[99]

Second, he confirmed that an enemy alien in a declared War (perhaps surprisingly) need not necessarily be either alien or an enemy, stating that '[a]

---

[97] *Amin v Brown* [2005] EWHC 1670 (Ch) [12].
[98] Ibid [46].
[99] Ibid [23].

British citizen or neutral who is voluntarily resident in the enemy country is also treated as an alien enemy.[100]

In order to understand the full rationale for the rule, we should take a moment to comprehend what it means to be voluntarily resident in the enemy country, and consider how this applies to corporate persons. The leading case concerned a Dutch ship-owning company, which had chartered a ship before the outbreak of the Second World War to a Russian company. In 1940, the Dutch company sought to go to arbitration in London under a clause in the charterparty. As the company was domiciled in enemy-occupied territory, the House of Lords determined that the Dutch company fell foul of the enemy alien rule. The rationale is explained by Viscount Simon as 'for if the claimant succeeds an asset in the form of an award or a judgment is created which the occupying power can appropriate and which is calculated to increase the enemy's resources.'[101]

Although there was a keen sense of the injustice of this result, Lord Wright's opinion in particular allows one to get a feel for the way in which the priority of winning a War, such as the Second World War, becomes an overriding objective even for the judicial branch. War trumps fairness:

It was accepted that metropolitan Holland had been occupied by and was under the dominion of the Germans. It is true that the Dutch government has been established in and recognized by Great Britain, and is the government to which, in theory, all Dutch subjects owe obedience, but in Holland itself that obedience cannot be enforced nor can that government protect its subjects resident there. Allegiance is generally dependent on reciprocal protection by the state. The Dutch government can give no such protection to its subjects in Holland. They are under the dominion and control of the Germans, who exploit them, plunder them, and tyrannize over them for the benefit of the German Reich. It is clear that the Germans do not intend to relinquish their possession unless forced to do so. However high may be the patriotic fervour of that loyal and valiant race and their devotion to the Allied cause, the Dutch, so far as they are in Holland, must, until the day of deliverance, submit to the German yoke and also accept the comparatively minor affliction of being described for limited purposes and occasions as being in law enemies vis-à-vis Great Britain. Such is the effect of

---

[100] Ibid [22].
[101] *Sovfracht v Van Udens Scheepvaart En Agentuur Maatschappij* [1943] AC 203, 212 (footnote omitted).

the common law of England. They cannot sue or appear as actors in the English courts, they cannot trade with England, their property in England is subject to the Trading with the Enemy Act and regulations. They are shut off from intercourse with Britain. The reason is that, while the occupation lasts, they are on the wrong side of the line of hostile demarcation, the line of war which shuts off those on that side of the line from communication and intercourse and commercial dealing with those on our side in substantially the same way as if they were originally enemies as nationals of, or resident in, the enemy state. This rule is only concerned with relations across the line of war.[102]

A moment's reflection makes it clear that extending this rule so that it covers not just declared War, but also other forms of armed conflict would cause considerable injustice and would be hard to square with modern human rights law. For example, the Iraqi and Afghan nationals who complained in the English courts of human rights violations at the hands of British troops would be procedurally barred from raising their cases as they could be classed as enemy aliens. Any business entity based in enemy countries, including territory occupied by the enemy, would be unable to access the UK courts for as long as the conflict continued. The default rule, which sought to ensure that all benefits were denied to the enemy, looks likely to be applicable now only in very exceptional circumstances, and would need an explicit certification that the United Kingdom is at War.

Let us now consider the separate statutory framework for trading with the enemy. The rule just described is mainly procedural, preventing access to the courts for the duration of the War; the law on trading with the enemy has a substantive dimension that can 'destroy the cause of action once and for all'.[103]

5.2.2 Trading with the Enemy and the UK Law

In Britain and the United States, trading with the enemy became illegal under the Common Law on the outbreak of War, unless there was a special

---

[102] Ibid at 229. In fact it remains possible to seek a royal licence; the plea was not barred only in abatement. It is suggested that such a licence would carry with it the right to sue in court (even if the plaintiff remained an enemy alien); see McNair and Watts (n 89) at 363.

[103] See *Chitty* (n 88)vol 1 at para 11-032, citing *Schmitz v Van der Veen & Co* (1915) 84 LJKB 861, 864; *Rodriguez v Speyer Bros* [1919] 59, 122; and see McNair and Watts (n 89) at 347.

licence.[104] In the First World War, both states introduced legislation under the title 'Trading with the Enemy Act'. And in both cases this legislation has been updated over the years. Germany and France introduced similar provisions into their law.[105]

Trading with the enemy remains contrary to public policy under the Common Law, and so no subject can contract to do anything detrimental to the interests of the country in time of War, or for the benefit of the enemy.[106] The contract is not merely suspended during hostilities, it becomes unenforceable. This means 'a contract by a British subject to insure an enemy against loss through capture by British ships is unenforceable ab initio, even though it was entered into before the commencement of hostilities'.[107] As with the rule on enemy aliens being prevented from accessing the courts in time of War, there is no evidence that this rule prohibiting trading with the enemy has been extended, or is likely to be extended, beyond situations where there is an actual State of War. In other words, for these rules to apply, one would need a declared War or a situation where the Foreign Office certifies that the country is in a 'State of War'.

The Trading with the Enemy Act 1939 statutory scheme creates offences and makes provision for an agency to deal with enemy property.[108] A person is deemed to have traded with the enemy if they have 'had any commercial, financial or other intercourse or dealings with, or for the benefit of, an enemy'. There are exceptions, for example, for anything done under authorization from the Government. In this context

> ... the expression 'enemy' for the purposes of this Act means—
> (a) any State, or Sovereign of a State, at war with His Majesty,
> (b) any individual resident in enemy territory,
> (c) any body of persons (whether corporate or unincorporate) carrying on business in any place, if and so long as the body is controlled by a person who, under this section, is an enemy,
> (d) any body of persons constituted or incorporated in, or under the laws of, a State at war with His Majesty; and

---

[104] Lauterpacht (ed) (n 84) at 319.

[105] Ibid at 320-21.

[106] *Chitty* (n 88) at para 16.026.

[107] Ibid, referencing *Furtado v Rogers* (1802) 3 Bos & Pul 191; *Ertel Bieber & Co v Rio Tinto Co* [1918] AC 260, 273, 289–90.

[108] For an early examination, see Parry, 'The Trading with the Enemy Act and the Definition of an Enemy', 4 *MLR* (1941) 161–82.

(e) as respects any business carried on in enemy territory, any individual or body of persons (whether corporate or unincorporate) carrying on that business;

but does not include any individual by reason only that he is an enemy subject.[109]

While:

'enemy subject' means—

(a) an individual who, not being either a British subject or a British protected person, possesses the nationality of a State at war with His Majesty, or

(b) a body of persons constituted or incorporated in, or under the laws of, any such State...[110]

And

'enemy territory' means any area which is under the sovereignty of, or in the occupation of, a Power with whom His Majesty is at war, not being an area in the occupation of His Majesty or of a Power allied with His Majesty.[111]

The Executive, in the form of the Board of Trade, retains the right to order that the provisions 'shall apply in relation to any area',[112] or 'direct that any person specified in the order shall, for the purposes of this Act, be deemed to be, while so specified, an enemy'.[113] The idea was floated by McNair and Watts in 1966 that it might be theoretically possible for the Board of Trade to use such provisions to extend the scope to the legislation to situations of armed conflict that are not Wars.[114] This seems unlikely to happen at the present time, and they were clear that, in any event, the Common Law rules on trading with the enemy seem to be dependent upon there being an actual War.[115]

---

[109] Trading with the Enemy Act 1939, s 2(1).
[110] Ibid, s 15(1).
[111] Ibid.
[112] Trading with the Enemy Act 1939, s 15(1A).
[113] Ibid, s 2(2).
[114] McNair and Watts (n 89) at 364.
[115] Ibid.

5.2.3 The Enemy Alien Disability Rule and the Alien Enemy Act in the United States

The procedural bar for enemy aliens would apparently also apply in the courts of the United States, where there would be a need for 'some determination by the political department of the government evidencing the existence of such a condition [of War]'.[116] A non-resident enemy alien will therefore not have access to the courts in time of declared War. As explained, however, by Vladeck, this 'enemy alien disability' rule does not preclude an enemy alien from challenging before the courts whether or not they can be considered an enemy alien,[117] or, we might add, whether there is actually a declared War that triggers the inability to sue in the first place.[118]

But the much more controversial aspect of the enemy alien idea in the United States is the rule that, in the words of Justice Jackson, 'The resident enemy alien is constitutionally subject to summary arrest, internment, and deportation whenever a "declared war" exists.'[119] Congress passed the Alien Enemy Act in 1798, and the Supreme Court has so far interpreted this statutory war power as exclusively applicable to declared War, which continues until the political branches hold that there is a Peace. The power continues even after the cessation of hostilities as long as there is a declared War.

So a German national, Mr Ludecke, was unable to claim that the War was over when there was an order in 1946 that he be deported to Germany. The Supreme Court considered it was for the political branches to determine when the War was over, and at that time they had not so determined:

> The Court would be assuming the functions of the political agencies of the Government to yield to the suggestion that the unconditional surrender of Germany and the disintegration of the Nazi Reich have left Germany without a government capable of negotiating a treaty of peace. It is not for us to question a belief by the President that enemy aliens who were justifiably deemed fit subjects for internment during active hostilities do not

---

[116] *Verano v De Angelis Coal Co (No 1)* [1941] ILR 435, 435–36; 41 F Supp 954 (held no condition of war between the United States and Italy in November 1941).

[117] 'Enemy Aliens, Enemy Property, and Access to the Courts', 11 *Lewis and Clark Law Review* (2007) 963–96 at 965.

[118] *Johnson v Eisentrager*, 339 US (1950) 763, per Justice Jackson at 775: 'Courts will entertain his plea for freedom from Executive custody only to ascertain the existence of a state of war and whether he is an alien enemy and so subject to the Alien Enemy Act. Once these jurisdictional elements have been determined, courts will not inquire into any other issue as to his internment.'

[119] Ibid at 775. See 50 US Code § 21 below.

lose their potency for mischief during the period of confusion and conflict which is characteristic of a state of war even when the guns are silent but the peace of Peace has not come.[120]

The 1798 Alien Enemy Act, as amended, reads in part:

Whenever there is a declared war between the United States and any foreign nation or government, or any invasion or predatory incursion is perpetrated, attempted, or threatened against the territory of the United States by any foreign nation or government, and the President makes public proclamation of the event, all natives, citizens, denizens, or subjects of the hostile nation or government, being of the age of fourteen years and upward, who shall be within the United States and not actually naturalized, shall be liable to be apprehended, restrained, secured, and removed as alien enemies.[121]

Proclamations were issued in the 1812 War with Great Britain, and in the First and Second World Wars. In the Second World War, proclamations were issued by President Roosevelt in 1941 with regard to Japanese, Germans and Italians, with detailed restrictions on what they could do. These included a prohibition on possessing firearms, cameras or taking airplane flights. Although the Act makes no provision for a hearing, the Attorney-General considered that internees should be able to question whether they should interned, and over '100 Enemy Alien Hearing Boards, composed of community leaders working without pay, were established to make internment recommendations to the Attorney General'.[122] According to the National Archives:

Furthermore, on the basis of hemispheric security, the United States offered to intern allegedly dangerous enemy aliens living in Latin American countries and even recommended which enemy aliens should be interned. Over fifteen Latin American countries accepted the offer and eventually deported a total of over 6,600 individuals of Japanese, German, and Italian

---

[120] *Ludecke v Watkins*, 335 US (1948) 160 at 170; for some of the implications of this line of case-law for the war powers exercised in the war on terror and the open-ended nature of the 2001 Congressional authorization to use military force, see Vladeck, '*Ludecke's* Lengthening Shadow: The Disturbing Prospect of War Without End', 11 *Lewis and Clark Law Review* (2007) 963–96.

[121] 50 US Code § 21.

[122] Sidak, 'War, Liberty, and Enemy Aliens', 67 *New York University Law Review* (1992) 1402–31; for the details see ibid at 1414–19.

ancestry, along with some of their families, to the US for internment. Few, if any, of those deported received any sort of a hearing so many did not know the specific reasons for their deportation. Often these individuals were deported based on hearsay or for other political reasons.

By the end of the war, over 31,000 suspected enemy aliens and their families, including a few Jewish refugees from Nazi Germany, had been interned at Immigration and Naturalization Services (INS) internment camps and military facilities throughout the United States.[123]

As we saw above with regard to Mr Ludecke's *habeas corpus* application, heard before the Supreme Court in 1948 (he had been arrested in 1941), the Court held it is for the Executive to determine when these war powers are no longer applicable, and further held there could be no judicial review over the Executive's action. The President had delegated the power to remove, whenever the enemy alien was 'deemed by the Attorney General to be dangerous'; it was not apparently necessary that there be a finding that the alien was actually 'dangerous'. For the Supreme Court this meant that any such deeming by the Attorney-General could not be subject to the scrutiny of the courts; this was a war power of the President that was not subject to judicial review.[124] At this point, the Supreme Court mentions that it was aware that 530 alien enemies had been ordered to depart the United States, 'whose disposition awaits the outcome of this case'.[125]

For a sense of how War, and in this case the Second World War, brought its own justification for such incursions into individual liberty, we might just mention a comment on these cases from a member of the UN secretariat (in a personal capacity) written in 1950:

In all cases it is a question of prosecuting a successful war and taking no chances with 'dangerous' or 'doubtful' enemy aliens, rather than exercising too many scruples over constitutional provisions and safeguards. In such matters it is best to err on the severe side: legal laxities in time of war reap little reward.[126]

---

[123] 'World War II Enemy Alien Control Program Overview', available at https://www.archives.gov/research/immigration/enemy-aliens-overview.html.

[124] *Ludecke v Watkins* (n 129) at 165–66.

[125] Ibid at fn 2.

[126] Brandon, 'Legal Control Over Resident Enemy Aliens in Time of War in the United States and in the United Kingdom', 44 *AJIL* (1950) 382–87 at 387.

The Alien Enemy Act has not been used since its application was terminated through the Proclamation of the end of the War in October 1951.[127] The *Ludecke* showdown nevertheless provided for vigorous dissents, questioning why these powers should be operative in the absence of hostilities[128] and defending constitutional rights. Three dissenting Justices stated:

> The notion that the discretion of any officer of government can override due process is foreign to our system. Due process does not perish when war comes. It is well established that the war power does not remove constitutional limitations safeguarding essential liberties.[129]

Turning to the treatment of those from Japan or of Japanese descent, orders were given under a separate legal basis that allowed for exclusion orders, curfews and internment. This not only applied for West Coast Japanese citizens, but also extended to American citizens of Japanese ancestry. This led to the eventual internment of around 110,000 persons, of whom around 70,000 were US citizens of Japanese ancestry. The most controversial aspect of the operation of the Executive Orders promulgated by the Commanding General in 1942 was the overt racism that was entailed. United States citizens of German or Italian descent were not affected by the key measures. A series of cases came before the courts. In *Korematsu*, the majority of the Supreme Court upheld the constitutionality of the orders and Korematsu's conviction for breaching an exclusion order. In the words of the judgment:

> Korematsu was not excluded from the Military Area because of hostility to him or his race. He was excluded because we are at war with the Japanese Empire, because the properly constituted military authorities feared an invasion of our West Coast and felt constrained to take proper security measures, because they decided that the military urgency of the situation demanded that all citizens of Japanese ancestry be segregated from the West Coast temporarily, and, finally, because Congress, reposing its confidence in this time of war in our military leaders – as inevitably it must – determined that they should have the power to do just this.[130]

---

[127] President Truman, Proclamation 2950 – Termination of the State of War with Germany, 24 October 1951.

[128] *Ludecke v Watkins* (n 120) per Justices Black, Douglas, Murphy and Rutledge.

[129] Ibid at 187 per Justices Douglas, Murphy and Rutledge.

[130] *Korematsu v United States* 323 US (1944) 214 at 223.

Justice Murphy's dissent pulled no punches. He started out '[the] exclusion goes over "the very brink of constitutional power," and falls into the ugly abyss of racism'.[131] He pointed to the absence of any reliable evidence that that could support the General's report, depicting 'all individuals of Japanese descent as "subversive," as belonging to "an enemy race" whose "racial strains are undiluted," and as constituting "over 112,000 potential enemies . . . at large today" along the Pacific Coast'.[132] And he makes some fundamental points about a society committed to inherent individual rights:

> No one denies, of course, that there were some disloyal persons of Japanese descent on the Pacific Coast who did all in their power to aid their ancestral land. Similar disloyal activities have been engaged in by many persons of German, Italian and even more pioneer stock in our country. But to infer that examples of individual disloyalty prove group disloyalty and justify discriminatory action against the entire group is to deny that, under our system of law, individual guilt is the sole basis for deprivation of rights. Moreover, this inference, which is at the very heart of the evacuation orders, has been used in support of the abhorrent and despicable treatment of minority groups by the dictatorial tyrannies which this nation is now pledged to destroy. To give constitutional sanction to that inference in this case, however well intentioned may have been the military command on the Pacific Coast, is to adopt one of the cruelest of the rationales used by our enemies to destroy the dignity of the individual and to encourage and open the door to discriminatory actions against other minority groups in the passions of tomorrow.[133]

Although Korematsu's conviction was vacated in 1983, and he was awarded the Presidential Medal of Freedom in 1988, the ideas from this case (and the *Ludecke* case), that times of War call for exceptional inroads against an enemy defined according to race, religion or nationality, continue to have a powerful appeal.[134] On the one hand, the name of Korematsu is invoked and celebrated by those taking inspiration from a civil rights activist who,

---

[131] Ibid at 233.

[132] Ibid at 236.

[133] Ibid at 240.

[134] For some of the related legal developments and references to these cases, see Vladeck, 'Ludecke's Lengthening Shadow' (n 120); Cole, 'Enemy Aliens', 953 *Stanford Law Review* (2002) 953–1004; Sidak, 'War, Liberty, and Enemy Aliens', 67 *New York University Law Review* (1992) 1402–31.

in his eighties, filed *amici* briefs to the Supreme Court warning of the parallels between the internment of the Japanese Americans and the detentions in Guantánamo. On the other hand, the precedent set in the *Korematsu* case continues to bolster those looking for legitimacy when proposing exceptional measures that target particular religions, races or nationalities.[135]

5.2.4 Trading with the Enemy Act (US)

The Trading with the Enemy Act (1917) in the United States was modelled on the United Kingdom's Act discussed in section 5.2.2 above.

Coates explains the Act's original purpose:

> In the beginning, the Trading with the Enemy Act had two primary functions: to prevent Germany from mobilizing American resources and to 'conscript' German property for the benefit of the US war effort. The latter entailed seizing 'enemy' funds – 'enemy' referring to anyone living in the territory of the Central Powers, including American heiresses who had the misfortune of marrying Austro-Hungarian nobles – and investing them in US liberty bonds. The act also allowed US firms to license German chemical patents – no small thing in an age when German firms dominated synthetic chemistry. The patent for Salvarsan, then the most effective treatment for syphilis, was especially important considering the combination of war-induced pharmaceutical shortages and US government fears about the sexual behavior of its new soldiers.[136]

In the end, although the plan had been to return seized assets, the United States retained certain enemy property, including German patents that were sold on to American companies. Coates continues the story:

> The Trading with the Enemy Act also boosted US corporate fortunes. On November 4, 1918 – a week before the armistice – an amendment allowed Palmer [the Alien Property Custodian] to permanently repossess German chemical patents. In April 1919, his successor Francis P Garvan sold 4,500

---

[135] Yamamoto, Berti and Tokioka, ' "Loaded Weapon" Revisited: The Trump Era Import of Justice Jackson's Warning in *Korematsu*', 24 *Asian American Law Journal* (2017) 5–47.

[136] Coates, 'The Secret Life of Statutes: Century of Trading with the Enemy Act', 1 *Modern American History* (2018) 151–72 at 156 (footnotes omitted).

patents to the newly formed Chemical Foundation, of which Garvan was president. Though their value was estimated at up to $8 million, they were transferred for only $250,000. The Foundation then licensed them to US chemical firms, helping to jumpstart the postwar US chemical industry, which eventually emerged as a challenger to German concerns.[137]

During the Second World War, the Act allowed the Executive to freeze or vest assets in the Alien Property Custodian. Hundreds of millions of dollars worth of German and Japanese property was affected, leading to complex litigation. Again the confiscation included the taking of the patents from companies such as IG Farben. Together with the frozen assets, the programme affected property of around $8 billion.[138] Unlike the rules on internment, the rules on trade relating to property were not extended to German and Japanese nationals who were residents in the United States.[139] It seems unlikely that the Act's wartime powers over private assets would be used in the contemporary world, and we need not delve into the complex case-law, which often involved determining whether there was enemy 'control' over a corporation on the facts of the case.[140]

In 1933 the Act was amended to allow the President to extend the powers beyond times of declared War to other periods of national emergency declared by the President. And in 1977 the Act was amended again, limiting the powers once more to situations of declared War. It now almost exclusively applies to situations of declared War. It is still in force, and in the definitions it states that 'The words "the beginning of the war," as used herein, shall be deemed to mean midnight ending the day on which Congress has declared or shall declare war or the existence of a state of war.'[141] This last amendment did not affect the inclusion in 1962 of Cuba within the scope of the Act. Cuba is now the only remaining state covered by the Act; its inclusion has been renewed each year by the President, who merely has to certify that this is in the 'national interest'.[142]

---

[137] Ibid at 158–59 (footnotes omitted).

[138] Bishop, 'Judicial Construction of the Trading with the Enemy Act', 62 *Harvard Law Review* (1949) 721–59 at 722.

[139] Ibid at 753.

[140] Ibid.

[141] 50 US Code § 4302, 'Definitions'; note also 'The words "end of the war," as used herein, shall be deemed to mean the date of proclamation of exchange of ratifications of the treaty of peace, unless the President shall, by proclamation, declare a prior date, in which case the date so proclaimed shall be deemed to be the "end of the war" within the meaning of this Act.'

[142] See, eg, the renewal in 2019, available at https://www.whitehouse.gov/presidential-actions/memorandum-continuation-exercise-certain-authorities-trading-enemy-act/.

5.2.5 The UK Foreign Enlistment Act 1870 and Similar Legislation in Other Jurisdictions

The Foreign Enlistment Act 1870 was enacted in the aftermath of the dispute between Great Britain and the United States over the fitting out of ships for the Confederate forces in the American Civil War. But it included provisions to prevent British citizens from becoming involved in the looming Franco–Prussian War. In addition to creating offences regarding shipbuilding – such as that covering anyone who 'Builds or agrees to build, or causes to be built any ship with intent or knowledge, or having reasonable cause to believe that the same shall or will be employed in the military or naval service of any foreign state at war with any friendly state'[143] – the Act (which is still in force) provided that an offence would be committed:

> If any person, without the license of Her Majesty, being a British subject, within or without Her Majesty's dominions, accepts or agrees to accept any commission or engagement in the military or naval service of any foreign state at war with any foreign state at peace with Her Majesty.[144]

Although there are clear references to engagement with a 'foreign state at war', the Act's definition of 'foreign state' suggests that internal armed conflicts could be covered, and that there could be an offence of engagement with a non-state actor.[145] Under the Act:

> 'Foreign state' includes any foreign prince, colony, province, or part of any province or people, or any person or persons exercising or assuming to exercise the powers of government in or over any foreign country, colony, province, or part of any province or people . . .[146]

In later years, the British Government was keen to be seen to be keeping out of the Spanish Civil War, and wanted to prevent people from leaving for Spain to fight. In particular, the Government sought to prevent the

---

[143] Foreign Enlistment Act 1870, s 8(1).

[144] Ibid, s 4.

[145] McNair and Watts concluded that the term 'war' here is not limited to the technical international sense of War but could include armed conflicts between states, civil wars, and even conflicts between states and non-recognized rebels or insurgents who have not been recognised as belligerents. *The Legal Effects of War* (n 89) at 451–52.

[146] Foreign Enlistment Act 1870, s 30.

Communist Party of Great Britain from helping people get to Spain in order to fight for the Republican side against General Franco's forces. Ministers and others had some doubts over whether the Act could be applied to the situation in Spain. The Foreign Office nevertheless issued a press notice stating that it was illegal to recruit or volunteer for the armed forces of either side in the Spanish conflict.[147] No one was ever prosecuted, in part due to the difficulty of getting evidence and in part due, it seems, to a fear that the courts might not uphold the applicability of the Act to the Spanish Civil War.[148] The Government were not keen to recognize Franco's forces in a way that would clarify the legal situation. In Canada similar legislation was invoked to prevent Canadians from fighting in the Spanish Civil War. This time it was assumed that the legislation only applied to conflicts between states, and the situation was clarified with an Order in Council stating that it was an offence to recruit, enlist or fight on either side in the Spanish Civil War.[149] No one was prosecuted.

In 1976, a report by the Committee of the Privy Council in the United Kingdom on the topic of mercenary activity opined that the Act was not clear enough to create criminal offences related to internal conflicts without actual recognition by the Government of *de facto* forces.[150] This opinion implies that, should the Act be applied today to those fighting for groups such as the so-called 'Islamic state', this would require the UK Government to

---

[147] Mackenzie, 'The Foreign Enlistment Act and the Spanish Civil War, 1936–1939', 10 *Twentieth Century British History* 1 (1999) 52–66 at 58.

[148] Ibid.

[149] Wentzell, 'Canada's *Foreign Enlistment Act* and the Spanish Civil War', 80 *Journal of Canadian Labour Studies* (2017) 213–46 at 229–31. At one point the legislation was entitled 'An Act respecting Participation in certain Foreign Wars by Canadian Nationals': ibid at 225.

[150] 'Report of the Committee of Privy Counsellors appointed to inquire into the recruitment of mercenaries', Cmnd 6569 (1976) at para 34: 'The expanded definition of "foreign state" prevents its being confined to a government that is recognised by HM Government as the *de jure* sovereign government over a particular area. It is, and was no doubt intended by the draftsman to be, broad enough to make it an offence to enlist in armed forces raised by rival governments in a civil war such as that which had been waged in the United States of America, or forces such as those which had been raised by insurgents in the Spanish American colonies in their recent struggles for independence. But the questions whether and, if so, when the Act becomes applicable to particular cases of internal struggles for power between rival factions within a state in the varied circumstances in which such struggles may arise today, are capable of raising so many doubts as to make this part of the Act unsuitable, in our opinion, to continue to be used as a penal statute.' See further Arielli, Frei and Van Hulle, 'The Foreign Enlistment Act, International Law, and British Politics, 1819–2014', 38 *The International History Review* (2015) 636–56. *Halsbury's Laws of England* (2019) vol 3 'Neutrality and Illegal Activities: 12. Foreign enlistment', footnotes the word 'war' in this context and states 'Since the Foreign Enlistment Act 1870 is a criminal statute it is uncertain whether "war" for these purposes includes an international armed conflict which has not resulted from a declaration of war or a non-international armed conflict (given the definition of a "foreign state" in s 30 …).' At fn 6.

recognize the Islamic state as a *de facto* insurgency, something that would be likely misconstrued as suggesting some sort of legitimacy or entitlement to international law rights.

Australia has legislation that avoids references to war and the forces of a foreign state. The legislation creates the offence of *engaging in a hostile activity* in a foreign country.[151] And more recently Australia has added an offence committed when the person enters, or remains in, an area in a foreign country and that area is one that has been 'declared' by the Foreign Affairs Minister.[152] Declarations have been made for Al-Raqqa in Syria (no longer in force) and for Mosul in Iraq (first made in 2015 and renewed in 2018).

Other jurisdictions, such as the Maldives (from where a high number of fighters leave for the conflicts in Iraq and Syria), have similar legislation under the heading of prevention of terrorism. Regarding the 2019 amendments to the Maldives Prevention of Terrorism Act, it was reported that 'The amendment also criminalises the act of departing for war zones without authorisation by the administration. While the current Act recognises partaking in a foreign conflict as a crime, the new changes criminalise all unauthorised attempts to go to any war zones.'[153]

Today, worldwide, most prosecutions and administrative sanctions, such as the removal of passports or nationality, take place in the context of counterterrorism legislation,[154] rather than by reference to the older offences related to foreign enlistment, which were conceived against a background of the need to ensure respect for the obligations connected to Neutral Status[155] and

---

[151] See, for the detail, Criminal Code Act (1995), s 117.1 et seq.

[152] Ibid, s 119.2.

[153] 'Parliament passes amendments to Prevention of Terrorism Act', *The Edition* (20 September 2019), available at https://edition.mv/news/12678.

[154] For a review, see Paulussen and Pitcher, 'Prosecuting (Potential) Foreign Fighters: Legislative and Practical Challenges', International Centre for Counter-Terrorism, January 2018.

[155] In Japan, Art 94 ('Violations of Neutrality Orders') of the criminal code still contains the following offence: 'A person who violates an order of neutrality in a war between foreign states shall be punished by imprisonment without work for not more than 3 years or a fine of not more than 500,000 yen.' The last Neutrality Order was issued in 1911 with reference to the 1911–12 Turco–Italian War; no new order has been issued under the 1947 Constitution. (With thanks to Hibiki Urano.) For foreign enlistment, and crimes of fitting ships, etc for a foreign nation at peace with the United States, see 18 US Code §§ 951–970; compare §2339A (Providing material support to terrorists). In *Oppenheim's International Law*, Lauterpacht (n 82) at 668 states that 'Neutrality Laws are latent in time of peace; but their provisions become operative *ipso facto* by the respective States making a declaration of neutrality to their officials and subjects.' Today one might still expect a declaration of neutrality before such criminal law provisions could apply. International armed conflicts break out quite regularly; unless there was some sort of neutrality order, how would a citizen know that their activity would suddenly become criminal? See section 2.3.4.

to prevent a neutral state's territory being used for recruitment in an inter-state War.

5.3 Internment of Enemy Aliens under the Royal Prerogative in the United Kingdom

We have seen that, with regard to the *procedural bar on enemy aliens* having access to the courts, the concept of enemy alien is quite narrowly defined. A person with permission to be in the country is considered 'in protection', and therefore *not* an enemy for procedural purposes. But when it came to internment during the Second World War, the 'unwritten law' applied by the Home Secretary led to 23,000 male refugees from Germany being in-discriminately interned 'solely on the ground of their present or former nationality'.[156]

The *power to detain* in this context seems to be derived from the Royal Prerogative in time of War. Such a use of the Prerogative was considered unreviewable by the courts in one key case, when a German resident in England for many years sought to challenge his internment. In 1946, Mr Kuechenmeister was faced with the use of the Royal Prerogative to detain him in War, coupled with a statement from the Secretary of State, dated 2 April 1946, confirming that the Second World War continued. The Court of Appeal was not ready to review either of these executive acts. The details are worth recalling, as they remind us that even if these war powers were always applied out of a sense of necessity, they came with indiscriminate, devas-tating effects for foreign nationals from the enemy nation:

He came to England in 1928 and was granted the right of permanent resi-dence in 1931. He then married an Englishwoman, by whom he had three children, all born in England. In May, 1939, he applied for British nation-ality. In August of that year he was asked by the Home Secretary to leave the country. He thereupon went to Eire, where he remained until December, 1939, when he was informed by the Home Office that he might return to England to appear before an advisory committee on the question of his

---

[156] Cohn, 'Legal Aspects of Internment', *MLR* (1941) 200–09 at 203–04. For the situation in France (before and during occupation), Italy and Germany, see Koessler, 'Enemy Alien Internment: With Special Reference to Great Britain and France', 57 *Political Science Quarterly* (1942) 98–127; see also section 9.1.3.1 below.

internment. He did so, and was sent to Australia for internment. He remained there until 1945, when he returned to England, being sent to the internment camp at Beltane School on his arrival.[157]

Kuechenmeister argued that even if there might have been some unwritten power to intern an enemy alien during the War, the complete surrender of Germany in 1945, and the assumption of government there by the Allied Control Commission, meant there could no longer be a War between the UK Government and Germany. The Court of Appeal rejected his arguments and chose to rely on the Executive's certificate that a State of War continued. His internment under the Royal Prerogative could not be challenged. Lord Justice Asquith speculated that even after the defeat of the armed forces and the end of hostilities, there might be a continuing justification to intern enemy aliens: 'the combatant forces of Germany having been utterly defeated, no means remain to her for pursuing the struggle beyond underground agencies in Allied countries, acting by way of espionage, propaganda and the like'.[158]

The internment of enemy aliens *as prisoners of war* rests on the same legal foundations of the Royal Prerogative. In the 1991 Iraq war, 35 members of the Iraqi armed forces, who found themselves in the UK at the outbreak of the armed conflict, were interned as prisoners of war. Despite the absence of a Declared War, the Royal Prerogative seems to have been applied on the basis that

the courts today would doubtless accept that international law has developed since *Kuechenmeister*, and that the concept of 'armed conflict' has to some extent at least superseded that of 'war'. If so, the courts would be likely to regard a state of armed conflict as equating, for prerogative purposes, to a state of war, thereby confirming the right to intern prisoners of war as an act of state.[159]

---

[157] *R v Bottrill, ex parte Kuechenmeister* [1947] 1 KB 41, 42; 13 ILR, Case 132, 312.

[158] Ibid at 57; today a refugee could not be interned solely on the basis of nationality, see GC IV Art 44 and the Convention Relating to the Status of Refugees (1951) Art 8.

[159] Risius (Colonel), 'Prisoners of War in the United Kingdom', in Rowe (ed), *The Gulf War 1990–91 in International and English Law* (1993) 289–303 at 294 (fn omitted); for further detail on the situation of these prisoners, see Hampson, 'The Geneva Conventions and the Detention of Civilians and Alleged Prisoners of War', *Public Law* (1991) 507–22. Hampson highlights that there were some confusing references to detention under immigration rules with a view to deportation, and that this sits uncomfortably with the status of prisoner of war. She suggests that it would have been preferable to ask Parliament for specific legislation to detain such enemy aliens. When it comes to challenging detention in the English courts, the doctrine of 'act of state' may play a large role when coupled with the idea of the Executive having the power and responsibility with regard to 'making war'; see MacLachlan, 'The Foreign Relations Power in the Supreme Court', 134 *LQR* (2019) 380–406 at 400–02.

Of course, at the international level, the application of the Third Geneva Convention on Prisoners of War needs no Declaration of War for it to be applicable, yet it contains some gaps with regard to its arrangements for challenges by internees who wish to deny that they can be considered prisoners of war. Some of the Iraqis interned in 1991 denied that they were members of the armed forces of Iraq and asked to be released. Strictly speaking, the tribunal for hearing such a complaint only need be established where the person in custody 'has committed a belligerent act' before capture by the enemy.[160] Nevertheless, Boards of Inquiry were established 'in order to follow the spirit of the Convention'.[161] Three of the internees were subsequently released, as it was concluded they were not members of the Iraqi armed forces. The others remained interned as prisoners of war in a prisoner of war camp until the end of hostilities. None chose to be repatriated to Iraq and they were released with vouchers to buy train tickets to their chosen destinations.

5.4 Detention by the United States in the War on Terror

When the full prisoner of war regime is applied in the way just described, the laws of war seem relatively protective and unproblematic. But the problem comes when that regime is not applied with all the in-built procedural and substantive protections. In the United States the idea has been promulgated that detention is simply an inherent aspect of war. In this way, detention is impliedly authorized for those considered at war with the United States. This category now includes an expanding number of groups and their sympathizers.

In the United States, the authority to detain in the post-9/11 period has been implied through the Authorization for the Use of Military Force (AUMF) passed by Congress and signed by the President in 2001. The extent to which the protections in the Geneva Conventions ought to apply to detainees such as those captured during the invasion of Afghanistan will be

---

[160] See GC III, Art 5; and the Royal Warrant governing the Maintenance of Discipline among Prisoners of War, First Schedule, Prisoner of War Determination of Status Regulations (1958) reg 1, para 1. For the situation in the United States, Australia, Canada, New Zealand and Israel, see Naqvi, 'Doubtful Prisoner-of-War Status', 84 *International Review of the Red Cross* (2003) 571–95; and for a full overview of the legal issues, see Tougas, 'Determination of Prisoner of War Status', in Clapham, Gaeta and Sassòli (eds), *The 1949 Geneva Conventions: A Commentary* (2015) 939–55.

[161] Risius, 'Prisoners of War' (n 159) at 296; see the Army Act 1955, s 135.

dealt with later.[162] The issue I want to highlight now is how the courts have discovered a power to detain *incidental to the conduct of war*.

In 1942, German submarines deposited eight saboteurs on the coast of the United States. Four men landed on Long Island and four in Florida; their mission was to destroy various targets in the United States. They landed in the uniform of the German Marine Infantry and brought with them explosives, fuses and timing devices. Two of them quite quickly turned themselves in to the FBI and provided the information that led to the arrest of the other six. These two claimed that they had always been ready to sabotage the sabotage mission. They claimed they were anti-Nazi and pro-American. One was actually a US citizen, while the other had completed all the steps for citizenship but had apparently not turned up for the swearing ceremony.[163]

The US President created a Military Commission, and all the men were tried and convicted. All were sentenced to death. The two who had cooperated had their sentences commuted by the President to hard labour for life and for 30 years, while the other six were electrocuted less than two weeks after the end of the trial in the Military Commission.

The contemporaneous decision of the Supreme Court that approved the use of the Military Commission by the President is remarkable for a number of reasons, not least because it is frequently cited as part of the argumentation about the authority to detain, prosecute and even execute those held in Guantánamo as part of the detention programme related to the war on terror. For the moment, let us consider the way the proclamation of the President draws on the notion of War to establish the military jurisdiction over the saboteurs. The President was keen to ensure the death penalty, and had been told by his Attorney-General that a Military Commission would be a better route, as the death penalty could be imposed by a two-thirds majority and the civil courts might have trouble finding the men guilty of sabotage as they never actually achieved any damage. The Proclamation was issued within a week of the capture of the saboteurs:

> *Whereas,* the safety of the United States demands that all enemies who have entered upon the territory of the United States as part of an invasion or

---

[162] For an expert appraisal regarding this phase in Afghanistan, see Aldrich, 'The Taliban, Al Qaeda, and the Determination of Illegal Combatants', 96 *AJIL* (2002) 891–98; for further discussion, see Chs 7, 9 and 10 below.

[163] See the entertaining account by G Cohen, 'The Keystone Kommandos', *The Atlantic* (February 2002), available at https://www.theatlantic.com/magazine/archive/2002/02/the-keystone-kommandos/302405/

predatory incursion, or who have entered in order to commit sabotage, espionage, or other hostile or warlike acts, should be promptly tried in accordance with the Law of War;

Now, Therefore, I, Franklin D Roosevelt, President of the United States of America and Commander in Chief of the Army and Navy of the United States, by virtue of the authority vested in me by the Constitution and the statutes of the United States do hereby proclaim that all persons who are subjects, citizens, or residents of any Nation at war with the United States or who give obedience to or act under the direction of any such Nation and who during time of war enter or attempt to enter the United States or any territory or possession thereof, through coastal or boundary defenses, and are charged with committing or attempting or preparing to commit sabotage, espionage, hostile or warlike acts, or violations of the law or war, shall be subject to the law of war and to the jurisdiction of military tribunals...[164]

According to Fisher, 'Reference to the "law of war" was crucial. Had Roosevelt cited the "Articles of War", he would have triggered the statutory procedures established by Congress for courts-martial.'[165] This departure from the statutory law paved the way for the Commission to be able to sentence to death by a two-thirds majority rather than by unanimity, and for generous rules for the admission of prosecution evidence.[166] The Supreme Court explained that the President could establish the Military Commission under his war powers:

The Constitution thus invests the President, as Commander in Chief, with the power to wage war which Congress has declared, and to carry into effect all laws passed by Congress for the conduct of war and for the government and regulation of the Armed Forces, and all laws defining and punishing offenses against the law of nations, including those which pertain to the conduct of war.[167]

---

[164] Proclamation 2561 – Denying Certain Enemies Access to the Courts, 2 July 1942.

[165] Fisher, *Nazi Saboteurs on Trial: A Military Tribunal and American Law* (2003) at 50. There were four Charges: the first was 'Violations of the Law of War', essentially being enemies of the United States and going behind the defences of the United States for the purpose of committing acts of sabotage, espionage and other hostile acts; the second and third Charges related to the 81st and 82nd Articles of War, covering communicating intelligence to the enemy; while the fourth was conspiracy to commit the other acts.

[166] Ibid at 52–53; and see the Military Order issued by the President, F Fed Reg 1503 (1942).

[167] *Ex parte Quirin et al*, 317 US (1942) 1 at 26.

The Military Commission was therefore constitutional, according to the Supreme Court, based on the idea that such Commissions are prosecuting offences under 'the law of nations'.[168] The assumption in the Supreme Court seems to be that espionage, landing and proceeding disguised as civilians could be considered as violations of the laws of war (in fact these acts are not violations or crimes under the international law of war; as we shall see, such acts simply remove combatant immunity and the right to prisoner of war status).[169]

Whether or not the confusion created by the Supreme Court in *Quirin*, including through a reference to the 'common law of war', will provide a precedent for the prosecution of those who are being tried in the Guantánamo Military Commissions for conspiracy (not known in international war crimes law) is still being debated in the courts.[170] Our interest here is in a different passage, which was used in passing by the Supreme Court and which has been taken up in other contexts.

The Court stated:

> An important incident to the conduct of war is the adoption of measures by the military command not only to repel and defeat the enemy, but to seize and subject to disciplinary measures those enemies who in their attempt to thwart or impede our military effort have violated the law of war.[171]

The idea has taken hold that this sentence helps bolster the idea that today, those who are now named 'unlawful combatants' could be lawfully detained as part of the Congressional authorization to use force in the wake of 9/11.[172]

---

[168] Ibid at 26–29.

[169] Ferrell (Major), 'No Shirt, No Shoes, No Status: Uniforms, Distinction, and Special Operations in International Armed Conflict', 178 *Military Law Review* (2003) 94–140; Baxter, 'So-Called "Unprivileged Belligerency": Spies, Guerrillas, and Saboteurs', 28 *BYBIL* (1951) 323–45; see section 7.1 below.

[170] See the scholarly and detailed discussion by Ohlin, who traces this phrase back to the idea of Vattel that there was a common law of war applicable to both sides in a civil war based on natural law and his maxims of 'humanity, moderation, and honour': Ohlin, 'The Common Law of War', 58 *William and Mary Law Review* (2016) 493–533 esp at 519–23; he is also clear that the expression 'common law' here should not be confused with the idea of Common Law under English Law. For the detail on the charges in the Guantánamo Military Commissions, see Brenner-Beck, 'Trial and Punishment for Battlefield Misconduct', in Corn et al, *The War on Terror and the Laws of War: A Military Perspective*, 2nd edn (2015) 193–236.

[171] *Ex parte Quirin et al* (n 167) at 28–29.

[172] Eg in *Hamdi v Rumsfeld*, 542 US (2004) 507 at 518, 'that detention of individuals falling into the limited category we are considering, for the duration of the particular conflict in which they were captured, is so fundamental and accepted an incident to war as to be an exercise of the "necessary and appropriate force" Congress has authorized the President to use. The capture and detention of lawful combatants and the capture, detention, and trial of unlawful combatants, by

The problem here is that the authorization to use force against those who attacked the United States in September 2001 has been combined with the Supreme Court's justification for prosecuting German military saboteurs, who either confessed or were caught red-handed, during the Second World War. This idea that detention is an incident to the conduct of war is now used to detain an expanding range of individuals as law-of-war detainees, with no end in sight.

The issue was memorably explained by Harold Hongju Koh at the end of his time as Legal Advisor in the Obama Administration. Koh had been grappling with this issue for four years when he left in 2013, but the issues remain just as intractable and inadequately addressed by either national or international law:

> [T]he key question going forward will thus be whether or not we treat new groups that rise up to commit acts of terror as 'associated forces' of Al Qaeda with whom we are already at war. The US Government has made clear that an 'associated force' must be (1) an organized, armed group that (2) has actually entered the fight alongside al Qaeda against the United States, thereby becoming (3) a co-belligerent with al Qaeda in its hostilities against America. Just because someone hates America or sympathizes with Al Qaeda does not make them our lawful enemy. Under both domestic and international law, the United States has ample legal authority to respond to new groups that would attack it without declaring war forever against anyone who is hostile to us. But make no mistake: if we are too loose in who we consider to be 'part of' or 'associated with' Al Qaeda going forward, then we will always have new enemies, and the Forever War will continue forever.[173]

There has been no new legislation that would extend the 2001 authorization for the use of force against Al-Qaeda to the fight with the so-called 'Islamic state'. Detention and use-of-force questions both depend on an expanded interpretation of this legislation, and yet there seems little appetite in Congress to set any new boundaries for the Executive in this context.[174] In the

---

"universal agreement and practice," are "important incident[s] of war." *Ex parte Quirin, supra,* at 28, 30.'

[173] Oxford Union, 7 May 2013, available at http://opiniojuris.org/wp-content/uploads/2013-5-7-corrected-koh-oxford-union-speech-as-delivered.pdf.

[174] For detail, see Ford, 'War by Legislation: The Constitutionality of Congressional Regulation of Detentions in Armed Conflict in Armed Conflicts', 110 *Northwestern University Law Review*

meantime, those taken to Guantánamo between 2001 and 2008 look likely to remain in indefinite detention, likened by analogy to prisoners of war and detained, according, to Congress, 'under the law of war without trial until the end of the hostilities authorized by the Authorization for Use of Military Force'.[175] There are around 20 individuals held in Guantánamo Bay who are not scheduled to be tried and are now known as 'forever prisoners'.[176]

One such Guantánamo detainee, captured in 2001 in Pakistan and accused of fighting with Al-Qaeda and the Taliban in Afghanistan, tried to claim that he should no longer be held as an enemy combatant as that conflict is now over. His claim failed in the US Supreme Court. Despite President Obama's 2015 statement that 'our combat mission in Afghanistan is over, and America's longest war has come to a responsible and honourable end', the lower courts considered that the continuing conflict and counter-terrorism operations against the Taliban and the remnants of Al-Qaeda meant there was continuing authority to detain.[177] Although the Supreme Court declined to hear the appeal in 2019, Justice Breyer made a statement highlighting the problems associated with such an evolving notion of a war, the vaguely defined executive war powers, and a law of war informed by other sorts of conflict. In his words:

> al-Alwi faces the real prospect that he will spend the rest of his life in detention based on his status as an enemy combatant a generation ago, even though today's conflict may differ substantially from the one Congress anticipated when it passed the AUMF [2001 Authorization for Use of Military

(2016) 119–36; Ingber, 'Co-Belligerency', 42 *Yale Journal of International Law* (2016) 67–120. For the suggestion that all such authorizations for the use of force should contain 'sunset' clauses, see Ackerman and Hathaway (n 12).

[175] As part of the National Defense Authorization Act for Fiscal Year 2012, Congress includes authority for the armed forces to engage in such detention, see § 1021 (c)(1); for a discussion of these issues, see Bradley and Goldsmith, 'Obama's AUMF Legacy', 110 *AJIL* (2016) 628–45; for an example of how the logic of war led to an implied authority to detain in the wake of September 11, see the Supreme Court in *Hamdi v Rumsfeld*, 542 US (2004) 507 at 517: 'In light of these principles, it is of no moment that the AUMF [2001 Authorization for Use of Military Force] does not use specific language of detention. Because detention to prevent a combatant's return to the battlefield is a fundamental incident of waging war, in permitting the use of "necessary and appropriate force," Congress has clearly and unmistakably authorized detention in the narrow circumstances considered here.'

[176] See at https://www.miamiherald.com/news/nation-world/world/americas/guantanamo/article2203501.html; a current list is maintained at https://www.nytimes.com/interactive/projects/guantanamo/detainees/current.

[177] See *Al-Alwi v Trump*, 236 F Supp 3d 417 (2017); 901 F 3d 294 (2018).

Force], as well as those 'conflicts that informed the development of the law of war.'[178]

5.5 The Political Question and Enemy Property Doctrines

We have already seen how the judiciary in the United States have been careful not to get involved with policy choices, leaving these either to Congress or to the President.[179] Judges have not been willing to patrol the boundaries between Congress and the Executive over war powers as set out in the War Powers Resolution or the Constitution. A new set of arguments about war, however, arose in the litigation surrounding the bombing of the El-Shifa Pharmaceutical factory in Sudan in 1998.

Following the bombing of the US Embassies in Kenya and Tanzania, President Clinton responded by launching missile strikes against 'terrorist facilities and infrastructure' in Afghanistan and the El-Shifa factory in Sudan. He explained the same day that the factory was 'associated with the bin Ladin network' and 'involved in the production of materials for chemical weapons'.[180] A letter was sent to Congress, 'consistent' with the War Powers Resolution, reporting that the strikes were a necessary and proportionate response to the threat of an imminent threat of future attacks by terrorists on the United States and its personnel and facilities.

The litigation arose because the owner of the factory, which was said to be producing more than half the pharmaceuticals used in Sudan, sued the US Government for the mistaken destruction of his property (claiming damages of $50m), for defamation and for a declaration that the denial of compensation violated the law of nations. He claimed that there was no evidence that the factory had any links to chemical weapons or Osama bin Laden. The Government contested that the courts had jurisdiction to hear such complaints, and the cases proceeded on the assumption that the Sudanese owner's claims were true: that there were no links to terrorism or the production of chemical weapons.

---

[178] *Al-Alwi v Trump*, 587 US _ (2019) at 2.

[179] The six formulations that could point to a political question are set out in *Baker v Carr*, 369 US 186 (1962) 210 at 217.

[180] Address to the Nation on Military Action Against Terrorist Sites in Afghanistan and Sudan, 20 August 1998.

The judgments are interesting for the way they identify what are political questions: 'the President's extraterritorial enemy property designation'[181] and 'the merits of the President's decision to launch an attack on a foreign target'.[182] Essentially, the result is that there is no recourse to the US courts for a complaint that the President mistakenly destroyed property abroad as a target. There is some debate as to whether these issues really are covered by the political question doctrine, or are better described as operational decisions that the courts feel unwilling or unable to second guess.[183] What interests us here is the way the judges deal with the ideas discussed above: the concept of the enemy and the notion that action is justified as a fundamental incident of war.

The litigation has drawn critical commentary due to the repeated reference to an 'enemy property doctrine', as if this were an established precedent.[184] The Court of Appeals, dealing with the claim for the taking of property in violation of the Constitution, referred nine times to the 'enemy property doctrine'. The cases relied on by the Court involved: the destruction of property (belonging to US nationals) in the context of the destruction of a Nicaraguan city in 1854; the destruction of 13 bridges by the Union forces in Missouri in 1864 in the middle of the Civil War; and, more recently, the destruction of oil terminals in the Philippines in the context of Japanese troops advancing on Manila following the attack on Pearl Harbour in 1941. Such destruction

---

[181] *El-Shifa Pharm Indus v United States*, 378 F 3d (2004) 1346 at para 105; see also the case before the US Court of Federal Claims, *El-Shifa Pharm Indus v United States*, 55 Fed Cl 751 (2003) at 752, where it was held that 'the US Constitution's Fifth Amendment "just compensation" clause does not extend to claims arising out of the destruction of a purported enemy warmaking instrumentality through American military action'. The reasoning relies on the fact that those making the claims were 'enemies, not merely aliens' at 761, and that the property was 'an asserted enemy weapons factory' (ibid at 767). It was the logic that one does not pay for damage in war that seems to have driven that decision, and that 'as the President as Commander in Chief can conclusively designate by his actions a state of war, so he can also designate as Commander in Chief the identity of the enemy targets for the purposes of applying military force or engaging in combat activities' (ibid at 772). The war in question was considered against the backgrounds to the 1998 attacks on the US Embassies in Kenya and Tanzania by Al-Qaeda earlier in the same months that saw the attack on the pharmaceutical factory.

[182] *El-Shifa Phar Indus v United States*, 607 F 3d (2010) 836, No 0705174, at p 15.

[183] See in particular the separate opinions in the 2010 appeal *El-Shifa Pharma Ind v United States*, US F 3d 836: 'It is not the role of judges to second-guess, with the benefit of hindsight, another branch's determination that the interests of the United States call for military action.' Per Griffith at 844; and 'the Supreme Court has invoked the political question doctrine only in cases alleging violations of the Constitution. This is a statutory case. The Supreme Court has never applied the political question doctrine in a case involving alleged *statutory* violations. Never.' Per Kavanaugh at 856.

[184] Vladeck, 'Enemy Aliens, Enemy Property, and Access to the Courts', 11 *Lewis and Clark Law Review* (2007) 963–96; Tabacinic, 'The Enemy-Property Doctrine: A Double Whammy?', 62 *University of Miami Law Review* (2008) 601–23.

was said to be necessary in order that the oil and facilities should not fall into enemy hands. The US Army did compensate for the oil and transportation destroyed (but not for the actual facilities).

The concept of enemy property (as historically applied), however, came with a number of safeguards that allowed the enemy owners to have their assets unfrozen, or in many cases their vested property returned to them after the War by the Alien Property Custodian. Under this regime mistakes could certainly be challenged. This enemy property regime last operated in a full-scale total war with over 50 million deaths. The questions around the attack on the factory in Sudan are really nothing to do with the complex legal regime that allowed for the seizure of enemy property as part of an overall policy of defeating the enemy in a war such as the Second World War. It is this confusion that the present book is trying to lay bare. The targeting decisions may at a pinch be tangled up with operations involving something that looks like warfare, but this is something completely different from the arrangements for dealing with the seizure of the property of enemy aliens in time of a War such as the Second World War.

The Court refers back to the Constitution's reference to the functions of the Executive in time of war, and the derived implied incidents to the conduct of war that were said to ground the President's right to detain, prosecute and execute saboteurs and spies in the *Quirin* case. Now, 60 years later, this incidental Wartime power to detain and prosecute would be expanded to an incidental power to destroy property without compensation when tackling a new enemy: Al-Qaeda:

In exercising the power to wage war, the President finds authorization in the Constitution itself to 'direct the performance of those functions which may constitutionally be performed by the military arm of the nation in time of war.' *Ex parte Quirin*, 317 US at 28, 63 S Ct 1. Within these functions are 'important incident[s] to the conduct of war' such as 'the adoption of measures by the military command ... to repel and defeat the enemy. . . .' *Id.*[185]

It is, according to the Court, the Commander in Chief's designation of targets that is actually unreviewable: 'In our view, the President's power to wage war must also necessarily include the power to make extraterritorial enemy property designations because such designations are also an important incident

---

[185] *El-Shifa Pharm Indus v United States* 378 F 3d (2004) 1346 at 1363.

to the conduct of war.[186] And it is the framing of the fight as *waging war* that justifies the widest ambit of what may be destroyed:

> The cases teach that the purpose of such designations is almost always to 'repel and defeat the enemy' by diminishing the sum of material resources it has at its disposal to prosecute hostilities against the United States and its citizens. Whether the private property destroyed as enemy property is a tank firing rounds at American forces, a bridge the enemy finds necessary to advance to the front, or a commodity, such as oil, imperiled by advancing forces, the aim is the same – to 'wage war successfully.'[187]

These ideas, drawn from the contexts of the Civil War (no compensation for destroyed bridges), the First World War (an implied Congressional power to 'wage war successfully'), and the Second World War (a decision, by a majority, to restrict rights to claim for destroyed facilities in the face of the oncoming Japanese Army), illustrate how Wartime law has permeated decision making that relates to precluding accountability for the use of force in situations, which, perhaps, should not be so quickly assimilated to these Wars.

The Wartime decision of the Supreme Court in 1952, concerning the destroyed property in the Philippines, contains one passage (which resonated in the *El-Shifi* Appeal[188]) that explains how the judiciary see destruction in war as the responsibility of war itself rather than that of any government:

> The terse language of the Fifth Amendment is no comprehensive promise that the United States will make whole all who suffer from every ravage and burden of war. This Court has long recognized that, in wartime, many losses must be attributed solely to the fortunes of war, and not to the sovereign.[189]

5.6   Treason

Treason in the United Kingdom is covered in part by the Treason Act 1351 (as amended), which contains the offences of levying 'War against our Lord the King in his Realm' and being 'adherent to the King's Enemies in his

---

[186] Ibid at 1364.
[187] Ibid.
[188] *El-Shifa Pharm Indus v United States* 378 F 3d (2004) 1346 at 1360.
[189] *United States v Caltex*, 344 US (1952) 149 at 156.

Realm, giving to them Aid and Comfort in the Realm, or elsewhere'. These are the two offences that have been the inspiration for the crimes of treason in other jurisdictions such as the United States: levying war against the state and aiding the enemy.

This ancient UK Act of Parliament includes other offences that are not related to war or even armed conflict, and thus a person is guilty of treason who:

- compasses or imagines the death of the Sovereign;
- compasses or imagines the death of the King's wife or of the Sovereign's eldest child and heir;
- violates the King's wife or the Sovereign's eldest daughter unmarried or the wife of the Sovereign's eldest child and heir;
- endeavours to deprive or hinder any person who is next in succession to the Crown for the time being from succeeding after the demise of the Sovereign to the Crown and the dominions and territories belonging to the Crown and attempts the same maliciously, advisedly and directly by overt act or deed; or, knowing such offence to be done, is an abettor, procurer and comforter of the offender;
- slays the chancellor, treasurer, or the king's justices, being in their places, doing their offices.[190]

The offence of treason requires not only the act of treason, but also allegiance owed to the Sovereign.[191] According to *Halsbury's Laws of England*, this covers not just British citizens everywhere but also residents and some alien enemies:

> Natural allegiance is due from all British citizens at all times wherever they may be; local allegiance is owed by an alien under the protection of the Crown so long as he is resident within the realm and by a resident alien who goes abroad leaving his family or effects within the realm or goes abroad in possession of a British passport. An alien enemy may also be convicted of treason if has accepted British protection during a war. An ambassador

---

[190] *Halsbury's Laws of England*, vol 25 (2016) '7. Offences against the state or security', para 419 (footnotes omitted); the original Act is not in modern English and the *Halsbury* enumeration is widely used. Geoffrey Robertson QC seems to have considered that James Hewitt, the lover of Princess Diana, was 'bang to rights' and could have been prosecuted and executed in 1995 for adultery with the wife of the Monarch's heir: *Rather His Own Man: In Court with Tyrants, Tarts and Troublemakers* (London: Biteback, 2019) at 303.

[191] See *Joyce v DPP* [1946] AC 347, 365 per Lord Jowitt LC, 'An act, it is said, which is treasonable if the actor owes allegiance, is not treasonable if he does not.'

who is not a subject of the state to which he is accredited does not owe any temporary allegiance to that state.[192]

It is assumed that an enemy prisoner of war on British territory could not be prosecuted for treason against the United Kingdom.[193] During the Second World War, the Treachery Act 1940 allowed for the prosecution and execution of those who had secretly entered the country to commit acts of sabotage and were therefore considered to owe no allegiance. Over a dozen people were tried and executed, including German, Dutch, Swiss and Belgian nationals. The crime was defined in section 1 of the 1940 Act as follows:

> If, with intent to help the enemy, any person does, or attempts or conspires with any other person to do, any act which is designed or likely to give assistance to the naval, military or air operations of the enemy, to impede such operations of His Majesty's forces, or to endanger life, he shall be guilty of felony and shall on conviction suffer death.

The convicted saboteurs were mostly rather ill-prepared to go incognito in Britain at that time. One aroused suspicion by entering a pub at breakfast time and ordering a type of champagne cider that had not been available for years. He was tried for treachery at the Central Criminal Court and hanged.[194] Josef Jakobs parachuted in with a radio and civilian clothes under his flying suit.[195] He broke his ankle on leaving the plane and hurt his leg on landing. He surrendered and was prosecuted for treachery, in that he descended by parachute with intent to help the enemy. He was convicted and executed by firing squad at the Tower of London, as it seems he was considered a member of the enemy's armed forces and so treated to a firing squad rather than being hanged like the others convicted of treachery at that time.

The case-law concerning treason consistently confines 'levying war' to acts of insurrection. In one definition it encompasses 'armed resistance made on political grounds to the public order of the realm'. The Law Commission quotes approvingly from a major treatise:

---

[192] *Halsbury's Laws of England* (n 190) at para 420 (footnotes omitted). For misprision of treason, treason felony, assaults on the Sovereign and contempt of the Sovereign, see ibid paras 421–425. See also the Treason Act 1842 and the Treason Felony Act 1848.

[193] Law Commission 'Working Paper 72: Treason, Sedition and Allied Offences' (1977) at 22 fn 17.

[194] Storey, *Beating the Nazi Invader* (2020) at 97.

[195] Ibid at 134–38; and for details, see the blog prepared by his granddaughter at http://www.josefjakobs.info/p/blog-page.html

'War', here, is not limited to the true 'war' of international law, but will include any foreseeable disturbance that is produced by a considerable number of persons, and is directed at some purpose which is not of a private but of a 'general' character, eg to release the prisoners in *all* the gaols.[196]

So the concept of war here is used neither in the technical sense of a State of War between states, nor in the sense of a material war between states, nor even in the sense of a civil war or armed conflict of any kind. Levying war here means threatening the general policies or laws of the state through a show of force. It differs from riot in that the demand is general rather than with regard to a specific perceived injustice.[197] Treason was considered so serious that the penalty was death, and for a while a particularly gruesome, prolonged form of execution involving dragging the prisoner to the gallows, partially hanging him (women were to be burned), then disembowelling him, beheading him and cutting the body into four quarters. The pieces were then put on public display.[198] The exceptional forms of execution were generally abolished by 1870. Nevertheless, it was often difficult to secure convictions for treason due to the harsh penalties, which, in addition to the death penalty, involved forfeiting to the Crown all assets, including houses and land.

As we saw in Chapter 1, the Indian Penal Code has adapted the idea of treason and includes in its Penal Code the offence of 'waging war' against India. India prosecuted these crimes in the context of various terrorist attacks. With regard to the attacks on hotels in Mumbai, the Appellate Court stated:

> Thus, to constitute offence of 'waging war', it is not necessary that any particular number of persons is necessary. The mode and the manner of waging war is not defined. The war contemplated by this offence is not necessarily a traditional war. There need not be a declaration of war. Two countries may not be at war involving conventional military operations. A stealthy operation carried out by the terrorists to strike terror and to overwhelm the armed or other personnel can amount to waging war. Certain terrorist acts do fall within the ambit of the term 'waging war'. The intention of perpetrators to strike at the sovereign authority of the State is important. The

---

[196] Law Commission, 'Working Paper 72' (n 193) at 11, quoting *Kenny's Outline of Criminal Law* (original emphasis).

[197] *Kenny's Outline of Criminal Law*, 18th edn (1962) at para 406; for some of the contentious cases and the borderline with riot, see *Kenny's Outline of Criminal Law*, 5th edn (1911) Ch VII.

[198] More details are to be found in *Kenny's* 18th edn (n 197) at para 419.

purpose must be intended to be achieved by use of force and arms in defiance of armed and other security personnel. Even a limited number of persons who carry powerful explosives and missiles without regard to their own safety can cause more devastating damage and that will manifest their intention to wage war. If such desperadoes hold the Government at ransom, by keeping foreign nationals as hostages and try to dictate terms to the Government that would amount to waging war. Places where the attackers launch the attack are also an indication of this offence. If a public place like a railway station which is under the Central Government's command is attacked, if hotels in which foreign nationals stay are attacked, if people particularly foreign nationals are kept hostages so as to bring the Government down on its knees, that would amount to waging war. It is not necessary that the object of the perpetrators should be to overthrow the existing Government and substitute it with other authority. Even foreign nationals who do not owe allegiance to the Government can be held guilty of waging war. It is the intention to imperil the safety of the people to destabilize the Government with use of force, it is the intention to make the Government helpless by adopting devious means such as keeping people as hostages so that it would succumb to the illegal demands of the perpetrators which gives the offence the character of the offence of 'waging war'.[199]

Turning to the *aiding the enemy* offence of treason in the UK Treason Act 1351, this refers to an actual State of War as understood in international law and throughout this book. The Law Commission is clear: 'The meaning of "enemies" here is to be taken in the strict sense which international law gives the word and depends upon the existence of a state of war'.[200] A case might turn on whether the defendant knew about a Declaration of War.[201] The mental element is 'an intention to aid an enemy contrary to the defendant's duty of allegiance'.[202]

---

[199] *The State of Maharashtra v Mohammed Ajmal Mohammad Amir Kasab @ Abu Mujahid,* Confirmation Case No 2 of 2010 in Sessions Case No 175 of 2009, Criminal Appellate Jurisdiction Bombay, 21 February 2011, at para 571.

[200] 'Working Paper 72' (n 193) at para 24.

[201] Ibid at paras 26–27, referencing *R v Ahlers* [1915] 1 KB 616, where the jury did not believe that the German Consul in Sunderland (a British national) did not know that War had been declared. In making a proposal for a new crime of treason in 'time of war', the Commission explains (at para 55) that 'A person who, for example, is living on a remote island and does not know war has broken out would not have the required intent to aid the enemy'.

[202] 'Working Paper 72 (n 193) at para 29.

The last person to be tried for treason in the UK was William Joyce (aka Lord Haw-Haw), an American citizen, resident in Britain, who, having obtained a British passport (by lying about his status), travelled to Germany in 1939 and during the Second World War was employed by the German radio company of Berlin, where (according to the count in the indictment) he broadcasted 'to the subjects of our Lord the King propaganda on behalf of the said enemies of our Lord the King'.[203] He was hanged for High Treason in 1946.

Recently, in the light of British nationals going to fight for the so-called 'Islamic state' and other groups, there have been suggestions to decouple the aiding-the-enemy head of treason from the idea of a public War between states, and to create a new offence 'to aid a state or organisation that is attacking the UK or preparing to attack the UK or against which UK forces are engaged in armed conflict'.[204] The advocates for such a development point to developments in other states, such as Canada, Australia and New Zealand.

According to Canada's Criminal Code:

46 (1) Every one commits high treason who, in Canada . . .
(b) levies war against Canada or does any act preparatory thereto; or
(c) assists an enemy at war with Canada, or any armed forces against whom Canadian Forces are engaged in hostilities, whether or not a state of war exists between Canada and the country whose forces they are.

This last offence would seem to be limited (outside War) to assistance to the forces of another state and would not necessarily cover assistance to an armed non-state actor.[205] The Code also adopts the concept of 'alien enemy', and adapts it, making it an offence to assist 'an alien enemy to leave Canada'. The alien enemy is with reference back to the elements of treason as a subject of (i) a state that is at war with Canada, or (ii) a state against whose forces Canadian Forces are engaged in hostilities, whether or not a state of war exists between Canada and the state whose forces they are.[206]

---

[203] *Joyce v DPP* (n 191) at 348. For a study of two other 20th-century treason trials, see Weale, *Patriot Traitors: Roger Casement, John Amery and the Real Meaning of Treason* (2001).
[204] See Ekins, Hennessey, Mahmood and Tugendhat, *Aiding the Enemy: How and Why to Restore the Law of Treason* (2018) at 6; on 11 May 2021 the Government announced in the context of the Queen's Speech and a future Counter-State Threats Bill that 'We are also considering whether there is a case to be made for criminalizing other harmful activity conducted by and on behalf of states, including the consideration of updating treason laws.'
[205] See also Elkins et al (n 204) at 23.
[206] Criminal Code of Canada, s 50.

The Australian Criminal Code Act (as amended in 2018) states that a person commits the offence of treason if 'a party (the *enemy*) is engaged in armed conflict involving the Commonwealth or the Australian Defence Force' and the enemy is declared in a Proclamation made by the Governor-General.[207] A separate question arose under Australian law with regard to whether sedition requires a war. The Australian Communist newspaper *The Tribune* was convicted of sedition on the basis of various articles published concerning the hostilities in Korea. The publisher appealed against the conviction, arguing that the articles could not be seditious if the war in Korea was illegal. He claimed it was illegal due to the absence of the Soviet Union from the Security Council at the time of the vote. After hearing from the Australian Foreign Office, the Court held that Australia was 'at war with Korea, whether it is a *de facto* war or some other kind of conflict'.[208]

New Zealand's Crimes Act 1961 provides:

> Every one owing allegiance to the Sovereign in right of New Zealand commits treason who, within or outside New Zealand
>
> . . .
>
> (b) levies war against New Zealand; or
>
> (c) assists an enemy at war with New Zealand, or any armed forces against which New Zealand forces are engaged in hostilities, whether or not a state of war exists between New Zealand and any other country; or
>
> (d) incites or assists any person with force to invade New Zealand; or
>
> (e) uses force for the purpose of overthrowing the Government of New Zealand . . .[209]

The trend in these Commonwealth countries seems to be away from premising the aiding-the-enemy element of treason on a State of War. Nevertheless, the idea of an enemy is drawn quite strictly, and would seem to be limited to declared enemies or a particular identified armed force.

The idea of treason as rebellion is also prevalent in various constitutions, and remains very relevant as states use treason or sedition charges to suppress varying forms of dissent. Recently, the concept of treason as 'levying war in the realm' has been used to argue for extradition from Scotland to Spain of Professor Ponsatí in connection with her role in the Catalan referendum. The

---

[207] Australian Criminal Code Act, ss 80.1.AA and 80.1AB (original emphasis).
[208] *Burns v The King* [1951] ILR 596, 598.
[209] Crimes Act 1961, s 73.

Prosecution argued that treason is the equivalent, for double criminality purposes, of the Spanish charges of rebellion.[210]

In the United States, the definition of treason in the US Code reads:

> Whoever, owing allegiance to the United States, levies war against them or adheres to their enemies, giving them aid and comfort within the United States or elsewhere, is guilty of treason and shall suffer death, or shall be imprisoned not less than five years and fined under this title but not less than $10,000; and shall be incapable of holding any office under the United States.[211]

Congressional power over the definition of treason is limited by the Constitution.[212] The Constitution cut out the most brutal and draconian aspects of punishment for treason under English law and introduced some procedural protections. The case-law on the two types of treason carried over from England mirrors the scope of these crimes under English law explained above. Charles Warren put it succinctly:

> [T]reason by levying war is more generally committed in internal insurrections directed against the government by persons in the United States; whereas giving aid and comfort is generally committed in connection with a war waged against the United States by a foreign power.[213]

Allegiance is a necessary element for both forms of treason, but is again defined broadly, and the notion of obedience is often included. So it has been stated at the level of the Supreme Court that every foreigner 'residing in a country owes to that country allegiance and obedience to its laws so long as he remains in it.'[214]

---

[210] BBC, 'Ancient treason law to be used in Clara Ponsati extradition case', 5 July 2018, at https://www.bbc.com/news/uk-scotland-scotland-politics-44726376; the case is suspended at the time of writing in order to resolve the question of the Professor's immunity as an MEP.

[211] 18 US Code § 2381.

[212] See also Art III of the US Constitution and Larson, *On Treason: A Citizen's Guide to the Law* (2020); Crane, 'Did the Court Kill the Treason Charge?: Reassessing *Cramer v United States* and Its Significance', 36 *Florida State University Law Review* (2009) 635–96.

[213] 'What is Giving Aid and Comfort to the Enemy?', 27 *Yale Law Journal* (1918) 331–47 at 332.

[214] Justice Field delivering the opinion of the Supreme Court in *Carlisle v United States*, 83 US 147 (1872) at 155, quoting Secretary of State Webster from 1851, and cited by Warren (n 213) at 346–47. The elements from the two types of treason are sometimes confused in the United States due to the cases concerning both types of treason that relate to the Civil War, which was considered a State of War under international law due to the recognition of Belligerency (see section 6.4 below).

The fascinating history of treason trials in the United States is engagingly told by Carlton Larson. He recounts how Jefferson Davis, the President of the Confederate States, avoided prosecution for treason as he had already been punished enough through exclusion from office, how John Brown's attempt to trigger a slave revolt with an assault on the federal arsenal in Virginia led to his trial for treason and execution by hanging, and how resistance to the return of slaves under the Fugitive Slave Act was not in the end found to constitute treason, the Judge finding 'that the term "levying war" should be confined to insurrections and rebellions for the purpose of overturning the government by force and arms'.[215]

No one has been successfully prosecuted for treason in the United States since the cases that relate to the Second World War. In 2005, however, an American member of Al-Qaeda was indicted for treason. Adam Gadahn (aka Azzam al-Amriki) was charged that he, 'owing allegiance to the United States, knowingly adhered to an enemy of the United States, namely, al-Qaeda, and gave al-Qaeda aid and comfort, within the United States and elsewhere, with intent to betray the United States'.[216] It was alleged he had appeared in an Al-Qaeda video and made a number of statements, including saying:

People of America . . . you too shall pay the price for the blood that has been spilled. . . . I remind you of the weighty words of our leaders Sheik Usama bin Laden and Doctor Ayman al-Zawahiri that what took place on September 11th was but the opening salvo of the global war on America. . . . The magnitude and ferocity of what is coming your way will make you forget all about September 11th.[217]

---

[215] , Larson, *On Treason* (n 212) at 78–79 quoting Justice Grier in the trial of Castner Hanway in 1951; see, for a full range of case-law, Larson, 'The Forgotten Constitutional Law of Treason and the Enemy Combatant Problem', 154 *University of Pennsylvania Law Review* (2006) 863–926; for the separate crimes of rebellion and insurrection see 18 US Code § 2383 'Whoever incites, sets on foot, assists, or engages in any rebellion or insurrection against the authority of the United States or the laws thereof, or gives aid or comfort thereto, shall be fined under this title or imprisoned not more than ten years, or both; and shall be incapable of holding any office under the United States.' See also Section 3 of the 14th Amendment to the Constitution. President Trump was impeached for 'incitement of insurrection' by the House of Representatives on 13 January 2021. The Senate voted on 13 February 2021 by 57 to 43 to convict, but 67 votes were needed for a conviction, so the judgment of the Senate was that Trump was acquitted on the one charge of incitement of insurrection.

[216] Indictment available at https://www.justice.gov/sites/default/files/opa/legacy/2006/10/11/adam_indictment.pdf.

[217] Ibid.

Gadahn was never tried as he was killed (along with an American and an Italian hostage) in a US drone strike in 2015 on an Al-Qaeda compound.[218]

As a last example of treason charged in recent times, let us consider the case of the former Argentinian President, Cristina Fernandez de Kirchner (2007–15), her Foreign Minister, and other former officials and allies. In 2017 they were charged, *inter alia*, with treason.[219] They were accused of 'uniting' with Iran to undermine a criminal investigation into the suicide bombing of the building of the Argentine Israelite Mutual Association (AMIA) in Buenos Aires. The attack killed 85 people and injured 300 others.

The Constitution of Argentina provides in Article 119:

> Treason against the Nation shall only consist in rising in arms against it, or in joining its enemies, supplying them with aid and assistance. Congress shall by a special law determine the punishment for this crime; but the penalty shall not extend beyond the person of the convicted, nor shall this dishonor be transmitted to relatives of any degree.

The Criminal Code defines the crime of treason in Article 214.[220] This would cover any Argentine or person who owes allegiance to the country due to their employment or public function, who takes up arms against the nation, or unites with its enemies or gives them help or assistance.

At first instance the judge found the Declaration of War had fallen into desuetude since the Second World War. He noted that there had been no Declarations of War for Korea and Viet Nam, and that, as concerns Argentina, there had been no Declaration of War since 1945. He went on to say that with regard to the Malvinas (Falkland Islands), Argentina occupied the islands in 1982

---

[218] 'Americans Warren Weinstein and Adam Gadahn Killed in US Drone Strikes', NBC News, 23 April 2015, at https://www.nbcnews.com/news/us-news/warren-weinstein-adam-gadahn-killed-u-s-operation-n346861. Larson suggests that had Gadahn been tried, 'his lawyers would have objected that aiding a terrorist group cannot amount to treason': *On Treason* (n 212) at 197.

[219] See Center of Judicial Information, 'Resolution of Judge Bonadio regarding the indictment with pre-trial detention of Cristina Kirchner in the case of the complaint presented by Nisman about the memorandum with Iran' at https://www.cij.gov.ar/nota-28791-Resoluci-n-del-juez-Bonadio-que-dispuso-el-procesamiento-con-prisi-n-preventiva-de-Cristina-Kirchner-en-la-causa-por-la-denuncia-de-Nisman-por-el-memor-ndum-con-Ir-n.html, 7 December 2017.

[220] Será reprimido con reclusión o prisión de diez a veinticinco años o reclusión o prisión perpetua y en uno u otro caso, inhabilitación absoluta perpetua, siempre que el hecho no se halle comprendido en otra disposición de este código, todo argentino o toda persona que deba obediencia a la Nación por razón de su empleo o función pública, que tomare las armas contra ésta, se uniere a sus enemigos o les prestare cualquier ayuda o socorro.

without any prior notice, and it 'would not be credible for someone to question legally the status of war between the United Kingdom and Argentina'.[221]

The Appeals Court revoked the treason charges. It stated that the crime of treason required a State of War declared by the Argentine National Congress, or a belligerent response from the Argentinian Government:

> One of the parties to the dispute (the victims' lawyer (*querella*)) has since the beginning of the dispute sought that the case be qualified as 'treason' (Art 214 of the Criminal Code). In addressing this issue, the lower-level judge opted for a favourable view of that position, after carrying out an interpretation of the normative requirements in the law.
>
> We will adopt a different interpretation.
>
> Indeed, the idea of uniting or giving support or providing any help or assistance to the *enemies of the nation* presupposes, on the view of this tribunal, a status of exterior or international war.
>
> And the declaration of war – through a formal act or through certain actions – is trusted, under the National Constitution, to the political powers, who have the sole power to take any decision regarding its initiation or duration. This issue is foreign to any interference or analysis by courts of justice.
>
> That said, the case does not fit into the discussed criminal definition, since, even if one would consider that the terrorist attack against the AMIA fits within the concept of 'aggression' (an idea widely discussed by the lower-level judge), the fact is that the response by Argentina's political powers was not belligerent.[222]

[221] Decision of Judge Bonadio, 6 December 2017, at 274 (author's translation) ['sin embargo en Malvinas (1982) Argentina ocupó las islas sin ningún tipo de aviso previo y no es creíble que alguien cuestione jurídicamente el estado de guerra entre el Reino Unido y Argentina'] available at Justice Information Centre (Centro de Información Judicial) at https://www.cij. gov.ar/nota-28791-Resoluci-n-del-juez-Bonadio-que-dispuso-el-procesamiento-con-prisi-n-preventiva-de-Cristina-Kirchner-en-la-causa-por-la-denuncia-de-Nisman-por-el-memor-ndum-con-Ir-n.html.

[222] I am grateful to Juan Pappier for bringing this case to my attention and for his translation from the Spanish of this part of the ruling at p 37 (original emphasis), available from the Centro de Información Judicial at https://www.cij.gov.ar/nota-28956-La-C-mara-Federal-ratific--el-procesamiento-y-prisi-n-preventiva-de-Cristina-Kirchner-en-la-causa-por-la-denuncia-de-Nisman-por-el-memor-ndum-con-Ir-n.html.

5.7 A Word of Warning about Inherent War Powers

In closing this long chapter, the warning from Justice Jackson of the US Supreme Court bears repeating:

> The Solicitor General lastly grounds support of the seizure upon nebulous, inherent powers never expressly granted, but said to have accrued to the office from the customs and claims of preceding administrations. The plea is for a resulting power to deal with a crisis or an emergency according to the necessities of the case, the unarticulated assumption being that necessity knows no law.
>
> Loose and irresponsible use of adjectives colors all non-legal and much legal discussion of presidential powers.
>
> 'Inherent' powers, 'implied' powers, 'incidental' powers, 'plenary' powers, 'war' powers and 'emergency' powers are used, often interchangeably and without fixed or ascertainable meanings.[223]

---

[223] *Youngstown Sheet & Tube Co v Sawyer*, 343 US (1952) 579 at 646–47; Jackson also highlighted that Congress should control any use of the war powers when it came to domestic policy (ibid at 644). This was picked up by the Court of Appeals in *El-Shifa*, 378 F 3d (2004) 1346 at 1369, where the Court surmised that the outcome of that case (refusing to allow a claim for damage for the mistaken destruction of the pharmaceutical factory) 'might have been different if the appellants' property were located within the borders of the State rather than in Sudan'.

6

Triggering the International Law of Armed Conflict

The next four chapters deal with the application of the law of armed conflict to the actual conduct of war. This is often known as the *jus in bello*. This international law applies to all parties to the conflict, whether they consider themselves to be fighting a just war or not. This law applies whether or not the conflict is accepted as having given rise to a State of War. The threshold for triggering the modern international law of armed conflict is not set out in the treaties. In the past this law of war obviously applied when states were in a State of War, and the rules came to be applied in the American Civil War. But today the situation is complicated, not only because the treaties provide little guidance, but also because states may wish to deny that the law of armed conflict applies to their operations, or that armed groups have taken control of territory. Moreover, where an armed conflict qualifies as an armed conflict between states, captured armed forces will be entitled to prisoner of war status and to be released at the end of the conflict. In all situations where the international law of armed conflict applies, certain violations will constitute war crimes (although the list of war crimes for international armed conflicts is longer than for non-international ones). So the legal consequences of triggering the threshold for the application of this international law can be significant. One needs to determine: first, what kind of conflict we are dealing with; and, second, what the appropriate threshold of violence is that would trigger the law of armed conflict for such an armed conflict.[1]

I think for present purposes seven different situations can be helpfully separated out:

---

[1] These questions have generated a huge amount of doctrine and analysis: Wilmshurst (ed), *International Law and the Classification of Conflicts* (2012) 117–45; Zamir, *Classification of Conflicts in International Humanitarian Law: the Legal Impact of Foreign Intervention in Civil Wars* (2017); Lubell, 'Fragmented Wars: Multi-Territorial Military Operations against Armed Groups', 93 *International Law Studies* (2017) 215–50; Kleffner, 'The Legal Fog of an Illusion: Three Reflections on "Organization" and "Intensity" as Criteria for the Temporal Scope of the Law of Non-International Armed Conflict', 95 *International Law Studies* (2019) 161–78.

1. Declared War.
2. Armed conflicts between states.
3. Belligerent occupation.
4. Recognized Belligerencies.
5. National Liberation Movements under Additional Protocol I.
6. Non-international armed conflicts.
7. Conflicts involving forces under UN command and control where the United Nations is as a party to the conflict.

6.1 Declared Wars

Today neither a Declaration of War, nor war in the material sense is a necessary condition for the application of the laws of war (also known as the law of armed conflict (LOAC), or international humanitarian law (IHL)).[2] Even where older treaties on the laws and customs of war on land state that the treaty is 'only binding on the Contracting Powers, in case of war between two or more of them',[3] today the rules in such treaties are applied to all armed conflicts between states, and the equivalent customary international law does not require that the armed conflict counts as a War.[4]

---

[2] The choice of which phrase to use may reflect the personal appreciation of the purpose of this branch of international law. For example, Dinstein, *Non-International Armed Conflicts in International Law* (2014) at 3 explains that in his books, he prefers references to the law of armed conflict, as it has 'dispassionate connotations' and 'avoids a false impression (implicit in the "humanitarian limb" of IHL) that the rules governing non-international armed conflict hostilities are *de rigueur*, humanitarian in nature. It is an irrefutable fact that, even though humanitarianism is always a consideration, many of these rules are engendered primarily by military necessity.' He has also explained that 'The use of the adjective "humanitarian" occasionally misleads the uninitiated to confuse IHL with human rights law.' Dinstein, *The Conduct of Hostilities under the Law of International Armed Conflict*, 3rd edn (2016) at 20. Solis suggests that 'civilians' refer to the law of armed conflict as international humanitarian law: *The Law of Armed Conflict: International Humanitarian Law in War* (2010) at xxix. Military manuals tend to present all these expressions as synonymous: see, eg, US Department of Defense, *Department of Defense Law of War Manual* (2016) at para 1.3.1.2 UK Ministry of Defence, *The Manual of the Law of Armed Conflict* (2004) at para 1.2.
[3] Eg Laws and Customs of War on Law (Hague II, 1899) Art 2.
[4] See UK *Manual* (n 2) at 28–29; US *Manual* (n 2) at 79–82; Kalshoven and Zegveld, *Constraints on the Waging of War: An Introduction to International Humanitarian Law*, 4th edn (2011) 30–32; Dinstein, *International Armed Conflict* (n 2) 20–22. We suggested, however, in Ch 2 that in order to trigger the obligations of Neutral Status under treaties such as Hague (1907) V and XIII, it maybe that the non-participating state would have to consider the armed conflict a War and declare a that it has Neutral Status. When it comes to the 1907 Hague Conventions VI and XI concerning capture of merchant ships, it may be that they would only be applied in time of a formal State of War or an inter-state conflict of certain intensity and duration; see Ch 8 below for a full discussion of the appropriateness of continuing the idea of capture of merchant ships in Naval economic warfare as a question of Belligerent Rights.

As we have seen, states and international organizations have been keen, for different reasons, to avoid describing various conflicts as Wars. But this was not really to avoid the protective law that we are now interested in. States wanted to be able to continue to trade and import and export arms without fear of breaching rules regarding to Neutral Status. Organizations such as the League of Nations did not want to qualify a conflict as War, only to then seem to everyone be impotent to stop it under their new arrangements designed to impose sanctions on those who resort to War.[5]

It would be misleading to suggest that Japan, in denying the existence of War with China in 1937, was simply seeking to avoid the obligations found in the law of war treaties that protected prisoners of war and those under occupation. In fact, by the beginning of 1942 Japan had agreed to apply the relevant Prisoner of War Convention (which it had not ratified) with regard to American, British, Canadian and New Zealand prisoners of war, even extending it to civilian internees in order to gain reciprocal advantages for the protection of captured or interned Japanese.[6] In any event, the Tokyo Tribunal applied the laws of war to the killing and mistreatment of prisoners of war and civilians.[7] The situation with regard to the denial of War is more complex than any apparent wish to avoid constraints on how the enemy should be treated.

The issues emerge in the proceedings in Tokyo at the International Military Tribunal for the Far East. Two defendants told the Tribunal that 'it was officially decided in 1938 to continue to call the war in China an "Incident" and to continue for that reason to refuse to apply the rules of war to the conflict'.[8] Judge Pal, from the Tokyo International Military Tribunal, who considered that the hostility between China and Japan in 1937 'cannot be denied the name of "war"',[9] sets out his speculations on why states chose to deny the existence of War:

---

[5] See Ch 3 above.

[6] Pritchard and Zaide (eds), *The Tokyo War Crimes Trial* (1981) vol 22 at 49,711–31.

[7] The Defence argued, therefore, that the Chinese troops who resisted the Japanese Army were not lawful combatants and could be treated as bandits. The Judgment refers to the inauguration of a 'ruthless campaign for the extermination of these "bandits"'. Pritchard and Zadie at 49,600-01. In addition, when fighting broke out in Mukden in 1932, over 2,700 civilians accused of harbouring bandits were machine-gunned or bayoneted to death. The 'Rape of Nanking' from 1937 was said by the Tribunal to involve the killing of 12,000 non-combatants in the first few days of occupation, and the rape of 20,000 women during the first month. Overall, the Judgment refers to an estimate of 200,000 civilians and prisoners of war murdered during the first six weeks of occupation.

[8] Ibid at 49,602.

[9] Ibid at 1,015.

Japan did not give the hostility the name 'war' perhaps because she thereby expected to elude the constraints of the Kellogg-Briand Pact, perhaps she thought that simply by omitting to issue a declaration it would be possible for her to avoid the opprobrium of waging war, and to avoid the duties imposed by international law for the conduct of war.

Japan says that she was anxious to localize the matter. Of course, it must be said that by not declaring the hostility to be war, Japan deprived herself of certain valuable rights of belligerency also, like rights of blockade, etc.

China also did not want to give the name of 'war' to this hostility before Japan became involved in war with the United States of America by her attack on Pearl Harbour.

China did not give it the name 'war' perhaps because she needed the assistance of the so-called neutral countries who were anxious to avoid being openly at war.

America also did not give it that name: perhaps because she desired to escape the disabilities of her neutrality legislation whereby the shipments of arms and munitions of war to belligerents were automatically forbidden. America certainly could have openly acknowledged a state of war.[10]

Since the Second World War, states have hesitated when it comes to declaring War or accepting that they are in a State of War. Again, this is not usually connected to any attempt to avoid the rules for the protection of victims of war. Rather this relates now to the reluctance to trigger the effects in national law that we discussed in the previous chapter. With regard to the Malvinas/Falklands conflict in 1982, the UK Government chose not to declare War to avoid the consequences for British citizens under the Trading with the Enemy Act and the general international opprobrium that would accompany any contemporary Declaration of War.[11]

A Declaration of War by one state against another will nevertheless still trigger the application of the law of armed conflict, even in the absence of hostilities. This is explicitly stated in the 1949 Geneva Conventions for the protection of war victims, and the 1954 Hague Convention on the Protection of Cultural Property in Armed Conflict.[12] It is also explicitly stated that

---

[10] Ibid at 1023–24.
[11] Fazal, *Wars of Law: Unintended Consequences in the Regulation of Armed Conflict* (2018) at 103–7; see also the statement by Speaker Foley with regard to the 1991 conflict with Iraq in section 5.1.1 above.
[12] See GCs (1949) Common Art 2, and Hague (1954) Art 18.

these treaties apply even if the State of War is not recognized.[13] Multiple other treaties, including those prohibiting certain weapons, incorporate this trigger of Declared War by referencing the key provision of the Geneva Conventions.[14] The relevant common paragraph in all four of the 1949 Geneva Conventions reads:

> In addition to the provisions which shall be implemented in peacetime, the present Convention shall apply to all cases of declared war or of any other armed conflict which may arise between two or more of the High Contracting Parties, even if the state of war is not recognized by one of them.[15]

The last uncontroversial Declaration of War with legal effect is sometimes said to be the one made by the Soviet Union on Japan on 8 August 1945.[16] However, references are often made to the insistence by Egypt that it considered it was at War with Israel when it came to certain matters related to the Suez Canal,[17] and the claim by Pakistan in 1965 that it was at War with India. But these instances have not led all outside decision-makers to consider that real Declarations of War had been issued with any legal effects beyond what would apply in any armed conflict.[18] Schindler's study concluded that 'State

---

[13] The Hague Convention is explicit that it applies even if the state of war is not recognized by 'one or more of' the states parties. The Geneva Conventions state that they apply 'even if the state of war is not recognized by one of them', but this has been interpreted as covering the situation where all states parties to the conflict deny that there is a war. Clapham, 'The Concept of International Armed Conflict', in Clapham, Gaeta and Sassòli (eds), *The 1949 Geneva Conventions: A Commentary* (2015) 3–26 at 5; ICRC, *Commentary on the First Geneva Convention*, 2nd edn (2016) (hereinafter *Commentary GC I* (2016)) at 213.

[14] See Additional Protocol (AP) I of 1977, Convention on Prohibitions or Restrictions on the Use of Certain Conventional Weapons Which May be Deemed to be Excessively Injurious or to Have Indiscriminate Effects (1980).

[15] Art 2 first para.

[16] Turns, 'The Law of Armed Conflict (International Humanitarian Law)' in Evans (ed), *International Law*, 5th edn (2018) 840–76 at 844, who suggests that 'the association of such declarations with the appearance of an unlawful use of force under the Charter, or an act of aggression, has led to the procedure becoming defunct'.

[17] Khadduri, 'Closure of the Suez Canal to Israeli Shipping', *Law and Contemporary Problems* (1968) 147–57; Avram, *The Evolution of the Suez Canal Status from 1869 up to 1956: A Historico-Juridical Study* (1958). See also Rosenne, 'Directions for A Middle East Settlement – Some Underlying Legal Problems', 33 *Law and Contemporary Problems* (1968) 44–67 at 52, writing from an avowedly Israeli perspective, who stated 'As a matter of principle we believe that the very existence of a state of war is utterly incompatible with membership in the United Nations and the obligations imposed by the Charter.' See further Baxter, *Humanizing the Laws of War: Selected Writings of Richard Baxter* (2013) at 198ff, for a discussion of the rights of Egypt in this context and the relevance of a state of war or peace.

[18] Schindler, 'State of War, Belligerency, Armed Conflict', in Cassese (ed), *The New Humanitarian Law of Armed Conflict* (1979) 3–20 at 9–11.

practice since 1945 shows that, in a state of war, third parties do not act in a different way than in an armed conflict.'[19] As we saw in the Preface, there have been significant references to 'Declarations of war' by Al-Qaeda and the so called 'Islamic state'. Any such declarations by armed groups are of no effect in terms of bringing into force the humanitarian law treaties under consideration in this chapter. For a declaration of war to trigger the 1949 Geneva Conventions, it would have to be a formal unilateral Declaration of War issued by the appropriate authority of a state declaring War on another state.

There is no particular form that that the Declaration of War need take, but political statements will not today be assumed to be the equivalent of a Declaration of War. In the Eritrea/Ethiopia Arbitration, the Commission rejected Eritrea's argument that a Resolution of the Ethiopian Council of Ministers and Parliament condemning the Eritrean invasion of the day before (12 May 1998) could be taken as a Declaration of War. Even though the Resolution made clear that Ethiopia would act in self-defence, the Commission stated that the essence of a Declaration of War 'is an explicit affirmation of a state of war between belligerents'.[20] Some would consider that a declaration of a Blockade could still count as an act of War, or trigger a State of War.[21] Leaders and politicians are often quoted as calling a situation war, complaining of 'acts of war', or even referring to being in 'a state of war',[22] but from a legal perspective such statements have rarely been found to have any legal effect.

The validity of a purported Declaration of War was considered in some detail in the 1976 Arbitral Award by Pierre Lalive in an arbitration in Geneva between an Indian cement company and the National Bank of Pakistan. The Bank argued that there was a 'State of War' between India and Pakistan due to the 'hostile acts of India in the form of an invasion'. And that, in addition, there had been a 'Declaration of War by the President of Pakistan' in a radio

---

[19] Ibid at 15.

[20] 26 RIAA, 19 December 2005, Partial Award, *Jus Ad Bellum – Ethiopia's Claims 1–8* at para 17.

[21] See section 8.2.1 below. See also ICRC, *Commentary GC I* (2016) (n 13) at para 223, suggesting that a declaration of air or naval blockade would be sufficient to create an armed conflict to which humanitarian law would apply. It is also worth noting that the French *Manuel de droit des conflits armés* (2012) states (at 27), without particular explanation, 'Le blocus est un acte de guerre'. Compare Heintschel von Heinegg, 'Naval Blockade', 75 *International Law Studies* (2000) 203–30 at 204; and similarly see 'Blockade', *MPEPIL* (2015) at para 5.

[22] For a suggestion that the North Korean leader had apparently declared war in 2013, see Casey-Maslen and Haines, *Hague Law Interpreted: The Conduct of Hostilities under the Law of Armed Conflict* (2018) at 27.

broadcast. Lalive found that the broadcast did not constitute a Declaration of War:

> In the official copy of this broadcast ... are to be found, inter alia – with a criticism of Indian 'aggression' and attack, which was made 'without a formal declaration of war' – the words 'We are at war' and a statement to the effect that Pakistan is invoking its right of self-defence under the UN Charter.
>
> Whether or not the facts or claims referred to in the broadcast are suf-ficient evidence that a 'state of war' came into existence, a distinct ques-tion remains: can the President's statement be considered as a 'declaration of war' ...? The answer, in my opinion, must be in the negative. In the words of a leading authority much relied upon by both parties (Oppenheim-Lauterpacht, *International Law*, Vol II, 7th ed, § 94, p 293), a declaration of war is:
>
> 'a communication by one State to another that the condition of peace between them has come to an end and a condition of war has taken place'.
>
> It is obvious that the President's speech of September 6, 1965, addressed to his 'dear countrymen' in no way was, or purported to be, a 'communica-tion' to India. The official text produced by the President, moreover, con-tains, neither in its title nor elsewhere, the terms 'declaration of war'.[23]

Although in the present context we are examining the possibility of a declared War triggering the 1949 Geneva Conventions and other treaties covering the law of armed conflict, Lalive's separate examination of whether there could nevertheless have been a 'State of War' in the post-UN Charter world is also worth examining. His reticence to finding a State of War explains in part the high threshold needed to assume a Declaration of War, or indeed to assume the existence of a War in the legal-technical sense:

> The *obligations* of both India and Pakistan under the Charter – a text which purports to prohibit or at least regulate the use of force – are bound to have *some* effect and *some* relevance upon the question whether a 'state of war' came into existence on September 6, 1965. This minimum effect may be described as follows: *in case of doubt* as to the answer to be given to that question, the answer should be negative rather than affirmative, for the

---

[23] *Dalmia Cement Ltd v National Bank of Pakistan*, 18 December 1976, 67 ILR 611 at 615–16 (paras 8 and 9).

existence of a state of war can certainly *not be presumed* between members of the UNO. On the contrary, it must be presumed, *in dubio*, that each Member State, if and when it is using force, intends to use it in a manner consistent with its obligations under the Charter (especially under article 2(4)).[24]

Lalive then turns to the legal argument and the words used by the President of Pakistan at the end of same radio broadcast examined above:

'*We are invoking the United Nations Charter to exercise our inherent rights of individual and collective self-defence recognised in Chapter VII of the Charter.*' It is clear that this right of self-defence can be exercised not only when an armed attack initiates a 'war' but also in cases of armed conflicts short of war. The fact that Pakistan referred to Article 51 of the UN Charter and, eventually, on September 21, 1965, complied with the Security Council Resolution on a cease-fire indicates that it did intend to fulfil its obligations and exercise its right of Member of the UNO. One is therefore tempted to draw the conclusion that, if any 'presumption' may be based on the use of force by the attacked State, it is a presumption rather against than in favour of the will to wage 'war', a presumption that self-defence will be limited and the use of force kept within the general limits of the Charter, pending action by the Security Council.[25]

A court may well follow Lalive's lead and presume that in most cases there is no War in the international legal sense, ambiguous declarations of war (or even claims about a state of war) being seen as extremely unlikely to be of legal effect in the contemporary world. In the present context, therefore, we should conclude that it is more likely that the law of armed conflict would be triggered by an actual conflict between states than by reference to a supposed declared War.

---

[24] Ibid at 619 (para 27) (original emphasis). The question under national law would most likely be decided by a binding certificate on the courts, issued by the Executive; Lalive discusses this and concludes that the English Common Law on this point would have been applicable in India and Pakistan, but held as an international arbitrator he was not bound to follow any certification. See also McNair and Watts, *The Legal Effects of War*, 4th edn (1966) at 457–58.

[25] *Dalmia Cement* (n 23) at 622–23 (para 41).

6.2 Armed Conflicts between States

The Geneva Conventions state, as we have seen, that they apply to 'any other armed conflict which may arise between two or more of the High Contracting Parties'. These Parties now include all UN member states, as well as the State of Palestine, the Holy See and the Cook Islands. We can conclude that these treaties are of universal application and would apply to any armed conflict between two or more such Parties. Other treaties with a more limited range of states parties will apply to armed conflicts between those states parties. So, for example, armed conflicts under Additional Protocol I include inter-state conflicts covered by the 1949 Geneva Conventions where both states are parties to this Protocol. In practice, some states may choose to apply this more protective regime to a conflict even where they are not bound to do so.[26] The customary international law of international armed conflict will also apply to any armed conflict between two or more states.[27]

The next question, then, is what constitutes an armed conflict in this context? We can afford to be brief: the short answer is that the threshold is low. Where there is an intention by one state to engage with force against another state, the humanitarian protections in the law of armed conflict will be triggered. So the first wounded or captured person will be covered by the relevant protective regime. On the other hand, it seems clear that mistakenly 'invading' a territory due to a GPS mix up, or drunken wanderings over the border, would not trigger an armed conflict.[28] I have sought to set out criteria elsewhere for understanding this threshold:

---

[26] So a state might chose to apply AP I in a conflict where the other party had not ratified the Protocol or made a declaration. It would seem that Australia applied AP I in determining what would constitute a lawful target in its conflict with Iraq in 2003 (Iraq was not a party to the treaty at that time); see Henderson (Flight Commander), *The Contemporary Law of Targeting* (2009) Ch 1; interestingly, the Swedish International Humanitarian Law Committee suggested that 'Above all, a state that has ratified the protocol should not too readily and categorically choose a line of non-application in relation to an adversary that has not ratified. The principle of reciprocity is intended to give reasonable protection against obvious military disadvantages (a "safety net"), not to be an unconditional mechanism for setting aside the provisions of the protocol.' Report reproduced in part in Sassòli, Bouvier and Quintin, *How Does Law Protect in War?* 3rd edn (2011) vol II, document 76, electronic version only, available at https://www.icrc. org/en/download/file/19456/icrc-0739-part-ii-vol-i.pdf. See also AP I Art 96(2), which allows for the application of the Protocol as a matter of law where a state that is not a party accepts and applies its provisions.

[27] See further Henckaerts and Doswald-Beck, *Customary International Humanitarian Law, vol 1: Rules* (2005).

[28] See eg Rogers, *Law on the Battlefield,* 3rd edn (2012) at 3, where he states 'an accidental border incursion by a military aircraft caused by navigational error would not amount to armed conflict'; ICRC, *Commentary GC I* (2016) (n 13) at para 241. And see more generally, for the factors that constitute an international armed conflict, paras 210–244.

For such low-level hostilities between states to trigger the application of the Geneva Conventions, one might take into account factors such as whether the use of force was undertaken by the military and targeted at the other state's military, or is harmful to the state or to those under its jurisdiction, the extent of the damage or casualties, the location of the incident (an attack on the territory of the state carrying particular significance), the level of control exercised over any non-state groups involved in the hostilities, and the significance of any target. This does not represent a scientific formula, but we can see that, for example, a deliberate and attributed attack on a single warship, even with no casualties, could trigger the application of the law of [international armed conflict], while a cross-border skirmish involving some over-excited customs officers may not. While the subjective approach of the two states concerned is not determinative, in many situations the admission that the incursion or damage was a mistake may resolve dubious cases.[29]

The problems in this area tend to turn less on whether the minimal threshold has been reached, and more on whether the actions of non-state armed groups operating in one state should be considered as under the control of another state so that the situation can be considered as part of an international armed conflict.[30] This is a controversial area, complicated by the fact that there may be overlapping conflicts, one between the two states and another between a state and an armed group.[31] Confusion arises because there

[29] Clapham, 'The Concept of International Armed Conflict' (n 13) at 16.

[30] For the purposes of international criminal law, the international criminal tribunals have developed a test, sometimes known as the 'overall control test', that suggests that once a state is in overall control of a non-state armed group engaged in an armed conflict in another state, this can trigger the application of the law of international armed conflict so that a wide set of war crimes come into play. This has not yet been adopted by the International Court of Justice for the test as to whether or not a state supporting an armed group can be accused of an armed attack (see Ch 4 above), nor as the test for attribution (see International Court of Justice, *Application of the Convention on the Prevention and Punishment of the Crime of Genocide (Bosnia and Herzegovina v. Serbia and Montenegro)*, Judgment of 26 February 2007, para 404 and see rule 4 below). For references to such internationalized conflicts in the context of international war crimes trials, see *Prosecutor v Bemba* ICC-01/05-01/08, 21 March 2016, at para 130. The Prosecutor facing the need to choose charges under international or non-international armed conflict for the purposes of a war crimes prosecution would seem to be more likely to consider the nature of the entities that are fighting than the doctrinal possibilities offered by the idea of conceiving such an 'internationalized' armed conflict. See the ICC Prosecutor in Prosecution's Closing Remarks, ICC-01/04-01/06, 1 June 2011, *Situation in the DRC, Prosecutor v Lubanga*, who states in such a context that the conflict is internationalized 'as long as sovereign nation States are opposed to each other' (at para 32) and '[t]he character of the conflict is to be determined by reference to the parties involved rather than the territory on which the conflict takes place' (at para 34).

[31] Some authors consider that at one point the conflicts merge into one single international armed conflict (see, eg, ICRC, *Commentary GC I* (2016) (n 13) at paras 265–273). See also

are, as we saw in Chapter 4, parallel rules determine the permissible reactions by one state to another state's support to an armed group. These depend on the type of support that is proffered.

Let me recall the separate rules:

1. The sending of armed groups into another state can be considered an act of aggression and an armed attack, generating the right to self-defence against the sending state.

2. Where the state is merely supporting an armed group fighting another state, this may be considered a use of force, but not an act of aggression; this would not be considered an armed attack, and there would be no right for the victim state to engage in the use of force against the other state in self-defence. The rationale is that one should not let states too easily claim the right to use force in self-defence.

3. Where the state engages in an armed conflict with such an armed group, the law of armed conflict for a non-international armed conflict should apply.[32]

4. Where a state is in effective control of, or instructing or directing, the operations of an armed group, and in the course of those operations the group or its fighters commit violations of international law, then those acts are attributable back to the state that bears international responsibility for such violations of international law.[33]

the detailed discussions in Sassòli, *International Humanitarian Law* (2019) (hereinafter *IHL*) at paras 6.13–6.21; Mačák, *Internationalized Armed Conflicts in International Law* (2018) Ch 3; Carron, 'When is a Conflict International? Time for New Control Test in IHL', 98 *IRRC* (2016) 1019–41; and see further Gill, 'Classifying the Conflict in Syria', 92 *International Law Studies* (2016) 353–80; Ferraro, 'The ICRC's Legal Position on the Notion of Armed Conflict Involving Foreign Intervening and on Determining the IHL Applicable to this Type of Conflict', 97 *IRRC* (2015) 1227–52; Milanovic and Hadzi-Vidanovic, 'A Taxonomy of Armed Conflict', in Henderson and White (eds), *Research Handbook on International Conflict and Security Law* (2013) 256–313.

[32] For further suggestions on how individuals should be treated in these complex proxy conflicts, see Clapham 'The Concept of International Armed Conflict' (n 13) at 17ff. There may also be an international armed conflict between two states, and for that conflict the laws of international armed conflict would apply. If the armed group is operating from occupied territory, the conflict between the occupier and the armed group will only be international if the armed group is fighting 'on behalf of the territorial government or in the exercise of a right to self-determination'. Prosecutor's Closing Remarks ICC ICC-01/04-01/06, 1 June 2011, *Situation in the DRC, Prosecutor v Lubanga* at para 50. See section 6.5 below.

[33] See *Military and Paramilitary Activities in and against Nicaragua (Nicaragua v USA)*, ICJ judgment of 27 June 1986, at paras 109 and 115; Art 8 of the ILC Articles on State Responsibility (2001); and *Case Concerning the Application of the Convention on the Prevention and Punishment of the Crime of Genocide (Bosnia and Herzegovina v Serbia and Montenegro)*, judgment of 26 February 2007, at para 400.

The modern and complex question concerns the situation where a state attacks an armed group in the territory of another state without that state's permission. One view holds that this can constitute an international armed conflict,[34] while this 'does not exclude the existence of a parallel non-international armed conflict between the intervening State and the armed group'.[35] Lubell stresses, however, that Article 2 of the Geneva Conventions applies to an armed conflict that 'arises between two or more' states. So he concludes that 'it is submitted that the notion of "between" still carries weight, as it can be understood as pointing to the combination of the objective and subjective aspects of belligerent intent and *animus belligerandi*'.[36] He, and others, such as Gill, would separate out cases where there was obviously an international armed conflict, 'due to the nature of the activities and the amount of harm caused',[37] from other uses of force directed against a non-state actor where there is no intent to engage the host state in an armed conflict. For Dinstein, 'The legal position is transformed only if States become entangled in combat with each other'.[38]

In sum, when an armed conflict arises between states, the amount of force necessary to trigger the international humanitarian law of armed conflict is low; one does not need to conceive of the inter-state violence as something that looks like war. This has a very meaningful rationale: from the outset the first wounded and captured benefit from the full legal protection offered by the Geneva Conventions. When it comes to the separate conflicts with armed groups, as we shall see, the threshold of violence for the application of the law of armed conflict may be higher. Separating out these conflicts is challenging not only for lawyers – the political dimension will play a real role.

Political leaders may prefer not to refer to an 'international armed conflict', let alone a 'war'. Lawyers working within ministries of defence nevertheless will usually be keen to accept that humanitarian law applies, not least for the protection it will offer their own side in the event of capture. Goodman, who worked as Special Counsel in the US Department of Defense, offers these pertinent insights:

---

[34] ICRC, *Commentary GC I* (2016) (n 13) at paras 237 and 262.

[35] Ibid at para 261.

[36] Lubell, 'Fragmented Wars: Multi-Territorial Military Operations against Armed Groups', 93 *International Law Studies* (2017) 215–50 at 236.

[37] Ibid at 233; and Gill, 'Classifying the Conflict in Syria', 92 *International Law Studies* (2016) 353–80 at 373, who lists a number of factors he considers are more persuasive than the issue of consent.

[38] Dinstein, *International Armed Conflict*, (n 2) at 36.

The Administration might be reluctant to admit these events amount to an armed conflict with Syria, because such an admission could lead to an uncontrolled escalation of hostilities. If the President walked out onto the Rose Garden tomorrow and announced that the United States was in an armed conflict with Syria, just imagine the results.

...

To say we are in an armed conflict, however, is not to say we are at war. The definition of an 'armed conflict', which preoccupies humanitarian lawyers who want to know if the Geneva Conventions apply, is not the same as the political state of affairs involved in 'war'. Remember even the detention of a single soldier would presumably be enough to trigger the protections of the POW [Prisoner of War] Convention, yet that is nowhere near a sufficient amount of force to be considered a war between two states. Indeed, as odd as it might sound to a policymaker, a detained soldier may properly be classified as a 'prisoner of war' even when there isn't a war.[39]

6.3 Belligerent Occupation

Armed resistance by government forces to an occupation by another state should be considered an international armed conflict. According to the Geneva Conventions, even where there is no armed resistance to an occupation, as long as the host state has not consented to the presence, the Geneva Conventions apply.[40] An occupation need not involve an invasion. Foreign forces that started out in another state with the consent of the host state could refuse to leave and then go on to establish an occupying force, triggering the application of the relevant international law of armed conflict. Occupation is defined by Article 42 of the 1907 Hague Regulations, which reads:

Territory is considered occupied when it is actually placed under the authority of the hostile army. The occupation extends only to the territory where such authority has been established and can be exercised.

---

[39] 'Is the United States Already in an "International Armed Conflict" with Syria?', 11 October 2016, available at https://www.justsecurity.org/33477/united-states-international-armed-conflict-syria/; and see the response by Gabor, 'Letter to the Editor: Not So Fast on Calling it an "Armed Conflict" Between the US and Syria', 13 October 2016, available at https://www.justsecurity.org/33546/letter-editor-fast-calling-armed-conflict-syria/.

[40] See Common Art 2 para 2 to the 1949 Geneva Conventions; Sassòli, *IHL* (n 31) at 6.22 et seq stresses that the Hague Regulations (1907) on occupied territory would also apply.

In recent times, consideration has been given to a state of occupation's continuing even where the occupying power remains outside the occupied territory yet remains in effective control.[41] The Prosecutor of the International Criminal Court considered in 2014 there 'is a reasonable basis upon which to conclude that Israel continues to be an occupying power in Gaza despite the 2005 disengagement'.[42] Among other things, she noted:

> Israel's exercise of control over border crossings, the territorial sea adjacent to the Gaza Strip, and the airspace of Gaza; its periodic military incursions within Gaza; its enforcement of no-go areas within Gaza near the border where Israeli settlements used to be; and its regulation of the local monetary market based on the Israeli currency and control of taxes and customs duties.[43]

6.4 Recognized Belligerency

Aside from the regimes established by the multilateral treaties, the laws of international armed conflict have been applied by states to conflicts that were fought against groups that were not considered nation states at that time. In the 19th century, when international law contained no specific rules for civil wars, the idea of recognizing as Belligerents the non-state party in a civil war meant that the international laws of war would apply to both parties. There were conditions for recognition, essentially that there was: (i) a 'civil war' with 'a state of general hostilities'; (ii) territory controlled by the non-state party to the conflict and with 'a measure of orderly administration' and (iii) observance of the 'rules of warfare' under a 'responsible authority'.[44]

Sivakumaran has detailed the various claims by entities, such as Franco's Nationalists, to a 'right' to be recognized as Belligerents with Belligerent Rights,[45] and yet it seems that recognition has been rarely granted by the state

---

[41] For a detailed look at the criteria for occupation in this context, see ICRC, *Commentary GC I* (2016) (n 13) at paras 285–341.

[42] 'Report on Situation on Registered Vessels of Comoros, Greece, and Cambodia', 6 November 2014, paras 25–29 at 29.

[43] Ibid at para 27.

[44] See Lauterpacht (ed), *Oppenheim's International Law: a Treatise (Disputes, War and Neutrality)*, 7th edn (1952) vol II at 249, discussed by Sivakumaran, *The Law of Non-International Armed Conflict* (2012) at 9–20.

[45] My use of capitals (upper case) is to show that the term 'Belligerent' is not just descriptive but refers to the type of entity that has Belligerent Rights and obligations that flow from that state recognition. The recognition turns a belligerent armed group into a Belligerent. An unrecognized armed group cannot claim the Belligerent Rights that a state enjoys. The same logic applies

fighting an insurgency. It is hard to see that there really is a right to be recognized as a Belligerent. It was more common for a state not associated with the conflict to act on their interests and recognize a belligerent entity in order to convert a civil war into an international War with rights and obligations for non-participating states which could thereby enjoy Neutral Status. Such a recognition, while it risked being seen as an unfriendly act, did not change the application of the law of armed conflict between the insurgents and the state they were fighting. So the laws of war regarding neutrality, search and seizure of contraband, even Prize Law, would apply between the insurgents and the recognizing state and its nationals, but not between the parties to the civil war.[46] In this area national courts are unlikely to have much room for discretion. For the English courts, a certificate relating to Belligerency (as for War, or Neutrality) would be issued by the Executive, and that would be binding on the court.[47]

Where things became famously dramatic was the Belligerency that was implied by President Lincoln's Blockade of Confederate ports in the American Civil War, which in turn allowed Great Britain to ensure its own rights related to its Neutral Status: ensuring goods carried on its neutral ships would be immune from seizure. As Witt explains, in his very engaging book *Lincoln's Code*, it seems clear that President Lincoln did not intend to recognize the Belligerency of the Southern States and apply the international laws of War to them; he only wanted to turn his closure of Southern ports into a 'Blockade', as that term was understood under international law. This was in order to mollify Great Britain and others who feared for the safety of their nationals under the criminal law covering port closures, and for their trade, as well as their access to the cotton and other goods exported from the Southern States.[48]

In Witt's telling, Lincoln assumed that the United States could apply the laws of War between itself and states such as Great Britain, and at the same

---

to the capitalization of 'War' and 'Blockade'. It is the status that these institutions have under international law that gives rise to rights and obligations. A *de facto* war or blockade would not have the same legal effects.

[46] 'When the insurgents are sufficiently well organized, conduct hostilities according to the laws of war, and have a determinate territory under their control, they may be recognized as belligerents whether or not the parent state has actually or impliedly recognized that status, as by establishing a maritime blockade against ports under their control. With the recognition of belligerency, the third state assumes the obligations of neutrality, just as in a war between two states.' Jessup, *A Modern Law of Nations* (1948) at 53.

[47] Mann, *Foreign Affairs in English Courts* (1986) 4, 47–48.

[48] Witt, *Lincoln's Code: The Laws of War in American History* (2012) at 141–51.

time treat the rebellious Southerners as criminals, rather than as soldiers of war entitled to be prisoners of war under the laws of war. This 'mixed theory' allowed for the situation to be both rebellion and War.[49] The US Supreme Court, when faced with challenges from the owners of ships seized for running the Blockade, found that the President had the executive power to treat this as a War, even though there was no fight with a foreign nation:

> If a war be made by invasion of a foreign nation, the President is not only authorized but bound to resist force by force. He does not initiate the war, but is bound to accept the challenge without waiting for any special legislative authority. And whether the hostile party be a foreign invader or States organized in rebellion, it is nonetheless a war although the declaration of it be 'unilateral.'[50]

However, it was apparent there was an inconsistency between treating the rebels as criminals and seeing the British as entitled to rights flowing from their Neutral Status in War. And in the end the Confederate Forces were treated to the privileges that would have been accorded to forces from a foreign state at War with the United States. The British Declaration of Neutrality of 1861 is taken as a recognition of the Confederate States as Belligerents under international law. But that British Declaration did not constitute a recognition of international statehood for the Confederate States – such a recognition would have been considered by the United States as grounds for War with Great Britain.[51]

After the American Civil War, the US Army continued its wars with American Indians, including the Plains Indians. For decades the execution of Native Americans had been commonplace, and seen as outside the formal structures of the laws of war (their nations not being seen as sovereign states). The plight of US soldiers captured by the Confederate forces in the Civil War, and the emerging notions that there were limits prescribed by law of war manuals such as the Lieber Code, forced a rethink on how captured prisoners should be dealt with. Witt recounts how, in 1862, Dakota warriors associated with the Sioux Nation were tried, convicted and sentenced to death by Military Commissions for murder, rape and robbery. But President Lincoln

---

[49] Ibid at 151; Witt references Sumner speaking in the Senate, calling it a 'double' case: 'you may call it Rebellion or War, as you please, or you may call it both'.

[50] *Prize Cases*, 67 US (1862) 635 at 668.

[51] Arielli, Sadler and Frei, 'The Foreign Enlistment Act, International Law, and British Politics, 1819-2014', 38 *The International History Review* (2015) 636–56.

separated out those who had merely fought against his soldiers and they were interned.[52] Similarly, Witt highlights that the Apache leader, Geronimo, captured in 1886, was eventually sent, together with his fellow fighters and the women and children, to a camp in Florida, where they remained as prisoners of war for 25 years.

The invocation of the laws of war with regard to the battles between the Native Americans and the US armed forces is part of the background against which the laws of war are sometimes seen in the United States. Solis recounts how the notion of war was central to the trial of Senika-Wakan-Ota, aka 'Plenty Horses'. What follows is a précis of his gripping account.

Fearing a massacre similar to the one meted out at Wounded Knee, the Brulé Sioux took up position in order to fight the US soldiers. Lieutenant Casey went to meet the Sioux, and after briefly talking with Plenty Horses, he turned to leave, at which point Plenty Horses shot him. Plenty Horses was later arrested and tried for murder. The Prosecutor called on the US Army to testify that that there had been no State of War with the Sioux. Interestingly, General Miles reportedly advised the Prosecutor 'My boy it was a war.'[53] Addressing the jury, the Judge said that 'it clearly appears that on the day when Lieutenant Casey met his death there existed in and about the Pine Ridge Agency a condition of actual warfare between the Army of the United States ... and the Indian troops'. Casey was unquestionably a combatant and could be killed by the enemy. The Judge reminded the jury that if Casey had killed Plenty Horses while reconnoitering his camp, he would surely not have been tried with murder, and that if the attack on Wounded Knee was not a wartime event then all the US soldiers involved should be tried for murder. He directed the jury to conclude the killing had to be an act of war. They did – and Plenty Horses was acquitted.

The episode serves as an important reminder for the contemporary context: if one is to rely on Belligerent Rights derived from War-time, then one should accept that these Belligerent Rights will apply to one's enemies. The traditional approach is neatly expressed by Castrén in his seminal 1966 book on *Civil War*: 'If a lawful Government has not recognized insurgents as belligerents, it cannot itself exercise belligerent rights'.[54]

---

[52]   Witt, *Lincoln's Code* (n 48) at 330–36.
[53]   Solis, *The Law of Armed Conflict: International Humanitarian Law in War* (2010) at 32.
[54]   Castrén, *Civil War* (1966) at 99; for Castrén's distinctions between civil war, insurrection, riot, and rebellion, see ibid 26–33.

Today it is unlikely that a state would seek to recognize as Belligerents any non-state group fighting against it and thereby entitle the rebels to the privileges of a combatant when those rebels kill the state's own soldiers. To recognize an armed group under the formal regime of Belligerency, in effect, gives the Belligerent non-state actor most of the rights and obligations associated with the armed forces of a state in an inter-state armed conflict.[55] Such recognition would mean that those taking up arms against the state could not be prosecuted for the fact of fighting but would have to be interned as prisoners of war until the end of hostilities, after which they would have to be released. In an inter-state armed conflict such prisoners are for the most part repatriated to the other state. If a Belligerency were to be recognized, all those prisoners of war would have to be 'released onto the streets', potentially dangerous and able to regroup in the future and fight once more against the state. Similarly, it seems unlikely today that another state would declare its Neutral Status, and thus indirectly recognize certain Belligerent rights for the rebel group in the interaction with the Neutral state that chose to recognize the group.[56] What has emerged more recently has been the recognition in Latin America of armed groups fighting for freedom under dictatorships. As Gurmendi has documented, the Andean Pact recognised the belligerency of the Sandinistas in 1979. The issue was not neutral rights. In Gurmendi's words, 'The recognition itself was rather part of a toolbox designed to directly interfere in the Nicaraguan conflict and bring about the end of the Somoza dictatorship, in the name of human rights.'[57]

Whether or not there is any recognition of belligerency, the Geneva Conventions nevertheless specifically encourage the parties to a non-international armed conflict to adopt special agreements to bring into force all or part of the Conventions,[58] and indeed states and armed groups can and do make declarations and enter into agreements that create obligations beyond what the treaties bind them to do.[59]

---

[55] For discussion of other rights related to, *inter alia*, treaties, occupation and reparations, see ibid at 152–67.

[56] For instances of 19th-century recognitions of Belligerency by belligerent states and neutral states, see Sivakumaran (n 44) at 17–20.

[57] 'The Last Recognition of Belligerency (and Some Thoughts on Why You May Not Have Heard of It)', 10 December 2019, at www.opiniojuris.org.

[58] See Vierucci, 'Applicability of the Conventions by Means of Ad Hoc Agreements', in Clapham, Gaeta and Sassòli (eds), *The 1949 Geneva Conventions: A Commentary* (2015) 509–21; see also the Hague Convention for the Protection of Cultural Property (1954) Art 19(2).

[59] See the collection of statements at http://theirwords.org/pages/geneva-call; and Bellal and Heffes, ' "Yes I Do": Binding Armed Non-State Actors to IHL and Human Rights Norms Through Their Consent', 12 *Human Rights and International Law Discourse* (2018) 120–36.

6.5 Wars of National Liberation under Additional Protocol I

There is another way in which an armed conflict between a non-state armed group and a state can become seen in law as an international armed conflict, triggering the application of the relevant international rights and obligations for both sides. When the Additional Protocols to the Geneva Conventions were negotiated and concluded in 1977, newly decolonized states, together with socialist states, succeeded in finding a way for Wars of National Liberation to be considered international armed conflicts. Such conflicts would involve the full application of the four Geneva Conventions of 1949 and the extensive provisions of Protocol I.

The key provision from 1977 applies Additional Protocol I and the Four Geneva Conventions to

> armed conflicts in which peoples are fighting against colonial domination and alien occupation and against racist régimes in the exercise of their right of self-determination, as enshrined in the Charter of the United Nations and the Declaration on Principles of International Law concerning Friendly Relations and Cooperation among States in accordance with the Charter of the United Nations.[60]

The states that were particularly targeted by this provision at that time, South Africa and Israel, rejected the notion that liberation movements could gain the rights applicable in international armed conflict against racist régimes or alien occupiers. After the transition in South Africa from apartheid

---

[60] Art 1(4). A similar provision applies under the Convention on Certain Conventional Weapons (1980), and the United States, Israel, Turkey, the United Kingdom and France have made reservations to that treaty to limit the possibility of being bound to apply all the provisions of the four Geneva Conventions and this treaty to an armed conflict with a group claiming to be acting as part of a self-determination struggle. A question mark remains over whether the law of international armed conflict could be triggered for a War of National Liberation under customary international law or otherwise. For early discussion, see Abi-Saab, 'Wars of National Liberation in the Geneva Conventions and Protocols', 165 *RCADI* IV (1979) 353–445; Abi-Saab, 'Wars of National Liberation and the Development of Humanitarian Law', in Akkerman et al (eds), *Declarations on Principles* (1977) 143–79; and Bothe, Partsch and Solf, *Commentary on the Two 1977 Protocols Additional to the Geneva Conventions of 1949*, 2nd edn (2013) at 45–51. Cf Prosecutor's Closing Remarks (n 32) at para 32 fn 30, where the Prosecutor considers this rule does not exist as a matter of customary international law. Mačák, *Internationalized Armed Conflicts* (n 31) at 7–75 has suggested that the wording of Protocol I implies that its provisions apply to the relevant state even before the declaration by the group concerned creates obligations for the group.

to multiracial democracy, South Africa joined the Protocol. States with colonial possessions, such as the United Kingdom and France, entered declarations when joining the treaty. These declarations essentially sought to
restrict the application of the provision to armed groups that these states
would in the future consider are legitimate self-determination movements.[61]

For a long time, this controversial provision was considered to be more
symbolic than anything else. But in 2015, the Polisario Front sent a unilateral declaration to the depositary (the Swiss Federal Council), stating that it
undertook to apply the four Geneva Conventions and the Protocol in its conflict in Western Sahara with Morocco (a party to the Protocol). Switzerland
notified the parties to the Geneva Conventions that the declaration had the
effect of immediate application of the Geneva Conventions and the Protocol
to both parties to the conflict.[62] Morocco has objected that Morocco is the
only representative of the population of the Sahara, that there is no armed
conflict and that Morocco has not been said in any of the UN documents to
be a *colonisateur*, or a *puissance occupante*, let alone a *régime raciste*.[63] The internal Swiss memorandum nevertheless explained that that it was sufficient
that Morocco was in occupation and that the self-determination issue had
been addressed in various General Assembly resolutions.[64] These treaties
governing international armed conflict therefore apply to any armed conflict
between Polisario and Morocco.

6.6 Non-International Armed Conflicts

The Geneva Conventions refer to these conflicts in the negative, in the
sense that they are 'not of an international character'.[65] There was little judicial determination of the threshold of violence that was needed to trigger
the application of this international humanitarian law until it became necessary for the purposes of the international prosecution of war crimes. The

---

[61] Available at https://ihl-databases.icrc.org/applic/ihl/ihl.nsf/States.xsp?xp_viewStates=X
Pages_NORMStatesParties&xp_treatySelected=470.

[62] For some of the practical implications, see Fortin, 'Unilateral Declaration by Polisario under
API accepted by Swiss Federal Council', available at https://armedgroups-internationallaw.org/
2015/09/02/unilateral-declaration-by-polisario-under-api-accepted-by-swiss-federal-council/.

[63] The letter of 30 June 2015 is available at https://www.dfae.admin.ch/dam/eda/fr/docu-
ments/aussenpolitik/voelkerrecht/geneve/150709-GENEVE-avec-ann_e.pdf.

[64] See Mačák, 'Wars of national liberation: the story of one unusual rule II', 30 July 2018, available at https://blog.oup.com/2018/07/wars-national-liberation-unusual-rule-part-2/.

[65] Common Art 3 of the 1949 Geneva Conventions.

international tribunals with jurisdiction over war crimes committed in non-international armed conflicts have developed criteria to determine whether there is an armed conflict to which the laws of war apply. We are discussing here an armed conflict between a state and an armed group, or between two armed groups. Defendants have sought in their criminal trials to show that the conditions for armed conflict and the attendant laws of war were not met. This is crucial for the defence at trial, because without an armed conflict that triggers the laws of war, there can be no prosecution for war crimes. In turn the international criminal tribunals have explained in some detail where the threshold is for the application of the law of war in an armed conflict where one or more of the parties is an armed group.

Two key criteria have emerged that take us over the threshold: the intensity of the violence, and the level of organization of the non-state armed group. Such requirements for the application of the customary international law of non-international armed conflict, and presumably for the application of Common Article 3 of the 1949 Geneva Conventions,[66] were spelt out in some detail by the International Criminal Tribunal for the former Yugoslavia. The first relates to intensity:

> Trial Chambers have relied on indicative factors relevant for assessing the 'intensity' criterion, none of which are, in themselves, essential to establish that the criterion is satisfied. These indicative factors include the number, duration and intensity of individual confrontations; the type of weapons and other military equipment used; the number and calibre of munitions fired; the number of persons and type of forces partaking in the fighting; the number of casualties; the extent of material destruction; and the number of civilians fleeing combat zones. The involvement of the UN Security Council may also be a reflection of the intensity of a conflict.[67]

The second criterion requires that the armed non-state actor has to fulfil certain organizational requirements:

> As for armed groups, Trial Chambers have relied on several indicative factors, none of which are, in themselves, essential to establish whether the

---

[66] See Moir, 'The Concept of Non-International Armed Conflict', in Clapham, Gaeta and Sassòli (eds), *The 1949 Geneva Conventions: A Commentary* (2015) 391–414 at 404–14.

[67] *Prosecutor v Haradinaj*, Case No IT-04-84-84-T, 3 April 2008, para 49; see also Vité, 'Typology of Armed Conflicts in International Humanitarian Law: Legal Concepts and Actual Situations', 91 *International Review of the Red Cross* (2009) 69–94.

'organisation' criterion is fulfilled. Such indicative factors include the existence of a command structure and disciplinary rules and mechanisms within the group; the existence of a headquarters; the fact that the group controls a certain territory; the ability of the group to gain access to weapons, other military equipment, recruits and military training; its ability to plan, coordinate and carry out military operations, including troop movements and logistics; its ability to define a unified military strategy and use military tactics; and its ability to speak with one voice and negotiate and conclude agreements such as cease-fire or peace accords.[68]

Whether or not the political purposes of the group are relevant remains controversial,[69] yet judicial statements have suggested that the motives of the parties are irrelevant.[70]

These thresholds were developed for the purposes of determining when individuals could be prosecuted for war crimes committed in a non-international armed conflict. They have come to be used as a general guideline as to when the protections in Common Article 3 of the Geneva Conventions apply, as well as for the customary international law applicable to both sides in a non-international armed conflict.

This leaves the question of when the treaty law contained in Additional Protocol II should apply. It is generally accepted that there needs to be control over territory and perhaps a higher degree of organization. The Protocol applies to non-international armed conflicts between the armed forces of a state party to the Protocol and 'dissident armed forces or other organized armed groups which, under responsible command, exercise such control over a part of its territory as to enable them to carry out sustained and concerted military operations and to implement this Protocol'.[71]

---

[68] *Haradinaj* (n 67) at para 60. And see further ICTY *Prosecutor v Boskoski*, Case No IT-04-82, 10 July 2009, para 175.

[69] See Vité, 'Typology of Armed Conflicts' (n 67) at 78; Sassòli, *IHL* (n 31) at para 6.38.

[70] See the cases and other references discussed by the ICRC *Commentary GC I* (2016) (n 13) at paras 447–51.

[71] AP II Art 1. Complex questions arise when states parties to AP II operate abroad: see Geiß, 'Has the Armed Conflict in Afghanistan Affected the Rules on the Conduct of Hostilities?', 93 *IRRC* (2011) 11–46 at 16; similarly Pejic, 'The Protective Scope of Common Article 3: More than Meets the Eye', 93 *IRRC* (2011) 189–225 at 201. *Contra* Bellal, Giacca and Casey-Maslen, 'International Law and Armed Non-State Actors in Afghanistan', 93 *International Journal of the Red Cross* (2011) 47–79 esp at 60–61; see also Hampson, 'Direct Participation in Hostilities and the Interoperability of the Law of Armed Conflict and Human Rights Law', 87 *International Law Studies* (2011) 187–213 esp fn 79 at 213: 'When the conflict is of the requisite intensity for Additional Protocol II to be applicable, but it is not applicable because the conflict occurs in the territory of a State not a party to the conflict, it should be treated as an Additional Protocol II conflict for these purposes. It is beyond the scope of this article to consider whether Article 1.1 of

Several commentators suggest that, in addition to the requirement that the organized armed group control territory, there should be a greater intensity of violence before the Additional Protocol applies.[72] But today one could ask whether the Protocol really requires a greater level of intensity of violence than that required to trigger Common Article 3. So far the International Criminal Court seems to have avoided creating two separate thresholds. The UK Military Manual seems only to demand that, to move from Common Article 3 to Additional Protocol II, the dissidents should 'achieve a degree of success and exercise the necessary control over a part of the territory.'[73] Dinstein nevertheless highlights the requirement under the treaty for 'sustained and concerted military operations'.[74] The *Manual on the Law of Non-International Armed Conflict* similarly suggests a 'higher' threshold for the Applicability of Additional Protocol II (AP II).[75]

There may be good arguments for insisting on a hierarchy of thresholds related to the level of military action, so that humanitarian protection for people in the hands of the other party is triggered at the lowest level of violence, and yet serious fighting is needed to trigger other provisions of the law of war related to targeting. It makes sense for us to consider a rather low threshold for those who have fallen into the hands of the enemy under Common Article 3, and a higher one for rules concerning the conduct of hostilities and some of the extra obligations we find in Additional Protocol II.[76]

Additional Protocol II should be amended to replace "its armed forces" by "the armed forces of a High Contracting Party."'

[72] Sandoz, Swinarski and Zimmermann (eds), *Commentary on the Additional Protocols of 8 June 1977 to the Geneva Conventions of 12 August 1949* (1987) at 1343ff; Hampson, 'Direct Participation in Hostilities'(n 71) 187–213 at 195–97 and 203; Dinstein, *Non-International Armed Conflicts* (n 2) 39–50; Abi-Saab, 'Les protocoles additionnels 25 ans après', in Flauss (ed), *Les nouvelles frontières du droit international humanitaire* (2003) 17–39 at 24–25; Clapham, 'Defining Armed Conflicts under the Additional Protocols: Is There a Need for Further Clarification?' in Pocar (ed), *The Additional Protocols 40 Years Later: New Conflicts, New Actors, New Perspectives* (2018) 33–42.

[73] UK *Manual* (n 2) at para 3.9.

[74] Dinstein, *Non-International Armed Conflicts* (n 2) at 46–47.

[75] Schmitt, Garraway and Dinstein, *The Manual on the Law of Non-Armed Conflict* (2006) at 3, available at https://www.scribd.com/document/108685710/Manual-on-the-Law-of-Non-International-Armed-Conflict-Prof-Michael-N-Schmitt.

[76] See in particular the point made by Hampson that some Hague-style rules in AP II can be read as *permitting* action to be taken, while the lower threshold for Common Article 3 only *protects* the victims of armed conflict. So suggesting that there is only one threshold with customary rules that apply to all non-international armed conflicts 'may imply a shift from a law and order paradigm to an armed conflict paradigm at an inappropriately low level of disruption. Since Geneva-law rules are focused on the protection of victims and bear a significant similarity to the approach of [human rights law], their applicability at the Common Article 3 threshold does not appear to be too problematic. It is specifically customary rules of Hague law that give

Also at a more political and journalistic level, there is still a sense that some conflicts move from rebellion, through insurgency into something called 'civil war'. In the past, this term was seen to have specific legal implications (and historically writers such as Vattel suggested that civil war denoted lawful resistance – while rebellion was unjust).[77] Today no humanitarian law expert suggests that labelling something a civil war triggers extra rights and obligations. Nevertheless, media entities such as Reuters, the BBC and the *New York Times* spend considerable time writing about whether the conflicts in Iraq or Syria constitute a civil war. Similarly, government authorities may choose, for political reasons, to deny that there is a civil war (rather than some sort of insurgency, conflict or series of terrorist attacks).[78] Acceptance that there is a 'civil war' is seemingly to admit that the government has lost control, and perhaps subliminally conjures up older notions that the parties have become, in Vattel's words, 'two independent parties, who consider each other as enemies, and acknowledge no common judge'.[79] Perhaps there is also still an understanding of civil war that suggests that each side may have just as much legitimacy as the other, and outside powers should refrain from any intervention and abstain from assistance to the government or the side claiming to be the government. In short, this second higher threshold for non-international armed conflict may matter, especially if it is consciously, or unconsciously, assimilated to civil war and all that that term conjures up.[80]

rise to this difficulty. More particularly, it is [law of armed conflict] rules that *permit* action to be taken, rather than [law of armed conflict] rules that prohibit attacks against certain types of targets or the use of certain weapons, that cause the problem.' Hampson, 'Direct Participation in Hostilities' (n 71) at 197. For a nuanced look at which rules involve varying degrees of permission, see Quintin, *The Nature of International Humanitarian Law: A Permissive or Restrictive Regime?* (2020). For those who consider that international humanitarian law in this context 'not only prohibits and prescribes conduct but also authorizes conduct (such as killing or depriving an enemy fighter of liberty)', there may be good policy arguments for fixing the threshold for the application of this law higher as, for such authors, human rights law would no longer be applicable when the Protocol (or even the customary international law equivalent) applies, and human rights law would have been more protective; see Sassòli, *IHL* (n 31) at paras 6.39, and 10.02–10.19. Compare Clapham, 'The Limits of Human Rights in Times of Armed Conflict and Other Situations of Armed Violence', in Fassbender and Traibach (eds), *The Limits of Human Rights* (2019) 305–17; and see further Shany, 'The End of the War/Peace Limit on the Application of International Human Rights Law: A Response to Andrew Clapham', ibid at 319–27.

[77] Vattel, *The Law of Nations (1797)*, eds Kapossy and Whatmore (2008) at 645 para 293.
[78] See, eg, Lozano and Machado, 'The Objective Qualification of Non-International Armed Conflicts: A Colombian Case Study', 4 *Amsterdam Law Forum* (2012) 58–77.
[79] *The Law of Nations* (supra) at para 293.
[80] See Armitage, *Civil Wars: A History* (2017) at 220–222. The latest *Department of Defense Manual on the Laws of War* (n 2) suggests that civil wars can lead to recognition of belligerency, which could in turn lead to the application of the laws of international armed conflict: at para 17.1.1.1, '*NIAC and Civil War*'. 'Civil war is a classic example of a non-international armed

6.7 Conflicts Involving UN Mandated Peacekeeping Operations

A complex set of questions concern the extent to which the United Nations, or any other intergovernmental organization, can be considered a party to a conflict, and so bound by the laws of war. As none of these entities can become parties to humanitarian law treaties such as the Geneva Conventions, they become bound by the relevant international law of armed conflict to the extent that this law applies to them as a matter of customary international law. In addition they may be bound by the fundamental rules and principles of humanitarian law as a result of their own internal regulations,[81] or through agreements entered into with host states.

The Convention on the Safety of United Nations and Associated Personnel foresees that the United Nations might become a party to an international armed conflict, at which point this Safety of UN Personnel Convention would no longer apply (the context would also have to be specifically a UN enforcement operation authorized by the Security Council under Chapter VII).[82] It seems clear that a conflict between the United Nations and the armed forces

---

conflict. For example, a non-international armed conflict could involve the open rebellion of segments of a nation's armed forces (sometimes called dissident armed forces) against the incumbent regime, each claiming to be the legitimate government. . . . In some cases of civil war, the insurgent party has been recognized as a belligerent, and, at least in some respects, the law of international armed conflict would be applied by the States choosing to recognize the insurgent party as a belligerent.' The footnote in the original reads: 'See, e.g., LIEBER CODE art. 150 ("Civil war is war between two or more portions of a country or state, each contending for the mastery of the whole, and each claiming to be the legitimate government. The term is also sometimes applied to war of rebellion, when the rebellious provinces or portions of the state are contiguous to those containing the seat of government.").' See also Luban, 'Military Necessity and the Cultures of Military Law', 26 *Leiden Journal of International Law* (2013) 315–49 at 324; Sassòli, 'The Convergence of the International Humanitarian Law of Non-International and International Armed Conflicts – The Dark Side of a Good Idea', in Biaggini, Diggelmann and Kaufmann (eds), *Polis und Kosmopolis -Festschrift für Daniel Thürer* (2015) 679–89; De Wett, *Military Assistance on Request and the Use of Force* (2020) at 19, who uses the expression 'civil war' in her study as synonymous with a conflict defined by AP II.

[81] See the UN Secretary-General's Bulletin, *Observance by United Nations Forces of International Humanitarian Law*, UN Doc ST/SGB/1999/13, 6 August 1999; Shraga, 'The Secretary-General's Bulletin on the Observance by United Nations Forces on International Humanitarian law: A Decade Later', 39 *Israel Yearbook of Human Rights* (2009) 357–77.

[82] Art 2(2): 'This Convention shall not apply to a United Nations operation authorized by the Security Council as an enforcement action under Chapter VII of the Charter of the United Nations in which any of the personnel are engaged as combatants against organized armed forces and to which the law of international armed conflict applies.' For the background, see Bloom, 'Protecting Peacekeepers: The Convention on the Safety of United Nations and Associated Personnel', 89 *AJIL* (1995) 621–31.

of a state would be an international armed conflict, such that the relevant protective rules from the Geneva Conventions should apply.

While the low threshold we discussed above applies to inter-state conflicts, doubts have been expressed as to whether this low threshold is workable where peacekeepers engage in the use of force with a state in the course of a mandate to protect civilians or provide humanitarian assistance. If an international armed conflict is triggered, say, by a small skirmish between the UN forces and government troops, then triggering the laws of war would imply the whole UN force would lose its protection from attack as the Safety Convention would no longer apply. Attacks on the UN mandated peacekeeping operations would no longer qualify as international crimes.[83]

As Greenwood points out, the drafters of that UN Safety Convention did not intend for UN forces to lose their protection in Bosnia and Herzegovina as a result of the use of force in self-defence.[84] We may have to accept that the threshold and criteria for triggering an international armed conflict may be different when a UN operation engages with the armed forces of a state in the course of such mandated operations. Greenwood predicted that 'A degree of violence which, in the past, would certainly have been regarded as sufficient to constitute an international armed conflict will come to be regarded as something of a lesser nature if it involves UN forces.'[85]

Caution over rushing to apply the law of armed conflict to UN forces is also premised on the fact that, in many cases, the UN forces will have multiple tasks, including humanitarian assistance, demining, protection of civilians, etc, and may be spread across a wide territory. The normal assumptions that the laws of war apply across a whole territory and allow for targeting of all members of the armed forces from the enemy party should not, in my view, be transposed to this situation.[86] As Bianca Maganza highlights, UN

---

[83] See further, for the perspective from the international criminal tribunals, Pacholska, '(Il)legality of Killing Peacekeepers: The Crime of Attacking Peacekeepers in the Jurisprudence of International Criminal Tribunals', 13 *JICJ* (2015) 43–72. The crime in the ICC Statute for both international and non-international armed conflicts is defined as 'Intentionally directing attacks against personnel, installations, material, units or vehicles involved in a humanitarian assistance or peacekeeping mission in accordance with the Charter of the United Nations, as long as they are entitled to the protection given to civilians or civilian objects under the international law of armed conflict': Art 8(2)(b)(iii) and (e)(iii).

[84] 'Protection of Peacekeepers: The Legal Regime' 7 *Duke Journal of Comparative and International Law* (1996) 185–207 at 202.

[85] Ibid. See also for a detailed discussion Ferraro, 'The Applicability and Application of International Humanitarian Law to Multinational Forces', 95 *IRRC* (2013) 561–612.

[86] Grenfell, 'Perspective on the Applicability and Application of International Humanitarian Law: The UN Context', 95 *IRRC* (2013) 645–52.

military vehicles, planes, helicopters bases, etc are used every day by humanitarian workers.[87] The idea that the United Nations could be considered at war could lead to catastrophic confusion over what could be targeted under the laws of war.

In the context of the applicability of the protective regime of the UN Safety Convention, the expert *Leuven Manual* clarifies:

> Acting in lawful self-defence does not constitute a hostile act or automatically result in becoming party to an armed conflict under IHL. Lawful self-defence includes protection of mission personnel and/or civilians from imminent physical danger and extends to proportionate action to counter attempts to disarm or otherwise incapacitate mission personnel or seize vital installations or equipment.[88]

The issue is further complicated by the fact that even UN forces nominally under the command and control of the United Nations will often still be, in fact, under the control of the sending state. This will be even more the case in a situation such as a NATO operation. States will in many cases retain international responsibility for the actions of their forces, even if the relevant international organization may also be responsible under what is known as 'dual attribution'.

The legal reasoning on this last point has been developed by a judgment of the Supreme Court of the Netherlands in a case brought by a specific victim from Srebrenica, concerning the conduct of the Dutch Battalion in the UN operation.[89] At one point it had been argued in this context, and elsewhere, that the behaviour of UN peacekeepers was exclusively attributable to the United Nations. The judgment, however, is clear that in such operations the sending state retains some effective control over its forces, and the sending state can be responsible for any unlawful acts. The key point is that the sending state will always retain 'disciplinary powers and criminal jurisdiction ("the organic command")'.[90] The United Nations has no criminal jurisdiction over such personnel, and so the control the sending state retains

---

[87] Maganza, 'From Peacekeepers to Parties to the Conflict: An IHL's Appraisal of the Role of UN Peace Operations in NIACs', 25 *JCSL* (2020) 209–36 at 232.

[88] Gill, Fleck, Boothby and Vanheusden (eds), *Leuven Manual on the International Law Applicable to Peace Operations* (2017) at 324.

[89] *Netherlands v Hasan Nuhanović*, Supreme Court of The Netherlands, Case No 12/03324, 6 September 2013.

[90] Ibid at para 3.10.2.

can lead to state responsibility, alongside any responsibility attributable to the United Nations or any other international organization.[91]

Therefore, in some cases, the participating state may well enter into an armed conflict with the host state in addition to any armed conflict between the United Nations and the state.[92] The humanitarian law treaties would apply to the state alongside the equivalent customary international law that might also bind the United Nations or other international organization. The humanitarian protections outlined in the following chapters would apply. What we would not have is a War, with the attendant ideas of enemy aliens, enemy property and so on. The language used in this context matters, as elucidated by the distinguished law of war scholar, LC Green:

> It should be noted that by using the term 'enforcement measures' or even 'armed conflict' rather than 'war' for incidents in which military action is taken in the name of the United Nations, there need be no debate whether the United Nations, not being a state, is able to engage in war and enjoy the rights of a belligerent.[93]

Opinion is divided on whether an armed conflict between the United Nations and a non-state armed group might be considered an international armed conflict where the United Nations is acting for neither side in any internal armed conflict. It is suggested here that it is not the international character of the United Nations that determines the classification of the conflict, but rather the non-state character of the opposing forces that means that the conflict is of a non-international character. Neither the United Nations nor the rebel group will have the international law rights associated with international armed conflict. Both sides are bound by the humanitarian law of armed conflict applicable to non-international armed conflict.[94]

---

[91] See especially the discussion at ibid paras 3.9.2–3.12.3.

[92] The legal framework will be dependent on the particular facts, see Sassòli, *IHL* (n 31) at paras 6.63–6.66; see also Nollkaemper, 'Dual Attribution: Liability of the Netherlands for Conduct of Dutchbat in Srebrenica', 9 *JICJ* (2011) 1143–57.

[93] *The Contemporary Law of Armed Conflict*, 3rd edn (2008) at 381; for a critical discussion of the extent to which Belligerent Rights can continue, at all see Ch 8.

[94] For the United Nation's own binding directives covering these obligations, see UN Doc ST/SGB/1999/13, 6 August 1999, ss 5–9; for the Bulletin on Special Measures for Protection from Sexual Exploitation and Sexual Abuse, see ST/SGB/2003/13, 9 October 2003.

7

Warfare – the Conduct of Hostilities

We have seen that under international law (and some constitutions) it is now illegal to go to war, and that a state is generally only entitled to use force against another state in self-defence in response to an armed attack, or with the authorization of the Security Council. War as an institution has been outlawed, even (I would say) abolished, and yet there are still rules for fighting wars: the laws of war. Let us unpack this conundrum. Those in the movement to outlaw war likened their quest to the abolition of slavery and duelling as institutions. It made no sense after abolition to continue to apply the rules for duels or enforce contracts for the sale of slaves. With abolition, the rules that bolstered the legal institution fell away. With the outlawing of war new rules indeed flowed that reinforced the prohibition: territory seized would not be recognized, treaties that were coerced would not be valid, wars of aggression became criminalized.[1] But states continued to engage in armed conflicts, whether they labelled them wars or something else. While the special rules for duelling and slavery fell away to be replaced by the regular national laws covering public order, violence and forced labour, the international treaties and law providing protection to the victims of war were still needed.[2]

Nevertheless, in the wake of the successful adoption of the UN Charter, which not only outlawed the use of force but also promised international peace and security through effective sanctions and the ready deployment of armed forces, there was queasiness about any international exercise aimed at codifying or adapting the old laws of war. The United Nations International Law Commission, meeting for the first time in 1949 in New York at Lake Success, determined not to tackle this topic. The Report shows that 'The Commission considered whether the laws of war should be selected as a topic

---

[1] As discussed in Ch 3, Hathaway and Shapiro term this the 'New World Order'; see their diagram in *The New Internationalists: And Their Plan to Outlaw War* (2017) at 304.

[2] The question of whether Belligerents' Rights that flowed from the State of War continue to exist today is something we shall tackle in the following chapter. We concentrate here on the obligations of the parties to armed conflicts during the conduct of hostilities, primarily on what may not be targeted and what weapons are prohibited. See also Neff, 'The Prerogatives of Violence – In Search of the Conceptual Foundations of Belligerents' Rights', 38 *GYBIL* (1995) 41–72.

for codification. It was suggested that, war having been outlawed, the regulation of its conduct had ceased to be relevant.[3] Brierly, the member from the United Kingdom, was among the most persuasive voices on this point. He is reported as saying the Commission should

> refrain from taking up the question of the laws of war because if it did so its action might be interpreted as a lack of confidence in the United Nations and the work of peace which the latter was called upon to carry out, and as a proof of the very relative value which might be attached to the obligation assumed by the signatories to the Charter to settle their disputes by peaceful means. Nothing would create a worse impression of the Commission's work, nothing would upset public opinion more.[4]

Of course part of the context was that the Swiss Government was convening, the next day, outside the United Nations, a 'Diplomatic Conference for the Establishment of International Conventions for the Protection of Victims of War'. Four months later, that Conference adopted the four 1949 Geneva Conventions (GCs I–IV). These new treaties had been developed by the International Committee of the Red Cross (ICRC) (in consultation with governments) following the Second World War. The Conference significantly produced a new treaty on the protection of civilians (particularly in occupied territory), a draft having been submitted by France at an earlier meeting in 1947. And the Conference further adopted revised versions of earlier Conventions covering the sick and wounded (adapting the rules to include the situation at sea) as well as prisoners of war. The Conventions now were adjusted to include a 'mini-convention', known as Common Article 3 to the Conventions, covering non-international armed conflicts.

Jean Pictet, writing in 1985 and at the time the Director of the ICRC, later explained a key change that took place in 1949:

> Another achievement of the 1949 Diplomatic Conference arose from the fact that a large number of prisoners of war had been refused the benefit of the 1929 Convention, their captors claiming that there was no war as defined in international law or denying that their adversary was a State, that

---

[3] UN Doc A/CN.4/13 at para 18, and Corr 1–3, Report of the International Law Commission on the work of its First Session, 12 April 1949, Official Records of the General Assembly, Fourth Session, Supplement No 10, at 281.
[4] UN Doc A/CN.4/SR.6 Summary record of the 6th meeting, p 52 para 55.

it was at war or even that it existed. This unhappy circumstance produced common Article 2, which stipulates that the Conventions shall apply not only to all cases of declared war but also to any other armed conflict, even if the state of war is not recognized. This means that the law must apply whenever there are victims, the only humane criterion. The ICRC, however, does not seek to exacerbate the situation by claiming that all armed clashes are wars.[5]

As we saw in the previous chapter, the Geneva Conventions and their 1977 Protocols now apply to different types of armed conflict, and there is no need for any such armed conflict to be recognized as a War.

Pictet recounts how the ICRC was thwarted after the Second World War in its attempt to tackle the bombardment of civilian populations. Essentially this was because powerful states were keen not to be prevented from using their newly found nuclear options. But by 1977, after four years of discussion, the Diplomatic Conference in Geneva was nevertheless able to adopt treaty provisions in the Protocols protecting the civilian population, regulating aerial bombardment and prohibiting bombardment for the purpose of spreading terror. Pictet rightly considered that such provisions 'represented a tremendous advance.'[6]

But not every humanitarian dream is protected in rigorous terms in the treaties. As Pictet puts it, this humanitarian law

results from the balance struck between the principle of humanity – that is, the imperative which drives a human being to act for the good of fellow beings – and the principle of necessity – that is, the duty of public authorities to preserve the State, defend its territorial integrity and maintain order.[7]

His formula for preparing such texts is as witty as it is revealing:

Briefly, in order to codify successfully, take two drops of dreams, one drop of madness and one hundred drops of realism, and blend thoroughly before serving. I make you a gift of the recipe.[8]

---

[5] 'The Formation of International Humanitarian Law', 25 *IRRC* (1985) 3–24 at 14.
[6] Ibid at 18.
[7] Ibid at 20.
[8] Ibid at 21.

These Geneva treaties, together with relevant Conventions adopted in The Hague and elsewhere, contain hundreds of Articles, and we will here only barely scratch the surface.[9] Traditionally, the law of armed conflict was broken into what was known as Hague law and Geneva law. Hague law covered the means and methods of warfare, or, in other words, the conduct of hostilities. Geneva law was said to be for the protection of the victims of war (eg the wounded, prisoners of war and civilians in occupied territory). These labels now make little sense, as the law of the Geneva Additional Protocols covers extensive rules related to the conduct of hostilities. The distinction nevertheless remains relevant to an understanding of the development of the law of armed conflict.[10] I have split our discussion into two parts, dealing first here with the conduct of hostilities and later (in Chapter 9) with the humanitarian protection of the victims of war.

7.1 Privileged Belligerents and Combatant Immunity

As we saw in the last chapter when we looked at the case of Senika-Wakan-Ota, aka 'Plenty Horses', behind the idea of war is an understanding that killing the enemy is not murder. This idea endures. I am continually surprised how often I come across claims that the laws of war entitle you to kill members of the enemy's armed forces. This is sometimes explained as exercising 'law of war authority', or as being justified as a 'lawful act of war'. More popularly, the idea is today often expressed as a 'licence to kill'; and I guess that we have the fictional James Bond and the film franchise to thank for that.

In fact, when the idea of the Double O signifier was invented for OO7 by Ian Fleming in 1953, it was explained by Bond himself as follows: 'A Double O number in our Service means you've had to kill a chap in cold blood in

---

[9] For a very clear, yet reflective, view of almost the entire set of rules applicable in times of armed conflict, see the important book by Sassòli, *International Humanitarian Law: Rules, Controversies, and Solutions to Problems Arising in Warfare* (2019) (hereinafter *IHL*).

[10] For a brief history of the 'convergence' of these 'currents', together with the suggestion of a third current from New York (human rights), see Kalshoven and Zegveld, *Constraints on the Waging of War: An Introduction to International Humanitarian Law*, 4th edn (2011); for war crimes, see Ch 10 below. Hampson suggests that the different currents address different actors: 'If Hague law is principally directed at the individual operator, Geneva law appears to focus more on the obligations of a party to the conflict. Geneva law provides answers or required outcomes, but Hague law provides tools enabling the operator to arrive at an answer in a specific situation.' Hampson, 'Direct Participation in Hostilities and the Interoperability of the Law of Armed Conflict and Human Rights Law', 87 *International Law Studies* (2011) 187–213 at 193–94.

the course of some job.'[11] Bond explains that his first was a Japanese cipher agent, operating on the 36th floor of the Rockefeller Building in New York, decoding British communications. Bond took a room on the 40th floor in the next door skyscraper and shot the Japanese agent through a hole in the window with a telescopic sight and silencer. The second was a Norwegian who had been acting as a double agent and working with the Germans. He was knifed in his hotel room in Stockholm. 'For those two jobs I was awarded a Double O number in the Service. Felt pretty clever and got a reputation for being good and tough.' But Bond tells the story at a time when he is considering resigning:

> Now . . . that's all very fine. The hero kills two villains, but when the hero Le Chiffre starts to kill the villain Bond and the villain Bond knows he isn't a villain at all, you see the other side of the medal. The villains and heroes get all mixed up. Of course . . . patriotism comes along and makes it seem fairly all right, but this country-right-or-wrong business is getting a little out-of-date. Today we are fighting communism. Okay. If I'd been alive fifty years ago, the brand of conservatism we have today would have been damn near called communism and we should have been told to go and fight that. History is moving pretty quickly these days and the heroes and villains keep on changing parts.[12]

The idea morphed even within the James Bond books,[13] and indeed some agents in real life have enjoyed immunity from prosecution in their own country. There are still books and films entitled *Licence to Kill*, but none of this contributes to the formation of international law. Should any government choose to have laws that immunize its agents from prosecution at home for murder (whether committed at home or abroad), it is clear that no other state would be obliged to recognize such a so-called 'licence to kill'.[14]

---

[11] Fleming, *Casino Royale* (1953) (London: Vintage, 2012) at 170.

[12] Ibid at 170–71.

[13] In *Dr No* (1958), the hard-earned double 'OO' prefix is linked to a licence to kill (Vintage, London, 2012) at 24.

[14] Diplomatic or other immunity under international law would be a separate question. The intelligence services do include their agents in diplomatic lists held by host states, thereby ensuring complete immunity from arrest or prosecution. The United Kingdom has a new statutory scheme to authorize criminal conduct in the course of certain covert operations, see Covert Human Intelligence Sources (Criminal Conduct) Act 2021. The Home Office's Explanatory Notes state that the power remains subject to safguards including the fact that: 'All public authorities are bound by the Human Rights Act to act in a way that is compatible with the rights protected by the European Convention on Human Rights. Rights that are protected by the

And yet the deeper idea of soldiers' being entitled to kill continues in multiple forms. General David Petraeus, the former Commander of US General Command, complaining about the influence of human rights law ('negative lawfare'), explained that 'under the Geneva Convention (which codified the law of armed conflict) lethal force is allowed as a matter of first resort against a clearly identified enemy'.[15] Now I realize that the expression 'Geneva Convention' is being used here loosely to invoke the law of armed conflict, and of course General Petraeus is expressing himself not as a lawyer, but rather in accessible shorthand to make a point, but in the present context I want to use his phrasing to make my own point. My point is that we should challenge this assumption that something called the 'Geneva Convention', or something called the 'laws of war', *authorizes* in broad terms lethal force as a matter of first resort against an identified enemy.

The codification in the 1949 Geneva Conventions grants no such permission to kill people. It actually contains prohibitions, including prohibitions on 'murder' of persons protected by those Conventions.[16] It will, of course, be argued that what is not prohibited is permitted (even authorized), but such an approach, while perhaps received wisdom in times when war was an acceptable way to resolve international disputes, should no longer apply to conflicts today. Now, both sides will be bound by the laws that confine the resort to the use of force,[17] and individuals are protected by multiple legal regimes, including human rights law.[18]

Convention include the right to life, and prohibition of torture or subjecting someone to inhuman or degrading treatment or punishment'.

[15] 'Human Rights Law is Harming Britain's Armed Forces', *The Times* (19 October 2018).
[16] See especially Common Art 3 to the 1949 Geneva Conventions, and paras 541, 596–600 of ICRC, *Commentary on the First Geneva Convention*, 2nd edn (2016); see also Knuckey, 'Murder in Common Article 3', in Clapham, Gaeta and Sassòli (eds), *The 1949 Geneva Conventions: A Commentary* (2015) 449–67.
[17] See Ch 4 for the law that binds states in the context of the use of force against another state. Non-state actors resorting to the use of force can hardly rely on humanitarian law to authorize their killing of soldiers from the state they are fighting against. Such acts remain crimes under national law. At the end of the conflict, states are encouraged under Additional Protocol (AP) II to the Geneva Conventions (1977) to grant an amnesty to those who 'have participated in the armed conflict', but this does not mean that the acts themselves were authorized by international law. Such an amnesty is not supposed to cover acts that constitute serious international crimes. See further Seibert-Fohr, 'Amnesties', *MPEPIL* (2018); and Schabas, *Unimaginable Atrocities: Justice, Politics, and Rights at the War Crimes Tribunals* (2012) Ch 7.
[18] See Clapham, 'The Limits of Human Rights in Times of Armed Conflict and Other Situations of Armed Violence', in Fassbender and Traibach (eds), *The Limits of Human Rights* (2019) 305–17.

If there is any so-called 'licence to kill', it is very tightly circumscribed. In fact the issue is better understood by considering the international rule concerning 'combatant immunity'. This is the rule that quickly gets translated into a vaguer, deeper idea about some right to kill. The parameters of the actual rule are important because, outside the bounds of those particular circumstances, a killing would quite possibly be a war crime, or a crime that could be prosecuted as murder under national law.

This an area of law that few humanitarian lawyers feel comfortable examining. It is easier to list the prohibitions than the permissions in the law of armed conflict. Humanitarian law feels not so humanitarian when it gets deployed to justify killing. Sean Watts has, however, grappled with the issues and researched the state practice. He finds in the context of inter-state armed conflict that 'The concept of combatant status has ancient law-of-war roots.'[19] Of course in ancient times combatant status might indeed have implied such a right to fight, but on capture under the ancient law of war one could also be enslaved, ransomed or simply slaughtered. This is not the case today. So ancient law-of-war roots are not enough to prove that a right continues unaltered over millennia. The ancient right to kill one's prisoners is obviously no longer valid. Turning to the treaties, Watts finds that they do not actually commit states to a clear set of rights and obligations for combatant status under international law. He concludes:

> States' apparent reluctance to commit combatant status fully to international law in IAC [international armed conflict] makes the prospect that they would do so in NIAC [non-international armed conflict] extremely unlikely. Nothing even approaching the partial coverage offered by Additional Protocol I appears in Additional Protocol II. Nor do any of the usual indicators of customary norms, such as military manuals or statements of *opinio juris*, indicate any State commitment of combatant status in NIAC to international law.[20]

Today, then, we can say with some certainty that states only accept that forces on the other side have combatant status *if they are part of the armed forces of another state*. On the other hand, states do not accept combatant status for rebel forces. States do not accept that rebel forces should merely

---

[19] Watts, 'Present and Future Conceptions of the Status of Government Forces in Non-International Armed Conflict', 88 *International Law Studies* (2012) 145–80 at 151.
[20] Ibid at 152.

be detained as prisoners of war, rather than prosecuted for shooting at or bombing the state's own forces. Shooting at the armed forces of a state is often criminalized by the law of that state (even if the rebels and others claim these are lawful acts of war).[21] In the contemporary world, shooting at the state's soldiers is likely to be criminalized as terrorism. At this point it is clear that the mantra that the law of war treats belligerents equally seems to have broken down. The state will not prosecute its own soldiers for shooting at armed groups fighting against them. But the same state will prosecute fighters from those armed groups for shooting at its troops. Of course an international lawyer can recount that the law of war treats both shootings equally (in that this law does not prohibit such killings), but this is of no interest at all to the rebel who is arrested and tried by the state for murdering the state's own troops (it is no defence to say 'I did not violate the law of war').

Such one-sidedness makes no sense if one starts from the idea that the law of war provides the 'rules of the game'. But in fact we should abandon the idea that the law of war provides such a 'level playing field', or that the rules treat parties equally irrespective of the purpose of the war. The law of war is better seen, as Sir Adam Roberts explains, as 'a modest and limited set of rules that establish certain limitations in war'.[22] For him it is a 'misleading assumption' that the law of war 'grants belligerents certain "rights", including the right to shoot at the soldiers of an opposing army'. Rather than deriving from the law of war, Sir Adam says 'the right to attack the armed forces of an adversary' is simply something 'intrinsic to war'.[23] How to explain this conundrum? In war one might assume that one must have a 'right' to shoot at the other side, and yet this is not a right derived from law, and certainly does not apply when

---

[21] For examples of national law in Australia, the Netherlands and the United Kingdom criminalizing violence by non-state actors 'without any exception whatsoever to accommodate armed conflict and the special regime of IHL' see B. Saul, 'Terrorism, Counter-Terrorism, and International Humanitarian Law', in Saul and Akande (eds), *The Oxford Guide to International Humanitarian Law* (2020) 403-23 at 417. For the jurisdiction asserted by the United States over 'unprivileged enemy belligerents' causing loss of life as 'murder in violation of the law of war' and 'terrorism' see Military Commissions Act of 2009, 10 USC § 950t(15) and (24) (2009). For the definition of 'unpriviledged enemy belligerent' see 10 USC § 948a(6) and (7). See also Watts (n 19) at 152.

[22] Roberts, 'The Equal Application of the Laws of War: A Principle Under Pressure', 90 *IRRC* 872 (2008) 931–62 at 935.

[23] Ibid. Roberts' main focus is, however, international armed conflicts (see Roberts (n 22) at 934), and he is addressing those who would seek to enhance the rights of those responding to aggression and addressing the plight of the 'innocent soldier' rather than building a case for a right to rebel; see further Roberts, 'The Principle of the Equal Application of the Laws of War', in Rodin and Shue (eds), *Just and Unjust Warriors: The Moral and Legal Status of Soldiers* (2008) 226–54.

one is a non-state actor, whether one is labelled an insurgent, a rebel or a terrorist.

We saw in the previous chapter that during the US Civil War, and even in some instances in the wars with different tribes of Native Americans,[24] privileged belligerency or combatant immunity was granted to those who fought against government forces. Today such grants of immunity would most likely be treated as privileges that were bestowed, rather than as legal rights that flow from the fact of war. So what exactly is the law that prevents a soldier who shoots their enemy from being tried for murder?

National law tends not to address this issue. In English law, murder is not defined by statute but is generally understood under the Common Law to cover unlawful killing with malice aforethought of someone 'under the Queen's Peace'. This last antiquated expression (dating from around four centuries ago) has recently been argued to mean that a killing of someone thought to be an enemy in war could not be murder.

The Court of Appeal did not entertain such a theory when it dealt with the killers of Lee Rigby. Fusilier Rigby had seen service for the British Army in Afghanistan and was a recruiter for the Army in the United Kingdom when he was attacked and brutally killed in a knife attack. His attackers produced a statement at the scene of the crime, stating that this knife attack was in retaliation for deaths in Muslim lands.[25] In court, the argument for one of the attackers was that murder under the law does not include killing in the course of a war. The situation was not under the Queen's Peace, it was argued, and therefore fell outside the definition of murder. The Defence stated:

> At all times the [applicant Adebolajo] honestly believed he was fighting a war. He believed he was a soldier fighting that war. He only targeted a serving member of the British armed forces because they were engaged in fighting an unjust war on behalf of the State.[26]

The Court of Appeal limited the discussion of the Queen's Peace to questions of jurisdiction over acts committed abroad, and saw no reason to discuss the issue of war.[27] To the extent that the Queen's Peace is a requisite element for the crime of murder, the judgment stated:

---

[24] For a list of the wars between US forces and Native American peoples between 1776 and 1890, see Vine, *The United States of War* (2020) Appendix.

[25] *R v Adebolajo and Anor* [2014] EWCA Crim 2779 [13].

[26] Ibid [17].

[27] Ibid [17] et seq.

Although the Queen's Peace may play some part still in the elements that have to be proved for murder as regards the status of the victim (and it is not necessary to examine or define the ambit of that), it can only go to the status of the victim; it has nothing whatsoever to do with the status of the killer.[28]

One can see why the Court did not want to countenance the idea that murder could be excused because someone considered they were in a state of war with their own state,[29] but some might still consider that in war, battlefield killings by members of the armed forces could not be considered murder. We should perhaps not lose sight completely of the idea that the inclusion of the phrase 'the Queen's Peace' in the definition of murder is seen by some as necessary. As Hirst explains:

The justification generally advanced for including reference to the Queen's peace in the definition of murder is that it is necessary in order to exclude the killing of enemy soldiers or rebels in battle from the ambit of the offence. The enemy soldier (so the argument goes) is not within the Queen's peace. Killing him cannot therefore be murder, unless he has surrendered, in which case he does come within the Queen's peace and enjoys the protection of English law.[30]

The law here is so untested that, in the run up to the United Kingdom's armed conflict with Iraq in 2003, the Legal Advisor to the Foreign Office could not say with certainty 'whether troops involved in conflicts which are unlawful under international law would be committing criminal offences in the UK'. In his preliminary views, responding to a request from the Foreign Secretary for an urgent note, he points to the two arguments that could be used to suggest that there would be no prosecution: that an alien enemy

---

[28] Ibid [33].

[29] The Court of Appeal explains (ibid [21]): 'It was not surprising it was submitted that this element of the offence of murder in relation to the Queen's peace did not normally feature in murder cases because prior to 1997 reliance by a defendant on a state of war would have been likely to involve an admission of treason. On the basis that this argument was available, Adebolajo was therefore entitled to put before the jury his defence that his killing of Lee Rigby was part of a war with the British Government, involving a people's struggle against forceful occupation and aggression; he had not been under the Queen's peace, but at war with the Queen.'

[30] 'Murder under the Queen's Peace', *Criminal Law Review* (2008) 541–46 at 542. Hirst considers this idea might be traced to a passage by Sir Matthew Hale, whose *History of the Pleas of the Crown* (1736) stated that 'If a man kill an alien enemy within this kingdom, yet it is felony, unless it be in the heat of war, and in the actual exercise thereof.' So for Hirst (ibid), 'killing in the heat of combat is not "unlawful" in the first place'.

would not be within the Queen's Peace, and that the Common Law 'will accept that belligerents in an armed conflict cannot be prosecuted for normal acts of conflict'. But he concludes that 'there must at least be uncertainty, arising from the fact that the law is nowhere laid down'.[31]

There is also considerable confusion in the United Kingdom when it comes to the immunity from suit before national courts for battlefield activity. This has nothing to do with the international rules on combatant immunity, and is confusingly referred to in the British context as 'combat immunity' (as opposed to *combatant* immunity under international law). Accordingly:

> Combat Immunity is a legal principle which provides an exemption from legal liability for members of the Armed Forces and the Government within the context of combat in armed conflict. So a soldier does not owe a fellow soldier a duty of care where a personal injury has resulted when either one or both of them is engaged with an enemy in the course of combat, and the Ministry of Defence is not under the normal duty to maintain a safe system of work for Service personnel engaged with an enemy in the course of combat.[32]

There is new legislation that extends this idea by amending the law relating to time limitations on legal actions for personal injury or death brought against the Ministry of Defence. Courts will not be allowed to permit cases to brought more than six years after the relevant date.

---

[31] Minute Wood to PS [Private Secretary FCO] 15 October 2002, at paras 5 and 6. Rowe also states in this context that '[t]here is no specific defence to the crime of murder given to a soldier during international armed conflict', and he has suggested ways to introduce combatant immunity in international armed conflict into national law. Rowe, *Legal Accountability for Britain's Wars 2000–2015* (2016) at 135–36. Rowe considers that there would be no combatant immunity for either side in a non-international armed conflict such as those involving British troops in Afghanistan from December 2001 and in Iraq in 2004 (ibid at 136–37). He discusses this point and some of the judicial comments from past cases further in Rowe, 'The Criminal Liability of a British Soldier Merely for Participating in the Iraq War 2003: a Response to Chilcot Evidence', *Criminal Law Review* (2010) 752–60. To the extent that the Common Law has been interpreted in the United States there is little authority. In one case, John Gut was convicted for the murder of Native Americans after they had been captured; at one point in the judgment it was stated 'The evidence offered to prove a state of war existed between the United States and Sioux, and that the State, though its legal authorities had offered a reward for the killing of any male of that tribe, was properly rejected. That it is legal to kill an alien enemy in the heat and exercise of war, is undeniable: but to kill such an enemy after he has laid down his arms, and especially when he is confined in prison, is murder.' *State of Minnesota v Gut*, 13 Minn (1868) 341 at 357.
[32] https://www.gov.uk/government/uploads/system/uploads/attachment_data/file/573565/20161128-Consultation_document_death_and_injury_compensation_scheme.pdf. At para 21.

The same legislation amends the Human Rights Act 1998, affecting the discretion to allow human rights cases to proceed beyond the normal time limit by asking the relevant court to have particular regard to 'the operational context' in overseas operations and 'the exceptional demands and stresses' on the members of the armed forces.[33] In a way these developments extend the idea of *combat immunity* in the UK legal order.

But let us return to the general situation seen from the perspective of international law. There are different ways of looking at the ways in which killing in war is not to be tried as murder. One way stresses that a lawful combatant cannot be prosecuted on capture by the enemy side for merely participating directly in hostilities. While this might seem inherent in some general conception of war, in fact today it can only really be said to apply to the armed forces in inter-state armed conflicts.[34] The sole reference to such a combatant immunity principle is found in Additional Protocol I (AP I), which applies only to inter-state conflicts, or conflicts between states and National Liberation Movements under certain conditions. The relevant provision states:

> Members of the armed forces of a Party to a conflict (other than medical personnel and chaplains covered by Article 33 of the Third Convention) are combatants, that is to say, they have the right to participate directly in hostilities.[35]

This right has to be respected by the other state that is a party to the inter-state conflict; to prosecute a combatant just for fighting in an inter-state conflict is therefore a violation of international law. The national law of murder may have been violated, but prosecutions cannot be brought against the combatant from the armed forces of the other state due to the international law of combatant immunity. The individual being prosecuted has, in the words of the treaty, 'the right to participate directly in hostilities'. Of course anyone captured may nevertheless be tried for war crimes.[36]

---

[33] Overseas Operations (Service Personnel and Veterans) Act 2021; for the background, see Mills and Dawson, 'Briefing Paper 8983', 22 September 2020; the Act also introduces the idea of a presumption against prosecution for relevant offences once a period of five years has expired, beginning with the day on which the alleged conduct took place. Sexual offences, genocide, crimes against humanity, torture and war crimes are exluded from the scope of this presumption.

[34] See also Rowe, *Legal Accountability for Britain's Wars 2000–2015* (2016) at 135–37.

[35] AP I Art 43(2).

[36] We will deal with the scope of these crimes and the possibilities for prosecution in Ch 10.

Another way to look at this is from the humanitarian point of view of the protection of those who fall into the hands of the enemy. As we shall see, various categories of persons, including combatants in an international armed conflict, are entitled to prisoner of war status, and this implies that the combatant will be held until the end of the conflict and not prosecuted for taking part in the conflict. The ICRC is clear that, under customary international law, the connected ideas of a right to participation in hostilities and the right to prisoner of war status apply only in conflicts between states: 'Combatant status ... exists only in international armed conflicts ... '[37]

> The implications of being recognised as a combatant in an international armed conflict are significant, as only combatants have the right to participate directly in hostilities . . . . Upon capture, combatants entitled to prisoner-of-war status may neither be tried for their participation in the hostilities nor for acts that do not violate international humanitarian law.[38]

To the extent that the concepts of combatant and prisoner of war status exist in customary international law, they only apply to international armed conflicts.[39]

Dinstein similarly asserts that international law simply protects the soldier from trial for murder:

> Warfare amounts to a series of acts that are generally forbidden – and subsumed as criminal – in the various domestic legal systems, eg murder, assault, and arson. When a combatant, John Doe, holds a rifle, aims it at Richard Roe (a soldier belonging to the enemy's armed forces) with the intent to kill him, pulls the trigger, and causes Richard Roe's death, what we have is a premeditated homicide fitting the definition of murder in most (possibly all) domestic penal codes. If upon being captured by the enemy, John Doe is not prosecuted for murder, this is due to one reason only. International law provides John Doe with a legal shield, protecting him

---

[37] Henckaerts and Doswald-Beck, *Customary International Humanitarian Law, vol 1: Rules* (2005) at 11 in the summary on Rule 3. Under this Rule 'All members of the armed forces of a party to the conflict are combatants, except medical and religious personnel' ; see also the introduction to Ch 33 at t 384.

[38] Ibid at 384.

[39] Henckaerts, 'Study on Customary International Humanitarian Law: A Contribution to the Understanding and Respect for the Rule of Law in Armed Conflict', 857 *International Review of the Red Cross* (2005) 175–212, rules 3, 4 and 106.

from trial and punishment, by conferring upon him the status of a prisoner of war.[40]

This legal shield or immunity can, however, be lost. A privileged belligerent, entitled as a member of the armed forces of a state fighting another state, can lose their combatant immunity if they fail to distinguish themselves from the civilian population when directly engaged in hostilities. If captured in such circumstances, they can be prosecuted under the national law of the other state for unlawful participation in the fighting. The UK's *Military Manual* states:

> The position of a person who takes a direct part in hostilities while failing to comply with the rule of distinction is as follows. If he falls into the power of the enemy while engaged in an attack or a military operation preparatory to an attack, and is not at that time complying with the requirements of the general rule (or, where applicable, the special rule . . .), he forfeits his combatant status and may be tried and punished for unlawful participation in hostilities.[41]

The overarching point is that, in an international armed conflict (whether considered a war or not), those entitled to fight on behalf of the state cannot

---

[40] Dinstein, 'The Distinction Between Unlawful Combatants and War Criminals', in Dinstein and Tabory (eds), *International Law at a Time of Perplexity: Essays in Honour of Shabtai Rosenne* (1989) 103–16 at 104.

[41] UK Ministry of Defence, *The Manual of the Law of Armed Conflict* (2004) at 43 para 4.6. For the special rule, see ibid at 42 paras 4.5 et seq. Looked at from the perspective of prisoner of war status, the result is similar. The ICRC's study on *Customary International Humanitarian Law* (n 37) states in Rule 106 that 'Combatants must distinguish themselves from the civilian population while they are engaged in an attack or in a military operation preparatory to an attack. If they fail to do so, they do not have the right to prisoner-of-war status.' In the past some saw belligerent acts by civilians as offences against the laws and customs of war, or even as war crimes; today such acts do not figure in the catalogues of international war crimes applied by international tribunals. For discussion of this point, and the related issue of spies, see Rogers, 'Unequal Combat and the Law of War', 7 *Yearbook of International Humanitarian Law* (2004) 2–34 at 21–27; Baxter, 'So-Called 'Unprivileged Belligerency': Spies, Guerrillas, and Saboteurs', 28 *BYBIL* (1951) 323–45; Dinstein, 'The Distinction between Unlawful Combatants and War Criminals' (n 40) at 109 makes the further distinction between a soldier removing his uniform during an operation, losing the status of lawful combatant but not becoming a war criminal, and a soldier instead putting on the enemy uniform and becoming a war criminal, as this would be an 'improper use' of the uniform of the enemy under Art 23(f) of the Hague Regulations. The precise application and acceptance of the special rules in Art 44 of AP I is complex and need not detain us here; see further Sassòli, *IHL* (n 9) at paras 8.58, 8.69, 8.70 and 8.83. He concludes that in international armed conflicts, 'although acts of hostility committed by persons who have lost or never had combatant status may be punished under the domestic law of the captor, such acts do not constitute war crimes' (ibid at para 8.112).

be prosecuted by the other state for simply engaging in hostilities in a regular way.

In recent times the combatant immunity rule has come under pressure from different quarters. Two approaches in particular seek to improve the humanitarian protection offered by the laws of war. A first set of suggestions revolve around the idea that combatant immunity should be extended to rebels in an internal armed conflict.[42] Under the current rule, rebels are detained and often prosecuted for having taken part in the rebellion. As they are likely to be imprisoned for long periods, or even executed for treason, sedition or rebellion, there is then, it is argued, little incentive to abide by the humanitarian law that protects civilians when rebels are engaged in armed conflict. For the present, however, governments simply have no appetite for any recognition of armed non-state actors as being entitled to any sort of combatant immunity.[43] During the conflict the armed group will most likely be labelled terrorist. It will not be accepted that they have a right to fight.

After the fighting, there may be some negotiated peace agreement that grants amnesties or pardons to those who merely took up arms and engaged on the battlefield. Such arrangements have been made in recent years for Colombia.[44] In other situations, such as South Sudan, the peace agreements simply make provision for the release by all sides of detained fighters.[45] So, in practice, there may be some sort of immunity depending on the distribution

---

[42] Emily Crawford suggests that even before a single regime is achieved for all armed conflicts, captured rebels should enjoy 'treatment' as prisoners of war, *The Treatment of Combatants and Insurgents under the Law of Armed Conflict* (2010) at 173; see further section 9.1.2 below.

[43] The only exception would seem to be the historical category of *levée en masse*. See Corn et al, *The Law of Armed Conflict: An Operational Approach* (2012) at 134 and 367; and Sassòli, *IHL* (n 9) at para 8.67.

[44] Consider the most recent arrangements in Colombia under the Amnesty Lei 1820 of 30 December 2016, which allows for pardons for political crimes related to the hostilities where these do not amount to war crimes or human rights violations. See, eg, Art 15: 'Artículo 15. Amnistía de iure. Se concede amnistía por los delitos políticos de "rebelión", "sedición", "asonada", "conspiración" y "seducción", usurpación y retención ilegal de mando y los delitos que son conexos con estos de conformidad con ley, a quienes hayan incurrido en ellos.' Thousands have been granted amnesty by the President for 'political crimes'. See at http://es.presidencia.gov.co/noticia/170710-Presidente-Santos-firmo-decreto-que-otorga-amnistia-a-3252-miembros-de-las-Farc-por-delitos-politicos.

[45] In the Biafra conflict, the Federal authorities and the opposition both treated captured fights as prisoners of war. Sivakumaran, *The Law of Non-International Armed Conflict* (2012) at 524. The various agreements entered into by the parties to the conflict in South Sudan foresee the release of those detained in relation to the conflict (often referred to as 'prisoners of war'). See, eg, Revitalised Agreement on the Resolution of the Conflict in the Republic of South Sudan, 12 September 2018, Art 2.1.6. See also the obligation under Art 6(5) of AP II: '5. At the end of hostilities, the authorities in power shall endeavour to grant the broadest possible amnesty to persons who have participated in the armed conflict, or those deprived of their liberty for reasons related to the armed conflict, whether they are interned or detained.'

of power at the end of the fighting. But rebel fighters have no way of knowing during the conflict whether there will be a negotiated peace of this sort. During the fighting the rebels might have to presume that on capture they will be tried and prosecuted for simply being fighters. Rebels have no combatant immunity as a matter of international law.

A second line of argument comes from those who, building on just war theory, question the morality of treating soldiers from the just and unjust sides in the same way. David Rodin has suggested that individual soldiers fighting an unjust war should and could be punished at the end of the war for their mere participation. This assumes that in any armed conflict one side is to blame, and therefore asks why we should not seek to minimize the chances of participation in such unjust wars by punishing those who fight on the wrong side. Rodin is aware that the law does not currently favour such an approach, and that there is no obvious impartial institution to determine which side is in the wrong, but he asks that we should be 'constantly seeking opportunities to align both legal norms and legal institutions more closely with moral considerations'.[46] He recounts that British and American officers told him they believed the 2003 invasion of Iraq was morally unjustified. He points to standard moral and legal concepts concerning reasonable belief and justification to suggest that soldiers could be punished for fighting an unjust war. He makes the point that 'War leaders are held responsible for the decisions they make in light of facts as they honestly and reasonably believed them to be. It is at the very least unclear why we should not hold soldiers responsible in the same way.'[47]

Ten years after Rodin wrote this, we now have, since 2018, the prospect of individual leaders being prosecuted in the International Criminal Court, or in various national jurisdictions,[48] for manifest violations of the UN Charter (the crime of aggression). Stepping back, it is perhaps not such a leap of logic to extend the idea of prosecution for aggression from leaders to commanders or soldiers, sailors and pilots. And yet such an idea would be met with howls

---

[46] Rodin, 'The Moral Inequality of Soldiers: Why *jus in bello* Asymmetry is Half Right', in Rodin and Shue (eds), *Just and Unjust Warriors: The Moral and Legal Status of Soldiers* (2008) 44–68 at 63–64.

[47] Ibid at 68.

[48] Hartig, 'Post Kampala: The Early Implementers of the Crime of Aggression', 17 *JICJ* (2019) 485–93. In many cases national jurisdictions already had the possibility to prosecute wars of aggression, but these laws have been adjusted in the light of the ICC Statute: see Hartig's examination with regard to Afghanistan, Croatia, Czech Republic, Estonia, Finland, Germany, North Macedonia and Slovenia; other states that have included the crime of aggression include Luxemburg, Ecuador and Samoa.

of protest not only from state representatives, but also from scholars. There is so much invested in the idea that the laws of war will apply equally to both sides, that few of the relevant legal experts will countenance the suggestion that the combatants from one side might lose their immunity from prosecution due to their knowing contribution to an aggression. As Weiler and Deshman have argued, opposition to mixing up the illegality of the war with the rights of those fighting it will be, in part, traceable to legal conservatism, and in part 'motivated by purely political calculations of what would increase the likelihood of moral, legal, or military victory', but the opposition 'can just as easily be driven by close emotional proximity to those who must live, fight, and die on one side of a conflict'.[49]

Moreover, the traditional humanitarian approach has been to remain impartial, treating everyone equally in time of war. Questions of the legality of the war (the *jus ad bellum*) are to be banished from the realm of the humanitarian law of armed conflict to another sphere. And yet Rodin, Weiler, Dashman and others are highlighting fundamental shifts that are going on:

> The normative perspectives of human rights and international criminal law have put a very particular lens on the current debate. Whereas pure humanitarianism tends to insist on absolute separation and simply protecting all humans caught up in war, the human rights framework imposes a more complex analysis.[50]

Human rights law demands that the taking of a life be necessary and not arbitrary.[51] Killings have to be justified. We will consider issues of necessity in the next section. For now, with regard to the need for killings to be lawful rather than arbitrary, let us note that the Human Rights Committee concluded in 2018 that 'States parties engaged in acts of aggression as defined in international law, resulting in deprivation of life, violate ipso facto article 6 of the Covenant [the right not to be arbitrarily deprived of one's life].'[52] In other words, members of the armed forces killed in action as the victims of an aggressor state's armed forces have had their human rights violated.

---

[49] Weiler and Deshman, 'Far Be It from Thee to Slay the Righteous with the Wicked: An Historical and Historiographical Sketch of the Bellicose Debate Concerning the Distinction between *Jus ad Bellum* and *Jus in Bello*', 24 *EJIL* (2013) 25–61 at 57.

[50] Ibid at 60.

[51] Clapham, 'The Limits of Human Rights' (n 18) at 306–07.

[52] General Comment No 36 (2018) on Article 6 of the International Covenant on Civil and Political Rights, on the Right to Life, UN Doc CCPR/C/GC/36, 30 October 2018, para 70.

In sum, the popular idea that war brings with it a licence to kill has no basis in law. The immunity from prosecution of soldiers is limited to those fighting for the armed forces of one state against another state. This combatant immunity is inapplicable if a soldier is caught attacking or spying out of uniform. The so-called equal application of the law of war does not prevent states from prosecuting rebels for taking up arms. Nor does equal application prevent leaders who plan or execute or assist others in an act of aggression from being prosecuted for the crime of aggression. Finally, even if killing the enemy is seen by some as simply a 'lawful act of war', from a different perspective the UN Human Rights Committee has now confirmed that when forces from the aggressor side kill anyone (combatants included) from the other side, that constitutes a violation of the victim's rights under international human rights law. Far from being licensed, the killing is unlawful.

7.2 Distinction

7.2.1 Military Objectives and Civilian Objects

International law now contains detailed rules on the obligation to distinguish between military objectives and civilian objects.[53] The rules apply to all parties to the conflict, and certain violations will constitute war crimes.[54] Today, for all operations that take effect on land, at sea, in the air or even in the context of a cyber operation, attacks must be directed at military objectives.[55]

---

[53] See eg AP I Arts 48–67; and Henckaerts and Doswald-Beck, *Customary International Humanitarian Law*, vol 1: *Rules* (2005) (n 37) Rules 1–56.

[54] See Ch 10 below; for an overview of some of the recent practice and war crimes trials before international tribunals, see Casey-Maslen and Haines, *Hague Law Interpreted* (2018) Chs 4–7.

[55] AP I Art 48; Schmitt, Garraway and Dinstein, *The Manual on the Law of Non-International Armed Conflict* (2006) at para 1.1.4; Doswald-Beck (ed), *San Remo Manual on International Law Applicable to Armed Conflicts at Sea* (1995) at para 39; The Program on Humanitarian Policy and Conflict Research at Harvard University (HPCR), *Manual on International Law Applicable to Air and Missile Warfare* (2013), Rule 10(a)(ii); Schmitt (ed), *Tallinn Manual 2.0 on the International Law Applicable to Cyber Operations* (2017) Rules 99–100. Sassòli and Quintin point out that certain cultural or medical objects, which might be seen as military objectives under the tests discussed below, are protected from attack under specific rules: 'Active and Passive Precautions in Air and Missile Warfare', 44 *Israel Yearbook on Human Rights* (2014) 69–123 at 91, referencing Arts 9 and 11 of the Hague Convention for the Protection of Cultural Property in the Event of Armed Conflict (1954) and Arts 12 and 13 of the 1999 Second Protocol to that Convention on Cultural Property; as well as Art 21 of GC I of 1949, Art 35 of GC II (1949) and Art 19 of GC IV (1949).

Attacks in this context mean 'acts of violence against the adversary, whether in offence or in defence'.[56]

What, then, constitutes a military objective? The concept has been codified in treaty law, and the rule is applied as a matter of customary international law to all armed conflicts.[57] The relevant provision in Additional Protocol I reads:

> Attacks shall be limited strictly to military objectives. In so far as objects are concerned, military objectives are limited to those objects which by their nature, location, purpose or use make an effective contribution to military action and whose total or partial destruction, capture or neutralization, in the circumstances ruling at the time, offers a definite military advantage.[58]

There is plenty of debate over how to interpret each and every aspect of this rule.[59] Some insight as to how part of this might be applied in practice is gleaned from this paragraph in the US Commander's *Handbook on the Law of Navy Operations*:

> An object is a valid military objective if by its nature (eg, combat ships and military aircraft), location (eg, bridge over an enemy supply route), use (eg, school building being used as an enemy headquarters), or purpose (eg, a civilian airport that is built with a longer than required runway so it can be used for military airlift in time of emergency) it makes an effective contribution to the enemy's war-fighting/war-sustaining effort and its total or partial destruction, capture, or neutralization, in the circumstance ruling at the time, offers a definite military advantage.[60]

Let us highlight three controversies related to what should constitute a military objective. The first one relates to the way in which the same *Handbook* and the US *Law of War Manual* seem to expand the idea of purpose. The

---

[56] AP I Art 49(1). For the discussion as to when a cyber attack leads to violence or the destruction of an object, and whether data can be considered objects, see Schmitt (ed), *Tallin Manual 2.0* (n 55) at 414–22.

[57] International Law Association Study Group on the Conduct of Hostilities in the 21st Century, 'The Conduct of Hostilities and International Law: Challenges of 21st Century Warfare', 93 *International Law Studies* (2017) 322–88 at 327.

[58] AP I Art 52(2).

[59] See Sassòli, *IHL* (n 9) at Ch 8.6.5; Casey-Maslen and Haines, *Hague Law Interpreted* (n 54) Chs 4 and 5; Boothby, *The Law of Targeting* (2012) at 98–111; Dinstein, *The Conduct of Hostilities under the Law of International Armed Conflict*, 3rd edn (2016) Ch 4.

[60] US Department of the Navy, NWP 1-14M, August 2017, para 5.3.1.

same paragraph from the *Handbook* continues: 'Purpose is related to use, but is concerned with the intended, suspected, or possible future use of an object rather than its immediate and temporary use.' This introduces considerable latitude. If a civilian object becomes a military objective simply due to some possible future use, this is potentially a 'disturbing loophole'.[61] Other Manuals seem to restrict the purpose criterion, so an attacker would need to have a reasonable belief that there is an *intention* to use the object for military purposes.[62] And Dinstein adds that 'most enemy intentions are not easy to decipher'.[63] He urges:

> When in doubt, caution is called for, especially where hospitals, schools, places of worship and cultural property are concerned. For instance, field intelligence revealing that the enemy intends to use a given school as a munitions depot does not justify an attack against that school as long as no practical steps have been taken to move the munitions in.[64]

A second issue relates to the insistence by a number of western states that here, and elsewhere in the Protocol, the reference to the military advantage 'anticipated from an attack is intended to refer to the advantage anticipated from *the attack considered as a whole* and not from isolated or particular parts of the attack'.[65] The United States, even though not a party to this treaty, has endorsed this understanding of the general rule. The relevant paragraph from the US *Law of War Manual* is worth quoting here, as it illustrates how the concept of the anticipated military advantage has become defined by the United States, first by the concept of the attack 'considered as a whole', and then seen against the 'full context of the war strategy':

> 'Military advantage' refers to the advantage anticipated from an attack when considered as a whole, and not only from its isolated or particular

---

[61] Casey-Maslen and Haines, *Hague Law Interpreted* (n 54) at 102.

[62] UK *Manual of the Law of Armed Conflict* at 56; see also Schmitt, Garraway and Dinstein, *The Manual on the Law of Non-International Armed Conflict* (2006) (n 55) at 6, ' "Purpose" indicates that it is known, based on reliable intelligence or other information, that the enemy intends to use (or abuse) the object militarily in the future.'

[63] Dinstein, *International Armed Conflict* (n 59) at 114.

[64] Ibid.

[65] From the understanding made by Canada at the time of ratification (20 November 1990) of AP I (emphasis added); see also the similar positions of Australia, Belgium, France, Germany, Italy, the Netherlands, New Zealand, Spain and the United Kingdom with regard to the idea of considering the attack as a whole and not just isolated parts of the attack.

parts. Similarly, 'military advantage' is not restricted to immediate tactical gains, but may be assessed in the full context of the war strategy.[66]

There is a real danger here that once the idea of an attack as a whole morphs into a 'war strategy', the range of military objectives becomes overly broad. Dinstein has stressed, however, that ' "an attack as a whole" must be a finite event, not to be confused with the entire war'.[67] Similarly, the latest New Zealand *Manual of Armed Forces Law* confirms the point: 'The term "operation as a whole" is to be assessed realistically and in good faith. It is not to be expanded to routinely refer to the entire war or campaign.'[68] Precisely because today permission to engage in warfare may be limited by the specific authorization of the Security Council, the concept of military advantage has to be seen as an aspect not of winning the war, but of fulfilling a limited objective.[69]

A third controversy is whether a military objective can cover objects that make 'an effective contribution to the enemy's war-fighting/war-sustaining effort'. The latest US *Law of War Manual* proposes that such objects are covered, but acknowledges that there is no explicit authority for such an expansive view:

Military action has a broad meaning and is understood to mean the general prosecution of the war. It is not necessary that the object provide immediate tactical or operational gains or that the object make an effective contribution to a specific military operation. Rather, the object's effective contribution to the war-fighting or war-sustaining capability of an opposing force is sufficient. Although terms such as 'war-fighting', 'war-supporting', and 'war-sustaining' are not explicitly reflected in the treaty definitions of military objective, the United States has interpreted the military objective definition to include these concepts.[70]

---

[66] *Department of Defense Law of War Manual* (2016) at para 5.6.7.3 (footnotes omitted).

[67] Dinstein, 'Legitimate Military Objectives Under Current Jus in Bello', 78 *International Law Studies* (2002) 139–72 at 145; and see also Dinstein, *International Armed Conflict* (n 59) at 108–09.

[68] *Manual of Armed Forces Law*, vol 4: *Law of Armed Conflict*, DM 69 (2nd edn) (2019) at para 8.6.5.

[69] See Henderson, *The Contemporary Law of Targeting* (2009) at 152–54.

[70] At para 5.6.6.2 (footnotes omitted); see also the Australian Manual (2006), *Law of Armed Conflict* at para 5.31, 'economic targets that indirectly but effectively support operations are also military objectives if an attack will gain a definite military advantage'. The differences between the Manuals is significant, the Australian Manual requires that there be effective support to 'operations', while the US *Manual* requires 'an effective contribution to the enemy's war-fighting/war-sustaining effort'.

Although reference is made here to the prosecution of a 'war',[71] the US authorities have in recent years been applying this expansive understanding of the objects that can be targeted to its attacks on objects sustaining non-state armed groups such as the so-called 'Islamic state'.[72] The argument emerges clearly from a 2016 speech given by the General Counsel of the US Department of Defence:

> First, the targeted object must make an effective contribution to military action. In the case of ISIL and the targeting of certain petroleum facilities it controls, petroleum is the principal source of support for ISIL's armed action. ISIL regularly uses petroleum to support its armed action, and, indeed the organization depends on it. The money it receives from sales of petroleum is used to purchase weapons and pay fighters. ISIL funnels petroleum revenues directly to the group's fighting forces. ... Given this analysis, certain petroleum facilities such as pumping stations or the transportation assets that take the oil either to its depots or to market to be sold make an effective contribution to ISIL's military action ...
>
> The second part of the legal test is that the complete or partial destruction of the object must offer a definite military advantage in the circumstances at the time. This requirement generally excludes attacks for which anticipated military gains are indeterminate or speculative. Because ISIL controls and depends on petroleum production, sales, and revenue for its military operations, the military advantage the United States gains from striking this infrastructure is not indeterminate or speculative. The United States eliminates not only the use of the petroleum for military purposes, but also the opportunity to sell the petroleum to create cash that will also be used for military purposes. Also, ISIL cannot easily substitute petroleum for other sources of ready fiscal income. So the military effects of damaging or destroying ISIL-controlled petroleum facilities will be more certain than

---

[71] We might note that in this context that, after referencing the US interpretation of military objectives as including economic targets that 'indirectly but effectively support or sustain the enemy's war-fighting capability', the distinguished drafters of the *Manual on the Law of Non-International Armed Conflict* considered that such a reading of military objective 'is not relevant to non-international armed conflicts': Schmitt, Garraway and Dinstein, *The Manual on the Law of Non-International Armed* (n 62) at 6 fn 3.

[72] Egan, 'International Law, Legal Diplomacy, and the Counter-ISIL Campaign: Some Observations', 92 *International Law Studies* (2016) 235–48 at 242.

they might otherwise be if ISIL could easily replace that revenue from other sources.[73]

This notion that fighting a war entitles parties to destroy those objects that can be considered as making an effective contribution to the war-fighting/ supporting/sustaining capabilities of the enemy may have existed in the past, and the United States points to the Lieber Code (1863),[74] but today this notion is rejected in a range of other Manuals.

Those who have sought to defend a wider understanding of military objectives have sometimes pointed to a paragraph in New Zealand's *Interim Law of Armed Conflict Manual* of 1992, which read:

> Economic targets that indirectly but effectively support enemy operations may also be attacked to gain a definite military advantage. For example, an 1870 international arbitral tribunal recognized that the destruction of cotton was justified during the American Civil War since the sale of cotton provided funds for almost all Confederate arms and ammunition. Authorization to attack such targets will be reserved to higher authority.[75]

But the current *Manual* (2019), which replaces the earlier one, has excised that paragraph and today makes no reference to economic targets or indirect support.[76]

The established expert manuals on armed conflict at sea, on air and missile warfare, on non-international armed conflict and on cyber operations have all rejected such an expansion of military objectives to those objects that contribute to the enemy's war-sustaining effort.[77] Kenneth Watkin (a retired Brigadier-General from the Canadian Forces and an experienced law of war commentator) has warned that 'Historically, this is an issue that stands at

[73] Jennifer M O'Connor (US General Counsel, Dept of Defense), 'Applying the Law of Targeting to the Modern Battlefield' (2016), available at https://dod.defense.gov/Portals/1/ Documents/pubs/Applying-the-Law-of-Targeting-to-the-Modern-Battlefield.pdf.

[74] Note the reference to the Lieber Code Art 15 in the US *Law of War Manual* at para 5.17.2.3.

[75] DM 112, para 515(5).

[76] *Manual of Armed Forces Law* (n 68).

[77] Doswald-Beck (ed), *San Remo Manual* (n 55) at 150; *Harvard Manual on Missile Warfare* (2013) (n 55) at 121:'The crux of the issue is related to revenues from exports of oil which is not put to military use by the enemy. The majority of the group of Experts took the position that the connection between revenues from such exports and military action is too remote. Consequently, it rejected the war-sustaining argument . . .' and 42 (commentary to Rules 24, and 1y). Also Schmitt (ed), *Tallinn Manual 2.0* (n 55) at 441; Schmitt, Garraway and Dinstein, *The Manual on the Law of Non-International Armed Conflict* (n 62) at 6 fn 3.

the edge of a very steep and slippery slope that has led directly to considerable humanitarian suffering.'[78] Other, similarly qualified writers have given examples of what cannot be targeted in this context. APV Rogers (a retired Major-General from the British Army) stated:

> If a country relies almost entirely on, say, the export of coffee beans or bananas for its income and even if this income is used to great extent to support its war effort, the opinion of the author is that it would not be legitimate to attack banana or coffee bean plantations or warehouses.[79]

Similarly Dinstein opines:

> It is true that revenues from export may sustain the war effort. Yet, enemy exports on board neutral vessels can be stopped or curtailed only through the imposition of a blockade on the enemy coast ... The link between crops for export and military action is too remote. For an object to qualify as a military objective, there must exist a proximate nexus to 'war-fighting'. Crops and other agricultural produce as such do not qualify as military objectives . . . In the same vein, the stock exchange, banking system and money markets of the enemy State – albeit, perhaps, vital to its economic staying power in the armed conflict – do not, as such, constitute lawful military objectives.[80]

Returning to the example of attacks on the oil tankers on land servicing ISIS, where the 'goal of the attacks is to stop refined oil from being supplied to Islamic State military forces', a case could indeed be made that such fuel makes an effective contribution to military action (war-fighting).[81] But a considerable bulk of expert opinion is against allowing for a more general campaign against objects that are merely war-sustaining (both with regard to inter-state conflicts and conflicts with non-state armed groups, including those labelled as terrorists). The International Law Association's Study Group issued the most recent unequivocal pronouncement:

[78] 'Targeting "Islamic State" Oil Facilities', 90 *International Law Studies* (2014) 499–513 at 513.

[79] Rogers, *Law on the Battlefield*, 2nd edn (2004) at 70-71.

[80] Dinstein, *International Armed Conflict* (n 59) at 199.

[81] For detail of the approach of the US Department of Defense see Goodman, 'The Obama Administration and Targeting "War Sustaining" Objects in Noninternational Armed Conflict', 110 *AJIL* (2019) 663–79 at 664 and 677. For arguments about targeting cash as 'war sustaining' or 'war supporting', see Schmitt and Merriam, 'The Tyranny of Context: Israeli Targeting Practices in Legal Perspective', 37 *University of Pennsylvania Journal of International Law* (2016) 53–139.

There is no indication in State practice that objects contributing to the enemy's war-sustaining effort qualify as such as military objectives and the [Study Group] believes that this position has no basis in the law as it stands today and should be clearly rejected.[82]

As we shall see in the next chapter, there is an idea that war, and especially total war,[83] justifies capturing enemy merchant ships on the high seas and cutting off an enemy nation (and its people) through Blockade. This thinking resulted in the 'unrestricted' submarine warfare against merchant shipping in the two World Wars leaving thousands of civilian crew from merchant ships killed, and millions of tons of shipping destroyed.[84] This practice from the Second World War is referenced in the 2017 US Naval Commander's *Handbook*. A legal explanation is given:

Initially, such acts were justified as reprisals against illegal acts of the enemy. As the war progressed, however, merchant vessels were regularly armed and convoyed, participated in intelligence collection, and were other-wise incorporated directly or indirectly into the enemy's war-fighting/

[82] 'The Conduct of Hostilities and International Law: Challenges of 21st Century Warfare', 93 *International Law Studies* (2017) 322–88 at 341.

[83] Total war, under one understanding, 'assumes the commitment of massive armed forces to battle, the thoroughgoing mobilization of industrial economies in the war effort, and hence the disciplined organization of civilians no less than warriors'. See Chickering and Förster, 'Are We There Yet? World War II and the Theory of Total War', in Chickering, Förster and Greiner (eds), *A World at Total War: Global Conflict and the Politics of Destruction (1937–1945)* (2005) 1–16 at 2. To be clear, claiming to be in a total war cannot suspend the laws of armed conflict: Rowe, 'Total War', in Gutman, Rieff and Dworkin (eds), *Crimes of War*, 2nd edn (2007) 402; the origins of the expression in the period between the World Wars is explained by Strachan, when it mainly referred to the demands likely to be made on the belligerent state. Nevertheless, he explains, 'When General Erich Ludendorff's *Der Totale Krieg*, first published in 1935, was trans-lated into English, its title was *The Nation at War*, and "der totale Krieg" was rendered much more accurately as "totalitarian" war. The German warlord's point was that the next war would require the mobilisation of the entire nation for the purposes of its prosecution: the political and social fabric of the state would be bent to the achievement of a single purpose. But between 1939 and 1945 total war acquired an additional and different meaning: it referred to the readiness to breach the principle of non-combatant immunity, one of the keystones of just war theory. It defined not what would be required of one's own population, but what one would inflict on the enemy's.' 'Strategic Bombing and the Question of Civilian Casualties up to 1945', in Addison and Crang (eds), *Firestorm: The Bombing of Dresden, 1945* (2006) 1–17 at 1.

[84] For the complex arguments about whether the merchant ships had become military ob-jectives by carrying arms for self-defence, whether such attacks were justified as reprisals, and whether the orders regarding submarine crew's obligations towards survivors were illegal see Tucker, *The Law of War and Neutrality at Sea* (1957) at 57–73; see also Goldie, 'Targeting Enemy Merchant Shipping: An Overview of Law and Practice', 65 *International Law Studies* (1993) 1–26; Heintschel von Heinegg, 'Submarine Operations and International Law', in Engdahl and Wrange (eds), *Law at War: The Law as Was and the Law as it Should Be* (2008) 141–62.

war-supporting/war-sustaining effort. Consequently, enemy merchant vessels were widely regarded as legitimate military targets subject to destruction on sight.[85]

The conditions for rendering a merchant ship or civilian aircraft a military objective have been codified in two expert manuals. Rather than referencing any such war-sustaining effort, they refer to 'making a contribution to military action eg carrying military materials'.[86] Once the line between military objectives and civilians involved in the war-sustaining effort is blurred, we clearly risk reducing the protection of civilians to vanishing point.[87]

Today it is certainly worth reinforcing the rule that a military objective is limited to those objects that both make an effective contribution to military action and whose destruction at that time offers a definite military advantage. We might also add that it is no longer accepted that a state can establish at sea a 'war zone' or 'exclusion zone' where any vessel (including merchant

---

[85] See para 8.6.2.2 (destruction by surface warships); para 8.7.1 (destruction by submarines); and para 8.8 (destruction by military aircraft).

[86] Eg *San Remo Manual* (n 55) para 60(g). The rules for attacks on enemy and neutral vessels and civil aircraft more generally are found ibid at paras 60, 63, 67 and 70, as well as at paras 38–46 and 72–77. The other criteria listed in para 60 include, for enemy merchant vessels: (a) engaging in belligerent acts on behalf of the enemy; (b) acting as an auxiliary to an enemy's armed forces; (c) being incorporated into or assisting the enemy's intelligence gathering system; (d) sailing under convoy of enemy warships or military aircraft; (e) refusing an order to stop or actively resisting visit, search or capture; (f) being armed to an extent that they could inflict damage to a warship. Passenger vessels carrying only civilian passengers may not be destroyed at sea: ibid at paras 140 and 152. Cf the International Law Association's Helsinki Principles on the Law of Maritime Neutrality, Principle 5.1.2 para 5, which seems to allow for an attack where passenger ships are 'incorporated into or assist the enemy's intelligence system'. See also the *Harvard Manual on Missile Warfare* (n 55), Rules 27 and 174, for enemy and neutral civilian aircraft; and for civilian airliners servicing passengers, see ibid Rules 58–63 and 68–70. For a detailed look at the traditional law, see Fenrick, 'Legal Aspects of Targeting in the Law of Naval Warfare', *Canadian Yearbook of International Law* (1991) 238–82; and Fenrick, 'The Merchant Vessel as Legitimate Target in the Law of Naval Warfare', in Delissen and Tanja (eds), *Humanitarian Law of Armed Conflict – Challenges Ahead: Essays in Honour of Fritz Kalshoven* (1991) 425–43.

[87] See the detailed criticism of such an approach by Busuttil, *Naval Weapons Systems and the Contemporary Law of War* (1998) at 143–48. See also Heintschel von Heinegg, 'Submarine Operations and International Law', in Engdahl and Wrange (eds), *Law at War: The Law as Was and the Law as it Should Be* (2008) 141–62 at 157–59; and Heintschel von Heinegg, 'The Law of Armed Conflict at Sea', in Fleck (ed), *The Handbook of Humanitarian Law in Armed Conflict*, 3rd edn (2013) 463–547 at 490, '"war material" may not be understood as comprising goods which have some tenuous relevance for the enemy's war efforts. Rather, the objects concerned must be directly apt for use by the enemy's armed forces.' And most recently Heintschel von Heinegg, 'Blockade', *MPEPIL* (2015) at para 54, 'the US position on targeting the enemy's war-sustaining effort has not found approval by other States, and it is therefore contrary to international treaty and customary law'. Dinstein is explicit in his exclusion of exports as an example of a contribution to military action; for a legitimate attack on an enemy or neutral merchant he gives the example of 'carrying military materials': Dinstein, *International Armed Conflict* (n 59) at 129–30.

vessels) can be attacked on sight.[88] The state's obligations under international humanitarian law continue to apply even in any such declared war zone.[89]

7.2.2 The Prohibition on Attacks on Civilians

Civilians enjoy protection from being the objects of attack, 'unless and for such time as they take a direct part in hostilities'.[90] This last concept of direct participation has also been stretched to attempt to include economic support, for example by drug traffickers with links to an insurgency.[91] Rather than examining the developing doctrine over what can be considered direct participation, it is suggested here that armed forces are more likely to consider the lists prepared in manuals, which limit what activity can be considered direct participation in hostilities. For example, the New Zealand *Manual* (2019 has a carefully considered list:

a. armed attack by whatever means, including shelling, bombardment, missile launch and small-arms fire;

b. aggressive manoeuvring, such as positioning and registration of mortars, taking up firing positions or moving in military configuration towards an objective;

c. positioning, emplacement and/or detonation of mines, booby traps or emplaced munitions;

d. conducting reconnaissance, surveillance or espionage on behalf of an opposing force;

e. passing targeting information to an opposing force or acting as a lookout or scout;

f. interdiction of logistic support;

---

[88] Sivakumaran, 'Exclusion Zones in the Law of Armed Conflict at Sea: Evolution in Law and Practice', 92 *International Law Studies* (2016) 153–203.

[89] See Doswald-Beck (ed), *San Remo Manual* (n 55) 181–83 esp at para 10.

[90] See API Art 51(3) and AP II Art 13(3); the interpretation of what constitutes direct participation remains controversial, see Melzer, 'Keeping the Balance Between Military Necessity and Humanity: A Response to Four Critiques of the ICRC's Interpretive Guidance on the Notion of Direct Participation in Hostilities', 42 *New York University Journal of International Law and Politics* 3 (2010) 831–916; further controversy surrounds the related concept of a 'continuous combat function' in an armed group, which is said to also remove protection from attack. See section 9.2.1 below. For criticism see Alston, 'Report of the Special Rapporteur on extrajudicial, summary or arbitrary executions: Study on targeted killings', UN Doc A/HRC/14/24/Add6 (2010) at paras 57–69.

[91] See Alston (n 90) at para 68.

g. deliberate interference with command, control, communications, computers or intelligence systems, whether by direct physical means, through information operations or cyber warfare;

h. interfering with lines of communication, eg by destroying roads, bridges, railway lines, etc;

i. clearing mines and other obstacles laid by a force (other than for humanitarian purposes) while they are of tactical importance;

j. capturing, holding and guarding [prisoners of war] PWs, detainees or hostages;

k. attempting to liberate PWs or detainees held by the force;

l. providing direct logistic support to an opposing force, eg carrying ammunition or other material, constructing and providing improvised explosive devices (IEDs);

m. denying access to military objectives or interfering with manoeuvre, eg deliberately blocking roads or bridges;

n. defending military objectives against attack;

o. commanding, directing or controlling military operations, including issuing orders and directives and making operational or tactical decisions;

p. planning military operations; and

q. gathering, analysing and transmitting tactical intelligence to an opposing force.[92]

Rogers sets out a similar list. He also gives an example of civilian activity that does *not* render the civilians legitimate targets: 'Working in commercial institutions that indirectly support the war effort by financing the government through taxation.'[93]

Let us now turn to the specific rules that protect civilians in the context of targeting military objectives. This means dissecting what is often known as the 'proportionality' rule and delving into ideas of excessive incidental loss of life, or injury to civilians or, as it is often termed, 'collateral damage'.[94]

---

[92] New Zealand, *Manual of Armed Forces Law* (n 68) at para 6.5.15 (footnotes omitted).

[93] Rogers, *Law on the Battlefield*, 3rd edn (2012) at 15.

[94] The expression 'collateral damage' is not defined in the treaties on the law of armed conflict, but it has entered the popular lexicon and may often now be perceived as a euphemism for civilian deaths in a military strike. The use of the term itself, however, does not determine whether or not the strike was legal or the deaths justified. The Elements of Crimes for the International Criminal Court Statute, adopted by the States Parties in 2002, uses the expression to explain that even where such incidental damage is acceptable as a matter of war crimes law, this does not mean that it necessarily legal under other rules (at fn 36, Art 8(2)(b)(iv)): 'The fact that this crime admits the possibility of lawful incidental injury and collateral damage does not in any

7.2.3 Indiscriminate Attacks and Proportionality

We set out above which objects that can be attacked as military objectives. Everything else is considered a civilian object.[95] Civilian objects cannot be attacked. Where the attack is indiscriminate, in that it is not directed at a specific military objective, or because of the weapons used cannot distinguish properly between military objectives and civilian objects, this too is prohibited. One type of such a prohibited attack is a disproportionate attack, as explained in Additional Protocol I:

> the following types of attacks are to be considered as indiscriminate:
>
> . . .
>
> (b) an attack which may be expected to cause incidental loss of civilian life, injury to civilians, damage to civilian objects, or a combination thereof, which would be excessive in relation to the concrete and direct military advantage anticipated.[96]

So where a legitimate military objective has been identified, those who are planning or deciding on the attack have to determine whether this proportionality test is met.[97] If it is not, the attack has to be cancelled or suspended.[98] A disproportionate attack will be a violation of the laws of war, and can be a war crime.[99] The nature of this test, however, makes it tricky to apply when it

way justify any violation of the law applicable in armed conflict. It does not address justifications for war or other rules related to *jus ad bellum*.' The *San Remo Manual* (n 55) uses the expression in order to include protected objects beyond civilians and civilian objects (such as wounded combatants and the environment): para 13(c) 'collateral casualties or collateral damage means the loss of life of, or injury to, civilians or other protected persons, and damage to or the destruction of the natural environment or objects that are not in themselves military objectives'. Such a use of the expression 'collateral damage' is in my view helpful, as it allows for such non-civilian protected persons to be included in the proportionality equation on the opposite side of the military advantage calculation rather than being ignored. On the issue, see International Law Association Study Group on the Conduct of Hostilities in the 21st Century, 'The Conduct of Hostilities and International Law: Challenges of 21st Century Warfare', 93 *International Law Studies* (2017) 322–88 at 357–59.

[95] We will deal with the specificities of who may be attacked as a combatants or fighters or civilians directly participating in hostilities in the sections below, even if some consider that such individuals constitute a military objective. Rogers, *Law on the Battlefield* (n 93) at 102.

[96] AP I Art 51(5)(b).

[97] AP I Art 57(2)(a)(iii).

[98] AP I Art 57(2)(b); for a detailed discussion of all the rules for precaution in attack and by the party subject to the attack, see Sassòli and Quintin, 'Active and Passive Precautions' (n 55).

[99] AP I Art 85(1) and 85(3)(b); ICC Statute Art 8(2)(b)(iv); and for customary international law, Henckaerts and Doswald-Beck, Customary International Humanitarian Law, (n 37) Rule 156 at 576 and 590.

comes to determining a violation or individual criminal responsibility. I do not wish to suggest that the test is unworkable or ignored. In fact, in contemporary conflicts, military commanders run sophisticated tests to determine the lawfulness of targeting, and there is plenty of evidence that attacks are called off when they do not pass the test.[100] But the nature of the present book is that we should point to some of the controversies and complications.

The first problem is that someone has to weigh the anticipated military advantage against the expected civilian damage and decide whether it is worth it. And anyone weighing these rather different considerations against each other is going to bring their own appreciation of what each is worth. What are the lives of 10 civilians worth in terms of an anticipated military advantage? Is the calculation different when the civilians are working in a munitions factory, or when they are children playing in an adjacent house? Are commercial premises worth less than a residential block? Does one take into account the future effect on the civilian population, or just the immediate damage?

We have perhaps reached the limits of what can usefully be set out as clear legal rules and ought to spend more time encouraging an ethical approach to such questions. Rather than thinking about whether targeting is allowed under this rule, it might be better to have policies that take into account a multiplicity of interests (without allowing for action that would violate the rule). So, for example, there is a good argument that the attacker should consider the longer-term effects of an attack for the civilian population. The expected destruction could be significant not only for the civilian population itself, but also for the longer-term political and military strategy of the attacker. The destruction could affect the prospects of alienation of the host population, and have major implications for reconciliation or reconstruction. Lawyers are reluctant to allow these future effects (sometimes known as 'reverberating harm'[101]) to be factored into the equation.[102]

The paucity of case-law probably means that prosecutors may prefer to charge an indiscriminate attack, or even a simple attack on civilians, rather than enter this terrain involving proportionality. In any event, it seems to me

---

[100] For an introduction to some of ways in which collateral damage is calculated, see Corn, Dapper and Williams, 'Targeting and the Law of Armed Conflict', in Corn, VanLandingham and Reeves (eds), *US Military Operations: Law, Policy, and Practice* (2016) 167–207; and see also Jones, *The War Lawyers: The United States, Israel, and Juridical Warfare* (2020).

[101] See Gillard, *Proportionality in the Conduct of Hostilities: The Incidental Harm Side of the Assessment* (2018) at 18–20; Gisel, *The Principle of Proportionality in the Rules Governing the Conduct of Hostilities Under International Humanitarian Law* (2018) at 44ff.

[102] Gisel (n 101) at 21 and 22.

that the key to this test is admitting that there may be a very different weight to be given to a military advantage depending on the context. The instinct of law of war lawyers is to banish discussions of the rationale for a war when discussing the laws of war. But today, as we have seen, conflicts are rarely fought as wars until one side is vanquished or conquered. A contemporary armed conflict involving such targeting decisions is more likely to have been undertaken for the protection of civilians, or to destroy weapons of mass destruction, or as part of a limited self-defence action against a terrorist group, or in order to restore law and order in the face of armed activities by an armed group (counter-insurgency). The aim of the military advantage may not be, as in the past, a step on the path to total victory over an enemy.

The most recent discussions regarding the proportionality test are starting to consider these issues. It may be admitted that what counts as a military advantage in the context of repelling the massed armed forces of a neighbouring state, bent on conquest, is very different from action that might create an advantage when faced with confronting a local group plotting to use home-made bombs against a peace enforcement mission.[103] In the latter case it is increasingly recognized that antagonizing the local population by killing innocent civilians as collateral damage in an attack on an amateur bomb-making facility, may simply represent a set-back rather than an advantage.[104] The same considerations would not apply to hitting a vital state munitions factory in enemy territory during a protracted inter-state war over disputed territory. On the other hand, if the whole point of the military campaign is the protection of civilians, the timely neutralization of the bomb-making equipment could save many civilian lives, and in such circumstances the protection of civilian lives can be seen today as a 'concrete and direct military advantage'.[105] It sometimes emerges that rather than seeking zero civilian casualties, guidelines allow for commanders to authorize strikes up to certain limits. With regard to US airstrikes on ISIS in 2016, it was reported that military leaders 'may authorize strikes where up to 10 civilians may be killed, if it is deemed necessary in order to get a critical military target'.[106]

---

[103] Blum, 'The Fog of Victory', 24 *EJIL* (2013) 391–421 at 420 asks what the aims of modern wars are, and illustrates the inadequacy of considering military advantage as the key concept: 'Consider, for instance, the "war over hearts and minds". To the extent that such a war exists, why would it make sense to weigh collateral harm against military advantage? Why would it not be weighed against popular perceptions of good and bad, the just and the unjust?'

[104] Ibid at 14, 21, 22, 55.

[105] Ibid at 29–31.

[106] Associated Press, 'New War Rules Emphasize Need to Avoid Civilian Casualties' (14 December 2016), attributing this to 'senior defense officials'. In the 2003 Iraq conflict it was

Higher numbers of civilians require higher authority. This approach seems to be more based on calculations of what public opinion will bear at any one time,[107] rather than an attempt to apply the spirit and purpose of the rule.

A second problem is that another facet of this test is that it can require a judge to consider what the decision-maker foresaw at the time, and then consider compliance with the benefit of judicial hindsight.[108] The proportionality rule demands that a prospective attacker (and of course this also applies to actions contemplated in defence) weigh two future variables, the *anticipated* military advantage and the *expected* civilian damage. By the time that a third party comes to judge the actions, either as a serious violation of international humanitarian law, or as a war crime, the damage will have been done, and the military advantage may or may not have materialized. States have been keen to emphasize that 'Military commanders and others responsible for planning, deciding upon, or executing attacks necessarily have to reach decisions on the basis of their assessment of the information from all sources which is reasonably available to them at the relevant time.'[109] Nevertheless, the concept of an anticipated 'concrete and direct military advantage' is explained in the British *Military Manual* as meaning

> that the advantage to be gained is identifiable and quantifiable and one that flows directly from the attack, not some pious hope that it might improve the military situation in the long term. In this sense it is like the term "definite" used in the definition of military objects.[110]

Third, a controversy surrounds how to factor in wounded military personnel and medical military personnel. Such persons may not be targeted and are protected – but they do not qualify, technically speaking, as civilians in the context of the treaty rule. The latest US *Law of War Manual* suggests

---

reported that 'Air war commanders were required to obtain the approval of Defense Secretary Donald L Rumsfeld if any planned airstrike was thought likely to result in deaths of more than 30 civilians. More than 50 such strikes were proposed, and all of them were approved.' Gordon, 'US Air Raids in '02 Prepared for War in Iraq', *New York Times* (20 July 2003).

[107] Gow, *War and War Crimes: The Military, Legitimacy and Success in Armed Conflict* (2013).
[108] The United States and other states have stressed that judges should not take into account information that was not available to the decision-maker at the time. See US *Law of War Manual* (2016) at para 5.3.2.
[109] From the UK Statement made at the time of ratification of AP I; see also US *Law of War Manual* (2016) at para 5.3.2; for further discussion of what sort of foreseeability is expected in this context, see Gillard, *Proportionality* (n 101) at 15–17.
[110] UK *Manual* (2004) at para 5.33.3.

that attacks cannot be prohibited on the grounds of incidental harm to wounded personnel due to 'the general impracticality of prohibiting attacks on this basis during combat operations'.[111] In other words, when targeting a military objective surrounded by wounded soldiers, those soldiers and their attendant medics are not to be considered when weighing up the expected collateral damage. Boothby is clear in his criticism: 'it cannot be right that expected injury or as the case may be damage is simply ignored in applying the proportionality rule'.[112]

Fourth, some have argued that civilians who act as human shields should not be counted as civilians, or should be given less weight, in the proportionality calculation.[113] When it comes to voluntary human shields, the argument may turn on whether they are considered as directly participating in hostilities, and for Sassòli this means the act must 'harm the enemy or its military operations through a chain of causality'.[114] He continues, however, to outline a number of reasons why one cannot distinguish voluntary from involuntary action in this context. With characteristic insight he points out that

> the distinction between voluntary and involuntary human shields cannot be readily determined in practice. How can a pilot or soldier launching a missile know whether the civilians he observes around a military objective are there voluntarily or involuntarily? What counts as a voluntary presence? Must a pilot observing a spouse accompanying a Taliban fighter in Afghanistan determine whether she was the victim of an arranged marriage or is engaged in a love match?[115]

Lastly, the issue of 'force preservation' has captured the imagination not only of lawyers, but also of philosophers. To what extent are the safety and lives of the attacking forces to be factored into the military-advantage side of the balancing equation. If flying lower when targeting means fewer civilian casualties due to better visibility, what weight should be given to the extra risk from anti-aircraft fire that could kill the pilots and crew? Are such

---

[111] US *Law of War Manual* (2016) (n 66) at para 5.10.1.2.

[112] Boothby, 'Aspects of the Distinction Principle under the US DoD Law of War Manual', in Newton (ed), *The United States Department of Defense Law of War Manual: Commentary and Critique* (2018) 161–200 at 193.

[113] See the discussion in Haque, *Law and Morality at War* (2017) Ch 9, and his criticism of the DoD Revised *Law of War Manual* (n 66) on this point at https://www.justsecurity.org/35589/human-shields-updated-dept-defenses-law-war-manual/.

[114] Sassòli, *IHL* (n 9) at para 8.35.

[115] Ibid.

military disadvantages to be placed on the scales? Should it make a difference if the forces are under attack?[116] Again, our approach to this quandary may alter depending on how we approach the actual armed conflict: is it on a war footing, or is it resorting to force for some limited reason?[117]

A recent meeting organized by the ICRC reported 'All the experts agreed that force preservation was a very important military consideration, as the purpose of war is to overcome the enemy and a belligerent needs to preserve its own forces to achieve this.'[118] But what if the military action is not really a war at all, but rather a rescue operation to extract children from the hands of an armed group in a civil war, or a raid on a terrorist cell in an urban centre as part of a continuing counter-insurgency effort? How much risk should we expect the military to take in such cases?

As a legal matter, we can simply say that the party is obliged to take as much risk as is necessary to ensure that there is no excessive collateral damage in achieving the legitimate military advantage foreseen in the proportionality test.[119] But there is now real political and ethical concern that, in many modern wars, all the risks of loss of life are being transferred from the military personnel belonging to powerful states on to the foreign civilian population. Martin Shaw calls this 'risk transfer-warfare'. Such warfare illustrates a shift,

> whereby the governments of advanced democracies, worried about the electoral impact of allowing the costs of war to fall on their citizens, transfer risks away from their combatants toward enemy combatants and noncombatants, minimizing their own casualties while causing excessive collateral damage.[120]

7.3 The Morality of Killing in Contemporary Warfare

Let us leave law for a while and take an excursion into moral philosophy. As Lazar points out in this context, 'People will be more motivated to obey

---

[116] For diverging arguments, see Gisel, *The Principle of Proportionality* (n 101) at 23–31.

[117] Kennedy, 'War and International Law: Distinguishing Military and Humanitarian Professions', 82 *ILS* (2006) 3–33 esp at 25–26.

[118] Gisel, *The Principle of Proportionality* (n 101) at 25.

[119] See the UK *Manual* (2004) at para 2.7.1.

[120] Lazar, 'War' in *International Encyclopedia of Ethics* (2013) at 12; see also Shaw, *The New Western Way of War: Risk-Transfer War and its Crisis in Iraq* (2005).

international law if it tracks our moral reasons than if it is just a useful proxy.[121] As already mentioned, there is considerable discussion on the topic of asymmetric warfare. The interesting thing here is that the word 'asymmetric' is used to evoke so many different conclusions depending on the context. For philosopher Michael Walzer, '[m]ost of the wars of the past several decades have been asymmetric; notably for American citizens';[122] he then suggests that just war theory was invented for 'conventional' warfare, and that such wars are 'not likely to happen anytime soon'.[123] He wants to argue that the same rules apply to both sides, even when only one warring party is an army 'organized, armed and disciplined by a modern state'.[124] But he picks out a dimension in modern conflicts that few lawyers want to address. He suggests that the insurgents stand to benefit from a state's killing of civilians, and therefore the dynamics have changed. Of course the law against killing civilians remains the same, but the political costs are now different. Let us consider his arguments in more detail:

> Many conventional wars have been fought in crowded urban neighbourhoods; we shouldn't expect insurgents to miss the opportunities offered by cities and also by towns and villages. There is, however, a difference here: a conventional army, fighting its way through a city, will probably kill civilians, but these killings do not benefit the opposing army. In asymmetric warfare, the army's killings definitely benefit the insurgents, who are therefore liable to the charge . . . that they deliberately expose civilians to enemy fire. But suppose they have the support of many of the men and women they expose, from whose homes and neighbourhoods they choose to fight. Then, indeed, the army responding to insurgent attacks will face a difficult and highly charged moral and political decision: how to deal with the 'people,' that is, with unarmed but possibly hostile civilians, who are indistinguishable from the insurgents.
>
> Here is what I take to be the central issue in asymmetric warfare (it's also an issue in conventional wars, but asymmetry gives it special significance): How should the army fight when its fighting puts 'enemy' civilians at risk? 'Enemy' is in scare quotes because, while some of these civilians may well sympathize with or actively support the insurgents (as the insurgents

[121] Lazar, *Sparing Civilians* (2015) at 143.
[122] Walzer, *Just and Unjust Wars: A Moral Argument with Historical Illustrations*, 5th edn (2015) at xiii.
[123] Ibid at xiv.
[124] Ibid.

claim), some of them do not; some of them just wish they were somewhere else. . . . The key moral issue can be specified more clearly: What risks should the army ask its soldiers to take in order to reduce the risks they impose on 'enemy' civilians?[125]

Walzer puts forward the moral argument that suggests such civilians 'should not be killed, and these soldiers have an obligation to do everything they can to avoid killing them'.[126] And then suggests that it is possible that 'the effective meaning of this obligation is that the soldiers won't be able to win asymmetric wars'.[127] Walzer and others are keen to find ways for armies to fight asymmetric wars and still remain within the law and morality.

On paper the legal test is quite straightforward. It is the rule of proportionality in attack (*jus in bello* proportionality) that we just discussed. As long as the civilian damage is not excessive with regard to the concrete and direct anticipated military advantage, it will not be illegal under this rule. But Walzer inserts the issue of risk undertaken by the army's soldiers to determine as a matter of morality who should get the blame for civilian deaths. In his hypothetical scenario, civilians are on a roof with Taliban insurgents (either dragged there by force, or willingly standing with the insurgents). He suggests an air strike would probably be a war crime, while he thinks there would be no crime if the state's soldiers get onto the roof of an adjacent building and fire at insurgents, killing civilians. Walzer believes 'that whenever soldiers have accepted risks in order to minimize the injuries they inflict on civilians, the blame should fall elsewhere'.[128]

There is no simple answer to the question of how much risk the armed forces are required to accept by law and morality. I would suggest, however, that one has to consider the context, including the reasons for the conflict in the first place. If the army is seeking to rescue a civilian population in imminent mortal danger, the morality of killing some civilians to save others must be different than a situation where civilians are killed to achieve objectives such as disrupting enemy supply lines, or reclaiming territory lost to irregular forces that have split from the army and are now in the opposition. We cannot engage with Walzer's scenarios unless we know why anyone is

---

[125] Walzer (n 122) at xviii–xix.
[126] Ibid at xx.
[127] Ibid.
[128] Walzer (n 122) at xxi.

being killed in the first place. For me it is no answer to say that as long as soldiers take risks, their killing is morally acceptable.

Such questioning of the purpose of the war itself is not only vigorously discouraged in textbooks on the law of armed conflict (we are constantly reminded that rules on *jus ad bellum* and *jus in bello* must be kept separate, the same rules apply to aggressor and defender and so on). Such an approach is also excluded by Walzer from his suggested morality of targeting. In the most recent edition he generalizes, in what I consider to be a rather particular way:

> The army is, as it were, already in power, serving a sovereign state whose political policies and moral authority are contested, rightly or wrongly. So it's the insurgents who usually start the war. Claiming the prerogatives that I have just described, they often attack civilian targets, inviting a military response, the more savage the better.[129]

For Walzer, 'what is critically at issue in asymmetric warfare is less the cause than the conduct of the war'.[130] I think we are off to a bad start with the idea that in modern wars the insurgents usually started it and deliberately seek to have a regular army inflict savage destruction on the civilian population. To understand the morality of killing civilians standing alongside Taliban fighters one needs to know what the Taliban is going to do next: set off a bomb in a crowded place, execute the said civilians, or enter peace talks with the attacking army.

So, on one view, asymmetric warfare apparently alters the equation for evaluating the morality of killing civilians because, it is assumed, insurgents have chosen to disrupt the normalcy of proper government and deliberately use civilians to shield their operations. At this point, at least according to Walzer, where regular soldiers assume greater risks to save some civilians, their actions should attract less blame than if they refuse to assume those risks.

But from another point of view there is considerable concern – not about the risk-taking by the soldiers on the ground, but rather about the absence of risk for modern-day pilots targeting people through remotely operated air strikes (drone operators). There are various concerns here, one being that this makes conflict and killing more likely and, second, that there is something unfair about killing defenceless people who do not

---

[129] Ibid at xvi.
[130] Ibid.

stand a fighting chance. In turn, this is apparently making it harder in the United Kingdom to retain drone crews. According to one researcher, 'Not many people want to sign up to sit in a cabin for eight hours at a time conducting mostly routine surveillance and sometimes killing people who can't fire back. It doesn't compare with the glamour and excitement of live flying.'[131]

In 2011, the UK Ministry of Defence addressed the first issue and seemed to accept, at the time, that the ability to use unmanned aircraft does indeed lead to more rather than fewer armed conflicts, to greater use of force and more likelihood of war:

> It is essential that, before unmanned systems become ubiquitous (if it is not already too late) that we consider this issue and ensure that, by removing some of the horror, or at least keeping it at a distance, that we do not risk losing our controlling humanity and make war more likely.
>
> For example, the recent extensive use of unmanned aircraft over Pakistan and Yemen may already herald a new era. That these activities are exclusively carried out by unmanned aircraft, even though very capable manned aircraft are available, and that the use of ground troops in harm's way has been avoided, suggests that the use of force is totally a function of the existence of an unmanned capability – it is unlikely a similar scale of force would be used if this capability were not available.[132]

This note was withdrawn, and in 2017 the replacement paper concluded 'For the UK, there is no evidence that availability of remotely piloted aircraft has lowered the threshold for the use of force.'[133]

However one evaluates the evidence, clearly it is arguable that it is easier to go to war or engage in lethal air strikes when there is minimal risk to one's own side.[134] These are not just philosophical conundrums for the classroom. In the end, the ability of a democracy to sustain a war will depend on public support. And it is the morality of war, just as much as the legality of it, that will in the end determine support for the war.

---

[131] Justin Bronk, quoted in Fisher, 'Stress of Killing from Afar Creates Shortage of MoD Drone Operators', *The Times* (13 January 2020).

[132] UKMOD, 'The UK Approach to Unmanned Aircraft Systems', Joint Doctrine Note 2/11, 30 March 2011, at para 517.

[133] 'Unmanned Aircraft Systems', JDP 0-30.2, August 2017, at 50.

[134] See the discussion by Blum, 'The Paradox of Power: The Changing Norms of the Modern Battlefield', 56 *Houston Law Review* (2019) 745–87.

For legal philosophers such as Paul Khan, risk is what defines war as opposed to other forms of state violence: 'Without the imposition of mutual risk warfare is not war at all.' Such 'riskless warfare' would resemble 'police enforcement', and here he succinctly explains a crucial moral difference: 'The moral condition of policing, however, is that only the morally guilty should suffer physical injury. ... Individuals are the targets of police action because of what they have done, not because of who they are.'[135]

States have tried nevertheless to defend the idea that an asymmetry where only one side is at risk can be justified. The UK 2011 note continued:

> The discussion . . . must be tempered however, by the fact that the moral responsibility on every commander to reduce loss of life – on both sides – is clear. The use of unmanned aircraft prevents the potential loss of aircrew lives and is thus in itself morally justified.[136]

Seen from within, one is protecting the lives of one's own troops by carefully tracking targets; by monitoring situations from an eye in the sky, one is engaged in more humane and reliable targeting decisions; and the strikes are all argued to be within the rule of law. But such reasoning does not really address the bigger moral debate seen from outside the armed forces.[137] There is still a sense that it is simply unfair to pick people off from behind a computer screen at no personal risk. Numerous films, plays and novels have highlighted this moral quandary.[138] Governments refute the accusation that they 'have created a disconnected "Playstation" generation of operators who are divorced from the reality of their activities'.[139] The United Kingdom's response to this is that 'Operators have "a strong sense of connection to the life and death decisions they are sometimes required to take . . . in stark contrast to the image portrayed by some pressure groups."'[140] Indeed it has been

---

[135] Khan, 'The Paradox of Riskless Warfare', 22 *Philosophy and Public Policy Quarterly* 3 (2002) 1–8 at 4.

[136] JDN 2/11 (n 132) para 517.

[137] Time and again the debate over drones is reduced to the idea that they are more accurate and less likely to make mistakes in the heat of battle. Drones are said, therefore, to bring better compliance with the law of war. But this manoeuvre avoids tackling the bigger question of whether the killing should be taking place at all. See Boyle, *The Drone Age* (2020) esp at 278–79.

[138] See, eg, Sutcliffe, *We See Everything* (2018) (book); *Good Kill* (2014) (film); *Grounded* (2012) (play).

[139] JDN 2/11 (n 132) at 49.

[140] Ibid at 50; see, for further discussion of the relationship between the US military and the gaming industry, as well as the effects of gaming training on the military, Bourke, *Wounding the World: How Military Violence and War-Play Invade Our Lives* (2014) Chs 6 and 7.

shown in a careful survey of the US Air Force that the level of mental-health issues, including post-traumatic stress, suffered by drone operators is similar to that suffered by those pilots deployed in manned aircraft in similar missions.[141] But none of this can take away the lingering idea that the rules of chivalry that once permeated the laws of war (or even the law of arms we encountered in section 2.1) would not accept such an uneven fight. In Singer's words, what 'gives war its humanity' is the 'willingness to bear the most horrible burdens, face the most terrible risks, and even make the ultimate sacrifice, for your nation or your buddies'.[142]

Walzer, by contrast, does not focus on mutual risk; he sees the obligation as stemming from the job of being a soldier, and rather wants to address the soldier's moral choices in war. For him, the 'war convention requires soldiers to accept personal risks rather than kill innocent people'.[143] He has been tracking the orders given to soldiers that suggested that soldiers accept 'some risk' in order to avoid killing civilians. Irrespective of the orders or rules of engagement, Walzer explains:

> I have talked to American and Israeli soldiers who firmly believe that taking risks to minimize civilian casualties is part of their job. It is crucial to the pride they take in doing their job.
>
> But to what extent is this their job? Taking risks to save lives is required in certain professions – it is a central feature of the fireman's professional code, for example, and this is true whether the people at risk are citizens or foreigners, relatives, friends, or personal enemies. But rescuing people trapped in burning buildings is the most important job of the fireman. The military profession is different. The most important job of the soldier is to win the war or to accomplish a military mission that is closely connected to winning the war. It is commonly taken for granted that some number of civilian deaths is 'not disproportionate' to the value of that mission. We want soldiers to minimize that number as best they can, even at some risk to themselves. But the risk-taking can't undermine or endanger the mission.

---

[141] Otto and Weber, 'Mental Health Diagnoses and Counselling Among Pilots of Remotely Piloted Aircraft in the United States Air Force', Medical Surveillance Monthly Report, US Armed Forces Health Surveillance Centre, available at https://health.mil/Reference-Center/Reports/2013/01/01/Medical-Surveillance-Monthly-Report-Volume-20-Number-3.

[142] Singer, *Wired for War: The Robotics Revolution and Conflict in the Twenty-first Century* (2009) at 432.

[143] Walzer, *Just and Unjust Wars* (n 122) at 305.

This military target is so important (we believe) that we will allow some collateral damage in order to capture or destroy it.[144]

Walzer's argument, in this piece and elsewhere, is that there is a strong moral argument that soldiers should accept this risk as part of their role.

Not everyone agrees.[145] In particular, his approach has been challenged head on by Kasher and Yadlin, who focus on examples from Israel's activity in the Gaza Strip.[146] They contextualize the issue and dismiss Walzer's idea as 'unrealistic', particularly because they say one should include in the equation the value of the civilian lives they are defending:

> [A]ssuming 'some risk' to soldiers' lives would take the form of taking prior action designed to separate terrorists from their neighbors before carrying out the required engagement with the terrorists. Obviously, such prior action would affect the possibility of the soldiers to accomplish their mission because it would eliminate the element of surprise, reveal the soldiers' positions, and so on. If 'some risk' taking should not affect the possibility of accomplishing the mission, we must conclude that 'some risk' taking should not be assumed, because it interferes with the possibility of the soldiers of successfully carrying out their mission.
>
> Therefore, we do not believe there is any moral validity to Walzer's priorities, which are based on an unrealistic view in which battling terrorists is akin to jousting or based on a mistaken comparison between the risks to which soldiers are exposed and the risks to which terrorists' neighbors are exposed.[147]

From another perspective, McMahan wants to go further and distinguish between, those innocent civilians who are likely to benefit from the attacker's humanitarian intervention, and innocent civilians in other situations. He

---

[144] Walzer, 'The Risk Dilemma', 44 *Philosophia* (2016) 289–93 at 292–93; and see Kasher and Yadlin, 'Human Life in the War on Terrorism: a Response to "the Risk Dilemma" by Michael Walzer', ibid at 295–308; and Walzer, 'Response to Asa Kasher and Amos Yadlin', ibid at 309–11.

[145] See Frowe, *Defensive Killing* (2014) Ch 8, who argues that those acting in self-defence may avoid harm to themselves by harming those non-combatants who knowingly contribute to an unjust war; compare Kamm, *The Moral Target* (2012) Ch 4 and Haque, *Law and Morality at War* (n 113) Appendix.

[146] See Kasher and Yadlin, (n 145) ; and Walzer, 'Response to Asa Kasher and Amos Yadlin' (n 145). For a legal analysis of the way the Israeli Defense Forces include an aversion to the risk of a soldier's being captured when considering proportionality calculations and acceptable civilian damage, see Schmitt and Merriam, 'The Tyranny of Context' (n 81) esp at 128–31.

[147] Kasher and Yadlin (n 144) at 304–05.

argues that the civilians who are the 'expected beneficiaries of the war' can expect to have extra risks imposed on them by the combatants fighting to save them.[148] This reasoning, while philosophically eye-catching (as with McMahan's related idea that some civilians can be targeted as morally responsible),[149] not only cuts across the contemporary understanding of the need to distinguish between military objects and civilians in the law of armed conflict, but also challenges normal ideas of human rights. If all the civilians liable to be killed as collateral damage have the human right to life, and are to be considered worthy of protection due to the need to respect their individual dignity, it cannot be compatible with such a view of human rights that some civilians on one side should be instrumentalized for the greater good of those on the other side.[150]

But thinking about this quandary in human rights terms also forces us to think about the human rights of the attacking soldiers, who are being asked to risk their own lives. Benvenisti accepts that that there may be a 'moral duty of *combatants* to consider taking some risks to reduce the harm to enemy civilians, but not a duty to actually risk themselves.'[151] He accepts the legal duty 'to reduce harm to enemy civilians', but determines that the dignity principle that underpins human rights means that this duty 'does not entail an obligation to assume personal life-threatening risks'.[152] The important conclusion

---

[148] McMahan, 'The Just Distribution of Harm Between Combatants and Non-combatants', 38 *Philosophy and Public Affairs* (2010) 342–79 at 359.

[149] '[A] person is morally liable to attack in war by virtue of being morally responsible for a wrong that is sufficiently serious to constitute a just cause for war, or by being morally responsible for an unjust threat in the context of war.' McMahan, 'The Morality of War and the Law of War', in Rodin and Shue (eds), *Just and Unjust Warriors: The Moral and Legal Status of Soldiers* (2008) 18–43 at 22. McMahan also suggests that there is a case for distinguishing between just and unjust combatants when it comes to their liability to attack: McMahan, *Killing in War* (2009) 25. For example, McMahan suggests that there is a case for distinguishing between just and unjust combatants when it comes to their liability to attack ibid at 25. Frowe takes this further and would render non-combatants liable to attack even for contributions that do not directly cause a threat. She challenges the 'widespread acceptance of the principle of non-combatant immunity', because a consequence is that 'it undermines the moral pressure on non-combatants to think about the justness of their country's war': Frowe, *Defensive Killing* (n 145) at 185. Some of these arguments are addressed by Haque, *Law and Morality at War* (n 113).

[150] Similarly from a philosophy of just war perspective, see Margalit and Walzer, 'Israel: Civilians and Combatants', *New York Review of Books* (14 May 2009) at 21–22. In this piece they advocate the following guideline (at 22): 'Conduct your war in the presence of noncombatants on the other side with the same care *as if* your citizens were the non-combatants.' For a thoughtful and detailed look at how these moral concerns map on the international law, see Luban, 'Risk Taking and Force Protection', in Benbaji and Sussmann (eds), *Reading Walzer* (2014) 277–301.

[151] Benvenisti, 'Human Dignity in Combat', 39 *Israel Law Review* (2006) 81–109 at 90 (original emphasis).

[152] Ibid at 93.

is about how alien a human rights approach still is in this context, in part due to the way politicians and the military have come to view their enemies:

> For many armies it is difficult to subscribe to the human dignity principle because they indoctrinate their combatants on an opposite perception, one that dehumanizes the enemy. They coach their soldiers to fear and hate the enemy out of their belief that portraying adversaries as evil and malicious creates feelings that make killing easier. This approach seeks to prevent the recurrence of the behavior of Allied soldiers during the two World Wars, most of whom balked at firing at the enemy even when attacked. American troops in Vietnam acted differently, suggesting that new training methods fostering aggressive behavior have been effective and leading psychologists to conclude that soldiers who dehumanize the enemy fight better. Commanders and soldiers who are goaded to view their enemy as subhuman will find it enormously difficult to risk their lives to save those they had been told are unworthy creatures. And, of course, they believe that their – subhuman – opponent is equally motivated to kill them and their civilians.[153]

7.4 Necessity

7.4.1 Necessity as an Excuse

The concept of 'necessity in war' or 'military necessity' is complicated by the fact that its meaning has radically changed over time. In Chapter 1 we saw how the concept of being at war involved the idea that the associated death and destruction were not murder and arson but justified as lawful acts of war. Allied with this was a conception that 'military necessity' provided an excuse, especially in a total war, to violate what would otherwise be enforceable protective rules. The latest version of the New Zealand *Military Manual* addresses the point:

> The principle of military necessity is not the same thing as the nineteenth-century doctrine, 'necessity in war overrules the manner of warfare', which held that any measure was justified in order to defeat the enemy. In German: '*Kriegsraeson geht vor Kriegsmanier*'. These views, not unique to

---

[153] Ibid at 93–94 (footnotes omitted).

the German states, find much support in the writings of other military theorists, generals, admirals and jurists. Nor is modern military necessity to be confused with military expediency or convenience.[154]

This old doctrine of military necessity is no longer acceptable, and has been roundly rejected in various contexts.[155] Dinstein confirms its obsolescence as follows:

> In the past, it was often claimed that a belligerent party is at liberty to deviate from the law of international armed conflict when military necessity – especially in dire circumstances – so demanded. This claim, which actually means that military necessity is superior to the law, is now completely defunct.[156]

We know, then, that military necessity cannot be used as an argument to override existing rules of international law. But the concept continues to play a significant role in our understanding of rights and obligations in war, even though it is nowhere properly defined in international law. As with the concept of war, the concept of 'necessity in war' or 'military necessity' needs to be treated with care. On the one hand, it is claimed that the 'principle' is a *right*: it *justifies* what is necessary to win the war (within the law); but (confusingly) on the other hand, and at the same time, the same principle is seen as including an *obligation*: it provides an additional *restraint* on the warring parties. At one level this makes sense, if you have a right to do something up to a point, then you may also have an obligation not to do that thing if you go beyond that point. But the aim of the following discussion is to show that there are choices about how we present this 'doctrine' on military necessity, and the choices we make can have concrete consequences – not least in the way that members of the armed forces and their commanders perceive their duties in warfare.

On reading military manuals one gets the impression that military necessity justifies action and creates rights for the military. The US *Manual on the Laws of War* (2016) takes this a little further and places necessity against the context of winning the whole war: '*military necessity* justifies those measures

---

[154] At para 4.2.3 fn 6; and see the similar statement in the US *Law of War Manual* (2016) at para 2.2.2.1.

[155] For an overview of some of the cases and discussions, see Solis, *The Law of Armed Conflict* (2010) at 258–69.

[156] Dinstein, 'Military Necessity', *MPEPIL* (2015) at para 8.

necessary to achieve the object of war, and the object of war is not simply to prevail, but to prevail as quickly and efficiently as possible'.[157] The UK *Manual* has been amended to incorporate a form of the NATO definition and elaborate on it:

> Military necessity is now defined as 'the principle whereby a belligerent has the right to apply any measures which are required to bring about the successful conclusion of a military operation and which are not forbidden by the laws of war'. Put another way, a state engaged in an armed conflict may use that degree and kind of force, not otherwise prohibited by the law of armed conflict, that is required in order to achieve the legitimate purpose of the conflict, namely the complete or partial submission of the enemy at the earliest possible moment with the minimum expenditure of life and resources.[158]

But such an approach is at risk of orientating the concept of military necessity into something that excuses action that would otherwise be illegal.

It is true that the expression 'military necessity', or variations such as the 'necessities of war', is found explicitly incorporated into certain treaty provisions of the laws of war, including provisions that are specifically aimed at humanitarian protection, designed for strictly humanitarian purposes. In these specific contexts, military necessity may indeed justify a departure from the rule. The list of provisions of law of war treaties that specifically reference military necessity, or a similarly phrased exception, includes, for example, a restriction on choosing where to visit prisoners of war:

> Representatives and delegates of the Protecting Powers shall have full liberty to select the places they wish to visit. The duration and frequency of these visits shall not be restricted. Visits may not be prohibited except for reasons of imperative military necessity, and then only as an exceptional and temporary measure.[159]

Similarly, consider the rule prohibiting the destruction of property in occupied territory:

---

[157] *Manual* (n 41) at para 2.2.3.1 (original emphasis).

[158] At para 2.2, as amended September 2010 (footnotes omitted). The excerpt quotes the *NATO Glossary of Terms and Definition* AAP-06 (2019) at 82.

[159] GC III Art 126 para 2.

Any destruction by the Occupying Power of real or personal property belonging individually or collectively to private persons, or to the State, or to other public authorities, or to social or cooperative organizations, is prohibited, except where such destruction is rendered absolutely necessary by military operations.[160]

We could easily list the other main provisions that explicitly allow exceptions to the party's obligations for reasons of military necessity, military considerations, imperative military reasons, the needs of the army of occupation and the necessities of war.[161]

But outside these specific rules that contain such explicit limitations, *there is no room for implied exceptions for reasons of military necessity or the necessities of war.* For a well-known example, consider the rule that states that if a group of armed forces captures an enemy combatant during an operation, and they are unable to intern or evacuate that person due to the nature of the operation, they then have to release the captured person – they cannot claim military necessity and kill the prisoner (however much they feel that releasing the captive will endanger the operation).[162] In short, you cannot invoke military necessity to get around a rule from the laws of war.

A second confusion sometimes arises when people refer to the plea of necessity under general international law. This plea means that a state can avoid its international obligations where its act 'is the only means for the State to safeguard an essential interest against a grave and imminent peril'.[163] But this general rule is not available to states in the present context. It cannot be used to justify force, even for the purposes of humanitarian intervention,[164] and it cannot be used to avoid the rules in the law of armed conflict. The International Law Commission's Commentary explains that the general rule on necessity does not cover the 'doctrine of "military necessity"', as that doctrine is the underlying criterion for 'a series of the substantive rules of the law

---

[160] GC IV Art 53.

[161] GC I Arts 8, 12, 32, 33, 42, 50; GC II Arts 8, 28, 51; GC III Arts 23, 126; GC IV Arts 16, 18, 27, 49, 51, 53, 55, 83, 108, 143, 147; AP I Arts 54(5) 62(1), 67(4), 71(3). See also Hague IV (1907) Regulations Art 23(g). Note also in the ICC Statute Art 8(2)(a)(iv) 'military necessity'; Art 8(2)(b)(xiii) 'necessities of war'; and Art 8(2)(e)(xii) 'necessities of the conflict'.

[162] See AP I Art 41(3), which is confirmed as a rule of customary international law; see Dinstein, *International Armed Conflict* (n 59) at 11–12.

[163] ILC Articles on State Responsibility (2001) Art 25(1)(a).

[164] See Crawford, *The International Law Commission's Articles on State Responsibility* (2002) at 185 para 25; and see also ILC Articles (n 163) Art 26.

of war and neutrality', as well as being specifically mentioned in 'a number of treaty provisions in the field of international humanitarian law'.[165]

We can summarize the situation so far. The principle of military necessity:

(a) does not override the laws of war;
(b) is said to encapsulate a right to apply required measures for a successful operation;
(c) operates to limit force to that required to defeat the enemy and involving the minimum loss of life and resources (usually focused on one's own side);[166]
(d) has already been implicitly or explicitly been built into the laws of war; in the absence of an explicit exception for military necessity or an equivalent phrase, one cannot rely on military necessity (or necessity as a general plea) to excuse behaviour that is otherwise in violation of the laws of war.

7.4.2 Necessity is Rejected in Submarine Warfare Against Merchant Ships

Perhaps to get a better sense of how the necessity excuse may be rejected, let us consider the early controversy over submarine attacks on merchant ships. As already mentioned, the degeneration into unrestricted submarine warfare led to considerable loss of life. For some this was seen as justified by the necessity of winning the war. As Fenrick explains:

> Although the use of submarines and aircraft to sink merchant vessels on sight was inconsistent with the pre-1914 law of naval warfare, there were militarily important reasons for doing so. As the World Wars tended towards totality, merchant shipping was incorporated into the belligerent war effort, and it was reasonable to conclude that, in general, merchant vessels

---

[165] Crawford (n 164) at 185–86 para 21, see also para 19. See also Sassòli, *IHL* (n 9) at paras 5.51–5.55. For discussion of the implicit and explicit references to military necessity in the all treaties dealing with the law of armed conflict, see Dinstein, 'Military Necessity' (n 156).

[166] The New Zealand definition of 'military necessity' includes the sentence 'The principle of military necessity holds that a State involved in armed conflict is justified in using such lawful force as is necessary to bring about the submission of the enemy at the earliest possible moment and with the least possible cost to itself in terms of lives and resources. LOAC [the Law of Armed Conflict] does not require a State to allow itself to be destroyed.' See NZ *Manual of Armed Forces Law* (n 68) at 4.2.1.

did not travel to and from belligerent states unless they carried cargoes that would either improve the ability of a belligerent to make war or provide revenue to bolster the belligerent's war economy. As the submarine was a small vessel and, with the exception of torpedoes, weakly armed, it was not able to perform the traditional tasks of visit and search of merchant vessels once the opposing belligerent began to arm merchant vessels and to order them to act aggressively in self-defence by ramming. Further, the British tactic of using Q-Ships, warships disguised as merchant vessels which would attempt to lure submarines within range of their weapons and then disclose their identity and attack, did not provide an incentive for submarines to comply with traditional practices.[167]

The trial of Admiral Dönitz before the International Military Tribunal in Nuremberg revealed the practices on both sides. The Nuremberg Tribunal mitigated the punishment of Admiral Dönitz for certain specific violations of the laws of war in this context, on the premise that both sides had engaged in such violations.[168] It also declined to find him guilty for attacks on British merchant ships, due to the fact that the British Admiralty had armed the merchant vessels, was using intelligence from them on the position of sighted enemy submarines and had ordered them to ram German U-boats if possible.[169]

Nevertheless Dönitz's infamous orders against rescuing survivors led in part to his conviction for war crimes. War Order 154 is worth reproducing for what it tells us about the idea of war at that time:

Do not rescue any men; do not take them along; and do not take care of any boats of the ship. Weather conditions and proximity of land are of no consequence. Concern yourself only with the safety of your own boat and with efforts to achieve additional successes as soon as possible. We must be hard in this war. The enemy started the war in order to destroy us, and thus nothing else matters.[170]

---

[167] Fenrick, 'Legal Aspects of Targeting in the Law of Naval Warfare' (n 86) at 247.

[168] 'In view of all the facts proved and in particular of an order of the British Admiralty announced on the 8th May, 1940, according to which all vessels should be sunk at sight in the Skagerrak, and the answers to interrogatories by Admiral Nimitz stating that unrestricted submarine warfare was carried on in the Pacific Ocean by the United States from the first day that Nation entered the war, the sentence of Dönitz is not assessed on the ground of his breaches of the international law of submarine warfare.' *Prosecutor v Goering et al*, Judgment of the IMT, 1 October 1946, Official Text, at 313.

[169] Ibid at 312.

[170] As read out at the *Nuremberg Trial Proceedings*, vol 5, Thursday, 9 May 1946, at 218.

Later in the War, Dönitz issued the *Laconia* order, which again reveals the war sentiment and the failure to balance the demands of military necessity with any recognition of a principle of humanity:

1. No attempt of any kind must be made at rescuing members of ships sunk; and this includes picking up persons in the water and putting them in lifeboats, righting capsized lifeboats and handing over food and water. Rescue runs counter to the rudimentary demands of warfare for the destruction of enemy ships and crews.
2. Orders for bringing in captains and chief engineers still apply.
3. Rescue the shipwrecked only if their statements will be of importance to your boat.
4. Be harsh, having in mind that the enemy takes no regard of women and children in his bombing attacks on German cities.[171]

Sentencing Dönitz to 10 years' imprisonment (the shortest of the sentences handed down, most of the defendants were hanged), the International Military Tribunal was clear that there is no room for the argument that force security, military necessity or the necessities of war override a clear humanitarian prohibition set out in the London Protocol of 1936:

> The argument of the Defense is that the security of the submarine is, as the first rule of the sea, paramount to rescue, and that the development of aircraft made rescue impossible. This may be so, but the Protocol is explicit. If the commander cannot rescue, then under its terms he cannot sink a merchant vessel and should allow it to pass harmless before his periscope. These orders, then, prove Dönitz is guilty of a violation of the Protocol.[172]

---

[171] Ibid at 220.

[172] *Prosecutor v Goering et al* (n 168) at 313. See also Boothby and Heintschel von Heinegg, *The Law of War: A Detailed Assessment of the US Department of Defense Law of War Manual* (2018) at 333, who conclude that 'the sinking of an enemy merchant vessel without having first placed passengers, crew and documents in a place of safety for the sole reason that capture and sending the vessel into port is impossible or unfeasible because of military considerations will most probably be considered a war crime'. Doswald-Beck has pointed out that the absolute rule in the 1936 Protocol actually concerns removal of passengers from a merchant ship after capture rather than the idea of rescue from a sinking warship: 'The International law of Naval Armed Conflicts: The Need for Reform', VII *Italian Yearbook of International Law* (1986/7) 251–82 at 257. For the expectations on submarine commanders in the context of rescue, see ICRC, 'Article 18' in *Commentary on the Second Geneva Convention*, 2nd edn (2017) at paras 1642, 1644, 1652.

7.4.3 Necessity as an Extra Layer of Restraint in Warfare

The concept of necessity (sometimes distinguished from military necessity) is also seen by key commentators, but not all,[173] as providing an extra layer of restraint. We have already seen that necessity operates in the context of self-defence to limit the options of the state acting in self-defence, or under authority from the Security Council, or indeed under any claim to be acting legally.[174] So experts such as Greenwood and Garraway have consistently suggested that 'far from justifying a state in acting contrary to humanitarian law, the principle of necessity operates as an additional level of restraint by prohibiting acts which are not otherwise illegal, as long as they are not necessary for the achievement of legitimate goals'.[175]

More recently, Adil Ahmed Haque has argued that, with the abolition of the sovereign right to go to war, 'we must understand military necessity in a fundamentally different way, not as an authorizing principle entitling both sides to fight, but as a constraining principle prohibiting both sides from inflicting excessive harm'.[176]

Let us consider the scenario provided by Steven Haines. Today a warship can be

taken out of contention by a single hit from a missile. This can result in a catastrophic failure of the warship's power and essential fighting systems, severely disabling the vessel and rendering it incapable of further involvement in combat operations, despite the majority of the crew itself remaining physically capable of doing so.[177]

---

[173] The idea of military necessity as an extra layer of restraint is rejected by Hayashi, 'Basic Principles', in Liivoja and McCormack (eds), *Routledge Handbook of the Law of Armed Conflict* (2016) 89–105 at 92; and for more detail see Hayashi, *Military Necessity* (2020).

[174] Greenwood, 'International Humanitarian Law (Laws of War)', in Kalshoven (ed), *The Centennial of the First International Peace Conference* (2000) 161–259 at 181–84.

[175] Greenwood, 'Historical Development and Legal Basis', in Fleck (ed), *The Handbook of Humanitarian Law in Armed Conflicts* (1995) 1–38 at 33; ibid, 2nd edn (2007) 1–43 at 38; and the sentence is carried over into the 3rd edn (2013) by O'Connell, 'Historical Development and Legal Basis' 1-42 at 37. See also Garraway, 'International Humanitarian Law in Self-Defence Operations', in Gill and Fleck (eds), *The Handbook of the International Law of Military Operations* (2010) 213–15, 'the principle of necessity can operate as an additional level of restraint in that acts which might otherwise be legal under international humanitarian law may be prohibited if they are not necessary for the pursuance of legitimate goals'.

[176] 'Indeterminacy in the Law of Armed Conflict', 95 *International Law Studies* (2019) 118–60; and see also Haque, *Law and Morality at War* (n 113) at 32–34, where he rejects the claim that military necessity can justify or permit certain acts.

[177] Casey-Maslen and Haines (n 54) at 299.

For Haines, an attack on enemy naval units has to be limited to 'that which is necessary to render the target incapable of engaging in hostilities', and launching further attacks on a severely disabled warship would be an unnecessary act.[178]

A fierce controversy has developed around the idea of necessity's being considered an extra layer of restraint in a series of operational settings. One could choose to see this in part as a struggle for the legal high ground between humanitarians and military lawyers.[179] But the commentators represent multiple, even shifting, positions on a wide spectrum. Indeed one of the foremost among them has admitted to having changed his mind: having asserted in 1997 that military necessity is a 'principle of limitation, not authorization',[180] he now claims that it 'is not, as sometimes asserted, a limitation on military operations. Instead the principle recognizes the appropriateness of considering military factors in setting the rules of warfare.'[181]

This is an area of law and moral philosophy that is far from stable.[182] In fact, the idea that necessity is a rule of restraint rather than a permission is not as modern as is often suggested. Even at the beginning of the 19th century, necessity in war was not universally seen as a way around the rules. Necessity was seen by some as a restraint on waging war. The historian Geoffrey Best has helpfully reproduced the following statement by Napoleon:

> My great maxim has always been, in politics and war alike, that every injury done to the enemy, even though permitted by the rules, is excusable only so far as it absolutely necessary; everything beyond that is criminal.[183]

Gérard de Rayneval reflected the legal point in his 1803 book *Institutions du droit de la nature et des gens*: 'The law of war rests on this fundamental and

---

[178] Ibid.

[179] For a detailed look at the competing approaches, see Luban, 'Military Necessity and the Cultures of Military Law', *Leiden Journal of International Law* (2013) 315–49.

[180] Schmitt, 'Green War: An Assessment of the Environmental Law of International Armed Conflict', 22 *Yale Journal of International Law* (1997) 1–109 at 54.

[181] Schmitt, 'Military Necessity and Humanity in International Humanitarian Law: Preserving the Delicate Balance', 50 *Virginia Journal of International Law* 4 (2010) 795–839 at 799.

[182] For an introduction to the debate in modern just-war theory pitting the traditional approach of Walzer against revisionists such as McMahan and Rodin with his concept of 'reductive individualism', see Lazar, 'Method in the Morality of War', in Lazar and Frowe (eds), *The Oxford Handbook of Ethics of War* (2018) 21–40.

[183] Best, *Humanity in Warfare: The Modern History of the International Law of Armed Conflicts* (1980) at 49; the translation is by Best, who includes the French (ibid at 335) 'Ma grande maxime a toujours été qu'en politique comme en guerre que tout mal, fût-it dans les régles, n'est excusable qu'autant qu'il est absolument necessaire; que tout ce qui est en delà, est crime.'

sacred maxim: do to your enemy as much harm as is necessary for force to be just, but go no further.'[184]

For a very clear contemporary assertion that the principle of necessity works to restrict the acts of a party to a conflict, consider this passage from Kolb and Hyde:

> The aim of the war should not be seen as the destruction of as much of the adverse belligerents property and killing of as many members of the adverse armed forces as possible; rather the aim is to destroy and to kill as few as possible and to cause such damage only to the extent necessary to overpower the enemy. That idea was aptly expressed in the 1868 St Petersburg Declaration. Where it is stated:
>
> That the only legitimate object which States should endeavour to accomplish during war is to weaken the military forces of the enemy; That for this purpose it is sufficient to disable the greatest possible number of men; That this object would be exceeded by the employment of arms which uselessly aggravate the sufferings of disabled men, or render their death inevitable.
>
> Thus, there is a hierarchy of acts allowed: one should capture rather than wound; one should wound rather than kill; one should kill less persons rather than kill more persons and so on. It is often possible to obtain the same military result by placing the military personnel of the enemy *hors de combat* rather than killing them. In operation, the principle of necessity therefore requires that the least destructive measure that gains the same military advantage should be preferred. This rule is expressed in Article 57(3) of Additional Protocol I . . . [185]

The objections to such an approach are particularly engaged when it comes to the idea that there is an obligation on soldiers to capture rather than kill.[186]

The ICRC has stated that the principle of military necessity implicitly contains a principle of humanity, which complements it and limits the kind and degree of force that is permissible. This position came in the

---

[184] Allain, *The Last Waltz of the Law of Nations: A Translation of the 1803 Edition of The Institutions of Natural Law and the Law of Nations by Joseph-Mathias Gérard de Rayneval* (2019) Book III, Ch V, §1, 'On the Effects of War', at 153.

[185] Kolb and Hyde, *An Introduction to the International Law of Armed Conflicts* (2008) at 47 (footnote reference omitted).

[186] Goodman, 'The Power to Kill or Capture Enemy Combatants', 24 *EJIL* 3 (2013) 819–53; Schmitt, 'Wound, Capture, or Kill: A Reply to Ryan Goodman's "The Power to Kill or Capture Enemy Combatants"', 24 *EJIL* 3 (2013) 855–61; Goodman, 'The Power to Kill or Capture Enemy Combatants: A rejoinder to Michael N Schmitt', 24 *EJIL* 3 (2013) 863–66.

context of its 'Interpretative Guidance on the Notion of Direct Participation in Hostilities'.[187] In the process of consultations on how to interpret this notion in the law of armed conflict, we find, on one account, 'academicians' fundamentally disagreeing with 'military experts',[188] and the 'the preeminent international humanitarian law organization' (the ICRC) being accused of failing to take account of the expert views of those from 'states with the greatest involvement in contemporary armed conflict'.[189] These fundamental, and deeply felt disagreements, can also be seen as part of the battle over 'who owns the rules of war'.[190]

The opposition to the idea of a necessity principle that limits permissible force in this context is articulated in different forms. First, it is claimed that the principles of military necessity and humanity 'do not operate as independent legal norms in and of themselves'.[191] Second, it is suggested that the laws of warfare on the conduct of hostilities already contain within themselves a balance between humanitarian considerations and military necessity, so there 'can be no appeal to military necessity outside the formulation of the rule'.[192] Third, there is an objection that the rule that limits attacks on military objects to those that contribute to military action, and destruction of which offers a definite military advantage, does not apply to combatants as they are objectives rather than objects.[193] Fourth, the norm that prohibits employing weapons and methods of warfare of a nature to cause superfluous injury or unnecessary suffering is said to be 'shrouded in mystery', and thus there is no evidence that states would interpret this norm to require the least harmful means.[194] Fifth, we find the objection that such a 'least-harmful-means theory is a creature of human rights law, and it has won no place in the law of war'.[195] Lastly, it is said such a rule is impracticable, in part because the

---

[187] 'Interpretive Guidance on the Notion of Direct Participation in Hostilities under International Humanitarian Law: Adopted by the Assembly of the International Committee of the Red Cross on 26 February 2009', 90 *IRRC* (2008) 991–1047 at 1040–44.

[188] Parks, 'Part IX of the ICRC "Direct Participation in Hostilities" Study: No Mandate, No Expertise, and Legally Incorrect', 42 *New York University Journal of International Law and Politics* 3 (2010) 769–830 at 784.

[189] Schmitt, 'Military Necessity and Humanity in International Humanitarian Law: Preserving the Delicate Balance', 50 *Virginia Journal of International Law* 4 (2010) 795–839 at 835.

[190] Anderson, 'Who Owns the Rules of War?', *New York Times Magazine* (13 April 2003).

[191] Kleffner, 'Section IX of the ICRC Interpretive Guidance on Direct Participation in Hostilities: The End of *Jus in Bello* Proportionality as We Know It?', 45 *Israel Law Review* (2012) 35–52 at 41.

[192] Hampson 'Direct Participation in Hostilities' (n. 10) at 194.

[193] Parks, 'Part IX' (n 188) at 803.

[194] Kleffner, 'Section IX' (n 191) at 44–45; see also Ohlin, *The Assault on International Law* (2015) at 186–87.

[195] Ohlin (n 194) at 187.

soldier cannot be expected to carry a collection of weapons, just as a golfer carries a range of golf clubs.[196]

So from the side of the military experts we have a plea for simplicity, and essentially the idea that some individuals will have assumed a status that means they can be targeted as such. Others seek to suggest that some killing of those directly participating in hostilities may be unnecessary and that the law of armed conflict demands that such targeting must be necessary for it to be legal.[197] Nevertheless, the idea of 'classic large-scale confrontations' (aka wars) with a reduced role for limiting ideas related to necessity, proportionality and humanity hovers in the background, and seems to encourage an acceptance that the balance can be tipped in favour of what is said to be required by military necessity and away from concerns over humanity.[198] However we see the limits of military necessity, we have definitely come some way from the 19th-century idea that 'extreme necessity could deprive the laws of war of their binding force'.[199] To be clear, there is now complete agreement that we cannot accept the idea of any return to the *Kriegsräson* doctrine that was understood as stating that 'necessities of war take precedence over the rules of war'.[200]

To get a better sense of the necessity debate let us leave the law and return to questions of morality.Now might be a good time to examine the paradigmatic example of the sleeping soldier. Law of war textbooks invariably reference the idea that it is not a violation of the law of war for one soldier to kill a sleeping enemy soldier. This image remains seared in the minds of those who come across this cliché. I know because it is repeated back to me on an annual basis. The time has come to expose this dangerous trope as a cheeky way to get students' attention, rather than as a helpful way to understand the laws of war.

---

[196] Parks, 'Part IX' (n 188) at 786–87, referencing Kalshoven, 'The Soldier and His Golf Clubs', in Swinarski (ed), *Studies and Essays in International Humanitarian Law and Red Cross Principles: Essays in Honour of Jean Pictet* (1984) 360–76.

[197] Some of the points raised by the military experts have been addressed in detail by Melzer, who was responsible for the ICRC expert process and is the author of its Interpretive Guidance. Melzer, 'Keeping the Balance Between Military Necessity and Humanity: A Response to Four Critiques of the ICRC's Interpretive Guidance on the Notion of Direct Participation in Hostilities', 42 *New York University Journal of International Law and Politics* 3 (2010) 831–916; Melzer, *Targeted Killing in International Law* (2008).

[198] Note the admission in the ICRC Guidance (n 187) at 1043, that 'In classic large-scale confrontations between well-equipped and organized armed forces or groups, the principles of military necessity and of humanity are unlikely to restrict the use of force against legitimate military targets beyond what is already required by specific provisions of IHL.'

[199] Schmitt, 'Military Necessity' (n 189) at 796–97.

[200] Kleffner, 'Section IX' (n 191a) at 41 fn 29; see also Hayashi, 'Basic Principles' (n 173) at 91.

Gabriella Blum has suggested that even if the current law might allow for the targeting of a soldier who is swimming naked, or sleeping, or sitting cooking, or even retreating, we should move away from questions of legality and consider the morality of such killing. She argues that the existing rules on distinction and necessity can be reinterpreted. She would adjust the rules on distinction, so that non-threatening individuals, including combatants, 'who pose no real threat would be spared from direct attack'. And the principle of military necessity would introduce 'a least-harmful-means test, under which an alternative of capture or disabling of the enemy would be preferred to killing whenever feasible'. She accepts that this would involve extra risk for soldiers, but considers such concern for enemy combatants involves 'moral, cultural, and aesthetic sensibilities' that could possibly 'drive other militaries – although certainly not all fighting forces – to adopt similar doctrines'.[201]

We might take a moment to consider the idea of shooting a naked soldier referenced by Blum. She is in turn using Walzer's reference to the war mémoire by Robert Graves, *Goodbye to All That*. Graves' queasiness, I feel, reveals a lot about why we might want to forbid unnecessary killing in war:

> I only once refrained from shooting a German I saw, and that was at Cuinchy . . . While sniping from a knoll in the support line, where we had a concealed loop-hole, I saw a German, perhaps seven hundred yards away, through my telescopic sights. He was taking a bath in the German third line. I disliked the idea of shooting a naked man, so I handed the rifle to the sergeant with me. 'Here take this. You're a better shot that I am.' He got him; but I had not stayed to watch.[202]

Sassòli has his own explanation of why some militaries object to the idea of necessity playing a limiting role in this context. His insight comes from many years of interacting with the military, and warrants repeating here:

> The underlying reason for such resistance against a rule, which corresponds to basic moral imperatives . . . may be the military's fear that – if the rule is not clear-cut – soldiers will hesitate to use lethal force and retroactively

---

[201] Blum, 'The Dispensable Lives of Soldiers', 2 *Journal of Legal Analysis* 1 (2010) 69–124 at 69 and 107; see also Blum, 'The Paradox of Power: The Changing Norms of the Modern Battlefield', 56 *Houston Law Review* (2019) 745–87 at 776 on the impact of social and cultural norms; see further Ohlin and May, *Necessity in International Law* (2016) at 184.

[202] *Goodbye to All That* (1929) (New York: Everyman's Library, 2018) at 136.

second guess their decision, leading them to them feel guilty for having killed another human being.[203]

7.5 The Weapons of War

Today, weapons are only permitted where they can distinguish between military objectives and civilian objects. The International Court of Justice confirmed this in its opinion on the legality of nuclear weapons: 'States must never make civilians the object of attack and must consequently never use weapons that are incapable of distinguishing between civilian and military targets.'[204]

But the law of war contains a second fundamental principle, and this one covers attacks even where they only affect the *armed forces* of the enemy. In the words of the Court, 'it is prohibited to cause unnecessary suffering to combatants: it is accordingly prohibited to use weapons causing them such harm or uselessly aggravating their suffering.'[205] The application of this rule requires a contextual reading as to what sort of military necessity or advantage was being weighed at the time.[206] And because a number of weapons have been specifically outlawed against this background, there can be a temptation to suggest that what has not been specifically outlawed is permitted. But there is evidence that the rule prohibiting unnecessary suffering to combatants can and does influence behaviour, even in the absence of a prohibition of a specific type of weapon.[207]

---

[203] Sassòli, *IHL* (n 9) at para 8.373; a related point is the idea that it is better to have clear guidance than to leave the rules so open-ended that they cannot be applied by soldiers on the ground. See for example Dill 'Towards a Moral Division of Labour between IHL and IHRL during the Conduct of Hostilities' in Bohrer, Dill, and Duffy, *Law Applicable in Armed Conflict* (2020) at 197–265 esp at 220.

[204] *Legality of the Threat or Use of Nuclear Weapons*, Advisory Opinion, 8 July 1996, at para 78.

[205] Ibid.

[206] See Judge Higgins' Dissenting Opinion in the *Nuclear Weapons Opinion* (n 204) at paras 10–20; for an overview of all the Opinions, see O'Connor, 'Nuclear Weapons and the Unnecessary Suffering Rule', in Nystuen, Casey-Maslen and Golden Bersagel (eds), *Nuclear Weapons under International Law* (2014) 128–47.

[207] See the discussion by Sassòli, *IHL* (n 9) at 8.368–8.372; for a detailed look at some of the parameters of this rule and the history of the discussions around it, see Casey-Maslen and Haines, *Hague Law Interpreted* (n 54) Ch 8; Meyrowitz, 'The Principle of Superfluous Injury or Unnecessary Suffering: From the Declaration of St Petersburg of 1868 to Additional Protocol I of 1977', 34 *IRRC* (1994) 98–122.

Starting perhaps with ancient prohibitions on poison weapons,[208] the unnecessary suffering norm has been behind the expanding list of weapons that are prohibited under international law. In particular, we might mention the following prohibitions: on explosive or expanding bullets; on weapons that injure with non-detectable fragments; and on blinding laser weapons. At the same time, some weapons have been prohibited with more regard to their indiscriminate effects. We might mention chemical weapons, bacteriological weapons, anti-personnel landmines and cluster munitions. Some rules do not actually ban weapons but rather restrict the ways in which they can be used. These rules also create obligations that continue after the arms have been deployed. Here we might mention sea mines, torpedoes, incendiary weapons (including napalm and flamethrowers), booby traps and obligations concerning the 'explosive remnants of war'.

Some of these prohibitions apply to all states and the opposing armed non-state actors in all conflicts (such as chemical weapons); other prohibitions may only be binding for those states that have accepted the relevant treaty (such as cluster munitions).[209] The extent to which such prohibitions

---

[208] This rule can be traced to the Laws of Manu, in Asia (circa 200 BCE), Ch VII, para 90. When a King 'fights with his foes in battle, let him not strike with weapons concealed (in wood), nor with (such as are) barbed, poisoned, or the points of which are blazing with fire.' While the Laws of Manu reference the duty of honourable warriors, in Europe in the 17th century, Grotius considered the ban on poison originated with kings who were less safe from poison – see Kalmanovitz, *The Laws of War in International Thought* (2020) at 65 fn 101; the prohibition nevertheless evolved into something aimed at unnecessary suffering for those subjected to poisoned weapons – see Casey-Maslen and Haines, *Hague Law Interpreted* (n 54) at 212, where they highlight the suffering caused by the use of bamboo punji sticks placed in traps in Viet Nam.

[209] The relevant treaties are as follows: 1868 St Petersburg Declaration Renouncing the Use, in Time of War, of Explosive Projectiles under 400 Grammes Weight; 1899 Hague Declaration 2 Concerning Asphyxiating Gases; 1899 Hague Declaration 3 Concerning Expanding Bullets; 1907 Hague Convention VIII Relative to the Laying of Automatic Submarine Contact Mines; 1925 Geneva Protocol for the Prohibition of the Use in War of Asphyxiating, Poisonous or Other Gases, and of Bacteriological Methods of Warfare; the 1972 Convention on the Prohibition of the Development, Production and Stockpiling of Bacteriological and Toxin Weapons and their Destruction; 1993 Convention on the Prohibition of the Development, Production, Stockpiling and Use of Chemical Weapons and their Destruction; 1997 Convention on the Prohibition of the Use, Stockpiling, Production and Transfer of Anti-Personnel Mines and on their Destruction; 1980 UN Convention on Prohibitions or Restrictions on the Use of Certain Conventional Weapons which May be Deemed to be Excessively Injurious or to Have Indiscriminate Effects, amended in 2001, and its protocols: 1980 Protocol I on Non-Detectable Fragments; 1980 Protocol II on Mines, Booby Traps and Other Devices, amended 1996; 1980 Protocol III on Incendiary Weapons; 1995 Protocol IV on Blinding Laser Weapons; and 2003 Protocol V on Explosive Remnants of War; 2008 Convention on Cluster Munitions; and most recently the (2017) Treaty on the Prohibition of Nuclear Weapons discussed below. For an overview, see Sassòli, *IHL* (n 9) at paras 8.366–8.407; and for a detailed examination, see Boothby, *Weapons and the Law of Armed Conflict*, 2nd edn (2016); Casey-Maslen, *The Treaty on the Prohibition of Nuclear Weapons* (2019).

and restrictions apply in non-international armed conflicts and to the non-state actors party to the conflict is complicated due to the multiple treaties and amendments involved.[210] In fact, whether or not the armed group is prohibited from using such weapons as a matter of international law, in practice multiple armed groups have entered into commitments to destroy their stockpiles of landmines and refrain from using such weapons.[211]

When it comes to weapons of mass destruction, there is a universal ban on states 'providing any form of support to non-State actors that attempt to develop, acquire, manufacture, possess, transport, transfer or use nuclear, chemical or biological weapons and their means of delivery'.[212]

National jurisdictions will criminalize the use or stockpiling or transfer of certain weapons in those states that have joined the relevant treaties. Such offences will apply to everyone, irrespective of whether there is any sort of armed conflict or war.[213]

At the international level, the Statute of the International Criminal Court foresees six types of weapons that can lead to the prosecution of war crimes for those who employ them in the context of an armed conflict:

- poison or poisoned weapons;
- asphyxiating, poisonous or other gases, and all analogous liquids, materials or devices;
- bullets which expand or flatten easily in the human body, such as bullets with a hard envelope which does not entirely cover the core or is pierced with incisions;
- employing weapons, which use microbial or other biological agents, or toxins, whatever their origin or method of production;
- employing weapons the primary effect of which is to injure by fragments which in the human body escape detection by x-rays;
- employing laser weapons specifically designed, as their sole combat function or as one of their combat functions, to cause permanent

---

[210] See for the details, see Boothby (n 209) Ch 18; Sivakumaran, *The Law of Non-International Armed Conflict* (n 45) 392–412.

[211] See at https://www.genevacall.org/.

[212] Security Council Resolution S/RES/1540 (2004) para 1, and note the definition included for the purposes of this Resolution only, 'Non-State actor: individual or entity, not acting under the lawful authority of any State in conducting activities which come within the scope of this resolution.' See also S/RES/2325 (2016). For the general prohibition on states regarding transfers of weapons to non-state actors seeking to overthrow another government, see section 4.3.2 above.

[213] See, eg, s 2 of the UK's Landmines Act 1998.

blindness to unenhanced vision, that is to the naked eye or to the eye with corrective eyesight devices.[214]

With regard to the second and third crimes, it is understood that the use of tear gas and expanding bullets for *law enforcement purposes* would not constitute a war crime.[215] It may seem strange that a bullet could be completely prohibited in times of war due to its capacity to cause unnecessary suffering and yet be legal in times of peace. The reality is that, in situations such as hostage-taking, an expanding bullet is considered the best way to immobilize the hostage-taker without risking injury to the hostages. Experienced commentators have asked whether the comprehensive ban on the use of such bullets in the law of war still makes sense, and whether there may be a rationale for allowing expanding bullets in certain types of urban warfare, where there can be equivalent risks to civilian bystanders.[216]

Although the use of chemical weapons was not explicitly included as a war crime in the Statute of the International Criminal Court, it can be argued that some forms of chemical and biological weapons are included in the war crime related to the use of asphyxiating gases.[217] In any event, under the Chemical Weapons Convention (CWC) (1993), states are expected to create relevant offences under national law – and indeed do so.[218] The absence of these weapons

---

[214] See ICC Statute Art 8(2)(b)(xvii)–(xix), (xxvii)–(xxix) and (e)(xiii)–(xviii). Some of these crimes represent amendments, so the jurisdiction of the Court will be limited where the state party has not ratified the necessary amendment or the employment takes place in the territory of a non-state party; see further Casey-Maslen, Clapham, Giacca and Parker, *The Arms Trade Treaty: A Commentary* (2016) at 240–41. See also ICC Statute Art 8(2)(b)(xx), but no annex has been adopted.

[215] Casey-Maslen et al (n 214) at 240–41.

[216] See Casey-Maslen and Haines (n 54) at 216–19, 230–31; Boothby, *Weapons* (n 209) 139–44.

[217] There is little doubt that the use of biological or chemical weapons is a violation of customary international law; this was never questioned when Syria (at the time not a party to the Chemical Weapons Convention) was condemned for violating international law. Whether or not such weapons can fall within the crime related to poisonous gases and the jurisdiction of the Court depends on how much one considers that a treaty is to be interpreted according to its ordinary meaning or by reference to the drafting history. See the various views of Alamuddin and Webb, 'Expanding Jurisdiction over War Crimes under Article 8 of the ICC Statute', 8 *JICJ* (2010) 1219–43; Boothby, *Weapons* (n 209) at 125 considers that 'certain chemical substances' would be covered by the crime of employment of poison or poison weapons; Naqvi outlines multiple possibilities for prosecuting the use of chemical weapons: 'Crossing the Red Line: The Use of Chemical Weapons in Syria and What Should Happen Now', 99 *IRRC* (2017) 959–93.

[218] See Art VII of the CWC; and see, eg, the UK's Chemical Weapons Act 1996. See also the Decision of the Executive Council of the Organisation for the Prohibition of Chemical Weapons, EC-86/DEC.9, 13 October 2017, which urged states parties to enact penal legislation; a compendium of national legislation can be found at https://www.opcw.org/resources/national-implementation/legislation-compendium.

from the language of the Statute can be traced to the heated debate over whether to include nuclear weapons in the Statute of the International Criminal Court.[219]

The absence of nuclear weapons from the Statute of the International Criminal Court has not prevented a number of states from pursuing treaties to outlaw their use. The Treaty on the Prohibition of Nuclear Weapons entered into force on 22 January 2021. There are now 50 States Parties to the treaty. Of course nuclear weapon states, their allies and those under their protection have distanced themselves from this process. The United States, the United Kingdom and France have stated that they would not accept 'any claim that this treaty reflects or in any way contributes to the development of customary law'.[220]

The Treaty extends beyond the issue of the *use* of nuclear weapons. It starts:

Each State Party undertakes never under any circumstances to:
(a) Develop, test, produce, manufacture, otherwise acquire, possess or stockpile nuclear weapons or other nuclear explosive devices;
(b) Transfer to any recipient whatsoever nuclear weapons or other nuclear explosive devices or control over such weapons or explosive devices directly or indirectly;
(c) Receive the transfer of or control over nuclear weapons or other nuclear explosive devices directly or indirectly;
(d) Use or threaten to use nuclear weapons or other nuclear explosive devices;
(e) Assist, encourage or induce, in any way, anyone to engage in any activity prohibited to a State Party under this Treaty;
(f) Seek or receive any assistance, in any way, from anyone to engage in any activity prohibited to a State Party under this Treaty;
(g) Allow any stationing, installation or deployment of any nuclear weapons or other nuclear explosive devices in its territory or at any place under its jurisdiction or control.

The resistance of the states with nuclear weapons should not blind us to the fact that any use of such weapons will almost certainly be a violation of the laws of war and a war crime, due either to the unnecessary suffering imposed

---

[219] See Schabas, *The International Criminal Court* (2010) at 243–47; for an account of the investigations into the use of chemical weapons in Syria and elsewhere see the autobiographical book by de Bretton-Gordon, *Chemical Warrior: Syria, Salisbury and Saving Lives at War* (2020).

[220] Press Statement, 7 July 2017; for further background and statements, see Mills and Culpin, 'A Treaty on the Prohibition of Nuclear Weapons', Briefing Paper No 7986, 9 October 2018, House of Commons Library.

on combatants, or to the excessive loss of life or injury to civilians or civilian objects (which is now seen as including the natural environment).[221]

7.6 The Necessity of Shortening the War

Thinking about nuclear weapons forces us to confront the argument that such a weapon might shorten a war thus saving thousands of lives. The law is clear that targeting civilians is never justified by claims that more lives will be saved in the long run. This has been reaffirmed recently in the context of the law on cyber operations.[222] Of course, as we have already seen, the more complex point comes when the attacker claims that the target is a military objective (broadly defined) and the collateral damage is proportionate to the anticipated military advantage. Throughout this chapter we have seen that the more states seek to expand the definition of military objective, the more one finds recourse to the concept of *war*. The idea becomes seductive that to defeat the enemy, one must be able to eliminate, not only targets that contribute to war-fighting, but also those that sustain the war. Attacks and military advantages start to become associated with a fuller 'war strategy'.

We should not allow the practice and thinking from Wars past, when the distinction between combatants and civilians was almost abandoned, to shape our approach today.[223] The civilian damage and loss of life that was

---

[221] See, eg, the International Court of Justice in the *Nuclear Weapons Opinion* (n 20) at para 95: '[M]ethods and means of warfare, which would preclude any distinction between civilian and military targets, or which would result in unnecessary suffering to combatants, are prohibited. In view of the unique characteristics of nuclear weapons, to which the Court has referred above, the use of such weapons in fact seems scarcely reconcilable with respect for such requirements. Nevertheless, the Court considers that it does not have sufficient elements to enable it to conclude with certainty that the use of nuclear weapons would necessarily be at variance with the principles and rules of law applicable in armed conflict in any circumstance.' See further ibid at para 30, and under the Art 8(2)(b)(iv) of the ICC Statute, which covers international armed conflict and includes in the proportionality equation 'or widespread, long-term and severe damage to the natural environment'. For a detailed look at questions of the environment in this context, see Dinstein, *International Armed Conflict* (n 59) Ch 7; and Henckaerts and Constantin, 'Protection of the Natural Environment', in Clapham and Gaeta (eds), *The Oxford Handbook of International Law in Armed Conflict* (2014) 469–91. For discussion of when the use of a tactical nuclear weapon would not violate the laws of war, see Haines, 'The Developing Law of Weapons: Humanity, Distinction, and Precautions in Attack', in Clapham and Gaeta (eds), *The Oxford Handbook of International Law in Armed Conflict* (2014) 273–95 at 283–84 fn 27.

[222] The most recent manual on cyber operations reiterates the point that 'an attack against a civilian object would be unlawful even if it shortened the course of the conflict and thereby saved civilian lives': Schmitt (ed), *Tallinn Manual 2.0* (n 55) at 422.

[223] The practices developed in the Second World War, seen through the phenomenon of total war, led Hersch Lauterpacht, writing in 1952, to consider that the distinction between

witnessed in the area bombing of Coventry, Hamburg, London and Dresden, as well as the catastrophes visited on Tokyo, Hiroshima and Nagasaki, should be recalled before anyone considers allowing the contemporary law of war to justify attacking economic targets.[224]

The idea that 'vigorous wars' are better for humanity has been with us since at least 1863.[225] In 1945, the idea of shortening the War was famously used in an attempt to justify the use of atomic bombs on the people of Hiroshima and Nagasaki.[226] One must hope that we will never see this sort of planned annihilation again. But there is constant temptation to frame the rules for today's armed conflicts in terms of what is necessary to win the war, rather than in terms of eliminating unnecessary suffering to combatants while respecting the rights of those who are posing no immediate threat. The logic of war is changing. Today, there is no room for the once popular idea that one can shorten the war by weakening civilian morale through bombing campaigns, the primary purpose of which is spreading terror in the civilian population. Creating such terror is now outlawed and can no longer be defended.[227]

combatants and civilians had been reduced to a 'hollow phrase', and that the role played by the 'economic weapons' in modern war rendered it 'practically impossible' to differentiate 'between civilians and combatants': 'The Problem with the Revision of the Law of War', 29 *BYBIL* (1952) 360–82 at 364.

[224] For the reasoning deployed in the United Kingdom and the background legal norms, see Best, *Humanity in Warfare* (n 183) 262–85; for a discussion of why this topic has often been suppressed, see Maier, 'Targeting the City: Debates and Silences about the Aerial Bombing of World War II', 87 *IRRC* (2005) 429–43; Addison and Crang (eds), *Firestorm: The Bombing of Dresden* (2006); Grayling, *Among the Dead Cities* (2007), Overy, *The Bombing War* (2014); see also Henderson, 'The Firebombing of Tokyo and Other Japanese Cities', in Tanaka, McCormack and Simpson (eds), *Beyond Victor's Justice? The Tokyo War Crimes Trial Revisited* (2010) 311–21.

[225] See Witt, *Lincoln's Code* (2012) at 184, 278–90; The Lieber Code, General Orders No 100, 1863, Art 29, famously stated 'The more vigorously wars are pursued, the better it is for humanity. Sharp wars are brief.'

[226] See Cassese, *Violence and Law in the Modern Age* (1988) 17–21.

[227] See Parks, 'The Protection of Civilians From Air Warfare', 27 *Israel Yearbook on Human Rights* (1997) 65–111 at 77–84; this is a longstanding debate, but even in 1938 the position was clearly stated by the British Prime Minister, Neville Chamberlain: '[W]e cannot too strongly condemn any declaration on the part of anybody, wherever it may be made and on whatever side it may be made, that it should be part of a deliberate policy to try and win a war by demoralising the civilian population through a process of bombing from the air. That is absolutely contrary to international law . . .' *Hansard*, HC Deb 21 June 1938, vol 337, col 934.

8

Belligerent Rights and the Future of Naval Economic Warfare

8.1 Introduction to Naval Warfare and the Capture of Property at Sea

This chapter highlights how old ideas of what is permitted in War continue to play a role when it comes to the use of force against merchant shipping and seizing such ships and their cargo on the high seas.

The powerful naval states have, through their state practice, established so-called 'Belligerent Rights' in War, and imposed rules for economic warfare that now look inappropriate for a world in which War has been outlawed. Moreover, today, the owners and crew of private cargo ships, as well as their states of nationality, have expectations as to their own rights under international law.

Prize Courts are central to the story in this chapter. Neff traces Prize Courts to the unilateral measures taken by England in the 13th century and by France in 1400; they were essentially courts set up by the Sovereign to adjudicate over captures at sea. 'The original function of prize courts was to compile an official inventory of captured goods, to ensure that the government received its full share of any booty.'[1] Such jurisdiction in more recent centuries has, in the United Kingdom, been dependent on a specific declared War. The last time it was used followed the 1939 Order issued by King George VI. That in turn was authorized by powers under the 1894 Prize Courts Act, which states that the Court shall act only upon a 'proclamation' that War has 'broken out'.[2] The earlier Order in Council authorizing the Commissioners to apply prize law for the First World War refers to 'a state of war between this Country and the German Empire'.[3] King George VI's Order of 5 September 1939 contains only two operative paragraphs, and might helpfully be

---

[1] Neff, *The Rights and Duties of Neutrals* (2000) at 24–5.
[2] Prize Courts Act 1894, s 2(1)–(3).
[3] Anderson, *The Navy and Prize: An Essay* (1917) at 16.

reproduced here in part (not least because it was quite tricky to find) in order to get a flavour of what it means to trigger the law of Prize and Prize Court jurisdiction. The text essentially states that, because of the State of War, the United Kingdom can, in the context of naval warfare, lawfully seize everything belonging to the enemy state, its nationals and inhabitants. It then establishes Prize Court jurisdiction to adjudicate these matters:

> WHEREAS a state of war now exists between this Country and the German Reich so that His Majesty's Fleets, Ships and Aircraft may lawfully seize all ships, vessels, aircraft and goods belonging to the said German Reich or to the Citizens and Subjects thereof, or other persons inhabiting within any of the countries, territories, or dominions of the said German Reich, and bring the same to judgment in any such Courts as shall be duly commissioned to take cognizance thereof ...
>
> We do hereby authorize and enjoin you ... to take cognizance of and judicially proceed upon all and all manner of captures, recaptures, seizures, prizes and reprisals of all ships, vessels, aircraft, and goods already seized and taken, and which hereafter shall be seized and taken, and to hear and determine the same, and according to the course of Admiralty and Law of Nations, and Statutes, Rules, and Regulations for the time being in force in that behalf, and goods as shall belong to the said German Reich or to the Citizens or Subjects thereof, or to any other persons inhabiting within any of the countries, territories, or dominions of the said German Reich or which are otherwise condemnable as Prize.[4]

In a separate Proclamation on the same day the King specifies what the United Kingdom would treat as 'Contraband of War':

> Whereas a state of War exists between Us, on the one hand, and Germany on the other:
>
> And Whereas it is necessary to specify the Articles which it is our intention to treat as Contraband of War:
>
> ... the Articles in Schedule I hereto will be treated as Absolute Contraband [arms, ammunition etc fuel of all kinds, means of transportation and components thereof, all means of communication, coin currency etc, metal, machinery etc,] the Articles in Schedule II hereto will be treated

---

[4] Statutory Rules and Orders (1939) vol II, 3605.

as Conditional Contraband . . . All kinds of food, foodstuffs, feed, forage, and clothing and articles and materials used in their production.[5]

The key controversies are covered by customary international law, and are not likely to be dealt with in any new treaty-making process. Ronzitti's evaluation from the 1980s remains realistic:

> Modernization is, however, a difficult task. The great maritime Powers seem to be happy to live with the old law rather than embark on a process of revision which would involve States with insignificant navies and even land-locked countries.[6]

While there is some existing treaty law and, as we saw in the last chapter, there have even been prosecutions for breaches of the rules of naval warfare amounting to war crimes,[7] the contemporary law with regard to Blockade, seizure of enemy merchant shipping and goods, seizure of neutral merchant ships, seizure of enemy state-owned military equipment, the operation of Prize Courts and the rights of neutral shipping, is in all cases relatively uncertain and contested. Moreover, just because certain action was accepted as legal as recently as the last two World Wars, does not necessarily mean that we should automatically accept that the same rules continue to apply to all armed conflicts today.[8]

---

[5] Ibid 3605–06.

[6] Ronzitti, 'The Crisis of the Traditional Law Regulating International Armed Conflict at Sea and the Need for Revision', in Ronzitti (ed), *The Law of Naval Warfare: A Collection of Agreements and Documents with Commentaries* (1988) 1–58 at 51. See more recently, making the same point, Roach, 'Submarine Warfare', *MPEPIL* (2017) at para 34: 'Such a conference would presumably be open to representatives from all nations and non-governmental organizations who would not, for the most part, have significant interests as potential participants and would have little or no practical experience in the conduct they would seek to regulate. Of the more than 150 coastal and island States, only a small fraction have a significant naval capacity or experience in naval warfare. Another 40 States are landlocked. Consequently, unless the rules of procedure of such a conference provided for all decisions, particularly on matters of substance, to be taken by consensus, or unless the conference could be limited to significant naval powers, those States without significant interests at stake would probably have the votes to decide matters of vital importance to naval powers without their consent.' Heintschel von Heinegg suggested that some of the necessary updating to the rules could be accomplished through a meeting of experts to revise the *San Remo Manual*: 'The Development of the Law of Naval Warfare from the Nineteenth to the Twenty-First Century – Some Selected Issues', 30 *Yearbook of International Humanitarian Law* (2014) 69–93; such an exercise is currently underway.

[7] For a look at some of the war crimes trials in the 20th century, see Fenrick, 'Legal Aspects of Targeting in the Law of Naval Warfare', 29 *Canadian Yearbook of International Law* (1991) 238–82 esp at 244–55.

[8] There are almost no treaties in force that cover these areas. Past initiatives that sought to codify and develop the law include Institut de droit international (IDI), *Règlement international*

In the previous chapter we already challenged the idea that the logic of war grants permission to attack without warning merchant ships or aircraft that are considered to have become military objectives through their contribution to the enemy's war-sustaining effort.[9] Now the focus will be on whether the law of war still entitles a state on the high seas to search for and appropriate through capture the property of other states and private third parties.

Unlike the contemporary law on land warfare, the practice of maritime warfare in international armed conflicts (and most would agree that this law of naval economic warfare is limited to international armed conflicts)[10] would at first glance seem to involve some pretty draconian apparent rights for belligerent states with regard to merchant (civilian) ships, their crew and the property of foreigners. In part, this is sometimes explained by the idea that land warfare takes place 'within the territory of some state, whereas naval warfare is very largely carried on in the "no man's land" of the high seas'.[11] But it must also be explained today by the continuing grip of naval powers over the law-making arena and the absence of relevant treaty law governing many of these aspects of naval economic warfare.

The history of the thinking on these topics considers a 'right to fight' alongside a competing 'right to trade'. As Smith explained in 1948, 'At bottom it is the question of trying to reconcile two conflicting rights, each in itself quite legitimate – the right of the belligerent to defeat his enemy and the right of the neutral to carry on his normal trade.'[12] But I wonder if such an unqualified belligerent right to defeat the enemy can continue to exist now that we have abolished the right to go to War?

The questions we will be asking in this chapter are these: is it legitimate in the 21st century for a state that has decided to go to war (or initiate an international armed conflict) to continue to claim such 'Belligerent Rights', based

---

des prises maritimes (1897) and IDI, *Manual of the Laws of Naval War* (1913), the London Declaration concerning the Laws of Naval War (1909) (an unratified treaty signed by 10 naval powers), and the Harvard Draft Convention on Rights and Duties of Neutral States in Naval and Aerial War, 33 *AJIL* (Supplement) (1939) 175–203. More recently see Doswald-Beck (ed), *San Remo Manual on International Law Applicable to Armed Conflicts at Sea* (1995) (hereinafter *San Remo Manual*); and The Program on Humanitarian Policy and Conflict Research at Harvard University, *Manual on International Law Applicable to Air and Missile Warfare* (2013) (hereinafter *Harvard Manual on Air Warfare*).

[9] See the discussion in section 7.2.1; and with regard to the US *Law of War Manual* (2016) see the criticism in Boothby and Heintschel von Heinegg, *The Law of War: A Detailed Assessment of the US Department of Defense Law of War Manual* (2018) at 335–36.

[10] See, eg, Boothby and Heintschel von Heinegg (n 9) at 326.

[11] Smith, *The Law and Custom of the Sea* (1948) at 64

[12] Ibidem.

on a 'right' to defeat an enemy state, so that the rights or expectations of neutrals or 'enemy nationals' to trade in goods unrelated to direct military action are extinguished? Should a belligerent state be entitled to acquire property rights over every enemy ship and plane (along with its enemy cargo) just because this belligerent state has the capacity to capture them? My answer starts from the idea that international law can hardly outlaw the recourse to war and then reward those who violate that rule with so-called 'Belligerent Rights' over neutrals and those from the victim state.

The idea of Belligerent Rights in naval warfare includes capturing enemy ships and their cargoes on the high seas. The idea is that the property rights in the vessels and the cargo are then acquired by the capturing belligerent state after condemnation (aka confiscation) in a Prize Court.[13] No one now accepts that one can seize private enemy property on land, so what rationale remains for seizing on the high seas private enemy ships and their cargo, while also retaining the right to intern their crew as prisoners of war?[14]

It may be that in the past it was accepted that the Law of Nations entitled the aggrieved side to retake in reprisal (*repriser*) what is owed to them. And it was once accepted that states authorized privateers (private individuals in charge of private ships) in time of War to seize those enemy goods by using their merchant ships and crew.[15] But today such authorization of private force against foreign ships is outlawed for such purposes. The state can no longer, since the Paris Declaration of 1856, authorize privateers to carry out such seizures. Moreover, at least since the UN Charter in 1945, the state itself is no longer entitled to engage in forceful reprisals to right a wrong.[16]

It may also be that historically it was considered that all merchant sailors could be easily redeployed to the armed forces, and that merchant ships could potentially easily be requisitioned for the war effort, but can such rationales for capturing merchant ships still stand? And does not this blurring of the distinction between military and civilian objects hinder rather than help

---

[13] See, eg, UK *Manual of the Law of Armed Conflict* (2004) paras 13.99–13.104; *San Remo Manual* (n 8) at paras 135–140.

[14] For a traditional statement of the law, see Colombos, *The International Law of the Sea*, 6th edn (1967) at 491: 'All private property on land, enemy and neutral, is free from confiscation, but all is equally subject to requisition. On the other hand, enemy merchant ships and goods at sea are liable to capture.' He then goes on to explain the 'ancient principle' regarding interning enemy merchant crew as prisoners of war. Compare Art 105 UN Convention on the Law of the Sea (1982) with regrd to seizure in the context of piracy.

[15] For detailed study in one particular context, see Kert, *Prize and Prejudice: Privateering and Naval Prize in Atlantic Canada in the War of 1812* (1997).

[16] See section 4.1 above.

uphold modern international humanitarian law, which starts out by stressing the need to distinguish between combatants and civilians?

Challenging the idea of these Belligerent Rights derived from War need not throw into chaos the whole of the laws of war. We could confine ourselves at this stage to rethinking some of the rules related to traditional maritime warfare as they relate to capture of enemy and neutral ships. My complaint with the traditional law as currently understood is that we cannot reward the aggressor state with Belligerent Rights that states have accumulated under the old legal institution of War.

I will not, however, be suggesting that such Belligerent Rights cannot be claimed by the aggressor but should remain unaffected for the state acting in self-defence. As is well known, all states claim to be acting in self-defence or for some other legitimate cause. What I will suggest is that, with regard to private property, no seizure or capture rights for any belligerents should flow merely from the fact of being in a State of War or in an international armed conflict. This focus on private property at sea may seem to be a rather niche preoccupation, but the idea that a belligerent state is entitled to seize the private property of the enemy at sea, and the vessels of neutrals accused of breaching blockade or carrying contraband, has significant knock-on effects.

For example, refusing visit or capture exposes merchant ships to attack. Moreover, the rules that are said to allow for capture also allow for the destruction of enemy civilian aircraft and neutral merchant ships where capture and adjudication for Prize are not feasible.[17] Perhaps the time has come to remove the idea that, in war, the high seas involve a battle for private property and the means to strangle the enemy's economy. To continue to countenance such old rules related to the capture of merchant ships in a State of War is to encourage a state of mind whereby the enemy is much more than the military forces one faces in battle.

To the extent that navies resort to inspection, interception, diversion, capture, seizure, confiscation or acquisition against private ships on the high seas, I would suggest that the legal basis for such action ought to be confined to the international law covering self-defence, and not ancient traditions dressed up as 'Belligerent Rights', even if the thinking that attempts to justify such rights goes back centuries.[18]

---

[17] For the rules proposed relating to destruction as an 'exceptional measure', see para 151 of the *San Remo Manual* (n 8) (for neutral vessels) and Rule 135 of the *Harvard Manual on Air Warfare* (n 8) (for captured enemy civilian aircraft).

[18] One might also inquire if such rights ever had any credible foundation as a matter of morality or universal law. Neff's conclusion is clear, '[t]he concept of belligerents' rights

Henry Maine, Whewell Professor of International Law at the University of Cambridge, sought in his lectures in 1887 on international law to explain the rationale for an international law right for a belligerent state to seize private enemy property on the high seas. His reasoning traces the idea back to Roman law:

> The elements of the subject are simple. When two states go to war, the ships, public and private, of one are, relatively to the other, so many articles of movable property floating on the sea. The capture of one of them by a ship of the other belligerent is *prima facie* regulated by the same principle as the seizure on land of a valuable movable by a soldier or body of soldiers. The law on the subject descends to us directly from the Roman Law. The property of an enemy is one of those things which the Roman Law in one of its oldest portions considers to be *res nullius* – no man's property. It may be taken just as a wild bird or wild animal is taken, by seizing it with the intention to keep it . . . [19]

We have argued throughout this book that we should now abandon the idea of an institution of War that leads to the notion that everyone on the other side becomes an enemy with minimal rights. I wonder if today a lecturer could really explain the right to seize private property by analogy to the Roman law right to seize wild animals. But today the law books and manuals see no need to explain this ancient Belligerent Right. The Belligerent Right to capture enemy property on the high seas apparently continues, carried over each time a law of war manual is updated.[20]

Maine himself introduces his lectures by referencing William Whewell's testament, and the related regulations for his own professorship in international law, stating that he 'should make it his aim, in all parts of his treatment of the subject, to lay down such rules and suggest such measures as might tend to diminish the evils of war and finally to extinguish war among nations'.[21] Perhaps with this injunction in mind, Maine asks whether there

is a delusion': 'The Prerogatives of Violence – In Search of the Conceptual Foundations of Belligerents' Rights', 38 *GYBIL* (1995) 41–72 at 71.

[19] Maine, *International Law: A Series of Lectures Delivered before the University of Cambridge, 1887* (1888) at 94–95.
[20] See, eg, UK *Manual* (n 13) at paras 12.91–12.96 and 13.99–13.104; *San Remo Manual* (n 8) at paras 135–145; *Harvard Manual On Air Warfare* (n 8) Rules 49 and 134.
[21] Maine, *International Law* (n 19) at 1.

should not be new treaty law that would 'exempt all private property from capture'.[22] He sets out multiple reasons for Great Britain to encourage such a change: at the time Great Britain had the largest merchant navy and therefore more to lose, as ships were then being built of iron rather than timber, and Britain was overtaking Russia, the Netherlands and the United States in shipbuilding. Most importantly, Britain was increasingly dependent on food arriving by sea.[23] Maine ended his lecture encouraging adoption of the American proposal to exempt all private property from capture, adding:

> Of course I am aware of the objections which might be made. It may be asked whether it would tend to diminish wars if economical loss were reduced to the lowest point, and if hostility between nations resolved itself into a battle of armed champions, of ironclads and trained armies, if war were to be something like the contests between the Italian States in the Middle Ages, conducted by free companies in the pay of this or that community. I think that, even thus modified, war would be greatly abated. But this is a subject which ought not to be taken for granted without discussion, and I hope in some future lecture to take it up and go into it completely.[24]

Unfortunately he died a few months later. Over a hundred years on, the law remains largely unreformed. Let us go into some of the detail of these rules for economic warfare at sea and then reflect on the contemporary legal situation with a view to its radical overhaul.

8.2 Angary

We might briefly set the scene by considering the historical claimed right of angary. War historically was said by some to entitle a belligerent state to seize neutral property, including merchant ships and their crew, and put them to work for the war effort. The practice fell out of use in the 18th and 19th centuries. States entered into treaties to renounce the right to seize one anothers' vessels, but a variant of this old right of angary was relied on again during the two World Wars, with no claim now to any right to commandeer the neutral crew. This right of angary is explained as 'a right deriving from the law of war',

---

[22] Ibid at 117.
[23] Ibid at 199–22.
[24] Ibid at 122.

and may or may not still exist under international law.[25] In its more recent form it essentially applied to taking with full compensation merchant ships belonging to neutrals found in the harbours of a belligerent state, where the transport is necessary for the belligerent's war effort.[26] At the end of the War the property should be returned to the neutral.[27]

Whether or not such a right can exist today, expert commentary on this customary international law right states that it only applies where the objects are 'urgently needed'[28] or for 'strategic purposes of immediate necessity',[29] and where they are 'serviceable to military ends and wants'.[30] It would be odd if this Belligerent Right could be applied in a brief international armed conflict in the absence of a Declaration of War. Nationals from neutral states would have no notice that their vessels, aircraft and equipment, etc could be acquired through angary, and it is unlikely that there would be the requisite element of urgency or necessity.[31] Nevertheless, for some, angary may still exist as a right: 'In large-scale armed conflicts of a longer duration, however, it is conceivable that belligerents will be forced to seize neutral objects because their resources will not suffice to sustain the war effort.'[32]

---

[25] Lauterpacht (ed), *Oppenheim's International Law: a Treatise*, vol II: *Disputes, War and Neutrality*, 7th edn (1952) 759–766 at 765.

[26] See Lauterpacht, 'Angary and Requisition of Neutral Property', 27 *BYBIL* (1950) 455–59, who suggests angary gives rise to full compensation in comparison with requisition, which could be used where the neutral property was voluntarily in the territory of the belligerent state; requisition in occupied territory is covered by separate rules, for occupied territory see Regulations Hague Convention IV (1907) Arts 52 and 53. For the UK legislation on requisition generally, see Compensation (Defence) Act 1939 and Defence (General) Regulations 1939; and for discussion of some case-law, see Fitzmaurice, 'Some Aspects of Modern Contraband Control and the Law of Prize', 22 *BYBIL* (1945) 73–95 at 79–82; Colombos, *Law of the Sea*, (n 14) at 570–78.

[27] For the practice of subsequently seizing the same vessel when the neutral state entered the War, see Colombos, *Law of the Sea* (n 14) at 576.

[28] Heintschel von Heinegg, 'Angary, Rights of', *MPEPIL* (2009) at para 16.

[29] Colombos, *A Treatise of the Law of Prize*, 3rd edn (1949) at 315.

[30] Lauterpacht (ed), *Oppenheim* (n 25) at 762.

[31] Although some of the state practice and case law might arguably suggest that 'a very high degree of convenience to the belligerent Power would be sufficient'. See the explanation by Lord Parker in *The Zamora* [1916] 2 AC 77, 101–03.

[32] Heintschel von Heinegg, 'Angary, Rights of', *MPEPIL* (2009) at para 22. Compare Verzijl on 'the so called "right" of angary practised by Belligerent Governments with regard to neutral ships lying in their ports ... Instead of being the exercise of an internationally recognized right, it is no more than a fossilized abuse from the past.' Verzijl, *International Law in Historical Perspective: Part IX-B The Law of Neutrality* (1979) at 243. *Halsbury's Laws of England*, vol 3 (2019) at para 10 seems to confine a continuing right of angary to time of war: '(2) Prerogative Powers in Wartime 10. Blockade and angary; damage to and seizure of property. ... The Crown has also, by right of its prerogative, a jus angariae, that is to say a right to appropriate the property of a neutral where necessity requires in time of war.'

I would suggest that, as is evident from the last extract, deeper notions about what a belligerent needs to do in war continue to play a role in the thinking about the rights of belligerent naval powers. Let us turn to dissect the other more familiar concepts of naval warfare.

8.3 Booty

Most readers will have a sense of what is meant by war booty. 'The concept of war booty is as old as recorded history. It has developed over a period of many centuries from the ancient practice by which the individual soldier was considered to be entitled to take whatever he could find and carry away, to the modern rule under which only the state is entitled to seize property as war booty.'[33] In naval warfare, in the past 'everything above the gun deck was the property of the captors, aught else had to be brought into the Prize Court.'[34]

The contemporary law of war foresees, in treaty law dating from 1907, that in an inter-state armed conflict, an 'army of occupation' can take possession of the cash, movable property, arms, means of transport and supplies that belong to the enemy *state* 'which may be used for military operations'.[35] Transport vehicles, weapons and munitions, as well as appliances for the transmission of news, belonging to *private persons* 'may be seized', but 'they

---

[33] Downey (Maj), 'Captured Enemy Property: Booty of War and Seized Enemy Property', 44 *AJIL* (1950) 488–504 at 490. For an interpretation of GC II Art 18 concerning the obligation to protect the shipwrecked from pillage, see ICRC, *Commentary on the Second Geneva Convention*, 2nd edn (2017) at para 1669 (fn omitted), which states that 'there is a recognized right in international armed conflict to capture as war booty any movable property belonging to the enemy State. Booty of war covers all types of enemy movable public property that can be used for military operations, such as arms and munitions. If individuals were to take these types of public goods from a wounded or sick person in a situation of armed conflict at sea, it might not amount to pillage if it is handed over to the State. If such goods are taken for private use, however, that would constitute pillage and would contravene the prohibition in Article 18.' The *Commentary* also suggests that a civilian aircraft temporarily used for exclusively medical purposes could be taken by the enemy state through condemnation through Prize Court, while a military aircraft in the same situation could be captured as 'booty of war' (ibid at para 2621).

[34] Anderson, *The Navy and Prize* (n 3) at 28, this right was abolished in favour of a share for the captors, see also at 5, 'The practice of pillage, however, led to great abuse and was abolished by an Act passed in the reign of William and Mary.' For the rule relating to this right to everything the gundeck see Rule 10 in the 'Black Book of the Admiralty' (section 8.5.1 below) translated (at 55): 'In the case of any ship or vessel of the enemy being taken as prize by any ship of our fleet, then the captors shall have for their own use all manner of goods and furniture found above the hatches, and the forecastle or the poop of the said vessels, saving always the ancient customs and usages of the sea.'

[35] Art 53 Regulations annexed to Hague Convention IV (1907) (Hague Regulations). See further Van Engeland, 'Protection of Public Property', in Clapham, Gaeta and Sassòli (eds), *The 1949 Geneva Conventions: A Commentary* (2015) 1535–50 esp at 1545–46.

must be restored and compensation fixed when peace is made.[36] The old law of war institution of 'booty' has been mostly overtaken by these treaty rules, but the concept of booty is still used in military manuals to outline the rules applicable to property seized on the battlefield (and not as part of an occupation). In particular, the booty of war is used with regard to certain property found on prisoners of war.[37] So the UK *Manual* refers to 'booty of war' when explaining that personnel who find sums of money belonging to the enemy state on a prisoner of war, in fact have to hand over the money to the capturing government. Such money becomes 'booty of war' and the property of the capturing government.[38] Battlefield booty is arguably not constrained by the rule that the property 'may be used for military purposes'.[39] But the uniforms, articles for personal use and private property of prisoners of war are protected,[40] as is other enemy private property (with the possible exception of privately-owned weapons, etc).[41]

More significantly, it is understood under customary international law that warships, military aircraft and other vessels (including their cargo) belonging to the state can be captured by the enemy state, and ownership passes immediately to the capturing state. Some authorities still refer to such captures as 'booty of war'.[42] The property can be sold, and the only exception to capture in this context would be cultural property.[43] This customary rule is stated in the ICRC study on customary international humanitarian law as

[36] Art 53 Regulations Hague Convention IV (1907). See further Art 52 for requisitions; and see Arai-Takahashi, 'Protection of Private Property', in Clapham, Gaeta and Sassòli (eds), *The 1949 Geneva Conventions: A Commentary* (2015) 1515–34, esp at 1521–24.

[37] Some manuals still refer to state property seized by an occupying army as 'booty of war', see *German Law of Armed Conflict Manual* (2013) at para 553.

[38] UK *Manual* (n 13) at para 8.25(g).

[39] See Lauterpacht (ed), *Oppenheim* (n 25) at para 139; and see ibid at para 144 for private property.

[40] See GC III Art 18, Hague Regulations (1907) Art 4; and GC I Arts 15, 16 and GC II Arts 18 and 19 for property on the wounded, sick and dead in the field, and on the shipwrecked.

[41] The US *Law of War Manual* (n 9) states at para 5.17.3 (footnote omitted) 'In general, enemy *private* movable property on the battlefield may be seized if the property is susceptible to direct military use, *ie*, it is necessary and indispensable for the conduct of war. This includes arms, ammunition, military papers, or property that can be used as military equipment (*eg*, as a means of transportation or communication).' The French *Manuel de droit des conflits armés* (2012) allows for 'butin de guerre' taken from private persons where this constitutes 'matériel de guerre'. See also Dinstein, 'Booty in Warfare', *MPEPIL* (2015) at para 8. The latest New Zealand *Manual of Armed Forces Law*, vol 4: *Law of Armed Conflict*, DM 69 (2nd edn) (2019) excludes, however, all private property from being considered booty. See at paras 8.10.35 and 12.3.17.

[42] German *Law of Armed Conflict Manual* (n 37) at paras 1025 and 1129; US *Law of War Manual* (n 9) paras 13.4.3 and 14.3.1.

[43] See Zhang, 'Customary International Law and the Rule Against Taking Cultural Property as Spoils of War', 17 *Chinese Journal of International Law* (2018) 943-89; Convention on the Protection of Cultural Property in the Event of Armed Conflict (1954).

Rule 49, 'The parties to the conflict may seize military equipment belonging to an adverse party as war booty.'[44] It should be stressed that the customary rules that entitle parties to seize and take ownership of 'war booty' are confined to international armed conflicts – conflicts between states.[45] So property belonging to the other side always refers to state property.

Interestingly, various government manuals, and even the ICRC study on customary international humanitarian law, refer to such property as 'war booty' or 'booty of war', or 'butin de guerre' in French. On reflection this makes some sense; one needs the concept of *war* here to help justify the rule, with its associated idea that the winner takes it all, or at least as much as is necessary to continue to wage war and pay for the occupation. One can hardly derive such a rule from principles of humanity or some humanitarian imperative. The rule must derive from ancient practices in war; but having outlawed going to war, alongside the institution of War, how can states retain such Belligerent Rights? The idea of booty of war forces us to ask ourselves today, with the outlawry of war and the criminalization of aggression, why does the same international legal order authorize either state to acquire and keep such war booty?

Having outlawed recourse to war, and rendered illegitimate the legal acquisition of territory through force, it seems anomalous that states can still acquire ownership of the movable property of the enemy state through the institution of 'war booty'. This not only covers military equipment, arms and ammunition, but also can include cash, securities and even horses considered part of the army. In 1945, the US Army famously took over 100 Hungarian thoroughbred horses, 'captured in combat' from the German Army, who had in turn captured the horses in Hungary and removed them to Germany. The horses were then shipped in a stormy Atlantic crossing to the United States for a US Army breeding programme. A request from Hungary for their return

---

[44] Henckaerts and Doswald-Beck, *Customary International Humanitarian Law, vol 1: Rules* (2005) at 174: 'With respect to non-international armed conflicts, no rule could be identified which would allow, according to international law, the seizure of military equipment belonging to an adverse party, nor was a rule found which would prohibit such seizure under international law.'

[45] *Military Manual on international law relevant to Danish armed forces in international operations* (2016) Ch 10: para 2.8 '10.7 A party to a conflict in IAC may lawfully seize and confiscate war booty.' and 'Confiscation of war booty in NIACs is not clearly authorised in international law.' See also Henckaerts and Doswald-Beck (n 44) at 174: 'With respect to non-international armed conflicts, no rule could be identified which would allow, according to international law, the seizure of military equipment belonging to an adverse party, nor was a rule found which would prohibit such seizure under international law.' This is part of the commentary to Rule 49 quoted above.

was heard in a special subcommittee of the US Senate, and the thoroughbred horses were understood as a matter of law to be war booty.[46] One might also mention French wine vats seized by the German Army in the Second World War and sold on to a private buyer,[47] and even the 2 million cigars destined for the German Army, along with tobacco leaf for 4 million more cigars.[48]

While there may have been a case that the courts recognized such seizure as lawful after the Second World War, even for the unlawful belligerent,[49] there is a very good case that we should no longer consider that the law on such war booty is good law.[50] The time has surely come to move beyond the idea that war should be allowed to legalize theft by states.[51]

---

[46] The full details emerge from the Hearings before a Subcommittee of the Committee on Armed Services United States Senate on Determining the Basis of the Contemplated Return to Hungary of Certain Horses Said to Have Been Brought to the United States as captured War Matériel, 3–23 December 1947 (1948); the total number of horses was higher than the 100 or so Hungarian horses mentioned above – the details are to be found at p 12 of the Senate Hearings; see also Downey (Maj), 'Captured Enemy Property' (n 33) at 497 and 503–04; *Bessenyey v Commissioner of Internal Revenue*, 45 TC 261 (1965) 17 December 1965; Letts, *The Perfect Horse: The Daring US Mission to Rescue the Priceless Stallions Kidnapped by the Nazis* (2016) Ch 27.

[47] *Etat français v Etat Monmousseau*, 37 *Revue critique de droit international privé* (1948) 311–15.

[48] Smith, 'Booty of War', 23 *BYBIL* (1946) 227–39 at 233, 'in this case both the manufactured cigars and the leaf were clearly booty of war'; Downey (Maj), 'Captured Enemy Property' (n 33).

[49] Baxter, 'The Definition of War', 16 *Revue égyptienne de droit international* (1960) 1–14 at 9.

[50] In *Kuwait Airways Corporation v Iraqi Airways Company and Republic of Iraq* [1995] 1 Lloyd's Rep 25 (CA), Leggatt LJ stated that 'From earliest times the concept of plunder, booty and the spoils of war has been amongst the most basic. The seizure by one state of goods belonging to another represents an act of conversion as obvious as it is flagrant.' Such a seizure could be covered by war risks insurance, which covers seizure in this context as a Prize (see *Kuwait Airways Corporation v Kuwait Insurance Company* [1999] 1 Lloyd's Rep 803, HL, 11 March 1999, per Lord Hobhouse), but the English courts would not recognize as legal the Iraqi seizure of the Kuwaiti planes on grounds of public policy: 'Iraq's invasion of Kuwait and seizure of its assets were a gross violation of established rules of international law of fundamental importance. ... Such a fundamental breach of international law can properly cause the courts of this country to say that, like the confiscatory decree of the Nazi government of Germany in 1941, a law depriving those whose property has been plundered of the ownership of their property in favour of the aggressor's own citizens will not be enforced or recognised in proceedings in this country. Enforcement or recognition of this law would be manifestly contrary to the public policy of English law. ... International law, for its part, recognises that a national court may properly decline to give effect to legislative and other acts of foreign states which are in violation of international law.' *Kuwait Airways Corporation v Iraqi Airways Company*, [2002] UKHL 19 [29], per Lord Nicholls. In this situation the illegality of Iraq's action was also based on the binding nature of the relevant Security Council Resolutions.

[51] See also the suggestion by Hersch Lauterpacht that 'a state waging an unlawful war does not obtain or validly transmit title with respect to property acquired in connexion with the conduct of war regardless of whether such title is otherwise acquired in accordance with the law of war'. 'The Problem with the Revision of the Law of War', 29 *BYBIL* (1952) 360–82 at 378 fn 2; Baxter, 'The Definition of War' (n 49) at 9 fn 38, claimed that Lauterpacht peddled back from this view as a description of the actual law, referencing Lauterpacht, 'The Limits of the Operation of the Law of War', 30 *BYBIL* (1953) 206–43 at 233. To be clear, I am suggesting that today, neither side

8.4 Bounty

Another familiar term related to wartime is 'bounty'. This refers to the money paid to the officers and crew present on a warship successful in battle. It was calculated according to the number of enemy sailors on a warship that had been captured, burned, destroyed or sunk (and in earlier times this included 'private ships of war' with letters of *marque*). Elaborate procedures determined what counted as evidence for calculating the number of personnel on board the sunken or captured ship.[52] It has been said that bounty was intended to encourage 'personal gallantry and enterprise'.[53]

In the United States, this bounty money meant that the crew could expect, for a ship that had been destroyed or sunk, $100 per enemy sailor if the American naval power was superior, and $200 if the American force was smaller or equal to that of the enemy. For a captured warship ordered to be destroyed, the bounty was $50 per enemy head on board at the time of capture. Knauth provides some examples, such as the Battle of Manila Bay in 1898, where the American force won with superior armaments, leading to an award of $191,400 based on destroyed vessels that had 1,914 crew members.[54] The Admiral's share in turn was 5% of the total, and the rest shared according to a scale fixed in prize law. The actual provision, which was abolished in 1899, gives us a flavour of the complexities of the reward structure, and reads in part:

> A bounty shall be paid by the United States for each person on board any ship or vessel of war belonging to an enemy at the commencement of an engagement, which is sunk or otherwise destroyed in such engagement by any ship or vessel belonging to the United States or which it may be necessary to destroy in consequence of injuries sustained in action, of one hundred dollars, if the enemy's vessel was of inferior force, and of two

ought to be able to permanently acquire booty of war, even if there is obviously a case that military equipment need not be immediately returned to the adversary during the armed conflict.

[52] For example, the numbers were in the first instance 'proved by the oaths of three or more of the chief officers or men belonging to the said hostile ship or ships of war or privateers'. These oaths were to be sworn before a British Mayor or, if in a neutral port, before a British Consul or Vice-Consul. See Horne, *Compendium of the Statute Laws, and Regulations of the Court of Admiralty Relative to Ships of War, Privateers, Prizes, Re-Captures, and Prize Money* (1803) Ch VII at 89–90.

[53] Anderson, *The Navy and Prize* (n 3) at 27.

[54] For further detail and examples, see Knauth, 'Prize Law Reconsidered', 46 *Columbia Law Review* 1 (1946) 69–93 at 70.

hundred-dollars, if of equal or superior force, to be divided among the officers and crew in the same manner as prize-money; ... and there shall be paid as bounty to the captors of any vessel of war captured from an enemy, which they may be instructed to destroy, or which is immediately destroyed for the public interest, but not in consequence of injuries received in action, fifty dollars for every person who shall be on board at the time of such capture.[55]

In the United Kingdom, an equivalent provision provided for payment of £5 sterling and read as follows, until it was repealed in 1948:

If, in relation to any war, Her Majesty is pleased to declare, by proclamation or Order in Council, Her intention to grant Prize bounty to the officers and crews of Her ships of war, then such of the officers and crew of any of Her Majesty's ships of war as are actually present at the taking or destroying of any armed ship of any of Her Majesty's enemies shall be entitled to have distributed among them as Prize Bounty a sum calculated at the rate of five pounds for each person on board the enemy's ship at the beginning of the engagement.[56]

Awards during the First World War to British Naval Service personnel ran to quite large sums, which could be the equivalent of three years' salary for an Able Seaman.[57] In the absence of hard evidence, the awards of bounty handled by the courts would sometimes estimate upwards the number of enemy crew on a destroyed battleship.[58]

---

[55] Rev Stat (1873) § 4635.

[56] Naval Prize Act 1864, s 42, repealed by the Prize Act 1948, s 9(2).

[57] For some detail of head money at £5 a head paid in 1916 to British submarine crew, see Ballantyne, *The Deadly Trade: The Complete History of Submarine Warfare from Archimedes to the Present* (2018) at 115, where it is recorded that the Crew of the B11 received £3,500, meaning that in fact an Able Seaman, after deduction of the prize agent's fee and apportionment, would receive '£120 6s 1d. the equivalent of three years' pay'. For the detail of some of the bounty money awarded during the First World War, see *Fleet Annual and Naval Year Book* (1917) available at https://archive.org/stream/fleetannualnaval00coveuoft/fleetannualnaval00coveuoft_djvu.txt.

[58] The crew of the B11 benefitted from Sir Samuel Evans rounding up the size of the crew on the enemy battleship to 700. In his award of 24 July 1916, Sir Samuel Evans stated 'I declare the officers and crew of submarine B 11 are entitled to prize bounty as being the only vessel present that brought about the destruction of the Turkish battleship "Mesudieh," and I think I am justified in adding a percentage to the complement ordinarily carried by that battleship. I declare the number on board to be 700. Nobody can say I am wrong, and I hope I am right. The prize bounty awarded will be £3,500.' See *Fleet Annual and Naval Year Book* (1917) (n 57) at 16.

While such bounty or 'head money' is no longer paid under the US or UK legislation, and no other states are known to have awarded such bounty,[59] the implications for the development of naval warfare may have been quite far-ranging. Seen from the perspective of incentives, some scholars have speculated that the system of rewards might have meant that commanders selected their battles and the way they fought in order to maximize not just bounty, but also the prize money that would be shared according to the values of the captured ship and cargo. Prize money (as opposed to 'head money' or bounty) was calculated according to the value of the warship, merchant ship and relevant cargo. Restraint in attack in order to ensure a more valuable prize could explain some tactics in limited wars until prize money was no longer distributed between the capturing state and the naval personnel. Allen's study of incentives in the British Navy in the 18th-century age of sail highlights how such rewards were essential not only for the lower ranks, but also for admirals. 'At a time when an admiral of the fleet might earn £3,000 per year, some admirals amassed £300,000.'[60] Let us look at the concept of Prize Law more closely.

8.5 Prize

In addition to the Belligerent's Right to capture and keep enemy property, such as warships (booty of war), maritime warfare has traditionally included a Belligerent Right to capture enemy merchant (civilian) ships and aircraft. Property passes to the capturing state after adjudication by a Prize Court. The origins of the idea of Prize Law are related to the idea of *seizing* enemy property; as Kraska explains, the 'English word "prize" or French "*prise*" is derived from the Latin verb "*prehendere*", which means to seize.'[61] Grotius opined in his *Commentary on the Law of Prize and Booty* (1603) that the idea of seizing and acquiring enemy property goes to the very purpose and rationale of just war:

> But war is just for the very reason that it tends toward the attainment of rights; and in seizing prize or booty, we are attaining through war that

[59] See Anderson, *The Navy and Prize* (n 3) at 57, for the history of bounty see 27-39 and for salvage and recapture see 40-53.

[60] Allen, 'The British Nay Rules: Monitoring and Incompatible Incentives in the Age of Fighting Sail', 39 *Explorations in Economic History* (2002) 204–231 at 213.

[61] 'Prize Law', *MPEPIL* (2009) at para 1.

which is rightfully ours. Consequently, I believe those authorities to be entirely correct who hold that the essential characteristic of just wars consists above all in the fact that the things captured in such wars become the property of the captors: a conclusion borne out both by the German word for war, [*krieg* from Middle High German *kriec(g)*, which means 'exertion', 'endeavour to obtain something',] and by the Greek word for Mars, since Ἄρης, ['Ares', ie 'Mars',] is apparently ἀπὸ τοῦ αἴρειν, 'derived from ἀείρειν', [which means 'to take away', 'to seize']. Therefore, the seizure of spoils of war is necessarily just on some occasions; and furthermore, it must be just in regard to the same persons and by that same criterion of all law, embraced in our demonstration of the justice of war.[62]

8.5.1 Reprisals, Letters of Marque, Prize and the distribution of Prize Money

One way into understanding Prize Law is to consider and contrast the history of reprisals. As already mentioned, in the Middle Ages reprisals were the chosen method for righting a wrong done to a national by a foreigner or foreign government. As Neff explains:

> When a person was injured by a foreigner and was unable for some good reason, to obtain compensation from the very person who committed the wrong, satisfaction could be had, as a last resort, by seizing property belonging to any fellow-national of the wrong-doer.[63]

The victim would need a 'letter of reprisal' from their sovereign, and should the reprisal be effected against innocent fellow nationals, they would, in theory, be 'entitled to be indemnified by the original wrong-doer'.[64] These private or particular wars look more like law enforcement until they relate to action abroad. At this point they start to look more like war, and the letters were known as 'letters of *marque*', letters of reprisal being considered an authorization to seize goods within the jurisdiction, whereas letters of *marque* 'permitted such capture *beyond* the borders'.[65]

---

[62] Grotius, *Commentary on the Law of Prize and Booty* (1603) ed Van Ittersum, tr Williams (Indianapolis, IN: Liberty Fund, 2005) at 68–69 (footnotes omitted).

[63] Neff, *War and the Law of Nations* (2005) at 77.

[64] Ibid at 78.

[65] Horne, *Compendium* (n 52) at 2, where the footnote reads '[t]he term *marque* is derived from the antiquated word *marche*, denoting a boundary or limit'. See also Neff (n 63) at 81, 'This

Only the letters of *marque* separated these authorized 'privateers' from pirates whose acts would be illegal. The logic of these private wars is found in just war doctrine and the justifications given for Wars between sovereigns. Nevertheless, the separate institution of Prize Law developed in time of War meant that enemy property and enemy vessels on the high seas could be captured and condemned through adjudication by a Prize Court. The captured property might also include enemy goods on neutral vessels, neutral goods on enemy vessels, contraband of war or vessels caught breaching a Blockade.

The Prize was claimed as a sovereign right of a belligerent state at War. By the beginning of the 19th century, some saw this as a universally accepted right that flowed from sovereignty and the need to acquire such property in time of war. The issue is no longer the recuperation of what has been wrongfully taken (reprisal) but a Belligerent Right based on ancient practice to take and keep all such foreign property captured on the high seas in time of War. Any connection to a just war cause is by this time severed. As Sir William Scott (later Lord Sewell), sitting as a judge in Prize Court, explained in an 1804 judgment:

> The right of making war and peace is exclusively in the Crown. The acquisitions of war belong to the Crown; and the disposal of these acquisitions may be of the utmost importance for the purposes of both war and peace.[66]

The value of the ship and the cargo taken in War was divided between the state (the Crown) and the crew and officers of the relevant authorized ships.[67] As with bounty (or prize bounty), there were complex rules that applied to

---

expression apparently derives from the German word *Mark*, meaning frontier, referring to the right to take action beyond the frontier of the issuing state.' See further, for other suggestions of the relevance of the term *marque*, based on the Latin *marchare* to seize as a pledge, Clark, 'The English Practice with Regard to Reprisals by Private Persons', 27 *AJIL* (1933) 694–723.

[66] *The Elebe*, 19 December 1804, reproduced in Roscoe (ed), *Reports of Prize Cases: 1745 to 1859* (1905) vol I, 441–55 at 447; see also Hazlitt and Roche, *A Manual of the Law of Maritime Warfare* (1854) at 374.

[67] Articles of Agreement would set out the division of Prize between the owner of the ship and the Captain, officers and crew. For example, for the *Mars* in New York (1762), the owner was to get half, the other half to be divided between the Captain (6 shares), Lieutenants and Master (3 shares), Captain's Clerk, Mates, Steward, Prize-Master, Gunner, Boatswain, Carpenter and Cooper (2 shares), their Mates (1½ shares), Doctor (3 shares) and the rest of the Company deemed Able Seamen (1 share). Jameson, *Privateering and Piracy in the Colonial Period* (1923) at 581–82.

the distribution of prize money with regard to the value of the captured ship. For the United States:

> The net proceeds of all property condemned as prize, shall, when the prize was of superior or equal force to the vessel or vessels making the capture, be decreed to the captors; and when of inferior force, one-half shall be decreed to the United States and the other half to the captors, except that in case of privateers and letters of marque, the whole shall be decreed to the captors, unless it shall be otherwise provided in the commissions issued to such vessels.[68]

The British rules on distribution have been traced back to early in the reign of Henry VIII (1511) when, for one expedition, they were divided between the King and the Admiral. The rules reach a consolidated form under Queen Anne, in 1708, when they were transferred completely to the captors (with nothing left to the sovereign). Those rules can be summarized as providing for a Captain 'actually on board at the time of the prize' to be allowed three-eighths; Lieutenants one-eighth; gunners, carpenters, surgeons and chaplains one-eighth; gunner's mates, surgeon's mates, etc one-eighth; trumpeters, barbers, cooks, etc two-eighths.[69]

Today, Prize in the United States, or in the United Kingdom, would belong exclusively to the state, but in the 18th and 19th centuries the sums that would accrue to the officers or crew could be enormous. The record sum probably goes to the 1762 capture of the Spanish frigate *Hermione*, loaded with treasure, which led to each seaman's getting £485, a sum which would perhaps be worth close to £100,000 in 2021. The Captains received around £65,000 each, a sum equivalent to around £13,000,000 today.[70] One can see why the state had an interest in ensuring that it got its fair share of the proceeds through careful application of the law in Prize Courts. The Prize Courts also operated as courts applying international law (the Law of Nations) and/or national law, to protect the rights of those who risked having their property seized and eventually condemned.[71]

---

[68]   See Rev Stat (1873) § 4630 for an overview of the distribution in the British, Italian, Russian and French systems; see Anderson, *The Navy and Prize* (n 3) 54–57.

[69]   For the Cruizers Act 1708 and the Proclamation issued by the Queen following the Statute, see Anderson, *The Navy and Prize* (n 3) at 6–7.

[70]   For further details, see at https://en.wikipedia.org/wiki/Action_of_31_May_1762; and for the salaries at the time see http://warfareofficers.org.au/members/engage/2013-September.pdf.

[71]   For a full explanation, see Verzijl, Heere and Offerhaus, *International Law in Historical Perspective: Part IX-C The Law of Maritime Prize* (1992); for the controversy as to whether Prize

The rules relating to the character of the goods that could be captured were set out as far back as the 13th century in well-known books for traders, such as the *Consolat de Mar* (originally in Catalan), and in the following centuries from the British Navy's perspective in the *Black Book of the Admiralty* (in ancient French). According to the *Consolat de Mar*, property belonging to enemies on neutral ships could be captured by a belligerent state in time of War, while it was prohibited to capture neutral property when capturing an enemy ship. Not all states respected this rule, and various powers came to different arrangements for different Wars. In the run-up to the Crimean War, Sweden (united with Norway at that time) and Denmark declared their Neutral Status and sought exemption from capture of enemy goods on neutral vessels. In turn the British and French, who were joining the War against Russia on the side of Turkey, agreed to such a waiver of rights. In the words of the British Declaration of War on Russia, 'Her Majesty is willing, for the present, to waive a part of the belligerent rights appertaining to Her by the law of nations. ... Her Majesty will waive the right of seizing enemy's property laden on board a neutral vessel, unless it be contraband of war.'[72]

Following the 1856 Congress of Paris, which brought the Crimean War to an end, the participants adopted the Declaration of Paris (as a legally binding treaty), and in an early commitment to multilateralism opened the treaty up to states that were not at the Congress. This treaty stated that it was prohibited to capture two categories of non-contraband goods: enemy goods on neutral ships; and neutral goods on enemy ships.[73]

But even after the 1856 Paris Declaration offered protection for neutral goods and ships, there was still unease with the idea that the fact of a War (in the technical legal sense) could allow a state (with the requisite naval capacity) to seize and capture enemy goods on enemy ships on the high seas. Not only were such goods seized along with the ships, but through the institution of Prize Courts, the seizing state could acquire property rights over

---

Courts really apply only international law, or are in the end municipal courts that will apply national law when ordered to do so, see ibid at 596–601.

[72] *London Gazette* (28 March 1854).
[73] Art 2, 'The neutral flag covers enemy's goods, with the exception of contraband of war'; Art 3, 'Neutral goods, with the exception of contraband of war, are not liable to capture under enemy's flag'. See Fujita, 'Commentary to the 1856 Paris Declaration', in Ronzitti (ed), *The Law of Naval Warfare* (1988) 66–75; although some may not have considered that this sort of exception from capture should apply beyond the states parties (see Piggott, *The Declaration of Paris* (1919)), the Declaration is today widely seen as reflecting customary international law, see Roberts and Guelff (eds), *Documents on the Laws of War*, 3rd edn (2001) at 47.

such goods, and a title to such goods valid against the whole world. While there might once have been some strategic rationale for cutting off trade from the enemy state, including food and other goods, over time, with the advent of new forms of transport (railways meant that many ports were no longer dependent on ships for supplies), such seizures start to look more like benefitting from the fortunes or spoils of war – in other words, another form of war booty (even if not falling into that technical category under most definitions).

A joint resolution of the US Congress in 1904 stated that

> it is desirable, in the interest of uniformity of action by the maritime states in the world in time of war, that the President endeavor to bring about an understanding among the principal maritime powers with a view of incorporating into the permanent law of civilized nations the principle of the exemption of all private property at sea, not contraband of war, from capture or destruction by belligerents.[74]

This was not the first time the United States sought to swim against the tide of allowing rights of capture of private enemy property. Already in its 1785 treaty with Prussia, it protected private trading vessels from interference or capture on the high seas, but, as Verzijl's historical accounts show, subsequent attempts by the United States and others, such as France, Italy, Austria, Prussia, China and the Institut de droit international, all failed to enshrine a lasting ban on capture of private property at sea.[75] In Paris, the United States proposed to abolish privateering in return for a new rule that the private property of the subjects of a belligerent power should not be seized by the other belligerent unless it be contraband.[76] The US case was that 'The prevalence of Christianity and the progress of civilization have greatly mitigated the severity of the ancient mode of prosecuting hostilities. War is now an affair of Governments.' And so it was argued that there was a received rule,

> at least as operations upon land are concerned, that the persons and effects of non-combatants are to be respected. The wanton pillage or

---

[74] 33 Stat 592 (1904).

[75] Verzijl et al (n 71) 275–79; and his examination of the Institut's texts from the meetings in the Hague (1875), Zurich (1877) and Turin (1882), which were, as he explains, all 'in favour of the abolition of the capture and confiscation of private enemy property in naval war' (ibid at 278).

[76] Piggott (n 73) at 146; the official proposal is reproduced ibid at 398–404.

uncompensated appropriation of individual property by an army, even in possession of an enemy's country, is against the usage of modern times. Such a mode of proceeding at this day would be condemned by the enlightened judgment of the world, unless warranted by special circumstances. Every consideration which upholds this sentiment in regard to the conduct of a war on land favours the application of the same rule to the persons and property of citizens of the belligerents found upon the ocean.[77]

This was not acceptable to the other states in Paris, or when proposed in a new treaty the following year.[78] Nevertheless, in the American Civil War, both the North and the South formally approved the rules prohibiting the seizing of enemy property on neutral ships, and neutral property on enemy ships, in their relations with neutral shipping from France and Great Britain.[79]

A subsequent American proposal to the 1907 Hague Peace Conference, which would have demanded respect for enemy property on the high seas, attracted 21 votes, with 11 votes against, 11 not responding, and one abstention. To pass the proposal would have required 23 votes among the 44 participating states.[80] The United States unsuccessfully invoked the following ideas in favour of abolition of the right to capture enemy property on the high seas: there was minimal military advantage to be gained by capturing enemy goods; reasons of humanity; and the existing prohibition of pillage in land warfare.[81]

Although the British delegation had instructions to support such an initiative, as the Government appreciated that changing the rules to grant immunity to enemy merchant ships and property at sea would possibly

---

[77] Marcy (US Secretary of State), Note of 28 July 1856 at 397.

[78] Stockton, 'The Declaration of Paris', 14 *AJIL* (1920) 356–68.

[79] Ibid at 366–67; Pigott (n 73) at 411ff. See the proposed Art I, 'That privateering is, and shall remain, abolished, and the private property of subjects or citizens of a belligerent, on the high seas, shall be exempted from seizure by the public armed vessels of the other belligerent, except it be contraband.' Letter from Dallas to Clarendon (1857), Pigott (n 73) at 407.

[80] In favour, USA, Germany (with reservations due to the uncertain nature of the law on contraband and blockade), Austro-Hungarian Empire, Belgium, China, Cuba, Denmark, Ecuador, Greece, Haiti, Italy, Norway, Netherlands, Persia, Romania, Siam, Sweden, Switzerland, Turkey; against, Colombia, Spain, France, Great Britain, Japan, Mexico, Montenegro, Panama, Portugal, Russia, Salvador; abstention Chile. Min. des affaires étrangères, *La deuxième conférence international de la paix 1907* (1908) at 102.

[81] Ibid at 101. The rhetorical point that capture of enemy property at sea is essentially piracy was similarly unpersuasive; the Colombian delegate, Triana, reportedly said that war was organized murder. Westlake, *International Law: Part II War* (1907) at 311 fn 1. The Belgian and Brazilian proposal that the Conference should adopt a *voeu* (recommendation) that the property should be returned after the War was similarly unsuccessful (ibid at 314).

benefit Great Britain and represent a restraint on acts of war and a 'step to-wards the abolition of all war', diminishing in turn expenditure on arms, the Government also considered that, logically, immunity for merchant ships would involve 'the abolition of the right of commercial blockade'. Bearing in mind that the Government considered at that time that '[t]he British navy is the only offensive weapon which Great Britain has against Continental Powers', the Government was clear that it did not authorize the delegation to 'agree to any Resolution which would diminish the effective means which the navy has of bringing pressure to bear upon an enemy'.[82] Naval powers were, in the end, unwilling to abolish their acquired Belligerent Rights. One has to ask whether such rights for states can continue to exist today. Mainstream opinion suggests that they do. The manuals state that a belligerent state is entitled to capture and confiscate enemy goods on enemy ships along with the ships, as well as enemy aircraft with enemy goods.[83] Title will pass following condemnation by a Prize Court after it is determined that the capture is 'good prize'.[84]

I would suggest that rather than suggesting such Belligerent Rights apply in all armed conflicts, we should accept that they can no longer be upheld in the face of states' obligations under the UN Charter. A state should no longer be able to seize and confiscate a foreigner's private property, whether or not there is a Declaration of War, and whether or not it sets up a Prize Court.

Although the British and Germans resorted to capture and prize during both World Wars, the United States, despite passing a series of laws, has not used Prize Law since around 1903. Congress abolished bounty and prize money in 1899. The French law from 1939 regulating maritime prize was updated in 2014, and now excludes enemy warships seized during hostilities.[85] The remaining prize jurisdiction over other ships and their cargo would require a State of War (état de guerre).[86] Interestingly, merchant ships and

---

[82] The full instructions are reproduced in Pearce Higgins, *The Hague Peace Conferences* (1909) 614–25, the quotations are taken from paras 18–20.

[83] Capture must take place outside neutral waters or airspace; see, eg, UK *Manual* (n 13) at paras 12.91–12.96 and 13.99–13.104; *San Remo Manual* (n 8) at paras 135–145.

[84] The procedural rules for the standing of an enemy alien before a Prize Court vary from state to state, and justice would clearly demand that the Prize Court should be able to hear the point of view of the enemy whose property has been captured. Colombos, *A Treatise on the Law of Prize* (supra) at 349–55.

[85] Décret-loi du 1er septembre 1939 relatif aux prises maritimes, as amended.

[86] I am extremely grateful to Commissaire-Général Jean-Louis Fillon for guiding me though the French legislation. He concludes, 'L'application de la législation des prises relève bien d'un cadre juridique différent, celui du temps de guerre qui dans notre droit constitutionnel reste formellement marqué par la déclaration de guerre.' See Fillon, 'A propos du Conseil des prises et de la déclaration de la guerre: Etude sur l'obsolescence du droit de la guerre navale', *Revue*

their goods captured by the French maritime armed forces, if condemned in the *Conseil des prises*, would be divided among all the armed forces taking part (including the army and air force). One quarter would go to the captors or their heirs, and three-quarters to the Treasury of the French State. The captors' share would in turn be divided among the officers and crew, one-quarter going to the officers and three-quarters to the crew, according to weighted percentages, with vice admirals getting twice as much as commanders, and first mates getting four times more than sailors. The relevant rank is the rank at the time of capture.[87]

8.5.2 Contraband of War as Prize

A further aspect of Prize Law relates to the law on contraband of war. This meant that belligerent states considered they had Belligerent Rights to stop and search neutral ships for contraband (certain goods destined for use by the enemy). There were eventually attempts to draw up rules distinguishing Belligerent Rights with regard to absolute contraband (arms, ammunition, etc) from conditional contraband (food and provisions destined for the army).[88] The concept of 'continuous voyage' meant one could presume that even goods to be unloaded in a neutral port were destined for the enemy.[89]

Today, the traditional law states that neutral ships carrying contraband can be captured outside neutral waters.[90] Contraband has been defined in the

---

Maritime 516 (March 2020) 126–133 at 133. A key text is the Ministerial Instruction No 2380/EMM/2 of 31 December 1964 on the Application of International Law in the Event of War (l'instruction sur l'application du droit international en cas de guerre) (last amended in 1969).

[87] Décret-loi du 1er septembre 1939 relatif aux prises maritimes (last amended 2014).

[88] London Declaration Concerning the Laws of Naval War (1909) Arts 22–44. This distinction is no longer deemed particularly relevant, as today states would draw up specific lists of contraband; see *San Remo Manual* (n 8) at paras 147–150.

[89] See Schaller, 'Contraband', *MPEPIL* (2015) at para 14; and London Declaration (1909) Art 30. For the legal effects on British subjects, see Proclamation of King George V, 5 August 1914, reproduced in Clements and Waterson, *Commercial Law in War Time: A Book for Business Men* (1914) at 67; note the Proclamation starts by announcing that 'a state of War exists between Us on the one hand and the German Empire on the other'. This book also covers the effect in English law of a Declaration of War for British nationals, alien enemies and alien friends (subjects of states allied with Great Britain or neutral) on contract law, patents and insurance. As seen in Ch 5 of the present book, the definition of 'alien enemy' under English law is not solely related to a persons's nationality but rather connected to their 'war domicil'. See Page, *War and Alien Enemies: The Law Affecting their Personal and Trading Rights, and Herein of Contraband of War and the Capture of Prizes at Sea*, 2nd edn (1915) at 4ff.

[90] *San Remo Manual* (n 8) at para 146.

San Remo Manual (1994) as 'goods which are ultimately destined for territory under the control of the enemy and which may be susceptible for use in armed conflict'.[91] And the *Manual* states that in order for there to be a right of capture for the contraband goods or neutral vessels, the belligerent must have published contraband lists.[92]

8.5.3   Attacks on Merchant Vessels

Merchant ships flying the flag of the enemy and their enemy cargo have been captured, diverted or, in exceptional circumstances, destroyed.[93] The property passed to the capturing state following adjudication by a Prize Court of the capturing state (all efforts to have an International Prize Court have been stalled since the non-entry into force of the Hague Convention XII (1907)). Resisting visit, search and capture meant a merchant ship could be attacked. Captured vessels could be destroyed in cases of military necessity. Even the civilian crew on board could be interned as prisoners of war, in part to forestall their future use as sailors in the navy.[94] Some vessels, such as hospital ships and small fishing boats, etc, are exempt from capture under certain conditions.[95]

More generally in this context, the purpose of sea warfare became, in Oppenheim's words, 'annihilation of the enemy merchant fleet'.[96] It was the

---

[91]   Ibid at para 148.

[92]   Ibid at para 149. The *Manual* seems to draw a distinction between capture and condemnation in this context: ibid at 213–14. Whether the goods or vessels can actually be condemned in this context by a Prize Court is not certain, see Lauterpacht (ed) (n 25) Ch V; views differ on the relevance of the knowledge of the master or the owner of the character of the cargo as contraband and of the outbreak of war. This idea, which centres on the 'state of mind of the neutral claimant', can be traced back to the time when carrying contraband in breach of neutrality was a crime. See Colombos, *Law of Prize* (n 27) Ch V. Today it is difficult to see why neutral vessels or the goods they are carrying should be condemned in a punitive way either for carrying contraband, or for unneutral service. But see the *Harvard Manual on Air Warfare* (n 8) at 348–53, which assumes that neutral airplanes and their cargo can be condemned in Prize Courts.

[93]   *San Remo Manual* (n 8) at paras 135–140; for an early work highlighting some of the practice and controversies, see Smith, *The Destruction of Merchant Ships under International Law* (1917).

[94]   See GC III Art 4A(4) and, for the 'more favourable treatment' referred to there, Arts 5 and 6 of Hague Convention IX Relative to Certain Restrictions with Regard to the Exercise of the Rights of Capture in Naval War (1907): 'Art 6. The captain, officers, and members of the crew, when nationals of the enemy State, are not made prisoners of war, on condition that they make a formal promise in writing, not to undertake, while hostilities last, any service connected with the operations of the war.'

[95]   See *San Remo Manual* (n 8) at paras 136 and 137; see also Hague Convention XI (1907).

[96]   (n 25) at 458.

nature of the World Wars that explains the erosion, or absence, of rules that protected merchant shipping. This particularly applied to submarine warfare against merchant shipping. The war logic in part is that merchant ships, their civilian crew and indeed all enemy vessels, including private yachts, etc, are presumed to be potentially part of the enemy's naval fleet.[97] The institution of War meant that captures could be made even after the end of hostilities, as long as there was a formal State of War.[98] Moreover, in the World Wars the belligerent states did assume control over merchant vessels to the extent that they were seen as naval auxiliaries.[99]

The two World Wars were total or 'totalitarian' wars. They came to involve almost all the Powers and all, or almost all, of their populations and re-sources so that each of them strained every resource to ensure victory. As the contest increased in intensity, resort was made to additional and more ruthless means and methods of fighting as the conflict escalated. ... For each side, the war was, in a very real sense, 'to the death', and because more and more of each nation's resources were sucked into the fight, the escalation became a function of each side's desperation.[100]

Despite this history of 'unrestricted' attacks on merchant shipping in situ-ations of total war, as well as the more recent practice in the Iran–Iraq War, the fundamental rules that determine if and when a merchant ship has be-come a military objective remain in force. Today, such targeting rules must not depart from the established rule requiring that in order for objects to be attacked they must be military objectives,

---

[97] Colombos, *Law of the Sea* (n 14) at 551–52.

[98] Heintschel von Heinegg makes the point that the confiscation of private property in War continues even after an armistice: 'Visit, Search, Diversion, and Capture in Naval Warfare: Part I, The Traditional Law', 30 *Canadian Yearbook of International Law* (1992) 283–329 at 305; see also Colombos, *Law of the Sea* (n 14) at 548, 'The outbreak of war immediately confers on a bel-ligerent the right to seize and confiscate enemy merchant vessels on all areas of the sea outside neutral territorial waters.'

[99] 'In a general war, the true merchant vessel is rarely to be found because the belligerent states normally assume such a degree of control over their own vessels and neutral vessels en-gaged in trading with them as to convert them into *de facto* naval auxiliaries. As *de facto* naval auxiliaries, they should be subject to the same treatment as *de jure* naval auxiliaries, that is, they may be sunk on sight outside of neutral waters.' Fenrick, 'Legal Aspects of Targeting' (n 7) at 253.

[100] Goldie, 'Targeting Enemy Merchant Shipping: An Overview of Law and Practice', 65 *International Law Studies* (1993) 1–26 at 19.

which by their nature, location, purpose or use make an effective contribution to military action and whose total or partial destruction, capture or neutralization, in the circumstances ruling at the time, offers a definite military advantage.[101]

As we shall see, retaining the rules on search, capture and blockade engenders further rules on resistance to capture and breach of blockade, which in turn lead to a claimed right to attack such merchant ships.[102]

8.5.4 Modern Prize Court Legislation

In the interests of clarity, it is worth explaining at this point that a significant stream of the commentary in English has distinguished 'capture' from 'seizure'.[103] Capture is used to denote that full legal ownership passes to the state taking control. This is said to be the case for enemy warships or other enemy ships employed in public service.[104] Captured warships would more properly therefore be considered booty of war, and were put in to Prize Court 'for the purpose of prize money only [bounty], as property passes immediately on capture'.[105] Strictly speaking, then, these sorts of captures do not form part of contemporary Prize Law, as they are not adjudicated and condemned through Prize Courts.[106] 'Seizure' refers to the situation where the act does not transfer ownership; this happens only after adjudication and condemnation (aka confiscation) by a Prize Court. The international usage today is, however, not consistent, so the terms in this chapter have had to be used somewhat interchangeably.

'The Law of Prize' (as already explained, from the French 'prise' meaning 'seize'), comprises rules that were central to the laws of war and were administered by national courts, under which vessels, aircraft and goods were seized and then liable to be condemned by the national Prize Court of the captor state, with the result that the title to property would pass to the captor

---

[101] *San Remo Manual* (n 8) at para 40.
[102] Ibid at paras 98, 52 and 67.
[103] See Smith, *The Law and Custom of the Sea* (n 11) at 93–94.
[104] Ibid at 94; compare *Oxford Manual of the Laws of Naval War* (1913) definitions.
[105] Colombos, *Law of Prize* (n 27) at 51.
[106] Capture with immediate transfer of ownership and without reference to Prize Court is said to apply to enemy and neutral merchant vessels and aircraft that have become military objectives. See Doswald-Beck (ed), *San Remo Manual* (n 8) at 187.

Belligerent State if the seizure was good Prize.[107] The most recent entry on the 'Law of Prize' in *Halsbury's Laws of England* seems to assume a State of War:

> Capture is lawful from the outbreak of war, the exact moment of which is usually stated in the declaration of war by the belligerent power, until the final termination of the war, which is not necessarily synonymous with the total cessation of hostilities unless accompanied by a declaration on the part of the victorious power that the war is ended.[108]

Indeed when writing about Prize Law, commentators often reference wars and warfare, but some will imply that Prize Law can apply beyond declared war to international armed conflicts more generally (even though all commentators exclude its application to non-international armed conflicts).[109]

India, however, in reaction to the establishment of Prize Courts by Pakistan in 1965, argued not only that Prize Courts could only be established in the context of a declared War,[110] but that as War was now banned under the UN Charter, so too must Prize Courts now be illegal:

> [P]rize court action is contrary to the international law as at present established under the regime of the United Nations Charter. It is well known that the United Nations Charter has banned war and no country can, therefore,

---

[107] For a study on the law applied by a wide variety of states and the implications for international law, see Sico, *'Toute prise doit être jugée': Il guidizio delle prede nel diritto international* (1971).

[108] *Halsbury's Laws of England* (2012) vol 85, para 609 (footnotes omitted).

[109] See Kraska, 'Prize Law', *MPEPIL* (2009) para 1: 'In modern usage the term "prize" means a ship or property captured at sea under the laws of war. A prize is a legal capture at sea during wartime. The concept of prize law arose in customary international law in connection with the seizure at sea of enemy property in naval warfare, which may include ships and cargo at sea during times of international armed conflict.' See also 'There is no concept of prize law in non-international armed conflict': Harvard, *Manual on Air Warfare* (n 8) at 338. For the law of Prize is said to be 'applicable in international armed conflict only': Heintschel von Heinegg, 'Blockades and Interdictions', in Weller (ed), *The Oxford Handbook of the Use of Force in International Law* (2015) 925–46 at 940. See also Dederer, 'Enemy Property', *MPEPIL* (2015), who contemplates the use of Prize Law for enemy merchant ships and enemy property, but confines the term *enemy* to international armed conflict, while non-international armed conflicts involve *adversaries* rather than enemies.

[110] Heintschel von Heinegg, 'Visit, Search, Diversion, and Capture in Naval Warfare: Part II, Developments since 1945', 30 *Canadian Yearbook of International Law* (1992) 89–136 at 96 explains that Pakistan exercised Prize Court jurisdiction over 50 ships and their cargoes (mostly the cargoes consisted of tea belonging to Indian owners or British corporations). India protested the seizure of Indian cargo on neutral ships, 'asserting that the laws of prize can be exercised in a formal state of war only'.

legally declare a war. Without such declaration of war, prize court action is illegal. If any country declares a war, it establishes its naked aggression. In the circumstances, contraband control and prize court action stand illegal.[111]

The Indian Naval and Aircraft Prize Act, 1971, in an apparent change of approach, now specifies that India's Prize Court has 'exclusive jurisdiction in respect of each prize and each proceeding for the condemnation of property as prize, whether such prize is taken before or after the commencement of this Act'.[112] Jurisdiction also extends to all ships, aircraft, cargo, etc 'as may be captured or seized as prize during a war or as a measure of reprisal during an armed conflict or in the exercise of the right of self-defence'.[113] When asked in Parliament why India had not passed similar legislation in 1965, the Minister responded that no goods had been captured on the high seas.[114] The measure was welcomed by one Member of Parliament, 'as we are certain that we are going to have a rich haul of enemy property'.[115] In the brief debate on the legislation, Members of Parliament do refer to 'a state of belligerency at the outbreak of war', 'powers with whom we are in a state of belligerency', 'a state of belligerency and hostility', and of the need to check neutral ships when 'we are at war with Pakistan'.[116] One Member of Parliament urged the Government that, 'having been fortified with this law, they should at no cost return the enemy property captured by us during this war with Pakistan'. He continued, 'I have referred to this in particular because we cannot afford to commit the same mistake again.'[117] The Minister responded to a number of points, explaining that property belonging to the state of Pakistan would not be subjected to the Prize Courts but would be simply captured as booty of

---

[111] Statement of 26 March 1966, quoted in McNair and Watts, *The Legal Effects of War* (4th edn) (1966) at 457. They state that 'the Government of India announced that cargoes detained in India and belonging to third countries would be returned to them' (ibid). The Indian Ministry of Defence's official *History of the Indo-Pak War, 1965* (1992) suggests that plans were made to seize Pakistani merchant ships but not to sink them (Ch 10 at 284).

[112] Section 4(1) goes on to outline the conditions for bringing the prize within the jurisdiction of the Prize Court.

[113] Section 4(3).

[114] Shri Vidya Charan Shukla, Parliamentary Debates, 15 December 1971, Fifth Series, vol XX No 24, col 70.

[115] Shri Somnath Chatterjee, ibid at cols 60–61.

[116] Parliamentary Debates (n 114) at cols 61, 62, 64 and 66.

[117] Shri JM Gowder, ibid at col 66.

war;[118] the legislation was said to be primarily aimed at contraband on neutral ships headed to Pakistan.

In the 1971 conflict with Pakistan (which is said to have been considered a War by the parties and the United States[119]), India captured four Pakistani navy vessels (ships of war), a number of Pakistani merchant ships, declared a blockade of Eastern Pakistan, published lists of contraband (as did Pakistan) and adjudicated contraband cargo unloaded from Danish ships.[120]

The historical regime covering 'enemy property' applies mainly to property left behind in India by those who departed and took Pakistani nationality. It is not connected to naval warfare or Prize Court jurisdiction. Under the Defence of India Acts, an 'enemy' is defined as:

(*i*) any person or country committing external aggression against India;

(*ii*) any person belonging to a country committing such aggression;

(*iii*) such other country as may be declared by the Central Government to be assisting the country committing such aggression;

(*iv*) any person belonging to such other country . . .[121]

The concept of an enemy for the purposes of the historical disputes over assets in India remains linked in the legislation to foreign nationals connected to particular acts of aggression.[122]

It is rather difficult to draw definitive conclusions from these various Indian texts. It seems likely that Indian Prize Court jurisdiction would only cover Declared War and international armed conflicts of a certain duration, and would apply the international customary rules on Prize.[123]

[118] See Section 12 of the 1971 Act, 'Prize proceedings not to apply to enemy warships and military aircraft.'

[119] See Heintschel von Heinegg, 'Introductory Report I', in Heintschel von Heinegg (ed), *Visit, Search, Diversion and Capture: The Effect of the United Nations Charter on the Law of Naval Warfare* (1995) 1–91 at 56.

[120] Ibid; and Goel, 'Comment No 4', in Heintschel von Heinegg (ed) (n 119)at 103–06.

[121] Defence of India Act, 1962, Section 2(c), and Defence of India Act, 1971, Section 2(b) respectively. For the application, see now the Enemy Property Act, 1968 and the Enemy Property Rules, 2015 and the Enemy Property (Amendment) Rules, 2018. For a recent order under the Enemy Property Act, see Ministry of Home Affairs Order SO 292 E, 22 January 2020. I am grateful to Abhimanyu George Jain for pointing me to the Indian legislation and for guiding me through the context, as well as for the references to the 1971 Parliamentary Debates and the official history of the 1965 conflict.

[122] Under the Enemy Property Act, 1968, Section 2(b), ' "enemy" or "enemy subject" or "enemy firm" means a person or country who or which was an enemy, an enemy subject or an enemy firm, as the case may be, under the Defence of India Act, 1962, and the Defence of India Rules, 1962 or the Defence of India Act, 1971 and the Defence of India Rules, 1971, but does not include a citizen of India.'

[123] See Section 4(4).

A more recent example of Prize Court legislation is that of Iran, which sought to condemn, through a Prize Court, property seized in its conflict with Iraq. Although this Court never came into effect, it is interesting that Iran would have authorized acquisition of property from 'States at war' with Iran under Article 3(a) of the 1987 Iranian law regarding 'War Prizes', thus limiting enemy property taken as Prize to property owned by states. Certain other property, including that owned by nationals of the enemy state, would be confiscated as war contraband involving, under Article 3(b), a contribution to the combat power of the enemy. This last category is said to be intended to go beyond the idea of absolute contraband and reflect the practice of Iran of seizing 'any merchandize benefitting the war effort of the enemy, either directly or indirectly'.[124] For the property of enemy states at War with Iran, and objects that Iran had forbidden to be transported to enemy territory, the confiscation could, according to this law, have taken place without the intervention of the judge.[125]

The Iranian 'Law Regarding the Settlement of Disputes over War Prizes', ratified by the Constitutional Council on 31 January 1988 to apply as an experiment for five years, included the following provisions:

Article 3: According to this law, the following goods, merchandise and means of transport shall be considered as war prizes:
(a) All goods, merchandise, means of transport and equipment belonging to a State or to States at war with the Islamic Republic of Iran.
(b) Merchandise and means of transport in paragraph (a) belonging to neutral States or their nationals, or to nationals of the belligerent State if they could effectively contribute to increasing the combat power of the enemy or their final destination, either directly or via intermediaries, is a State at war with the Islamic Republic of Iran.
(c) Vessels flying the flag of a neutral country as well as vehicles belonging to a neutral State transporting the items set out in this article.
(d) Merchandise, means of transport and equipment which the Islamic Republic of Iran forbids from being transported to enemy territory.
Article 4: All goods, merchandise and means of transport indicated in paragraph (a) of Article 3 will become the property of the Islamic Republic of Iran. All goods, merchandise and means of transport indicated in

---

[124] See the explanation in Momtaz, 'Iran' in De Guttry and Ronzitti (eds), *The Iran–Iraq War (1980–1988) and the Law of Naval Warfare* (1993) 19–53 at 26.
[125] Ibid at 27.

paragraphs (b) and (c) of Article 3 will be confiscated by the Government of the Islamic Republic of Iran. ... The means of transport indicated in paragraph (d) of Article 3 will become the property of the Islamic Republic of Iran or be confiscated according to circumstances. Any person contesting this must appear before the Tribunal.[126]

This War Prizes Tribunal was premised, then, on the notion or fact of one or more states being in a State of War with Iran. The jurisdiction of the Tribunal was dependent on the State of War.

As we saw above, the UK and US Prize Courts, for example, have been institutionalized as part of the national legal orders and, as with other states, no longer require to be commissioned through an express instrument.[127] There have been no instances of American or British Prize Courts since the Second World War, leaving the situation a little uncertain. Certainly the famous judgments of the highest courts in these two states have historically conceived of the international law applied by Prize Courts as related to 'acts done by the sovereign power in right of war',[128] 'the acts of a belligerent Power in right of war',[129] 'capture at sea during war',[130] 'prize of war'[131] and 'the immunity of fishing boats in time of war'.[132] So, while Prize Courts may now be established as temporarily dormant institutions, rather than created for each and every War, it remains unclear whether national Prize Courts would operate outside a situation of a formal State of War.

The practice in the United Kingdom has been for Prize jurisdiction to be exercised following a special commission 'upon the outbreak of every war'.[133] The US Code provides that the federal district courts have exclusive jurisdiction over prize,[134] and on the substance states that 'This chapter applies to all

---

[126] Ibid at 39–40.
[127] See further Colombos, *Law of the Sea* (n 14) at 804 and 812 for the United Kingdom and the United States; and for brief references to France, Belgium, Italy, Germany, Japan, China, USSR, Thailand, Austria, Turkey, Greece, Romania, the Netherlands and Norway, see Colombos, *Law of Prize* (n 27) at 36–47. For further detail, see Haines and Martin, 'Prize Courts: Their Continuing Relevance', in Stephens and Stubbs (eds), *The Law of Naval Warfare* (2019) 267-82; see also, for the Prize Court in the United Kingdom, *Halsbury's Laws of England*, vol 85 (n 108) at para 645.
[128] *The Zamora* [1916] 2 AC 77, 91 (PC).
[129] Ibid at 92.
[130] Ibid at 94.
[131] *The Paquete Habana*, 175 US (1900) 677 at 678 (US Supreme Court).
[132] Ibid at 702.
[133] Colombos, *Law of the Sea* (n 14) at 804.
[134] 28 US Code §1333: 'The district courts shall have original jurisdiction, exclusive of the courts of the States, of: ... Any prize brought into the United States and all proceedings for the condemnation of property taken as prize.'

captures of vessels as prize during war by authority of the United States or adopted and ratified by the President.'[135]

In the context of the discussion over the legal consequences of a blockade of Cuba by the United States in 1961, it seems to have been assumed by the Assistant Attorney-General that captured ships accused of attempting to breach such a blockade 'could be treated as prizes and placed within the prize jurisdiction of the federal district courts, provided the captures could be deemed to have been made "during war" '.[136]

The idea of Prize Court jurisdiction is to ensure that the draconian rights of the belligerent state are not applied against totally innocent parties. A hearing before a Prize Court is a chance for the parties affected to claim that the Belligerent Rights related to capture have been abuses, and that the property should not be condemned (and pass to the Blockading state) but rather be restored to its owner. There may even be related issues concerning compensation to the shipowners for visit, search and seizure where such action could not be based on a reasonable belief on the part of the belligerent state.[137] As we have seen, Prize Court jurisdiction has been asserted only very rarely since the Second World War, and some national legal orders probably require a Declaration of War before a Prize Court can sit. Heintschel von Heinegg is unequivocal that the law of Prize is 'applicable in international armed conflict only'.[138]

In the 20th century, Prize Courts were commissioned against a background of Belligerent Rights in a State of War.[139] Modern military and expert

---

[135] 10 USC § 8851 (2018).

[136] 'Authority of the President to Blockade Cuba: Memorandum Opinion for the Attorney General', 25 January 1961, Robert Kramer, Assistant Attorney-General, Office of Legal Counsel, reproduced in *Supplemental Opinions of The Office of Legal Counsel* (2013) vol 1, 195–205 at 200; see also 'Legal and Practical Consequence of a Blockade of Cuba: Memorandum' (unsigned), 19 October 1962, ibid at 486–92.

[137] For detail of the different approaches of British and German Prize Courts with regard to the burden of proof on the award of damages where there was unfounded reasonable suspicion on the side of the captor, see Wendel, *State Responsibility for Interferences with the Freedom of Navigation in Public International Law* (2007) at 236–40; see also London Declaration 1909 (not in force) Art 64; Colombos, *Law of the Sea* (n 14) 775–825.

[138] Heintschel von Heinegg, 'Blockades and Interdictions' (n 109) at 940.

[139] The Security Council, with regard to Israel and Egypt in 1951, considered the Armistice Agreement to be of a 'permanent character', so that 'neither party can reasonably assert that it is actively a belligerent or requires to exercise the right of visit, search and seizure for any legitimate purpose of self-defence' (Resolution 95 (1951)). The most extensive debate on this topic took place in 1951 in the Security Council with regard to the claim of Egypt that it enjoyed Belligerent Rights under a state of War with Israel, notwithstanding the Armistice. The Security Council found that neither Israel nor Egypt was an active belligerent, and that neither of them could reasonably assert that they were required 'to exercise the right of visit, search and seizure for any legitimate purpose of self-defence'. See Resolution 95 (1951). While several Council members emphasized the permanent nature of the Armistice, Israel also argued that 'the claim to

manuals, however, assume that the armed forces can as a matter of extant international law capture and divert vessels for adjudication and condemnation in Prize Court, whether or not they are dealing with a recognized State of War between two states or simply an international armed conflict.[140] And yet the same manuals make no reference to the ways in which Prize Court jurisdiction is to be established, or the prospect that under national law today these may still be premised on a Declaration or State of War.

8.6   Blockade

We came across the legal institution of Blockade when we looked at how War came to be outlawed. We saw that, in order to avoid the legal consequences

---

belligerency cannot be sustained by the United Nations'. Ambassador Eban of Israel continued, 'The Charter has created a new world of international relations within which the traditional "rights of war" cannot be enthroned. It is no accident that belligerent rights have never been recognized or mentioned either by the Charter or by any organ of the United Nations. Members of the United Nations are pledged to refrain entirely in their international relations from the threat or use of force, except on behalf of the purposes of the United Nations. There can therefore be no room within the régime of the Charter for any generic doctrine of belligerency, since belligerency is nothing but a political and legal formula for regulating the threat or use of force.' SCOR, 6th year, 549th meeting, 26 July 1951, UN Doc S/PV.549, 11 at para 40, see also the rest of the debate in S/PV.550-553 and S/PV.555. Whether or not belligerent rights existed, several delegations would seem to limit them to rights that would be exercised in self-defence following an armed attack. Egyptian Prize Courts may have continued to operate on the assumption that there was a State of War: *The Lea Lott*, United Arab Republic, Prize Court, 16 December 1959, 28 ILR 652; *The Esperia*, United Arab Republic, 26 February 1959, 28 ILR 656; *The Fjeld*, Egypt Prize Court of Alexandria, 4 November 1950, 17 ILR 345; *The Flying Trader*, Egypt, Prize Court of Alexandria, 2 December 1950, 17 ILR 440. However, one Prize Court later additionally referred to the fact that the measures were only taken in areas of sovereign territory rather than under the 'rules of war on the high seas', and that, in any event, the Constantinople Treaty of 1888 'gives Egypt the right to take all necessary measures for the maintenance of public order in time of peace and for her defence in time of war': *The Inge Toft*, United Arab Republic, Prize Court, 10 September 1960, 31 ILR (1966) 509, 518.

---

[140] See, eg, US Navy, US Marine Corps, US Coast Guard, *The Commander's Handbook on The Law of Naval Operations* (2017) at para 5.2; US *Law of War Manual* (n 9) at para 3.4.1.1; UK *Manual* (n 13) at para 12.78.1. Note that the 2007 amendments to the UK Manual (n 13) delete the words 'the United Kingdom has not used prize courts for many years and is unlikely to do so in the future'. See Farrant, 'Modern Maritime Neutrality Law', 90 *International Law Studies* (2014) 198–306 at 305; Haines, 'The United Kingdom's Manual of the Law of Armed Conflict and the San Remo Manual: Maritime Rules Compared', 36 *Israel Yearbook of Human Rights* (2006) 89–118 at 100–01. In the Netherlands, Art 14 of the Prize Regulations states that 'The Right of Capture may be exercised during the period in which the Netherlands is in a state of war or armed conflict with another Power'. Zeeman, 'The Netherlands, The Law of Neutrality, and Prize Law', in van Panhuyst et al (eds), *International Law in the Netherlands* (1980) 337–71 at 361. We will consider the recent use of Prize Court jurisdiction by Israel in section 8.6.4 below.

of War, states sought to portray their blockades of foreign ports as 'pacific blockade', the idea being that the action (arguably in reprisal) was only being taken against ships from the blockaded state, which could be 'seized and sequestrated' but not 'condemned and confiscated'.[141] The ships of third states were free to pass through the blockade to the blockaded port.[142] Where action was desired against neutral shipping, a pacific blockade would have to be converted into a Blockade proper, with an accompanying State of War. An act of blockade,[143] whatever the intention, could become an act of War when either side considered the legal situation to be one of a State of War.[144]

Generations of lawyers have studied *The Prize Cases* decided by the US Supreme Court. This judgment concerned the Civil War between the Northern States loyal to the Union (the North) and the Confederate States (the South) that had broken away. In this situation, the US Supreme Court considered that 'The proclamation of blockade is itself official and conclusive evidence to the Court that a state of war existed which demanded and authorized a recourse to such a measure under the circumstances peculiar to the case.'[145] This was in a way a recognition of the Belligerency for the rebel forces of the Confederate States, creating an international armed conflict out of a civil war, with the attendant rules that applied in time of War (for the belligerent parties and for states with Neutral Status).

Today a series of questions arise that are not easily answered. First, can one institute a blockade without also accepting that one has created a State of War? And, second, in the absence of a recognition of Belligerency, is the

---

[141] Lauterpacht (ed), *Oppenheim* (n 25) at 148, for examples of pacific blockade and the reactions of third states, which drew a distinction between the rights of states in pacific blockade and Blockade in a State of War: see ibid at 144–49.

[142] Heidelberg Resolution of the Institut de droit international, 'Déclaration concernant le blocus en dehors de l'état de guerre' (1887) para 1.

[143] A blockade has been explained as 'a belligerent operation to prevent vessels and/or aircraft of all nations, enemy and neutral, from entering or exiting specified ports, airports, or coastal areas belonging to, occupied by, or under the control of an enemy nation. The purpose of establishing a blockade is to deny the enemy the use of enemy and neutral vessels or aircraft to transport personnel and goods to or from enemy territory.' Heintschel von Heinegg, 'Blockade', *MPEPIL* (2015) at para 1. I am using a capital 'B' for Blockades to signify that these Blockades were recognized as part of a State of War in the technical sense, giving rise to Belligerent Rights for states. The capital letters signify that the International Law of War, in the technical sense of a State of War, gave rights to Belligerents in International Law. These rights were assumed to flow from International Law as such (or the Law of Nations) and not from national law or any particular treaty.

[144] See McNair and Watts, *The Legal Effects of War*, 4th edn (1966) at 20, suggesting that pacific blockade 'does not *ipso facto* give rise to a state of war, although even if the blockading State is acting *sine animo beligerendi*, it will amount to an act of force which the blockaded State may elect to regard as creating a state of war'.

[145] 67 US 635 at 670.

declaration or establishment of a blockade, with the traditional associated rights and obligations, applicable to a non-international armed conflict? If so, does such an application of the law of blockade still imply a recognition of Belligerency, as it did at the time of the American Civil War?

8.6.1 Is Blockade Limited to a State of War (in the Legal Sense)?

The idea that today, maritime warfare rules related to blockade require a State of War has been rejected in broad terms by Heintschel von Heinegg: 'The existence of a state of war is not a precondition for the legality of certain methods and means of warfare anymore.'[146] At one level this seems sensible. After all, it ought to be possible to judge the legality of a blockade by the modern humanitarian law standards that relate to its effect on the civilian population, and not simply according to whether there is a War on or not. One might be able to determine the limits of this method of warfare using the customary principles applicable to warfare more generally, the distinction between civilian objects and military objectives, the prohibition on disproportionate damage to the civilian population, and agree that there is a prohibition on blockades the sole purpose of which is 'starving the civilian population or denying it other objects essential for its survival'.[147] More generally there is a prohibition of starvation of civilians as a method of warfare.[148]

But, seen from another perspective, Blockade is inextricably associated with the old institution of War, and beyond the legality of the means and methods of warfare, the institution of Blockade is said to bring with it certain traditional customary rights for the Blockading state that affect the economic rights of neutral and enemy nationals. These rights belonging to the Blockading state are mostly unregulated by treaty, and traditionally flow from being in a State of War. One has to ask, therefore, whether the *rights* of a Blockading state (as opposed to the *obligations* imposed by international

---

[146] Heintschel von Heinegg, 'Naval Blockade', 75 *International Law Studies* (2000) 203–30 at 204; and similarly see Heintschel von Heinegg 'Blockade' (n 143) at para 5; see also Green, *The Contemporary Law of Armed Conflict*, 3rd edn (2008) at 204–07; Drew, *The Law of Maritime Blockade: Past, Present, and Future* (2017).

[147] *San Remo Manual* (n 8) para 102.

[148] See Heintschel von Heinegg, 'The Law of Armed Conflict at Sea', in Fleck (ed), *The Handbook of Humanitarian Law in Armed Conflict*, 3rd edn (2013) 463–547 at 532–38 esp at 535, where he states that 'If a blockade has the effect of starving the civilian population it becomes illegal according to Article 49 para 3, and Article 54, para 1 AP I.'

humanitarian law) can continue with the withering away of the institution of War?

At the time of the Cuban missile crisis, legal advisors within the US Administration studied the implications of declaring a Blockade of Cuba. The US *Law of War Manual* quotes part of one unsigned memorandum:

> The declaration of a state of war was helpful in ascertaining the rights and obligations of neutrals in a given situation. Apart from this, however, it served little function. War itself, whatever its reason, was legal self-help, and so were lesser measures if such could be said to exist. Whether or not a nation declared a state of war it would be found by others to exist if that state were claiming rights, such as blockade, normally associated with war.[149]

The memorandum goes on, however, to explain:

> One could deduce a state of war from the existence of a blockade. And one could not conceptually claim rights of blockade without acknowledging its relationship to war.

And then the unsigned memorandum states:

> I would recommend, therefore, that if we declare a blockade, we simply claim all the rights a blockading nation would have if a state of war existed. This clarifies our position sufficiently for legal purposes. A number of states will say this amounts to a declaration of war against Cuba, but that could scarcely be avoided under any circumstances.

The summary conclusion that heads the memorandum reads 'a blockade could be regarded by Cuba and other Soviet Bloc nations as an act of war'.

A similar legal opinion from 1961 explained that Prize Courts could operate to treat neutral ships breaching the blockade as prize, 'provided the captures could be deemed to have been made "during war"'.[150] The opinion also stated 'In the absence of a state of war, it might also be possible for Cuban nationals to resort to our courts for the purpose of testing the legality of the

---

[149] The US *Law of War Manual* (n 9) includes references to a legal opinion of 19 October 1962, para 3.4.1.1 fn 59. This is an unsigned, unaddressed memorandum, 'Legal and Practical Consequences of a Blockade of Cuba', see n 136.

[150] Authority of the President to Blockade Cuba, of 25 January 1961, from Robert Kramer, Assistant Attorney-General for the Office of Legal Counsel (n 36).

blockade.' The United States ultimately instituted a 'quarantine', which only focused on certain goods; precisely, it seems to avoid the legal implications that flow from Blockade's being bound up with a State of War.[151]

Traditionally, we find that the Blockading state had, in the case of breach of Blockade, the right to seize vessels and goods from ships flying the flag of any state. The idea that neutral vessels can be seized in some circumstances, and that the property rights pass permanently to the seizing state (even an aggressor Blockading state), must lead us to question whether these days the formal institution of Blockade, with its attendant rights, can be established without the formal State of War from which those rights flowed. And even if one imagines such a formal State of War today, how can Blockade at the same time not only be considered an act of aggression under the UN Charter,[152] and a crime of aggression under the Statute of the International Criminal Court,[153] but also give rise to a UN member state's *right* to seize and permanently keep the property and vessels of neutrals? International law surely cannot outlaw such acts of war as aggression under the UN Charter, criminalize such acts of aggression for the leaders who ordered the blockade and then reward the perpetrators by sanctioning that they may keep anything they seize while carrying out the international crime?

Remarkably, the military manuals and expert textbooks that I have been able to consult seem untroubled by this contradiction. I suppose that the authors of such military manuals always consider themselves to be imposing Blockade for justified reasons, and are concerned to maintain the legitimacy of this method or tactic of warfare. The most recent *Manual*, published by New Zealand in 2019, comes closest perhaps to recognizing the modern tension. It states early on that '[a] blockade is an act of war'[154] and that New Zealand 'is unlikely to be enforcing a blockade other than as part of a coalition operation.'[155] But it goes on nevertheless to outline the rules for capture of ships breaching blockade, and for attacking ships resisting visit, search or capture, and for confiscation of neutral property in the context of breach or attempted breach. And yet the hesitation is clear when the *Manual* later

---

[151] See further US Navy et al, *The Commander's Handbook* (n 140) at para 4.4.8 'Maritime Quarantine'; for the international law on the quarantine, see Wright, 'The Cuban Quarantine', 57 *AJIL* (1963) 546–65 and see also Wilson, 'International Law and the United States Cuban Quarantine of 1962', 7 *Journal of Inter-American Studies* (1965) 485–92.

[152] 'The blockade of the ports or coasts of a State by the armed forces of another State' qualifies as an act of aggression: 'Definition of Aggression', UN GA Resolution 3314 (1974) Art 3(c).

[153] ICC Statute (as amended) Art 8bis (2)(c).

[154] New Zealand *Law of Armed Conflict* (n 41) at para 10.5.1.

[155] Ibid at para 10.5.2.

addresses the idea of exercising Prize jurisdiction in order permanently to confiscate ships or goods: 'It is generally not now appropriate for a State to profit financially from the waging of armed conflict, although it will still wish to be compensated for its losses.'[156]

There has also been some hesitation among other states over the idea that Blockade can simply be decoupled from the institution of War. This could be for either of two reasons. First, a non-participating state today may wish to avoid Belligerent Rights being exercised by the Blockading state over their ships and cargoes. Speaking about the UK Government's approach to the conflict between Iran and Iraq in the 1980s, Greenwood explained as follows:

> [T]he Foreign Office and Ministry of Defence recently have avoided any references to a war in the Gulf. Although originally British spokesmen talked about the United Kingdom being 'neutral' in the 'war' between Iraq and Iran, since 1986 the tone of statements has changed. Reference is made instead to an 'armed conflict' in which Britain is 'impartial'. This is more than just the British love of understatement. It represents, in part, an attempt to ensure that the law of blockade will not be applied to the detriment of British shipping.[157]

Second, it may be that states contemplating establishing a Blockade still see Blockade as associated with formal War and aggression. For them this means Blockade has to be justified under the UN Charter.[158] Haines, who was involved in the British Ministry of Defence discussions over the appropriateness of a Blockade of the Montenegrin port of Bar during the NATO armed conflict over Kosovo in 1999, recounts that there 'was a marked reluctance on the part of many within NATO, first to admit that the Alliance was actually in a state of war with Serbia and second, that belligerent blockade was an acceptable way of controlling access to Bar'.[159] Speller, similarly, suggests

---

[156] Ibid at para 10.6.16 fn 126.

[157] He continued, 'Whether it is right to assume that the law of blockade would be applicable in a state of war, and would not be applicable if the conflict was not recognized as war, remains a much more complicated question.' Greenwood, 'Remarks', *Proceedings of ASIL* (1988) 158–61 at 158–59.

[158] There were apparently internal British Government discussions on the decision not to declare War or impose a blockade (as it seemed to them that blockade could not be undertaken without War) in the context of the conflict with Argentina over the Falklands/Malvinas; see Fazal, *Wars of Law: Unintended Consequences in the Regulation of Armed Conflict* (2018) at 103–07.

[159] Haines, 'The United Kingdom's Manual of the Law of Armed Conflict and the San Remo Manual: Maritime Rules Compared', 36 *Israel Yearbook of Human Rights* (2006) 89–118 at 108.

that 'In 1999 NATO was unwilling to declare a blockade of the port of Bar in Montenegro (during the Kosovo conflict), because it was not formally at war with Yugoslavia.'[160] Ronzitti puts it slightly differently, explaining 'During the NATO intervention against the Federal Republic of Yugoslavia in 1999, the United States proposed the blockade of the port of Bar, but the proposal was not endorsed by France and Italy as they deemed it required authorization by the UN Security Council.'[161]

The issue is that blockade is not just a method or tactic of warfare; blockade in itself has to be justified as compatible not only with humanitarian rules for the protection of the civilian population, but also with the UN Charter. So Greenwood, even though he considered the NATO aerial attacks legal and justified as humanitarian intervention, considered that any naval blockade would still have to be judged against the claimed justification for what would otherwise be a breach of the rule in the UN Charter prohibiting the use of force.[162] He is making an important point for the purposes of our present inquiry. He is saying that a state establishing a blockade only has rights over neutral shipping to the extent that these are necessary for its legitimate purpose in resorting to force in the first place.

I would suggest then that a state cannot claim that because there is an armed conflict, or a War, the state has Belligerent Rights at sea that flow from the old institution of Blockade in War. Its rights do not stem from the institution of War, or the fact of blockade, but are rather dependent on the UN Charter rules governing resort to force and the maintenance of peace and security.[163] On this reading, a state choosing to impose a blockade without UN

---

[160] Speller, *Understanding Naval Warfare*, 2nd edn (2019) at 138–39.

[161] Ronzitti, 'Naval Warfare', *MPEPIL* (2009) at para 17.

[162] Greenwood, 'The Applicability of International Humanitarian Law and the Law of Neutrality to the Kosovo Campaign', 78 *International Law Studies* (2002) 35–69 at 56–57.

[163] Of course an embargo at sea authorized by the UN Security Council would be legal but would not necessarily give rise to the rights to confiscate permanently the property of neutral states, as was foreseen under the old law of Blockade. In recent cases the situation between the naval states enforcing the embargo through interdiction measures has not been covered by the laws of war, as there has been no armed conflict between these states and the states under embargo or those involved in the transport being interdicted. See Frostad, 'United Nations Authorized Embargoes and Maritime Interdiction: A Special Focus on Somalia', in Andreone (ed), *The Future of the Law of the Sea* (2017) 213–37 at 226: 'As the embargo enforcers are not party to the noninternational armed conflict in Somalia, or in an armed conflict with the weapons and charcoal transporters, the reference to international humanitarian law would seem unnecessary.' Frostad (at 234) further suggests that although the Security Council authorizes seizure, destruction and sale of vessels and prohibited items, these would have to be compliant with international human rights law; and that where items are seized in a UN operation, the United Nations could consider a sanctions panel, which could operate 'in a prize court fashion', for the disposal of seized items. See also Geiß and Petrig, *Piracy and Armed Robbery at Sea* (2011) at 131–35. For other UN-authorized interdiction operations, see Fink, who explains how

authorization, as a simple act of war or aggression, should therefore have no Belligerent Rights over neutral shipping, while a state acting in self-defence has only those rights that are necessary and proportionate to its defence. Greenwood's important, and to my mind convincing, argument has only rarely been made and will be reproduced here at some length:

> The need to comply with the *jus ad bellum* is particularly important when the measures in question are taken against neutral States. An oil embargo of the FRY [Federal Republic of Yugoslavia] would have involved enforcing restriction on the exercise by the shipping of neutral States of the normal rights of freedom of navigation under international law. Accordingly, while it is necessary to show that those restrictions were compatible with the *jus in bello*, it is not sufficient to do so; they must also be within the limits of the *jus ad bellum*.
>
> The uncertainty about the possible imposition of an oil embargo was therefore, for many, the reflection of their uncertainty about whether NATO had a solid legal justification for resorting to force at all. In addition, even if international law does recognize a right to use force by way of humanitarian intervention, it is still necessary to ask whether that extends to the exercise of belligerent rights over the shipping of neutral States. As was made clear earlier in this paper, the present writer is firmly of the view that there is a right of humanitarian intervention in an extreme case. Moreover, if international law permits States to use force in such a case against the State responsible for the humanitarian crisis, then it is logical that it should also permit the taking of action which is both necessary and proportionate against neutral shipping to prevent that State from acquiring supplies needed to continue its human rights abuses or resist attempts to prevent them. But it is in considerations of this kind, and not just in references to the traditional rights of belligerents at sea, that the justification for an oil embargo needed to be found.[164]

---

the language of the Security Council Resolutions with regard to Libya did not relate to the idea of blockade and a mandate to 'halt all inward and outward shipping' but was focused on arms and measures necessary to protect civilians. 'UN-Mandated Maritime Arms Embargo Operations in Operation Unified Protector', 50 *Military Law and Law of War Review* (2011) 237–60.

[164] Greenwood, 'Applicability' (n 162) at 56–57; see also his study Greenwood, 'The Effects of the United Nations Charter on the Law of Naval Warfare' in Heintschel von Heinegg (ed), *Visit, Search, Diversion and Capture: The Effect of the United Nations Charter on the Law of Naval Warfare* (1995) 133–76 at 167: 'Measures taken against neutrals must be taken in accordance with the laws of neutrality but the justification for taking them rests today in the law of self-defence rather than in any concept of belligerent rights necessarily inherent in a state of war.' He

So, even if blockade can arguably be declared and established without a formal State of War, we should consider that, when imposed with regard to another state, it will be seen, if not as an 'act of War', then as an act of aggression, unless there is a justification to ensure that not just the blockade, but also its manner of establishment is legal under the UN Charter.

8.6.2   Do the Belligerent Rights in Blockade Apply Beyond Inter-State Armed Conflicts?

Let us turn to the other question posed above: does the institution of Blockade apply where one or more of the parties is a non-state actor? Heintschel von Heinegg is again emphatic, 'It is to be emphasized that blockade is a method of warfare recognized to apply in international armed conflicts only.'[165] The US *Law of War Manual* (2016) contains sections on the right to blockade, but defines blockade as applying only where one state blockades the port, coast, etc of another *state*.[166] The commentary to the *Harvard Manual on Air Warfare* is clear that '[a]erial blockade is a method of warfare exclusively applicable in international armed conflicts'.[167]

While some might consider that the international law on blockade imposed by Israel should give Israel Belligerent Rights in the context of Gaza, even if this were to be considered a non-international armed conflict,[168]

concludes (ibid at 154 (footnote omitted)) that 'While the state of war may survive in a technical sense after the conclusion of an armistice or permanent ceasefire, the continued assertion of belligerent rights cannot be justified as a necessary measure of self-defence and will therefore be unlawful.' And it is suggested that even in the absence of a cease-fire or armistice, 'the exercise of belligerent rights after it has become clear that active hostilities have ceased is no longer lawful, even if a state of war remains in existence' (ibid at 155). Smart seems to separate Belligerent Rights in 'wars declared formally' from maritime interdictions in other conflicts that depend on the UN Charter provisions on self-defence: 'Maritime Interdiction Operations', in Corn, Van Landingham and Reeves (eds), *US Military Operations: Law, Policy, and Practice* (2016) 729–56 at 741–42, and see 736 and 740–43.

[165]   Heintschel von Heinegg, 'Blockade', (n 143) at para 25; see also Frostad, 'Naval Blockade', 9 *Arctic Review on Law and Politics* (2018) 195–225 at 200.
[166]   US *Law of War Manual* (n 9) at para 13.10: 'A blockade is an operation by a belligerent State to prevent vessels and/or aircraft of all States, enemy as well as neutral, from entering or exiting specified ports, airfields, or coastal areas belonging to, occupied by, or under the control of an enemy belligerent State.'
[167]   *Harvard Manual on Air Warfare* (n 8) at 358.
[168]   See *The Public Commission to Examine the Maritime Incident of 31 May 2010* (the Turkel Commission) at 45–49 esp at 49, 'the Commission would have considered applying the rules governing the imposition and enforcement of a naval blockade even if the conflict between Israel and the Gaza Strip had been classified as a non-international armed conflict'. See also Farrant, 'The Gaza Flotilla Incident and the Modern Law of Blockade', 66 *Naval War College*

others are just as adamant that no Belligerent Rights flow from such a blockade in a non-international armed conflict.[169]

No state is likely to accept that a non-state actor involved in blocking access to its own ports can assert legal rights over any shipping, whether flagged by that blockaded state or by neutral states.[170] The *Tallinn* expert manual on cyber operations is clear 'Non-state actors are not entitled to establish and enforce a naval, aerial, or *a fortiori*, cyber blockade.'[171] On reflection, therefore, there seems little room for extending the Belligerent Rights associated with Blockade to non-international armed conflicts.[172] This conclusion is further supported by the absence of any state seeking to apply the law of Blockade to the control measures taken off the coast of Yemen, notwithstanding that the action is popularly referred to as the blockade of Yemen.[173]

It is true that the international community of states came to accept that the traditional Belligerent Rights associated with naval Blockade in a formal War between states, meant there would be interference with neutral shipping and their right to trade. But there is no evidence that states have accepted that neutral shipping can be interfered with, or that global trade (unrelated to supplies directly related to the conflict) can be blocked as a result

---

Review (2013) 81–98 at 94; and Shamir-Borer, 'The Revival of Prize Law – An Introduction to the Summary of Recent Cases of the Prize Court in Israel', 50 *Israel Yearbook on Human Rights* (2020) 349–71 at 362–66; *The State of Israel v The Ship Marianne*, Case No 7961-07-05, Maritime Court Haifa, summarized by J Lahav, 'Summary of Recent Cases of the Prize Court in Israel', 50 *Israel Yearbook on Human Rights* (2020) 373–447 at 418–41 esp at 424; discussed in section 8.6.4.

[169] See *Turkish National Commission of Inquiry* (2011) 61–63, Buchan, 'The Palmer Report and the Legality of Israel's Naval Blockade of Gaza', 61 *ICLQ* (2012) 264–73 at 268.

[170] *Harvard Manual on Air Warfare* (n 8) at 358; Ronzitti, 'The Crisis' (n 6) at 12–13.

[171] See also Schmitt (ed), *Tallinn Manual 2.0 on the International Law Applicable to Cyber Operations* (2017) at 507.

[172] It is sometimes suggested that the *San Remo Manual* left open the possibility of applying the rules on blockade in non-international armed conflict. See, eg, the New Zealand *Law of Armed Conflict* (n 41) at para 10.5.1 and the Report of the UN Secretary-General's Panel of Inquiry on the 31 May 2010 Flotilla Incident, July 2011, Appendix I paras 23–24 (which represents an account by the Chair and Vice-Chair of the principles of public international law but not the opinion of the other two members). The bulk of opinion since the publication of the *San Remo Manual* would nevertheless suggest that the international law on blockade does not apply to non-international armed conflicts. This does not mean, however, that the humanitarian law that protects the civilian populations from the effects of a naval or aerial action designed to cut off trade from the port or coast is not relevant, as we shall see below. Whether or not the action qualifies as a 'blockade' under international law should not affect the question whether the effects of the action can be judged for compliance with humanitarian law rules concerning starvation and disproportionate damage for the civilian population.

[173] For the conclusion that there can be no legal application of the Belligerent Rights of states related to Blockade in this non-international armed conflict, see Fink, 'Naval Blockade and the Humanitarian Crisis in Yemen', 64 *Netherlands International Law Review* (2017) 291–307 at 296–97.

of a state's declaring a blockade in its non-international armed conflict with a non-state actor.[174] Of course a state is entitled to restrict access to its own territory at any time, including during a non-international armed conflict, and a state may have claims related to self-defence against foreign shipping under the UN Charter, but these rights do not flow from the legal institution of Blockade.[175]

8.6.3 The Impact of Blockade

It is often suggested that blockade (even if it is not a proper Blockade in legal terms) has become seen as 'a blunt instrument', which 'can have an impact on the innocent as much (often rather more) than enemy belligerents'.[176] It was estimated that around 763,000 wartime deaths could be attributed to the 'five-year economic strangulation' of Germany during the First World War.[177] Drew points out that the 'Hunger Blockade' of Germany 'was responsible for the deaths of more German civilians than was the Allied strategic bombing campaign of World War II'.[178]

Blockade is often presented as just another method of warfare. But, like siege on land, it has often been aimed at deliberately creating suffering.[179] As Dinstein explained:

A blockade applies even to cargoes destined for the civilian population, and should this population be dependent on the importation of foodstuffs for

---

[174] Guilfoyle, 'The *Mavi Marmara* Incident and Blockade in Armed Conflict', 81 *BYIL* (2011) 171–223 at 191ff. But see his tentative suggestion (ibid at 194) 'On the basis of relevant state practice one can at most hazard a suggestion that irrespective of the precise classification of a conflict, states are likely to tolerate the assertion of a blockade only in cases of higher-intensity conflicts on a par with the traditional understanding of war.'

[175] Heintschel von Heinegg, 'Blockades and Interdictions' (n 109) esp at 931–32 and 939–41.

[176] Speller, *Understanding Naval Warfare* (n 160) at 139.

[177] Drew, 'Can We Starve the Civilians? Exploring the Dichotomy between the Traditional Law of Maritime Blockade and Humanitarian Initiatives', 95 *ILS* (2019) 302–21 at 309 fn 34.

[178] Ibid.

[179] One legitimate aim of a siege is said to be to limit supplies reaching the enemy forces in order to force the enemy to surrender. See Gillard, 'Sieges, the Law and Protecting Civilians', Chatham House Briefing (2019). International humanitarian law would prohibit a deliberate attempt to starve the *civilian* population or the starvation of civilians as a method of warfare, as well as, as we saw above, disproportionate incidental effects on the civilian population. See also OHCHR, 'International Humanitarian Law and Human Rights Law Relevant to Siege Warfare' (2017) at https://www.humanitarianresponse.info/sites/www.humanitarianresponse.info/files/documents/files/sieges_legal_note_-_final_-_en_1.pdf.

its survival, the blockade may utilize the populace's suffering as a lever to pressure the enemy into surrender.[180]

Recent practice, with regard to the conflict in Yemen, has resulted in the conclusion by the UN Group of Eminent Experts that the proportionality rule, usually associated with attacks, can apply to the effects of a blockade, or a similar action, whether it can be called a Blockade under international law or not. They 'find persuasive the argument for a broader interpretation of "attacks", where the requisite violence for an attack can be found in the consequences of an operation.[181] They went on to find that the effects of the embargo/blockade could not be justified:

> No possible military advantage could justify such sustained and extreme suffering by millions of people. When the coalition was able to assess that the naval restrictions were causing harm to the civilian population that was excessive in relation to the anticipated concrete and direct military advantage of those restrictions, the coalition was required by law to cancel or suspend those restrictions. It has failed to do so.[182]

8.6.4 The Israeli Prize Court Adjudication over the Protest Ships attempting to Reach Gaza

In the 21st century, Israel has exercised Prize Court jurisdiction and condemned two ships captured while they were engaged in protesting the blockade of Gaza.[183] The Court ordered that the proceeds of the sale of the

---

[180] Dinstein, 'Sea Warfare', in Bernhardt (ed), *Encyclopedia of Public International Law* (1982) vol 4, 201–12 at 204.

[181] UN Doc A/HRC/39/43, 17 August 2018, at 29; see also Drew, *The Law of Maritime Blockade* (n 146) Ch 7; *The German Commander's Handbook: Legal Bases for the Operations of Naval Forces* (2002) states (at para 298, original emphasis) 'A blockade must never be devoted to the sole objective of starving the civilian population or depriving it of vital items (*prohibition of the so-called hunger blockade*). A blockade is also inadmissible, if it is certain or to be anticipated that the negative effect on the civilian population is out of all proportion to the concrete and direct military advantage anticipated.'

[182] UN Doc A/HRC/39/43 (n 181) at 32. If a state were to impose a blockade in an international armed conflict (unless this was specifically authorized by the Security Council), the effect of the blockade would also have to comply with the necessity and proportionality requirements of self-defence under the UN Charter; see Greenwood, 'Applicability' (n 164) at 55–57; Heintschel von Heinegg, 'Blockades and Interdictions' (n 109) at 931.

[183] According to a newspaper report, the Swedish Ministry of Foreign Affairs protested its view of the incident to Israel. The report states that only the flag state can interfere with a ship in international waters. 'Ship to Gaza: Sex släppta', *Österbottens Tidning* (30 June 2015).

ships (one under Swedish flag and the other flagged in the Netherlands) be transferred to the State of Israel.[184] An earlier case concerned the *Estelle*, a Swedish-owned, Finnish-flagged ship, which had sailed from Finland and was said to have been attempting to breach the naval blockade of Gaza. The Haifa Maritime Court and the Israeli Supreme Court found that the State of Israel had initiated Prize proceedings 10 months after seizure, that this delay exceeded the accepted international norms in this area and that the State had not contacted the owners or responded to their inquiries, and thus the State of Israel, had, through these failures, deprived the owners of their right to submit their claims. The Supreme Court therefore ordered the release of the *Estelle* and for Israel to pay the ship's costs.[185]

The two Israeli judgments in the case of the *Estelle* were the first to grapple with the question of whether such a Prize jurisdiction actually existed as a matter of Israeli law. It was argued that the Prize jurisdiction for Israel applied due to the extension of the UK Naval Prize Act 1864 to Palestine through the UK Prize Act 1939, with the associated Supreme Court of Palestine (Prize) Order in Council of 1939 (which vested Prize Court authority in the High Commissioner)[186] and the UK's Order in Council of 1939 Declaring War that we looked at above. Such a Prize jurisdiction was originally dependent on a Declaration of War (in this case the United Kingdom's 1939 Declaration of War on Germany). The District Court heard from Israel that it now had an independent power to continue this Prize jurisdiction and that the blockade of Gaza should allow not only for seizure, but also for confiscation. According to the 2014 judgment in the Haifa District Court:

> The State did not present a proclamation about the outbreak of war as it ostensibly was required for the establishment of the authority according to the King's Order of 1939, but argues that there is no need for such a proclamation. The state believes that the King's Order does not depend

---

[184] *The State of Israel v The Ship Marianne*, Case No 7961-07-05, Maritime Court Haifa, summarized by Lahav, 'Summary of Recent Cases' (n 168) at 418–41 esp at 441; *The State of Israel v The Ship Zaytouna-Oliva*, Case No 19424-10-16 in Lahav 441-7 esp at 447.

[185] *State of Israel v the Ship Estelle*, Original petition, Claim in Rem, 26861-08-13, ILDC 2299 (IL 2014), 31 August 2014; CA7307/14, Supreme Court, 8 August 2016; for commentary in English, see Ruth Levush, 10 August 2016, Library of Congress Legal Monitor, available at https://www.loc.gov/law/foreign-news/article/israel-supreme-court-orders-release-of-ship-captured-attempting-to-break-gaza-blockade/; and a detailed comment by the lawyers for the ship https://shiparrested.com/wp-content/uploads/2015/11/The-Awekening-of-the-Prize-Court.pdf.

[186] See also the UK's Supreme Court of Palestine (Prize) Order 1939 No 1137, 2 September 1939, *Statutory Rules and Orders*, 1939, vol II, at 2906-07; and the UK's Prize Act 1939, s 2(1).

on the authority of a future publication of a proclamation, but rather on the declaration of war, which, as we know, broke out shortly before the publication of the King's Order (the outbreak of World War II on 9/1939). The State also contends that with the establishment of the State and the publication of the Order of Government and Law Ordinance, 5748-1948, there is no longer a need to obtain the approval or authorization of the Secretary of the British King and that all the powers have been transferred to the State of Israel. Lastly, it was claimed, that there is no need to proclaim a war for the purpose of starting the procedure of confiscating a ship, it is enough that an armed conflict exist, and the existence of such a conflict is not disputed.[187]

In the Supreme Court we find a similar statement that '[t]he existence of a state of war or at least an armed conflict between Israel and the residents of the Gaza Strip is not controversial'.[188] The Maritime Court and the Supreme Court on appeal nevertheless ordered the release of the *Estelle* due to the delay of 10 months in seizing the Prize jurisdiction.

The Israeli judges determined that no link to the 1939 Declaration of War was necessary. This was because they found the authority of the Prize Court established by the British King at the outbreak of the Second World War had been bestowed on the State of Israel. The lower Court found it had jurisdiction to operate as a Prize Court and authority to interpret the Naval Prize Act of 1864 and the 1939 Regulations;[189] and as we saw, it referenced the existence of a state of war, or at least an armed conflict, between Israel and the residents of Gaza. In a concurring opinion in the Supreme Court, Justice Meltzer stated that the Minister of Defence's declaration of the Gaza blockade 'renewed the continuum (even if severed) and is sufficient for our needs'.[190]

Although the Haifa Court determined that it could operate as a Prize Court under Israeli law, for all three ships it stressed the need for legislation, stating that 'leaving such an important chapter as far as maritime laws and

---

[187] *State of Israel v the Ship Estelle*, 31 August 2014 (n 185) at para 31, English translation with the assistance of Dr Sharon Weill.

[188] The Supreme Court judgment, 8 August 2016, continues (at para 56) '(see, for example, the court's statement in HC 769/02, Public Committee Against Torture in Israel v Government of Israel [6], at p 2003); HCJ 201/09 Physicians for Human Rights v Prime Minister [1], at p 534 (2009))'.

[189] Lahav, 'Summary of Recent Cases' (n 168) at 396.

[190] Ibid at 416.

prize laws practically hidden from the public's view is contrary to the principle of legality'.[191] The judges were also aware that it is not clear how a contemporary application of Prize Law could be squared with expectations of protection of individual and property rights as well as freedom of navigation.[192] In the subsequent rulings the Court applied a series of considerations that were not derived from the ancient law of Blockade. The Court stated that it would examine, *inter alia*, 'whether the ship itself or its cargo is intended to be used or can be used as part of the enemy combat equipment' and 'whether there is an affinity between the shipowner and the activity intended to violate the blockade and consider whether this affiliation is sufficient to justify the expropriation of property'.[193]

In the two later cases of the protest ships in the Maritime Court, such considerations did not, however, prove an obstacle to condemnation. The Court also considered its condemnation as justified when weighed against the right to protest. According to the summary of the judgment in *The Marianne*:

> The flotilla organizers, including the shipowners and the STG [Ship to Gaza] organization, which includes the current flotilla organizers, have a right to protest and protest Israeli operations in the Gaza Strip, anywhere and in any other legal way. However, the attempt to violate the naval blockade as a means of protest violates the public interest and harms the purpose of imposing the blockade and, in particular, the purpose of weakening Hamas in the Gaza Strip. The entrance of ships for the purpose of protest will encourage the population, strengthen the power of Hamas and damage the blockade objectives.
>
> In these circumstances, where the purpose of the ship's journey is merely a protest, and when it is proven that the ship was on its way to violate the blockade, the State of Israel was entitled to seize it and there is cause to order the condemnation of the ship.[194]

---

[191] Ibid at 397.

[192] District Court Judgment (n 185) at para 46, citing Lieblich, 'Yet Another Front in Israel/Palestine Lawfare – International Prize Law', available at http://opiniojuris.org/2014/01/13/lieblich-guest-post-yet-another-front-israelipalestinian-lawfare-international-prize-law/; and Heintschel von Heinegg, "Developments since 1945' (n 110); see also Lahav, 'Summary of Recent Cases' (n 168) at 385 and 391.

[193] Lahav, 'Summary of Recent Cases' (n 168) at 438 and 445–47.

[194] Ibid at 440 (*The State of Israel v The Marianne*).

8.6.5   Final Thoughts on Blockade

In concluding this section on blockade, we can welcome the important re-strictions highlighted by the UN Group of Eminent Persons concerning the blockade of Yemen. But the existence of such protection does not re-solve the tension that we find with the rights of neutral shipping, encoun-tered in the most recent cases concerning Gaza. Under the traditional idea of Blockade, ships of all states (including neutral states) can be blocked from approaching or leaving the enemy coast or a part of it; and merchant ves-sels believed to be breaching a blockade can be seized along with their cargo. We have questioned whether this can still be correct. The *San Remo Manual* reiterates the traditional Belligerent Right: 'Merchant vessels believed on reasonable grounds to be breaching a blockade may be captured. Merchant vessels which, after prior warning, clearly resist capture may be attacked.'[195] Accordingly, on this reading of the law, any ship in the world that is reason-ably believed to be breaching the blockade can be captured and condemned in Prize Court, with the property title passing to the capturing blockading state. It is this last draconian set of Belligerent Rights relating to attack and confiscation that I would call into question.[196]

With regard to seizure for breaching Blockade, the leading scholar in the field, Heintschel von Heinegg, has even raised doubts whether the old rule remains valid:

> Under the traditional law (Art 21 London Declaration of 1909) a vessel found guilty of breach of blockade may be condemned, ie, subject to the decision of a prize court, and property of the vessel or aircraft may be trans-ferred to the capturing State. It is doubtful whether that rule continues to be valid today. In any event, the capturing State is entitled to repress the air-craft or vessel for the duration of the international armed conflict.[197]

---

[195] *San Remo Manual* (n 8) at para 98. See also ibid at para 67: 'Merchant vessels flying the flag of neutral States may not be attacked unless they: (a) are believed on reasonable grounds to be carrying contraband or breaching a blockade, and after prior warning they intentionally and clearly refuse to stop, or intentionally and clearly resist visit, search or capture...'

[196] The experts assembled in San Remo were apparently divided on the continuing existence of the international law related to blockade: 'Although a minority believed that the traditional rules for formal blockade were in complete desuetude, a majority believed the occurrence of a number of incidents subsequent to the Second World War, in which States engaged in actions adopting some or all of the traditional rules of blockade, indicated that the doctrine still had utility as a coercive instrument.' Doswald-Beck (ed), *San Remo Manual* (n 8) at 176.

[197] Heintschel von Heinegg, 'Blockade' (n 143) at para 41; in France, as we shall see below, it is uncertain how capture in blockade could be legalized in the absence of a prize jurisdiction, which in turn requires a Declaration of War: Fillon, 'A propos du Conseil des prises et de la

Other scholars have, at least since 1862, voiced doubts over whether a commercial blockade should take priority over the rights of neutral states and their nationals.[198] We have to conclude that there is real uncertainty over whether a state could, today, rely on traditional so-called 'Belligerent Rights', which belonged to a state at War, to seize and permanently confiscate neutral vessels in the context of breach of blockade.[199]

8.7 Some Suggestions for Reform

We should now draw a few conclusions with regard to the viability of this kind of economic warfare in the contemporary world.

I have come to conclude that there is indeed, as Elih Lauterpacht put it, 'a genuine measure of absurdity in suggesting that a legal system which has excluded the right to have recourse to force should nonetheless permit the wrongdoer to assert belligerent rights arising out of his own wrongdoing'.[200] I think it would be better to deny states (whether engaged in an act of aggression or acting in self-defence) the traditional Belligerent Rights to acquire property rights against the civilian owners of ships, vessels and aircraft. In other words, we need to reconsider the traditional rule that is said to allow for any state at war with another state to capture and (following condemnation in the captor state's own Prize Court) acquire title over privately-owned

---

déclaration de la guerre: Etude sur l'obsolescence du droit de la guerre navale', *Revue Maritime* 516 (March 2020) 126-133.

[198] See, eg, Macqueen, *Chief Points in the Laws of War and Neutrality, Search and Blockade* (1862) at 30–31: 'It may be said that to abolish blockades would be a hardship upon belligerents. But may it not be answered, that to continue blockades would be a greater hardship upon neutrals? Who are the most entitled to favour – the bulk of mankind, who are at peace, or the small, ill-conditioned portion who fight for an idea? Even supposing war to be a necessary evil, the struggle should be to make its mischiefs as small as possible to those not engaged in it.' See also Westlake, 'Note on Belligerent Rights at Sea', in Latifi, *Effects of War on Property* (1909) at 152; Westlake, *War* (n 81) at 164ff, but see ibid, 2nd edn (1913) at 263; and Ch IX; and the discussion in Lauterpacht (ed), *Oppenheim* (n 25) at 770ff.

[199] See Gioia and Ronzitti, 'The Law of Neutrality: Third States' Commercial Rights and Duties', in Dekker and Post (eds), *The Gulf War of 1980-1988* (1992) 221–42 at 232–33. Heintschel von Heinegg, while considering that a formal State of War is relevant neither for blockade nor for Prize Law, seems to accept that prize measures may not create permanently valid titles where the seizing state is acting beyond what is permitted by the necessities of self defence; see 'The Current State of International Prize Law', in Post (ed), *International Economic Law and Armed Conflict* (1994) 5–34, at 34 fn 163.

[200] 'The Legal Irrelevance of the "State of War"', 62 *Proceedings of the American Society of International Law* (1968) 58–68 at 63.

enemy merchant ships, enemy aircraft and enemy goods on board either ships or planes.[201] The rule seems even more ripe for review when one remembers that the same manuals insist that such civilian ships and aircraft can be destroyed, having secured the safety of the passengers and crew, where 'military circumstances preclude taking the aircraft [vessel] for prize adjudication'.[202] How feasible will it be today for naval powers during a war to bring a prize into their own ports for condemnation in Prize Court? Destruction will remain a very real option.

Even if these traditional rules applied to both World Wars, and even if states might come to agree that the rules are different in a total war, today the idea that an aggressor state, in any international armed conflict, can seize and keep such property seems to contradict the modern law that prohibits recourse to war to settle disputes. The idea of a state's claiming Belligerent Rights simply because it is at war seems completely at odds with the UN Charter and the prohibition of aggression.

Any attempt, however, to reserve the right to seize private ships and aircraft only to the state said to be acting in self-defence is doomed to failure. First, all states will claim they are acting in self-defence; and, second, there is no overarching international umpire to determine which side started it. Prize Courts may be applying some sort of international law, but they traditionally will not enter into who was the aggressor and who was the innocent party. In any event, as national courts they could not credibly make such a determination.

Several authors have pointedly burst the fictitious bubble that suggests that Prize Courts simply apply the Law of Nations. Not only will a Prize Court ultimately have to follow rules or legislation laid down by its own government, but where there are differences between different states on the substantive rules, one has to expect that Prize Court Judges will be more likely to follow the local interpretation, especially where they are bound to do so by national precedent or legislation.[203] The British concern over Russian Prize Courts led to the proposal for an International Prize Court and the eventual adoption of

---

[201] See, eg, *Oxford Manual of Naval War* (1913) Art 33; *San Remo Manual* (n 8) at para 135; *Harvard Air Warfare Manual* (n 8) Rule 134.

[202] *Harvard Air Warfare Manual* (n 8) Rule 135; and *San Remo Manual* (n 8) at paras 139 and 140.

[203] See Brierly, *The Law of Nations*, 5th edn (1955) at 89–90 esp at 89: 'But when we remember that the question upon which Lord Stowell was deciding concerned the resistance to visit and search by a British warship on the part of a Swedish ship sailing under convoy, and that the right of convoy was one on which the British and Swedish views were at that time diametrically opposed, it is hard to believe that Lord Stowell really thought that a Swedish judge, sitting in Stockholm, would have been likely to decide the case in the way in which he proposed to decide it himself.' See also Verzijl et al (n 71) at 596–601; 'The Case of the Zamora', 30 *Harvard*

Hague Convention XII (1907).[204] But the failure to ratify the 1909 London Declaration Concerning the Laws of Naval War (1909), which would have determined rules that such an International Prize Court would apply, meant that the Court was never established.

Given these problems, an alternative could be to say that because the defending state needs these Belligerent Rights, we have to be pragmatic and allow such rights to both sides. But even the defending state is limited as to how it can interfere with the rights of other states, bound as it is by the UN Charter's limitations of proportionality and necessity. It is hard to see how those limits can be read as authorizing the permanent confiscation of foreigners' property, in effect punishing individuals for the actions of their state.[205]

We are left not only with considerable uncertainty concerning the applicable treaty law on Prize (all relevant treaties are strictly speaking dependent on a State of War, and mostly only applicable where all parties to the War are parties to the treaties),[206] but also with no specialized international judicial or arbitral body to ensure the impartial application of this law beyond what is decided by national jurisdictions. It is suggested that rather than continuing to quest for an international jurisdiction to ensure an impartial application of the rules, the uncertain nature of the rules themselves needs to be revisited to see if such rules should be upheld at all. The time has come to overhaul the presumptions that suggest a belligerent state can acquire through the Law of Prize (applied by its own courts) title to private enemy or neutral property.

As a matter of treaty law, then, there seems to be no treaty authorization for the seizure of private enemy property, whether as a ship, an aircraft or as enemy goods on board. The authority comes from the general assumption (including among most scholars) that these rules continue as a matter of

---

Law Review (1916) 66–68; *The Zamora* [1916] 2 AC 77; Foxton, 'International Law in Domestic Courts: Some Lessons from the Prize Court in the Great War', 73 *BYBIL* (2002) 261–91.

[204] Kalshoven, 'Commentary to the 1909 Declaration', in Ronzitti (ed), *The Law of Naval Warfare: A Collection of Agreements and Documents with Commentaries* (1988) 257–75 at 257.
[205] I am grateful to Sandesh Sivakumaran for these points.
[206] See, eg, Paris Declaration Respecting Maritime Law (1856), Hague Convention VI Relating to the Status of Enemy Merchant Ships at the Outbreak of Hostilities (1907), Hague Convention VII Relating to the Conversion of Merchant Ships to War-ships (1907), Hague Convention XI Relative to Certain Restrictions with Regard to the Exercise of the Right to Capture in Naval War (1907), Hague Convention XIII Concerning the Rights and Duties of Neutral Powers in Naval War (1907), Havana Convention on Maritime Neutrality (1928), London Procès-Verbal Relating to the Rules of Submarine Warfare Set Forth in Part IV of the Treaty of London of 22 April 1930 (1936).

customary international law. The rules are detailed in expert manuals, alongside military manuals from powerful states, and they are usually stated to be a reflection of customary international law. Commentators such as Sassòli come close to questioning the continuing validity of such rules, by referring, in this context, to law from before the First World War that 'allegedly still applies'.[207] He also describes the rules as 'outdated' due to the changes we outlined above regarding the way goods are now shipped around the world, but also to 'changes in moral perception'.[208]

He is right: the rules (at least those relating to seizure, condemnation and exceptional destruction of private enemy ships, planes and goods[209]) must now be seen as not only outdated and unworkable, but also immoral, and moreover a sure way to undermine the distinction between military objectives and civilian objects.

But denying these so-called 'Belligerent Rights' to keep other people's property need not leave states unable to defend themselves. Rather than seeing interception, search and seizure as an economic warfare right undertaken to weaken the war-making capacity of the enemy, one can simply see them as related to the right to self-defence under the UN Charter.[210] Seizing guns destined for the enemy could be excused as a proportionate and necessary measure of self-defence. But confiscating tea exports, or any ships seeking to trade by breaching blockade, widens the concept of war-like activity for both sides. This legitimization of economic warfare certainly risks blurring the distinction between a civilian object and military objectives, leading to a wider range of objects being considered to be engaged in war-sustaining activity and perhaps turning them into apparent military objectives.

Stripping away a customary international law right to confiscate on the high seas all enemy property and certain neutral property need not interfere with the right of a state to defend itself. The British Chief Naval Judge Advocate, while not purporting to reflect the views of the Ministry of Defence, made a similar point when evaluating the state of the law in 1997:

---

[207] Sassòli, *International Humanitarian Law* (2019) at para 8.434.

[208] Ibid at para 8.440.

[209] The rules relating to seizure and condemnation of enemy merchant ships and neutral ships, etc accused of carrying contraband to an enemy state, or breaching blockade or engaging in unnatural service, may also need revisiting and are discussed below.

[210] See Art 21 of the ILC Articles on State Responsibility and the explanation in the Commentary that this justification or excuse of self-defence applies where non-performance of the obligation is related to a breach of Art 2(4) and it foresees action in self-defence may have effects vis-à-vis third states. Crawford, *The International Law Commission's Articles on State Responsibility* (2002) at 166–67.

It is entirely possible that under the modern conditions of economic warfare at sea, depriving the enemy of the necessary arms and war materials is sufficient belligerent action, and the capture and condemnation, and thus benefit to the capturing belligerent, of the ship and/or cargo, is unnecessary in furthering that belligerent's war aims. It would also obviate, it would seem, the necessity for establishing a Prize Court in accordance with the traditional law, and thus it may well be, if the law develops in this direction, that Prize Courts and Prize Law become obsolete.[211]

This may seem radical, but in fact these belligerent rights have not been the subject of a Prize Court condemnation since the India–Pakistan conflicts in 1965 and 1971. Specific national legislation was last adopted in the 1980s for the Iran–Iraq conflict, and even then, the jurisdiction of the proposed 'War Prizes Tribunal' was never actually established by Iran.

Today we also have to counter the impracticality of applying many of these rules in the context of modern maritime commerce. Haines explains:

Searching a container ship would be impossible. The characteristics of the majority of merchant ships today make it extremely difficult to divert them to convenient ports because few ports will be able to take them. This is especially the case with container vessels, which require specialist container terminals. It would also be difficult to put together a prize crew capable of operating a modern merchant vessel. It also seems most unlikely that the lawful destruction of very large container vessels on the high seas would be regarded as appropriate, either politically, or economically or environmentally.[212]

Let me now separate out suggestions for reform into questions of (i) seizure for breach of blockade; (ii) visit, search and seizure of neutral ships and goods in connection with breach of rules on contraband; and (iii) the seizure of enemy merchant ships and enemy property at sea.

---

[211] Humphrey, 'Belligerent Interdiction of Neutral Shipping in International Armed Conflict', 2 *Journal of Conflict and Security Law* (1997) 23–44 at 39–40.

[212] Casey-Maslen and Haines, *Hague Law Interpreted: The Conduct of Hostilities under the Law of Armed Conflict* (2018) at 306.

8.7.1 Seizure for Breach of Blockade

The modern expert manuals on conflict at sea and air warfare still reiterate that neutral merchant ships and aircraft are subject to seizure if caught breaching blockade.[213] The ships and aircraft are then be adjudicated in Prize Court and condemned – the property titles passing to the captor state. For some time, leading experts have been tentatively expressing doubts as to the continuing validity or feasibility of maintaining the existence of such a right for states. In the words of Heintschel von Heinegg, 'It is doubtful whether that rule continues to be valid today. In any event, the capturing State is entitled to repress the aircraft or vessel for the duration of the international armed conflict.'[214]

I think it is indeed important to state clearly that this rule allowing for capture for breach of blockade should no longer apply.[215] Obviously the execution of such claimed Belligerent Rights can lead to international friction with states that are not parties to the conflict. More fundamentally, it is difficult to understand why the property rights of individuals and companies should be overridden because a state has decided to enforce a Blockade outside its territory. But beyond these traditional objections, I should like to highlight a few further reasons why the institution of Blockade should no longer give rise to a Belligerent Right to seize merchant ships or aircraft.

The manuals (and here I am referring to the expert manuals on conflict at sea and air warfare, as well as the various military manuals published by states that address this issue) are explicit that a merchant vessel or aircraft (for aerial blockade) may be attacked if, after prior warning, it clearly resists capture or an order to land.[216] Some states (such as Canada) may consider that

---

[213] *San Remo Manual* (n 8) at paras 98 and 146(f), 153(f); *Harvard Air Warfare Manual* Rule 140(f).

[214] Heintschel von Heinegg, 'Blockade' (n 143) at para 41.

[215] The regulation of Blockades in 1856 was to prevent long-distance or paper blockades by demanding that a Blockade be effective. Paragraph 4 of the Paris Declaration of 1856 provided that 'Blockades, in order to be binding, must be effective, that is to say, maintained by a force sufficient really to prevent access to the coast of the enemy.' See also *San Remo Manual* (n 8) at paras 93–104; for the earlier history and the Declaration of 1780 by Catherine II of Russia, see Scott (ed), *Armed Neutralities of 1780 and 1800: A Collection of Official Documents Preceded by the Views of Representative Publicists* (1918) at 273ff. See also Moore, *International Law and Some Current Illusions* (1924) 40–80 at 48, for whom, once it was clear that Blockade had to be effective, the 'conflict between belligerent right and neutral right' moved to the domain of contraband. In turn, once the list of contraband was made long enough, in his words, 'the rule becomes a farce' (ibid at 50). Moore appends various treaties with lists of contraband from 1659 through to the US proposition for a definition of contraband in 1907.

[216] *San Remo Manual* (n 8) at paras 67(a) and 98.

breach of blockade is in itself a ground to attack such a vessel.[217] Others (such as the United Kingdom and Germany) may consider that breach of blockade converts the merchant vessel into a military objective.[218] Whichever way this is reasoned, the resulting deaths of civilians seem hard to justify as a general matter of morality, and attacks such as these would certainly undermine the general idea that civilians are immune from attack.

The right to capture a neutral vessel for breach of blockade is, then, inextricably bound up with a right to attack for resisting capture. It is also directly linked to the exceptional right to destroy such a captured ship 'when military circumstances preclude taking or sending such a vessel for adjudication as an enemy prize'.[219] So resisting capture can end in attack, and in some exceptional circumstances, even compliance with capture can result in destruction. Such destruction is supposed to take place only once the 'safety of passengers and crew is provided for'.[220]

When this rule on the permissible attacks on neutral vessels was being codified at the expert level in San Remo in 1994, there were some doubts as to why a neutral vessel could be attacked at all, considering that the Charter only allowed the use of force in self-defence,[221] and the majority view was that 'the definition of military objectives did not apply to the relationship between belligerents and neutrals'.[222] Nevertheless, a group of participants felt that 'States could not be expected to accept rules that would force them to lose the war'.[223] So, in the end, the participants seemed to have relied on the idea that capture for breach of blockade was foreseen in the London Declaration of 1909, and the practice of attacking neutral shipping in both World Wars led to the formulation of a rule that neutral ships can be attacked for breach of blockade.[224]

It seems the idea remains that if you want to strangle another state's economy and deprive its people of imports and exports, that is fair and just

---

[217] Canadian Joint Doctrine Manual *Law of Armed Conflict* (2003) at para 719(3)(a).

[218] UK *Manual* (n 13) at para 13.47(a); *German Law of Armed Conflict Manual* (n 37) at para 1017: 'Blockades are not a prize measure. Vessels breaching a blockade may, however, be confiscated in accordance with prize measures. Vessels which, after prior warning, clearly resist capture become a military objective.'

[219] *San Remo Manual* (n 8) paras 151 and 152.

[220] Ibid at para 151; and see the discussion of submarine warfare and the difficulty of securing passengers' safety in this context in section 7.4.1 above.

[221] Doswald-Beck (ed), *San Remo Manual* (n 8) at 156 para 67.3.

[222] Ibid at 157 para 67.7.

[223] Ibid at 157 para 67.8.

[224] Ibid at para 67.19.

because states still have some sort of 'right to win a war'. This to me makes no sense in a world where war has been outlawed.

The reader may feel that this complex rulebook seems of little relevance today, with blockade a relative rarity and economic warfare at sea looking increasingly unlikely. Wars look more and more like counter-terrorism operations rather than the naval strategies of yesteryear. But the destruction of merchant shipping in the relatively recent 'tanker war' between Iran and Iraq in the 1980s was considerable – by one estimate with over 200 mariners killed in attacks on over 400 ships, 31 merchant ships sunk, with another 50 so damaged as to be declared total losses.[225] This destruction and killing was not confined to rules concerning blockade, but related more generally to a disregard for the rules on distinction and a conflation of all the rules relating to economic warfare and merchant shipping.

In the end, the continuing idea that international law authorizes blockade with associated rights for states to engage in visitation, search and seizure, as well as attacks for resistance, and exceptionally destruction, can only lead to confusion and the erosion of the rules designed to minimize the suffering and destruction in war. The apparent rules that allow for capture (and associated attack and destruction) for breach of Blockade should be revisited to see if they can really still be applicable in the contemporary world. These rules are not contained in treaties but are derived from practices that have nothing to do with the humanitarian dimension that ought now to drive the development of the laws of war.[226] Rather than allowing them to gradually 'slip away',[227] a more concerted effort should be made to state clearly that international law no longer confers such Belligerent Rights on warring states. But of course, as stated at the beginning of the chapter, this means a few powerful states accepting that they may be giving away some rights that they might want to rely on later.

---

[225] Walker, 'Guerre de Course in the Charter Era: the Tanker War, 1980–1988', in Elleman and Paine (eds), Commerce Raiding: Historical Case Studies, 1755–2009 (2013) 239–52 at 249.

[226] For a forensic analysis of how law-making in the 19th century was focused more on preserving the interests of powerful states than on anything that we might call humanitarian concerns, see Benvenisti and Lustig, 'Monopolizing War: Codifying the Laws of War to Reassert Governmental Authority, 1856–1874' 31 EJIL (2020) 127–69.

[227] I am grateful to Steven Haines for this turn of phrase to describe the changing nature of some of these naval warfare rights. Private email correspondence 2020.

8.7.2 Interference with Neutral Shipping and Seizure of Contraband Goods and Neutral Ships

The point of a Belligerent Right to search neutral ships is to ascertain if there is contraband aboard. The idea of contraband was, however, expanded through extensive lists of items constituting contraband. Neff recounts how France declared that rice destined for China would be considered contraband as it was so important for the Chinese in 1885, as otherwise France said they 'would run "the risk of depriving themselves of one of the most powerful means of coercion" '.[228] Contraband was also expanded, as we saw, through the use of the notion of 'continuous voyage' and, lastly, through the idea of contraband infecting other goods on board so that the whole cargo and ship could be captured and condemned as prize.[229] Even today, the *San Remo Manual* foresees destruction in certain circumstances where the contraband is reckoned to form more than half the cargo.[230]

The United Kingdom, in particular, has come in the last decades to focus on the rights of neutrals, and no longer asserts Belligerent Rights against neutrals as it did in the past. In 1986, in the context of the Iran–Iraq war, the United Kingdom asserted that any Iranian right to stop and search was bounded by the right to self-defence.[231] The idea that the international law relating to the use of force adds cumulative restrictions on top of those obligations found in the traditional law of naval warfare is now replicated in the UK *Manual*.[232] A detailed study in 2010 suggested that when states came

---

[228] Neff, 'The Prerogatives of Violence' (n 18) at 51.

[229] The *San Remo Manual* (n 8) at paras 146(a) and 153(a) states that neutral vessels and aircraft are subject to capture for carrying contraband; see also *Harvard Air Warfare Manual* (n 8) Rule 140(a).

[230] Destruction is foreseen for captured neutral merchant vessels. The captured vessel may 'as an exceptional measure, be destroyed when military circumstances preclude taking or sending such a vessel for adjudication as an enemy prize', the conditions to be met beforehand including that '(a) the safety of passengers and crew is provided for'. For vessels carrying contraband, '[a] vessel may not be destroyed under this paragraph for carrying contraband unless the contraband, reckoned either by value, weight, volume or freight, forms more than half the cargo': *San Remo Manual* (n 8) at para 151. This provision did not garner full support from the experts involved in adopting the *Manual* – see Doswald-Beck (ed), *San Remo Manual* (n 8) at 218–19. See also Art 40 of the London Declaration 1909, 'A vessel carrying contraband may be condemned if the contraband, reckoned either by value, weight, volume, or freight, forms more than half the cargo.'

[231] Statement by the Minister of State to the House of Commons, reproduced in 57 *BYBIL* (1986) 583.

[232] See UK *Manual* (n 13) at para 13.3 and Greenwood, 'Self-Defence and the Conduct of International Armed Conflict', in Dinstein and Tabory (eds), *International Law at a Time of Perplexity: Essays in Honour of Shabtai Rosenne* (1989) 273–88 at 283–88; *contra* Heintschel von Heinegg, ' "Benevolent" Third States in International Armed Conflicts: The Myth of the Irrelevance of the Law of Neutrality', in Schmitt and Pejic (eds), *International Law and Armed*

to exercise rights of search of merchant shipping, they prioritized the international law of self-defence as the justification rather than the traditional law of maritime warfare.[233] Ronzitti now concludes that the practice is orientated towards reducing belligerents' rights so that they conform to rights exercised in self-defence, and that only action compatible with the law on self-defence would be within the law.[234]

At the opening of the 1907 Hague Peace Conference, the United Kingdom sought a new treaty that would abolish the principle of contraband, declaring:

> In order to diminish the difficulties encountered by neutral commerce in time of war, the government of HBM [His Britannic Majesty] is prepared to abandon the principle of contraband in case of war between powers which may sign a convention to that effect. The right of visit would be exercised, only in order to ascertain the neutral character of the merchantmen.[235]

When this initiative failed to garner a consensus and attracted negative votes from France, Germany, Russia, the United States and Montenegro, the British delegation sought to take the initiative outside the Hague Conference (which was supposed to operate at something approaching unanimity).

The support for the British initiative then fell away as it was seen as inappropriate to agree to a Convention at the Conference but outside the rules for the Conference. The proposed text would have stated 'Goods belonging to a subject of a neutral contracting power on board neutral or enemy ships cannot be condemned as being contraband'.[236] The proposal was dropped due to the opposition concerned with the venue. Westlake hoped that the Convention could nevertheless be adopted at 'an early date' through the 'ordinary methods of diplomacy'.[237] This did not happen.

Half a century later, in the wake of the Second World War and the prohibition on resorting to any use of force by UN member states against any other

---

Conflict: Exploring the Faultlines (Essays in Honour of Yoram Dinstein) (2007) 543–68 esp at 561–65. For an expansive view of belligerent rights, see generally Heintschel von Heinegg, 'International Economic Relations and Armed Conflict', in de Guttry, Post and Venturini (eds), *The 1998–2000 War between Eritrea and Ethiopia* (2009) 371–87.

[233] Upcher, *Neutrality in Contemporary International Law* (2020) at 167–78.
[234] 'La prassi sembra, infatti, decisamente orientata a far discendere i diritti di belligeranza compatabili con l'esercizio di questo diritto sono ritenuti legittimi.' Ronzitti, *Diritto internazionale dei conflitti armati*, 6th edn (2017) at 149.
[235] Westlake, *War* (n 81) at 298.
[236] Ibid at 299.
[237] Ibid at 300.

state, Lauterpacht ended his edited volume of *Oppenheim's International Law* with the words:

> To the existing ingredients of prize law recent developments in International Law have added one consideration of vital significance, namely, that as a rule the war will be waged on one side in violation of a legal obligation of a fundamental nature. In such a contingency the guilty belligerent will not be able to claim the benefit of the doubt in a branch of law in which so much is controversial and unsettled.[238]

Forty years later, Heintschel von Heinegg suggested that 'With regard to measures directed against neutral vessels (aircraft), the law may be in a state of change.'[239] But he offered only the following guide to the future:

> It is suggested, then, that the general status of neutral merchant shipping in an armed conflict *de lege ferenda* is as follows. At the outset, there is a rebuttable presumption for their general exemption from capture. The reasons justifying capture (and probably diversion) will depend on the policy of the flag state. If its policy is not to support any of the belligerents with war material, strong reasons will be needed to justify capture. Minor standards will apply if the flag state's policy is otherwise. Where the flag state is neither able nor willing to exercise the necessary control, belligerents will be entitled to exercise all those rights conferred upon them by the traditional law.[240]

Again, as with capture for breach of blockade, the time has come to relate the draconian nature of these rules not just to the UN Charter, but to our desire to separate out the use of force that is necessary in self-defence from what states would like to do to win a war. Once we accept the right of capture and condemnation in prize for contraband violations, we end up accepting, it seems, the contingent rights to attack neutral vessels where they are believed to be carrying contraband and, 'after prior warning they intentionally and clearly refuse to stop, or intentionally and clearly resist visit, search or capture.'[241] Civil aircraft can be attacked where they

---

[238] Lauterpacht (ed), *Oppenheim* (n 25) at 878.
[239] Heintschel von Heinegg, 'Developments Since 1945' (n 110) at 135.
[240] Ibid at 128–29.
[241] *San Remo Manual* (n 8) at para 67(a), but note that paras 68 and 40 require that the target fulfil the requirements of being a military objective.

are believed on reasonable grounds to be carrying contraband, and, after prior warning or interception, they intentionally and clearly refuse to divert from their destination, or intentionally and clearly refuse to proceed for visit and search to a belligerent airfield that is safe for the type of aircraft involved and reasonably accessible . . .'[242]

As we saw above, the wide nature of the contemporary understanding of contraband includes goods destined for the enemy, 'which may be susceptible for use in armed conflict'. The uses and customs on contraband of war, according to Pyke, 'have been created by the action of belligerent rather than neutral states, and with a view to extending and not restricting the advantages that accrue to a belligerent from the possession of a predominant command of the sea'.[243] For him, writing in 1915, it was impossible for 'nations at war to exercise the power and force required for the purpose of overthrowing each other without inflicting injury and loss upon the trade of other nations'.[244] Today, we no longer believe that nations have any business overthrowing each other, and so states should not be accorded the necessary rights against neutrals to do this. And yet the old rules apparently endure, with nefarious consequences. I would suggest that a belligerent state should no longer be able to claim that international law authorizes it to capture and permanently confiscate through a Prize Court the neutral ships and aircraft found to have been carrying contraband or engaging in unneutral service.[245]

This is not only a question of respecting the rights of individuals and the rights of non-participating (neutral) states. As already stated, the rights to search and capture quickly turn into a right to target under certain conditions. So for example, a neutral civilian aircraft apparently becomes 'a military objective' because it is suspected of carrying contraband and refusing to divert from its destination.[246] I am not convinced by the orthodox argument that by behaving in this way, the ship or an aircraft has become a military objective and the crew are no longer protected civilians because they are 'directly participating in hostilities'.

---

[242] Ibid at para 70(a), and see paras 71 and 40.

[243] Pyke, *The Law of Contraband of War* (1915) at vi.

[244] Ibid at 1.

[245] For the different types of unneutral service leading to capture as prize, 'transport of troops or military men', and 'carriage of dispatches', see Verzijl et al (n 71) at 456–70 and Colombos *Law of Prize* (n 27) Ch VI.

[246] See *Harvard Manual Missile Warfare* (n 8) Rule 174(a); UK *Manual* (n 13) at para 12.43.1(a).

The old Belligerent Rights need to be revised so that searching for contraband comes closer to law enforcement. Allowing the current regime to remain in place can only reinforce the mistaken idea that merchant shipping and civil aircraft might be fair game when it comes to capture, targeting and destruction.

8.7.3 Seizure of Enemy Merchant Ships, Aircraft and Cargo

Turning away from neutral property (or property belonging to individuals from non-participating states) and looking to private property belonging to enemy nationals, we might recall that there is no right for a belligerent to capture on land private property belonging to enemy nationals. The time has come to reject the idea that enemy commercial maritime traffic is so essential to winning the war that it should be not only seized, but also condemned and permanently acquired by the seizing state.[247] As mentioned above in section 8.5.1, at one point the British Government would have considered joining in the American idea of abolishing this Belligerent Right of capture at sea. The instructions to the British Delegation in 1907 started by stating:

> Anything which restrains acts of war is in itself a step towards the abolition of all war, and by diminishing the apprehensions of the evils which war would cause, removes one incentive to expenditure upon armaments. It is also possible to imagine cases in which the interests of Great Britain might benefit by the adoption of this principle of immunity from capture.[248]

But as explained previously, the utility of Blockade was considered too strategically important: 'The British navy is the only offensive weapon which Great Britain has against Continental Powers. The latter have a double means of offence: they have their navies and they have their powerful armies.'[249]

In the end, the eventual Hague Convention VI on Enemy Merchant Ships at the Outbreak of Hostilities (1907) only states that 'it is desirable' that a merchant ship of a belligerent state be allowed to depart an enemy port after a

---

[247] The law may be based on long-established custom, but there are no relevant treaties that authorize such seizures, only attempts to prevent some merchant ships being seized or requisitioned at the outbreak of hostilities.

[248] Pearce Higgins (n 82) at para 19.

[249] Ibid at para 20.

period of grace, and it provides that certain merchant ships that were unable to leave, or ignorant of the outbreak of hostilities at the time of encounter with the enemy navy on the high seas, may not be confiscated but only detained and restored after the war without compensation, or alternatively requisitioned or destroyed with compensation.

The United States refused to join the treaty on the grounds that customary international law was already more protective of merchant shipping than the proposed treaty. James Brown Scott made the point that 'it rarely happens that a vessel is provided on the outbound voyage with sufficient coal for the return'.[250] This means that on the outbreak of War, whether it continues on to the belligerent port or attempts to return home, the enemy merchant ship risks being captured. Moreover, he added even if it is indeed ignorant of the outbreak of hostilities at the time of being seized,

> it may be detained subject to restoration at the end of the war without compensation. The value of the vessel may be seriously depreciated in case of a long war. If requisitioned, it is unlikely that the transaction will be profitable to the original owner, and if destroyed it is improbable that the compensation will at all be adequate. The article in question, therefore, can not be considered an advance; it is a distinct limitation of customary rights.[251]

On the other hand, the treaty was seen as too protective of merchant shipping by Russia and Germany. Both states formulated reservations as they felt disadvantaged; not having 'naval stations in different parts of the world' that could receive the seized vessels, they would 'find themselves compelled to destroy them'. Japan became a party, while the United Kingdom and France eventually renounced the treaty, in 1925 and 1939 respectively.

In 2020 there were only 31 states parties to this treaty. At the time of its drafting commentators simply stated 'It is a well recognized rule of international law that private property belonging to the enemy on the sea is liable to capture.'[252] The treaty merely regulates the exceptions, in order to 'ensure the security of international commerce against the surprises of war'. One such exception is that there can be no capture where the enemy merchant ship is met at sea and is ignorant of the outbreak of hostilities. Neither this

---

[250] 'Status of Enemy Merchant Ships', 2 *AJIL* (1908) 259–70 at 269.
[251] Ibid.
[252] Higgins (n 82) at 300; Scott, 'Status of Enemy Merchant Ships' (n 250) at 259, 'private property of the enemy upon the high seas is subject to capture'.

treaty, nor any other multilateral treaty in force,[253] would seem to grant the Belligerent Right to capture enemy merchant ships.

The Hague Convention VI (1907) details which merchant ships *cannot* be captured. I do not see how such a treaty (which most experts consider is no longer in force), or the Hague Convention XI (1907) that, *inter alia*, exempts coastal fishing vessels from capture (and has only 32 states parties), could justify a continuing universal right of any state to capture all other enemy merchant ships and aircraft.[254]

---

[253] The Declaration of London 1909 of course covered enemy property in Arts 57–60, but this treaty never entered into force. The Declaration of Paris 1856 starts 'That maritime law, in time of war, has long been the subject of deplorable disputes; That the uncertainty of the law and of the duties in such a matter, gives rise to differences of opinion between neutrals and belligerents which may occasion serious difficulties, and even conflicts'; it then limits what goods cannot be captured on the high seas, ie 'The neutral flag covers enemy's goods, with the exception of contraband of war' and 'Neutral goods, with the exception of contraband of war, are not liable to capture under enemy's flag'. It seems a convoluted legal logic to suggest that such a prohibition from over 160 years ago could generate a universal permission in international law today. For the conclusion that the 'mere existence of regulations' under international humanitarian law 'should not be understood as creating strong permissions', see Quintin, *The Nature of International Humanitarian Law: A Permissive or Restrictive Regime?* (2020) at 10. One might question whether such a treaty is really just a negotiated bargain between belligerents and neutral states, rather than part of the corpus of humanitarian law, but there are passages addressed to the safety of persons on board the merchant ships. These restrictions on capture and condemnation from 1907 should not be read as today providing evidence that the right to capture enemy ships and goods remains unaffected by the outlawing of war and the ban on the use of force.

[254] It has been suggested that Hague VI (1907) has fallen into desuetude and is therefore of no legal effect for the states that remain parties: Casey-Maslen and Haines, *Hague Law Interpreted* (n 212) at 285 fn 36; see also Roberts and Guelff (n 73) at 95, who point to the failure of states to follow the Convention in the Second World War and the facility with which merchant ships can be converted into warships or used as auxiliary vessels to service warships. The use by the United Kingdom of cruise liners to transport troops in the Falklands/Mavinas conflict is a reminder of how useful merchant ships could be to a belligerent. Andrea de Guttry considers that the treaty can, however, still prohibit confiscation for certain ships and their cargo, even if in general states are no longer enthusiastic about protecting enemy merchant ships due to the decisive contribution merchant shipping can make to a belligerent's economy and the 'war effort': de Guttry, 'Commentary to the 1907 Hague Convention VI Relating to the Status of Enemy Merchant Ships at the Outbreak of Hostilities', in Ronzitti (ed), *The Law of Naval Warfare: A Collection of Agreements and Documents with Commentaries* (1988) 102–10 at 109. To the extent that the Convention's preamble refers to ensuring 'the security of international commerce against the surprises of war', one could assume that this treaty would only apply in a formal State of War, even if certain provisions reference the commencement of hostilities. de Guttry certainly makes reference to the significance of a captain's 'ignorance of a state of war' (ibid at 104) and to the status of enemy ships in 'time of war' (ibid at 106). Because the treaty covers obligations related to the outbreak of hostilities, it seems sensible not to limit the treaty to the period when a Declaration of War takes effect but to address the 'surprises of war'. Nevertheless, because the treaty adjusts vulnerability to confiscation of enemy ships, it should be seen as applying in the context of a formal State of War (if indeed it continues to apply at all). The experts in San Remo considered it had fallen into desuetude, and therefore did not include vessels in port and mail ships as exempt from capture in their *Manual*: Doswald-Beck (ed), *San Remo Manual* (n 8) at 207.

I suppose some will argue for a continuing general customary right for states to capture enemy merchant ships (notwithstanding the limited significance of these treaties). They will claim it is for those who no longer believe in the right of capture to show that it has fallen into disuse, or been overtaken by the laws that outlaw war and prohibit the use of force. When we recall the longstanding nature of this right to capture rule, we might remember that enemy goods in the past included slaves, being transported on enemy ships or belonging to the enemy. In fact in the 18th-century, members of the crew on any captured ship that were Black or mixed race would be presumed to be slaves, even where they might have evidence they were free. Captured and sold as prize, such crew members proved useful to captains either as income or as additions to the crew. Prize Law has an inglorious past. Charles Foy concludes his study:

> For Obadiah Gale and the hundreds of other black mariners sold into slavery during the American Revolution, the newly established American prize system was little different from its British colonial predecessor. Both systems presumed that blackness equaled enslavement. ... With both systems predicated upon a desire to develop maritime forces through awarding prize monies, little priority was given to black mariners' individual liberty. As a result, British and American prize systems ensured that going to sea involved anxiety for black seamen and their loved ones.[255]

Returning to the present day, modern academic commentary on the capture of enemy property at sea is sparse, but again, Heintschel von Heinegg admits that the rule concerning capture and confiscation of enemy merchant ships and cargo may need to be reinterpreted or restricted in the light of the UN Charter's restriction on the resort to force:

> In this context, one may consider exempting from capture passenger vessels that are transporting civilians and no contraband articles,

---

[255] Foy, 'Eighteenth Century "Prize Negroes": From Britain to America', 31 *Slavery and Abolition* (2010) 379–92 at 388–89; even where states were legislating against the importation of slaves, Prize Law was used to get around such restrictions, with slaves being sold on after condemnation as good prize captured in war, see van Niekerk, 'Judge John Holland and the Vice-Admiralty Court of the Cape of Good Hope, 1797–1803: Some Introductory and Biographical Notes (Part 1)', 23 *Fundamina* (2017) 176–210 at 186–95. I am grateful to Alessandro Marinaro for raising this issue and leading me to inquire further.

because capture always implies certain hazards for the ship concerned. If a belligerent wishes to make use of such a vessel, it can be requisitioned. Enemy merchant vessels in enemy port at the outbreak of hostilities, however, are not, and never have been protected by any binding rule. Today, because it is possible to integrate almost any merchant vessel into naval forces without major technical difficulties, states will be even less willing to agree to such a rule than they were in 1907. Nevertheless, if the direct influence of the United Nations Charter on the law of economic warfare at sea is accepted, the legality of condemning enemy property will probably have to be reconsidered. If all measures have to meet the principles of necessity and proportionality set out in the Charter, it is doubtful whether the acquisition of all enemy property at sea is legally justified.[256]

The most recent military *Manual* of New Zealand (2019) makes it clear that such a use of prize law is no longer considered normal in the contemporary context:

Due to the nature of modern armed conflict, in particular the need to limit conflict as much as possible and return to peaceful conditions quickly, the exercise of prize jurisdiction for the purposes of permanently acquiring the ships and property of another State is almost unknown. It is generally not now appropriate for a State to profit financially from the waging of armed conflict. New Zealand warships may seize enemy merchant vessels and submit them for prize arbitration only with the express authority of CDF [Chief of Defence Force]. If practicable, the advice of an NZDF LEGAD [New Zealand Defence Force Legal Adviser] is to be obtained before a vessel is seized as a prize. A ship that is captured may, however, be held until the end of hostilities, which may require that it is tied up in a foreign port.[257]

This captures perfectly the point with which I should like to conclude this chapter. If we have outlawed War as an institution at the disposal of states then we have to abolish the Belligerent Rights of states to benefit from War,

---

[256] Heintschel von Heinegg, 'Developments Since 1945' (n 110) at 134.
[257] New Zealand *Law of Armed Conflict* (n 41) at para 10.6.15 (footnote omitted).

or indeed any sort of armed conflict. It makes no sense to say that you cannot resort to armed conflict against another state and yet, if you do, you can keep the old Belligerent Rights that belonged to those that went to War. We do not outlaw burglary but then tell the law-breaker and home owner that they can keep what they find in the other's house.

9

Victims of War

The branch of the laws of war that focuses on the victims of war is known in some circles as Geneva law, in contrast to Hague law (which traditionally dealt with the conduct of hostilities, also known as the means and methods of warfare, and which we covered in the previous two chapters). Strictly speaking, today the labels Geneva law and Hague law make less and less sense, since the Additional Protocols to the Geneva Conventions include rules previously associated with Hague law and the conduct of hostilities. But the deeper structure of the laws of war is still based on the different logics found in these different branches. For Françoise Hampson, Geneva law focuses on the potential victim, while Hague law guides the decision making of the perpetrator:

> Hague law is directed to the military operator. It guides his decision making at the time. It deals principally with the places where, and times when, fighting is occurring. The rules tend to identify the considerations that must be taken into account and provide guidance as to how they are to be balanced, rather than simply prohibiting a particular outcome [fn An obvious exception is the absolute prohibition of intentional attacks against civilians and the civilian population]. The rules are a detailed articulation of general principles, such as the principles of distinction, proportionality and military necessity. Geneva law, on the other hand, is focused on the actual or potential victim, rather than the perpetrator. Many, but by no means all, of the issues that it addresses arise away from the immediate field of battle. The law tends to prohibit certain results or outcomes, usually by requiring certain forms of behavior.[1]

Similarly, the law-making dynamic is different. We considered the efforts to protect wartime maritime trading rights through some of the treaties discussed in the previous chapter; the impetus is different when it comes to the

---

[1] Hampson, 'Direct Participation in Hostilities and the Interoperability of the Law of Armed Conflict and Human Rights Law', 87 *ILS* (2011) 187–213 at 193.

treaties that protect the victims of war. As Kalmanovitz puts it in his historical study:

> In Paris, when delegates agreed that destroying a state's foreign trade should not be a legitimate war strategy, they acted old style, out of sheer state interest. In Geneva and Saint Petersburg, when delegates agreed on measures to ameliorate the suffering of soldiers in the battlefield, and to prevent it by banning the use of explosive projectiles, they were motivated by charity and respect for the inviolability of the human person.[2]

We will be stressing again in this chapter that there is a need to separate out international from non-international armed conflicts. In my teaching and practice I find that many people understandably lose patience with the idea of such a formalistic distinction in today's world. The situations in Syria, Ukraine, Palestine, Yemen, Afghanistan and so on can surely hardly be described as anything but international? And when it comes to the victims of war, why should they suffer from reduced protections due to some drafting decisions taken by states in 1949? Moreover, the International Criminal Tribunal for the former Yugoslavia, I am often told, has 'dissolved the difference'; and the judgment presided over by my former thesis director as President of the Tribunal, the late Judge Antonio Cassese, is quoted back at me:

> [E]lementary considerations of humanity and common sense make it preposterous that the use by States of weapons prohibited in armed conflicts between themselves be allowed when States try to put down rebellion by their own nationals on their own territory. What is inhumane, and consequently proscribed, in international wars, cannot but be inhumane and inadmissible in civil strife.[3]

As we saw in Chapter 7, there are indeed prohibitions on weapons that apply in both types of conflict, but here the Judges of the Tribunal were looking to discern customary crimes under international law rather than explain the overall framework of the laws of war. Moreover, states have deliberately amended the scope of the weapons treaties and the International Criminal Court to outlaw these weapons in situations of non-international

---

[2] *The Laws of War in International Thought* (2020) at 142.
[3] *Prosecutor v Tadić*, Case IT-94-1, 2 October 1995, para 119.

armed conflict (although many states have not yet adopted these amendments).[4] But when it comes to the protective regime for the victims of war, the different types of conflict remain, as a matter of law, stubbornly separate. Although some states have chosen to extend the weapons law regime (as well as the protection of cultural property[5]) to non-international armed conflicts, the Geneva Conventions of 1949 have not been amended in the same way. While many of the essential protections apply as customary international law in both kinds of conflict,[6] we will nevertheless distinguish between the separate international and non-international regimes. My insistence on this distinction is related to the significance that the distinction can play in quite specific legal contexts.

First, the war crimes regimes are not the same. A prosecutor or a defence lawyer in a criminal trial will be concerned to concentrate on the crime as it appears in the relevant statute or law. Some violations of international humanitarian law have not been criminalized by treaty as statutory war crimes. An attempt to prosecute for a crime not recognized in the relevant legal order would fail. Similarly, the regime for grave breaches of the Geneva Conventions and Protocol I creates not only war crimes specifically applicable only in international armed conflict, but also other obligations in this context, including an obligation to prosecute or extradite someone alleged to have committed such a war crime.[7] While states may be entitled, or even obliged, to prosecute or extradite those accused of war crimes in a non-international armed conflict, the legal basis will not be an enforceable treaty obligation under the Geneva Conventions of Protocol I. For a prosecutor, or those seeking to ensure the prosecution or extradition of a suspected war criminal, the categorization of a conflict as international may be essential to their case; by contrast, if the defendant can show the conflict is non-international, there may be no war crime to answer for in that particular jurisdiction.

---

[4] See the 2001 amendment to the Convention on Certain Conventional Weapons (1980) entered into force in 2004; in 2019, 86 of the 125 parties to the Convention had agreed to the amended treaty.

[5] See Henckaerts, 'New Rules for the Protection of Cultural Property in Armed Conflict', 835 *International Review of the Red Cross* (1999) 593–620.

[6] For an accessible list of the rules that apply in non-international armed conflict, as well as those where they 'arguably' apply, see Henckaerts, 'Study on Customary International Humanitarian Law: A Contribution to the Understanding and Respect for the Rule of Law in Armed Conflict', 857 *International Review of the Red Cross* (2005) 175–212 esp at 198–212.

[7] Gaeta, 'Grave Breaches of the Geneva Conventions', in Clapham, Gaeta and Sassòli (eds), *The 1949 Geneva Conventions: A Commentary* (2015) 615–46.

Second, there may be other regimes, such as the Arms Trade Treaty (2013), that contain specific obligations that apply with regard to the future possibility of violations of international humanitarian law. Where the obligations relate to grave breaches, it remains the case that such breaches can only be committed in an international armed conflict.[8]

Third, human rights case-law, especially before the European Court of Human Rights, has developed so that in a situation of international armed conflict where protective regimes co-exist, the human rights regime that covers the deprivation of liberty may *accommodate* 'the taking of prisoners of war and the detention of civilians who pose a risk to security'.[9] But when it comes to non-international armed conflicts, national courts have been reluctant to extend to governments such a right to intern people without trial.[10]

Precisely because the law of non-international armed conflict is less developed and does not comprise such a comprehensive protective regime, today the potential target or internee may want to rely on the protections that normally apply outside an inter-state conflict, which can include more protective human rights law, constitutional law, principles of law enforcement and habeas corpus.[11] This is a controversial and contested area of the law. For a government, these legal protections can be seen as serious obstacles to military operations and winning the war.[12] For those being targeted by the government, asserting the right not to be targeted is a matter of life and death.

My point is that it is too simplistic to state that one or the other regime is more protective, or to claim that we can and should apply rules for inter-state conflict to civil war by analogy; rather, we have to acknowledge that when the arguments start in concrete disputes, the stakes will be different for each party to the argument, and the policy implications of applying one or the other regime are context dependent.[13]

---

[8] For the detail see the discussion of Art 6(3) in Casey-Maslen, Clapham, Giacca and Parker, *The Arms Trade Treaty: A Commentary* (2016) 229–43.

[9] See *Hassan v UK*, European Court of Human Rights, 16 September 2014 at para 104.

[10] See generally Hill-Cawthorne, *Detention in Non-International Armed Conflict* (2016), and in particular the litigation that culminated in *Serdar Mohammed v Secretary of State for Defence* [2017] UKSC 2.

[11] Farrell, *Habeas Corpus in International Law* (2017); Tyler, *Habeas Corpus in Wartime: From the Tower of London to Guantanamo Bay* (2017).

[12] See Aughey and Sari, 'Targeting and Detention in Non-International Armed Conflict: *Serdar Mohammed* and the Limits of Human Rights Convergence', 91 *ILS* (2015) 60–118; Olson, 'Practical Challenges of Implementing the Complementarity between International Humanitarian and Human Rights Law – Demonstrated by the Procedural Regulation of Internment in Non-International Armed Conflict', 40 *Case Western Reserve Journal of International Law* (2009) 437–61.

[13] For the detail of some of the differing effects on human rights regimes depending on whether the conflict is international or non-international see Clapham, 'The Complex

What follows in no way attempts to describe (or even summarize) the range of the protections and obligations contained in the contemporary international humanitarian law. The reader is referred to the comprehensive manuals written by established experts in the field.[14] Here I want simply to explain the legal significance of some of the key terms and highlight a few ongoing controversies.

9.1 Protected Persons and Property in International Armed Conflict

In an international armed conflict, the Geneva Conventions of 1949 and Protocol I together provide a protection regime, sometimes delineating exactly who counts as a 'protected person' and what should be considered 'protected property'. These terms are used on some occasions as terms of art, prescribing a particular group that qualifies for this 'status', and at other times as a reference to the floor of protection that is offered even to those who do not qualify strictly speaking for the status of protected person.[15] The consequences of being a protected person, or not, are sometimes treated today as of less practical significance, as the basic protections will apply either through treaty or customary international law. But let me enumerate a few legal consequences of being a 'protected person'.

First, the International Committee of the Red Cross (ICRC) has the right to have access to certain protected persons as a matter of international treaty law under the 1949 Geneva Conventions. This is an obligation on every state, as all states are now parties to the Geneva Conventions. This right of access includes the right for the ICRC to interview prisoners of war and internees

Relationship between the 1949 Geneva Conventions and International Human Rights Law', in Clapham, Gaeta and Sassòli (eds), *The 1949 Geneva Conventions: A Commentary* (2015) 701–35.

[14] See especially Sassòli, *International Humanitarian Law* (2019) (hereinafter '*IHL*'); and Fleck (ed), *The Handbook of Humanitarian Law in Armed Conflict*, 4th edn (2021).

[15] See, eg, Art 75 of Additional Protocol I (AP I), discussed below. Note this statement from the US *Law of War Manual* (2016) at para 8.1.4.2 (footnotes omitted, emphasis added): 'Article 75 of AP I reflects fundamental guarantees for the treatment of persons detained during *international* armed conflict. Although not a Party to AP I, the United States has stated that the US Government will choose out of a sense of legal obligation to treat the principles set forth in Article 75 as applicable to any individual it detains in an *international* armed conflict, and expects all other nations to adhere to these principles as well. This statement was intended to contribute to the crystallization of the principles contained in Article 75 as rules of customary international law applicable in *international* armed conflict.'

without witnesses,[16] as well as rights for certain protected persons to communicate with the ICRC and other organizations.[17] Second, the Geneva Conventions prohibit any renunciation or restriction of the rights by protected persons.[18] Third, the grave breaches regime, as well as the Statute of the International Criminal Court, requires that the victim of the offence be a protected person or that the act be committed against protected property.[19] Fourth, reprisals are explicitly forbidden against persons and property protected by the Conventions and Additional Protocol I.[20]

So, for example, to understand what constitutes the war crime of a grave breach of the Geneva Conventions under the International Criminal Court Statute, one has to determine what is meant by an act 'against persons or property protected under the provisions of the relevant Geneva Convention'.[21] The persons and property so protected as such have been helpfully listed in the specialist commentary.[22]

Let us separate out the different fields of protection by grouping them under three headings: (i) medical personnel and equipment, the wounded, sick and shipwrecked; (ii) prisoners of war; and (iii) civilians.

---

[16]   See GC III Art 126; and GC IV Arts 76 and 143.

[17]   See GC IV Art 30; Van Der Heijden, 'Other Issues Relating to the Treatment of Civilians in Enemy Hands', in Clapham, Gaeta and Sassòli (eds), *The 1949 Geneva Conventions: A Commentary* (2015) 1241–68 at 1254–55.

[18]   See Common Arts 6/6/6/7 and 7/7/7/8 of the Four Geneva Conventions 1949 explained by Casey-Maslen, 'Special Agreements in International Armed Conflicts', in Clapham, Gaeta and Sassòli (eds), *The 1949 Geneva Conventions: A Commentary* (2015) 135–44; and d'Argent, 'Non-Renunciation of the Rights Provided by the Conventions', ibid at 145–53.

[19]   See Arts 50/51/130/147 of the Four Geneva Conventions and Arts 8, 11 and 85 of AP I. See eg ICRC, *Commentary on the First Geneva Convention*, 2nd edn (2016) at MNs 2926–2928 for those persons and property protected under that Convention. See also Art 8(2)(a) of the ICC Statute.

[20]   See Arts 46/47/13/33 of the 1949 Geneva Conventions, and Arts 20 and 51–56 of AP I.

[21]   Art 8(2)(a).

[22]   See Dörmann, Doswald-Beck and Kolb, *Elements of War Crimes under the Rome Statute of the International Criminal Court: Sources and Commentary* (2003) at 29 and 33: protected property includes those things that cannot be attacked as specified in Arts 19 and 33–35 of GC I (medical units, transports, etc and the property of aid societies); Arts 22, 24, 25 and 27 of GC II (1949) (hospital ships, etc); Arts 18, 19, 21, 22, 33, 53 and 57 of GC IV (eg hospitals and medical transports, etc; property of protected persons; public and private property in occupied territory). Loss of protection and exceptions for military necessity are discussed below and specifically dealt with in the relevant articles – see, eg, Art 53 of GC IV. Protected persons would include those covered by Arts 13, 24, 25 and 26 of GC I (wounded and sick from the armed forces or a *levée en masse*, medical personnel), Arts 13, 36 and 37 of GC II (at sea, the shipwrecked, sick and wounded members of the armed forces or a *levée en masse* and medical personnel), Art 4 of GC III (prisoners of war), Arts 4, 13 and 20 of GC IV (eg those in the hands of the enemy and hospital staff). See also Arts 8, 44, 45, 73 and 85(3)(e) of AP I.

9.1.1 Medical Personnel and Equipment, the Wounded, Sick and Shipwrecked (International Armed Conflict)

The detailed regime protecting medical personnel and the wounded contained in the Geneva Conventions can be directly traced back to 1859 and a celebrated episode in Solferino (about 90 miles from Milan). Henri Dunant, a businessman from Geneva, was looking for Napoleon III in order to get him to sign some papers related to Dunant's business in Algeria. This led him to the battlefield of Solferino, and more specifically to the village of Castiglione, where he found himself confronted with the realities of around 9,000 wounded and dying soldiers. He tried to help but was overwhelmed by the utter inadequacy of the facilities and assistance available to the wounded all around him. Famously, it was said there were more veterinary surgeons for the horses than doctors for the soldiers.

On his return to Geneva, Dunant wrote a small book, which he sent around to his impressive list of contacts, ensuring it got into the hands of a number of key sovereign leaders. Not only did he describe his feelings of despair and outrage, but he also asked 'Would it not be possible, in time of peace and quiet, to form relief societies for the purpose of having care given to the wounded in wartime by zealous, devoted and thoroughly qualified volunteers?'[23] This idea was the germ that led eventually to the first Geneva Convention (1864) and the creation of the ICRC, as well as the Red Cross and Red Crescent Movement.[24] An essential aspect of this experience was his determination that the wounded from both sides should be treated equally according to their wounds and not their allegiance – friend and enemy alike. In his words:

> How many young men of eighteen and twenty come reluctantly here, from the depths of Germany or from the Eastern Provinces of the immense Austrian Empire – and some of them, perhaps, under rude compulsion – were forced to suffer not only physical pain, but also the ill-will of the Milanese, who have a profound hatred for their race, for their leaders, and for their Sovereign. These men could count on little sympathy until they should reach French soil. Ah poor mothers in Germany, in Austria,

---

[23] Dunant, *A Memory of Solferino* [1862] (1959) at 115.
[24] See Bugnion, *The International Committee of the Red Cross and the Protection of War Victims* (2003); Durand, *Henry Dunant* (2011).

in Hungary and Bohemia, how can one help thinking of their agony, when they hear that their sons are wounded and prisoners in this hostile land!

But the women of Castiglione, seeing that I made no distinction between nationalities, followed my example, showing the same kindness to all these men whose origins were so different, and all of whom were foreigner to them. 'Tutti fratelli' [all are brothers], they repeated feelingly. All honour to these compassionate women, to these girls of Castiglione! Imperturbable, unwavering, unfaltering, their quiet self-sacrifice made little of fatigue and horrors, and of their own devotion.[25]

Dunant ended his booklet by asking 'we hear so much these days of progress and civilization, but unfortunately we still cannot avoid wars, should we not urgently try, in a genuine spirit of humanity and civilization, to prevent, or at least to alleviate, the horrors of war?'[26] He was awarded the first Nobel Peace Prize in 1901, along with Frédéric Passy, a French peace campaigner and founder of the Inter-Parliamentary Union.

Today multiple provisions of the Geneva Conventions and their Protocols, alongside customary international law,[27] address protection for medical personnel, the wounded sick and shipwrecked, as well as the relevant hospitals, medical transports and equipment.[28] The essential obligations are to search for and collect the wounded, and to protect and care for them without any discrimination. Medical personnel, the wounded, sick and shipwrecked are to be respected and may not be attacked.

Although the wounded and sick were originally categories confined to military personnel, today it is accepted that the obligations should extend to everyone. The UK *Manual* uses a definition taken from Additional Protocol I, stating that

the wounded and sick are 'persons, whether military or civilian, who, because of trauma, disease or other physical or mental disorder or disability, are in need of medical assistance or care and who refrain from any act of hostility'.

---

[25] Dunant, *A Memory of Solferino* (n 23) at 71–72.

[26] Ibid at 127.

[27] See Henckaerts and Doswald-Beck, *Customary International Humanitarian Law*, vol 1: *Rules* (2005).

[28] For a useful overview of the main protections, see Melzer, *International Humanitarian Law: A Comprehensive Introduction* (2016) Ch 4; for further detail, see Sassòli, *IHL* (n 14) Ch 8.1.

The definition goes beyond persons wounded on the battlefield to encompass anybody in need of medical treatment. That includes 'maternity cases, new-born babies and other persons who may be in need of immediate medical assistance or care, such as the infirm or expectant mothers' who refrain from any act of hostility. Those who carry on fighting despite their wounds are not included in the wounded and sick category.[29]

Medical facilities and medical transports have to be respected,[30] even though some might see them as military facilities providing an advantage to the enemy. Conflicts in Gaza, Syria and Yemen have all seen strikes on medical facilities, and these have contributed immeasurably to the tragic humanitarian situation.[31] In light of some of the confusion that sometimes surrounds this topic, we will set out the scope of limitations on this protection in some detail.

This special protection can be lost if the facilities 'are used to commit, outside their humanitarian duties, acts harmful to the enemy'.[32] Crucially, an extra layer of protection exists here, and Article 21 adds that protection can only end 'after a due warning has been given'. This obligation exists for military and civilian facilities,[33] and in all types of conflict,[34] as well as in occupied territory.[35] It is specified that the warning must set 'in all appropriate cases, a reasonable time limit', and protection is only lost 'after such warning has remained unheeded'.[36]

The treaties explain that the fact that personnel are armed for their own self-defence, or to defend the sick and wounded in their charge, does not deprive them of their special protection.[37] Similarly, the presence for medical reasons of combatants in the facility is also not to be considered an act harmful to the enemy.[38]

---

[29] Paras 7.2 and 7.2.1, referencing Art 8(a) of AP I.
[30] See Arts 21 and 35 of GC I (1949) and Arts 8, 21–31 of AP I (1977).
[31] See further Watkin, 'Medical Care in Urban Conflict', 95 *International Law Studies* (2019) 49–93.
[32] GC I (1949) Art 21.
[33] AP I (1977) Art 13(1).
[34] See also AP II Art 11(2) and Henckaerts and Doswald-Beck, *Customary International Humanitarian Law* (n 27) at 97; and Wilmshurst and Breau (eds), *Perspectives on the ICRC Study on Customary International Humanitarian Law* (2007) Ch 7 at 169–78.
[35] GC IV (1949) Art 19.
[36] GCs I and IV Arts 21 and 19; see also AP II Art 11(2).
[37] Eg GC I (1949) Art 22; see also GC IV (1949) Art 19.
[38] AP I Art 13(2).

The 2016 ICRC *Commentary* elaborates on what could actually constitute using the facilities to commit acts 'harmful to the enemy':

> Examples of such use include firing at the enemy for reasons other than individual self-defence, installing a firing position in a medical post, the use of a hospital as a shelter for able-bodied combatants, as an arms or ammunition dump, or as a military observation post, or the placing of a medical unit in proximity to a military objective with the intention of shielding it from the enemy's military operations. Furthermore, scenarios that are recognized as being 'acts harmful to the enemy' in the context of hospital ships under the Second Convention (transmitting information of military value) and of civilian hospitals under the Fourth Convention (use of a civilian hospital as a centre for liaison with fighting troops) may also constitute 'acts harmful to the enemy' in the context of military medical establishments and units under the First Convention. Engaging in such acts may not only lead to a loss of protection, but may also qualify, where the establishments and units were displaying the distinctive emblems, as improper use of the emblems or as the war crime of perfidy, if done in order to kill or injure an enemy combatant.[39]

It is worth stressing that this loss of special protective status does not turn the object into a military objective that can necessarily be attacked.[40] The rules on precaution, distinction, proportionality and necessity would still apply and demand compliance. Medical facilities and transports should benefit from a presumption against attack. Medical personnel should remain protected from attack unless they pose an immediate threat to the lives of others,[41] and any attack on medical personnel should similarly require an appropriate warning, as in the case of medical facilities. Instructions to issue warnings before attacking medical personnel who have lost their protection

---

[39] ICRC, *Commentary on the First Geneva Convention* (2016) (n 19) at MN 1842 (footnotes omitted).

[40] Melzer, International Humanitarian Law (n 28) at 145.

[41] The US *Law of War Manual* suggests (at para 7.8.3, footnote omitted) that medical and religious personnel may be made the object of attack if they 'participate in hostilities or otherwise commit acts harmful to the enemy. For example, weapons may not be used by medical and religious personnel against enemy military forces except in self-defense or defense of their patients.' Rather than a vague reference to acts harmful to the enemy, a better conclusion is that medical personnel can only be attacked where they pose an immediate threat rather than representing some harmful act for the attacking forces.

can be found in recent Military Manuals.[42] The protections at sea for the sick, wounded and shipwrecked also cover those civilians who may have been accompanying the armed force or belong to merchant ships or civilian aircraft (to the extent they are not covered by more favourable provisions of international law).[43]

The obligations with regard to submarines have been referred to in section 7.4.2 in the context of the limited possibilities for commanders to rely on the idea of necessity. . A complex point arises from the limited ability of a submarine to collect and care for the shipwrecked, sick and wounded due to their limited space and their vulnerability to attack. The Geneva Convention provisions limit the obligations to search for and collect the shipwrecked 'after each engagement' to 'all possible measures'.[44] Nevertheless, the rules on the conduct of hostilities apply to attacks from submarines, so there would be obligations of precaution in attack to avoid civilian injury even when targeting a military objective.[45] Those ordering an attack should be able to estimate the expected civilian injury, and would have to determine that such injury was not excessive when compared to the anticipated military advantage. Even where no civilians are involved at all, today parties to the conflict are obliged to take all possible measures to search for and collect the shipwrecked, even if this cannot feasibly be undertaken by the submarine crew themselves.[46]

9.1.2   Prisoners of War (International Armed Conflict)

The protection offered by the Third Geneva Convention on Prisoners of War only applies in inter-state armed conflicts. A completely different regime applies for non-international armed conflicts involving armed groups (see

---

[42] See the New Zealand *Manual of Armed Forces Law*, vol 4: *Law of Armed Conflict*, DM 69 (2nd edn) (2019) at para 11.5.13; Australian Manual (2006), *Law of Armed Conflict*, ADDP 06.4, at para 9.6.9.

[43] GC II (1949) Arts 13(5) and 16.

[44] GC II Art 18; compare GC I Art 15, which includes an obligation to search for and collect the wounded and sick on land 'at all times'.

[45] Heintschell von Heinegg, 'The Law of Armed Conflict at Sea', in Fleck (ed), *The Handbook of Humanitarian Law in Armed Conflict*, 3rd edn (2013) 463–547 at 478–82. The same author has pointed out that 'Submarines are highly sophisticated and expensive weapon platforms and most counties would be rather hesitant to use them against merchant shipping.' See his discussion in Heintschel von Heinegg, 'Submarine Operations and International Law', in Engdahl and Wrange (eds), *Law at War: The Law as Was and the Law as it Should Be* (2008) 141–62 at 143ff.

[46] See further ICRC, *Commentary on the Second Geneva Convention* (2017) at MN 1616–1702.

section 9.2 below).[47] I have lost count of the times I am asked 'Why not apply the protective regime for prisoners of war in non-international armed conflicts?' The stock response is simply stated: the Prisoner of War Convention requires release and repatriation without delay after the cessation of active hostilities.[48] Any government will want to reserve the right to incarcerate those who took up arms against it and prosecute them for terrorism, rebellion, sedition and so on. In an inter-state conflict, repatriation means the prisoners are normally transported across a border to a state that is no longer hostile. At the end of an internal conflict, the detainees who had taken up arms against the government would be 'back on the streets'. Furthermore, as we saw in Chapter 7, the prisoner of war regime is closely associated in the doctrine with the idea of combatant immunity. So, by implication, for many people, having prisoner of war status suggests that they cannot be prosecuted for having taken up arms against the state. In fact it is a bit more complex.

When the laws of war are taught in military academies, the armed forces are typically told 'The law of war recognizes the combatant's privilege to lawfully target enemy combatants and civilians while the latter are taking a direct part in hostilities and, conversely, to be targeted by lawful enemy combatants.'[49] But this privilege only extends to 'lawful enemy combatants', which does not include those who are not acting on behalf of a government: 'law of war denies the combatant's privilege and entitlement to prisoner of war status to private citizens (other than members of a *levée en masse*) who resort to armed violence without government authority'.[50] Combatant privilege and prisoner of war status are therefore reserved in broad terms for those acting for a government, and are denied to private citizens (also known as insurgents, non-state actors, rebels or terrorists). This is the standard approach,[51] and it has the merit of clarity, especially when one needs to reduce the logic of the rules down to basic obligations and protections, but we need

---

[47] Exceptionally, in situations where there is a recognition of belligerency by the government of the opposition forces, the Convention could be applied so that prisoners are treated as prisoners of war; according to Sivakumaran, such formal recognition has not been seen since the adoption of the 1949 Geneva Convention: *The Law of Non-International Armed Conflict* (2012) at 19. Nevertheless, even without a formal state of Belligerency, the Convention was applied in the Nigerian civil war over Biafra, explained by Bugnion as flowing from recognition: 'Jus ad Bellum, Jus in Bello and Non-International Armed Conflicts', VI *Yearbook of International Humanitarian Law* (2003) 167–98 at 181.

[48] GC III Art 118.

[49] Parks, 'Teaching the Law of War: A Reprise', *IDF Law Review* (2007) 9–24 at 10.

[50] Ibid at 11; for the definition of *levée en masse*, see GC III Art 4A(6) below.

[51] See the discussion in section 7.1 and the references therein.

not necessarily see combatant privilege as tied up with prisoner of war status in this way.

The present book has kept combatant immunity and prisoner of war status in separate chapters. In fact, when we get into the detail, there are some people entitled to prisoner of war status who are not entitled to target the enemy, and so who do not enjoy combatant immunity; well-known examples are war correspondents and the civilian members of the crew of merchant ships and civil aircraft.[52] It is suggested here that a better approach is not to connect combatant immunity with prisoner of war protection; this way the path is opened for the better protection of detainees using the norms of the prisoner of war regime, without any perceived risk of according some 'right to fight' or 'licence to kill' to the non-governmental opposition.[53]

Sivakumaran has detailed how various governments have accorded (at least in theory) prisoner of war treatment (but not status) to the non-governmental opposition in certain conflicts over the last 90 years: Spain (1936), France in Algeria (1958), Nigeria (1967), Federal Republic of Yugoslavia (1991), Bosnia-Herzegovina (1992), Philippines (1996) and Libya (TNC) (2011).[54] And the Geneva Conventions themselves encourage the parties to a non-international armed conflict to adopt 'special agreements' that would bring into force the protection offered by the provisions of the Prisoner of War Convention.[55]

Why, then, was there so much resistance by the United States Presidency to the application of the Prisoner of War Convention to those in the hands of the US at the start of the Afghanistan conflict in 2001? We will enter into some of the detail here, as it helps to understand the central theme of this book: how changing conceptions of war are undermining established legal protections for the victims of armed conflict.

The White House Legal Counsel Alberto Gonzales wrote the following in a memorandum to President George W Bush, explaining that the denial of the protection of the Prisoner of War Convention 'preserves flexibility', because:

---

[52] GC III Art 4A(4) and (5); Note the *ICRC Commentary to GC III* (2020) at para 1058 states 'The ICRC is of the view that persons entitled to prisoner-of-war status on the basis of Article 4A(5) are only those members of the crew whose professional activities are directly linked to the military activities of the armed forces. This includes all members of the crew involved in operating the vessel or aircraft.'

[53] See also Watts, 'Who Is a Prisoner of War?', in Clapham, Gaeta and Sassòli (eds), *The 1949 Geneva Conventions: A Commentary* (2015) 889–910 at 909–10.

[54] Sivakumaran (n 47) at 523–25.

[55] GC III 3 para 3; see further Vierucci, 'Applicability of the Conventions by Means of Ad Hoc Agreements', in Clapham, Gaeta and Sassòli (eds), *The 1949 Geneva Conventions: A Commentary* (2015) 509–21.

As you have said, the war against terrorism is a new kind of war. It is not a traditional clash between nations adhering to the laws of war that formed the backdrop for [the Geneva Convention on Prisoners of War] GPW. The nature of the new war places a high premium on other factors, such as the ability to quickly obtain information from captured terrorists and their sponsors in order to avoid further atrocities against American civilians, and the need to try terrorists for war crimes such as wantonly killing civilians.

The memorandum goes on, under a separate heading, to explain that such a denial of application of the Geneva Convention 'Substantially reduces the threat of domestic prosecution under the War Crimes Act (18 USC 2441).' The fear for the White House lawyer was that US prosecutors and courts would misapply or misconstrue the War Crimes Act based on undefined language in the Geneva Convention, such as 'outrages on personal dignity' and 'inhuman treatment', with dramatic consequences. Punishments for US personnel under paragraph 2441 of the Act included the death penalty. In a chilling sentence, the Legal Counsel advises 'A determination that the GPW [Geneva Convention on Prisoners of War] is not applicable to the Taliban would mean that Section 2441 would not apply to actions taken with respect to the Taliban.'[56]

In response to the possible counter-argument that denying the application of the Convention would put US personnel at risk should they be captured, it was claimed that 'we can still bring war crimes charges against anyone who mistreats US personnel'. This is a remarkable approach. It was argued that US prosecutors should not be given the possibility to prosecute war crimes for any alleged US mistreatment of the Taliban, yet the same prosecutors would apparently be able to prosecute as war criminals those Taliban who mistreated US personnel.

It was therefore, according to this material, the fear of national war crimes prosecutions against US military personnel (and their leaders) that drove the convoluted reasoning that attempted to disapply the protection of the Geneva Convention to such detainees.[57] In fact, one cannot simply shield one's own personnel from war crimes prosecutions by declining to apply the

---

[56] Memorandum of 25 January 2002, 'Decision re application of the Geneva Convention on Prisoners of War to the conflict with Al Qaeda and the Taliban', available at https://nsarchive2.gwu.edu/NSAEBB/NSAEBB127/02.01.25.pdf.

[57] For the subsequent litigation before the Supreme Court and the change in policy, see Hodgkinson, 'Detention Operations: A Strategic Overview', in Corn, Van Landingham and Reeves (eds), *US Military Operations: Law, Policy, and Practice* (2016) 275–305.

Geneva Conventions. Prosecutors in international courts or from other jurisdictions will be able to bring war crimes prosecutions based on whether the Conventions and any customary international law apply as a matter of law based on the facts, and not on whether the detaining power chose to apply the Conventions.[58]

Moving on from this controversy, what are the actual protections that apply, not just as principles[59] but as a matter of law? And what consequences flow from breaches of these provisions of the Geneva Conventions?

In order to be a protected prisoner of war in the context of this treaty, one must actually qualify as a prisoner of war in an inter-state conflict, as defined in Article 4 of the Prisoner of War Convention. As explained above, from this status flows an entitlement to private visits from the ICRC or a Protecting Power,[60] as well the fact that the following acts, when committed against a prisoner of war, will constitute a grave breach of the Convention: 'wilful killing, torture or inhuman treatment, including biological experiments, wilfully causing great suffering or serious injury to body or health, compelling a prisoner of war to serve in the forces of the hostile Power, or wilfully depriving a prisoner of war of the rights of fair and regular trial prescribed in this Convention'.[61] The commission of such a war crime leads to a universal obligation on all states to search for and prosecute or extradite an alleged perpetrator or anyone alleged to have ordered such a grave breach.

Article 4 defines who qualifies as a prisoner of war.[62] The key point is that members of the armed forces are entitled to prisoner of war status on capture,

---

[58] The ICC Appeals Chamber has authorized an investigation into the situation in Afghanistan since May 2003 and into other crimes connected to the conflict in other states since July 2002, ICC-02/17-138, 5 March 2020. The allegations concern: (i) the Taliban and affiliated groups for crimes against humanity and war crimes; (ii) the Afghan National Security Forces for war crimes; (iii) the armed forces of the United States and its Central Intelligence Agency (CIA) for war crimes.

[59] The White House Counsel memo of 25 January 2002, referred to above, argued that while the Geneva Convention should not be applied, the US would continue to treat detainees in a manner consistent with the 'principles' of the Prisoner of War Convention.

[60] GC III Art 126.

[61] GC III Art 130.

[62] Art 4 provides:

A. Prisoners of war, in the sense of the present Convention, are persons belonging to one of the following categories, who have fallen into the power of the enemy:

(1) Members of the armed forces of a Party to the conflict as well as members of militias or volunteer corps forming part of such armed forces.

(2) Members of other militias and members of other volunteer corps, including those of organized resistance movements, belonging to a Party to the conflict and operating in or outside their own territory, even if this territory is occupied, provided that such militias or volunteer corps, including such organized resistance movements, fulfil the following conditions:

or having surrendered to the enemy state. Accepted exceptions include those who are caught engaging in espionage (spies),[63] mercenaries,[64] and those members of the armed forces who fail to distinguish themselves from the civilian population when engaging in an attack or in a military operation preparatory to an attack.[65]

The concrete protections are complex and can be only summarized here as comprising humane treatment and protection from violence, insults and public curiosity, with an explicit prohibition on reprisals.[66] Interrogation is not prohibited, but the prisoner of war is only obliged to give 'his surname, first names and rank, date of birth, and army, regimental, personal or serial number, or failing this, equivalent information.'[67]

The detaining state is to establish an Information Bureau and cooperate with the ICRC Central Prisoners of War Information Agency. Cards are sent

> (a) that of being commanded by a person responsible for his subordinates;
> (b) that of having a fixed distinctive sign recognizable at a distance;
> (c) that of carrying arms openly;
> (d) that of conducting their operations in accordance with the laws and customs of war.
> (3) Members of regular armed forces who profess allegiance to a government or an authority not recognized by the Detaining Power.
> (4) Persons who accompany the armed forces without actually being members thereof, such as civilian members of military aircraft crews, war correspondents, supply contractors, members of labour units or of services responsible for the welfare of the armed forces, provided that they have received authorization from the armed forces which they accompany, who shall provide them for that purpose with an identity card similar to the annexed model.
> (5) Members of crews, including masters, pilots and apprentices, of the merchant marine and the crews of civil aircraft of the Parties to the conflict, who do not benefit by more favourable treatment under any other provisions of international law.
> (6) Inhabitants of a non-occupied territory, who on the approach of the enemy spontaneously take up arms to resist the invading forces, without having had time to form themselves into regular armed units, provided they carry arms openly and respect the laws and customs of war [levée en masse].
> The categories of resistance movement (Art 4A(2)) and levée en masse (Art 4A(6)) are narrowly interpreted and applied; see, for a very clear explanation, Kolb, *Advanced Introduction to International Humanitarian Law* (2014) at 124–34. See also Art 67(2) of AP I for military personnel serving within civil defence organizations having the right to be prisoners of war.

[63] See Hague IV Regulation Art 29 and AP I Art 46; ICRC Customary IHL Rule 107 (n 27); Sassòli, *IHL* (n 14) at para 8.73.

[64] AP I Art 47; ICRC Customary IHL Rule 108 (n 27); Sassòli, *IHL* (n 14) at para 8.72.

[65] The ICRC Customary IHL Rule 106 (n 27); AP I Art 44; and UK *Manual of the Law of Armed Conflict* (2004) at paras 4.4–4.12; US, *Law of War Manual* at para 4.17.5; see also Sassòli, *IHL* (n 14) at para 8.58; for a useful explanation of the limited applicability of Art 44, see Kolb (n 62) at 134–42.

[66] GC III Art 13.

[67] GC III Art 17.

to the family through the Central Agency. Successful escapees are not liable to punishment on recapture.[68] And there are detailed rules on evacuation, internment, labour, financial resources, tobacco, pay, relations with the exterior, complaints, fair trial, release and repatriation at the end of hostilities.

Since the 1949 Geneva Prisoner of War Convention was adopted, human rights law has developed so that the human rights of prisoners of war have been taken into consideration. Some of the provisions in the Prisoner of War Convention need now to be read against modern approaches to the human rights of people with disabilities. So 'isolation wards' for people with 'mental disease' could lead to violations of those persons' rights and render the detention arbitrary or illegal.[69] Moreover, the concept of 'reasonable accommodation' favours repatriation.[70]

Human rights and refugee law have also affected the detaining state's duty to repatriate. The Prisoner of War Convention has now been interpreted against the background of any prisoner of war's human right not to be returned where there is a substantial risk of torture or ill-treatment. As Sassòli's detailed study makes plain, such a prohibition on return should extend to cover

> threats of punishment for the mere fact of having been captured and interned as a POW . . . [I]t is hardly conceivable that 196 states could be party to a Convention the very purpose of which is to protect POWs in the power of the enemy, if they considered that the mere fact of having been made a prisoner by the enemy could entail legitimate punishment after repatriation.[71]

9.1.3 Civilians in the Hands of the Enemy (International Armed Conflict)

Chapter 7 outlined two cardinal rules of armed conflict. First, civilians can never be the object of direct attack and, second, civilians are protected by the law on precaution in both attack and defence, as well as the specific

---

[68] GC III Art 91.

[69] See Priddy, *Disability and Armed Conflict* (2019) 65–72.

[70] Ibid at 69.

[71] Sassòli, 'Release, Accommodation in Neutral Countries, and Repatriation of Prisoners of War', in Clapham, Gaeta and Sassòli (eds), *The 1949 Geneva Conventions: A Commentary* (2015) 1039–66 at 1054.

prohibitions on indiscriminate and disproportionate attacks. In this section we address the specific regimes applicable in international armed conflict that protect civilians in the hands of the enemy (as opposed to protection from attack). In particular we will examine the context of civilians considered as enemy aliens in the territory of a state party to an international armed conflict, as well as civilians in occupied territory. While a number of provisions protect civilians in both these categories,[72] and indeed civilians more generally,[73] we will concentrate on the protected persons regimes for those considered alien, enemy and hostile, as it is here that one finds the remnants of a logic of war that considers groups of foreigners as enemies.

Notwithstanding Rousseau's definition of war encountered in Chapter 1, that war is purely the relationship between enemy states and not between individuals, the protections in the Fourth Geneva Convention focus on protecting foreign civilians who are in the hands of the enemy. We should perhaps already clarify that, although the Fourth Geneva Convention speaks of individuals being in 'enemy hands' or in the 'hands of a Party to the conflict or Occupying Power', this is understood widely. The *Pictet Commentary to Geneva Convention IV* (1958) explains that 'the expression "in the hands of" need not necessarily be understood in the physical sense; it simply means that the person is in territory which is under the control of the Power in question'.[74]

9.1.3.1 Civilian Aliens in the Territory of the Enemy (International Armed Conflict)

Civilians in enemy territory are now protected specifically by Articles 34 to 46 of the Fourth Geneva Convention. In Chapter 5 we examined the legality under the US Constitution of interning persons of Japanese descent during the Second World War. The rules under the Fourth Geneva Convention (1949) protect only those who are not nationals of the state with control over them. Part of the Convention addressed the plight of those interned during the Second World War as enemy aliens. This protection regime now gets little

---

[72] See GC IV Arts 27–34.

[73] GC IV Arts 13–26; AP I Arts 48–79; ICRC Customary IHL Rules 87–138.

[74] Pictet (ed), *Geneva Convention Relative to the Protection of Civilian Persons in Time of War: Commentary* (1958) (hereinafter '*Pictet Commentary to Geneva Convention IV*') at 47; for subsequent confirmation in the case law of the international criminal tribunals, see Salmón, 'Who Is a Protected Civilian?' in Clapham, Gaeta and Sassòli (eds), *The 1949 Geneva Conventions: A Commentary* (2015) 1135–53 at 1142.

attention, but the background deserves highlighting for what it tells us about attitudes in war.

The following factsheet explains part of the history concerning internment in the UK during the Second World War.

At the outbreak of war there were around 80,000 potential enemy aliens in Britain who, it was feared, could be spies, or willing to assist Britain's enemies in the event of an invasion. All Germans and Austrians over the age of 16 were called before special tribunals and were divided into one of three groups:

- 'A' – high security risks, numbering just under 600, who were immediately interned;
- 'B' – 'doubtful cases', numbering around 6,500, who were supervised and subject to restrictions;
- 'C' – 'no security risk', numbering around 64,000, who were left at liberty. More than 55,000 of category 'C' were recognised as refugees from Nazi oppression. The vast majority of these were Jewish.

The situation began to change in the spring of 1940. The failure of the Norwegian campaign led to an outbreak of spy fever and agitation against enemy aliens. More and more Germans and Austrians were rounded up. Italians were also included, even though Britain was not at war with Italy until June. When Italy and Britain did go to war, there were at least 19,000 Italians in Britain, and Churchill ordered they all be rounded up. This was despite the fact that most of them had lived in Britain for decades.

Thousands of Germans, Austrians and Italians were sent to camps set up at racecourses and incomplete housing estates, such as Huyton outside Liverpool. The majority were interned on the Isle of Man, where internment camps had also been set up in World War One. Facilities were basic, but it was boredom that was the greatest enemy . . .

That many of the 'enemy aliens' were Jewish refugees and therefore hardly likely to be sympathetic to the Nazis, was a complication no one bothered to try and unravel – they were still treated as German and Austrian nationals. In one Isle of Man camp over 80 per cent of the internees were Jewish refugees.

As regards British citizens interned by the Nazis, in September 1942 the Germans sent 2,000 British-born civilians from the Channel Islands to internment camps in Germany. Another 200 were deported in January 1943, as a reprisal for a British commando raid.

In 1941–2 approximately 130,000 civilians from Allied countries living and working in colonies invaded by the Japanese were interned. These included men, women and children from the Netherlands, the UK, Australia, New Zealand and the USA . . .

Internment was also carried out in the USA after the Americans entered the war in December 1941. Some 100,000 Japanese-Americans living on the west coast of America were interned, often in very poor conditions.[75]

The injustice and absurdity of such internment is wonderfully captured by Ali Smith in her recent novel *Summer*, where she describes the arrival of a group of German internees on the Isle of Man:

The local island people lining the road as they marched up the hill were watching them with their mouths hanging open.

I think they think we're Nazis, Daniel said. They think we're Nazi prisoners of war.

See, I never would've imagined the NCO marching alongside them said then, that there'd be so many of you Jews who was Nazis. I can't comprehend it. Why would you like the Nazis so much when the Nazis don't like *you* so much?

We're not Nazis, Daniel said. You couldn't get more opposite from Nazis. Didn't they brief you?

Briefed us nothing the soldier said.

We're the ones who thought we'd got away from the Nazis, the man next to Daniel said. We're doctors, teachers, chemists, shopkeepers, labourers, factory workers, you name it. What we're not is Nazis.

Told us nothing, the soldier said. Enemy aliens is what they said. Are you not the Germans then?

The Germans are not all Nazis, the man said.[76]

Even after the internment of these 'enemies', the fear of an enemy within persevered. Neil Storey's book on the mounting fears of invasion in 1940 excerpts the following briefing by the secret service to senior police officers in 1940, giving a sense of the mood of a country at War:

---

[75] BBC Factfile: Civilian Internment 1939–1945, available at https://www.bbc.co.uk/history/ww2peopleswar/timeline/factfiles/nonflash/a6651858.shtml.

[76] *Summer* (London: Hamish Hamilton, 2020) at 147–48.

Racial Minorities of Doubtful Loyalty

1. Irish: This is the only section likely to take extensive action to assist the Germans.
2. Scottish and Welsh Nationalist Movements: Some evidence of German penetration, especially among the Welsh.
3. Germans: None still at large except some women of German nationality or extraction. Might give aid on a small scale to parachutists.
4. Other Refugees: 10,000 Czechs, 20,000 Dutch and Belgians. Some may be considered anti-Nazi. British refugees 6,000 to 7,000 returned from the Low Countries many unable even to speak English.
5. Italians: Most of the members of the Italian Fascist Party have either left the country or been arrested.[77]

The protective regime in the Fourth Geneva Convention now applies some general protections to all civilians.[78] But for a particular set of protected persons (enemy aliens) it provides specific protection, whilst also authorizing internment for such individuals. The condition in the Convention now stipulates that internment is authorized 'only if the security of the Detaining Power makes it absolutely necessary'.[79] This is an objective rather than a subjective test.[80] Nothing more severe than internment or assigned residence is permitted as a measure of control.[81] Today there are specific rules that preclude a state from treating refugees as security risks purely on the basis of their nationality.[82]

Stripped of its historical context and the particular regime of the Fourth Geneva Convention, this power to intern gets invoked or alluded to in the contemporary world in order to justify wide-ranging security detention in all sorts of situations, including counter-terrorism operations and non-international armed conflicts. On balance, it is probably better that this internment regime should be restricted to the situation carefully circumscribed by the treaty, with the attendant full protection found in the Geneva Convention, and not applied by analogy in other circumstances where the full protective regime will not be carried over.[83] It is suggested that we should

---

[77] *Beating the Nazi Invader* (2020) at 178.
[78] GC IV Arts 13–26.
[79] GC IV Art 42.
[80] See Hill-Cawthorne (n 10) at 41.
[81] GC IV Art 41.
[82] GC IV Art 44; Convention Relating to the Status of Refugees (1951) Art 8.
[83] Hill-Cawthorne (n 10) at 74; for a careful look at the advantages and disadvantages of applying this regime by analogy to a non-international armed conflict, see Olson, 'Admissibility

stick to a strict legal interpretation here in order to avoid abusive use of this kind of security internment by governments and non-state actors. If states and other actors want to intern outside this context, they need to find separate legal authority to do this.

Who, then, is a protected person who can be interned under the regime prescribed in this Geneva Convention? The treaty definition is difficult to understand on first reading, but the essential elements are that:

1. There is an international armed conflict between two or more states.
2. The person is in non-occupied territory and under the control of the territorial state.
3. The person is not a national of the detaining state.
4. The person is not a national of a neutral state or of a co-belligerent state with the detaining state, as long as the state of which they are a national has normal diplomatic representation in the state in whose hands they are.
5. The person is not protected under any of the other three Geneva Conventions of 1949 (discussed above).[84]

The attendant protections include the right to access ICRC representatives,[85] a detailed regime concerning treatment of internees almost as comprehensive as that for prisoners of war,[86] and the right to have the detention reconsidered with a review of the admissibility of the internment at least twice a year.[87] In addition, 'unlawful confinement' in this context is a grave breach of this Geneva Convention and a war crime. The crime will be committed either in the context of an initial unlawful detention, or through a failure to apply the periodic procedural protections with a view to possible release.

The International Criminal Tribunal for the former Yugoslavia explained that unlawful confinement occurred:

---

of and Procedures for Internment', in Clapham, Gaeta and Sassòli (eds), *The 1949 Geneva Conventions: A Commentary* (2015) 1327–47 at 1342–44.

[84] See GC IV Art 4, see also the *Pictet Commentary to Geneva Convention IV* (n 74) at 45–51; also explained by Sassòli, *IHL* (n 14) at paras 8.149–8.158; for a discussion of protection for those with the same nationality but different allegiance or ethnicity from the Power in whose hands they find themselves, see Salmón (n 74) at 1142–45.

[85] GC IV Art 143.
[86] GC IV Arts 79–135.
[87] GC IV Art 43.

(i) when a civilian or civilians have been detained in contravention of Article 42 of Geneva Convention IV, *ie*, they are detained without reasonable grounds for believing that the security of the Detaining Power makes it absolutely necessary; and

(ii) where the procedural safeguards required by Article 43 of Geneva Convention IV are not complied with in respect of detained civilians, even where their initial detention may have been justified.[88]

In the *Čelibići Camp* case, the Trial Chamber judgment of the same Tribunal found that the Commission established by the War Presidency in Konjic did not meet the requirements of Article 43, and that the *de facto* commander Mucić was guilty of the war crime of unlawful confinement. The procedural safeguards have to be meaningful:

An initially lawful internment clearly becomes unlawful if the detaining party does not respect the basic procedural rights of the detained persons and does not establish an appropriate court or administrative board as prescribed in article 43 of Geneva Convention IV.[89]

However, it was clear to the Trial Chamber that this Commission did not have the necessary power to decide to order the release of prisoners whose detention could not be considered as being justified for any serious reason. To the contrary, the power of this Commission was limited to initiating investigations of the prisoners and conducting interviews with prisoners in order to obtain relevant information concerning other individuals suspected of armed rebellion outside the prison camp. It was not possible for the members of the Commission to supervise the actual release of prisoners who were suggested for release by its members.[90]

For this crime, participation as a camp guard through mere presence may not be enough to find direct reasonability for committing the war crime. As the Appeals Chamber explained:

[T]he fact alone of a role in some capacity, however junior, in maintaining a prison in which civilians are unlawfully detained is an inadequate basis

---

[88] *Prosecutor v Kordić et al*, IT-95-14/2-T, 26 February 2001, at para 291.

[89] *Prosecutor v Delalić et al*, IT-96-21-T, 16 November 1998, at para 583 (the *Čelibići Camp* case).

[90] Ibid at para 1137.

on which to find primary criminal responsibility of the nature which is denoted by a finding that someone has *committed* a crime. Such responsibility is more properly allocated to those who are responsible for the detention in a more direct or complete sense, such as those who actually place an accused in detention without reasonable grounds to believe that he constitutes a security risk; or who, having some powers over the place of detention, accepts a civilian into detention without knowing that such grounds exist; or who, having power or authority to release detainees, fails to do so despite knowledge that no reasonable grounds for their detention exist, or that any such reasons have ceased to exist.[91]

To be clear, this type of internment covers a narrow category of individuals: for example, it would cover Iraqis in the United States or the United Kingdom during the armed conflicts between those states and Iraq. And of course it would cover Americans and British civilians interned by the Iraqi authorities in Iraq. But, as explained above, nationals of neutral states or co-belligerents could not be interned under this regime. Nor can this regime be applied by analogy to a global war on terror. It is confined to armed conflicts between two states.

9.1.3.2 Civilians under Occupation (International Armed Conflict)

As explained in earlier chapters, in the past, wars led not only to conquest and subjugation, but also to acquisition of territory. Occupation was a temporary situation while the victor negotiated what territory might be acquired, and even the payment owed by the vanquished for the cost of the war. It was only with the emergence in Europe of ideas of national self-determination and sovereignty for European states,[92] that the foundations of occupation law started to go beyond general principles of sparing the civilian population, and included the notion of conserving the political and economic system of the nation under occupation.[93]

---

[91] *Prosecutor v Delalić et al*, IT-96-21-A, 20 February 2001, at para 342.

[92] For the complexity of the scope of the right to self-determination, see Fisch, *The Rights of Self-Determination of Peoples: The Domestication of an Illusion*, tr Mage (2015); Miller, *Is Self-Determination a Dangerous Illusion?* (2020).

[93] For a scholarly coverage of these origins, see Benvenisti, *The International Law of Occupation*, 2nd edn (2012); Arai-Takahashi, 'Preoccupied with Occupation: Critical Examinations of the Historical Development of the Law of Occupation', 94 *IRRC* 885 (2012) 51–80.

Today, as we saw in section 3.6, it is not possible legally to acquire territory by force. Suffice it to recall the words of the Friendly Relations Declaration, adopted by all UN Member States in 1970: 'The territory of a State shall not be the object of acquisition by another State resulting from the threat or use of force. No territorial acquisition resulting from the threat or use of force shall be recognized as legal.'[94]

The modern international law on occupation aims in part at conservation of the legal system of the occupied party,[95] and is supposed to protect the population under occupation, including their public and private property.[96] Contemporary controversy concerns this first aim, and the debate turns on what has become known as 'transformative occupation'.[97] This is where the occupier seeks to change the law of the country under occupation beyond certain limits. The situation is complicated by the fact that the occupier may well be able to argue that the changes are for the good, that they better conform with the occupier's human rights obligations or with democratic principles.[98] The occupier may even argue that it is working for self-determination and liberation of the people. But of course these changes may be mainly for the benefit of the occupier and its nationals (sometimes settled in the occupied territory).[99] Benvenisti's book-length study of occupation highlights how the international legal duties imposed on the occupier were 'transformed into a legal tool extensively invoked by occupants in those areas in which they wished to intervene'. He continues, 'My analysis of occupation shows – and this should not be surprising – that social decisions taken and implemented in occupied territories were never incompatible with outcomes sought by occupants.'[100]

Clearly the changes brought about by the occupying Allies in Germany and Japan at the end of the Second World War went beyond the 'conservationist'

---

[94] A/RES/25/2625. See also Security Council Resolution 242 (1967) preambular para 2.

[95] See Art 43 of the Regulations Respecting the Laws and Customs of War on Land annexed to Hague Convention IV (1907) (hereinafter 'Hague Regulations'), and Arts 64 and 67 of GC IV.

[96] For the detail, see Arai-Takahashi, 'Protection of Private Property', in Clapham, Gaeta and Sassòli (eds), *The 1949 Geneva Conventions: A Commentary* (2015) at 1515–34; and Van Engeland, 'Protection of Public Property', ibid at 1535–50.

[97] Roberts, 'Transformative Military Occupation: Applying the Laws of War and Human Rights', 100 *AJIL* (2006) 580–622.

[98] Discussed in detail ibid and in Fox, 'Transformative Occupation and the Unilateralist Impulse', 94 *IRRC* 885 (2012) 237–66.

[99] See the insightful piece by Gross, especially with regard to decisions taken by the Israeli courts, 'The Righting of the Law of Occupation', in Bhuta (ed), *The Frontiers of Human Rights: Extraterritoriality and Its Challenges* (2016) 21–54.

[100] *The International Law of Occupation* (n 93) at 10–11.

idea and what was necessary to restore and ensure public order. This was acknowledged at the time, and said to be justified by the exceptional circumstances.[101] Today the tension may be expressed in terms of human rights obligations that require the occupier to replace discriminatory law, harsh punishments or inadequate due process rights. But, as just indicated, a critical approach demands careful scrutiny of changes brought about by the occupier and the limits that are imposed by the modern law of occupation.[102] The issue is not simple, as the law not only imposes limits but also requires that the occupier administer the occupied territory. Where significant changes that go beyond the limits imposed by international law are necessary, the preferred option for many commentators is that the Security Council should specifically authorize a departure from rules that limit the right of the occupier to introduce legal changes.

A major problem for the drafters in 1949 was the need to find compromises between the delegations from states that had been occupied during the Second World War, including France, who was also keen to legitimize the role of those engaged in an organized resistance, with those who had recently become occupiers and were more focused on the needs and protection of their military forces. This was, in a way, a departure from the law of war treaties adopted so far, as those earlier texts were concerned with the fate of combatants and associated medical personnel. The story is engaging told by the historian Geoffrey Best:

> Even if the members of opposed armed forces have a dislike, or are taught to have a dislike, for each other, the discipline to which they are normally subject may ensure some respect for law; besides which, the law-protected enemies they are most likely to encounter person-to-person are by definition the least likely to continue to threaten or bother them: surrenderers, prisoners, and the disabled. An army however stands in a different relationship towards an enemy civilian population. Instead of recognizable categories of fellow fighters, once seen never, probably, to be seen again, there is a mass of people alien in more than one sense to the soldiers who have to live among them. A perfectly docile occupied population is scarcely conceivable; and so far as it might exist, it would by most conventional canons

---

[101] Discussed by Roberts, 'Transformative Military Occupation' (n 97) at 601–03.

[102] For an examination of the steps taken by the occupiers in Iraq in 2003–04, see Sassòli, 'Legislation and Maintenance of Public Order and Civil Life by Occupying Powers', 16 *EJIL* (2005) 661–94; for an expert view on the legislation that can be applied by the military authority of the occupying power, see Sassòli, *IHL* (n 14) at paras 8.239–8.246.

of judgment (eg nationalist, patriotic, collectivist, tribal) be contemptible. There can hardly not be some hostility and resistance shown to the uninvited, forceful, menacing stranger.

The awkward questions were therefore inescapably posed: how much trouble should the occupier be prepared to put up with, and how tough was he allowed to get when the amount of trouble became unbearable? From some of the major war-crimes trials – the 'High Command' and 'Hostages' trials above all – came clearly the warning that the toughness could not lawfully go beyond a certain point; but in none of them was it suggested that he must passively submit to whatever indignities and inquiries the occupied population chose to inflict upon him.

The security- and order-maintaining parts of the Civilians Convention show how the Diplomatic Conference trod this tightrope. They were the necessary counterpart to the civilian-protecting parts, which otherwise and on their own must be considered pure fantasy. Much argument and a certain amount of unpleasantness had to be gone through before they were reached. The recently occupied countries found them bitter pills to swallow. The countries with experience as occupiers feared lest they were giving away too much.[103]

9.1.3.2.1 Internment and Punishment of Civilians in Occupied Territory

This balancing act is demonstrated by the regime for internment. As with enemy aliens in the territory of a belligerent state, those under occupation are susceptible to internment, and this is covered by a similar regime. Because the criteria are complex and slightly different from those outlined above, we might again list the criteria for being a protected person in the context of occupation.

1. There is a foreign occupation by a state of territory over which it does not have sovereignty (there need be no resistance) and the occupation continues as long as there is no consent to it.[104]

---

[103] Best, *War and Law Since 1945* (1994) at 124; the recent study by Longobardo concludes at one point that 'international humanitarian law offers scant indications regarding the implementation of the duty to restore and ensure public order': *The Use of Armed Force in Occupied Territory* (2018) at 184.

[104] For what constitutes an occupation, see Sassòli, 'The Concept and Beginning of Occupation', in Clapham, Gaeta and Sassòli (eds), *The 1949 Geneva Conventions: A Commentary* (2015) 1389–419. For the controversy concerning the applicability of the wording of Common

2. The person is in occupied territory and under the control of the occupying state.
3. The person is not a national of the occupying state.
4. The person is not a national of a co-belligerent state with the occupying state, as long as the state of which they are a national has normal diplomatic representation in the state in whose hands they are.
5. The person is not protected under any of the other three Geneva Conventions of 1949 (discussed above).[105]

Internment of security detainees is foreseen under the following conditions:

If the Occupying Power considers it necessary, for imperative reasons of security, to take safety measures concerning protected persons, it may, at the most, subject them to assigned residence or to internment.

Decisions regarding such assigned residence or internment shall be made according to a regular procedure to be prescribed by the Occupying Power in accordance with the provisions of the present Convention. This procedure shall include the right of appeal for the parties concerned. Appeals shall be decided with the least possible delay. In the event of the decision being upheld, it shall be subject to periodical review, if possible every six months, by a competent body set up by the said Power.[106]

Interestingly, when it came to negotiating the Civilians Convention after the Second World War, it was admitted that the people under occupation could not be expected to respect the occupier as they would their own government. While the rules that recognize the right of members of an organized resistance movement to prisoner of war status are dealt with in the Prisoner of War

---

Art 2 to the Geneva Conventions to the Israeli occupation of Palestinian territory, see the 2004 Advisory Opinion of the International Court of Justice discussed below. For the arguments as to why the law of occupation continues to apply with regard to Gaza, see Dinstein, *The International Law of Belligerent Occupation*, 2nd edn (2019) at 296–303; see also the 'Report of the detailed findings of the independent international Commission of inquiry on the protests in the Occupied Palestinian Territory', UN Doc A/HRC/40/CRP.2, 18 March 2019 at paras 59–67 (original: English).

[105] See GC IV Arts 2 and 4; see also the *Pictet Commentary to Geneva Convention IV* (n 74) at 45–51; also explained by Sassòli, *IHL* (n 14) at paras 8.149–8.158; for a discussion of protection for those with the same nationality but different allegiance or ethnicity from the Power in whose hands they find themselves, see Salmón (n 74) at 1142–45.

[106] GC IV Art 78; the internment regime can also be applied to benefit those who have been convicted of certain offences against the occupier – see Art 68.

Convention,[107] provisions were also made that recognized the general lack of allegiance to the occupier for those under occupation. A second provision provides for detention limited in proportion to the offence committed where

> [p]rotected persons ... commit an offence which is solely intended to harm the Occupying Power, but which does not constitute an attempt on the life or limb of members of the occupying forces or administration, nor a grave collective danger, nor seriously damage the property of the occupying forces or administration or the installations used by them.[108]

The use of the death penalty is limited, and the same provision states:

> The death penalty may not be pronounced against a protected person unless the attention of the court has been particularly called to the fact that since the accused is not a national of the Occupying Power, he is not bound to it by any duty of allegiance.

In addition, the occupier cannot impose the death penalty for spying, sabotage or intentional acts causing death, where the death penalty did not exist in the law of the occupied state before occupation. This was fiercely resisted by the United Kingdom and the United States, along with some of their allies. Schabas recounts how they argued that 'if the death penalty in an occupied territory were eliminated, it would only provoke soldiers in the occupying army to take matters into their own hands and summarily execute civilians rather than arrest them and turn them over to the judicial authorities'.[109] As the historian Geoffrey Best points out, this sort of provision divided 'those who had experienced the nastiest sort of military occupation' from those 'who resignedly assumed that military occupation could never be nice'. For the British and the Americans it 'seemed lunacy', as it 'appeared to mean that a capital-punishment State could protect its occupation-resisting civilians – even those who killed any number of occupying troops, etc – by the neat expedient of declaring the death penalty abolished just before the occupying forces arrived'.[110] In the end, the provision was put to the vote and, having

---

[107] See GC III Art 4A(2); and see also AP I Arts 43 and 44.

[108] GC IV Art 68; and see *Pictet Commentary to Geneva Convention IV* (n 74) at 344, explaining that the idea is to give persons guilty of minor offences the benefit of the conditions in Arts 79 et seq, and that the provision is a 'humane one and was intended to draw a distinction between such offenders and common criminals'.

[109] Schabas, *The Abolition of the Death Penalty in International Law*, 2nd edn (1997).

[110] Best, *War and Law Since 1945* (n 103) at 126.

lost the vote, a number of states entered formal reservations to the treaty to ensure they could impose the death penalty in such circumstances.[111] These remain in place for the United States, South Korea, Pakistan, Suriname and Uruguay. The United Kingdom and a number of other states have withdrawn their reservations on this point.

My aim here is to illustrate that this new Fourth Geneva Convention (the Civilians Convention) was conceived as covering protected civilians who would engage in acts of sabotage and resistance. On capture and trial they remain civilians protected by the Convention. If they are not civilians, they must be members of the armed forces of a state, or members of an organized resistance movement belonging to a state party to the conflict, and they would find protection under the Prisoner of War Convention.[112] A protected person who is a civilian does not lose their civilian status through any acts or activity.[113] The idea of a third category of person who is neither a combatant/ fighter nor a civilian makes no sense in the context of protecting those in the hands of the enemy. The introduction of such a third category of persons 'engaging in hostilities' in the US *Law of War Manual* has been roundly criticized as not only engendering confusion, but also suggesting the absence of protection, leading to a result that 'directly contravenes the letter and spirit' of the international law of armed conflict.[114]

9.1.3.2.2 Deportations and Transfers

A last topic related to occupied territory is deportations and transfers. The Convention generally prohibits forcible transfers in the territory, as well as deportations of protected persons out of the occupied territory.[115] Unlawful

---

[111] Eg 'The United States reserve the right to impose the death penalty in accordance with the provisions of Article 68, paragraph 2, without regard to whether the offences referred to therein are punishable by death under the law of the occupied territory at the time the occupation begins.' *Final Record of the Diplomatic Conference of Geneva of 1949*, vol I, Federal Political Department, Berne, p 346.

[112] GC III Art 4; and see Del Mar, 'The Requirement of "Belonging" under International Humanitarian Law', 21 *JICJ* 1 (2010) 105–24.

[113] See Dörmann, 'Unlawful Combatants', in Clapham and Gaeta (eds), *The Oxford Handbook of International Law in Armed Conflict* (2014) 605–23 esp at 607–13. Of course if a civilian does not qualify as a protected person due to their nationality then they would not be protected by the detailed regime of the Civilians Convention but rather by customary international law and AP I Art 75. For those outside occupied territory, see below.

[114] Blank, 'Muddying the Waters: The Need for Precision-Guided Terminology in the DoD Law of War Manual', in Newton (ed), *The United States Department of Defense Law of War Manual: Commentary and Critique* (2018) 261–81 at 274.

[115] GC IV Art 49.

transfers and deportations are grave breaches of the Convention (war crimes).

The Convention also states that 'The Occupying Power shall not deport or transfer parts of its own civilian population into the territory it occupies.'[116] It is this prohibition that renders illegal the establishment of settlements in occupied territory, and which is invoked in the context of the Israeli settlements in the territories they occupy. In addition, the International Criminal Court Statute includes a war crime of 'The transfer, directly or indirectly, by the Occupying Power of parts of its own civilian population into the territory it occupies, or the deportation or transfer of all or parts of the population of the occupied territory within or outside this territory'.[117]

The Israeli authorities and courts have claimed that the prohibition on transfer into occupied territory in the Geneva Convention is not applicable to Israel. This claim involves various arguments: first, that the Civilians Convention of 1949 does not apply as a matter of law to the occupation of the West Bank because Israel does not consider that the territory belongs to another state; second, Israel considers that this provision should only apply to *forcible* transfers of their population into the occupied territory; and, lastly, Israel argues that the Convention (even if it were applicable) and any relevant customary international law have not been incorporated into Israeli law, and therefore no prohibition could be enforced in the domestic courts of Israel.

The arguments that the Fourth Geneva Convention does not apply in this context and that the prohibition only relates to forced transfers have been convincingly rebutted, including in the findings of the International Court of Justice in its Advisory Opinion on the *Legal Consequences of the Construction of a Wall in the Occupied Palestinian Territories*.[118] The Court also stated with regard to the prohibition on transfers into occupied territory:

---

[116] GC IV Art 49(6).

[117] ICC Statute Art 8(2)(b)(viii); see also AP I Art 85(4)(a).

[118] 'The Court notes that, according to the first paragraph of Article 2 of the Fourth Geneva Convention, that Convention is applicable when two conditions are fulfilled: that there exists an armed conflict (whether or not a state of war has been recognized); and that the conflict has arisen between two contracting parties. If those two conditions are satisfied, the Convention applies, in particular, in any territory occupied in the course of the conflict by one of the contracting parties. The object of the second paragraph of Article 2 is not to restrict the scope of application of the Convention, as defined by the first paragraph, by excluding therefrom territories not falling under the sovereignty of one of the contracting parties. It is directed simply to making it clear that, even if occupation effected during the conflict met no armed resistance, the Convention is still applicable.' Advisory Opinion of 9 July 2004 at para 96. For further detail, see Meron, 'The West Bank and International Humanitarian Law on the Eve of the Fiftieth Anniversary of the Six-Day War', 111 *AJIL* (2017) 357–75 at 361–64.

That provision prohibits not only deportations or forced transfers of population such as those carried out during the Second World War, but also any measures taken by an occupying Power in order to organize or encourage transfers of parts of its own population into the occupied territory.[119]

More recently, Theodor Meron, who was the Legal Advisor of the Israel Ministry of Foreign Affairs in 1967, has revisited these issues, referencing the legal opinions he gave at the time and explaining the flaws in the reasoning of the Israeli authorities and judges. At one level he engages in a forensic interpretation of the international treaties involved, and points to the 'erroneous' interpretations offered by others. At another level he highlights the humanitarian nature of the Convention, and the way it provides for inalienable rights. In his expression, it is a 'people-oriented convention' unconcerned with legal claims to territory.[120] He makes the important point that the Convention references rights and privileges for protected persons that cannot be simply restricted, overridden or eliminated. The occupier owes a special duty under international law to foreigners under its occupation:

There is no question, as the Supreme Court has acknowledged on many occasions, that members of the Arab population of the West Bank are persons protected by the Convention. Conversely, however, Jewish settlers on the West Bank, as citizens of the occupant, to whom they owe allegiance, are not protected persons. Any discrimination between the two groups can only be justified when the Arab population, as constituting protected persons, benefits from additional rights accorded by the Convention. In reality, however, it is the Arab population that is subjected to discrimination.[121]

In sum, the regime for occupied territory has multiple aspects that need to be reconciled while respecting the rights of protected persons. First, the Hague Regulations recognize that the occupier shall take all 'measures in his power to restore, and ensure, as far as possible, public order and safety',[122] and the Geneva Civilians Convention states that the occupier 'may take such

---

[119] Advisory Opinion of July 2004 at para 120.

[120] Meron, 'The West Bank' (n 118) 366–67.

[121] Ibid at 369 (footnote omitted).

[122] Hague Regulations (n 95) Art 43; note the only authentic version of the treaty (French) uses an expression 'l'ordre et la vie publics', which is considered as covering a wider range of matters; see Arai-Takahashi, 'Law-Making and the Judicial Guarantees in Occupied Territories', in Clapham, Gaeta and Sassòli (eds), The 1949 Geneva Conventions: A Commentary (2015) 1421–53 at 1426.

measures of control and security in regard to protected persons as may be necessary as a result of the war'.[123] Second, the category of protected persons is defined as those who are foreigners in the eyes of the occupier; their rights are inalienable and cannot be bargained away or surrendered.[124] Third, the occupier is obligated to respect, 'unless absolutely prevented, the laws in force in the country',[125] while at the same time having a responsibility for the welfare of the population under occupation,[126] which over time inevitably means expanding duties towards the population in occupied territory.[127] For Greenwood there is also a 'duty to prevent economic collapse as well as a breakdown of law and order. This duty probably extends to requiring the occupant to ensure that there is a functioning currency in the occupied territory and that essential services are maintained'.[128] Lastly, the 1949 Civilians Convention and Additional Protocol I have created a grave breaches regime.[129] This legal regime not only criminalizes certain acts related to occupied territory, but also creates an obligation to search for, prosecute or extradite those alleged to have committed or ordered such grave breaches. We will examine these obligations in more detail in the following chapter on war crimes.

9.1.4 Civilians in Unoccupied Territory Undergoing Hostilities (International Armed Conflict)

There is some debate over the protective reach of the Civilians Convention to civilians caught up during an 'invasion phase' and before an occupation has been established.[130] Sassòli has suggested that civilians in invaded

---

[123] GC IV Art 27(4).

[124] For detail see d'Argent (n 18).

[125] Hague Regulations (n 95) Art 43. For detailed look at the scope of this phrase and the limits of what an occupier can do, see Benvenisti, *The International Law of Occupation* (n 93) at 89–95.

[126] See in particular GC IV Arts 50–63.

[127] Benvenisti grounds this in Art 43 of the Hague Regulations and goes on to say that 'This obligation is more pronounced in occupations where the occupant becomes actively involved in managing daily life and controls the institutions that run local public institution, and the local population thus becomes reliant on them.' *The International Law of Occupation* (n 93) at 87.

[128] Greenwood, 'The Administration of Occupied Territory in International Law', in Playfair (ed), *International Law in the Administration of Occupied Territories* (1992) 241–66 at 246.

[129] GC IV Arts 146 and 147; and AP I Art 85.

[130] For a full articulation of the debate, see Zwanenburg, Bothe and Sassòli, 'Is the Law of Occupation Applicable to the Invasion Phase?', 94 *IRRC* 885 (2012) 29–50.

(as opposed to occupied) territory must have some protection under the Convention:

> Most of the rules of Convention IV benefit only 'protected civilians', as defined in Article 4, who 'find themselves, in case of a conflict or occupation, in the hands of a Party to the conflict or occupying power of which they are not nationals.' When inhabitants of an invaded territory fall under the control of invading forces, such as by arrest and detention, they are without a doubt in the hands of a party to the conflict of which they are not nationals and are therefore protected persons. As such, they must benefit from some rules of Part III of Convention IV dealing with the 'status and treatment of protected persons'.[131]

The problem is that these civilians are strictly speaking in neither of the two categories of protected persons we dealt with above: they are neither enemy aliens in the territory of a party to the conflict (like the Germans interned in the UK), nor are they non-nationals in the hands of an occupying power. Furthermore, some of the far-reaching obligations of the occupier could not be fulfilled during the invasion phase (eg support for educational institutions). Sassòli's solution is a shift to 'functional occupation', with a 'sliding scale' of obligations. For him 'the very concept of occupation itself can also be understood using a functional approach under which a territory may be considered occupied along a sliding scale for the purpose of the applicability of certain rules of IHL of military occupation but not for others'.[132]

In any event, any civilians, or indeed members of the armed forces, would be protected by Article 75 of the Additional Protocol of 1977, which is considered, including by the United States, which is not a party, to contain a set of binding obligations.[133] These human rights-style protections are comprehensive and deserve to be constantly recalled. They include the right to be treated humanely, protection from indecent assault and threats to the life or well-being of persons, separate quarters and supervision for female detainees, prohibitions on the taking of hostages, collective punishment, and arbitrary detention, as well as guarantees for a fair trial.

---

[131] Sassòli, *IHL* (n 14) at para 8.217.

[132] Ibid at para 8.221.

[133] 'The US Government will therefore choose out of a sense of legal obligation to treat the principles set forth in Article 75 as applicable to any individual it detains in an international armed conflict, and expects all other nations to adhere to these principles as well.' White House, 'Fact Sheet: New Actions on Guantanamo and Detainee Policy', 7 March 2011.

9.2 Protection in a Non-International Armed Conflict

While the basic protections for all those in the hands of the enemy also apply in non-international armed conflict – guarantees of humane treatment and fair trial for offences related to the conflict[134] – the treaties make no provision for combatant immunity or internment without trial in non-international armed conflicts. The issues of targeting and detention therefore require separate discussions, not least because of the controversies that surround the unwritten law in this area. It bears repeating at this point that around 90% of the armed conflicts in the world have to be classed as non-international armed conflicts.[135]

9.2.1 Fighters, Direct Participation in Hostilities and Continuous Combat Function

We saw in Chapter 7 that a military objective is limited to those objects that both make an effective contribution to military action and whose destruction at that time offers a definite military advantage. We also saw that civilians can lose their protection from attack where they engage in a variety of acts harmful to the enemy. These acts could include: an armed attack by whatever means; taking up firing positions or moving in military configuration towards an objective; positioning, emplacement and/or detonation of mines, booby traps or emplaced munitions; conducting reconnaissance, surveillance or espionage on behalf of an opposing force, and so on. On the other hand we also concluded, along with General Rogers, that civilian activity that does not render the civilians legitimate targets includes 'Working in commercial institutions that indirectly support the war effort by financing the government through taxation.'[136]

---

[134] See Common Art 3 to the Four Geneva Conventions of 1949 (reproduced below) and AP II of 1977. In addition most of the rules of customary international law apply, see Henckaerts and Doswald-Beck, *Customary International Humanitarian Law* (n 27); the exceptions relate mostly to combatant immunity, prisoners of war and the law covering occupation – see further Sassòli, *IHL* (n 14) at paras 7.44 et seq.

[135] Cameron (ICRC), 'The Geneva Conventions: 150 Years of Codification of the Laws of War' in Hazan, Berchtold, Ducimetière and Imperiali (eds), *War and Peace* (2019) 122–27 at 126; for one recent listing of the different conflicts around the world divided according to the legal classification of the Geneva Conventions as international or non-international, see Bellal (ed), *The War Report: Armed Conflicts in 2018* (2019), which lists 7 active international armed conflicts, 11 belligerent occupations and 51 non-international armed conflicts.

[136] Rogers, *Law on the Battlefield*, 3rd edn (2012) at 15.

The tricky question, then, is how to describe those who can be targeted in a non-international armed conflict. States will not accept that the armed forces of the non-state actor are to be seen as *combatants* in a legal sense, as this implies a right to fight, immunity from prosecution for fighting and prisoner of war status on capture. As we shall see, they might be labelled 'fighters', but this does not really help in practical terms. In a conflict involving non-state actors, it will usually be difficult to determine who really is a member of the armed forces of the non-state group as opposed to a local inhabitant or a supporter.

This problem is explicitly recognized in the US *Law of War Manual*:

> Whether a person has joined a non-State armed group may be a difficult factual question. Non-State armed groups may not use formal indicia of membership (*eg*, uniforms or identity cards), or members of these groups may seek to conceal their association with the group. It may be appropriate to use circumstantial or functional information to assess whether a person is part of a non-State armed group.[137]

The terminology for those fighting against the armed forces of a state in a non-international armed conflict is convoluted and confusing. As already mentioned, most states and manuals will avoid the expression 'combatants' to avoid giving the impression that the person has a right to fight and combatant immunity. Additional Protocol II outlaws attacks on civilians and then states that this protection does not apply 'for such time as they take a direct part in hostilities'.[138] The US *Manual* uses the term 'private persons who engage in hostilities';[139] The expert *Manual on the Law of Non-International Armed Conflicts* refers to 'fighters' for the armed forces of both sides, and in that context 'civilians who actively (directly) participate in hostilities are treated as "fighters"'.[140]

In their national law and military manuals, states employ various terms such as 'unlawful combatants', 'unprivileged belligerents', 'enemy combatants', 'rebel forces', 'armed rebels', 'insurgents', 'enemy armed forces', 'enemy soldiers' and 'soldiers in the enemy army'.[141] The idea of labelling all members of the

---

[137] At para 4.18.4.1, 'Being Part of a Hostile, Non-State Armed Group' (footnote omitted).

[138] AP II Art 13(3).

[139] See para 4.18.1.

[140] Schmitt, Garraway and Dinstein, *The Manual on the Law of Non-International Armed Conflict: With Commentary* (2006) at paras 1.1.2 and 1.1.3.

[141] See the examples collected at https://ihl-databases.icrc.org/customary-ihl/eng/docs/v2_rul_rule1, esp part B.

armed forces of the non-state side as 'fighters' is tempting, as it implies that they are doing something violent and could therefore be liable to attack, but as the ICRC points out, the term 'fighter' 'would be translated as "combatant" in a number of languages and is therefore not wholly satisfactory'.[142] Nor is it satisfactory when it is a way of legitimizing the killing. According to the US *Law of War Manual*, 'belonging to an armed group makes a person liable to being made the object of attack regardless of whether he or she is taking a direct part in hostilities';[143] such an individual simply standing queuing for food or sleeping 'remains the lawful object of attack'.

The scope of activity that renders you liable to be labelled (and by implication targetable) as a 'fighter', 'unprivileged combatant', 'exercising a continuous combat function' or part of 'hostile forces' is extremely controversial, and there is no guidance in international treaties. Where labelling leads to targeting, it should in my view be rejected. The latest New Zealand *Manual* (2019) captured the point well with this paragraph:

DIRECT PARTICIPATION IS NOT A STATUS

6.5.3 'Direct participation in hostilities' refers to the actions of a person; it does not confer a separate legal status. Some of New Zealand's coalition partners use the terms *unlawful combatants* or *unprivileged belligerents* to describe persons who are not combatants but who take a direct part in hostilities. These terms are not used in this manual to avoid any suggestion that such persons fall between combatant and civilian status and can be denied fundamental rights as a result. Terms such as 'insurgent', 'freedom-fighter', 'jihadi', 'terrorist' or 'rebel' are commonly used to describe persons who do not have combatant status but who take a direct part in the hostilities. None of these terms define the legal status of the person concerned under LOAC [the law of armed conflict]. Terms such as 'counter-insurgency operations' relate to a method of operation rather than the legal status of the persons concerned.

The point is that, in certain non-international armed conflicts, care should be taken before resorting to status-based killing where it is unclear who belongs to the armed forces on the rebel side or is directly participating in hostilities. We should hesitate before accepting assertions that someone is alleged to be a combatant, fighter, exercising a continuous combat function, directly

---

[142] Henckaerts and Doswald-Beck, *Customary International Humanitarian Law* (n 27) at 13.
[143] At para 5.7.1.

participating in hostilities or substantially contributing to the enemy's capacity to engage in combat.

A recent reminder of how such terms come to be read as justifying unjustified lethal violence emerged from the inquiry into allegations against Australian forces in Afghanistan:

> Direct participation in hostilities. Dr Crompvoets [a sociologist from the Australian National University] was told that 'Direct participation in hostilities' was another tool used by Australian Special Forces to commit 'just about any atrocity that took their fancy'. One example of this related to 'squirters' – a reference to villagers running away when a force was inserted by helicopter. The scenario conveyed to Dr Crompvoets was that Special Forces would open fire, killing many men (and sometimes women and children) as they ran away. She was told that Special Forces would then contrive a plausible excuse, such as the squirters 'were running away from us to their weapons caches'. These were, she was told, 'sanctioned massacres'.[144]

Following a long series of discussions from 2003 to 2009, the ICRC concluded its interpretative guidance, which features two categories of persons (in addition to the armed forces of a state) it is said can be targeted under international humanitarian law. At the same time it suggests there is an additional level of restraint based on necessity and other branches of international law.[145] The guidance separates those directly participating in

---

[144] 'Report of Inquiry under Division 4a of Part 4 of the Inspector-General of the Australian Defence Force Regulation 2016 into Questions of Unlawful Conduct Concerning The Special Operations Task Group in Afghanistan' (2020) at 120, para 7b.

[145] The guidance includes such a condition in Principle IX, 'Restraints on the use of force in direct attack: In addition to the restraints imposed by international humanitarian law on specific means and methods of warfare, and without prejudice to further restrictions that may arise under other applicable branches of international law, the kind and degree of force which is permissible against persons not entitled to protection against direct attack must not exceed what is actually necessary to accomplish a legitimate military purpose in the prevailing circumstances.' The inclusion of this principle was, however, rejected by certain military experts who had participated in the process (see the discussion of military necessity in section 7.4 above), and the US *Manual on the Law of War* explicitly rejects the idea of necessity creating an obligation to capture rather than kill (see para 2.2.3.1 esp fns 44 and 45). For a theoretical discussion of the normative process and the subsequent impact of the guidance at the national level, see Yip, 'The ICRC's Interpretive Guidance on the Notion of Direct Participation in Hostilities: Sociological and Democratic Legitimacy in Domestic Legal Orders', 8 *Transnational Legal Theory* (2017) 224–46. She argues (at 234) that even if the rule contains a degree of determinacy that leads to certainty, nevertheless, 'where legitimate targets are not hors de combat and yet are in a situation where their threats can easily be neutralised through capture, killing them seems repugnant to an ordinary sense of justice'.

hostilities from those members of the armed group who can be targeted due to their 'continuous combat function'. Those who fall into the latter group are assumed to be targetable even in the absence of a hostile act:

> Continuous combat function requires lasting integration into an organized armed group acting as the armed forces of a non-State party to an armed conflict. Thus, individuals whose continuous function involves the preparation, execution, or command of acts or operations amounting to direct participation in hostilities are assuming a continuous combat function. An individual recruited, trained and equipped by such a group to continuously and directly participate in hostilities on its behalf can be considered to assume a continuous combat function even before he or she first carries out a hostile act.[146]

This explanation of status-based targeting is not universally accepted. For some it widens the range of people who can be targeted too far. For others, including various military experts, as well as some armed forces (primarily the United States and Israel), the category created by this test is too narrow. They claim that, as a matter of law, the armed forces of the state are entitled to target those who are simply members of the military wing of organized armed groups.[147] The explanation given is that limiting those who can be targeted to those who are continuously involved in the military operations of the rebel side is unfair on the non-involved members of the armed forces of the state who, it seems, can be targeted at any time under the rule. One prominent critic explains it thus:

> [B]y limiting continuous loss of protection to members of organized armed groups with a continuous combat function, the ICRC gives regularly participating civilians a privileged, unbalanced, and unjustified status of protection in comparison to members of the opposing armed forces, who are continuously targetable.[148]

---

[146] Melzer, *Interpretive Guidance on the Notion of Direct Participation in Hostilities under International Humanitarian Law* (2009) at 34.

[147] See for example the findings in Schmitt and Merriam, 'The Tyranny of Context: Israeli Targeting Practices in Legal Perspective', 37 *University of Pennsylvania Journal of International Law* 1 (2015) 53–139 at 112–13.

[148] Boothby, '"And For Such Time As": The Time Dimension to Direct Participation in Hostilities', 42 *New York University Journal of International Law and Politics* 3 (2010) 741–68 at 743; the same point is made by the Israeli Defense Forces in Schmitt and Merriam (n 147) at 113.

This complaint is, in a way, surprising, as the armed forces of a state do not really consider that their forces are targetable at all. Each attack on the armed forces is considered by the state as an act of sedition, or terrorism, and criminal. No one captured for attacking the armed forces of a state in a non-international armed conflict is today considered to have done no wrong.

At the least protective end of the spectrum of ideas as to who can be targeted we see the US *Manual*, extending the meaning of taking a direct part in hostilities so that this activity

> extends beyond merely engaging in combat and also includes certain acts that are an integral part of combat operations or that effectively and substantially contribute to an adversary's ability to conduct or sustain combat operations. However, taking a direct part in hostilities does not encompass the general support that members of the civilian population provide to their State's war effort, such as by buying war bonds.[149]

The US *Manual* has been specifically criticized by Adil Ahmed Haque as it 'broadly construes taking a direct part in hostilities to include making a *particularly valuable* contribution to the war effort'.[150] He also questions the myth of the 'farmer by day, guerrilla by night', and suggests that there is no need to weaken the rule that protects civilians by resorting to metaphors such as the 'revolving door'. As he explains:

> Simply put, a civilian who is in fact a 'farmer by day, guerrilla by night' will look like a guerrilla and be treated as such. In those exceptional cases in which an attacker has such detailed information about an individual that she determines that the individual is repeatedly fighting for an armed group but is *not* a functional member of that group, the attacker likely has effective control over the area or is monitoring the individual using a remotely piloted vehicle. If the attacker has effective control over the area, then typically she can arrest, detain, or intern the individual, and kill her if she forcibly resists. If the attacker is monitoring the individual using a remotely piloted vehicle, then typically she can continue to monitor the individual and kill her if and only if she again takes a direct part in hostilities.[151]

---

[149] US *Law of War Manual* (2016) at para 5.8.3 (footnote omitted).

[150] Haque, 'Misdirected: Targeting and Attack under the DoD Manual', in Newton (ed), *The United States Department of Defense Law of War Manual: Commentary and Critique* (2018) 225–60 at 236.

[151] Ibid at 241–42; *contra* Dinstein, who has argued 'When a person behaves as a "farmer by day, fighter by night" several times in a row, he can be considered DPIH [directly participating

Moreover, some human rights experts question the whole concept of continuous combat function as it, in effect, creates a 'status determination' that could lead to erroneous targeting where a fighter has disengaged. As Philip Alston cautions, 'If States are to accept this category, the onus will be on them to show that the evidentiary basis is strong.'[152]

Hampson has raised a more fundamental objection, questioning whether there ought not to be more recourse to a law-and-order paradigm that more closely follows the standards applicable under human rights law. This, she says, is particularly appropriate in smaller non-international armed conflicts:

> In low-intensity armed conflicts, the situation is likely to be made worse if armed forces target by reference to status rather than behavior. Mistakes and 'collateral casualties' may be even less well tolerated by the civilian population than in high-intensity NIACs [non-international armed conflicts]. The issue is not whether armed forces can be used to deal with organized armed violence during an emergency, but whether whatever forces are used are applying rules based on a law and order paradigm or an armed conflict paradigm.[153]

Turning to the ICRC's interpretive guidance on direct participation in hostilities, Hampson explains why the idea of continuous combat function does not necessarily flow from the concept of combatants and the law in the treaties:

> The status of combatant exists only in IACs [international armed conflicts]. While it is readily understandable that members of an organized armed group are not regarded as combatants, implying as it does an entitlement to fight, this does raise an interesting question about the status of members of the State's armed forces. . . . Although an individual has no right in international law to participate in a NIAC, he is not committing an international crime by doing so, but obviously he is very likely to be committing a crime

---

in hostilities] on a 24/7 basis. That is of tremendous practical import, since it may prove impossible to take the person out while he is lying in ambush.' ' "Direct Participation in Hostilities" ', 18 *Tilburg Law Review* (2017) 3–16 at 13.

[152] See Alston, *Report of the Special Rapporteur on extrajudicial, summary or arbitrary executions: Study on targeted killings*, A/HRC/14/24/Add.6, 28 May 2010 at para 66.

[153] 'Direct Participation in Hostilities and the Interoperability of the Law of Armed Conflict and Human Rights Law' (n 1) at 197.

under domestic law. Similarly, he will not commit an international crime if he kills a member of the State's armed forces or a member of another organized group, but he will commit an international crime if he breaches the rules on the conduct of hostilities by intentionally killing a civilian, for example.

The treaty rule that addresses DPH [direct participation in hostilities] is the same in IACs and NIACs. Civilians enjoy the protection afforded against the effects of hostilities 'unless and for such time as they take a direct part in hostilities.' Whatever the difficulties regarding the time during which a person can be attacked or the conduct that constitutes 'taking a direct part,' it is clear that the person has to be doing something that makes him a target of attack. In other words, that depends on behavior and not status.[154]

Sassòli, who has given the matter considerable thought, is very clear:

[T]he difficult and complex question arises in practice as to how government forces can determine that a person has a 'continuous combat function' for an armed group while he or she does not commit hostile acts. In my opinion, the enemy must base its targeting decisions on appearances except where very reliable intelligence information exists. Therefore, in the absence of sound intelligence information to the contrary, those who do not identify themselves as members of an armed group are civilians who may only be attacked if and for such time as they commit acts of direct participation.[155]

9.2.2 Detention in Non-International Armed Conflict

As we saw in sections 9.1.2 and 9.1.3, the Geneva Conventions specifically provide for internment regimes for prisoners of war and civilians constituting a security threat in international armed conflict. These regimes come with specific protections: there are procedures for reviewing the appropriateness of any individual internment[156] and for the ICRC to have access to internees,[157] as well as for certain protected persons to communicate with

---

[154] Ibid at 198 (footnotes omitted).
[155] Sassòli, *IHL* (n 14) at para 8.318.
[156] See Art 5 of GC III; and Arts 43, 68, 78 of GC IV.
[157] See Art 126 of GC III; and Arts 76 and 143 of GC IV.

the ICRC and other organizations.[158] The grave breaches regime applies to protected persons who are so interned, and operates to demand that all states search for and bring before their own courts anyone alleged to have committed such grave breaches against these internees. These regimes were not extended to non-international armed conflict in the humanitarian law treaties.

Nevertheless, a minimal protection regime is found in Common Article 3 to the Four Geneva Conventions and is universally applicable. Serious violations committed against persons taking no active part in the hostilities constitute war crimes at the international level. Common Article 3 provides in part:

> In the case of armed conflict not of an international character occurring in the territory of one of the High Contracting Parties, each Party to the conflict shall be bound to apply, as a minimum, the following provisions:
>
> 1) Persons taking no active part in the hostilities, including members of armed forces who have laid down their arms and those placed *hors de combat* by sickness, wounds, detention, or any other cause, shall in all circumstances be treated humanely, without any adverse distinction founded on race, colour, religion or faith, sex, birth or wealth, or any other similar criteria.
>
> To this end, the following acts are and shall remain prohibited at any time and in any place whatsoever with respect to the above-mentioned persons:
>
> *a)* violence to life and person, in particular murder of all kinds, mutilation, cruel treatment and torture;
>
> *b)* taking of hostages;
>
> *c)* outrages upon personal dignity, in particular, humiliating and degrading treatment;
>
> *d)* the passing of sentences and the carrying out of executions without previous judgment pronounced by a regularly constituted court, affording all the judicial guarantees which are recognized as indispensable by civilized peoples.
>
> 2) The wounded, sick and shipwrecked shall be collected and cared for.
>
> An impartial humanitarian body, such as the International Committee of the Red Cross, may offer its services to the Parties to the conflict.[159]

---

[158] See Art 30 of GC IV.
[159] Art 3 of GC II.

The controversy comes when this protective regime, which creates obligations for both the state and the non-state party to the conflict, is claimed by states to authorize detention abroad. In the past, a state that detained insurgents on its territory applied its national law to such detentions, and there would be a legal basis for detention in the law. If no national law authorized the detention it would be unlawful, and could be challenged using *habeas corpus* or a similar human rights claim. Now that states detain outside their national borders, most dramatically in Guantánamo, but also in places such as Afghanistan and Iraq, the question has arisen whether there is an inherent right to detain under the laws of war, or whether human rights law demands not just the right to challenge such a detention using a fair and accessible procedure, but also that the state find a legal basis for detention.

As with the issue of targeting fighters discussed above, the question of reciprocity lurks in the background. Just as states do not accept that it is acceptable for armed groups to target them with lethal force, nor do they lightly accept that armed groups can detain their soldiers until the end of the conflict. This is sometimes said to explain why there is no provision for internment in non-international armed conflicts.[160] Nevertheless, in the context of the military action in Afghanistan and Iraq, the claim has been made that the law of war contains an inherent right for states to detain fighters and others who pose a security risk. This has recently been challenged as contradicting the human right not to be arbitrarily detained.

The United Kingdom Supreme Court faced with such a challenge declined to find that international humanitarian law contained such an inherent right to detain. The majority chose instead to find that the Security Council had provided the necessary authority. Lord Sumption's judgment explains: 'I conclude that in both Iraq and Afghanistan, the relevant Security Council Resolutions in principle constituted authority in international law for the detention of members of the opposing armed forces whenever it was required for imperative reasons of security.'[161]

All forms of detention, whether by the government forces or by the armed opposition, will need to have a legal basis that allows for a degree of predictability so that the armed forces and inhabitants know what behaviour can

---

[160] *Serdar Mohammed v Secretary of State for Defence* [2015] EWCA (Civ) 843 (Eng) [178], and in the Supreme Court [2017] UKSC 2 [10], [127], [158] and [263]; and see the references in Clapham, 'Detention by Armed Groups under International Law', 93 *International Law Studies* (2017) 1–44 at 8–9.

[161] *Serdar Mohammed v Secretary of State for Defence* [2017] UKSC 2 [30].

lead to detention and how any detention can be challenged.[162] As the ICRC explains, even if one considers there is an inherent power to detain, 'additional authority related to the grounds and procedure for deprivation of liberty in non-international armed conflict must in all cases be provided, in keeping with the principle of legality'.[163]

Clearly there is no escaping the centrality of detention in all forms of armed conflict. The challenge is to agree on how to bring all such detention within the rule of law so that detainees (who are not being prosecuted for a criminal offence) are not only treated humanely, but also able to challenge on a regular basis the necessity for their detention.[164]

I would suggest that the basic principles are simple, well known and have already been articulated in the cases that deal with the legality of detention. They could also be applied where individuals are detained by non-state actors. With regard to the body entitled to order release, there must be 'guarantees of impartiality and fair procedure to protect against arbitrariness. Moreover, the first review should take place shortly after the person is taken into detention, with subsequent reviews at frequent intervals'.[165] With regard to the detainee, they have some basic rights. In the words of Lord Sumption, the minimum conditions of fairness would be:

(i) that the internee should be told, so far as possible without compromising secret material, the gist of the facts which are said to make his detention necessary for imperative reasons of security;

---

[162] For suggestions as to how this should work, in particular with regard to detention by non-state forces, see Clapham, 'Detention by Armed Groups under International Law' (n 160).

[163] ICRC, *Commentary on the First Geneva Convention* (2016) (n 19) at para 728; for a full explanation of the ICRC position, see Rodenhäuser, 'Legal Basis, Grounds and Procedures for Detention in Non-International Armed Conflicts', in *Legal and Operational Challenges Raised by Contemporary Non-International Armed Conflicts: Proceedings of the Bruges Colloquium* (ICRC, 2019) 63–74 at 71 (original emphasis): 'Invoking such inherent power to intern *alone*, however, would not be sufficient to make internment lawful. In keeping with the principle of legality, the detaining power needs to have defined grounds and procedures for internment. In other words, for internment to be lawful, there needs to be not only a legal basis but also grounds and procedures that are spelled out in a binding instrument. In traditional NIACs, such grounds and procedures would be defined in national law. When States operate extraterritorially, a binding instrument setting out grounds and procedures for internment could be an agreement among the parties involved, or the law of the intervening State, or binding Standard Operational Procedures (SOP).'

[164] Hampson, 'Administrative Detention in Non-International Armed Conflicts', in Lattimer and Sands (eds), *The Grey Zone: Civilian Protection Between Human Rights and the Laws of War* (2019) 157–78; for the situation under the International Covenant on Civil and Political Rights, see Shany, 'A Human Rights Perspective to Global Battlefield Detention: Time to Reconsider Indefinite Detention', 93 *ILS* (2017) 102–31.

[165] *Hassan v UK* (n 9) at para 106.

(ii)   that the review procedure should be explained to him;

(iii) that he should be allowed sufficient contact with the outside world to be able to obtain evidence of his own; and

(iv)   that he should be entitled to make representations, preferably in person but if that is impractical then in some other effective manner.[166]

9.3 The Role of the International Committee of the Red Cross

We recounted at the beginning of this chapter how the origins of the ICRC were inspired by Henri Dunant's experience when confronted with the inadequate arrangements for treating the wounded on the battlefield of Solferino. The mission statement of the ICRC today explains that it is 'an impartial, neutral and independent organization whose exclusively humanitarian mission is to protect the lives and dignity of victims of armed conflict and other situations of violence and to provide them with assistance'.[167] The history of this organization is rich and fascinating, and the reader is referred in particular to Bugnion's massive study, *The International Committee of the Red Cross and the Protection of War Victims*, and to Moorehead's *Dunant's Dream*.

The ICRC states that is has 20,000 staff working in over 100 countries around the world, and the organization had a budget of around $2billion. If we consider the larger Red Cross and Red Crescent Movement, which includes not only the ICRC, but also 192 National Societies and their International Federation of Red Cross and Red Crescent Societies (IFRC), it is said to be made up of 'nearly 100 million members, volunteers and supporters'.[168] In situations of armed conflict the ICRC takes the lead.[169] For

---

[166] *Serdar Mohammed v Secretary of State for Defence* [2017] UKSC 2 [107]; later applied in *Alseran et al v Ministry of Defence* [2017] EWHC 3289 (QB) at [91] so, for example, Al-Waheed was awarded £3,300 for his unlawful detention in violation of human rights law from 23 February to 28 March 2007 at [17]. It was found at [703] that 'His detention during that period therefore lacked any lawful basis and was contrary to article 5(1) [ECHR].' And the procedural guarantees were not met under article 5(4) ECHR, at [704] to [712].

[167] See at https://www.icrc.org/en/mandate-and-mission.

[168] From the Movement's site at https://www.ifrc.org/en/who-we-are/the-movement/ accessed 29 January 2020.

[169] Art 5 of the *Agreement on the Organization of the International Activities of the Components of the Red Cross and Red Crescent Movement* (1997), *IRRC* No 322 (1998) 159–76.

present purposes we will briefly consider just a few legal aspects of the role played by the ICRC and the emblem.

9.3.1 ICRC Access and Visits

We have already mentioned that in international armed conflicts there is a treaty obligation on states to allow ICRC delegates access to persons protected under the Conventions. In non-international armed conflicts the ICRC can offer its services, and according to the ICRC it 'sytematically requests access to persons deprived of their liberty in connection with non-international armed conflicts, and such access is generally granted'.[170] The ICRC's customary law study explains the separate rules as follows:

> Rule 124 A. In international armed conflicts, the ICRC must be granted regular access to all persons deprived of their liberty in order to verify the conditions of their detention and to restore contacts between those persons and their families.

> Rule 124 B. In non-international armed conflicts, the ICRC may offer its services to the parties to the conflict with a view to visiting all persons deprived of their liberty for reasons related to the conflict in order to verify the conditions of their detention and to restore contacts between those persons and their families.

The ICRC must be able to interview detainees in private without witnesses, and the purposes of these visits are partly humanitarian and partly to implement

> rules of customary international law, including the prevention of enforced disappearances, extrajudicial executions, torture and other cruel, inhuman or degrading treatment or punishment, monitoring the standard of detention conditions and the restoration of family links through the exchange of Red Cross messages.[171]

---

[170] Henckaerts and Doswald-Beck, *Customary International Humanitarian Law* (n 27) at 444.
[171] Ibid.

9.3.2 Confidentiality, the Privileged Status of ICRC Information and Evidence, and the Option of Denunciation

Obviously the information gathered during such ICRC visits is helpful not only to establish family contact and improve conditions, but also potentially for the purposes of obtaining accountability and even the prosecution of war crimes. The ICRC's methodology for conducting interviews with detainees and others is, however, premised on the idea of confidentiality. Parties to a conflict are promised that any report made by the ICRC will be passed to the detaining party and not to anyone else. This is designed to ensure that access is permitted and return visits are ensured. Evidence gathering and denunciation for violations of the laws of war is primarily left to other bodies such as the UN or regional organizations, primarily through Commissions of Inquiry or mandated experts,[172] or to non-governmental organizations and the media. The ICRC explains the method and rationale for its approach as

> aiming to put a stop to current violations and prevent potential future ones. As such, its focus is rectification rather than retribution. If violations of the law are alleged or observed, ICRC delegates document such information and – where applicable, with the consent of the person making the allegation – bring it to the attention of responsible authorities. The latter are then responsible – if the information is confirmed – for changing relevant practices, including, if necessary, by applying disciplinary or penal sanctions vis-à-vis those responsible.[173]

The detaining party is not free to share the information with the media, or even with its parliament or judiciary or in any legal proceedings, without written consent from the ICRC.[174]

The issue has arisen as to whether the ICRC could rely on its special role should its staff be compelled to testify or produce documents before an

---

[172] See Harwood, *The Roles and Functions of Atrocity-Related United Nations Commissions of Inquiry in the International Legal Order* (2020); Alston and Knuckey (eds), *The Transformation of Human Rights Fact-Finding* (2016).

[173] ICRC Blog post at https://blogs.icrc.org/law-and-policy/2019/01/31/5-things-make-icrc-confidential-information-unsuitable-legal-proceedings/: 'The ICRC does not perform the role of a commission of inquiry and, as a general rule, neither the organization nor its staff will participate in inquiry procedures.' Melzer, *International Humanitarian Law* (n 28) at 327.

[174] ICRC, 'The ICRC's Privilege of Non-Disclosure of Confidential Information', 97 *IRRC* (2016) 433–44.

international criminal court. The situations with regard to national courts will usually be regulated by separate agreements between the ICRC and the authorities or specific national law.[175] Several international tribunals have agreed that the ICRC has a right not to divulge information related to its activities.[176] This right is considered by the ICRC a 'form of testimonial immunity'. At the International Criminal Court, a specific sub-Rule states that, should the ICRC information be of great importance for a particular case, consultations will be held to resolve the matter, taking into account the respective functions of the Court and the ICRC, and the interests of justice and of victims.[177]

The ICRC itself explains that the confidentiality approach is not an 'inalienable principle' but rather applied for the objective benefit of the victims of violence. Its policy document states that 'It can never serve to justify, by silence, an unsatisfactory and static situation that is unlikely to change for the better in any significant way.' It has a policy that that it 'must be in a position deliberately to breach its undertaking of confidentiality in exceptional cases in which the approach runs counter to the interests of the victims'.[178]

Any such exceptional public denunciation would happen in accordance with the ICRC's specific policy on violations:

Public condemnation
The ICRC reserves the right to issue a public condemnation of specific violations of international humanitarian law providing the following conditions are met:

(1) the violations are major and repeated or likely to be repeated;
(2) delegates have witnessed the violations with their own eyes, or the existence and extent of those violations have been established on the basis of reliable and verifiable sources;
(3) bilateral confidential representations and, when attempted, humanitarian mobilization efforts have failed to put an end to the violations;
(4) such publicity is in the interest of the persons or populations affected or threatened.[179]

---

[175] See further Debuf, 'Tools to Do the Job: The ICRC's Legal Status, Privileges and Immunities', 97 *IRRC* (2016) 319–44 at 324 fn 17.

[176] Ibid.

[177] See Rule 73(6) of the ICC Rules of Procedure and Evidence.

[178] ICRC, 'The International Committee of the Red Cross's (ICRC's) Confidential Approach', 94 *IRRC* (2012) 1135–44 at 1137.

[179] ICRC, 'Action by the International Committee of the Red Cross in the Event of Violations of International Humanitarian Law or of Other Fundamental Rules Protecting Persons in Situations of Violence', 87 *IRRC* (2005) 393–400 at 397. It is worth noting that it is stated that the

9.4 The Use and Misuse of Emblems

9.4.1 The Emblem of the Red Cross, the Red Crescent or the Red Crystal

The emblem of a red cross on a white background is described in the First Geneva Convention (1949) as 'a compliment to Switzerland' and a reversal of the Swiss colours.[180] It was introduced in 1863, to be worn on armbands of the voluntary medical corps called for by Henri Dunant's campaign.[181] The adoption of a uniform symbol for medical personnel on the battlefield resolved a long-standing problem where different armies were using different symbols and colours.[182] Today, the relevant military authorize and control the use of the red cross as a protective emblem for the armed forces' medical personnel, property, hospitals, ambulances and other medical forms of transport. It can also be used as a protective emblem for a variety of other medical establishments and personnel.[183] The red cross enjoys equal status with the red crescent and red crystal, and states can choose which emblem to adopt.[184] The medical services of armed non-state actors engaged in an armed conflict are also entitled to use the emblem as a protective device.[185]

As we saw at the beginning of the chapter, hospitals and medical personnel, etc are protected whether or not they display the emblem. This is often misunderstood:

> [W]hile the emblem makes it easier to identify a protected person or property, this person or property is protected independently of the emblem. For example, a hospital may not be attacked under the pretext that it was not marked by a red cross. Conversely, a red cross wrongly placed on a military target does not confer immunity on it.[186]

policy on violations applies beyond the specific rules related to the victims of war outlined in this chapter and extends to the law on the conduct of hostilities (ibid at 394); and that where international humanitarian law does not 'formally apply', the ICRC responds to 'violations of other fundamental rules protecting persons in situations of violence' (ibid at 398).

---

[180] Art 38 of GC I.

[181] ICRC, *Commentary on the First Geneva Convention* (2016) (n 19) at para 2532.

[182] Bouvier, 'The Use of the Emblem', in Clapham, Gaeta, and Sassòli (eds), *The 1949 Geneva Conventions: A Commentary* (2015) 855–86 at 857.

[183] For the detail, see ibid.

[184] ICRC, *Commentary on the First Geneva Convention* (2016) (n 19) at para 2532.

[185] Bouvier (n 182) at 868.

[186] Sandoz, 'Land Warfare', in Clapham and Gaeta (eds), *The Oxford Handbook of International Law in Armed Conflict* (2014) 91–117 at 103.

Today the problem is often that targeting is carried out from a distance, and the distinctive sign may not be visible in this context. Special provisions cover radio signals and blue flashing lights,[187] and the ICRC has a policy of communicating the GPS coordinates of its medical facilities to the parties.[188] But unfortunately identification is not always a solution. Some armed forces and non-governmental organizations have had to opt for camouflaging their hospitals, or leaving them unidentified for fear of attracting attacks or revealing information concerning tactical developments.[189] Although some attacks on hospitals may be due to negligence, recklessness or a confusion over coordinates, there is increasing concern that medical workers and hospitals are being targeted in order to grind down the morale of the civilian population, force displacement and dissuade those who 'put terrorists back on the battlefield'. Non-governmental organizations have found their hospitals repeatedly hit in Syria, leading to claims that hospitals were being deliberately targeted.[190] After hospitals were hit that were part of the UN's de-confliction mechanism in Syria, the UN Under-Secretary-General told the Security Council that 'A number of partners now feel that supplying geographical coordinates to be given to the warring parties effectively paints a target on their backs.'[191]

9.4.2 Other Emblems

The laws of war include a series of other emblems, such as the white flag of truce.[192] Under the Hague Regulations there is protection for 'a parlementaire who has been authorized by one of the belligerents to enter into communication with the other, and who advances bearing a white flag. He has a right to

---

[187] See Annex I to AP I, 'Regulations Concerning Identification'.

[188] Bouvier (n 182) at 881.

[189] Ibid at 882–83.

[190] See, eg, 'Strikes on Syrian Medical Facilities Appear Deliberate: UN', *Reuters*, 8 November 2019.

[191] Lowcock, 'Briefing to the Security Council on the Humanitarian Situation in Idlib', 18 June 2019. The UN Secretary-General subsequently set up a Board of Inquiry, see 'Summary by the Secretary-General of the report of the United Nations Headquarters Board of Inquiry into certain incidents in northwest Syria since 17 September 2018 involving facilities on the United Nations deconfliction list and United Nations supported facilities'; one recommendation to come out of this was that 'With regard to the "deconfliction mechanism" . . . OCHA [UN Office for the Coordination of Humanitarian Affairs] should consider renaming it as "Humanitarian Notification Mechanism" to highlight its distinct nature, in the overall framework of international humanitarian law . . .'.

[192] See Henckaerts and Doswald-Beck, *Customary International Humanitarian Law* (n 27) Rule 58 at 205ff.

inviolability, as well as the trumpeter, bugler or drummer, the flag-bearer and interpreter who may accompany him.'[193] A specific emblem for protected cultural property and personnel involved in its control or protection consists of a blue square shield pointing down on a white background.[194] Civil defence personnel, buildings and equipment, as well as civilian shelters, are identified by a blue triangle on an orange background.[195] Dangerous installations, such as dams, dykes and nuclear power stations, are identified by three orange circles on a horizontal axis.[196] It is prohibited to make improper use of these emblems, as well as unauthorized use of the distinctive emblems of the United Nations.[197]

9.4.3   Misuse of Emblems Constituting a War Crime

As we have seen, attacking hospitals and medical personnel is prohibited and can be prosecuted as a war crime. The Statute of the International Criminal Court includes the specific war crime of 'Intentionally directing attacks against buildings, material, medical units and transport, and personnel using the distinctive emblems of the Geneva Conventions in conformity with international law'.[198] Another crime applicable in international armed conflict relates to *misuse* of emblems, flags, insignia and uniforms, where this results in death or serious personal injury.[199] The misuse of an emblem or the white flag, or pretending to have civilian status or to be sick or injured, can also be considered perfidy.[200] Under Additional Protocol I, 'it is prohibited to kill, injure or capture an adversary by resort to perfidy'.[201] As opposed to simple misuse of an emblem, the 'essence of perfidy is thus the invitation to

---

[193] Hague Regulations IV Art 32; and see also Art 23(f).

[194] Arts 1, 16 and 17, Convention for the Protection of Cultural Property in the Event of Armed Conflict (1954); see also the decision in 2015 to add a symbol of a blue shield with a red border for enhanced protection under the Second Protocol of 1999. Decision 9.COM 4, CLT-14/9.COM/CONF.203/4/REV2 – annex, figure 6(b).

[195] AP I Arts 61–67, and Annex I Arts 14–15.

[196] AP I Art 56, Annex I Art 16; Art 15 of AP II; Henckaerts and Doswald-Beck, *Customary International Humanitarian Law* (n 27) Rule 42 at 139–42.

[197] AP I Art 38.

[198] ICC Statute Art 8(2)(b)(xxiv) and (e)(ii).

[199] ICC Statute Art 8(2)(b)(vii).

[200] AP I Art 37; Henckaerts and Doswald-Beck, *Customary International Humanitarian Law* (n 27) Rule 65 at 221–26; Hague IV Regulations Art 23(b).

[201] AP I Art 37. The United States does not recognize that the customary international law on perfidy prohibits operations for capture; see US *Law of War Manual* (2016) at para 5.22.2.1. For some of the issues related to undercover soldiers engaged in operations to kill or capture, see

obtain and then breach the adversary's confidence'.[202] Perfidy causing death or serious injury is criminalized as a grave breach of Protocol I,[203] can be prosecuted as an offence at the national level, and can constitute a war crime prosecuted in the International Criminal Court as 'killing or wounding treacherously individuals belonging to the hostile nation or army'.[204]

Let us now turn in Chapter 10 to look at war crimes and accountability more generally.

Rosenzweig, *Combatants Dressed as Civilians? The Case of Israeli Mista'arvim under International Law, The Israel Democracy Institute Policy Paper 8e* (2014).

[202] Henckaerts and Doswald-Beck, *Customary International Humanitarian Law* (n 27) at 223.
[203] AP I Art 85(3)(f).
[204] ICC Statute Art 8(2)(b)(xi) and (e)(ix); the Court's Elements of the Crime explains that the perpetrator 'invited the confidence or belief of one or more persons that they were entitled to, or were obliged to accord, protection under rules of international law applicable in armed conflict'.

10

Accountability for Violations of the Laws of War

The first half of this book concentrated on explaining how resort to war came to be outlawed in international law. The UN Charter now only allows for the use of force by one state against another in situations where either there has been an armed attack and the state acts in self-defence, or the Security Council has authorized the use of force where this is necessary to maintain or restore international peace and security. Where this prohibition on the use of force is violated by states and their leaders, it may be possible to have some sort of accountability. With regard to leaders, there were of course trials and convictions for 'crimes against peace' in Nuremberg and Tokyo after the Second World War. The crime of aggression has now been inserted into the Statute of the International Criminal Court (although, as we shall see, the likelihood of prosecutions under the eventual agreed arrangements are very slim). But accountability can go beyond individual criminal conviction. We will examine other possibilities involving compensation and memorialization.

The second half of this book examined the laws of armed conflict. Here too there may be possibilities to demand various forms of accountability. Some breaches of these rules are considered war crimes and can be prosecuted as such. Command responsibility will attach to those who were in control and failed to prevent or punish such war crimes. All violations of these rules can, in theory, lead to various legal consequences beyond prosecution, and we will look below at several such forms of accountability.

But – and readers will have guessed there must be a 'but' coming – there are multiple obstacles to ensuring the rule of law in time of war. National courts are unlikely to challenge the government's decision to resort to force against another state.[1] International courts or Commissions have rarely been

---

[1] As Simpson points out in looking at recent judgments, 'Matters of war and peace (even those encompassing possible breaches of fundamental human rights guarantees) were left to the realm of politics.' Simpson, *Law, War and Crime* (2008) at 23.

given jurisdiction over such matters (and even then enforcement of payment of compensation will be problematic). The UN Security Council and the General Assembly rarely find political agreement on whom to blame, or how to bring justice. Nation states hardly ever prosecute their own forces for war crimes,[2] or even under the ordinary criminal law. With regard to the rare criminal cases that were brought in recent years in the United States, related to killing of civilians in Afghanistan and Iraq, we have had the spectacle of members of the armed forces and private contractors being pardoned by President Trump.[3] At the judicial level, courts are hesitant to decide cases against their own side that question decisions made in battle. Moreover, where a claim is brought in the domestic courts of one state against another state, it can be thwarted by the application of the international law of sovereign state immunity.[4]

In the end, even where the political and technical obstacles can be overcome, wars do not easily lend themselves to litigation. There is an assumption among many lawyers that war damage is too big to be dealt with in courts. For Tomuschat, the

> harm resulting from armed conflict pertains to a specific class of damage originating from state conduct that by necessity causes mass injuries. Accordingly, the financial consequences of armed conflict cannot be dealt with as everyday problems that fit into the ordinary legal framework.[5]

Let us delve, however, into some ways in which a degree of accountability can in fact be achieved for violations of the laws of war. Before coming to the

---

[2] See, however, the approach of the Colombian judiciary, which has insisted on applying the law of armed conflict even in the face of opposition from President Uribe, who refused to acknowledge the fact of an armed conflict, simply branding the armed opposition 'terrorist' and discouraging others from using the language of war, conflict or even guerrilla. See Lozano and Machado, 'The Objective Qualification of Non-International Armed Conflicts: A Colombian Case Study', 4 *Amsterdam Law Forum* (2012) 58–77; for the subsequent appropriation by the military of the framework of international humanitarian law for its 'exculpatory and permissive' character, see Kalmanovitz, 'Entro el deber de protección y la necesidad militar: oscilaciones del discurso humanitario en Colombia 1991–2016', *Latin American Law Review* (2018) 33–60.

[3] See the Chair-Rapporteur of the UN Working Group on the use of mercenaries: Jelena Aparac, 'Pardoning the Blackwater contractors is an affront to justice and to the victims of the Nisour Square massacre and their families', UN Press Release, 30 December 2020; Goldenziel, 'War Has Rules: The United States Must Respect Them', *National Interest* (29 December 2020).

[4] For a careful look at the multiple obstacles facing litigants before national courts, see Tomuschat, 'State Responsibility and the Individual Rights to Compensation Before National Courts', in Clapham and Gaeta (eds), *The Oxford Handbook of International Law in Armed Conflict* (2014) 811–39.

[5] Ibid at 821.

contemporary situation, let us consider what happened in the wake of the two World Wars, as these arrangements continue to shape how many think about the prospects of accountability.

10.1 The First World War

When we considered War as an institution for settling disputes between states against the background of the doctrine of Just War, we came across the idea that – in War – the loser pays. Accounts were settled in such a way that the winner was even compensated for the cost of fighting the War. These war 'expenses' or 'indemnities' were variously justified by the writers of the 16th and 17th centuries. While for some, the side fighting a just war could legitimately claim their costs, others considered that, as with a duel, the loser had consented to whatever might come. Alternatively, it was thought that the overarching principle was that the victor should be able simply to impose such conditions as were necessary to ensure their future security.[6] By the 19th century, peace treaties would contain demands by the winner for huge sums in war reparations.[7] By the beginning of the 20th century, a leading British law book, describing the 'Laws of War in General', would reflect these priorities for the winner, deeming it unnecessary to take into account whether or not the winner had been fighting a just war. Westlake explains:

> [T]he object on the part of each belligerent is to break down the resistance of the other to the terms which he requires for peace. These are not necessarily limited to the concession of the demand or the satisfaction of the complaint out of which the war arose. They may include a demand for indemnity, for new arrangements promising greater security in future, or for new arrangements more pleasing to the stronger party for any other reason; and these may go so far as to include the cession of territory.[8]

This old orthodoxy helps us understand how people thought about war reparations as the First World War came to an end. But the Versailles Treaty nevertheless stopped short of punitive demands to prevent Germany's ever

---

[6] See the analysis by Neff, *War and the Law of Nations* (2005) at 156–58; Sullo and Wyatt, 'War Reparations', *MPEPIL* (2015) at para 2.

[7] d'Argent, *Les réparations de guerre en droit international public: la responsabilité internationale des Etats à l'épreuve de la guerre* (2002).

[8] Westlake, *International Law: Part II War* (1907) at 53.

again being a threat. Instead the idea was put forward that compensation should be based on fault and capacity to pay. This was in part self-serving, as the victors wanted to trade with a Germany actually able to pay, although, at the same time, the notion of 'war reparations' was talked up to satisfy domestic pressure. Squeeze the Germans till the 'pips squeak' was a celebrated refrain. The United States was, however, against the old idea of indemnities, or fines, whereby the loser pays the winner's costs and some more. One option might have been to focus on violations of the laws of war, but this would have left Belgium a beneficiary for having been invaded and occupied, as that invasion had been under international law a violation of its Neutral Status. France and Britain, however, would have received relatively little under any scheme which concentrated on violations of international law.[9] The focus therefore shifted to *damages*, as opposed to the costs of the whole War, and now the French and Belgians stood to gain more than the British.

In MacMillan's expert telling of events, it emerges that the moral high ground staked out by President Wilson for the United States, whereby the winners would not be indemnified for the cost of fighting the war, was eventually subverted. Compensation came to include not only the estimates of damage done to the lands of France and Belgium, but also the costs of War pensions for 'victims of war', which meant those members of the Allied armed forces 'whether mutilated, wounded, sick or invalided, and to the dependents of such victims'.[10] This considerably bolstered the share of reparations owed to Great Britain, a sum that would otherwise have been essentially limited to the value of the merchant shipping damaged by German submarines.[11]

In addition to monetary reparations (by 1932 Germany is said to have paid about $4.5 billion[12]), the Versailles Treaty 'called for Germany to give France and Belgium 120,000 sheep, 4,000 bulls, 140,000 dairy cows, and more than 40,000 horses'.[13] German borders were redrawn, and Germany's colonies in Africa and the Pacific were taken over by mandate holders under the League of Nations (including Belgium, France, the United Kingdom, South Africa and Australia). German-leased territory in China was controversially ceded to Japan, and the 'Shandong problem' was resolved by treaty only in 1922.

---

[9] Neff (n 6) at 288.

[10] See Treaty of Peace with Germany (Treaty of Versailles) (1919) Annex I para 5.

[11] MacMillan, *Paris 1919: Six Months That Changed the World* (2003) Ch 15.

[12] Ibid at 480; the final settlement of the First World War reparations only comes with the reunification of Germany – see Sullo and Wyatt (n 6) at para 16, where it is stated that the average amount suggested by experts is DM40 billion (circa €20 billion).

[13] Neiberg, *The Treaty of Versailles: A Very Short Introduction* (2019) at 73; for the exact breakdown details, see Annex IV to the Treaty.

There were also restrictions on the size of the German Army and Navy. The Treaty further included the following curiosities: 'Germany had to return all French flags captured during the 1870–71 war, give to the king of Hejaz a historic Koran that the Ottoman sultan had once given to Kaiser Wilhelm, and deliver to the British the skull of the east African king Mkwawa.'[14] The Peace Treaty is an amalgam of reparations for damage and indemnities for the cost of the war, symbolic fines and measures attempting to ensure security in Europe.

Mixed Arbitral Tribunals were set up to hear claims about war damage by nationals from the Allied or Associated Powers,[15] while those same Powers enshrined in Article 297 of the Treaty that the private property of Germans in Allied lands would be simply seized and retained. By this time such seizure was considered outrageous by some. The records of the 1924 meeting of the International Law Association in Stockholm include this intervention by Wyndam Bewes:

> [A]s internationalists, and as just men, we entirely repudiate the practice shown after this last war by every one of the warring States, by which they went back to forgotten practices of barbarism, which, I thought, had been eliminated for ever from the practices of civilised States – I mean the confiscation of the private property of the citizens of hostile States by the warring States in which they are found.
>
> (Hear, hear.)

He then convinced the meeting to adopt unanimously the following text, whereby they 'Resolved that this Conference is firmly of opinion that the revived practice of warring States by which they confiscate the available private property of alien citizens is a relic of barbarism worthy of the most severe condemnation.'[16]

---

[14] Neiberg (n 13) at 74.

[15] Mixed Arbitral Tribunals were set up with Germany by Belgium, Czechoslovakia, France, Great Britain, Greece, Italy, Japan, Poland, Rumania, Serb-Croat-Slovene State and Siam; similar tribunals were set up with Austria, Hungary, Bulgaria and Turkey, while the United States, declining to ratify the Versailles Treaty, set up a Mixed Claims Commission with Germany. See further Dolzer, 'Mixed Claims Commissions', *MPEPIL* (2011); Bank and Foltz, 'Lump Sum Agreements', *MPEPIL* (2013).

[16] *Report of the Thirty Third Conference* (1924) at 70 and 73. It is difficult to see how today such seizures could be considered as being in conformity with human rights law, or, as we shall see, that a state could extinguish the rights of its nationals though a peace treaty.

When considering accountability for going to War, two further provisions from the Treaty are constantly recalled. The first is known as the 'War Guilt Clause':

> The Allied and Associated Governments affirm and Germany accepts the responsibility of Germany and her allies for causing all the loss and damage to which the Allied and Associated Governments and their nationals have been subjected as a consequence of the war imposed upon them by the aggression of Germany and her allies.[17]

The same language was used in the peace treaties with Germany's allies Austria, Bulgaria, Hungary and the Ottoman Empire. The second famous provision was supposed to lead to a trial of Kaiser Wilhelm:

> The Allied and Associated Powers publicly arraign William II of Hohenzollern, formerly German Emperor, for a supreme offence against international morality and the sanctity of treaties.
>
> A special tribunal will be constituted to try the accused, thereby assuring him the guarantees essential to the right of defence. It will be composed of five judges, one appointed by each of the following Powers: namely, the United States of America, Great Britain, France, Italy and Japan.[18]

During the Peace Conference, there was some hesitation among the leaders of the victorious powers over the legality of prosecuting a Head of State before a tribunal. At one point the Prime Minister of Italy, Orlando (a Professor of law), pointed to the lack of precedent for the basis of such a right. The Prime Minister of France, Clemenceau, was not looking for a precedent but rather seeking to set a precedent in the face of unprecedented atrocities:

> We have today a glorious opportunity to bring about the transfer to international law of the principle of responsibility which is at the basis of national law.
>
> Is there no precedent? There never is a precedent. What is a precedent? I shall tell you. A man comes along; he acts, for good or evil. Out of what is good we create a precedent. Out of what is evil, the criminals, whether individuals or heads of States, create the precedent of their crimes. We have no

---

[17] Versailles Treaty (1919) Art 231.
[18] Versailles Treaty (1919) Art 227.

precedent? Why! This is our best argument. Was there in recent generations any precedent for the atrocities committed by the Germans in the present war, the systematic destruction of wealth to stifle competition, the torture of prisoners, the submarine piracy, the abominable treatment of women in the occupied countries? To these precedents, we will oppose a precedent of justice.[19]

This trial never took place, despite an amateur attempt to abduct the Kaiser from The Netherlands and bring him before a court, as engagingly told by Schabas in his book, *The Trial of the Kaiser*. Schabas highlights not only the hesitation of some leaders and Monarchs over the idea of prosecuting an Emperor for starting an unnecessary War, but also the unease in the legal community over prosecuting crimes that, at the time, had not been properly articulated as individual offences (as opposed to violations of the law of nations) and for which no penalties had been prescribed by law. Nevertheless, the discussion and preparation focused not only on punishing the violations of the guarantees to respect the Neutrality of Belgium and Luxembourg, but also on condemning what was seen by key players as a premeditated war of aggression,[20] as well as describing violations of the laws and customs of war as war crimes.[21]

The Treaty eventually included a provision whereby Germany recognized the right of the Allies to try 'acts in violation of the laws and customs of war', and an obligation for the German Government to hand over all persons accused of having committed such an act.[22] Germany later explained that, under its law, it could not transfer any German citizens. In the end around a dozen people were tried for war crimes in German courts in Leipzig. The acquittals and minimal sentences provoked derision in France; and as Kreß has highlighted, this contributed to the breakthrough represented by the international trial in Nuremberg after the Second World War, and more generally explains the whole point of international criminal law. In his words, 'state will to investigate and prosecute a case of alleged state-based crime is inherently fragile'.[23]

---

[19] Mantoux (ed), *Paris Peace Conference 1919: Proceedings of the Council of Four (March 24–April 18)* (1964) at 149–50, discussed further in the entry on 'International Crimes' in Marks and Clapham, *International Human Rights Lexicon* (2005) at 223–25.
[20] Schabas, *The Trial of the Kaiser* (2018) esp at 45–46, 128–29 and Ch 9.
[21] Ibid Ch 10.
[22] Versailles Treaty (1919) Art 228.
[23] Kreß, 'Versailles – Nuremberg – The Hague Germany and International Criminal Law', 40 *International Lawyer* (2006) 15–39 at 19.

10.2 The Second World War

The situation at the end of the Second World War was very different from that at the end of the First World War. Not only did the victors want to avoid a repeat of the Versailles experience,[24] but the tension between the West and the USSR meant that 'the Western powers were reluctant to establish a reparations regime that would have helped the Soviet Union to recover quickly from its losses'.[25] The result at the Potsdam Conference was a reparations regime that apportioned resources according to which occupation zone (Soviet or Western) they came under.[26] Again, the agreement highlights the collective responsibility for unleashing the War, stating that a guiding principle of the occupation would be

> [t]o convince the German people that they have suffered a total military defeat and that they cannot escape responsibility for what they have brought upon themselves, since their own ruthless warfare and the fanatical Nazi resistance have destroyed German economy and made chaos and suffering inevitable.[27]

This time, as d'Argent explains,

> dismantling of industrial plants was a way to exact reparations in the short term and at the same time to pursue a long term security goal by disarming the former enemies. ... The delivery of manufactured goods was a way to help local industry and to promote long term trade channels.[28]

The bulk of the reparations for the USA and the United Kingdom were taken in terms of industrial goods, shipping and intellectual property rights. In addition, the victors benefitted from German forced labour for a few years after the Second World War. German prisoners of war subjected to forced labour in the Soviet Union were only finally released in 1953. The British were

---

[24] Neiberg (n 13) at 114.
[25] d'Argent, 'Reparations after World War II', *MPEPIL* (2009) at para 2.
[26] Ibid at paras 4–17; for a full treatment of war reparations under international law, see d'Argent, *Les réparations de guerre* (n 7).
[27] The Berlin Conference of the Three Heads of Government of the USSR, USA, and UK (Potsdam Conference) 17 July to 2 August 1945, Conclusion, II The Principles to Govern the Treatment of Germany in the Initial Control Period A.3(ii).
[28] d'Argent (n 25) at para 37.

organizing hard labour for Japanese prisoners in Burma until 1947.[29] The last prisoners of war left Britain in 1948.[30]

Similarly, for Japan there was concern that they were unable to pay full compensation, and that the priority should be reconstruction of the economy.[31] Article 14 of the San Francisco Treaty stated:

> It is recognized that Japan should pay reparations to the Allied Powers for the damage and suffering caused by it during the war. Nevertheless, it is also recognized that the resources of Japan are not presently sufficient, if it is to maintain a viable economy, to make complete reparation for all such damage and suffering and at the same time meet its other obligations.

Therefore,

> 1. Japan will promptly enter into negotiations with Allied Powers so desiring, whose present territories were occupied by Japanese forces and damaged by Japan, with a view to assisting to compensate those countries for the cost of repairing the damage done, by making available the services of the Japanese people in production, salvaging and other work for the Allied Powers in question. Such arrangements shall avoid the imposition of additional liabilities on other Allied Powers, and, where the manufacturing of raw materials is called for, they shall be supplied by the Allied Powers in question, so as not to throw any foreign exchange burden upon Japan.[32]

And a specific class of violations of the laws of war was to be compensated:

> As an expression of its desire to indemnify those members of the armed forces of the Allied Powers who suffered undue hardships while prisoners of war of Japan, Japan will transfer its assets and those of its nationals in countries which were neutral during the war, or which were at war with any of the Allied Powers, or, at its option, the equivalent of such assets, to the International Committee of the Red Cross which shall liquidate such assets and distribute the resultant fund to appropriate national agencies, for the

---

[29] For a rare first-hand account by a Japanese prisoner in English, see Aida, *Prisoner of the British* (1966).

[30] See further Reynolds, 'Life in Britain for German Prisoners of War', 17 February 2011, available at http://www.bbc.co.uk/history/british/britain_wwtwo/german_pows_01.shtml.

[31] Ibid at paras 24–34.

[32] Treaty of Peace with Japan (1951) Art 14.

benefit of former prisoners of war and their families on such basis as it may determine to be equitable.[33]

At the time, prisoners of war were paid around £75 each from the resulting fund. An attempt by former prisoners to sue the Japanese Government in 1998 failed in the Japanese courts, on the ground that such claims were already settled through the peace treaty.[34] Similarly, claims on behalf of Korean and Filipino women forced into sex (so-called 'comfort women'), and other claims by Korean, Filipino and Chinese nationals, have been dismissed on the grounds that their claims are invalid due to legal agreements between Japan and Korea, the Philippines and China respectively.[35]

The final settlement of reparations from Germany had to await a comprehensive peace agreement with a unified Germany. In the meantime Germany entered into various treaty agreements with different states, which again have been seen as extinguishing any private claims. Italy, Finland, Hungary, Romania and Bulgaria all paid reparations to other states under a series of Peace Treaties (1947).[36] In the end, it is estimated that, by 1965, 'Germany had paid more than DM18 billion (US$4.5 billion), on January 1, 1986, that figure rose to more than DM59 billion (US$27.5 billion) and in 2000 it was estimated to have reached more than DM82 billion (US$38.6 billion)'.[37]

After reunification, Germany set up funds, for example for the Conference on Jewish Material Claims, and reconciliation foundations with Poland, Russia, Belarus and Ukraine, and a special fund to compensate those subjected to forced labour.[38] This last foundation included contributions from German industry (the Foundation Initiative) and totalled around €5.1 billion; it was administered by the International Organization for Migration.[39]

---

[33] Ibid Art 16, this resulted in a payment of £4.5 million, for details see Rey-Schyrr, *From Yalta to Dien Bien Phu: History of the International Committee of the Red Cross 1945 to 1955* (2017) at 146 ff.

[34] See at http://news.bbc.co.uk/2/hi/asia-pacific/222253.stm.

[35] For references, see Hofmann, 'Compensation for Personal Damages Suffered during World War II, *MPEPIL* (2013).

[36] For a summary of the terms, see von Puttkamer, 'Peace Treaties (1947)', *MPEPIL* (2001).

[37] Colonomos and Armstrong, 'German Reparations to the Jews after World War II: A Turning Point in the History of Reparations', in De Greiff (ed), *The Handbook of Reparations* (2008) 390–419 at 408.

[38] d'Argent, 'Reparations after World War II' (n 25) at para 19.

[39] Bank and Foltz, 'German Forced Labour Compensation Programme', *MPEPIL* (2013)

10.3 Claiming Reparations in the Contemporary World before National Courts

The particularities of the German and Japanese settlements have left some uncertainty over the question as to whether individuals can claim, as a right, compensation from a state for violations of the laws of war. The German and Japanese Governments, and the courts in those countries, consider that claims relating to the Second World War, including against corporations in Japan, can no longer be litigated in their courts due, in part, to the War Reparations Treaties that have been adopted. The German and Japanese courts say that these treaties extinguish or dissolve any ability to litigate parallel claims, and that this is, in part, due to the absence in international law of *individual rights* to compensation for violations of the Hague Regulations 1907, the law on forced labour or the violation of the prohibitions on sexual slavery.[40]

It is interesting to see how what I will call 'the logic of war' permeates some of the judgments. For example, in 2005, the Tokyo High Court, addressing allegations of rape of two Chinese women by Japanese soldiers, explained:

> Since modern wars cause significant damage to a large number of people in each opponent State, if each national continues to pursue his or her claims for war damages against opponent States, it can hardly be said that the state of war has been terminated.[41]

As we have seen, traditional ideas about war meant the winner would impose conditions on the loser. The issue of a reckoning for violations of the laws of war was not central. In time, however, starting with the Hague Convention IV (1907), some treaties referenced a liability to pay compensation for violations of related provisions.[42]

---

[40] The German case-law is discussed below; for the Japanese cases, see especially *X v Y*, Supreme Court, 27 April 2007, 61 *Minshu* (3) 1188 [2007], English translation in 51 *Japanese Yearbook of International Law* (2008) 518–32 (Chinese citizens claiming with regard to forced labour from 1944); *X v State of Japan and Y*, Nagoya High Court, 8 March 2010, English translation in 54 *Japanese Yearbook of International Law* (2011) 514–22 (recruitment of female forced labour); *X et al v the Government of Japan*, Tokyo High Court, 11 October 2001, HJ (1769) 61 [2002], English translation in 45 *Japanese Annual of International Law* (2002) 144–46 (Dutch prisoners of war).

[41] *X et al v State of Japan*, Tokyo High Court, 18 March 2005, 51 *Shomu Geppo* (11) 2813 [2005], English translation in 49 *Japanese Annual of International Law* (2006) 149–54 at 152.

[42] See Hague Convention IV (1907) Art 3 with regard to the provisions of the attached Regulations, and Additional Protocol I (1977) Art 91 with regard to provisions of the 1949 Geneva Conventions and the Protocol.

In the two World Wars, complex arrangements for reparations were developed. Several treaties, such as the San Francisco Peace Treaty with Japan (1951), were explicit that reparations claims by the nationals of Allied Powers were being waived with regard to 'any actions taken by Japan and its nationals in the course of the prosecution of the war'.[43] Not only does this mean that the courts of Japan have determined that claimants have lost the ability to bring claims before the relevant national courts, but it has also coloured how people think about the whole idea of claims based on violations of the laws of war. It is still often assumed that states have only undertaken to be liable or accountable for violations of the laws of war *to other states* (and not individuals).

But an alternative vision is gaining ground, based on separate, mutually reinforcing ideas. First, consideration of the drafting history of certain original provisions of the 1907 Hague Convention IV and the 1949 Geneva Conventions shows that some proponents were concerned to indemnify particular classes of individuals, even at a time when international law was primarily about bilateral relationships between states.[44] Moreover, it has been highlighted that certain provisions, such as those on the rights of prisoners of war, should be perceived as generating individual entitlements, especially as the Geneva Conventions provide that the rights of prisoners of war, as well as rights belonging to other protected persons, cannot be subject to special agreements between states that would adversely affect the situation of such persons,[45] nor may such persons 'renounce the rights secured to them'.[46]

Second, in 2005, an international instrument negotiated over a period of 15 years,[47] and adopted by all states without a vote, provided guidance and reaffirmed obligations to victims in this context. This text adopted by the UN

---

[43] Treaty of Peace with Japan (1951) Art 14(b).

[44] See Kalshoven, 'State Responsibility for Warlike Acts of the Armed Forces', 40 *ICLQ* (1991) 827–58; Greenwood, 'Expert Opinion: Rights to Compensation of Former Prisoners of War and Civilian Internees under Article 3 of Hague Convention No IV, 1907', in Hisakazu, Isomi and Kantaro (eds), *War and the Rights of Individuals: Renaissance of Individual Compensation* (1999) 59–71 at 63—65; Kalshoven and Zegveld, *Constraints on the Waging of War*, 4th edn (2011) at 75–77, 273–76; *contra* Tomuschat, 'Compensation Before National Courts' (n 4); see also Provost, *International Human Rights and Humanitarian Law* (2002).

[45] See Common Arts 6/6/6/7, explained by Casey-Maslen, 'Special Agreements in International Armed Conflicts', in Clapham, Gaeta and Sassòli (eds), *The 1949 Geneva Conventions: A Commentary* (2015) 135–44.

[46] See Common Arts 7/7/7/8 of the Four Geneva Conventions 1949, explained by d'Argent, 'Non-Renunciation of the Rights Provided by the Conventions', in Clapham, Gaeta and Sassòli (eds), *The 1949 Geneva Conventions: A Commentary* (2015) at 145–53; in more general terms, see Thürer, 'International Humanitarian Law: Theory, Practice, Context', 338 *RCADI* (2008) 9–370 at 51.

[47] Bassiouni, 'International Recognition of Victim's Rights', 6 *HRLR* (2006) 203–79.

General Assembly has the long title of the 'United Nations Basic Principles and Guidelines on the Right to a Remedy and Reparation for Victims of Gross Violations of International Human Rights Law and Serious Violations of International Humanitarian Law'. During its adoption, states were careful to make clear that the text contained no new obligations but rather identified ways of ensuring 'the effective implementation of existing obligations'.[48]

The text extends way beyond what are now sometimes labelled 'atrocity crimes', or issues of 'responsibility to protect'. Indeed Theo van Boven, one of the authors of the expert work that led to the adoption of this instrument, highlighted that 'While the Principles and Guidelines focus on "gross" and "serious" violations, it is generally acknowledged that in principle all violations of human rights and international humanitarian law entail legal consequences.'[49] And the text is careful to state that 'it is understood that the present Basic Principles and Guidelines are without prejudice to the right to a remedy and reparation for victims of all violations of international human rights law and international humanitarian law'.[50]

We also might mention that, at the same time, states have recognized in this text that individuals and non-state actors (including armed groups and businesses) may also have to provide reparations in this context.[51] Moreover, as pointed out by Mona Rishmawi, the Guidelines further extend the notion of 'victim' beyond individual human beings to 'collectivities' and 'indirect victims' such as family members, and on this point they have been influential in fora such as the International Criminal Court.[52]

---

[48] The Chilean Delegate (Muñoz) introducing the text on behalf of the sponsors in the Third Committee where it was adopted by consensus. UN Doc A/C.3/60/SR.39, Meeting 10 November 2005, at 2; the Basic Principles were adopted and proclaimed by General Assembly resolution A/RES/60/147 of 16 December 2005.

[49] Available at https://legal.un.org/avl/ha/ga_60-147/ga_60-147.html.

[50] Principle 26.

[51] Principle 15: 'In cases where a person, a legal person, or other entity is found liable for reparation to a victim, such party should provide reparation to the victim or compensate the State if the State has already provided reparation to the victim.' See also van Boven, 'Introductory Note' at https://legal.un.org/avl/ha/ga_60-147/ga_60-147.html 'While the Principles and Guidelines are drawn up on the basis of State responsibility, the issue of responsibility of non-State actors was also raised in the discussions and negotiations, notably insofar as movements or groups exercise effective control over a certain territory and people in that territory, but also with regard to business enterprises exercising economic power. It was generally felt that non-State actors are to be held responsible for their policies and practices, allowing victims to seek redress and reparation on the basis of legal liability and human solidarity, and not on the basis of State responsibility.'

[52] Principle 8 states: 'For purposes of the present document, victims are persons who individually or collectively suffered harm, including physical or mental injury, emotional suffering, economic loss or substantial impairment of their fundamental rights, through acts or omissions that constitute gross violations of international human rights law, or serious violations of

Nevertheless, in 2006, when a claim was made by 35 civilians in relation to the bombing of the Varvarin Bridge in Serbia by NATO, the German Federal Court of Justice held that 'With regard to violations of international law based on actions against foreign citizens, the person affected was not entitled to bring a claim, but rather his or her native country was.'[53] Moreover, the Court held that references in humanitarian law treaties to liability for payment of compensation 'only supported intergovernmental rather than direct individual restitution claims.'[54] It has been incisively pointed out that the German Court may have been overly focused on the rules developed by the International Law Commission for inter-state responsibility, and failed to take into account that these rules were developed without prejudice to other forms of responsibility and accountability towards actors other than states.[55] The case is now considered an exception to the modern trend to acknowledge reparations for victims of the law of armed conflict.[56]

In the last 15 years, expert opinion has continued to gravitate towards emphasizing that states should provide a remedy and compensation for victims of violations of humanitarian law.[57] This comes in the most considered form in the International Law Association's Declaration of International Law Principles on Reparation for Victims of Armed Conflict (2010). Article 6

---

international humanitarian law. Where appropriate, and in accordance with domestic law, the term "victim" also includes the immediate family or dependants of the direct victim and persons who have suffered harm in intervening to assist victims in distress or to prevent victimization.' The development of this principle and its subsequent application by the International Criminal Court is explained in Rishmawi, 'The Human Rights of Victims' in 'International and Transitional Criminal Justice & Human Rights: Essays in Memory of M Cherif Bassiouni (1937–2017)', 89 *Revue internationale de droit pénal* (2018) 77–87.

[53] *Varvarin Bridge Case, 35 citizens of the Former Federal Republic of Yugoslavia v Germany* (2006) BGHZ 166, 384 at para 6 (translation in IDLC 887 (DE 2006)).

[54] Ibid at para 13.

[55] As highlighted by Aust in ILDC (n 53) at A3. Art 33(2) of the ILC Articles on State Responsibility reads 'This part is without prejudice to any right, arising from the international responsibility of a State, which may accrue directly to any person or entity other than a State.' The ILC Commentary elaborates 'Individual rights under international law may also arise outside the framework of human rights. ... It will be a matter for the particular primary rule to determine whether and to what extent persons or entities other than States are entitled to invoke responsibility on their own account.' Crawford, *The International Law Commission's Articles on State Responsibility: Introduction, Text and Commentaries* (2002) 209–10.

[56] Commentary to ILA Declaration of International Law Principles on Reparation for Victims of Armed Conflict, 74 ILA *Reports of Conferences* (2010) 291–345 at 316 fn112.

[57] Ibid at 312ff; Gaeta, 'Are Victims of Serious Violations of International Humanitarian Law Entitled to Compensation?', in Ben-Naftali (ed), *International Humanitarian Law and International Human Rights Law* (2011) 305–27; Hill-Cawthorne, 'Rights under International Humanitarian Law', 28 *EJIL* (2017) 1187–215.

simply states 'Victims of armed conflict have a right to reparation from the responsible parties.' The Association's Committee on Reparation concluded:

> Whilst claims of the individual were traditionally denied, the dominant view in literature has increasingly come to recognize an individual right to reparation – not only under international human rights law, but also under international humanitarian law. The same shift is discernible in State practice.[58]

The Commentary also explains that 'The Committee can find no reason why the individual, who already enjoys strong protection under international human rights law, should have a weaker position under the rules of international law applicable in armed conflict.'[59] In this context it is being suggested that the compensation provisions in Hague Convention IV (1907) and Additional Protocol I (1977) 'should in the future be interpreted and applied in such a way as to accord an individual rights to compensation for violations of humanitarian law against the state responsible for the violations.'[60]

Paola Gaeta, after a careful scholarly examination of developments in the law of state responsibility beyond the rights of an injured state, is clear about what she considers should be the direction of travel:

> Under contemporary international law, individuals are no longer considered the 'objects' of rights accruing only to states, but are also considered to enjoy rights themselves vis-à-vis states under international law. It would therefore be preposterous to affirm that the position of the individual as a holder of rights dissolves when their need to be protected against abuses reaches its peak, ie in situations of armed conflict, when individuals are more vulnerable than ever. To state that the rules of IHL concerning the guarantees that belligerent parties must afford to civilians in combat operations and to persons in the hands of the enemy have a merely inter-state dimension amounts to asserting, that under this body of law, individuals are at the mercy of belligerents and entitled to protection only as mere objects of belligerents' rights. This construction would mean that the relevant rules of IHL, when they apply, dispossess individuals of their entitlements to be

---

[58] Commentary (n 56) at 312.
[59] Ibid at 318.
[60] Hofmann, 'The 2010 International Law Association Declaration of International Law Principles on Reparation for Victims of Armed Conflict', 78 *ZaöRV* (2018) 551–54 at 553.

protected against illegal conduct by belligerents; that they suppress individuals to a position no different from that of 'endangered species' in situations where, on the contrary, belligerents must not forget they are dealing with human beings.[61]

But the German courts have, so far, failed to revise their position that individual claims cannot be brought on the basis of violations of international humanitarian law.[62] A set of recent claims concern the 2009 German air strike on oil trucks in Afghanistan.[63] In the most recent decision on this incident, the highest Federal Court has pointed to the parallel regimes under human rights law and international criminal law to explain why national tort law should not be read as including a right to claim for violations of humanitarian law. The Court also rehearses the policy argument that, if German courts were to go out on a limb and allow the victims of violations of the laws of war to claim compensation, Germany would no longer be invited by NATO to participate in humanitarian operations:

> In this connection, it should also not be overlooked that the risk of a hardly assessable liability could lead to a reduction in or even a complete end to humanitarian armed deployments by the German armed forces [. . .]. In the eyes, for example, of NATO partners whose national legal systems do not provide for individual claims to compensation for violations of international humanitarian law by their armed forces [. . .], the German armed forces would be limited in their ability to form alliances and take part in combat missions, because of the Damocles sword of – joint and several – public liability hanging over them [. . .].[64]

---

[61] Gaeta, 'Victims of Serious Violations' (n 57) at 319; see also, from a philosophical perspective, Schulzke, *Just War Theory and Civilian Casualties: Protecting the Victims of War* (2017).

[62] See *Vavarin Bridge Case*, 2 BvR 2660/06 German Constitutional Court ILDC 2238 (DE 2013).

[63] Karlsruhe, Federal Court of Justice, Judgement of the 3rd Civil Panel of 6 October 2016, III ZR 140/15, case note explained by Galina Wedel with unofficial translation available at https:// casebook.icrc.org/case-study/afghanistan-bombing-civilian-truck.

[64] Ibid at para 38(b). The original reads: 'In diesem Zusam-menhang darf auch nicht übersehen werden, dass das Risiko einer kaum ab-schätzbaren Haftung dazu führen könnte, dass humanitär motivierte bewaffnete Auslandseinsätze der Bundeswehr reduziert oder gar gänzlich eingestellt würden (Jutzi aaO S. 44). Aus Sicht zum Beispiel der NATO-Partner, deren na-tionale Rechtsordnungen individuelle Schadensersatzansprüche wegen Ver-stößen ihrer Streitkräfte gegen das humanitäre Völkerrecht nicht vorsehen (Raap, NVwZ 2013 aaO S. 554; BWV 2016 aaO S. 130), wären die deutschen Streitkräfte auf Grund des Damokles-Schwertes der – auch gesamtschuldneri-schen – Amtshaftung nur noch bedingt bündnis- und kampfeinsatzfähig (vgl. von Woedtke aaO S. 324).'

In general, the judges and legislators of states currently involved in international armed conflicts seem unenthusiastic about developing remedies for claims for compensation in the context of armed conflict. Although a stream of academic commentary pleads for a recognition that the individual victims of violations of the laws of war should have a right to make claims as a matter of international rights before national courts, a number of counter-assumptions remain. First, that the law of armed conflict does not generate enforceable rights to compensation. Second, that national courts should not in general be considering the actions of the military abroad. And, third, even if there could be national public law reviews of administrative decisions related to targeting, judges cannot equate the decisions of an 'administrative officer' to those of a 'soldier in combat'.[65]

And not all academic commentary points to the desirability of 'humanizing' or 'individualizing' claims about violations of the laws of war. Commenting on the prospect of allowing tort law to be used to address breaches of the law of armed conflict in national courts, Gärditz opines:

> National courtrooms are not necessarily adequate forums for assessing state conduct in international affairs, in particular armed conflicts. The perspective of the judge deciding on tort (or criminal) liability is unavoidably of a discrete case where the parties present arguments and evidence. Armed conflicts, on the other hand, are usually widespread, complex, and highly political. Applying tort liability against the state for military operations entails the risk that macroconflicts will be broken down into separate cases that can be fought as microwars at court, bereft of their political character.[66]

The idea that war reparations are exclusively reserved to the state bringing a claim at the international level, is, however, likely to be rejected by a national court at some point. For the moment the German and Japanese courts continue to reject individual claims, many of which are said to be barred by waivers contained in peace treaties from the Second World War. The future success of claims by individuals beyond this context should be built on the growing recognition that states have to provide victims of certain violations a remedy,[67] that under the Geneva Conventions of 1949 states cannot override

---

[65] Ibid at para 33: 'Darüber hinaus kann die Entscheidungssituation eines verwaltungs-mäßig handelnden Beamten nicht mit der Gefechtssituation eines im Kampfein-satz befindlichen Soldaten gleichgesetzt werden.'

[66] Gärditz, 'Bridge of Varvarin', 108 *AJIL* (2014) 86–93 at 92.

[67] See the UN Basic Principles and Guidelines (2005) (n 48).

certain individual rights,[68] that states cannot absolve themselves from liability for grave breaches of the four Geneva Conventions,[69] and that, even if there might be national procedural bars to litigating these cases in national courts, the substantive international claims of victims and collectivities cannot be extinguished by treaties – as the international rights now belong to the individual victims and other entities and not exclusively to states.[70]

On this last point, the Japanese Supreme Court explicitly stated:

> Considering that the purpose of the waiver of claims under the Framework of the San Francisco Peace Treaty is to prevent issues concerning claims from being brought up in individual and ex-post civil litigation, the term "waiver of claims" in this context should be understood to mean not to extinguish substantive claims but to extinguish the ability to litigate such substantive claims.[71]

In other words, what is extinguished is the right of the victim to claim reparation in court (including compensation, restitution and guarantees of non-repetition).[72] Intriguingly, the same judgment ends with a reminder that nothing prevents the party being sued from satisfying the victims' claims; indeed the Supreme Court's judgment ends by stating that it expected this to happen:

> [E]ven under the Framework of the San Francisco Peace Treaty, the obligors are not prevented from voluntarily and spontaneously taking measures to satisfy specific claims. Taking into consideration various circumstances, for example, the Victims' tremendous mental and physical suffering, the considerable benefits enjoyed by the appellant by having Chinese workers engaged in forced labor under the aforementioned harsh working conditions, and the aforementioned compensation received by the appellants, we

---

[68] See Common Arts 6/6/6/7 and 7/7/7/8 of the Four Geneva Conventions 1949.

[69] See Common Arts 51/52/131/148 of the Four Geneva Conventions 1949.

[70] See, in this direction, Dinstein, *The Conduct of Hostilities under the Law of International Armed Conflict*, 3rd edn (2016) at 29; see also Greenwood, 'Rights at the Frontier – Protecting the Individual in Time of War', in Rider (ed), *Law at the Centre: The Institute of Advanced Legal Studies at Fifty* (1999) 277–93.

[71] *X v Y*, 27 April 2007 (n 40) at 526.

[72] See UN Basic Principles and Guidelines (n 48) principles 15–23; ILA Declaration of International Law Principles on Reparation for Victims of Armed Conflict, Arts 6–10; De Greiff, 'Justice and Reparations', in De Greiff (ed), *The Handbook of Reparations* (2008) 451–77.

expect the appellant and other parties concerned to make efforts to provide relief to the Victims.[73]

In this stream of litigation, one of the defendants was the Nishimatsu Construction Company, and the reference is to the financial benefits accrued by such companies in the context of forced labour during the Second World War. The detailed study by Webster explains the eventual settlements reached by the Nishimatsu Company, and highlights the importance of apology, acknowledgement of legal liability and memoralialization (involving not only physical memorials, but also commemorative rituals for the dead).[74]

The recent Mitsubishi Settlement Agreement (2016) is worth quoting to give a flavour:

Article 1 (Apology)
Party B [Mitsubishi Materials Corporation] apologi[z]es for this Case as follows, and Party A [YAN Yu Cheng [闫玉成]] accepts the sincere apology of Party B.

During World War II, about 39,000 Chinese laborers were kidnapped forcibly to Japan in accordance with the 'Resolution on the Importation of Chinese Labor to Japan' enacted by the Cabinet of the Government of Japan. Out of this group our company's predecessor Mitsubishi Mining Company and its contractors accepted 3,765 Chinese laborers at its facilities, and forced them to work under harsh conditions, resulting in the death of as many as 722 Chinese laborers. This issue remains unresolved to this day.

'A true mistake is having erred and not correct it.' Our company frankly and truthfully admit the historical fact that the human rights of these Chinese laborers were violated, for which we express deep remorse. These Chinese laborers were separated from their country and their families, and had to suffer great pain and suffering in a foreign land. For this, our company accepts the historical responsibility of those who used this labor, and

---

[73] *X v Y*, 27 April 2007 (n 40) at 532; a case note is also provided by Levin, '*Nishimatsu Construction Co v Song Jixiao et al*; *Kō Hanako et al v Japan*', 102 *AJIL* (2008) 148–54; the two cases (forced labour and sexual slavery) were dealt with together and the legal reasoning is the same.

[74] Webster, 'The Price of Settlement: World War II Reparations in China, Japan and Korea', 51 *New York University Journal of International Law and Politics* (2019) 301–84 at 356–65 and 318–29.

sincerely apologizes to these Chinese laborers and their survivors. We also deeply mourn those Chinese laborers who died.

'Past experience must be our guide for the future.' Our company admits to the above-stated historical fact and historical responsibility, and from the perspective of contributing to improved Japanese-Sino relationship, will make payments towards a fund for these Chinese laborers and their survivors as part of the final overall solution. To prevent a repeat of past mistake, our company will assist in the erection of a memorial, and promises to pass this fact down to future generations.

...

Article 3 (Payment to indicate sincere apology, establishment of a fund)
1. As an indication of a sincere apology in Article 1, Party B will pay each confirmed member of the 3,765 Chinese laborers (hereinafter called 'Original Laborers') RMB 100,000 through a fund established by the clause below (hereinafter referred to as "the Fund").... For each deceased Original Laborer, the Fund will pay RMB 100,000 to his/her survivors with the right to inheritance as defined according [to] the law of the People's Republic of China (hereinafter referred to as "Survivors with right of inheritance").[75]

Under Article 5, the Fund is to cover, *inter alia*, the memorial service to take place in Japan and the building of the memorial in Japan.

In parallel developments, the Supreme Court of Korea has held that it is not bound by the findings of Japanese courts that the Claims Agreement (1965) between the two states removed the possibility of claims by the victims of forced labour against Japanese companies. The Korean Supreme Court held that states could not, by treaty, waive without permission an individual's pre-existing rights.[76] In subsequent cases, the Supreme Court has upheld awards of compensation (circa $90,000) for each victim against the New Nippon Steel Corporation and Mitsubishi.[77] The claims go beyond

---

[75] English version available at http://www.10000cfj.org/en/wp-content/uploads/2016/09/SETTLEMENT-AGREEMENT.pdf, accessed 30 April 2020; for more detail and an explanation of the significance of the quotes in the Settlement, see Webster, 'The Price of Settlement' (n 74).

[76] 'Further, a country may not expire a citizen's individual right to claim without consent of an individual citizen by treaty where a diplomatic protection right is abandoned. It is against the principle of modern law.' See *Claims for damages and wage payment claims against Mitsubishi Heavy Industries brought by victims of Japan's forced mobilization, Park and ors v Mitsubishi Heavy Industries Limited*, 2009 Da 22549, ILDC 1909 (KR 2012), 24 May 2012, at para 60.

[77] *Yeo Woon Taek v New Nippon Steel Corporation*, Supreme Court of South Korea, 30 October 2018, 2013 Da 61381; discussed by Lee and Lee, case note, 113 *AJIL* (2019) 592–99; and see the report of the judgment concerning Mitsubishi, 'South Korea's top court orders Mitsubishi Heavy to pay compensation for wartime labor', *Japan Times* (29 November 2018).

questions of unpaid wages, and in the *Nippon Case* were described by the Supreme Court as concerning

> the forced mobilization victims' rights to claim solatium [compensation for emotional harm] against [the] Japanese corporation, premised upon the Japanese corporation's unlawful acts against humanity with direct links to the Japanese Government's unlawful colonial domination of the Korean Peninsula and waging of wars of aggression . . .[78]

Let us now consider two modern innovative international arrangements that addressed the issue of reparations for the victims of war. In the first case, this was because the UN Security Council took decisive action with regard to the damage caused by the Iraqi invasion of Kuwait; and in the second case, it was because the states of Ethiopia and Eritrea agreed to set up an Arbitral Commission.

10.4 The UN Compensation Commission

In October 1990, two months after Iraq invaded Kuwait, the Security Council condemned

> the actions by the Iraqi authorities and occupying forces to take third-State nationals hostage and to mistreat and oppress Kuwaiti and third-State nationals, and the other actions reported to the Council, such as the destruction of Kuwaiti demographic records, the forced departure of Kuwaitis, the relocation of population in Kuwait and the unlawful destruction and seizure of public and private property in Kuwait, including hospital supplies and equipment, in violation of the decisions of the Council, the Charter of the United Nations, the Geneva Convention relative to the Protection of Civilian Persons in Time of War.

The Council continued by

> Reaffirming that the above-mentioned Geneva Convention applies to Kuwait and that, as a High Contracting Party to the Convention, Iraq is

---

[78] Section 4(B)(1), *Nippon Stell Corp* (n 77) English translation from the Court's website.

bound to comply fully with all its terms and in particular is liable under the Convention in respect of the grave breaches committed by it, as are individuals who commit or order the commission of grave breaches.[79]

It then reminded Iraq

that under international law it is liable for any loss, damage or injury arising in regard to Kuwait and third States, and their nationals and corporations, as a result of the invasion and illegal occupation of Kuwait by Iraq; . . .[80]

In March 1991 the UN Security Council went further, and demanded that Iraq '[a]ccept in principle its liability under international law' for the invasion and illegal occupation.[81] One month later, in what is known as the 'cease-fire resolution',[82] the Council reaffirmed that Iraq was liable, referencing this time 'any direct loss, damage – including environmental damage and the depletion of natural resources'.[83] The following month the Council established its Compensation Commission.

Again we see here limitations placed on the mechanism in the light of the target state's capacity to pay. At first the Security Council decided that compensation should not exceed 30% of the value of Iraq's exports of petroleum and petroleum products, later reduced to 25% in 2000 and then again reduced to 5% in 2003.[84] There is also a reflection of the old idea that payment can be demanded for the costs of the winning side in the war. By now, however, this can no longer be seen as the 'loser pays in war' principle, but rather as a requirement that the aggressor pay for the actual damage caused by both sides:

---

[79] Resolution 674 (1990) preamble.

[80] Ibid at para 8.

[81] Resolution 686 (1991) para 2.

[82] See Mensah, 'United Nations Compensation Commission (UNCC)', *MPEPIL* (2011), who explains (at para 2) that the Security Council had demanded that Iraq accept its liability under international law as a condition of the cease-fire.

[83] Resolution 687 (1991) para 16; for discussion of some of the aspects relating to the environmental damage, see Boisson De Chazournes and Campanelli, 'The United Nations Compensation Commission: Time for an Assessment?', in Fischer-Lescano et al (eds), *Frieden in Freiheit – Peace in Liberty – Paix en liberté: Festschrift für Michael Bothe zum 70. Geburtstag* (2008) 3–17.

[84] For details, see Higgins et al, *Oppenheim's International Law: United Nations* (2017) at 1279–80.

> [T]he starting point is the existence in contemporary international law of a norm which *post bellum* permits or even demands the liability of the aggressor state, charging it with an obligation to make good not only the entire amount of damage caused by itself, but also damage arising from the legitimate exercise of self-defence by the state that is the victim of the aggression.[85]

Nevertheless, the Governing Council of the Commission (members of the Security Council) excluded from the compensation scheme 'the costs of the Allied Forces, including those of military operations against Iraq',[86] even though one distinguished commentator had argued that 'The element of calculated deliberate aggression by Iraq would necessarily seem to widen the responsibility for the consequences resulting from its act. Thus it seems difficult to exclude the Allies' costs of waging the war'.[87]

Today it seems unlikely that a state will be able to recoup the costs of going to war as a matter of right (eg authorized by the Security Council or as a matter of self-defence) before an international court. Nevertheless, the reticence of the Security Council to impose such an obligation on Iraq will have been partly influenced by Iraq's ability to pay; but a state that started an aggressive war could indeed find that the Council might nevertheless seek to recoup the entire cost of restoring international peace and security. The obligation to pay imposed by the Security Council will flow from UN membership under the Charter. Recouping your costs can therefore no longer be seen as confined to the defunct prerogative of the winner in war.

This UN Commission marks an important step, because the compensation was awarded on the basis of *damage caused* rather than the *costs of a War*. Moreover, the sums awarded are substantial, around $50 billion, and they have actually been paid. They were paid because a portion of Iraq's petroleum revenue was put aside by the Security Council in order to ensure sufficient funds. The situation remains rather exceptional, however, as Iraq accepted its liability for its violation of international law related to the invasion along with the damages that should be paid as a consequence.

---

[85] Gattini, 'The UN Compensation Commission: Old Rules, New Procedures on War Reparations', 13 *EJIL* (2002) 161–81 at 173.

[86] S/AC.26/Dec.19 (1994).

[87] Fox, 'Reparations and State Responsibility' in Rowe (ed), *The Gulf War 1990–91 in International and English Law* (1993) 261–86 at 277.

Lastly, the remedies remain one-sided. No violations of the laws of war by the Allied forces that succeeded in expelling Iraq from Kuwait could come within the scope of the work of the Commission.[88]

10.5 Eritrea–Ethiopia Claims Commission

The peace treaty that ended the conflict between Ethiopia and Eritrea in 2000 made provision for a Boundary Commission and a Claims Commission. Each state could file complaints against the other for violations of international law on its own behalf and on behalf of its nationals and corporations, or even on behalf of non-nationals of Ethiopian or Eritrean 'origin'.[89] This time the parties were clear on the costs of war: 'The Commission shall not hear claims arising from the cost of military operations, preparing for military operations, or the use of force, except to the extent that such claims involve violations of international humanitarian law'.[90] The two states nevertheless agreed that the Commission had jurisdiction over the legality of the use of force as a matter of *jus ad bellum* under the UN Charter.[91]

The Commission, having determined that the initial use of force by Eritrea constituted a violation of the UN Charter's prohibition on the use of force, had to determine how much of the damage from the resulting war could be billed to that state. Although the costs of self-defence were not in issue under the terms of the peace Agreement, Ethiopia sought damages, *inter alia*, for the displacement of civilians, civilian death at the war front, civilian property damage, the premature deaths of prisoners of war, loss of investment, loss of tourism and loss of profits for Ethiopian Airlines. Interestingly, the Commission, having found a *jus ad bellum* violation of the UN Charter, explained to the parties that the 'Commission does not regard its *jus ad bellum*

---

[88] Members of the armed forces of the Allied forces, however, were eligible for compensation related to mistreatment in violation of international humanitarian law as prisoners of war. UN Governing Council S/AC.26/1992/11, 26 June 1992.

[89] Art 5(9) of the of the Agreement between the Government of the State of Eritrea and the Government of the Federal Democratic Republic of Ethiopia, UN Doc A/55/686-S/2000/ 1183, 13 December 2000; see further Brilmayer, Giorgetti and Charlton, *International Claims Commissions: Righting Wrongs after Conflict* (2017) at 230, and Klein, 'Eritrea–Ethiopia Claims Commission', *MPEPIL* (2013) at para 11.

[90] Art 5(1) of the Agreement (n 89).

[91] Explained by Murphy, Kidane and Snider, *Litigating War: Mass Civil Injury and the Eritrea– Ethiopia Claims Commission* (2013) at 104ff.

finding as a finding that Eritrea initiated an aggressive war for which it bears the extensive financial responsibility claimed by Ethiopia.[92]

The Commission also highlighted that the reparations that followed the World Wars were not strictly speaking based on damages according to international law, but rather shaped by policies related to revenge against Germany for the First World War and economic reintegration in the context of the Second World War. And that, with regard that that War, the 'States deemed by the international community to be directly responsible for the war ultimately bore financial consequences that were modest in relation to the resulting damages.'[93] In any event, the Commission reminds us that 'Throughout history, indemnities frequently have been exacted from the losing parties in wars, but this has resulted from the exercise of power by the victor, not the application of the international law of State responsibility.'[94]

The Commission was then faced with how far the law of state responsibility should extend to the damage caused in this Etritrea–Ethiopia war. The Commission decided that it went beyond the damage caused by the initial Eritrean attack on the town of Badme, but it limited the award of damages under this *jus ad bellum* head to damage where there was a 'proximate cause', a concept and requirement advocated by Eritrea. In Decision No 7, the Commission explained:

> In assessing whether this test is met, and whether the chain of causation is sufficiently close in a particular situation, the Commission will give weight to whether particular damage reasonably should have been foreseeable to an actor committing the international delict in question.[95]

A second intriguing dilemma concerned the issue of damages for events that were illegal under both the UN Charter prohibition on the use of force and the law of armed conflict. The targeted destruction of a civilian building, or the bombing of a military object resulting in an expected, disproportionate number of civilian casualties, would be illegal under both branches of international law if undertaken by the state resorting to the unlawful use of force.

---

[92] See Decision No 7 (27 July 2007) 'Guidance Regarding *Jus Ad Bellum* Liability' at para 5. Eritrea-Ethiopia Claims Commission - Preliminary Decisions
August 2001, December 2005 and July 2007
XXVI RIAA (2009) 1-22 at 10-20.
[93] Ibid at para 24.
[94] Ibid at para 21.
[95] Ibid para 13.

The Commission was probably the first body to really grapple with this as a practical rather than a philosophical matter. It delayed determining the question of damages for the violation of the UN Charter until after it had dealt with the violations of the law of armed conflict, and it sought to avoid 'double counting'. This then left the question of assessing damages for acts that flowed from the violation of the UN Charter, but which were not in themselves violations of the laws of armed conflict. So, for example, the use of landmines by Eritrea was found not to be illegal under the *jus in bello* as Eritrea was not bound by the relevant treaty. On the other hand, the damage to Ethiopians from those mines was a reasonably foreseeable and proximate consequence of the violation of the Charter (*jus ad bellum*). Similarly, the displacement of civilians was not found to be a violation of the laws of armed conflict, but it was nevertheless the foreseeable result of the initial illegal use of force.

To rationalize the award of damages for the violation of the UN Charter, the Commission places this war in the context of our wider discussion of reparations in war:

> Eritrea's violation of the *jus ad bellum* in May 1998 as found by the Commission was serious, and had serious consequences. Nevertheless, that violation was different in magnitude and character from the aggressive uses of force marking the onset of the Second World War, the invasion of South Korea in 1950, or Iraq's 1990 invasion and occupation of Kuwait. The Commission believes that determination of compensation must take such factors into account. The Commission also considered whether an award of compensation should be limited as necessary to ensure that the financial burden imposed on Eritrea would not be so excessive, given Eritrea's economic condition and its capacity to pay, as seriously to damage Eritrea's ability to meet its people's basic needs.[96]

The Commission went on to explain how a reparations programme should not itself undermine a successful peace, referencing the Treaty of Versailles.[97]

Most interestingly, the Commission then explained its reasoning when it came to assessing damages for giving a violation of the UN Charter (*jus ad bellum*) less weight than the actual violations of the law of armed conflict (*jus in bello*). The damages were in the end to be rough approximations rather

---

[96] Final Award Ethiopia's Damages Claims, 17 August 2009, XXVI RIAA (2009) at 728 at para 312–313.

[97] Ibid at 729 para 315.

than an exact calculation of lost earnings, etc. But when dealing with death, destruction and displacement, why should it matter whether the damage comes from a violation of the UN Charter or the Geneva Conventions? Why not assess the harm done under each heading? The Commission explained its approach as follows:

> Imposing extensive liability for conduct that does not violate the *jus in bello* risks eroding the weight and authority of that law and the incentive to comply with it, to the injury of those it aims to protect. The Commission believes that, while appropriate compensation to a claiming State is required to reflect the severity of damage caused to that State by the violation of the *jus ad bellum,* it is not the same as that required for violations of the *jus in bello.*[98]

In other words, there was a fear that if it became understood that an aggressor state was liable for all the damage done, whether or not there was a violation of the law of armed conflict including war crimes, then there would be no incentive for that state to abide by the rules on targeting. If the state has to pay for all the damage done anyway, there would, according to this logic, be no incentive to distinguishing between civilian objectives and military objectives.

In the end the Commission was perhaps most influenced by the nature of the claims and the difficulty of assessing actual damage. A few examples will illustrate the challenge that will be faced by any body seeking to award reparations after a war. First, the Commission dealt with the claim concerning the internally displaced in Ethiopia, finding that 'Eritrea is liable for injury to Ethiopians who were internally displaced from those areas and during those times on account of the war.'[99] The claim for damages was that 349,837 Ethiopians had been displaced, and the award should be about $600 per individual, totalling about $209 million. In addition there was a claim for $1.3 billion in moral (punitive) damages. Although the claim for moral damages was rejected, the Commission took 'into account the evidence of the nature of [internally displaced persons'] injuries and experiences in considering the level of compensation.'[100] Ethiopia was awarded $45 million for the

---

[98] Ibid at 730 para 316.
[99] Ibid at 731 para 321.
[100] Ibid at 732 para 326.

human suffering and lost income associated with these internally displaced persons.[101]

Claims for loss of profits, development assistance and investment were difficult for the Commission, bearing in mind the tests of proximate cause and foreseeability. But some passages reveal a more general attitude to the perceived inherent problem of assessing war reparations:

> No system of legal liability can address all of the economic consequences of war. Costs and delays happen; business is injured; plans and expectations are disrupted. International law does not impose liability for such generalized economic and social consequences of war.[102]

Many of the claims were dismissed or reduced. To understand this emerging topic, we might highlight one claim that nevertheless succeeded in part.

Ethiopia claimed loss of profits for Ethiopian Airlines. Precisely because this was a state-owned carrier, and the planes were at risk of seizure as enemy public property under the law of war should they land in Eritrea, as well as the obvious fall off in passengers and difficulty of obtaining insurance, the Commission found Eritrea liable for the associated loss of profits. It concluded

> that documented lost profits from termination of the Addis Ababa–Asmara service were the proximate result of Eritrea's *jus ad bellum* breach. Clearly it was, or should have been, foreseeable to Eritrea's leaders that a likely result of Eritrea's action at Badme would be the interruption of commercial air service between the two capitals, with attendant economic injury to [Ethiopian Airlines].[103]

Ultimately, the overall total awarded in 2007 to Ethiopia was around $174 million, roughly half for Eritrea's violations of the law of armed conflict (*inter alia*, death, disappearance, destruction, damage and detention of civilians) and the slightly larger portion for the violations of *jus ad bellum* related to starting the war (*inter alia*, the suffering and economic losses of the internally displaced, the death and injury of civilians, damage from shelling, deaths from landmines, loss of profits for Ethiopian Airlines).[104] Eritrea was

---

[101] The details of all the categories of award are to be found ibid at 768ff.
[102] Ibid at 747 para 395.
[103] Ibid at 761 para 450.
[104] Ibid at 768–70.

awarded compensation for violations by Ethiopia of the law of armed conflict (*jus in bello*) of around $161 million, and an additional $2 million awarded to Eritrean nationals as claimants.[105]

Unfortunately the itemized claims and awards have so far not translated into actual compensation for the individuals, communities and organizations damaged by the war.[106] Nevertheless, the awards by the Commission have put paid to the idea of the impossibility of determining what reparations should be paid for violations of the laws of war, including the damages owed by the state that starts a war.

10.6 International Criminal Law

In my experience, when reporting on the horrors of war, journalists and others quickly want to know 'But is it a war crime, are we dealing with genocide?' Similarly, reframing violations of human rights as crimes against humanity grabs attention and moves a story closer to the headlines. The prospect of war criminals' facing justice is also often accompanied, consciously or subconsciously, with the grainy black and white photos of famous war crimes trials. Such predispositions to see all violations of the laws of war as leading to war crimes trials have been reinforced by the adoption at the United Nations in the 21st century of the 'Responsibility to Protect' agenda, which essentially creates an expectation that states will act when faced with the commission of such international crimes in other states.[107] Before we launch into an examination of the framework that exists for the prosecution of international crimes, it is worth pausing to reflect on what gets overlooked, covered up or simply ignored when dealing with violence in war.

The expression 'rape as a weapon of war' has tragically become all too familiar as a way of describing the horrific rates of sexual violence in recent armed conflicts. It was not always thus. Christina Lamb's recent book is entitled *Our Bodies Their Battlefield: What War Does to Women*. She stresses how often rape in war has been considered normal. She reminds us:

---

[105] Final Award Eritrea's Damages Claims, 17 August 2009, XXVI RIAA (2009) at 629-30.

[106] Brilmayer et al, *International Claims Commissions* (n 89) 240–44.

[107] See further Bellamy, *The Responsibility to Protect: A Defense* (2015); Orford, *International Authority and the Responsibility to Protect* (2011) Evans, *The Responsibility to Protect: Ending Mass Atrocity Crimes Once and for All* (2008).

The word rape comes from the Middle English *rapen, rappen* – to abduct, ravish, snatch. It originates from the Latin *rapere* which means to steal, seize or carry away, as if women were property, which is exactly what men thought for so many centuries.[108]

Lamb interviews survivors and victims from across the globe, and shares their frustration at the absence of meaningful justice. This is a reference not only to the scarcity of criminal prosecutions, but also to the inadequacy of arrangements for reparations, counselling, health care and admissions of responsibility. She also interviews those who have struggled to bring about healing and accountability. What came through to me was that rape is not just something that happens in war but may be part of the purpose of warfare; and, furthermore, the inability to end such sexual violence is linked to war as a state of mind.

Lamb spent time with Dr Mukwege in the Democratic Republic of Congo at his clinic. Here he told her, 'It's not a sexual thing, it's a way to destroy another, to take from inside the victim the sense of being a human, and show you don't exist, you are nothing'. He also explained the thinking behind such violence (and this applies in other contemporary conflicts as well):

It's a deliberate strategy: raping a woman in front of her husband to humiliate him so he leaves and shame falls on the victim and it's impossible to live with the reality so the first reaction is to leave the area and there is total destruction of the community. . . . Rape as a weapon of war can displace a whole demographic and have the same effect as a conventional weapon but at much lesser cost.[109]

The Guatemalan judge, Iris Yassmin Barrios Aguillar, also interviewed by Lamb, explained how women in Guatemala were 'seen as a military objective'.[110] And Navi Pillay, a judge on two international criminal tribunals, explained how the conviction and judgment in the *Akayesu* case focused on what rape meant for the women: 'Until then rape had been regarded as collateral damage'.[111] Pillay captures it brilliantly 'People think war authorises to kill, so raping women is nothing'.[112]

---

[108] Lamb, *Our Bodies Their Battlefield* (2020) at 201.
[109] Ibid at 304–05.
[110] Ibid at 381.
[111] Ibid at 148; the relevant judgment is *Prosecutor v Akayesu*, ICTR-96-4-T, 2 September 1998.
[112] Ibid at 399.

These insights help us see how rape and the inadequate responses to it are bound up with ingrained ways of thinking about war. At the same time, concentrating too much on rape as a weapon of war can skew attention away from the prevalent sexual violence carried out within society and especially in time of conflict.[113] The focus on the idea that rape should be seen as a weapon, or even a strategy or tactic, means that we ignore the multiple aspects of sexual violence in armed conflict,[114] much of it happening away from the fighting, in the home, on the edges of the village, in schools and workplaces, much of it exacerbated by the war but related to micro disputes not part of the overall war.[115] This is not only an issue of how we choose to look at rape, it is a question of resources, criminal prosecution priorities, access to justice and long-term reconstruction that deals with the structural issues in society necessary for a sustainable peace.[116] Attention is now turning to how to work on the factors that underlie gender power inequalities, which necessitates thinking beyond the binary of perpetrators and victims.[117]

The virtual absence of prosecution of sexual violence in wartime is due, in part, to a complete lack of political will and, in part, because such crimes may take place out of public sight or in ways that are considered too shameful for the survivors to recount. Gerry Simpson asks us not to focus on the precedents but rather on the 'unprecedents' – the times when war crimes were not

---

[113] Heaton, 'The Risks of Instrumentalizing the Narrative on Sexual Violence in the DRC: Neglected Needs and Unintended Consequences', 96 *IRRC* (2014) 625–39.

[114] For an overview of many of the issues and some of the debates in the feminist literature see Chinkin, 'Gender and Armed Conflict', in Clapham and Gaeta (eds), *The Oxford Handbook of International Law in Armed Conflict* (2014) 675–99 esp at 693ff. See also Wood, 'Conflict-related Sexual Violence and the Policy Implications of Recent Research', 96 *IRRC* (2014) 457–78; Henry, 'The Fixation on Wartime Rape: Feminist Critique and International Criminal Law', 23 *Social and Legal Studies* (2014) 93–111.

[115] Eriksson Baaz and Stern, *Sexual Violence as a Weapon of War? Perceptions, Prescriptions, Problems in the Congo and Beyond* (2013).

[116] Luedke and Logan, '"That Thing of Human Rights": Discourse, Emergency Assistance, and Sexual Violence in South Sudan's Current Civil War', 42 *Disasters* (2018) 99–118; see also Engle, *The Grip of Sexual Violence in* Conflict (2020) at 151, who is concerned that the focus on sexual violence has 'distorted the lens through which feminists understand, represent, and address issues of gender, sex, ethnicity, and armed conflict'. The responses that support militarized or criminalized responses 'have displaced attention to imperialist, economic distribution, and – relatedly – causes of the very armed conflict in which they aim to intervene'.

[117] Céspedes-Báez, 'A (Feminist) Farewell to Arms: The Impact of the Peace Process with the FARC-EP on Colombian Feminism', 52 *Cornell International Law Journal* (2019) 39–63; Korac, 'Feminists against Sexual Violence in War: The Question of Perpetrators and Victims Revisited', 7 *Social Sciences* (2018) 182.

prosecuted – as, just like monuments that 'un-remember' acts of history, so too 'trials sometimes erase those "crimes" not juridified'.[118]

Let us turn now to the prosecution of war crimes more generally. Crimes committed in wartime may not necessarily be prosecuted as war crimes. Even when states do discipline their troops, they rarely prosecute their *own* forces for war crimes (the same acts can usually be prosecuted under military justice codes or the ordinary criminal law).[119] This may be changing. The creation of the International Criminal Court is starting to affect how states inquire into their own forces' crimes and how they conduct military justice. The recent Inquiry into the killings by Australian forces in Afghanistan may lead to some of the first modern war crimes prosecutions by a state of its own forces. The Inquiry's report explains at several points how action in Australia would have to meet the standards set by the International Criminal Court, or otherwise that Court could exercise jurisdiction over the alleged war crimes. On the substance the Inquiry found:

> that there is *credible information* of 23 incidents in which one or more non-combatants or persons *hors-de-combat* were unlawfully killed by or at the direction of members of the Special Operations Task Group in circumstances which, if accepted by a jury, would be the war crime of murder, and a further two incidents in which a non-combatant or person *hors-de-combat* was mistreated in circumstances which, if so accepted, would be the war crime of cruel treatment. Some of these incidents involved a single victim, and some multiple victims.
>
> These incidents involved:
> a. a total of 39 individuals killed, and a further two cruelly treated; and
> b. a total of 25 current or former Australian Defence Force personnel who were perpetrators, either as principals or accessories, some of them on a single occasion and a few on multiple occasions.

---

[118] Simpson, 'Unprecedents', in Tallgren and Skouteris (eds), *The New Histories of International Criminal Law: Retrials* (2019) 12–29 at 24; see also Mégret, 'International Criminal Justice History Writing as Anachronism: The Past that Did Not Lead to the Present', ibid 72–89.

[119] For a rare exception, see Rasiah, 'The Court-martial of Corporal Payne and Others and the Future Landscape of International Criminal Justice', 7 *JICJ* (2009) 177–99; even here the author concludes (ibid at 195) 'the military court-martial is an inherently self-serving institution with a tendency to operate as a damage limitation mechanism, focussing responsibility on the lower ranks, characterizing criminality as the aberrant conduct of a few "bad apples", and failing to call the political and military elite to account for their role in the implementation of the systems that lead to or facilitated the crimes in question.'; for an introduction to the shortcomings of the US system, see Fidell, *Military Justice: A Very Short Introduction* (2016).

None of these are incidents of disputable decisions made under pressure in the heat of battle. The cases in which it has been found that there is credible information of a war crime are ones in which it was or should have been plain that the person killed was a non-combatant, or *hors-de-combat*. While a few of these are cases of Afghan local nationals encountered during an operation who were on no reasonable view participating in hostilities, the vast majority are cases where the persons were killed when hors-de-combat because they had been captured and were persons under control, and as such were protected under international law, breach of which was a crime.[120]

The international law on war crimes, in a great part thanks to the existence of the International Criminal Court, has moved to the forefront of how we react to allegations of violations of international humanitarian law. On hearing of a violation of the law of war, the automatic response is that there should be a trial of the suspected war criminal. Considering the prospect of prosecution of the perpetrator is an important aspect of accountability, but I want to outline the international criminal law as much for the other measures of liability that this branch of law can introduce.

For example, at the international level, in the context of UN peacekeeping, the United Nations has developed its own due diligence policy, which relies in part on international criminal law.[121] The international regime that prohibits certain arms transfers relies in part on a prohibition on any transfer where a state party has knowledge that the arms would be used in the commission of certain international crimes.[122] At the national level, individuals and companies that furnish arms, ammunition and fuel to parties in foreign conflicts could still find themselves held accountable for complicity in war crimes.[123]

And framing a violation as an international crime can mean that national statutes of limitation, which would preclude prosecutions after a certain period, do not apply.[124] The defence of superior orders could also be precluded,

---

[120] Report of Inquiry under Division 4a of Part 4 of the Inspector-General of the Australian Defence Force Regulation 2016 into Questions of Unlawful Conduct Concerning The Special Operations Task Group in Afghanistan (2020) at 29, paras 15–17.

[121] Human rights due diligence policy on United Nations support to non-United Nations security forces (2013) UN Doc A/67/775–S/2013/110, Annex paras 1 and 12.

[122] Arms Trade Treaty (2013) Art 6(3), explained in Casey-Maslen, Clapham, Giacca and Parker, *The Arms Trade Treaty: A Commentary* (2016) 229–43.

[123] Hathaway, Haviland, Kethireddy and Yamamoto, 'Yemen: Is the US Breaking the Law?', 10 *Harvard National Security Journal* (2019) 1–74.

[124] Cassese et al, *Cassese's International Criminal Law*, 3rd edn (2013) at 313–15.

while the possibility of prosecution for command responsibility is opened up.[125] Immunities that protect officials from prosecution abroad may not apply in the face of certain international crimes.[126] And the rule that prevents prosecution for an offence that was not criminal at the time it was committed, contains an exception where the individual is accused of international crimes.[127]

Lastly, as we shall see, under rules related to universal jurisdiction, acts that constitute international crimes may be prosecuted outside the state where they were committed. In the case of grave breaches of the Geneva Conventions and Protocol I, there will be an *obligation* on states to search for those suspected of having committed or ordered to be committed such grave breaches, and to prosecute or extradite such persons.[128] And states such as Switzerland can exercise criminal jurisdiction over war crimes committed in non-international armed conflicts by anyone anywhere. Such trials are not regular occurrences, but they are starting. The trial of Alieu Kosiah, a commander from the rebel group ULIMO in Liberia in the 1990s, concluded at the Swiss Federal Criminal Court in Bellinzona in March 2021.

10.6.1 The Nuremberg and Tokyo International Military Tribunals

The International Military Tribunals (IMTs) were set up by the Allies to try the 'major war criminals of the European Axis' in Nuremberg, and the 'major war criminals in the Far East' in Tokyo.[129] The Charters (with slightly different wording) focused on:

---

[125] Gaeta, 'International Criminalization of Prohibited Conduct', in Cassese (ed), *Oxford Companion to International Criminal Justice* (2009) 63–74.

[126] The proposal being discussed at the International Law Commission is that 'Immunity *ratione materiae* from the exercise of foreign criminal jurisdiction shall not apply in respect of the following crimes under international law: (a) crime of genocide; (b) crimes against humanity; (c) war crimes; (d) crime of apartheid; (e) torture; (f) enforced disappearance.' See 'Seventh Report on Immunity of State Officials from Foreign Criminal Jurisdiction', by Concepción Escobar Hernández, UN Doc A/CN.4/729, 18 April 2019, Draft Art 7 and Annex. For an example of a national tribunal's refusal to apply immunity for a former Minister of Defence when faced with war crimes in a non-international armed conflict (Algeria), see *A v Ministère public de la Confédération*, Swiss Federal Criminal Court, 25 July 2012.

[127] Clapham, 'Human Rights and International Criminal Law', in Schabas (ed), *The Cambridge Companion to International Criminal Law* (2016) 11–33.

[128] Gaeta, 'Grave Breaches of the Geneva Conventions', in Clapham, Gaeta and Sassòli (eds), *The 1949 Geneva Conventions: A Commentary* (2015) 615–46 at 628–40.

[129] See Art 1 of the Charter of the International Military Tribunal (IMT) and Art 1 of the Charter of the International Military Tribunal for The Far East (IMTFE).

(a) *Crimes against Peace*: [Tokyo version]
   Namely, the planning, preparation, initiation or waging of a declared
   or undeclared war of aggression, or a war in violation of international
   law, treaties, agreements or assurances, or participation in a common
   plan or conspiracy for the accomplishment of any of the foregoing;

(b) *Conventional War Crimes*: [Tokyo version] Namely violations of the
   laws and customs of war;

(c) *Crimes against Humanity*: [in the Nuremberg version]
   Namely, murder, extermination, enslavement, deportation, and other
   inhumane acts committed against any civilian population, before or
   during the war, or persecutions on political, racial or religious grounds
   in execution of or in connection with any crime within the jurisdiction
   of the Tribunal, whether or not in violation of the domestic law of the
   country where perpetrated.[130]

These became known (after the numbering of the subparagraphs in the
Charters) as Class A crimes (crimes against peace), Class B crimes (war
crimes) and Class C crimes (crimes against humanity).

The Tokyo Charter demanded that all defendants had to be charged with
'offenses which include Crimes against Peace'.[131] This led to the idea that
those convicted were 'Class A War Criminals', and indeed the Tribunal was
established for the 'just and prompt trial and punishment of the major war
criminals in the Far East'.[132] Confusingly, 'US Occupation authorities com-
municated to the Japanese authorities that the "B" would be applied to military officers who had formal responsibility for atrocities and that "C" would
refer to soldiers who had actually carried out criminal acts'.[133] Eventually,
around 5,700 Japanese defendants were tried in subsequent trials (known
sometimes as the Class B and C trials) held by various Allied states in the Far
East. There were over 900 executions and over 3,000 sentencings to terms of
imprisonment, which in the end were often commuted; and the last prisoners
were freed in 1958.[134]

---

[130] IMTFE Charter, Art 5; IMT Charter, Art 6.

[131] IMTFE Charter Art 5; Totani, 'The Case against the Accused', Tanaka, McCormack and
Simpson (eds), *Beyond Victor's Justice The Tokyo War Crimes Trial Revisited* (2010) 147–61.

[132] IMTFE Charter Art 1.

[133] Wilson et al, *Japanese War Criminals* (2017) at 7; for some of the consequences in Japan
surrounding these labels, see ibid at 191.

[134] See ibid at 270 and Ch 3 for the trials; in addition, there were trials by the USSR and the
People's Republic of China; see also Wilson, 'War Criminals in the Post-war World: The Case of
Katō Tetsutarō', 22 *War in History* (2015) 87–110.

The Nuremberg IMT sentenced 12 defendants to death, seven received prison sentences and three were acquitted. In addition, three organizations were declared criminal, while another three organizations were acquitted.[135] In Tokyo, seven defendants were sentenced to death, 18 received prison sentences and there were no acquittals. There were further trials conducted by the military powers in occupation in Germany and in the Far East (sometimes referred to as trials of Class B/C criminals). These led to thousands of further convictions and hundreds of executions both in occupied Germany and the Far East. Later, in the 1960s and 1970s, West Germany took up the challenge of investigating and prosecuting thousands more cases before they could become time-barred under German law in 1980.[136] The atmosphere of these trials is captured in the famous book and film, *The Reader*.

The controversies pertinent to our present focus were as follows:

- conviction for crimes against peace or waging a war of aggression was seen by some as creating new law, rather than the result of a trial for breaching existing law;
- the category of 'crimes against humanity' had to be created for the Nuremberg Tribunal so that the German leadership might be prosecuted for the atrocities committed against other Germans and the extermination of the German Jews;
- no prosecutions of individuals from the winning side were included, and indeed evidence and argument related to crimes committed by the Allied side were mostly excluded.[137]

Crimes related to aerial bombardment were not charged, thus defusing any discussion of the Allies' 'area bombing' of cities like Dresden. The Allied bombings ended not only in the firebombing of Tokyo, but also with the

[135] The Tribunal found the following were criminal organizations: the Leadership Corps of the Nazi Party, Die Geheime Staatspolizei (Gestapo) and Der Sicherheitsdienst des Reichsfuhrer SS (SD) (considered together), and the Die Schutzstaffeln der Nationalsozialistiscen Deutschen Arbeiterpartei (SS). The Tribunal declined to issue a declaration of criminality for the Die Sturmabteilungen der Nationalsozialistischen Deutschen Arbeiterpartei (commonly known as the SA), the Reich Cabinet (Die Reichsregierung) and the General Staff and High Command of the German Armed Forces.
[136] Weinschenk, 'Nazis Before German Courts: The West German War Crimes Trials', 10 *International Lawyer* (1976) 515–29.
[137] See Röling and Cassese, *The Tokyo Trial and Beyond* (1993) at 59–60; although, as we saw in section 7.4.1, Admiral Dönitz was not sentenced for unrestricted submarine warfare due to similar behaviour by the US Admiral Nimitz in the Pacific – see *Prosecutor v Goering et al*, Judgment of the IMT, 1 October 1946, Official Text, at 313.

atomic bombs dropped on Hiroshima and Nagasaki, leaving up to another 200,000 dead.

Sitting in Japan, some of the judges of the IMT were acutely aware of this anomaly. As the Dutch Judge Röling recounts, when asked if he ever discussed the atomic bombings with the US Supreme Commander General McArthur:

> I sometimes had contacts with Japanese students. The first thing they always asked was 'Are you morally entitled to sit in judgement over the leaders of Japan when the Allies have burned down all of its cities with sometimes, as in Tokyo, in one night 100,000 deaths and which culminated in the destruction of Hiroshima and Nagasaki? Those were war crimes.' I am strongly convinced these bombings were war crimes. It was terrorizing the civilian population with the purpose of making war painful beyond endurance so that the civilian population would urge the government to capitulate. It was terror warfare, 'coercive warfare'. And that is forbidden by the law of war, for sure. So why discuss it with the General? That would have been only embarrassing, I think.[138]

The judges in both Tribunals were perhaps also a little uneasy about sentencing individuals for the newly-coined 'crimes against peace' and the related offence of the 'planning, preparation, initiation, and waging of wars of aggression'. It is well known that no one received the death sentence for this crime alone; death sentences were only attached to findings of guilt related to war crimes and crimes against humanity.[139]

The Judgments are remembered beyond their historical significance for multiple legal advances. These include the rejection not only of the defence of *tu quoque* (in other words, 'the other side did it too'), but also of the Germans' defence that their acts were the acts of the state, and only the state could be held accountable. International law was said by the Tribunal to attach to the individuals themselves, and they could therefore be held accountable for violations of international law. The Tokyo Tribunal and the subsequent trial and execution of the Japanese General Yamashita following an American court-martial are often associated with the development of the thinking on 'command responsibility'. In other words, holding an individual accountable for

---

[138] Röling and Cassese (n 137) at 84.
[139] Ibid at 67 and 99; Totani, 'The Case against the Accused' (n 131) at 152.

failing to prevent or punish the war crimes committed by those under their control.[140]

10.6.2 Contemporary Prosecutions for International Crimes Committed in Times of Armed Conflict

Even after the end of the occupation of both Germany and Japan, there were occasional trials of international crimes related to violations of the laws of war and crimes against humanity in the Second World War. Notable trials in Israel and France included those of Eichmann, Demjanjuk, Barbie and Touvier, and there have been multiple lesser-known trials in China, Canada and Australia.[141] Prosecutions unrelated to the Second World War were more rare until the creation of the ad hoc International Tribunals for the former Yugoslavia and Rwanda in the 1990s, and the series of ad hoc hybrid tribunals that followed for Sierra Leone, Cambodia and Kosovo.[142] Most recently, we are faced with the prospect of prosecutions for war crimes related to the conflicts in the Central African Republic and South Sudan.[143]

In 1998, the adoption of the Rome Statute of the International Criminal Court codified a long list of international crimes, created an international court and generated new momentum for prosecutions of international crimes in national courts. As will be well known, the Court has been criticized for the small number of successful prosecutions, as well as for failing to tackle crimes committed by the armed forces of major powers. It is true that the handful of convictions mostly relate to commanders from rebel groups, and all, so far, come from Africa. But this can be partly explained by the early African enthusiasm for the Court's jurisdiction, and the cooperation

---

[140] Röling and Cassese (n 137) at 70–74; see further Cryer, Robinson and Vasiliev, *An Introduction to International Criminal Law and Procedure*, 4th edn (2019) 368ff; Jackson, 'Command Responsibility', in de Hemptinne, Roth and van Sliedregt (eds), *Modes of Liability in International Criminal Law* (2019) 409–31.

[141] Lafontaine, 'National jurisdictions', in Schabas (ed), *The Cambridge Companion to International Criminal Law* (2016) 155–77; Lafontaine, *Prosecuting Genocide, Crimes Against Humanity and War Crimes in Canadian Courts* (2012); Heller and Simpson (eds), *The Hidden Histories of War Crimes Trials* (2013).

[142] Romano, Nollkaemper and Kleffner (eds), *Internationalized Criminal Courts and Tribunals: Sierra Leone, East Timor, Kosovo, and Cambodia* (2004); Schabas, *The UN International Criminal Tribunals: the former Yugoslavia, Rwanda and Sierra Leone* (2006);

[143] Labuda, 'Open for Business': The Special Criminal Court Launches Investigations in the Central African Republic', *EJIL Talk*, 8 February 2019; Revitalised Agreement on the Resolution of the Conflict in the Republic of South Sudan (2018) Ch V section 5.3, 'Hybrid Court for South Sudan'.

of African states in ensuring cases could go ahead against the rebel leaders they had been fighting. The Court's docket is also skewed by the fact that the Security Council is selective as to which situations it chooses to refer to the Prosecutor. The Council has referred the situations in Darfur and Libya, and has refused to do so for situations like that in Syria. In recent years, however, the Court has started investigations concerning Russian troops in Georgia and US personnel in Afghanistan. There have been preliminary investigations into UK personnel in Iraq, and for Israeli nationals with regard to war crimes committed in Palestine, both in Gaza and in the West Bank.[144]

We have no room here to rehearse all the heated exchanges over whether the International Criminal Court should be dealing with these issues, or to explain the rules that determine which cases fall within the jurisdiction of the Court. The fact that states and others feel so strongly about the prospect of their nationals being prosecuted is testament to the idea that war crimes law has come of age. No one seeks now to brush off the allegations with assertions of military necessity, or claims that 'all's fair in love and war'. And no one can seriously claim today that the international crimes that the Court can prosecute were unknown or uncodified when the crimes were committed.

We have already dealt with the definition of the 'crime of aggression' in the Statute of the International Criminal Court (see Chapter 4). Suffice it to say that the crime is defined as 'an act of aggression which, by its character, gravity and scale, constitutes a manifest violation of the Charter of the United Nations', and that, in the absence of a Security Council referral, jurisdiction is limited to the rare cases where the person in a position controlling or directing the action of a state has the nationality of a state that has accepted the amendment on aggression, and the state that is the victim of the aggression has also accepted the amendment.[145] So the individual aggressor and the victim state must both come from a short-list of around 40 states.[146] Let us now look in turn at the other crimes in the Statute: war crimes; crimes against humanity; and genocide.

---

[144] The Court's jurisdiction is limited, apart from referrals by the Security Council; for the current details, refer to the information provided by the Office of the Prosecutor, available at https://www.icc-cpi.int/pages/situation.aspx and https://www.icc-cpi.int/pages/pe.aspx.

[145] See section 4.4.

[146] As of 29 April 2021: Andorra, Argentina, Austria, Belgium, Bolivia, Botswana, Chile, Costa Rica, Croatia, Cyprus, Czech Republic (now Czechia), Ecuador, El Salvador, Estonia, Finland, Georgia, Germany, Guyana, Iceland, Ireland, Latvia, Liechtenstein, Lithuania, Luxembourg, Malta, Netherlands, North Macedonia, Panama, Paraguay, Poland, Portugal, Samoa, San Marino, Slovakia, Slovenia, Spain, State of Palestine, Switzerland, Trinidad and Tobago, and Uruguay.

10.7 War Crimes

The idea that individuals should be prosecuted for violations of the laws of war goes back centuries. George Abi-Saab explains that while the 19th-century codifications of the laws of war foresaw individual punishment, and states could only prosecute individuals from other states by relying on international law in order to assert their jurisdiction, 'A quantum leap took place . . . when international law undertook to define "war crimes" directly, instead of leaving it to municipal law.'[147] The Charters and judgments of the International Military Tribunals marked this leap, and the law on international war crimes was developed so that individuals were seen as having obligations derived directly from international law. The advent of the UN Criminal Tribunals for the former Yugoslavia (ICTY) and Rwanda (ICTR) determined that the international law on war crimes also applies to non-international armed conflicts.

Not every violation of the laws of war constitutes a war crime; there needs to be a secondary rule that criminalizes the conduct. And not every crime committed in wartime is a war crime; there needs to be a nexus to the armed conflict and, in practice, the crime must deemed to be serious. To make things more complicated, not all war crimes generate the same effects in international law. Space does not permit a detailed description of war crimes law and the complexities that relate to the modes of liability, such as planning, inciting, ordering, aiding, abetting, assisting, joint criminal enterprise and command responsibility.[148] What we can do is sketch some broad categories of war crimes in international law (national legal orders may go further[149]). I have used these categories as they are associated with separate obligations for states with regard to prosecution, extradition, immunity and prohibitions on export in the context of arms transfers.

---

[147] Abi-Saab, 'The Concept of "War Crimes"', in Yee and Tieya (eds), *International Law in the Post-Cold War World: Essays in memory of Li Haopei* (2001) 99–118 at 104.

[148] de Hemptinne, Roth and van Sliedregt (eds), *Modes of Liability in International Criminal Law* (2019).

[149] Garraway warns against overly concentrating on international law, as some breaches of the law of armed conflict should be prosecuted at the national level even if they are not defined as war crimes at the international level or would not be considered serious enough violations. He gives the examples of misuse of the flag of truce and using prohibited weapons. Garraway, 'War Crimes', in Wilmshurst and Breau (eds), *Perspectives on the ICRC Study on Customary International Humanitarian Law* (2007) 377–98 at 386. In Switzerland, the courts have prosecuted war crimes based on international conventions – see Swiss judgment in the *Niyonteze case* (2001) at para 3, available at https://casebook.icrc.org/case-study/switzerland-niyonteze-case: 'In principle, the provisions of Articles 108 to 114 MPC apply where war has

10.7.1   Grave Breaches of the Geneva Conventions and Protocol I (International Armed Conflicts)

Grave breaches of the 1949 Geneva Conventions include certain violations against protected persons, for example wounded or shipwrecked members of the armed forces (Geneva Conventions I and II), or prisoners of war (Geneva Convention III), or civilians in the hands of the a party to the conflict or occupier (Geneva Convention IV). They apply only to situations of international armed conflict.

Those breaches that qualify as grave breaches are listed in the four 1949 Geneva Conventions in Articles 50, 51, 130 and 147, respectively. The grave breach has to be committed against persons or property protected under the provisions of the relevant Geneva Convention.[150]

It is a grave breach when these protected persons are subjected to any of the following acts:

- wilful killing
- torture or inhuman treatment, including biological experiments
- wilfully causing great suffering or serious injury to body or health.

been declared and to other conflicts between two or more States (Art 108 (1) MPC). However, Art 108 (2) MPC stipulates that breaches of international agreements are punishable if those agreements specify a broader field of application. It therefore follows that the "international conventions governing the conduct of hostilities and the protection of persons and property" that apply to non-international conflicts, and which hence have a wider field of application than those of the conventions applicable exclusively to international conflicts, also fall under the provisions of Art 109 (1) MPC. There is, however, a danger that national jurisdictions will claim to be prosecuting war crimes when the behaviour is not related to a violation of the law of armed conflict: in response to the US Supreme Court's claim to prosecute the German saboteurs for violations of the laws of war (discussed in section 5.4), Dinstein points out that 'a soldier removing his uniform in a military operation does not thereby violate the laws of war – and is not a war criminal': Dinstein, 'The Distinction Between Unlawful Combatants and War Criminals', in Dinstein and Tabory (eds), *International Law at a Time of Perplexity: Essays in Honour of Shabtai Rosenne* (1989) 103–16 at 109. The issue of what constitutes a war crime under international law is now particularly significant in the context of the Military Commissions set up in Guantánamo Bay, where the concept of war crimes under international law is important to avoid retroactive penal application of the law, and where some charges related to terrorism have been held not to constitute war crimes under international law – see Brenner-Beck, 'Trial and Punishment for Battlefield Misconduct', in Corn et al, *The War on Terror and the Laws of War: A Military Perspective*, 2nd edn (2015) 193–236 esp at 195.

[150] See section 9.1 for details.

In addition, with regard to prisoners of war, a grave breach also is constituted by:

- compelling a prisoner of war to serve in the forces of the hostile Power
- wilfully depriving a prisoner of war of the rights of fair and regular trial prescribed in the [Third] Convention.

Lastly, with regard to civilians under the control of a state in an international armed conflict or occupation, a grave breach is also constituted by:

- compelling a protected person to serve in the forces of the hostile Power
- wilfully depriving a protected person of the rights of fair and regular trial prescribed in the [Fourth] Convention
- unlawful deportation or transfer or unlawful confinement of a protected person
- taking of hostages.

Grave breaches against protected property cover, *inter alia*, medical establishments and vehicles used for medical transport, and hospital ships; and in occupied territory they also cover real and personal property, as well as property belonging to the state and other public authorities. The provisions reference 'extensive destruction and appropriation of property, not justified by military necessity and carried out unlawfully and wantonly'.[151] The ICTY has explained that 'A single act may, in exceptional circumstances, be interpreted as fulfilling the requirement of extensiveness, as for instance the bombing of a hospital'.[152]

Chapter 9 explained in some detail the criteria for qualifying as a protected person or protected property under the grave breaches regime of the Geneva Conventions. This grave breach regime is supplemented by the additional grave breaches listed in the Additional Protocol I of 1977. For the avoidance of doubt, the Protocol explains that grave breaches of the Conventions and Protocol 'shall be regarded as war crimes'.[153]

One key set of war crimes is defined in Article 85(3) of the Protocol. The crimes must be 'committed wilfully, in violation of the relevant provisions of this Protocol, and causing death or serious injury to body or health':

a) making the civilian population or individual civilians the object of attack;

---

[151] Common Arts 50 GC I; 51 GC II; 147 GC IV.
[152] ICTY, *Prosecutor v Naletilic*, Judgment (Case No IT-98-34-T), 31 March 2003, §576.
[153] AP I Art 85(5).

b) launching an indiscriminate attack affecting the civilian population or civilian objects in the knowledge that such attack will cause excessive loss of life, injury to civilians or damage to civilian objects, as defined in Article 57, paragraph 2 a) iii);

c) launching an attack against works or installations containing dangerous forces in the knowledge that such attack will cause excessive loss of life, injury to civilians or damage to civilian objects, as defined in Article 57, paragraph 2 a) iii);

d) making non-defended localities and demilitarized zones the object of attack;

e) making a person the object of attack in the knowledge that he is hors de combat;

f) the perfidious use, in violation of Article 37, of the distinctive emblem of the red cross, red crescent or red lion and sun or of other protective signs recognized by the Conventions or this Protocol.

The prohibitions on indiscriminate and disproportionate attacks are spelt out here, and in order to understand fully these crimes we need to reproduce Article 57(2)(a)(iii), on which the crimes listed in Article 85(3)(b) and(c) are dependent.

(2) With respect to attacks, the following precautions shall be taken:
   (a) those who plan or decide upon an attack shall:
       . . .
       (iii) refrain from deciding to launch any attack which may be expected to cause incidental loss of civilian life, injury to civilians, damage to civilian objects, or a combination thereof, which would be excessive in relation to the concrete and direct military advantage anticipated.

This is the rule we met when we considered the law on targeting and the questions of distinction and proportionality. It becomes a war crime and a grave breach when there is a wilful launch of the attack, with relevant knowledge, which causes death or serious injury.

Additional Protocol I also defines a further set of war crimes in Article 85(4) that, unlike the list from Article 85(3) quoted above, need not cause death or serious injury to body or health.

[T]he following shall be regarded as grave breaches of this Protocol, when committed wilfully and in violation of the Conventions or the Protocol:

a) the transfer by the Occupying Power of parts of its own civilian population into the territory it occupies, or the deportation or transfer of all or parts of the population of the occupied territory within or outside this territory, in violation of Article 49 of the Fourth Convention;

b) unjustifiable delay in the repatriation of prisoners of war or civilians;

c) practices of apartheid and other inhuman and degrading practices involving outrages upon personal dignity, based on racial discrimination;

d) making the clearly-recognized historic monuments, works of art or places of worship which constitute the cultural or spiritual heritage of peoples and to which special protection has been given by special arrangement, for example, within the framework of a competent international organization, the object of attack, causing as a result extensive destruction thereof, where there is no evidence of the violation by the adverse Party of Article 53, subparagraph (b), and when such historic monuments, works of art and places of worship are not located in the immediate proximity of military objectives;

e) depriving a person protected by the Conventions or referred to in paragraph 2 of this Article of the rights of fair and regular trial.

These crimes, together with the crimes in Article 11 of the Protocol related to the mistreatment of anyone deprived of their liberty, comprise a complete list of the war crimes in the grave breaches regimes of the Geneva Conventions and their Protocol.[154] The significance of separating them out in this way is in order to highlight that, because every state has become a party to the Geneva Conventions, the Conventions' grave breaches regime applies universally. This means that every state in the world has an obligation to search for those alleged to have ordered or committed the grave breaches of the Geneva Conventions, and either to prosecute or extradite the persons it detains. Furthermore, by becoming parties to these treaties, it may be presumed that states have waived claims to immunity over their officials should they be tried abroad.[155] Where Additional Protocol I applies as a matter of treaty law, the list of grave breaches is extended with the same effects.

---

[154] Most of these grave breaches, but not all, are included (with some slight modifications) in the ICC Statute.

[155] Gaeta, 'Grave Breaches of the Geneva Conventions', in Clapham, Gaeta and Sassòli (eds), *The 1949 Geneva Conventions: A Commentary* (2015) 615–46 at 628–38.

10.7.2   Other War Crimes in International Armed Conflicts

The adoption of the Statute of the International Criminal Court means that we now have a catalogue of war crimes that includes not only the adaption of the grave breaches regime from the Geneva Conventions, but also a long list of war crimes going beyond the protected persons and property of that regime and covering the conduct of hostilities more generally, as well as certain prohibited weapons.

Other serious violations of the laws and customs applicable in international armed conflict, within the established framework of international law, namely, any of the following acts: (i) Intentionally directing attacks against the civilian population as such or against individual civilians not taking direct part in hostilities; (ii) Intentionally directing attacks against civilian objects, that is, objects which are not military objectives; (iii) Intentionally directing attacks against personnel, installations, material, units or vehicles involved in a humanitarian assistance or peacekeeping mission in accordance with the Charter of the United Nations, as long as they are entitled to the protection given to civilians or civilian objects under the international law of armed conflict; (iv) Intentionally launching an attack in the knowledge that such attack will cause incidental loss of life or injury to civilians or damage to civilian objects or widespread, long-term and severe damage to the natural environment which would be clearly excessive in relation to the concrete and direct overall military advantage anticipated; (v) Attacking or bombarding, by whatever means, towns, villages, dwellings or buildings which are undefended and which are not military objectives; (vi) Killing or wounding a combatant who, having laid down his arms or having no longer means of defence, has surrendered at discretion; (vii) Making improper use of a flag of truce, of the flag or of the military insignia and uniform of the enemy or of the United Nations, as well as of the distinctive emblems of the Geneva Conventions, resulting in death or serious personal injury; (viii) The transfer, directly or indirectly, by the Occupying Power of parts of its own civilian population into the territory it occupies, or the deportation or transfer of all or parts of the population of the occupied territory within or outside this territory; (ix) Intentionally directing attacks against buildings dedicated to religion, education, art, science or charitable purposes, historic monuments, hospitals and places where the sick and wounded are collected, provided they are not military objectives;(x) Subjecting persons who are in the power of an adverse party to physical mutilation or to medical or scientific experiments of any kind which are neither justified by the medical, dental or hospital treatment of the person concerned nor carried out in his or her interest, and which cause death to or seriously endanger the health of such person or persons; (xi) Killing or wounding treacherously individuals belonging to the hostile nation or army; (xii) Declaring that no quarter will be given; (xiii) Destroying or seizing the enemy's property unless such destruction or seizure be imperatively demanded by the necessities of war; (xiv) Declaring abolished, suspended or inadmissible in a court of law the rights and actions of the nationals of the hostile party; (xv) Compelling the nationals of the hostile party to take part in the operations of war directed against their own country, even if they were in the belligerent's service before the commencement of the war; (xvi) Pillaging a town or place, even when taken by assault; (xvii) Employing poison or poisoned weapons; (xviii) Employing asphyxiating, poisonous or other gases, and all analogous liquids, materials or devices; (xix) Employing bullets which expand or flatten easily in the human body, such as bullets with a hard envelope which does not entirely cover the core or is pierced with incisions; (xx) Employing weapons, projectiles and material and methods of warfare which are of a nature to cause superfluous injury or unnecessary suffering or which are inherently indiscriminate in violation of the international law of armed conflict, provided that such weapons, projectiles and material and methods of warfare are the subject of a comprehensive prohibition and are included in an annex to this Statute, by an amendment in accordance with the relevant provisions set forth in articles 121 and 123; (xxi) Committing outrages upon personal dignity, in particular humiliating and degrading treatment; (xxii) Committing rape, sexual slavery, enforced prostitution, forced pregnancy, as defined in article 7, paragraph 2 (f), enforced sterilization, or any other form of sexual violence also constituting a grave breach of the Geneva Conventions; (xxiii) Utilizing the presence of a civilian or other protected person to render certain points, areas or military forces immune from military operations; (xxiv) Intentionally directing attacks against buildings, material, medical units and transport, and personnel using the distinctive emblems of the Geneva Conventions in conformity with international law; (xxv) Intentionally using starvation of civilians as a method of warfare by depriving them of objects indispensable to their survival, including wilfully impeding relief supplies as provided for under the Geneva Conventions; (xxvi) Conscripting or enlisting children under the age of fifteen years into the national armed forces or using them to participate actively in hostilities; (xxvii) Employing weapons, which use microbial or other biological agents, or toxins, whatever their origin or method of production [not yet in force for all states parties] (xxviii) Employing weapons the primary effect of which is to injure by fragments which in the human body escape detection by X-rays [not yet in force for all states parties]; (xxix) Employing laser weapons specifically designed, as their sole combat function or as one of their combat functions, to cause permanent blindness to unenhanced vision, that is to the naked eye or to the eye with corrective eyesight devices [not yet in force for all states parties].[156]

As explained by the ICRC customary law study, the war crimes in this list are mostly accepted as representing the customary international law of war crimes. The list is not complete, however, in the sense that a number of further customary crimes can arguably be said to constitute war crimes under customary international law.[157]

The key crimes not already mentioned in our discussion of grave breaches include traditional war crimes such the use of certain prohibited weapons; destroying or seizing the enemy's property, unless such destruction or seizure be imperatively demanded by the necessities of war; attacks on hospitals or buildings dedicated to religion, education, etc;[158] pillage; and other traditional war crimes related to acts that are prohibited methods of war, such as killing or wounding combatants who have surrendered or are *hors de combat*, ordering that there should be no survivors or prisoners taken, and perfidy

---

[156] Art 8(2)(b).

[157] Henckaerts and Doswald-Beck, *Customary International Humanitarian Law*, vol 1: *Rules* (2005) at 568–603, adding slavery and deportation to slave labour; collective punishments; despoilation of the wounded, sick, shipwrecked or dead; attacking or ill-treating a *parlementaire* or bearer of a flag of truce; unjustifiable delay in the repatriation of prisoners of war or civilians; the practice of apartheid or other inhuman or degrading practices involving outrages on personal dignity based on racial discrimination; launching an indiscriminate attack resulting in loss of life or injury to civilians or damage to civilian objects; launching an attack against works or installations containing dangerous forces in the knowledge that such attack will cause excessive incidental loss of civilian life, injury to civilians or damage to civilian objects. For a critical look at the ICRC approach to war crimes in this study, see Garraway, 'War Crimes' (n 149).

[158] In addition there are specific war crimes under the Hague Convention for the Protection of Cultural Property in Times of Armed Conflict of 1954 and its Second Protocol (1999) – see O'Keefe, 'Protection of Cultural Property', in Clapham and Gaeta (eds), *The Oxford Handbook of International Law in Armed Conflict* (2014) 492–520 at 511–16; see also O'Keefe, Péron, Musayev and Ferrari, *Protection of Cultural Property: Military Manual* (2016) at 5, para 16, which highlights the obligations under Art 28 of the Hague Convention (1954) and Art 21 of its Second Protocol (1999) to prosecute or punish certain serious violations related to cultural property. In 2016, the ICC sentenced Al Mahdi (allegedly a member of Ansar Eddine, a movement associated with Al Qaeda in the Islamic Maghreb) to nine years' imprisonment for the war crime of intentionally directing attacks against historic monuments and buildings dedicated to religion, including nine mausoleums and one mosque in Timbuktu, Mali. *Prosecutor v Al Mahdi*, ICC-01/12-01/15, 27 September 2016. The guilty plea perhaps meant that the appropriateness of this crime was not fully tested; see Schabas, 'Al Mahdi Has Been Convicted of a Crime He Did Not Commit', 49 *Case Western Reserve Journal of International Law* (2017) 75–102.

(misuse of the flag of truce or feigning some protected status resulting in death or injury). On the other hand, we find crimes that were included in the 1998 Statute in order to reflect modern concerns, for example the war crime of conscripting or enlisting children under the age of 15 years into the armed forces, or using them to participate actively in hostilities.

Lastly, we should highlight the modern formulation covering war crimes related to sexual violations: committing rape, sexual slavery, enforced prostitution, forced pregnancy, enforced sterilization or other forms of sexual violence. This last crime covers a situation where the 'perpetrator committed an act of a sexual nature against one or more persons or caused such person or persons to engage in an act of a sexual nature by force, or by threat of force or coercion', and along with rape and enforced prostitution could be committed by 'taking advantage of a coercive environment or such person's or persons' incapacity to give genuine consent'.[159]

10.7.3 Serious Violations of Common Article 3 (Non-International Armed Conflict)

Today it is widely accepted that serious violations of Common Article 3 to the 1949 Geneva Conventions applicable to non-international armed conflicts (including civil wars) are war crimes. Garraway further suggests that we should see these war crimes as also applicable in international armed conflict.[160]

Such war crimes concern violations against 'persons taking no active part in the hostilities, including members of armed forces who have laid down their arms and those placed "hors de combat" by sickness, wounds, detention, or any other cause'.[161] As with grave breaches, once one has determined

---

[159] Elements of Crimes under the Rome Statute (2002) Art 8(2)(b)(xxii)-6 War crime of sexual violence, para 1; with regard to rape, it has been argued that the coercive environment should be seen as evidence of lack of consent in contrat to the idea that rape can be defined without the element of lack of consent – see Dowds, *Feminist Engagement with International Criminal Law: Norm Transfer, Complementarity, Rape and Consent* (2019).

[160] Garraway, 'War Crimes' (n 149) at 388.

[161] With regard to the category of persons taking no active part in hostilities, the ICTY Appeals Chamber in *Stuger* stated 'As the temporal scope of an individual's participation in hostilities can be intermittent and discontinuous, whether a victim was actively participating in the hostilities at the time of the offence depends on the nexus between the victim's activities at the time of the offence and any acts of war which by their nature or purpose are intended to cause actual harm to the personnel or equipment of the adverse party.' Judgment (Case No IT-01-42-A), 17 July 2008, §178.

who is protected – in this case the answer is simply 'persons taking no active part in hostilities' – the next step is to look at the finite list of obligations. Common Article 3 prohibits:

a) violence to life and person, in particular murder of all kinds, mutilation, cruel treatment and torture;
b) taking of hostages;
c) outrages upon personal dignity, in particular humiliating and degrading treatment;
d) the passing of sentences and the carrying out of executions without previous judgment pronounced by a regularly constituted court, affording all the judicial guarantees which are recognized as indispensable by civilized peoples.

10.7.4 Other War Crimes in Non-International Armed Conflict

Again we can reference the catalogue of crimes in the Rome Statute for further war crimes that can be prosecuted in times of non-international armed conflict. The list is shorter, in part due to compromises made during the drafting of the Statute, and in part because some concepts do not apply in the same way in times of non-international armed conflict (eg the law of occupation, and certain rights related to foreign nationals). The crimes absent from the list are identified in the footnote for completeness,[162] but we might highlight a couple of glaring omissions.

There is no explicit mention of the war crimes that cover attacks against civilian objects and attacks with knowledge that there will be disproportionate damage or injury to civilians. The absence of these two specific crimes from the Rome Statute for non-international armed conflicts should not lead us to the conclusion that such acts are not war crimes under international law. Indeed a new treaty, adopted by African states at the AU Summit in Maputo

---

[162] The omissions concern mainly the war crimes in ICC Statute Art 8(2)(b)(ii), (iv), (v), (vii), (viii), (xiv), (xv), (xx), (xxi), (xxiii) (see section 10.7.2) some crimes are adapted to fit the context of non-international armed conflict, see for example Art 8(2)(e)(viii). For details of the scope of each crime see Dörmann, *Elements of War Crimes under the Rome Statute of the International Criminal Court* (2003); the Statute was amended in 2019 to include the war crime of starvation of civilians in non-international armed conflict Art 8(2)(e)(xix) (it will first come into force for New Zealand on 14 October 2021).

in 2014, foresees a criminal chamber for the future African Court of Justice and Human Rights, which would have jurisdiction over the war crimes in non-international conflict of '[l]aunching an indiscriminate attack resulting in death or injury to civilians, or an attack in the knowledge that it will cause excessive incidental civilian loss, injury or damage'.[163] We should stress that practice points to states and other International Tribunals treating such actions as war crimes.[164] The absence of a war crime from the Statute of the International Criminal Court should not be read as meaning that the war crime does not exist as a matter of international law.

On the other hand, the Judges at the Court have proved capable of expanding the understanding of war crimes law in new directions. Recently the International Criminal Court clarified in the *Ntaganda* case that war crimes related to sexual violence can be committed not only against enemy forces and civilians, but also with regard to those from one's own side. Non-international armed conflicts have been particularly plagued by the use of child soldiers and sexual violence.

In the *Ntaganda* case, these two issues came simultaneously before the Court. Ntaganda was a commander from a rebel group UPC/FPLC in the Democratic Republic of Congo. He was prosecuted, in addition to other crimes, for rape and sexual slavery with regard to two girls who were part of the armed group of which he was a commander. It had been argued extensively that war crimes and the laws of war applied to regulate behaviour towards the *enemy* and not with regard to one's own side. It is now clear, however, according to the Court, that

> provided there is a nexus to the armed conflict, rape and *sexual* slavery against any person is prohibited, and that therefore members of the same armed force are not per se excluded as potential victims of the war crimes of rape and sexual slavery.[165]

---

[163] Protocol on Amendments to the Protocol on the Statute of the African Court of Justice and Human Rights Art 28D(e)xviii; the Protocol also includes most of the customary war crimes referenced in the ICRC study on *Customary International Humanitarian Law* (n 157) that were omitted from the Rome Statute both for international and non-international armed conflict.

[164] La Haye, *War Crimes in Internal Armed Conflicts* (2008) at 144; Henckaerts and Doswald-Beck, *Customary International Humanitarian Law* (n 157) at 599–601; Cryer et al, *An Introduction to International Criminal Law and Procedure*, 3rd edn (2014) at 293.

[165] *Prosecutor v Ntaganda*, ICC-01/04-02/06, 8 July 2019, para 965 (original emphasis); see also the judgment in the Appeal Chamber ICC-01/04-02/06 A A2, 30 March 2021

The Court found that:

> Female members of the UPC/FPLC were regularly raped and subjected to sexual violence . . . by male UPC/FPLC soldiers and commanders . . . and, in relation to his female bodyguards, by Mr Ntaganda himself. This common practice was generally known and discussed within the UPC/FPLC. A number of these female members of the UPC/FPLC became pregnant during their time in the UPC/FPLC. As set out with more specificity in the cases discussed below, PMFs [*personnel militaire feminine*] who suffered acts of sexual violence as just described included girls under 15 years of age.[166]

The rape and sexual slavery of the girls in the particular case attracted sentences of 17 years and 14 years respectively.

This precedent has widened considerably the concept of war crimes beyond the traditional understanding, which conceived of war crimes as perpetrated against the enemy. There is here a clear shift in logic away from war crimes being derived from a law of war that demands a certain respect for the enemy, towards the protection of human beings as such. The Appeals Chamber considered that 'international humanitarian law not only governs actions of parties to the conflict in relation to each other but also concerns itself with protecting vulnerable persons during armed conflict and assuring fundamental guarantees to persons not taking active part in the hostilities.'[167]

10.8 Crimes Against Humanity

As already mentioned, the Nuremberg Charter included crimes against humanity in order to capture the atrocities committed by Germans against other Germans (and in particular German Jews) that would not be covered by the traditional law of war, which protected, at that time, only enemy nationals in wartime. Philippe Sands traces the history of this development in his book *East West Street*, and pinpoints the moment when Hersch Lauterpacht's idea

---

[166] *Prosecutor v Ntaganda*, ICC-01/04-02/06 at paras 407–408 (footnotes omitted).
[167] *Prosecutor v Ntaganda*, ICC-01/04-02/06 OA5, 15 June 2017, Judgment on the appeal of Mr Ntaganda against the 'Second decision on the Defence's challenge to the jurisdiction of the Court in respect of Counts 6 and 9' at para 57.

regarding crimes against humanity was included in the Charter. He references Prosecutor Jackson's communication to the Allies when proposing revisions to the Charter: 'We should insert words to make clear that we are addressing persecution, etc of Jews and others in Germany, as well as outside it . . . before as well as after commencement of the war.'[168]

At the time, in order for the Tribunal to prosecute these new crimes, they had to be in execution of, or in connection with, other crimes within the jurisdiction of the Nuremberg Tribunal, as so connected to the War. Some from the United States, including Prosecutor Jackson[169] and Secretary of War Stimson, were apparently fearful that a self-standing crime against humanity could be used to condemn racial discrimination in the United States.[170] The need for such a connection to the Second World War, or indeed to any armed conflict, was later dispensed with, and today there is no need for crimes against humanity to be connected to any war or armed conflict; they can be committed both during an armed conflict and in peacetime.[171]

While different international tribunals and national law have defined crimes against humanity with slight variations, for present purposes we can focus on the definition used in Article 7 of the Statute of the International Criminal Court. This definition states that crimes against humanity mean certain acts 'committed as part of a widespread or systematic attack directed against any civilian population, with knowledge of the attack'. The acts constituting crimes against humanity are listed as follows:

(a) Murder;
(b) Extermination;
(c) Enslavement;
(d) Deportation or forcible transfer of population;
(e) Imprisonment or other severe deprivation of physical liberty in violation of fundamental rules of international law;
(f) Torture;

---

[168] Sands, *East West Street: On the Origins of Genocide and Crimes Against Humanity* (2016) at 111 and 413 fn 111.

[169] See Schabas, *Genocide in International Law: The Crime of Crimes* (2000) at 35.

[170] Röling and Cassese (n 137) at 55.

[171] Clark, 'History of Efforts to Codify Crimes Against Humanity: From the Charter of Nuremberg to the Statute of Rome', in Sadat (ed), *Forging a Convention for Crimes Against Humanity* (2011) 8–27; ILC Draft Articles on Prevention and Punishment of Crimes Against Humanity, with commentaries, UN Doc A/74/10 (2019) 53.

(g) Rape, sexual slavery, enforced prostitution, forced pregnancy, enforced sterilization, or any other form of sexual violence of comparable gravity;

(h) Persecution against any identifiable group or collectivity on political, racial, national, ethnic, cultural, religious, gender as defined in paragraph 3, or other grounds that are universally recognized as impermissible under international law, in connection with any act referred to in this paragraph or any crime within the jurisdiction of the Court;

(i) Enforced disappearance of persons;

(j) The crime of apartheid;

(k) Other inhumane acts of a similar character intentionally causing great suffering, or serious injury to body or to mental or physical health.

These terms are further defined in the Statute. It is enough to explain here that ' "[a]ttack directed against any civilian population" means a course of conduct involving the multiple commission of acts referred to in paragraph 1 against any civilian population, pursuant to or in furtherance of a State or organizational policy to commit such attack'.[172] In fact the victim need not be a civilian; it is enough that the acts occur as part of a widespread or systematic attack against the civilian population. Given that such crimes can occur in peacetime, it has been suggested that the term 'civilian population' has a wide, non-technical meaning.[173] Similarly, the concept of an 'organizational policy' has been found to include 'any organization or group with the capacity and resources to plan and carry out a widespread or systematic attack'.[174] While the policy should be linked to the state or group, it need not be formally adopted or motivated.[175]

10.9 Genocide

Like the notion of crimes against humanity, genocide as a concept gained a foothold in the Nuremberg Tribunal. As Sands highlights, even if genocide was not

---

[172] ICC Statute Art 7.

[173] See further Schabas, *The International Criminal Court: A Commentary on the Rome Statute* (2010) at 154: 'Generally, the concept of "civilian population" should be construed liberally, in order to promote the principles underlying the prohibition of crimes against humanity, which is to safeguard human values and protect human dignity.' See also Cassese et al, (n 124) at 102–04.

[174] ILC Draft Articles on Crimes Against Humanity (n 171) at 40.

[175] Ibid esp at 39.

included in the Charter, Rafael Lemkin's campaign to prosecute genocide partly paid off, with its inclusion in the indictment. Sands references the indictment, which accused the defendants in the context of their occupations of

> deliberate and systematic genocide, viz, the extermination of racial and national groups, against the civilian populations of certain occupied territories in order to destroy particular races and classes of people and national, racial, or religious groups, particularly Jews, Poles, and Gypsies and others.[176]

The concept of genocide did not figure further in the judgment, or in sentencing, but genocide was affirmed to be a crime under international law by the UN General Assembly in 1946,[177] and was included (albeit with a slightly more restrictive definition) in the 1948 Genocide Convention.[178] In part there was a perceived need to remedy the fact that Nuremberg had not dealt with genocidal crimes committed before the outbreak of the War.[179] The states parties to the Convention confirmed that the 'that genocide, whether committed in time of peace or in time of war, is a crime under international law which they undertake to prevent and to punish'.[180]

The universal nature of the prohibition on genocide was quickly established when the International Court of Justice concluded in 1951 that 'the principles underlying the Convention are principles which are recognized by civilized nations as binding on States, even without any conventional obligation'.[181] The prohibition has also attained the status of a peremptory norm (*jus cogens*),[182] meaning there can be no derogation from this prohibition, even in times of war. And the prohibition of genocide gives rise to rights and obligations *erga omnes* (meaning that even a non-injured state can seek accountability through international law, including binding provisional

---

[176] IMT Judgment (n 137) at 43–44; see Sands, *East West Street* (n 168) Ch IV at 188.

[177] Resolution 96(I).

[178] 1948 Convention on the Prevention and Punishment of the Crime of Genocide. See, eg, Gaeta (ed), *The UN Genocide Convention: A Commentary* (2009).

[179] See Schabas, *Genocide in International Law: The Crime of Crimes*, 2nd edn (2009) at 52, referencing the presentation of a text in the UN General Assembly by the Cuban delegate.

[180] Genocide Convention Art 1.

[181] ICJ, *Reservations to the Convention on the Prevention and Punishment of the Crime of Genocide*, Advisory Opinion, 28 May 1951, p 12.

[182] *Case Concerning Armed Activities on the Territory of the Congo* (New Application: 2002) (*Democratic Republic of the Congo v Rwanda*), Jurisdiction of the Court and Admissibility of the Application, Judgment, 3 February 2006, para 64.

measures ordered by the International Court of Justice, as recently happened in the case brought by Gambia against Myanmar).[183]

The 1948 Convention sets out a definition of 'genocide' for the purposes of the Convention, but which is referred to as reflecting the customary international law '*both* at the interstate level and at the level of individual liability'.[184] Article II reads:

> In the present Convention, genocide means any of the following acts committed with intent to destroy, in whole or in part, a national, ethnical, racial or religious group, as such:
> (a) Killing members of the group;
> (b) Causing serious bodily or mental harm to members of the group;
> (c) Deliberately inflicting on the group conditions of life calculated to bring about its physical destruction in whole or in part;
> (d) Imposing measures intended to prevent births within the group;
> (e) Forcibly transferring children of the group to another group.

Genocide is stated to be an international crime, which can be committed by individuals who are to be punished according to Article IV of the Convention, 'whether they are constitutionally responsible rulers, public officials or private individuals'.

Well-known trials have been carried out at the national level. Israel prosecuted and executed Eichmann in 1962 on genocide-related charges, and more recently, in 2010, the Iraq Special Tribunal prosecuted and executed Al Majid (also known as Chemical Ali) for genocide, including the use of chemical weapons against the Kurds. Less well-known cases have been prosecuted in states such as Ethiopia and Brazil, sometimes using a wider meaning of 'genocide' than the one found in the Convention.[185]

At the international level, the UN Tribunals for the former Yugoslavia and Rwanda found a number of individuals guilty of genocide.[186] Prosecutions also took place in Rwanda and in states from the former Yugoslavia, such as Croatia and Bosnia and Herzegovina. Most recently, in 2010, the International Criminal Court issued a warrant of arrest including charges of

---

[183] Ibid; and *Application of the Convention on the Prevention and Punishment of the Crime of Genocide (The Gambia v Myanmar)*, *Provisional Measures*, Order of 23 January 2020 esp at paras 41–42.

[184] Cassese, 'Taking Stock of the Genocide Convention and Looking Ahead', in Gaeta (ed), *The UN Genocide Convention* (2009) 531–44 at 537 (original emphasis).

[185] For the detail, see Schabas, *Genocide* (n 179) Ch 8.

[186] For the detail, see ibid.

genocide in connection with Darfur for Al Bashir (President of Sudan 1989–2019). Such international prosecutions are complicated by the uncertain nature of the terms 'national, ethnical, racial or religious group' and the need to find the specific intent to destroy such a group in whole or in part.[187] While genocide may attract the greatest opprobrium and the highest sentences, prosecutors may in the end choose to prioritize prosecutions for crimes against humanity or war crimes.

But the obligation not to commit genocide as defined in the Convention is also an international obligation on states, and so prosecution is not the only form of accountability that is available. This was confirmed by the International Court of Justice in the case brought by Bosnia and Herzegovina against Serbia and Montenegro:

> Under Article I [of the Genocide Convention] the States parties are bound to prevent such an act, which it describes as 'a crime under international law', being committed. The Article does not *expressis verbis* require States to refrain from themselves committing genocide. However, in the view of the Court, taking into account the established purpose of the Convention, the effect of Article I is to prohibit States from themselves committing genocide.[188]

In this case we learn some of the parameters of what it means to have an obligation to prevent genocide. Although the Court did not find that Serbia had committed genocide, it did find that the state had failed in its obligation to prevent genocide:

> The Court has found that the authorities of the Respondent [Serbia and Montenegro] could not have been unaware of the grave risk of genocide once the VRS forces had decided to take possession of the Srebrenica enclave, and that in view of its influence over the events, the Respondent must be held to have had the means of action by which it could seek to prevent genocide, and to have manifestly refrained from employing them . . .

---

[187] For a detailed look, see Cryer et al, *Introduction* (n 164) Ch 10.

[188] *Application of the Convention on the Prevention and Punishment of the Crime of Genocide (Bosnia and Herzegovina v Serbia and Montenegro)*, Judgment of 26 February 2007, para 166; for discussion of the differences between state and individual genocide, see further Gaeta, 'Génocide d'État et responsibilité pénale individuelle', *Revue générale de droit international public*, 111 (2007) 631–48.

The obligation to prevent the commission of the crime of genocide is imposed by the Genocide Convention on any State party which, in a given situation, has it in its power to contribute to restraining in any degree the commission of genocide.[189]

10.10 Beyond Prosecution for International Crimes

We should turn now to look at some of the other ways in which states hold actors accountable for violations of international law in wartime. Today a wide range of options are advocated that bear little resemblance to the 'loser pays' principle we encountered up to the end of the Second World War. The logic of why states engage in armed conflict has changed. Ruti Teitel goes so far as to suggest that, precisely because some of today's inter-state wars are said to be fought for human rights, reparations will have to be paid by winners and losers. 'The justification for war, especially where humanitarian justice considerations are prominent, sets the stage for higher expectations of humanitarianism, both in relation to how war is waged and the responsibilities of the victors post-conflict.'[190]

A first alternative to prosecution is civil or tort accountability before national courts.[191] Rather than presenting claims based on international humanitarian law, which, as we have seen, may be considered non-justiciable at the national level, the victim of mistreatment in detention may be able to present the claim under human rights law.[192] Civil litigation is slow and expensive, though, and many states will present multiple barriers to access to justice in this context. Worldwide, accountability for violations of international law in times of armed conflict is mostly dependent on investigations carried out by the armed forces themselves, notwithstanding the obvious

---

[189] *Bosnia and Herzegovina v Serbia and Montenegro*(n 188) at para 461.

[190] Teitel, 'Rethinking *Jus Post Bellum* in an Age of Global Transitional Justice: Engaging with Michael Walzer and Larry May', 24 *EJIL* (2013) 335–42 at 342.

[191] For example, see the Torture Victim Protection Act 1991, 28 USC § 1350, Section 2:
  (a) Liability – An individual who, under actual or apparent authority, or color of law, of any foreign nation–
      (1) subjects an individual to torture shall, in a civil action, be liable for damages to that individual; or
      (2) subjects an individual to extrajudicial killing shall, in a civil action, be liable for damages to the individual's legal representative, or to any person who may be a claimant in an action for wrongful death.

[192] For cases in the United Kingdom known as the 'Iraqi civilian litigation', see *Alseran et al v Ministry of Defence* [2017] EWHC 3289 (QB).

obstacles to conducting such activity in wartime.[193] Recent interpretations of the right to life by the UN Human Rights Committee nevertheless set out how human rights law encompasses the prohibitive rules in the laws of war and adds a series of duties related to disclosure and investigation:

> [P]ractices inconsistent with international humanitarian law, entailing a risk to the lives of civilians and other persons protected by international humanitarian law, including the targeting of civilians, civilian objects and objects indispensable to the survival of the civilian population, indiscriminate attacks, failure to apply the principles of precaution and proportionality, and the use of human shields, would also violate article 6 of the Covenant [the right to life]. States parties should, in general, disclose the criteria for attacking with lethal force individuals or objects whose targeting is expected to result in deprivation of life, including the legal basis for specific attacks, the process of identification of military targets and combatants or persons taking a direct part in hostilities, the circumstances in which relevant means and methods of warfare have been used, and whether less harmful alternatives were considered. They must also investigate alleged or suspected violations of article 6 in situations of armed conflict in accordance with the relevant international standards.[194]

In addition to human rights claims before national courts, international courts may hear claims from individuals as well as from states. In the past there has sometimes been an assumption that matters concerning armed conflicts should be dealt with exclusively as a matter of international humanitarian law and not by human rights courts with a limited jurisdiction. Today, human rights courts and treaty bodies have affirmed that human rights law continues to apply in times of armed conflict, and they have interpreted the

---

[193] See Schmitt, 'Investigating Violations of International Law in Armed Conflict', 31 *Harvard National Security Journal*, 2 (2011) 31–84.

[194] General Comment No 36 (2018) on article 6 of the International Covenant on Civil and Political Rights, on the right to life, UN Doc CCPR/C/GC/36, 30 October 2018, at para 64 (footnotes omitted); see further Rishmawi, 'Protecting the Right to Life in Protracted Conflicts: The Existence and Dignity Dimensions of General Comment 36', 101 *IRRC* (2019) 1149–69; see also the finding by the European Court of Human Rights that in the context of a complaint about a violation of the right to life there is an obligation 'under customary international humanitarian law to investigate the airstrike at issue, as it concerned the individual criminal responsibility of members of the German armed forces for a potential war crime'. *Hanan v Germany*, 16 February 2021, at para 137. The procedural duties on the state have nevertheless to be applied 'realistically', see paras 198-236.

human rights treaties with reference to the interrelated humanitarian law treaties.[195]

With regard to the conflict in Nagorno-Karabakh, the European Court of Human Rights recently called for the parties to refrain from military action that might entail breaches of the human rights of the civilian population, and for compliance with their obligations concerning the human rights of those captured.[196] The bombardment of the population and the treatment of detainees (including prisoners of war) were seen by the Court as human rights issues, with accountability for states before this human rights court.

Claims for reparations before international courts will, however, be the exception rather than the rule. In many conflicts transitional justice mechanisms continue to evolve, including not only reparations at the end of internal conflicts, but also truth and reconciliation mechanisms.[197] Nevertheless, we have to be clear that reparations for the victims of today's civil wars have to be conceived of very differently from the claims related to the victims of the World Wars, or even for the transitions to democracy witnessed in the 20th century. Thinking about today's conflicts in the Democratic Republic of Congo, the Central African Republic, South Sudan or Syria requires creative forms of reparation beyond individualized packets of compensation. As De Greiff, a leading expert in this field, explains:

> In these contexts, drawing familiar lines between contending forces, between civilians and armed agents, and even between victims and perpetrators, becomes increasingly difficult. Similarly, participation in violence may be more widespread in weak States, making the attribution of responsibility more complicated. The larger universe of potential beneficiaries coupled with economic scarcity make comprehensive reparations

---

[195] Clapham, 'The Complex Relationship between the 1949 Geneva Conventions and International Human Rights Law', in Clapham, Gaeta and Sassòli (eds), *The 1949 Geneva Conventions: A Commentary* (2015) 701-35; for the recent limits developed by the European Court of Human Rights, to the understanding of jurisdiction over extraterritorial acts resulting in loss of life, see *Georgia v Russia (II)*, 21 January 2021, esp paras 125-144; the procedural human rights obligations to investigate violations of the right to life nevertheless continue even when the substantive jurisdiction is limited. See paras 328-337. For human rights cases in the United Kingdom related to detention see section 9.2.2.

[196] See press releases ECHR 265, 276, 310, 314 (2020).

[197] De Greiff, 'Justice and Reparations', in De Greiff (ed), *The Handbook of Reparations* (2008) 451-77; OHCHR, 'Rule-of-Law Tools for Post-Conflict States: Reparations Programmes' (2008) Sooka, 'Dealing with the Past and Transitional Justice: Building Peace through Accountability', 88 *IRRC* (2006) 311-25; and for some of the theoretical issues, see Stahn, Easterday and Iversom (eds), *Jus Post Bellum: Mapping the Normative Foundations* (2014).

much less feasible. The absence of a well established institutional setting also makes talk of reform much less convincing than that of 'institution-building' in its most literal sense.[198]

The expectation that victims (beyond states) are entitled to reparations from the parties to an armed conflict (including non-state actors) is evolving, and the trend, especially outside the Second World War-related claims brought in the German and Japanese courts, is towards recognizing individual claimants and a wider range of possible responses to these claims beyond the obvious routes that hold out the promise of compensation.

The complaints mechanism under the UN Convention against Torture, for example, has been successfully used by a victim of rape in the armed conflict in Bosnia and Herzegovina. Article 14 of the Convention states:

> Each State Party shall ensure in its legal system that the victim of an act of torture obtains redress and has an enforceable right to fair and adequate compensation, including the means for as full rehabilitation as possible.

The UN Committee recently found there had been a violation of this provision and that in addition to compensation, a state party is required 'to ensure that the complainant receives medical and psychological care immediately and free of charge; [and] offer public official apologies to the complainant'.[199]

Another overlooked international accountability activity is the monitoring and reporting work carried out by various bodies, including the special procedures and commissions of inquiry established by international organizations.[200] In turn, such work may feed into national accountability

---

[198] 'Report of the Special Rapporteur on the promotion of truth, justice, reparation and guarantees of non-recurrence', UN Doc A/HRC/36/50, 21 August 2017, at para 45.

[199] *A v Bosnia and Herzegovina*, UN Doc CAT/C/67/D/854/2017, 11 September 2019.

[200] Harwood, *The Roles and Functions of Atrocity-Related United Nations Commissions of Inquiry in the International Legal Order* (2020); Alston and Knuckey (eds), *The Transformation of Human Rights Fact-Finding* (2016). See also Zhu, 'International Humanitarian Law in the Universal Periodic Review of the UN Human Rights Council: An Empirical Survey', 5 *JIHLS* (2014) 186–212; and Heinsch, 'The Future of the International Humanitarian Fact-Finding Commission: A Possibility to Overcome the Weakness of IHL Compliance Mechanisms', in Djukić and Pons (eds), *The Companion to International Humanitarian Law* (2018) 79–97. A new Oxford Forum for International Humanitarian Law Compliance is set to be developed in 2021. On the history of the failed attempt to develop a 'Meeting of States on IHL' as well as other possibilities for compliance review, see Poulopoulou, 'Strengthening Compliance with IHL: Back to Square One', 14 February 2019, blog ejiltalk.org.

mechanisms, including prosecution.[201] The public reporting by such Commissions before the UN Security Council or Human Rights Council is keenly followed, and not only introduces accountability through a form of truth-telling, but also constitutes a form of leverage, as states and armed groups do adjust their behaviour (although not nearly enough) in order to avoid censure.

Alternatively, information about individual violations may be relevant for immigration decisions related to refugee status. The 1951 Convention Relating to the Status of Refugees does not apply to individuals where 'there are serious reasons for considering' a person has committed 'a crime against peace, a war crime, or a crime against humanity, as defined in the international instruments drawn up to make provision in respect of such crimes'.[202]

Furthermore, decisions on leave to remain, family reunification and immigration rights more generally are now looking to reports that reference violations of the laws of war and international crimes. The most dramatic recent decision relating to immigration and asylum procedures concerns the trial for fraud and perjury of 'Jungle Jabbah', a commander fighting against Charles Taylor in the Liberian civil war. He was sentenced in the United States in 2017 to 30 years' imprisonment for lying in response to the question 'Have you ever engaged in genocide, or otherwise ordered, incited, assisted or otherwise participated in the killing of any person because of race, religion, nationality, ethnic origin or political opinion?'[203]

Turning away from national law related to immigration and perjury, we can highlight the sanctions imposed by the Security Council, the European Union and individual states, such as the United States, Canada and the United Kingdom. Such sanctions aim to freeze assets and impose travel bans with regard to allegations of violations of international law, including those committed in times of armed conflict. These sanctions cover individuals, groups and business entities.[204]

---

[201] See in particular the work of the UN Investigative Mechanisms for Syria and Myanmar, and the UN Commission on Human Rights in South Sudan.

[202] Convention Relating to the Status of Refugees (1951) Art 1F(a). On the burden of proof, see *JS v Home Department* [2010] UKSC 15.

[203] See the indictment and explanations on the website of Civitas Maxima at https://www.civitas-maxima.org/en/trials/legal-monitoring-of-the-jungle-jabbah-case; see also the conviction of Thomas Woewiyu on similar charges, 'Delco Man Convicted of Hiding Past as Liberian War Criminal', *Philadelphia Inquirer* (3 July 2018) – in 2020 he died from COVID 19 and was never sentenced.

[204] On the question of criminal obligations of corporations under international law, see Nerlich, 'Core Crimes and Transnational Business Corporations', 8 *JICJ* (2010) 895–908; on the application of international humanitarian law to entities, see 'Ten questions to Philip Spoerri,

For an example, consider the work of the Security Council's Panel of Experts for South Sudan, which is tasked in Resolution 2428 (2018), *inter alia*, with looking to place on a list those individuals and entities 'responsible for or complicit in, or having engaged in, directly or indirectly, actions or policies that threaten the peace, security or stability of South Sudan'. Such actions and policies may include:

- Planning, directing, or committing acts that violate applicable international human rights law or international humanitarian law, or acts that constitute human rights abuses, in South Sudan;
- The targeting of civilians, including women and children, through the planning, directing, or commission of acts of violence (including killing, maiming, or torture), abduction, enforced disappearance, forced displacement, or attacks on schools, hospitals, religious sites, or locations where civilians are seeking refuge, or through conduct that would constitute a serious abuse or violation of human rights or a violation of international humanitarian law;
- Planning, directing, or committing acts involving sexual and gender-based violence in South Sudan;
- The use or recruitment of children by armed groups or armed forces in the context of the armed conflict in South Sudan;
- The obstruction of the activities of international peacekeeping, diplomatic, or humanitarian missions in South Sudan, including the Ceasefire and Transitional Security Arrangements Monitoring Mechanism or of the delivery or distribution of, or access to, humanitarian assistance.[205]

Similar sanctions apply with regard to hundreds of individuals, groups and business entities in the situations related to the Democratic Republic of Congo, Central African Republic, Guinea Bissau, Iraq, North Korea, Libya, Mali, Al-Qaeda, Sudan, Somalia, the Taliban in Afghanistan, and Yemen.[206] A panel of experts may determine that they have 'reasonable grounds to believe that an incident occurred', but when determining that the responsibility

---

ICRC Director for International Law and Cooperation', 94 *IRRC* (2012) 1124–34; for some recent developments, see Clapham, 'Human Rights Obligations for Non-State Actors: Where Are We Now?', in Lafontaine and Larocque (eds), *Doing Peace the Rights Way: Essays in International Law and Relations in Honour of Louise Arbour* (2019) 11–35.

[205] Resolution 2428 (2018) at para 14.
[206] The full list with the explanations is available at https://www.un.org/securitycouncil/sanctions/narrative-summaries.

for an incident lies with an individual perpetrator it could be that all five experts have to agree beyond reasonable doubt on the bases of corroborative evidence.[207] These reports are not prosecutions, but when used by the Security Council or others to impose sanctions, the effects on an individual (with regard to travel bans or asset freezes) can be significant.

The United Kingdom has recently implemented its own sanctions criteria for action beyond what has been agreed in the United Nations.[208] In July 2020, the Government announced asset freezes and travel bans on 25 individuals from Russia (in connection with the mistreatment and death of Sergei Magnitski), 20 individuals from Saudi Arabia (in connection with the unlawful killing of Jamal Khashoggi) and two Generals from Myanmar (in connection with serious human rights violations (including unlawful killings and systematic rape) against the Rohinga population by the army in Rakhine State), and asset freezes on two entities from North Korea (in connection with serious human rights in prison camps).

The relevant UK legislation allows for regulations based on all the norms discussed in the present book: compliance with UN obligations; promotion of the resolution of armed conflicts or the protection of civilians in conflict zones; accountability for torture or inhumane treatment; promotion of compliance with international human rights law and international humanitarian law; and contribution to multilateral efforts to prevent the spread and use of weapons and materials of mass destruction.[209] Of course the efficacy of such measures depends on whether or not individuals or entities have assets in the United Kingdom, or want to travel to the UK, but the sanctions themselves are premised on the international law obligations we have been analyzing, and, however selective, represent a form of accountability.

---

[207] See 'Final Report of the Panel of Experts on Yemen', UN Doc S/2019/83, 25 January 2019, Annex 1, para 4 and Appendix B para 2(e).

[208] For the full list of sanctions applicable in the UK (including UN and EU sanctions) https://ofsistorage.blob.core.windows.net/publishlive/ConList.pdf.

[209] Sanctions and Anti-Money Laundering Act 2018, s 1(2); Global Human Rights Sanctions Regulations 2020 (SI 2020/680) – in this instance, under reg 4, the purpose of the Regulations is to deter and provide accountability for activity that, 'if carried out by or on behalf of a State within the territory of that State, would amount to a serious violation by that State of an individual's— (a) right to life, (b) right not to be subjected to torture or cruel, inhuman or degrading treatment or punishment, or (c) right to be free from slavery, not to be held in servitude or required to perform forced or compulsory labour, whether or not the activity is carried out by or on behalf of a State.' In other words, according to the Explanatory Note to the Regulations, 'The activities could be carried out by a State or non-State actor.'

10.11 Belligerent Reprisals

Lastly, we have to consider reprisals as a way of enforcing the law in time of war. In a way this topic contains within it many of the aspects of the evolution of the law of war that we have been exploring. We have seen throughout this book how a theory of reprisals allowed for violence that would otherwise be unlawful. From the 13th century we have examples of the issuing of letters of reprisal by an English sovereign to right a wrong done to a subject. This was an act against a collectivity for a wrong done by a member of that society. So,

> it was not at all necessary for the person who had suffered a loss to con-
> fine his reprisals to the goods of the particular person or persons who had
> inflicted the loss. If an Englishman's goods were taken unlawfully by a
> Spaniard, for example, he might seize in reprisal the goods of the Spanish
> King or of any subject of that king.[210]

Such authorized reprisals are no longer possible in peacetime or in war. Nor can a state resort to armed reprisals of any kind to right a wrong.[211] And yet, once an international armed conflict starts, the idea endures that a state can take *belligerent reprisals* against another state in response to violations of the laws of war. Belligerent reprisals are separate from the reprisal action that was said to justify the war. They relate to a violation of the laws of war (*jus in bello*) during the course of the war. The sinking of the passenger liner *Lusitania* in 1915, with over 1,000 killed, was sometimes argued to be a re-prisal for the long-range starvation blockade of Germany by Britain (a close, effective blockade would have been considered legal) and sometimes to be a response to the alleged transport of war munitions. The unrestricted sub-marine warfare on merchant ships in both World Wars was said to be in re-prisal for violations of the law of war, whether it be violations of neutrality, the arming of merchant ships, or the effects of blockade. At the same time, we also saw how the law on reprisal was invoked by the United States to justify its unneutral behaviour at the beginning of the Second World War (reprisal for Germany's aggression). And then again, targeting merchant ships was a reprisal in response to the unneutral assistance being offered by the United

---

[210] Clark, 'The English Practice with Regard to Reprisals by Private Persons', 27 *AJIL* (1933) 694–723 at 697.
[211] See Ch 4.

States to the United Kingdom. The famous 'V' bombs rained on London were said to be Germany's reaction to area bombing in Germany – the 'V' standing for *Vergeltungswaffen*, variously translated as weapons of vengeance or retaliation or reprisal.

It is not hard to see how the notion of reprisal quickly becomes tangled up with counter-reprisal, and that allowing for reprisal in wartime means that unlawful acts of violence spiral out of any meaningful legal control.

The language used in the British Order in Council framing reprisals in 1939 is revealing in the way the action is explained as taken as a right of retaliation:

> Whereas His Majesty has been compelled to take up arms against Germany in defence of the fundamental right of nations to a free and peaceful existence:
>
> And whereas German forces have in numerous cases sunk merchant vessels, British, Allied and neutral, in violation of the rules contained in the Submarine Protocol, 1936, to which Germany is a party:
>
> . . .
>
> And whereas it is manifest that the German Government have deliberately embarked on a policy of endeavouring to destroy all seabourne trade between the Allied and other countries by a ruthless use of the forces at their disposal, contrary to the laws and customs of war, the rights of neutrals and the obligations of humanity:
>
> And whereas this action on the part of the German Government gives His Majesty an unquestionable right of retaliation . . .[212]

There are, today, however, limits to what action can be taken in the form of belligerent reprisals. International humanitarian law has taken an incremental approach, first outlawing reprisals against prisoners of war in the Geneva Convention of 1929, and then extending the prohibition to protected persons and property under the 1949 Geneva Conventions.[213] In addition, cultural property is now protected from reprisals under the 1954 Hague Convention, and there are restrictions on reprisals against civilians in the context of restrictions on the use of mines, booby traps and

---

[212] *Statutory Rules and Orders* (1939) vol II, 3606–07; the reprisals related to goods leaving enemy ports and enemy goods on neutral ships, all such goods to be placed in the custody of the Marshal of the Prize Court.

[213] See de Hemptinne, 'Prohibition of Reprisals', in Clapham, Gaeta and Sassòli (eds), *The 1949 Geneva Conventions: A Commentary* (2015) 575–96.

other devices.[214] Additional Protocol I of 1977 extended the lists of protected persons and property, and added a prohibition on reprisals constituting attacks against the natural environment.[215] Particular controversy,
however, surrounds the inclusion of a prohibition on attacks on the civilian
population or civilian objects by way of reprisal, and a number of states
made statements or formulated reservations or declarations concerning
this provision.[216]

But away from the technical details of what is allowed, or not allowed,
under the law of reprisals, one needs to get a sense of the bigger picture. It
takes a historian like Best to put the lawyers' talk into perspective:

> 'Reprisals' has always been a particularly tricky and controversial topic
> throughout the history of the law of war, because in practice it is difficult
> to distinguish between the motives for pursuing 'reprisals', 'retaliation', 'ret-
> ribution', and 'revenge' (and even 'retorsion'). But 'reprisals' has become
> the morally more elevated and juridically acceptable concept. ... 'Revenge'
> rings meanly in many civilized ears, and 'retaliation' lacks moral overtones.
> But 'reprisals' has acquired a character of active virtue: in contemporary
> international law parlance, it is an act, perhaps unlawful in itself, justifiably
> undertaken with the specific object of paining a law-neglecting enemy back
> into conformity with the law.[217]

Today it is difficult to conceive of a state's thinking it would be considered
acceptable to claim that the law on reprisals entitled it to order disproportionate attacks harming the civilian population of another state; although the
continuing argument that nuclear weapons may be permitted in self-defence
seeks to leave open this possibility.[218]

The UK *Manual of the Law of Armed Conflict*, having recalled its statement that seeks to reserve the right to take reprisals against a civilian population in the event of serious and deliberate attacks against its own civilian

---

[214] See Protocol II, and (Amended Protocol II) to the Convention on Certain Conventional
Weapons (1980) Art 3(2).

[215] See AP I Arts 20, 51–56.

[216] Greenwood, 'Belligerent Reprisals in the Jurisprudence of the International Criminal
Tribunal for the Former Yugoslavia', in Fischer, Kress and Luder (eds), *International and National
Prosecution of Crimes under International Law: Current Developments* (2001) 241–66; for a look
at some of the statements by states, see Henckaerts and Doswald-Beck, *Customary International
Humanitarian Law* (n 157) at 520–23.

[217] Best, *Humanity in Warfare* (1980) at 166–67.

[218] *Legality of the Threat or Use of Nuclear Weapons*, Advisory Opinion, 8 July 1996, at para 46;
Casey-Maslen and Haines, *Hague Law Interpreted* (2018) 337–44;

population,[219] carefully restricts the possible use of any such reprisal against the civilian population:

> [C]ommanders and commanders in chief are not to take reprisal action on their own initiative. Requests for authority to take reprisal action must be submitted to the Ministry of Defence and require clearance at Cabinet level.[220]

Looking to the future, it is occasionally argued that there are few rules prohibiting reprisals in non-international armed conflict, leaving the door open to reprisals as a means to enforce international law in non-international armed conflict.[221] This makes no sense to me. Whatever history there may be of reprisals being carried out in civil wars in previous centuries, there is no evidence that states consider that belligerent reprisal as a matter of international law can be invoked outside inter-state conflict. The idea that a terrorist armed group could point to a violation of the laws of war by a state to legalize its own violations of the laws of war would get short shrift. And to allow a state to point to a violation of international law by the armed group it is fighting and then, in turn, to claim that it is justified in violating the law of war in retaliation, would be to signal the end of the rule of law in war.[222]

---

[219] The relevant statement made on ratification of Additional Protocol I (1977), and extended to Overseas Territories in 2002, reads in part: 'If an adverse party makes serious and deliberate attacks, in violation of Article 51 or Article 52 against the civilian population or civilians or against civilian objects, or, in violation of Articles 53, 54 and 55, on objects or items protected by those Articles, the United Kingdom will regard itself as entitled to take measures otherwise prohibited by the Articles in question to the extent that it considers such measures necessary for the sole purpose of compelling the adverse party to cease committing violations under those Articles, but only after formal warning to the adverse party requiring cessation of the violations has been disregarded and then only after a decision taken at the highest level of government.'

[220] UK Ministry of Defence, *The Manual of the Law of Armed Conflict* (2004) at para 16.19.2.

[221] See the discussion of this topic in Casey-Maslen and Haines, *Hague Law Interpreted* (n 218) 343–44; ICRC, *Commentary on the First Geneva Convention*, 2nd edn (2016) paras 904–907 (Art 3); Bílková, 'Belligerent Reprisals in Non-International Armed Conflicts', 63 *ICLQ* (2014) 31–65; Henckaerts and Doswald-Beck, *Customary International Humanitarian Law* (n 157) at 526–29; Turns, 'Implementation and Compliance', in Wilmshurst and Breua (eds), *Perspectives on the ICRC Study on Customary International Humanitarian Law* (2007) 354–76 at 370–72; Darcy, *Collective Responsibility and Accountability Under International Law* (2007) 166–85; Zegveld, *Accountability of Armed Opposition Groups in International Law* (2002) esp at 89ff; Romani, *Belligerent Reprisals from Enforcement to Reciprocity: A New Theory of Retaliation in Conflict* (forthcoming CUP).

[222] See also de Hemptinne, 'Prohibition of Reprisals' (n 213) at 587–91.

10.12 War in the Mind of a War Criminal

Many have puzzled over why brutal war crimes are committed. Each context is different, of course, and there will be thousands of explanations. But one reflection I came across bears out the thesis of this book: that war can be understood as a state of mind.

The Japanese prisoner of war camp commander, Katō Tetsutarō, was tried as a war criminal by the United States, and at one point was sentenced to death. He wrote a famous memoir, which was later televised and made into various films, with the English title *I Want to be a Shellfish*. This memorable plea comes from Katō's story entitled *I Want to Become a Shellfish – A Cry of a BC Class War Criminal*. This idea of wanting to come back as a shellfish provides us with a first insight into the mindlessness provoked by war. In his story he imagines a secret last testament of a fictional executed prisoner, Sergeant Akagi:

Who on earth did we fight the war for? I believed that it was for the Emperor, but it seems this was not the case. The Emperor did not save me. I had always faithfully obeyed every order as coming from you – whether I hated it or not. And I always tried hard to internalise the spirit of the *Imperial Rescript*.[223] I had never shirked my military duties, and I became a sergeant.

Why did not you save me, your Majesty the Emperor? Perhaps you just had no idea of how much we suffered. I would like to believe this. But I can no longer believe in anything. When you say we are *enduring the unendurable and suffering the insufferable*, do you mean that I must die?

I will be executed. It has been decided. I have obeyed your orders up until my death, so I therefore owe you nothing.

In my view, what I did owe to you were only the 7–8 cigarettes provided on the front line in China and some snacks at a field hospital. Cigarettes were very expensive – I paid you back with my life and my long-suffering. So, I will no longer be deceived by your words. No matter how honey-tongued they are. We are even now, and so, I owe you nothing.

If I should be reborn as Japanese, I would never be obedient to you. I would never become a soldier. If I have to be reborn, I do not want to be Japanese. No, I would rather not be human. I would not want to be a cow or horse, for humans bully me.

---

[223] The Emperor's speech is available at https://www.pearlharborhistoricsites.org/blog/gyokuon-hoso-the-jewel-voice-broadcast.

If I have no choice but to be born again, I would rather be a shellfish. Stuck on the rock at the bottom of the ocean, a shellfish has nothing to worry about. There I would have nothing to know, no sorrow or pleasure, no pains and itches, no headache, no conscription, and no war.[224]

The films and the memoir are often seen as highlighting the sense of injustice that flowed from the war crimes prosecutions conducted by foreign powers, but the memoirs of such convicted war criminals in the end formed part of the Japanese peace movement. Katō's *Cry of a BC War Criminal* includes a second insight into the author's state of mind:

War makes people mad. In a desperate life-or-death situation, any system of values breaks down. In war, killing is considered the highest virtue. By killing people and seeing fellow soldiers killed by the enemy at war, people become deranged in the state of mind that they are forever in a situation where they either kill or are killed.[225]

---

[224] I am extremely grateful to Hibiki Urano for her translations of Katō Tetsutarō, *Watashi wa kai ni naritai – Aru BC kyu senpan no sakebi (I Want to Become a Shellfish – A Cry of a BC Class War Criminal)*, ed Fujiko Kato (Tokyo: Shunjusha, 2007) at 26–27.

[225] Ibid at 47. The original reads: 戦争は、人間を発狂させる。死ぬか生きるかという、せっぱつまったとき、あらゆる価値が転倒する。殺人がもっとも大きな美徳とされるのが戦争である。自分が人を殺す、また仲間の兵隊が敵に殺されるのを見る、そして自分もまた、いつなんどき殺されるかわからないという心理が支配的となったとき、人間は発狂するのである. This passage and the memoir were highlighted by Tachikawa Kyoichi in 'The Treatment of Prisoners of War by the Imperial Japanese Army and Navy Focusing on the Pacific War' 9 *National Institute for Defense Studies Security Reports* (2008) 45–90 at 71. For the connection between these writings and the peace movement, see Takeshi, 'A Foreign Country in Japan: Sugamo Prison: Review of Utsumi Aiko, Sugamo Prison: The Peace Movement of the War Criminals (Sugamo purizun – senpantachi no heiwa undo). Tokyo: Yoshikawa Kobunkan, 2004', 2(7) *The Asia-Pacific Journal* (2004), online at https://apjjf.org/-Ishida-Takeshi/2050/article.html.

Conclusion

At the start of this book it was suggested war was out of fashion. Today's armed violence is explained in terms of peace enforcement, law enforcement, counter-insurgency, counter-terrorism, self-defence, or as necessary to preserve the international rule of law.

States may no longer rationalize their violence against each other as part of a longstanding tradition of going to War, but the logic that justifies the killing, detention and destruction is still premised on the idea of the necessities of war. States no longer declare War, and yet governments claim belligerent rights to acquire territory and neutral ships, to destroy things they consider are part of the enemy's war-sustaining economy, and intern people as law of war detainees (in some cases, forever).

What went wrong?

This is obviously not just a problem of labelling or vocabulary, but rather an inability to chose peaceful over violent ways of resolving disputes. And, as we have seen throughout this book, maybe 'the reason why there are always wars [is] because you can never completely share the suffering of others'.[1] The point I want to highlight in this book is that old ideas about what is permissible in war have survived when many of them should have been buried along with the legal institution of War. Of course, some long-standing ideas about war are worth preserving: only take a life where this is necessary, do not use weapons that cause unnecessary suffering, never attack the civilian population, treat all those under your control with dignity and humanity. But other ancient ideas related to killing, keeping what you capture and dehumanizing individuals who are considered the enemy, have to be properly banished.

Part of the problem comes from the enduring influence of ideas of just war. The trope that being at war simply allows for prohibited behaviour is repeated by self-styled 'orthodox' just war theorists, who take as a starting point that soldiers are 'licensed to kill in wartime', claiming that this is 'widely familiar to citizens of liberal democracies and beyond'.[2] An alternative (some

---

[1] Remarque, *The Way Back* [1931], tr Murdoch (London: Vintage, 2019) at 29.
[2] Meisels, *Contemporary Just War: Theory and Practice* (2018) at 151.

say revisionist) way to ground the morality of killing is not by referencing wartime, but by looking for an unjustified and immediate threat.[3] Law of war 9 manuals and just war philosophers gravitate to killing the paradigmatic sleeping or naked soldiers to inculcate the idea of status-based killing. However, it is rarely necessary to kill such a soldier. I suggest a paradigm shift.

The ancient law of war entitled states to capture, condemn and permanently confiscate civilian enemy goods on civilian enemy ships and airplanes. At the same time, the law of nations meant that ships of any nationality could be acquired by the blockading state on the ground that they were caught breaching blockade. After reviewing these rules, I suggested that all such ancient rules related to the acquisition of enemy and neutral property should be radically rethought. International law cannot simultaneously outlaw recourse to war and leave untouched the rewards that attached to states engaged in the institution of War. Slavery and duelling were outlawed and abolished, with no privileges left for those who persisted in engaging in such activities. The abolition of War as an institution must have eliminated the old advantages that attached to states who went to War.[4]

---

[3] See Rodin, 'The Moral Inequality of Soldiers: Why *jus in bello* Asymmetry is Half Right', in Rodin and Shue (eds), *Just and Unjust Warriors: The Moral and Legal Status of Soldiers* (2008) 44–68 at 46. 'Even if one holds that normative relations in war are necessarily mediated through super-personal entities such as the state or nation, one must still explain why individual soldiers in war no longer possess their ordinary human right not to be killed.' (ibid at 47)

[4] In fact a claim that international law entitled an aggressor State at War to acquire property rights over enemy goods and ships belonging to enemy nationals could even be refused by national judges on the grounds that this would be to condone the illegal act of aggression. Consider the approach of the UK House of Lords in the context of a claim by Kuwait Airways over its planes seized by the Iraqi Government in the course of the aggression in 1990: 'Such a fundamental breach of international law can properly cause the courts of this country to say that, like the confiscatory decree of the Nazi government of Germany in 1941, a law depriving those whose property has been plundered of the ownership of their property in favour of the aggressor's own citizens will not be enforced or recognised in proceedings in this country.' *Kuwait Airways Corporation v Iraqi Airways Company* [2002] UKHL 19 [29], per Lord Nicholls. Similarly, see Hersch Lauterpacht's suggestion 'that a state waging an unlawful war does not obtain or validly transmit title with respect to property acquired in connexion with the conduct of war – regardless of whether such title is otherwise acquired in accordance with the law of war – and that this principle applies in particular to title claimed to have been acquired by requisition, by other forms of appropriation of public and private enemy property, or by condemnation in prize' : 'The Problem with the Revision of the Law of War', 29 *BYBIL* (1952) 360–82 at 378 fn 2; and Lauterpacht (ed), *Oppenheim's International Law: a Treatise*, vol II: *Disputes, War and Neutrality*, 7th edn (1952) 217–22 at 219. *Contra* Baxter, 'The Legal Consequences of the Unlawful Use of Force under the Charter', in Baxter et al (eds), *Humanizing the Laws of War: Selected Writings of Richard Baxter* (2013) 68–75 esp at 72; and Baxter, 'The Definition of War', 16 *Revue égyptienne de droit international* (1960) 1–14 at 9–10. See also H Lauterpacht, 'The Limits of the Operation of the Law of War', 30 *BYBIL* (1953) 206–43 esp at 226 and 232–33.

I should now like to highlight a number of conclusions that point in the direction of exposing war as a dangerous and deceptive concept in international life.

First, the concept of war suggests a total commitment to the defeat of an enemy. This quickly leads to the categorization of *individuals* from the other side as *enemies*, of those who disagree as engaged in treason and of others who fail to support the government as *enemies within*. The concept of war also engenders a determination not to be a loser – one has to *win the war*. This in turn precludes ideas of compromise, accepting partial gains and losses, and finding a formula for peace. As Jessup put it, 'One can negotiate for a limited objective but one does not resort to total war for a limited objective.'[5]

Second, we should tackle the lingering idea that a Declaration of War entitles a state to cast off from the moorings that apply to the use of force and the treatment of individuals under the rule of law. On visiting the 9/11 Memorial and Museum in New York, I heard over the soundtrack, and saw on the walls, references to the 'Declaration of War' authored by Osama bin Laden in 1996, as well as another declaration of war signed by bin Laden in 1998. This general background was explained under the heading 'war against the United States 1998–2000'.[6] Such declarations of war should not affect any applicable legal regime,[7] nor can they be invoked to suggest extraordinary departures from established rules. If international law has abolished War as a method for resolving disputes, or as an instrument of national policy,[8] then a Declaration of War (by any actor) cannot at the same time generate rights and obligations under that same general international law. More generally, we should confront head-on the popular idea that 'history teaches us that there is no moral

---

[5] 'Intermediacy', 23 *Nordisk Tidsskrift for International Ret* (1953) 16–26 at 25.

[6] The Museum's website lists as the first two primary sources, Osama Bin Laden's Declaration of Jihad Against Americans in 1996 and Osama Bin Laden's 1998 Fatwa, at https://www.911memorial.org/911-primary-sources; the teaching materials ask teachers to discuss with students 'is it a war?' – see at https://www.911memorial.org/sites/all/files/Pre-visit%20Materials_0.pdf. See also Mohammad-Mahmoud Ould Mohamedou's thoughtful discussion of how the 1996 'Declaration of War' in turn referenced the United States 'occupying the lands of Islam' and 'the protracted blockade' after the 1991 Gulf War, and the 'occupation of Jerusalem', and that such crimes committed by Americans were said in Bin Laden's Declaration to be 'a clear declaration of war' by the USA: Ould Mohamedou, *Understanding Al Qaeda: The Transformation of War* (2007) at 70–71; he highlights how parts of the US Administration decided they were at war with Al-Qaeda without considering the war aims of Al-Qaeda or the nature of any such war (see ibid esp at 52 and 12). According to him, 'Al-Qaeda was pushing war forward more innovatively than its opponents', and it reinvented 'terrorism as war': see Ould Mohamedou, *A Theory of ISIS* (2018) at 54–55.

[7] See the discussion in the Preface with regard to the Prosecution's reliance on the 1996 declaration for the war crimes trials in Guantánamo Bay.

[8] Kellogg Briand Pact (1928) Art II.

high ground in total war.'[9] War is not an excuse to abandon the rule of law and our morality.

Third, the concept of the *necessity of war* is in danger of morphing into a general excuse or defence to be deployed each time there is a complaint that the laws of war have been violated.[10] At the legal level, there are indeed some specific rules that allow for deviation from the rule for justified cases of military necessity, but it is no longer acceptable as a matter of law for a state, or anyone else, to claim that war entitles them to do things that are otherwise illegal. Such thinking should be roundly rejected.[11] Rather than see war as an excuse or justification to break the law, we should be demanding ever-higher ethical levels of behaviour. As Lord McDonald recently commented, 'There are many ways to judge a nation. One is by the manner in which it wages war.'[12]

Fourth, the rules on proportionality are in danger of being bent to accommodate a logic of war. Under the first rule – the obligation of proportionality in self-defence – there is a temptation to consider that the defending state might only have to remain within the boundaries of what is proportionate to its aim, and if that aim is to win a war, or even a total war, then the limits of proportionality start to recede. Rejecting the relevance of the concept of war in this context allows us to find the proposed proper limits of proportionality in self-defence.[13] In other words, force is permitted in self-defence to the extent that it is necessary and proportionate to repelling and halting the armed

---

[9] Letter to *The Times*, Sir David Lewis, 15 August 2020 (commenting on the atom bombs dropped on Japan).

[10] Complaints about the mistreatment of detainees may be met with the response that this is 'part of war'. 'Revealed: The Evidence of War Crimes Ministers Tried to Bury: Torture, Murder, Abuse, Beatings and Sexual Humiliation – Camp Stephen in Iraq was Britain's Abu Ghraib, Our Investigation Finds', *Sunday Times* (17 November 2019).

[11] Similarly, see Dinstein, 'Military Necessity', *MPEPIL* (2015) at para 8: 'In the past, it was often claimed that a belligerent party is at liberty to deviate from the law of international armed conflict when military necessity – especially in dire circumstances – so demanded. This claim, which actually means that military necessity is superior to the law, is now completely defunct. At present, it is indisputable that if "necessity knows no law", then – at bottom – there is no law.' See also Greenwood, 'Scope of Application of Humanitarian Law', in Fleck (ed), *The Handbook of Humanitarian Law in Armed Conflict*, 2nd edn (2007) 45–78 at 36–38.

[12] 'Cover-ups and Crime Thrive When Soldiers Who Do Wrong Escape Justice', *Sunday Times* (17 November 2019).

[13] On the dangers of self-defence becoming so pliable and open-ended that it simply replaces the institution of war, see Blum, 'The Internationalists Mini-Forum: Wars of Self-Defense, An Exception that Swallows the Rule', 16 November 2017, available at https://www.justsecurity.org/47087/internationalists-mini-forum-vague-definition-self-defense-war/.

attack, and not with regard to some larger objective of winning the war and disabling the enemy.[14]

Similarly, by taking the idea of war out of the equation, there is less temptation to consider the initial attack as an 'act of war' that requires a response in kind. The law of proportionality in self-defence is not about inflicting equal damage on the attacker. As Greenwood puts it,

> proportionality in self-defence is also a forward-looking requirement. Whether action purportedly taken in self-defence meets the requirement of proportionality is to be assessed not by reference to the degree of force which was employed in the initial armed attack, but rather the threat posed by the armed attack.[15]

Once this requirement is fulfilled, one can turn to the second rule of proportionality which states that in targeting military objectives, expected civilian damage must not be excessive when weighed against anticipated military advantage. If we allow military advantage to be expressed as the need to win a war then the protection left to civilians starts to evaporate before our eyes. Thought now needs to be given to considering the aims of the conflict when calculating what is an acceptable level of civilian death. This point has not been lost on the Generals reflecting on NATO's role in the bombing of Serbia:

> [T]hose who believe in the continuing relevance of the [just war] tradition may need to reflect further on how the concept of discrimination in targeting should be applied when the main aim is not to inflict military defeat but to change a government's behaviour.[16]

Fifth, just as throwing war into the proportionality equation makes a mockery of the modern rules designed to protect civilians, so too does an over-emphasis on the idea of war in related rules. Without the idea of a war, claims about 'law-of-war detainees' and the 'war-sustaining economy' lose

---

[14] See Higgins, *Problems and Process: International Law and How We Use It* (1994) at 231–32; for a summary of some of the other approaches to what proportionality should mean in this context and the way that the original harm done and the harm to be prevented can be seen as being taken into account, see Haque, 'Necessity and Proportionality in International Law', in May (ed), *The Cambridge Handbook of the Just War* (2018) 255–72 at 259–61.

[15] Greenwood, 'Self-Defence', *MPEPIL* (2011) at para 28.

[16] Guthrie and Quinlan, *Just War: The Just War Tradition: Ethics in Modern Warfare* (2007) at 37–38.

much of their apparent logic. Of course people can be detained in times of armed conflict, and targets can be selected as a proportionate response in self-defence, but such acts should be done according to the international rules, and not by reference to self-serving concepts evoking war that are not found in treaties or contemporary customary international law.

Sixth, the idea that a state of war can last for decades, and thus obviate the need to justify new rounds of armed attack, is no longer appropriate. Invoking a pre-existing war should not be a way to justify controversial attacks. So, in 2003, in the midst of the controversy over the attack on Iraq, US Government lawyers set the scene for such justifications by suggesting that 'few would criticize a strike in the midst of an *ongoing war* against a second state's program to develop new types of weapons.'[17] One lawyer explicitly argued that the US attack on Iraq in March 2003 was justified as, in the absence of a peace treaty, the United States had been in 'a state of war' with Iraq since 1990.[18]

In the United Kingdom, in the run-up to the same attack on Iraq, it was suggested that it was as if the Iraqi Government had violated the terms of an 'armistice', and so could be punished for that, just as Germany could have been punished for breach of the 1918 Armistice.[19] Dinstein has argued that this 2003 attack on Iraq should be seen as 'reopening of fire in an ongoing war' that started in 1991 and cannot be seen as a new armed attack.[20] This idea of justifying massive attacks by harking back to a so-called existing 'state of war', more than a decade after the end of hostilities, seems completely at

---

[17] Taft and Buchwald, 'Preemption, Iraq, and International Law', 97 *AJIL* 3 (2003) 557–63 at 557 (emphasis added).

[18] Yoo, 'International Law and the War on Iraq', 97 *AJIL* 3 (2003) 563–76 at 569.

[19] UK, House of Commons, Select Committee on Foreign Affairs, Minutes of Evidence, Professors Greenwood and Brownlie, 24 October 2002, Examination of Witnesses at Questions, paras 90–91. Greenwood responded that the analogy of the First World War Armistice did not work, as 'the law has changed since then as a result of the Charter', although he went on to say that 'the underlying point is the same, the Security Council laid down these terms, Iraq has not complied with them'.

[20] Dinstein, *War, Aggression and Self-Defence*, 6th edn (2017) at 64; see also ibid at 281, 344–51. He further argues that the Israeli attacks on the Iraqi nuclear reactor in 1981 and the Syrian nuclear installation in 2007 are to be examined in the context of Israel and Syria or Iraq being 'embroiled in a state of war'. Such a technical State of War is significant for Dinstein (ibid at 227): 'Had Israel been at peace with Iraq or Syria, the bombing of the respective nuclear facilities would have been prohibited, since (when examined by itself and out of the context of an ongoing war) it did not qualify as an admissible act of self-defence comporting with Article 51.' See further Dinstein, 'Comments on War', 27 *Harvard Journal of Law and Public Policy* (2003) 877–92; and Dinstein, 'The International Legal Dimensions of the Arab-Israeli Conflict', in Kellermann, Siehr, and Einhorn (eds), *Israel Among the Nations: International and Comparative Law Perspectives on Israel's 50th Anniversary* (1998) 137–54 esp at 143–50.

odds with a world that has outlawed war and set strict conditions on the use of force.

Even where both sides seek to rely on the concept of a state of war, contemporary international law now seeks to prevent rather than excuse violence. Writing about the relationship between Israel and Lebanon in 1982, Barry Levenfeld concluded:

> The subjective perception by the parties that a state of war exists encourages more frequent resorts to force and an escalation in the magnitude of force. A legal system should minimize the occasions of recourse to force and limit its intensity. Rather than providing the parties with a ready-made excuse to use whatever level of violence they choose, a legal system should regulate and confine the use of force. The state of war thesis must be rejected as inappropriate and dangerously destabilizing.[21]

I conclude that having outlawed the legal institution of War, it makes no sense to seek to justify recourse to force with the idea of an ongoing war or State of War due to the absence of a Peace Agreement. Similarly, in the absence of an armed attack, the breach of a peace treaty, an armistice or a cease-fire agreement does not today entitle a state to resort to force.

I have come to what might be a rather surprising final conclusion for a book on war. Instead of proposing yet another problematic definition of war,[22] and advocating a return to circumscribed rights and obligations that flow from a 'proper war', so defined, I am of the view that no international legal rights or obligations should flow merely from the idea of being in a State of War.

I have tried to separate the old idea of War with a capital 'W', which allowed states to claim Belligerent Rights based on ancient practice, from the modern reality that armed conflicts (whether we call them wars or not) are circumscribed and regulated by detailed treaty provisions. And I have argued that the prohibition on the use of force in the UN Charter means not only that a state can no longer acquire territory or property rights through armed conflict or war, but also that a state can no longer rely on customary Belligerent Rights to seize and capture ships, planes and goods to sustain its war effort.[23]

---

[21] Levenfeld, 'Israel's Counter-*Fedayeen* Tactics in Lebanon: Self-Defense and Reprisal under Modern International Law', 21 *Columbia Journal of Transnational Law* (1982) 1–48 at 25–26.

[22] On the complications of defining war more generally, see Vasquez, *The War Puzzle Revisited* (2009) Ch1.

[23] See generally Ch 8.

Not only has War been outlawed, but it has also been abolished as a regime or institution of Law with its own attendant Rights and Obligations. Moving from speaking about a State of War to a situation of armed conflict (or even war with a small 'w') should not mean that we carry over the Belligerent Rights that Warring States have acquired for themselves over centuries. Such a conclusion will not be shared by all, even as the entry on *war* disappears from the encyclopaedias and dictionaries of international law.[24]

Finally, I am not suggesting that we should avoid the word *war*, or expressions such as the laws of war, war crimes or prisoners of war. The word 'war' can remind us of the enormity of what is being undertaken and the horror associated with such activity. The rhetorical impact of the word 'war' not only serves to justify violence, but can also be appropriated by those who want to protest against it. Campaigns to 'Stop the War', 'Criminalize War'[25] or 'End Rape as a Weapon of War' lose their force if we shy away from the emotions generated by references to war. The Security Council can reference hunger in the context of humanitarian crises, or alternatively strongly condemn 'the use of starvation of civilians as a method of warfare', adding that that 'method of warfare may constitute a war crime'.[26] Words matter. Invoking war reminds us that we have warring parties, warriors, weapons of war and methods of warfare, and of course the prospect of war crimes trials. Similarly, there may be a need to point to an absence of 'war powers', or to claim that trade or assistance is 'fuelling the war', while those that engage in such trade are 'profiting from war'. Introducing the word 'war' should prick the moral conscience rather than muddy the legal waters.

In the end, not only do we need to challenge the over-reliance on war to generate rights and avoid obligations, but we also need to be careful about reimagining war as something else, and everything short of war as simply a stage on the way back to inevitable peace. One study of peace in the 19th century concludes that

---

[24] Readers may or may not consider it significant that, in contrast to the first two editions of the *Max Planck Encyclopedia of Public International Law*, the latest print and online versions contain no entry for 'War' (as of January 2021). The last entry in 2000 uses the contribution published in the 1982 edition: see Meng, 'War', in Bernhardt (ed), *Encylopedia of Public International Law*, vol 4 (2000) 1334–42, who at one point (ibid at 1337) concludes that it 'seems unhelpful to distinguish between war in a formal sense and war in a substantive sense'. See also Grant and Barker, *Parry and Grant Encyclopædic Dictionary of International Law*, 3rd edn (2008) at 669: 'The term [war] has no precise meaning – or consequences – in contemporary international law, and the term *"armed conflict"* is used instead.'

[25] See, eg, the Kuala Lumpur Declaration to Criminalize War (15 December 2005).

[26] Security Council Resolution 2417 (2018).

in ascribing such an unconditional value to peace, we not only run the risk of forgetting contentious nature of peace but of deflating the concept of war and inflating the concept of peace. The long-term outcome was a hypocritical use of language in which we are not talking about war anymore, but about 'humanitarian intervention', 'air strikes', 'stabilizing', and 'peacekeeping missions', and so forth, often carried out not by identifiable political actors but by an 'international community' as an abstractly universal agent of peace.[27]

Such acts might indeed trigger the laws of war applicable between defined parties.

So we should not systematically avoid the word 'war', but we should be worried about what happens when war becomes a state of mind. The more we emphasise that the use of violence is a war, the more we risk generating a mentality that encourages thoughts about eliminating the enemy and escalating egregious excesses. The inquiry into the Australian Special Forces killings in Afghanistan concluded:

> A substantial indirect responsibility falls upon those in Special Air Service Regiment who embraced or fostered the 'warrior culture' and the clique of non-commissioned officers who propagated it. Special Forces operators should pride themselves on being model professional soldiers, not on being 'warrior heroes'.[28]

In reaction to the publication of this report, Andrew Hastie, who served as a Commander with the Regiment and is now a Member of Parliament, cautioned against the 'repudiation of all warrior culture', but honestly reveals that 'The warrior ethos I sometimes saw was about power, ego and self-adulation. It worshipped war itself'.[29]

And all wars involve propaganda. Writing after the First World War, John Bassett Moore observed that such material was received with a 'state of mind' where 'no report is too improbable, no theory too extravagant, no hypothesis too unreal for belief'. He continued:

---

[27] Hippler and Vec, 'Peace as a Polemic Concept: Writing the History of Peace in Nineteenth Century Europe', in Hippler and Vec (eds), *Paradoxes of Peace in Nineteenth Century Europe* (2015) 3–16 at 8.

[28] Afghanistan Inquiry Report (2020) at 33, para 34; see also at 334, 499 and 501.

[29] 'SAS Must Put Honour before Glory', *The Australian* (24 November 2020).

[A]s the history of wars has shown, this psychopathological condition by no means readily disappears, the uncritical suppositions to which it gives rise, welded by constant repetition into the texture of current thought strongly tend to persist.[30]

My conclusion that War no longer gives rise to Belligerent Rights for states is, I hope, a little surprising – but it is not as new as one might think. Rosalyn Higgins concluded in 1963 (and in the particular context of the 1951 controversy over shipping in the Suez Canal) that there was 'considerable evidence' that 'a state of war is incompatible with the UN Charter'[31] and that UN practice pointed to war ending with the cessation of hostilities rather than a formal peace treaty. For her this meant 'The contention of any state that it acts under rights of belligerency is to be rejected as incompatible with the Charter and current international law.'[32]

Throughout the book, however, I have sought to go even further. I have tried to show that the claims of a belligerent state that a war or armed conflict gives that state the right to appropriate, detain, kill and destroy need to be treated as just those – claims – and not as self-evident rights under international law. Only the actual rules of armed conflict, and not some presumed law of war stemming from a State of War, or the fact of war, can determine the legality of a party's behaviour.

A last word should go to Svetlana Alexievich, who spent years interviewing Soviet women who had experienced war on the front line. She is thinking about how to explain to her daughter that she has to meet a woman to talk about her memories of the war:

And I was about to go to the park with my little girl. To ride the merry-go-round. How can I explain to a six-year-old what it is I do? She recently asked me: 'What is war?' How do I reply? ... I would like to send her out into this world with a gentle heart, and I teach her that one shouldn't simply go pick a flower. It's a pity to crush a ladybug, to tear the wing off a dragonfly. So how am I to explain war to the child? To explain death? To answer the question of why people kill? Kill even the little children like herself. We, the adults,

---

[30] Moore, *International Law and Some Current Illusions* (1924) at 4; more recently, see Werner, 'Just War Theory: Going to war and collective self-deception', in Allhof, Evans and Henschke (eds), *Routledge Handbook of Ethics and War: Just War Theory in the 21st Century* (2013) 35–46.

[31] Higgins, *The Development of International Law Through the Political Organs of the United Nations* (1963) at 215.

[32] Ibid at 216.

are as if in collusion. We understand what the talk is about. But what of children? After the war my parents somehow explained it to me, but I can't explain it to my child. Can't find the words. We like war less and less; it's more and more difficult to find a justification for it. For us it's simply murder. At least it is for me.[33]

This has been a book about war, and the consequences that used to flow from being in a State of War. Today one can no longer seize people, territory or property and simply claim that 'all's fair in love and war'. I have also sought to show that the idea of war leads to a particular state of mind. We should challenge this mind-set that accompanies war, and which leads to horrors inflicted on fellow human beings just because someone has made up their mind they are at war with an enemy.

---

[33] Alexievich, *The Unwomanly Face of War*, trs Pevear and Volokhonsky (2017) at xx.

Index

For the benefit of digital users, indexed terms that span two pages (e.g., 52–53) may, on occasion, appear on only one of those pages.